CHARLES HARRISON

ENGLISH ART AND MODERNISM 1900–1939

WITH A NEW INTRODUCTION

PUBLISHED FOR THE PAUL MELLON CENTRE
FOR STUDIES IN BRITISH ART
BY YALE UNIVERSITY PRESS
NEW HAVEN AND LONDON

First published in 1981
Second Edition published 1994 by Yale University Press

20 19 18 17 16 15 14 13 12 11 10 9 8 7 6 5 4 3 2

ISBN 0-300-05986-8; Library of Congress catalog card number: 80-8611

Set in Monophoto Photina
Printed in Hong Kong through World Print

ENGLISH ART AND MODERNISM

1900–1939

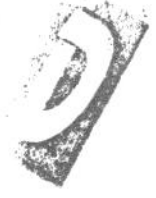

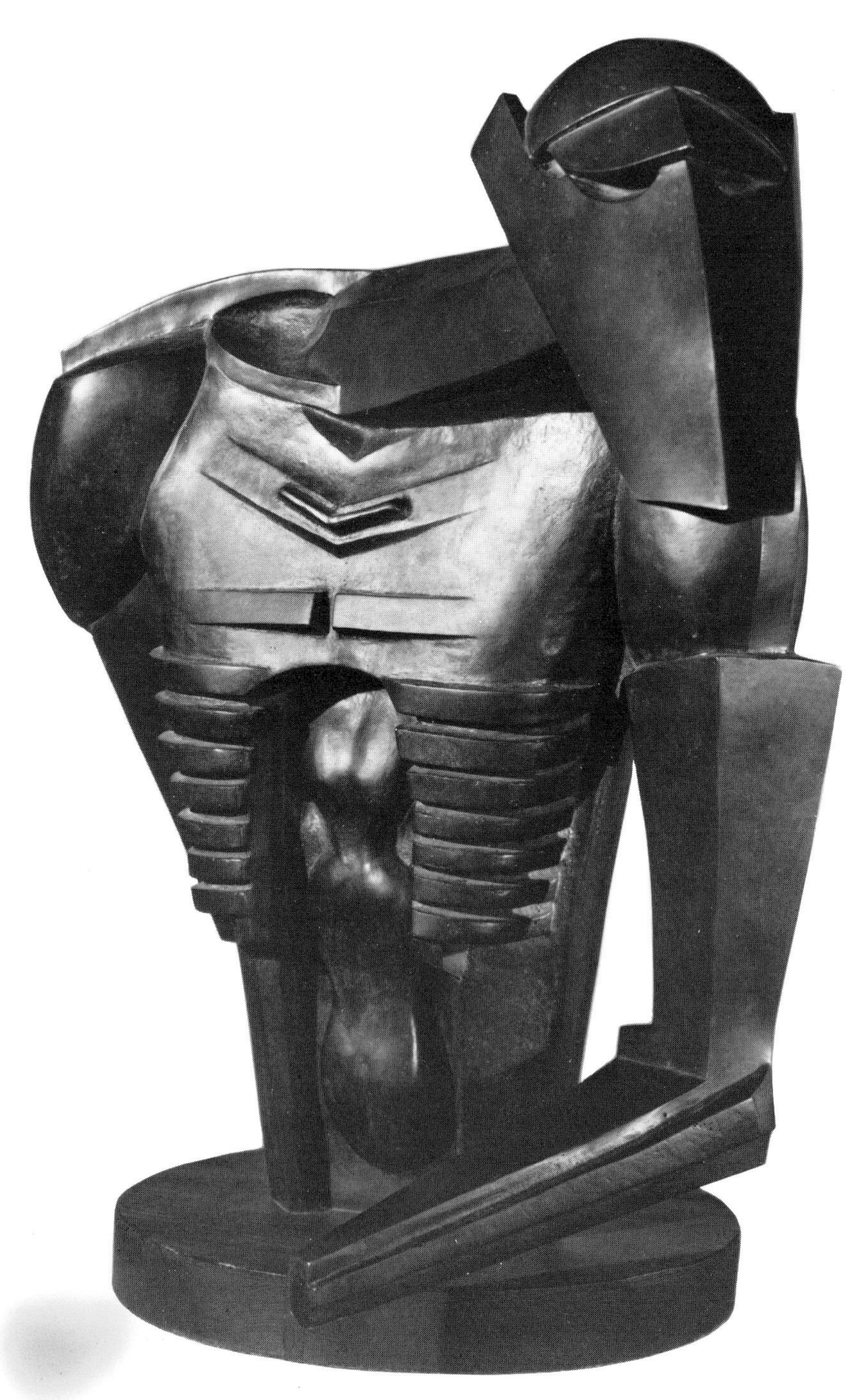

CONTENTS

Preface to the Second Edition vii

PART ONE: THE ORIGINS OF MODERNISM IN ENGLAND

1 Introduction: The Turn of the Century 13
2 From New English to Camden Town 19
3 'Post-Impressionism' and the 'New Movement' 45
4 Cubism, Futurism, Vorticism 75
5 The Great War 115

PART TWO: BETWEEN THE WARS

6 Hiatus: 1919–1924 145
7 Still Life and Landscape in the Twenties 167
8 The Development of Modernism in Sculpture 205
9 The Early Thirties: Unit One 231
10 'Abstract' and 'Constructive' Art 254
11 The Later Thirties: Surrealism, 'Realism', Romanticism 294
12 Postscript: The Euston Road School 333

Appendix: The Seven & Five Society 345
Notes 348
List of Illustrations 386
Selected Bibliography 395
Additional Bibliography, 1993 401
Index 402

PREFACE TO THE SECOND EDITION

This book was written with two principal purposes in mind. The first was that it should offer an informative and readable history of modern art in England during the first four decades of the twentieth century. In the course of a continuous narrative, I meant to make a case for the strengths of some early twentieth-century English art, and to support the view that those strengths are often considerable. The case still needs making. The sculpture of Henry Moore may now be ubiquitous, but Ben Nicholson and Barbara Hepworth are still widely treated as minor figures by comparison with a number of continental artists of lesser interest, while Walter Sickert, Harold Gilman and Paul Nash all remain largely unconsidered outside the British Isles, and virtually unrepresented in public collections outside the British Commonwealth, though each produced a distinctive body of painting in an individual modern vein.

The second purpose of the book was that it should serve to stimulate and assist inquiry into the nature of modernism itself. To pursue this second purpose was necessarily to acknowledge the limits of any history which concerns itself with English art alone, for there can be no adequate account of modernism in art which derives its critical interests and protocols from a survey of national tendencies alone. At the beginning of the twentieth century modern art very largely meant French art. By the time of the First World War, the idea of a modern movement had become an international preoccupation, but for the first three decades of the century at least there was to be no English contribution to this movement which a foreign observer would have regarded as central. To look for specifically English forms of modern art, then, is to examine the development of modernism within a provincial world. Unless pursued uncritically, a history of the modern in English art will inevitably concern itself on the one hand with achievements which were largely marginal, and on the other with a climate of persistent resistance and retrenchment in face of more uncompromising European developments.

To say this, however, is not to say that such a history must itself be marginal to the understanding of modernism in art. The preoccupation with modernity has in general been both inflating and deflating of the ambitions of art. Though it has served to encourage global and epochal visions, it has also entailed a sceptical attention to the actual conditions of practice. It needs to be born in mind that the grand modernist themes upon which art history tends to dwell were at specific moments and in specific places – not only in Paris or Munich or Moscow but also in Cumberland and St Ives – among the working materials of modest studios. If modernism is to be understood as historically specific, its larger pretensions must be studied in the light of clearly situated examples. The English art of the early twentieth century offers a fertile source of such examples.

To pursue the two purposes I mention requires of the book that it cope intellectually with the tension between them: that the larger questions of modernism and modernity should be kept in mind, but that the implications of those questions should be clearly exposed in discussion of local issues and incidental details. These implications are matters both of historical inquiry and of continual critical moment. To view a given work of art as 'English' or as 'modern' is to bring a range of valuations to bear – or a range of assumptions about what is and is not of value. To talk of a modern English art would normally be to convey a kind of double approval: to suggest that the work in question is at one and the same time modern in a culturally specific fashion, and representative of the national culture at its most progressive. It is also to imply that no contradiction is involved in this. But the evidence of history is that this last implication is by no means always a secure one. It is one clear lesson of the period under review – a lesson amply confirmed by the art history of the ensuing half century – that the meanings of modernism cannot always or often be made to coincide with the particular values generally associated with English culture. The resulting tensions are informative and interesting. The painter Paul Nash was one of those moved to speculation about the problems and possibilities of 'Going Modern and being British' – the title of an essay he devoted to the subject in 1932. This book offers some detailed material for the study of those problems and possibilities, though it does not pretend to resolve the former or to prescribe the latter.

A study with the aims I have specified could not conceivably be comprehensive. Nor could it be entirely objective in the selection of its material. To single out the modern from the national artistic culture is inevitably to discriminate, and to do so, moreover, in accordance with certain ideas both about the identifying characteristics of the national culture and about what is and is not modern. These ideas and discriminations will be open to question. The present study can lay claim to objectivity only to the extent that it is a history of a history: an account of what has already been singled out and considered as modern in the English art of the first four decades of the century. I do not pretend to neutrality, however, on those occasions when the 'English' and the 'modern' appear to be in conflict, nor are my own preferences altogether concealed from the reader. (It troubled some reviewers that they could not connect these preferences in terms of one coherent theoretical position – such as the 'marxist approach' attributed to the book by some. It did not trouble me.) In fact it is in the relatively circumspect manner in which many of its judgements are expressed that I would now see this book as most clearly marked by the conditions of its production. It was written as part of an enterprise on which several friends and colleagues and contemporaries were more or less consciously engaged during the 1970s: an attempt on various fronts to review the history of artistic modernism, and to recover a sense of the modern as a *contested* and contestable value. At the time it seemed important to resist that hegemonic and homogenizing representation of the modern tradition which had come to be identified as Modernism (with a capital M). That this was a necessary project was an intuition uniting certain groups and individuals in several countries who were variously engaged in art history, art criticism and the practice of art. It was a condition of this project that scepticism should be stepped up not only in face of the judgements of critics in the Modernist tradition, but also as regards the forms of art which those judgements had tended to approve. As a kind of corollary, the disparaged, the disregarded and the marginalised were viewed as the objects of prospective practical interest and as the potential bearers of critical virtue. In face of what seemed a Modernist co-option of the modern tradition, what we were looking for was a history to be going on with.

Since then, the rewriting of the history of modern art has proceeded apace, and the edifice of Modernist theory and criticism is widely supposed to have collapsed altogether under the incoming tides of the postmodern. During the period which separates the two editions of this book, it has been loudly claimed within the politics of culture that modernism itself is also passé, that is to say not only the tradition of critical methods and priorities but the whole modern phase in art which those methods and priorities served for better or worse to distinguish. Within the culture of politics over the same period it has also been loudly claimed that conservatism is modern.

What is clearer to me now than it was when the original text of this book was completed is that a third term is necessarily implicated in the conversation of values between modernism and Englishness. There can be no sensible sorting-out of the ground on which these values are related, that's to say, which does not recognise that each is inflected by the meaning accorded to conservatism. It is now necessary to make clear what it previously seemed possible to take for granted: that the critique of modernism (capitalised or not) has failed if all it does is usher in the conservative as a supposed form of modernity, irrespective of whether the conservatism in question is conceived in a political or in an artistic form.

This book is certainly designed to encourage a sceptical attitude towards some typical assumptions of Modernist theory. Among its other objectives, and against the dominant tendency of Modernist criticism, it is also intended to affirm the vividness of descriptive picturing as a mode of representation. But I did not imagine when I wrote it that it could be read either as a defence of cultural nationalism against the cosmopolitan tendencies of modernism, or as an argument for conservative forms of picturing in face of the difficulties of abstract art. There were reviewers who proved me wrong on both counts, however.

There is not much the writer can or should do to protect against those who read simply for confirmation of their own interests. But had I been able to anticipate the intellectual and political climate of the last dozen years I would have been more sceptical of the requirements of 'balance' in argument (though not of the requirements of logical adequacy), and less concerned about those of my preferences which comported with the judgements of earlier critics, Modernist or not. Were this to be a substantially revised edition I would not now wish significantly to revise its judgements upon the works of individual artists. But I would argue very much less circumspectly against the equation of Realism with an anti-modernist populism, and against the equation of cultural nationalism with a conservative virtue. For it remains the case that when either of these forms of equation is elevated on the cultural agenda, it is to some species of unmitigated modernism that we have to look for the renewal of critical values. (My circumspection was in part the consequence of the very enterprise I saw myself as engaged in at the time: an enterprise which required the maintenance of some distance from Modernist methods and judgements. It has to be acknowledged that if what is required is argument against anti-modernist populism or conservative cultural nationalism, the resources of Modernist criticism have still to be improved on.)

The writing of this book was part of my own process of learning about modern art in general. The most substantial conclusion I drew from it was that modernism and realism are mutually implicated terms if not coincidental as forms of description. To the extent that the virtues they stand for tend to converge upon the same range of objects, neither can be rendered consistent with conservatism. But the more the tokens of modernism and realism can be distinguished in practice, the more plausible it becomes to identify realism with conservatism, including those forms of conservatism which entail cultural nationalism. *English Art and Modernism* was not written in order to demonstrate a given pattern in these relations. But I hope that it will be found useful and interesting by those who wish to study them. And I hope it will serve as a reminder that the detail also matters.

It will quickly become clear to readers of the book that there is no way of using the designations 'modern', 'modernist' and 'Modernist' so as to avoid any overlap. They should be understood as adding various forms of stress to the discussion of ideas and examples. Throughout the book, 'modern' is used as a relatively weak and casual valuation – or at least as one which the reader might fairly take as reflecting my own views, however informally ordered and expressed. The term 'modernist' in the lower case is used to imply that some work or enterprise had been represented as modern in terms of a particular set of ideas and interests not necessarily compatible with the spirit of the text. The degree of coherence to be attributed to such ideas and interests is a critical issue for any history of modern art. A capitalized 'Modernism' and 'Modernist' is used where I intend reference to a self-conscious point of view or to the articulation of a purportedly consistent critique or theory. Thus a 'Modernist' form of criticism is one which offers to isolate and to identify 'modernist' art as a distinct qualitative presence within the modern. It was not my intention, however, to suggest that the relation between criticism or theory and art is necessarily intransitive.

The term 'avant garde' is used to signify a faction or aspect within a modern development which is nodal, often self-consciously so, since the formation of an avant garde implies the identification and expression of a common interest among a group of individuals. This study is largely concerned with those kinds of problems and interests which were distributed among various artists. This is not to say that individuals do not make history, or art history. But the book is not intended as an account of individual careers, and development in the work of individuals is for the most part considered with regard to the larger narrative. The need to advance this narrative is offered as justification for the scant attention paid to those artists such as Matthew Smith whose work was pursued during the period in question in circumstances of comparative isolation, apart from group activities. It is also the reason why no attempt was made to trace to the end of the period the careers of those such as Sickert and Wyndham Lewis who lived right through it.

It should be stressed that this book is concerned essentially with the arts of painting and sculpture and their near relatives, and with concepts of modernism in these arts specifically. Design and architecture are considered only when and in so far as they become implicated in discussions primarily relevant to painting and sculpture (as they do, for instance, in arguments about the nature of abstract art during the 1930s).

The pictures were chosen so as to provide adequate reference for the text without extending to illustrations of merely documentary interest. A decision not to include comparative works by non-English artists was taken for reasons of cost. In this second edition a major improvement has been effected through the reproduction of a number of works in colour.

I have corrected some errors of fact made in the first edition and I have extended the bibliography to take account of recently published material. I have also changed some misleading passages where I could do so without substantial alterations to the text. I have not attempted to revise my arguments or examples, however. To have done so would have been to produce a different book.

My considerable obligations to other writers are exposed in the Notes. Numerous individuals assisted my original researches by giving of their time in conversation, by responding to written inquiries, or by providing facilities and materials for study. At an early stage in the project from which this book developed I received hospitality and particular encouragement from Jim Ede, Ivon Hitchens, Ben Nicholson, Cyril Reddihough and Helen Sutherland. I remember each of them with gratitude. I would also like to thank those students of the Open University and of other institutions who put the first edition of this book to use in ways which have justified its reissue. My final and continuing debt is to the criticism and conversation of my friends.

Charles Harrison
October 1993

PART ONE

THE ORIGINS OF MODERNISM IN ENGLAND

I

INTRODUCTION: THE TURN OF THE CENTURY

Two significant and contrasting interests can be characterized in relation to English art in the later nineteenth century. On the one hand some concern was voiced for the social function of art within a society which derived much of its prosperity from industrial manufacture. At its crudest this was expressed in terms of a requirement that art should be morally uplifting to the population as a whole. During the second half of the century a great deal of priggish and sentimental art was produced, while some of the more worthy paintings of the same period, some works by Ford Madox Brown, Hubert von Herkomer and Luke Fildes, for instance, were designed to draw attention to the conditions of life of the working class (indirect though the artists' experience of their subjects must generally have been).

A better grounded response to a related set of concerns led William Morris to consider the condition of art and design in relation to the division of labour within modern society as a whole. Morris saw the 'degraded' condition of the great majority of contemporary art and design as a symptom of the degradation of personal and interpersonal values in nineteenth-century industrial society, and he believed that there was no prospect for the flourishing of a defensible and non-exclusive art without a revolution in society. The same technology which stimulated the development of design and architecture in the Modern Movement was seen by Morris and a few of his contemporaries as an overriding factor in the alienation of the artist from the world of values within which he had traditionally operated. Not that Morris regretted the technology; he regretted rather the development of a social and economic structure within which the effect of industrialization was to demean relationships of all kinds.

Morris's own 'medievalism' was in part an affirmation of the need for dignity in the labours of art. It was also a reflection of his desire to establish a context in which the artist's work might be seen in terms relevant to the criticism of social life and of conditions of labour in general. Art and design, by example, should affirm the entitlement of all men to a degree of that spiritual satisfaction which Morris saw as the privilege of a few.

> Unless something or other is done to give all men some pleasure for the eyes and rest for the mind in the aspect of their own and their neighbours' houses, until the contrast is less disgraceful between the fields where beasts live and the streets where men live, I suppose that the practice of the arts must be kept mainly in the hands of a few highly cultivated men, who can go often to beautiful places, whose education enables them, in the contemplation of the past glories of the world, to shut out from their view the everyday squalors that the most of men move in. Sirs, I believe that art has such sympathy with cheerful freedom, open-heartedness and reality, so much she sickens under selfishness and luxury, that she will not live thus isolated and exclusive. I will go further than this and say that on such terms I do not wish her to live. I protest that it would be a shame to an honest artist to enjoy what he had huddled up to himself of such art, as it would be for a rich man to sit and eat dainty food among starving soldiers in a beleaguered fort.[1]

In 1878, the year in which Morris delivered the lecture from which that passage was taken, James McNeill Whistler sued John Ruskin for libel. In a review of some paintings by Whistler exhibited at the Grosvenor Gallery the previous year, Ruskin had accused him of 'flinging a pot of paint in the face of the public'.[2] After a lengthy trial, Whistler was awarded a farthing damages. The payment of his costs for this Pyrrhic victory contributed largely to Whistler's subsequent bankruptcy, but history has tended to represent him as a martyr in the cause of modernism against moralizing Victorian reproof, and he might thus be said to have been vindicated.

Ruskin was on common ground with Morris in his belief that art could not, and should not, be considered as unconnected to political economy, nor as being in moral isolation from it. Whistler may be taken as representative of the contrasting point of view that art should be valued in terms of a set of culturally autonomous interests. In his evidence at the libel trial he described his reasons for titling the painting to which Ruskin appears to have taken particular exception, the *Nocturne in Black and Gold: The Falling Rocket* [1]:

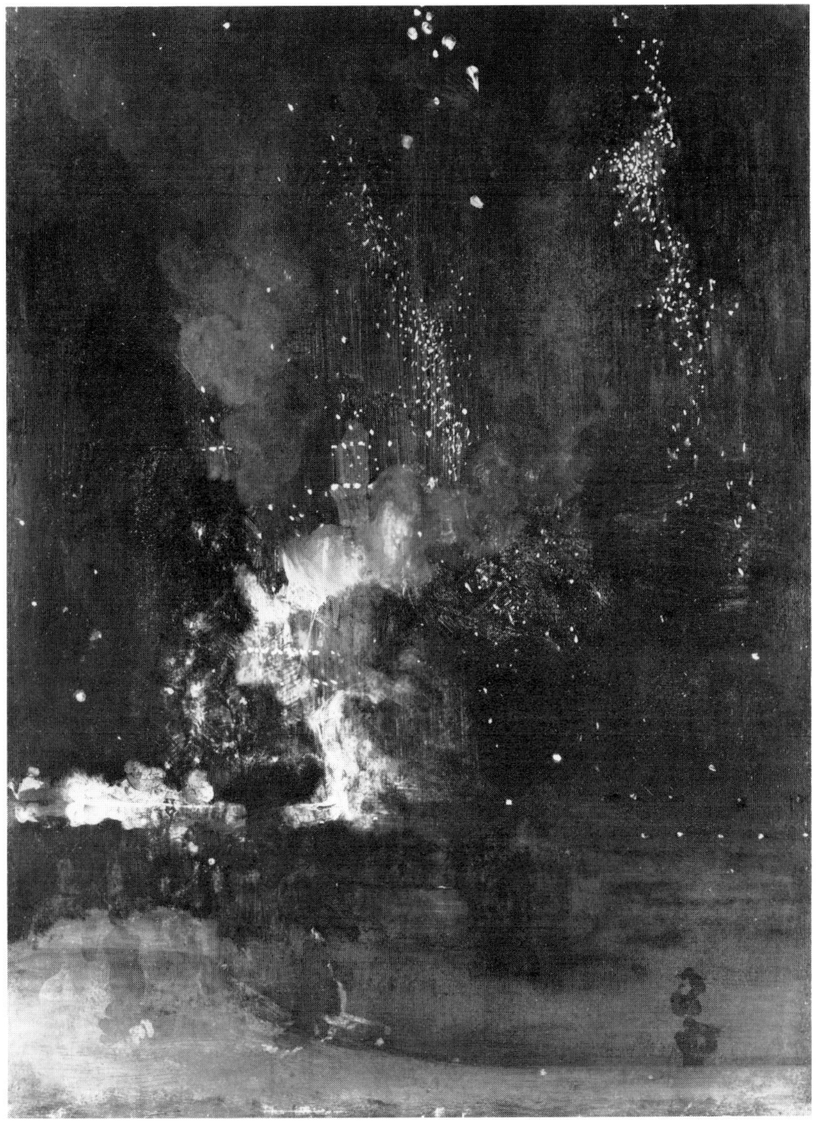

1. James McNeill Whistler: *Nocturne in Black and Gold: The Falling Rocket*, *c.* 1874. Oil on panel, $23\frac{3}{4} \times 18\frac{3}{4}$ in.

I have perhaps meant rather to indicate an artistic interest alone in my work, divesting the picture from any outside sort of interest which might have been otherwise attached to it. It is an arrangement of line, form and colour first, and I make use of any incident of it which shall bring about a symmetrical result. Among my works are some night pieces; and I have chosen the word Nocturne because it generalises and simplifies the whole set of them.[3]

The opposition of points of view is not always clearly expressed or perceived in the history of late-nineteenth-century art, nor in subsequent art history. In the 1860s Whistler had been a friend, and to a certain extent a disciple, of the French 'Realist' Gustave Courbet. After the period of comparative eclipse which followed the libel trial and his bankruptcy, he was re-established in England in 1892 by a retrospective exhibition of 'Nocturnes, Marines and Chevalet Pieces' at the Goupil Gallery. By this time he had become the principal representative in England for a point of view largely compatible with the positions of the French Symbolists and Nabis.[4] Edward Burne-Jones's retrospective at the New Gallery a year later might also have seemed to establish him as a kind of Symbolist. The works of both artists might be taken as illustrative of the view, typical of the Aesthetic Movement, that 'style' is something produced wilfully by gifted individuals.

Yet Burne-Jones had been a close friend and collaborator of Morris's since the 1850s and was lavishly praised by Ruskin. It would be a mistake to assume that there was somewhere a 'realist' art consistent with the ideas of Morris or Ruskin. Nor should we establish the contrast of interests simply as one which can be expressed in terms of some 'natural' distinction between the preoccupations of advanced 'artists' and 'practitioners' on the one hand, and of 'writers' and 'intellectuals' on the other, for all that this has become a well-rehearsed tactic in defence of modernist art. Morris was a professional artist and Ruskin a competent amateur. That there was no possibility of unity of theory with modern practice could be seen as a consequence of just that situation which Ruskin and Morris publicly lamented and which they worked to overcome.[5]

What distinguished Whistler, at least from our point of view, and what established his pre-eminence in English painting in the 1890s, was that he combined militant assertion of the autonomy of art with a practice which was seen to introduce his English audience to the technical interests of certain aspects of French painting about which they were curious.

> Art should be independent of clap-trap – should stand alone, and appeal to the artistic sense of eye or ear without confounding this with emotions entirely foreign to it, as devotion, pity, love, patriotism, and the like. All these have no kind of concern with it; and that is why I insist on calling my works 'arrangements' and 'harmonies'.[6]

In fact the assertion of works of art as 'arrangements' and 'harmonies' entailed an ideological and not merely a technical interest.

The influence of Impressionism in England was received by many of those who had been impressed by Whistler as confirmation of the notion that the art of the future was to be one in which a preoccupation with the relative significance of subject matter would give way to preoccupation with technique and with the expressive potential of surface. The weakness of the prevailing genres made this almost inevitable. By the 1880s the Royal Academy was already serving as the negative of ambition for the more 'advanced' artists, and academic style was identified in terms of technically conservative treatment of 'significant' subjects. With hindsight, and given that considerable interest in French Impressionism was aroused by exhibitions of Monet's works in London in 1887–9,[7] we can associate the proclamation of Modernism at the end of the nineteenth century with a concept of 'purity' in art, where purity entailed the pursuit of technical autonomy, a manifest if highly mediated interest in recent French art, and the avoidance of subjects which might conceivably be taken as moral exhortations.

This combination was one which a man of Ruskin's beliefs was bound to find offensive. The fact that much of the popular opposition to Whistler may have come from 'conservatives' and 'philistines', who would probably have been opposed to any significant technical change in art, should not mislead us as to the real value of Ruskin's case.

It was not a case which was to receive much support, however, in the ensuing half-century. The concept of 'art for art's sake', which had been promoted by the Aesthetic Movement in the last quarter of the nineteenth century, was the parent of the early-twentieth-century interpretation of 'art' as a condition of life virtually synonymous with 'civilization' (where the will to civilization was seen as being beyond the capacities alike of 'profiteer' and 'trade unionist'[8]). In the early years of the twentieth century commitment to the importance of French art of the later nineteenth became the avant-garde platform, and that commitment was proclaimed in terms of a strong belief in the autonomy of art. The typical slogans of those who occupied this platform were just such as would have earned Morris's whole-hearted condemnation.

> The artist and the saint do what they have to do, not to make a living, but in obedience to some mysterious necessity. They do not produce to live – they live to produce. There is no place for them in a social system based on the theory that what men desire is prolonged and pleasant existence. You cannot fit them into the machine, you must make them extraneous to it. You must make pariahs of them, since they are not a part of society but the salt of the earth.
>
> In saying that the mass of mankind will never be capable of making delicate aesthetic judgments, I have said no more than the obvious truth ... (Clive Bell).[9]

What is offensive about this is not that it was untrue but that its truth was empty and self-certifying. In the early 1900s, and for the rest of the first third of this century, successive waves of influence from recent European art raised matters of interest to other artists, specialists involved in the development of the technologies of painting and sculpture, and distracted the attention of all but a very few from the unresolved problems which lay at the root of the major controversies in the art and aesthetics of the nineteenth century. It is important to recognize that these problems thus remained unresolved. There was a spectre at the feast of early-twentieth-century English art, an untied loose end of that tradition of care for the representativeness of art's concerns which is often supposed to have been cut clean in Britain in the four years immediately preceding the First World War.[10]

The history of the art of the period under review can be interpreted by means of that schema according to which 'modernism' is characterized in various disciplines.[11] Modernist art is seen as restless, self-critical, self-determining. The artist who subscribes to the Modernist view of history values his practice in terms of its power to generate the sense of a need for progress, where progress is measured by the victory of one 'paradigm' of practice, one 'hypothesis', one 'concept of art', one manner over another less novel. As each manner achieves a measure of orthodoxy it is subject to increasing pressure from another or others, yet all within a somehow ineffable and socially autonomous value for the practice of 'art'. Controversy becomes a matter of opportunistic argument between practitioners rather than a matter of questioning the defensibility of the practice. 'Once we have judged a thing a work of art', according to Clive Bell writing in 1913, 'we have judged it ethically of the first importance and put it beyond the reach of the moralist.'[12] The alternative to compliance in this scheme soon becomes a matter of *de facto* resignation from the profession – or of dismissal by the equivalent of a bureaucracy.

Where this interpretation of history is adopted retrospectively, the Modernist critic or historian characteristically works to win for the subjects of his research the coveted status of 'most advanced', careless of the fact that they may have been best valued in their own time according to quite different criteria. Where the Modernist concept of progress is adopted in the practice and criticism of a current art the effect is to promote procedures for sorting 'progressives' from 'reactionaries' in terms provided by a pre-occupation with the formal characteristics of their work. During the years between 1900 and the outbreak of the First World War, the formulation in Britain of a Modernist interpretation of art led to the drawing of lines of demarcation according to novel types of distinction. These should not be regarded as any more defensible for the fact that they are now accorded the status of conventions within the writing of modern art history.

2

FROM NEW ENGLISH TO CAMDEN TOWN

The degree of support mustered then and now for Whistler's aesthetics as against Ruskin's, the comparative success (in the long term at least) of the former's appeals on behalf of his imagination,[1] the distinction accorded to John Singer Sargent simply by virtue of the facile elegance of his manner; these were all symptomatic of a change in the terms of reference for a concept of the artist's profession at the end of the nineteenth century. The typical British picture of the 1890s was of an unrealistic subject meretriciously painted. Whistler and Sargent, who were both American by birth, who both at times pursued careers in Paris, and who both had close links with French artists, were certainly more cosmopolitan than other artists in Britain around the turn of the century, but were as certainly not candidates for reprieve from William Morris's condemnation.

Whistler's atmospheric compositions had already by the end of the 1860s prepared ground in England for the acceptance of a manner of painting which, in the face of the natural or suburban world, served an interest in composing upon phenomena rather than in embodying significance. Sargent, twenty-two years the younger, was a close friend of Monet in the 1880s [2]. Sargent was among the founder members at the formation of the New English Art Club in 1886, and the example of Whistler was followed in the work of several of his fellows. These included Philip Wilson Steer, George Clausen, Sir John Lavery, Fred Brown, and the French painter Theodore Roussel. Sickert joined in 1888. The New English was founded by comparatively young men, largely to provide an alternative to the Royal

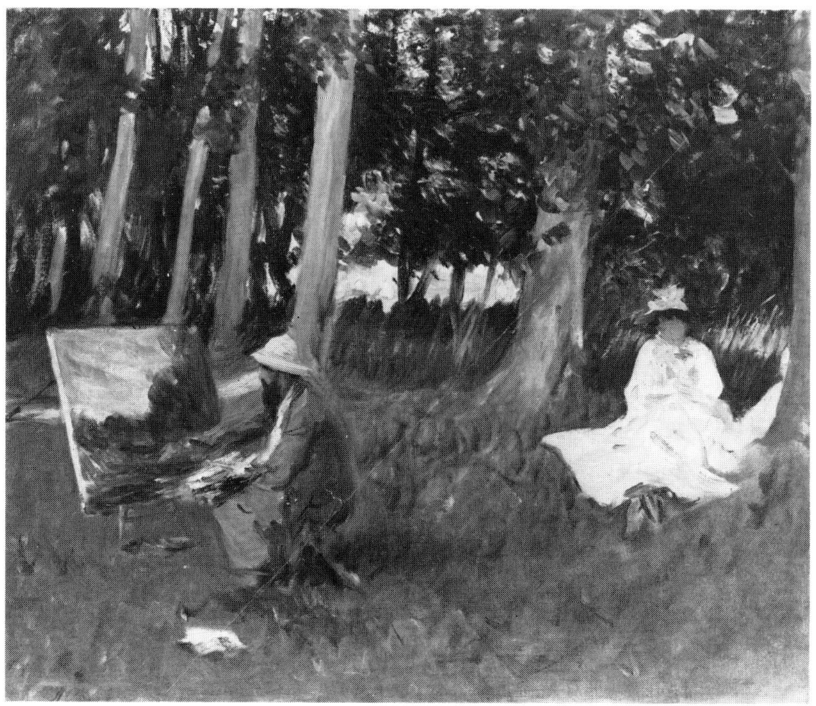

2. John Singer Sargent: *Monet painting at the Edge of a Wood*, 1888. Oil on canvas, $21\frac{1}{4} \times 25\frac{1}{2}$ in.

Academy, with which the majority of them felt out of sympathy at that stage in their careers. According to one witness the members were 'in utter revolt against the prettiness and anecdotal nature of the work at home, and enthusiastic for the impressionism of Monet, as well as for Manet'.[2] It had originally, and perhaps somewhat optimistically, been considered that the club should be called the Society of Anglo-French Painters. All the founder members had studied in Paris, though one has to exercise some caution against claiming too much for these studies. Wilson Steer, for instance, who was in Paris from 1882 to 1884, returned with virtually no understanding of the French language and with little enthusiasm for the Manet retrospective exhibition which he had seen at the end of his stay.

The strongest French influences on the majority of NEAC members were from men like Bastien-Lepage, Alphonse Legros and Carolus-Duran, all comparatively conservative painters by the standards of a Monet or a Renoir. Manet was generally admired both as an acceptable forerunner of Impressionism and as one who had paid due respect to the old masters and to Velazquez (then in vogue among painters in London and the subject of a study emphasizing the importance of technique[3]). It was, however, largely due to the influence of NEAC members that recent French studio practice and toned-down French 'plein-air' techniques were adopted in one or two of the more advanced art schools in London, notably at the Slade School, by far the most important college of art in London at the turn of the century. The most advanced students of the later 1890s, a group which included Augustus John, Harold Gilman and Spencer Gore, drew regularly from live models, painted direct from subjects rather than exclusively from drawings or sketches, employed 'daylight' tones and colours, and cultivated a certain informality.

Alphonse Legros held the chair at the Slade from 1873 to 1893 and was succeeded by Fred Brown, who immediately engaged his fellow NEAC member Wilson Steer to teach painting. Steer was one of those who made a sympathetic and original response to French Impressionism at the end of the century. During the 1890s he had painted some attractive sunlit beach scenes [3] with the bright colour and speckled brushwork typical of the later phase of Impressionism in France. These, and his informal figure subjects and nudes of the early 1890s, were his principal contributions to the development of modern art in England. By 1910 he was painting landscapes in a more informal manner, with more liquid paint and with more emphasis on tonality than brightness of hue. He turned increasingly to the use of watercolour. His career was typical of the main line of

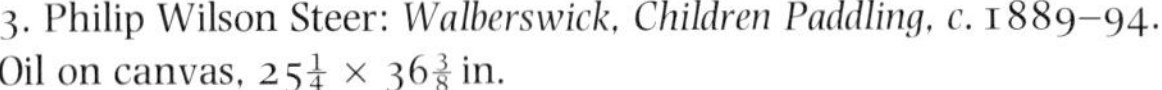
3. Philip Wilson Steer: *Walberswick, Children Paddling*, *c.* 1889–94.
Oil on canvas, $25\frac{1}{4} \times 36\frac{3}{8}$ in.

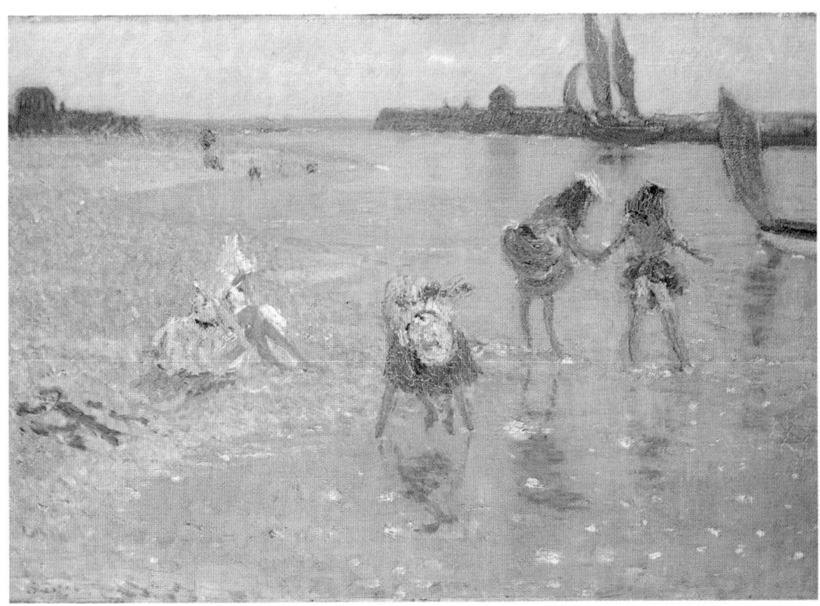

development within the NEAC: a gradual progress from moderate impressionism to moderate conservatism. It now seems more appropriate to see the work of his later years as a refined survival from the nineteenth century, an attenuation of the tradition of British landscape painting, than as a contribution to the development of art in the twentieth. But at the Slade his was the most 'modern' example among the principal members of staff.

Despite the innovations in studio practice and in the technology of painting, it was still considered by the majority that the principal obligation upon a school of art was that its students should become proficient in drawing (contrast Clive Bell's avant-garde assertion, 'All that the drawing-master can teach is the craft of imitation,' in *Art*, 1914), and the models of such proficiency were still considered to be the old masters. The dominating personality at the Slade, according to the testimony of Paul Nash[4] and many others, was Henry Tonks; and Tonks, though a New English member, taught drawing with an anatomist's rigour. Augustus John was considered one of the first of the Slade's 'modern' products, and during his student years, from 1894 to 1898, it was as an accomplished draughtsman that he starred. His facility in drawing was the foundation of his subsequent reputation and no doubt the main reason for his early success at a time when his more intelligent contemporaries were still unregarded.

Mary Chamot, herself a pupil of the Slade and of Tonks, wrote as late as 1937, in her *Modern Painting in England*, that John was 'undoubtedly a great artist. In the first quarter of the century the leader of all that was rebellious, independent and vital in British art.' (The emphasis upon rebellion is

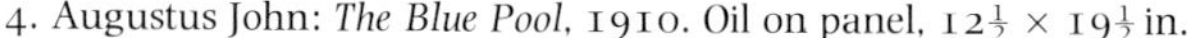

4. Augustus John: *The Blue Pool*, 1910. Oil on panel, 12½ × 19½ in.

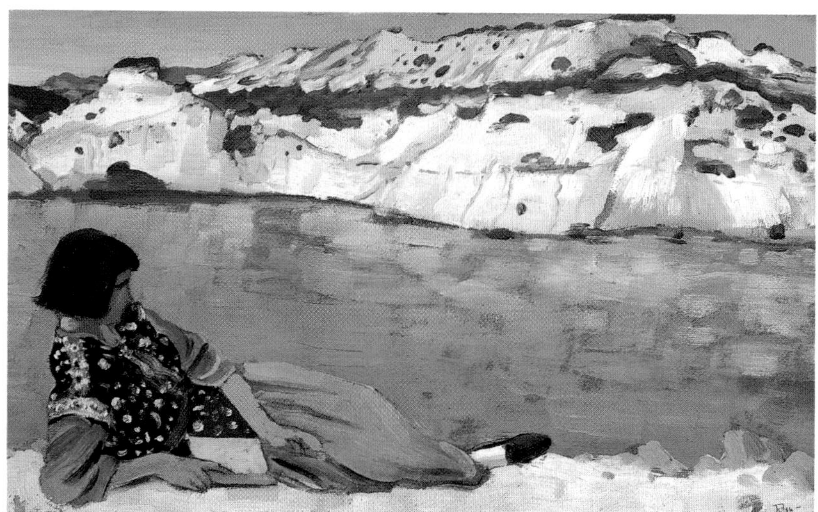

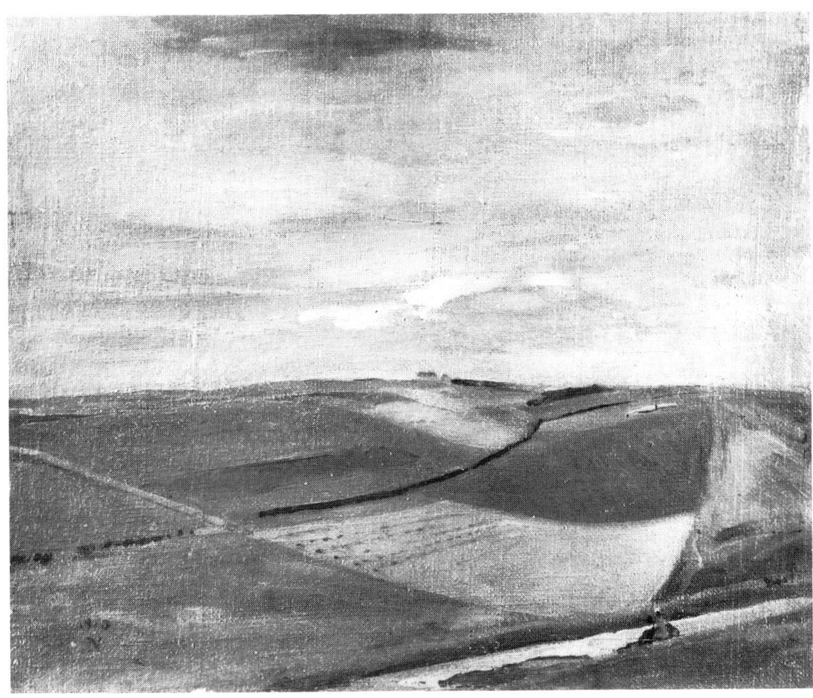

5. William Nicholson: *A Downland Scene*, 1910. Oil on canvas, 13 × 16 in.

significant. It was an aspect of the rejection of those moral values which were identified with the restrictions of the Victorian era, and we shall encounter it again in a different context.) John certainly conducted himself like a Bohemian, and for a while, from the time of his highly successful first exhibition in 1904 for half a dozen years, he might have looked to some like England's most modern artist – i.e., most like the image which the new French professionals were supposed to put across – but after 1910 no one as entirely unaffected by the art of Cézanne as John was and was to remain could fairly have claimed leadership of the avant garde. His small, idyllic oil paintings of 1910–14 [4], which were the prettiest he was to produce though he lived until 1961, testify to the endurance of a taste for lyrical subject painting untouched by French influences much beyond Manet.

The same might be said of the oil paintings of William Nicholson, a friend of John's and slightly older. His landscapes of the South Downs painted during the first dozen years of the century [5] have the same appearance of ingenuousness as John's figure-and-landscape paintings from Wales and the south of France; the former gain by an 'English' restraint and refinement of tone, the latter by a 'French' plein-air freshness of colour. John's and Nicholson's works, like Steer's after a certain date, stand apart from the main channels through which modern art developed, and they offer no alternative direction, but the most interesting of them (which are typically the most informal) are among the most literally attractive English paintings of the period. All three men continued for most of their lives to produce a fair number of good and professional paintings in comparatively conservative styles, and gradually fell from the view of modernist observers while many lesser painters became celebrated for their incompetent attempts to ape a modern manner.

Of all the established painters in England between 1900 and 1910, Sickert [6] best represented the case for the development of an independent art out of the influences of later-nineteenth-century French painting. This had much to do with the nature of his family background and early experience as a painter. His father was a Danish painter, himself the son of a painter, who emigrated to England in 1868 when Walter Richard Sickert was eight years old. His mother was half English and half Irish, brought up abroad. After a brief spell as an actor and a briefer one at the Slade he studied under Whistler in 1882–3. It is perhaps significant that he often

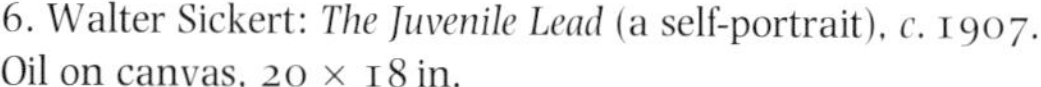

6. Walter Sickert: *The Juvenile Lead* (a self-portrait), *c.* 1907. Oil on canvas, 20 × 18 in.

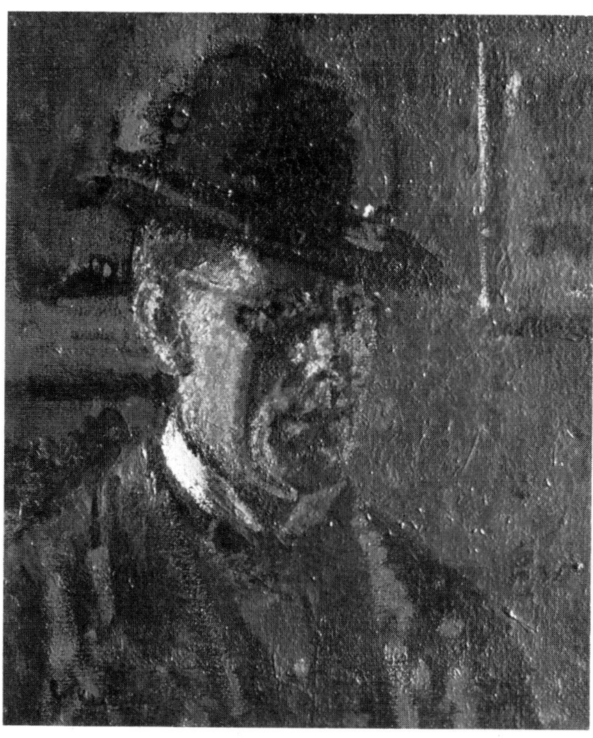

visited William Morris during the 1880s, in company with his first wife, the daughter of Richard Cobden, Liberal politician and free-trader. From 1883 until 1898 he was often abroad, and from 1898 to 1905 he lived in Dieppe, with long visits to Venice [7]. From his first meeting in 1883 for several years he was close to Edgar Degas, who must have provided a powerful antidote to the teaching of Whistler, and whose work, based as it was upon the study of the human figure in 'social' contexts, offered a strong alternative to the mainline of Impressionism. (Years later, in 1927, Sickert was to write of Degas as 'the greatest painter of the age'.[5]) Sickert's was a very 'modern' and a very cosmopolitan education for a painter in England in the late nineteenth century. Besides Degas, he came to know Monet, Pissarro, Gauguin, Signac, Bonnard and Vuillard. None of his English contemporaries could claim so extensive an acquaintance with the work of the French avant garde.

Although Sickert had soon gained a position at the forefront of the more progressive group within the NEAC, and although he had exhibited with a 'London Impressionist' group at the Goupil Gallery in 1889, he was no mere

7. Walter Sickert: *Mamma mia Poveretta*, 1903–4.
Oil on canvas, 18⅛ × 15 in.

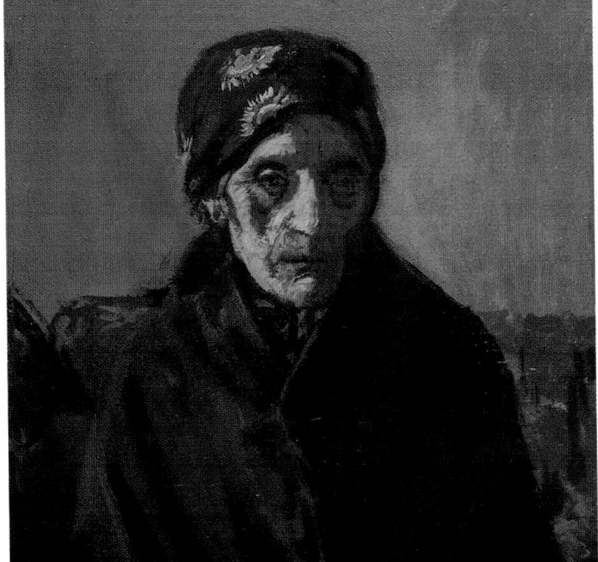

provincial Impressionist. He is impossible to pigeonhole. His introduction to the catalogue of the Goupil exhibition defines Impressionism in terms of a thoroughly Whistlerian aesthetic, as Wendy Baron has observed in her excellent monograph,[6] and yet in 1891 he was writing an article on 'Modern Realism in Painting' in defence of Millet and of painting from memory, as against the 'plein-air' technique which characterized the work of the Impressionists and the 'alla prima' touch employed both by the Impressionists and by Whistler.[7] He resigned from the New English in 1897, and thus, so far as younger painters were concerned, escaped identification with the increasingly conservative image of that body. Although he rejoined in 1906 after he returned to England, his contributions to the New English exhibitions must merely have made clear how much his work had developed meanwhile and how far his contemporaries had retrenched. It is also significant that Sickert remained virtually untouched by either Impressionism or Post-Impressionism in their more polar aspects. What he had developed was a procedure for making workmanlike modern paintings, palpably constructed, yet constructed on the basis of what he offered as faithful observation rather than proposed as mirrors of nature or reflections of the 'instantaneous'. He had learned from the 'documentary' quality of Degas' art and from the obstinate integrity of Pissarro's, and had also absorbed something from the early interiors of Bonnard and Vuillard, but there is little in his work that can be traced back to Monet, Renoir, Cézanne, Van Gogh, Seurat or Gauguin.

During a stay with Spencer Gore in Dieppe in 1906 it was clear that he had more to say about the academic artists of Victorian England than about the Post-Impressionists in contemporary France.[8] Sickert's continuing advocacy of the illustrative traditions of art, and his often teasing respect for ill-considered figures from the reviled Victorian era, were unfashionable at a time when modernist concepts of painting were increasingly gaining ground in England.[9] He was virtually alone in providing some means in his art by which a fraction of the more humanitarian concerns of the nineteenth-century artists might be transmitted to a minority among their early-twentieth-century successors. Although this was by no means the result of any kind of deliberate campaign on Sickert's part, his taste in art was certainly consistent with his social catholicity and with his natural inclination for what his contemporaries sometimes regarded as slumming.

Sickert first met Spencer Gore in Dieppe in 1904, when the young man came to visit him in company with William Rothenstein, an old friend and former pupil of Sickert's. The friendship between Sickert and Gore was crucial for the development of art in England in the decade before the first war. Sickert was forty-four at the time and Gore twenty-six, but the relationship which developed was not one as between master and apprentice. The previous winter, while staying in Venice, Sickert had embarked upon the series of paintings of figures in interiors which marks the beginning of his maturity as a painter, but he was later to pay generous tribute to Gore's influence upon his work immediately after their meeting.[10] Certainly by 1906, when Sickert loaned Gore his house at Neuville, the two men were close friends and were learning from each other, often painting together in the same studio.[11] Gore had recently adopted a method of composition of painting in which anecdotal or topographical detail was increasingly subordinated to the use of saturated colour, as a means of making vivid representations of brightly lit scenes. Sickert and Gore shared a love of the music hall and both painted some of their best pictures on music-hall themes [8]. So far as reconstitution of the drama of light and colour was concerned, Gore's was by far the more intense version, if not at the time of their meeting, then certainly by 1909. Gore learned from Sickert how to establish and explore a composition by means of preliminary studies, and Sickert learned from the younger man how to enrich and lighten his colours and how to use colour in aspects of his subjects which would

8. Walter Sickert: *Noctes Ambrosianae* (the gallery of the Middlesex Music Hall), 1906. Oil on canvas, 25 × 30 in.

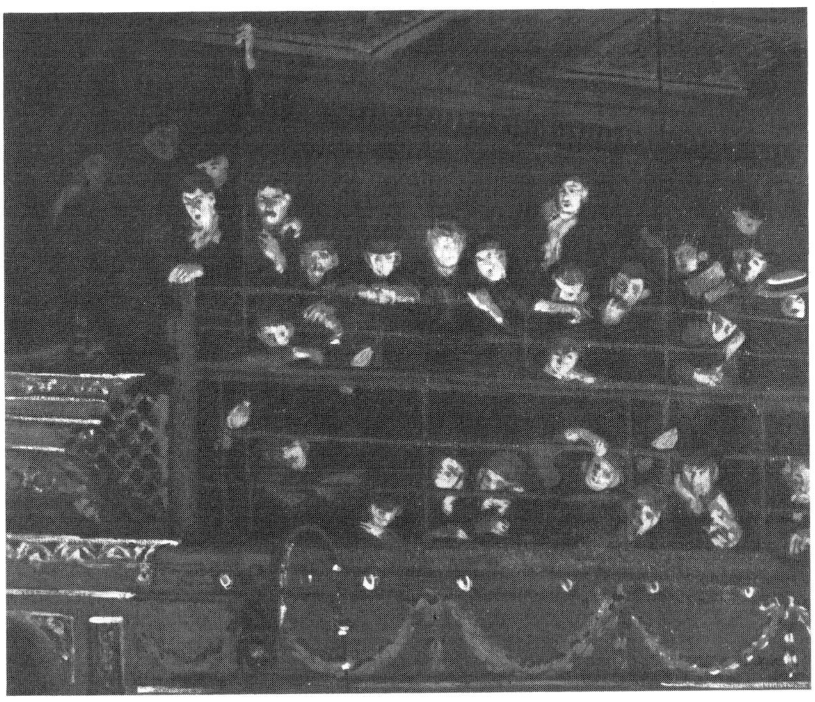

previously have been tonally described. Gore's paintings of the Alhambra Ballet, made in 1909–10, which already show an interest in the work of the Post-Impressionists such as Sickert never entertained, remain, in terms of vividness of colour and of atmosphere, among the most beautiful English paintings of this century [9].

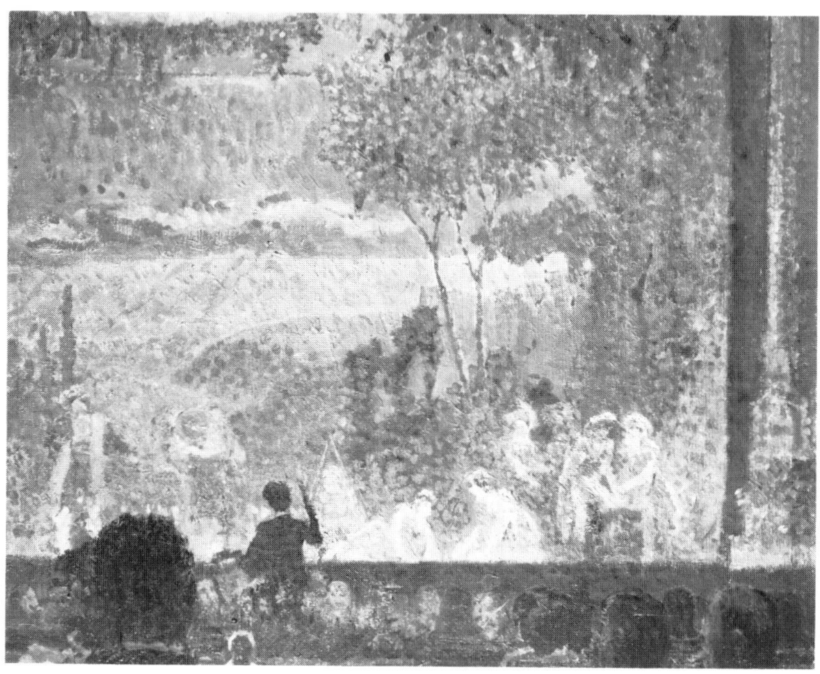

9. Spencer Gore: *Stage Sunrise, the Alhambra*, 1910. Oil on canvas, 16 × 20 in. (exhibited with the Camden Town Group, December 1911)

Sickert's return to England may have been prompted by hearing from Gore of the presence there of Pissarro's son Lucien, whom Sickert had met in the 1890s, and of the activity among younger painters interested in the development of an art beyond Impressionist influences. If so, his return served a mutual need. Gore had met Lucien Pissarro at about the same time as he met Sickert. The Impressionist's son had lived in England since 1890, and in 1900 had moved from Epping into London, where Gore had learned from him about the theoretical aspects of late-Impressionist and Divisionist approaches to colour and the transcription of light. Although Pissarro was exhibiting with the NEAC by 1906, it was probably Gore who renewed the contact between him and Sickert. It was around these three men – the two senior artists with unparalleled first-hand experience of late-nineteenth-century French art, and the alert and talented younger man – that a nuclear group of developing painters formed in the years between 1907 and the outbreak of war.

The principal meeting-place was the house at 19 Fitzroy Street in Bloomsbury where Sickert and Gore, together with the Rothenstein brothers and William Russell, had rented a couple of floors for exhibition

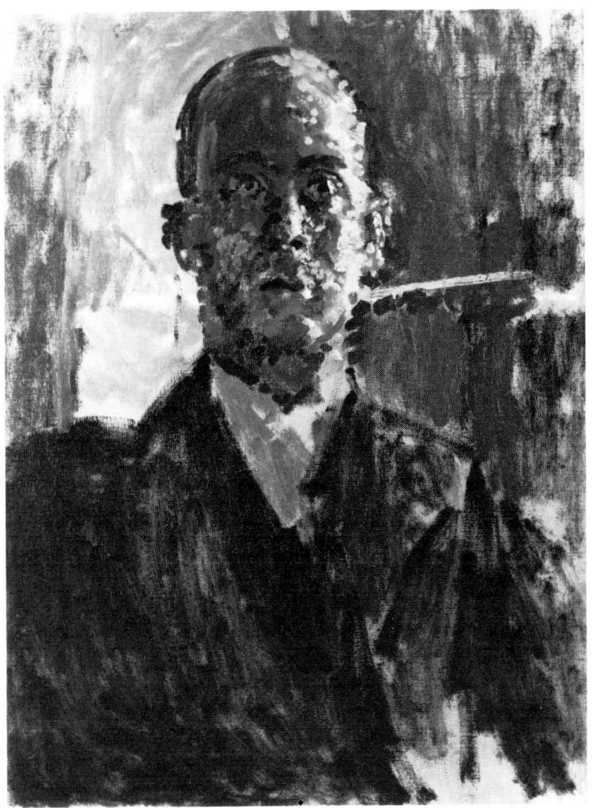

10. Walter Sickert: *Portrait of Harold Gilman*, c. 1912. Oil on canvas, 24 × 18 in.

and storage on behalf of the group as a whole. Harold Gilman [10], a close friend of Gore's since their student days at the Slade, became an early and regular visitor and was soon effectively a member of the core group. Walter Bayes was invited by Sickert, as were two women, Nan Hudson and Ethel Sands. Augustus John, Henry Lamb and J. B. Manson came occasionally. Rare appearances were made by Wyndham Lewis, with whom Gore had shared a studio on a trip to Madrid in 1902. Another frequent guest was the critic Frank Rutter, a supporter of the NEAC and organizer of the Allied Artists Association. The AAA was formed in 1908, with assistance from

Gore, Sickert and Pissarro, on the pattern of the French Salon des Indépendants, as a means of providing regular jury-free exhibitions. Its large, heterogeneous exhibitions at the Albert Hall (1908–14) provided a further source of recruits to be invited into the growing circle in Fitzroy Street. Robert Bevan and Charles Ginner were both introduced in this way, in 1908 and 1910 respectively.

Sickert himself provided an important point of focus for the younger artists. He was a highly articulate man, and his own views on art were obviously influential. He was also experienced in the kinds of machinations required to further a career or a cause in the social world of artists, dealers, critics and spectators, and he seems to have enjoyed putting this experience to work in the company of younger artists and on their behalf. He was particularly concerned for the circumstances under which art was viewed and purchased, and he was not one to avoid taking a platform. Though he had written often before, he began in 1910 to write regularly on art, mostly for the periodical *The New Age*. His essays are characterized by a tone of wry, commonsensical liberalism, often in correction of fashionable views: cutting John Singer Sargent down to size, but also castigating those inclined to scoff at Sir Edward Poynter, a senior academician and a painter of meticulous classical history-pieces.[12]

As a senior liberal, Sickert now held a position in relation to younger British artists comparable to that held in France at the end of the nineteenth century by Camille Pissarro, or at the beginning of the twentieth by Paul Signac, then president of the French Independents. He was particularly concerned lest the operations of dealers should force artists out of touch with those who might be prepared to buy their work for a modest sum, and who might offer exchanges of a different sort as well.

> Though I am a poor man, I can afford to buy a book of Hardy's a year, therefore I have had the opportunity of learning to love Hardy, but I doubt very much if the earnings of literature would enable Hardy to buy a picture by me or anybody else. Something in this system is wrong. It is not only their money we want, as the saying is. We believe our thoughts, which are not verbal thoughts, would be as interesting to them, are in fact as necessary to them, as theirs are interesting and necessary to us.[13]

Sickert particularly welcomed the foundation of the Allied Artists Association. Reviewing their exhibition of 1910 he wrote, 'Is the exhibition now open at the Albert Hall perhaps not a working object-lesson of the best elements of Socialism? Is it not a solvent, going concern founded by the poor to help themselves?'[14] (One should of course guard against establishing an image of Sickert as a consistent Socialist in practice or in principle.)

Through the gatherings in Fitzroy Street, Sickert was attempting to put into practice his belief in the need for 'a circle of devoted admirers' to buy works for their own houses ('small pictures for small patrons' as Louis Fergusson wrote[15]). As early as 1910 he was deploring the fact that the notion of the modern public picture for the public patrons of modern art (such as the municipal art galleries) was elevating the normal price of paintings beyond the reach of the average interested middle-class buyer, to the disadvantage of those artists who had yet to make the right kind of public reputation.[16] At 19 Fitzroy Street on Saturday afternoons, Sickert's associates among the younger painters, their supporters among the critics and their friends and potential buyers were invited to view the paintings displayed and to discuss them. In this way those involved found occasional sales free from dealers' commissions and were able to give some currency to their work, at least among the fellow members of that collaborative, interested community.

Sickert's prestige was of great importance in securing serious attention for the group of younger painters around him, and his concern for the survival of a certain dispassionate approach to subject-matter, a certain kind of painting, was undoubtedly transmitted to them. In particular it would be hard to overestimate the importance of Sickert's example in resisting the move towards 'alla prima' painting which the influence of Whistler and of the Impressionists (as their work was propagandized and received in England) had instigated among the majority of these new 'moderns'. The terms in which Sickert later came to express his disillusionment with the art of Whistler are significant of the sense of a need for consideration which he brought to all his own mature work:

> He accepted ... the very limited and subaltern position of a prima painter. These paintings are not what Degas used to call 'amenées', that is to say, brought about by conscious stages, each so planned as to form a steady progression to a foreseen end. They were not begun, continued and ended. They were a series of superimpositions of the same operation, based on a hope that the quality of each new operation might be an improvement on that of the last.[17]

The assertion of the need for a context within which deliberative criticism of the work can take place, in relationship to a plan, has since Sickert's day constituted perhaps the central critique of the practice of painting under Modernism.

Charles Marriot, author in 1920 of a history of *Modern Movements in Painting*, praised Sickert for his restraining influence on young painters in terms which make clear that it was no easier then that it is now to conscript

Sickert on to either side of the pseudo-war between modernism and traditionalism:

> ... Mr Sickert has come nearer than anybody to concealing the inevitable discrepancy between the facts and the medium. Or, to put it another way, to the theoretically impossible feat of using paint realistically and decoratively at the same time. It is only made possible by extreme selection of the facts and the nicest adjustment of natural rhythms – by the same expedients as good prose writing ... In order to design like Mr Sickert it is necessary to keep pretty close to the facts. That his influence is no check to originality is proved by the ... fact that several painters who have experienced it, directly or indirectly, have afterwards developed in a much more decorative manner. He compels the mastery of prose before experiments in verse. In view of modern tendencies he might be said to keep a hand on the brake of expression lest painting should run away into generalizations before it has made sure of its ground by the study of particulars.[18]

Marriot also praised Sickert for his domestication of French influences: 'He translates absinthe into beer.' Fourteen years later Virginia Woolf made use of a similar metaphor: 'He makes us aware of beauty,' she wrote, 'over the shoulders of the innkeeper ... The life of the middle classes interests him most – of innkeepers, shopkeepers, music-hall actors and actresses. He seems to care little for the life of the aristocracy whether of birth or of intellect.'[19] From a member of the intellectual aristocracy of Bloomsbury, the sister-in-law of Clive Bell, this was not necessarily the straightforward compliment it might seem.[20] In fact few of the figures which had come to populate Sickert's painting a couple of years before his return to England would have been accepted into British 'middle-class' society – even as characterized by Virginia Woolf. The superb paintings and drawings of nudes in interiors which he executed in Venice in 1903–4, in Dieppe in 1904–5, and in London from then until about 1910, represent the high point of Sickert's career and one of the high points of modern British art. I describe them as nudes, but they are perceived as unclothed women and unclothed girls, and they are painted with the same dispassionate but unconditional acceptance of fact as the portrait studies and theatre and street scenes which he produced during the same years.

These paintings are remarkable at once for their professionalism – for attention to the regulation of composition, to facture, to considerations of tonality, touch, etc. – and for their apparent lack of rhetorical devices. In favour of the tonal organization to which Degas largely adhered (and which is among the distinguishing characteristics of Cézanne's late work), Sickert avoided the early-Impressionist tendency to 'localize' subject-matter by making it entirely specific in terms of time, place and weather-conditions.

While the illustrative ingredients of the painting are generally specific – for instance the treatment of the individual painting recognizes the presence of a particular girl rather than hypothesizing a 'nude' – the overall composition, and particularly the disposition of tone, are attended to with the kind of deliberation reserved for attempts to establish value independent of occasion. The facticity of the surface is openly established, almost flaunted, the paint is always substantial and opaque (notably so in the paintings produced during his first four years back in England), yet the subjects remain entirely credible as representations. His paintings are evidently the works of a professional deeply engaged with the technology of painting, but none the less for that they embody a militant assertion, on Sickert's part, that, however much artifice may be required in their reconstruction and representation, the subjects for art should be generated from activities which are plausibly those of ordinary people. The paintings look like pictures of actual but undistinguished people in real but undistinguished places. As such they refer to a range of subjects and express a range of sympathies beyond what was generally deemed acceptable in English art at the time.

Sickert's paintings of the years 1903–10 take their place among the few modern paintings produced in Europe during this century which have been, at the time of their production, genuinely controversial in terms of subject-matter rather than merely in terms of treatment. In particular the group of two-figure compositions, with clothed man and naked woman, which culminated in the *Camden Town Murder* series of 1908–9 [11], incurred widespread disapproval and were regarded by many as blatantly pornographic. The measure of the price Sickert paid for his resistance to what he called 'puritan standards of propriety' is given by the response of his former friend and colleague at the NEAC, Fred Brown, principal of the Slade School, who wrote to Sickert that 'the sordid nature of his pictures since the Camden Town Murder series made it impossible for there to be any friendship between them'.[21]

It is perhaps again necessary to stress that Sickert's emphasis at this time (and it was a comparatively brief period) upon what his contemporaries for the most part regarded as 'sordid' subjects, was not the consequence of any 'social realist' conviction. If he admired painters like Millet and Courbet, as he certainly did, and as most of his contemporaries did not, it was partly in the context of his belief that 'the plastic arts ... fade at a breath from the drawing room',[22] but he would not have considered the expression of sympathy for the poor as any more likely a means to good art than the expression of adulation of the rich. He believed that the duty of the painter was faithfully to express a response to what he saw around him and to abstain from any practice aimed at the direction of sympathy. 'He [the

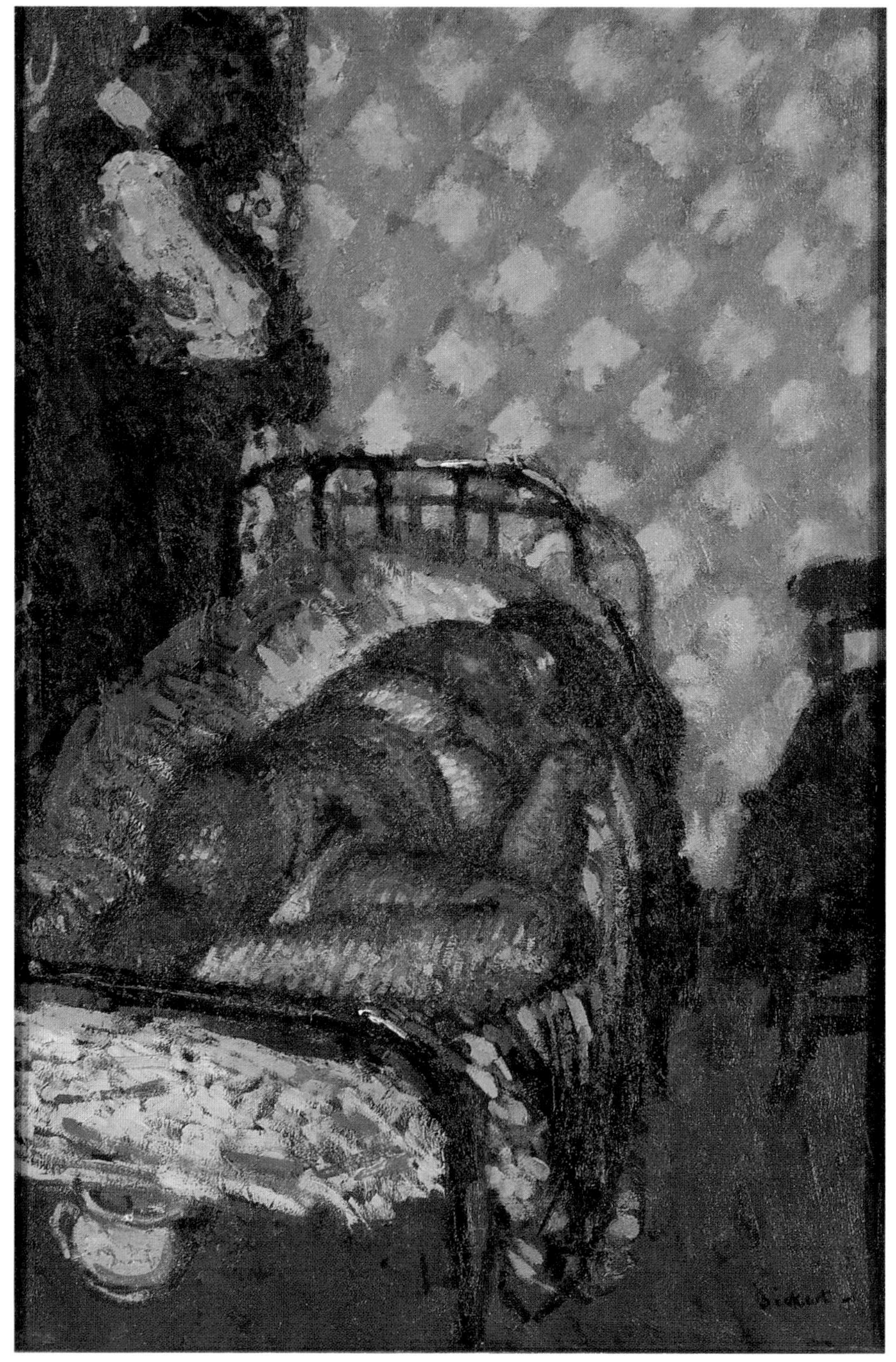

11. Walter Sickert: *L'Affaire de Camden Town*, 1909. Oil on canvas, $23\frac{1}{2} \times 15\frac{1}{2}$ in.

painter] has no business to have time for preferences,'[23] he wrote in rebuke of Whistler. But, of course, what you see when you look around you depends on where you are. And where you go is open to some choice and will follow from certain preferences. That the subjects of Sickert's paintings should have been asserted as representative of 'la moyenne de la vie', in itself constituted a criticism of established views as to where and how the painter should find his subjects, a powerful criticism, in fact, of other pictures. 'The more our art is serious, the more it will tend to avoid the drawing-room and stick to the kitchen. The plastic arts are gross arts, dealing joyously with gross material facts ...'[24]

In 1910, when Sickert came to review the achievements of the NEAC, he accorded due credit to that institution's influence upon the painting techniques of a whole generation: 'Technically we have evolved ... a method of painting with a clean and solid mosaic of paint in a light key'; but not surprisingly he found considerable fault with the NEAC approach to subject-matter: 'A glance round the walls of any NEAC exhibition does certainly not give us the sensation of a page torn from the book of life. There is an over insistence on two motifs. The one the august-site motif, and the other the smartened-up-young-person motif.'[25]

The NEAC was still recruiting from the Slade, and Gore was elected to membership in 1901, but as Sickert's criticism suggests, the club had failed to adapt to meet the needs of the new generation and had been becoming increasingly conservative. By 1910 many of its members had joined the very Academy they had originally banded together to oppose. Among younger painters like Gore, Gilman, Ginner and Bevan, 'Post-Impressionist' interests had come to supersede the now orthodox interest in Impressionism. An exhibition of 305 Impressionist paintings staged by Durand Ruel at the Grafton Galleries, with large representations of the work of Degas, Monet and Renoir, had passed without arousing much controversy in 1905. That was the penultimate year of Cézanne's life; Gauguin had been dead for two years and Seurat and Van Gogh for fifteen. Not before time, 'Post-Impressionism' had become a topic of interest. In 1911 Gilman and Ginner made a visit to Paris in the course of which they saw 'everything that could be seen'; this included paintings by Van Gogh, Douanier Rousseau, Vuillard, and even Picasso, Pellerin's Cézannes and the various holdings at Vollard's and Sagot's.[26] The formation of the AAA was a sign of the reluctance of younger artists to submit their work to the now established 'modern' institution. Harold Gilman, who tried, found that his work was rejected, and it was he who first suggested the formation of a new group. There was a strong need for a new organization in some context more public than that provided by the Fitzroy Street 'at homes', particularly after Roger Fry's exhibition of 'Manet and the Post-Impressionists' had opened in 1910. (The exhibition will be discussed in the next chapter.) In 1911 the more advanced nucleus of the wide Fitzroy Street circle was formalized into the Camden Town Group.

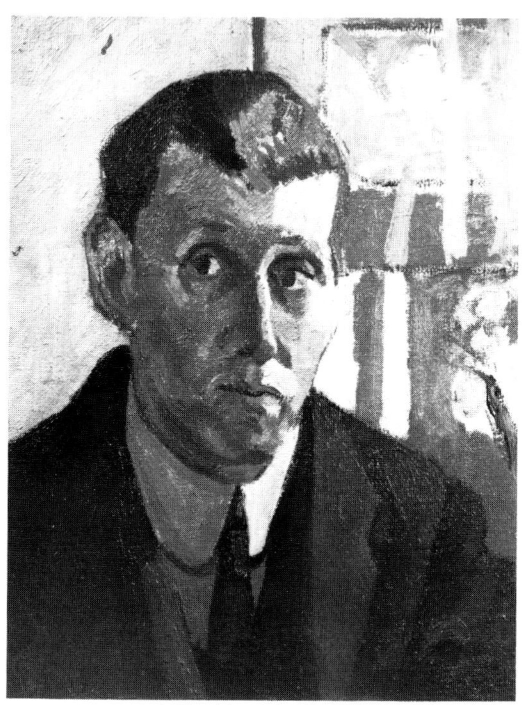

12. Spencer Gore: *Self-Portrait, c.* 1914. Oil on canvas, 16 × 12 in.

Gore [12], the most respected member among the advanced younger painters, was elected as president, and the other founder members were Manson (secretary), Bevan, Gilman, Ginner, Malcolm Drummond, Augustus John and his friend J. D. Innes (who died four years later), Henry Lamb, M. G. Lightfoot, Lucien Pissarro, William Ratcliffe, J. Doman Turner, Sickert, and Percy Wyndham Lewis (doubtfully accepted on Gilman's strong recommendation[27]). Lightfoot was replaced on his death a year later by Duncan Grant, a member of the Bloomsbury circle.

Although there was certainly no consensus of attitudes among them to French painting, the majority of these painters had studied or worked in France during a period when the work of the four principal Post-Impressionists, Cézanne, Van Gogh, Gauguin and Seurat, was already well established. Ginner had lived there until 1908; Gore had worked in Paris and Dieppe in 1904–6; Bevan had been to Pont-Aven in 1894, where he had met Gauguin; Grant and Lamb had both studied in Paris under Sickert's friend Jacques-Émil Blanche; John and Innes had both travelled and painted in France at various times; Lucien Pissarro had been involved in the development of Neo-Impressionism ('Divisionism' or 'Pointillism') almost since its beginning in Paris in the mid-1880s. The formation of the group reflected a new and growing desire for cosmopolitanism in British art. Although less than half of the founder members were to remain at all closely associated, that so diverse a number of painters should have banded together at all testified to an urge towards the centralization of the modern movement in England – a grouping of various forces towards some kind of common end. Such alliances were to become increasingly common, but for sheer weight of talent the Camden Town Group has remained unmatched to this day.

The group was formed primarily as an exhibiting society in face of the conservatism of the NEAC, and its first exhibition was held in June 1911. A second was staged in December of the same year, and a third, the last, one year later. Thanks no doubt to Sickert's prestige, all were held at the Carfax Galleries in London, and were followed there in 1913 by individual

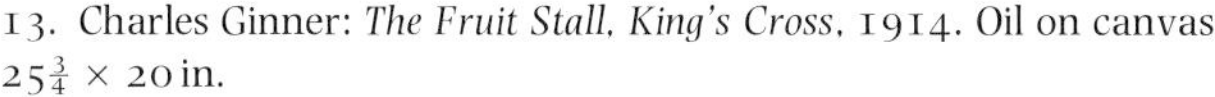

13. Charles Ginner: *The Fruit Stall, King's Cross*, 1914. Oil on canvas, $25\frac{3}{4} \times 20$ in.

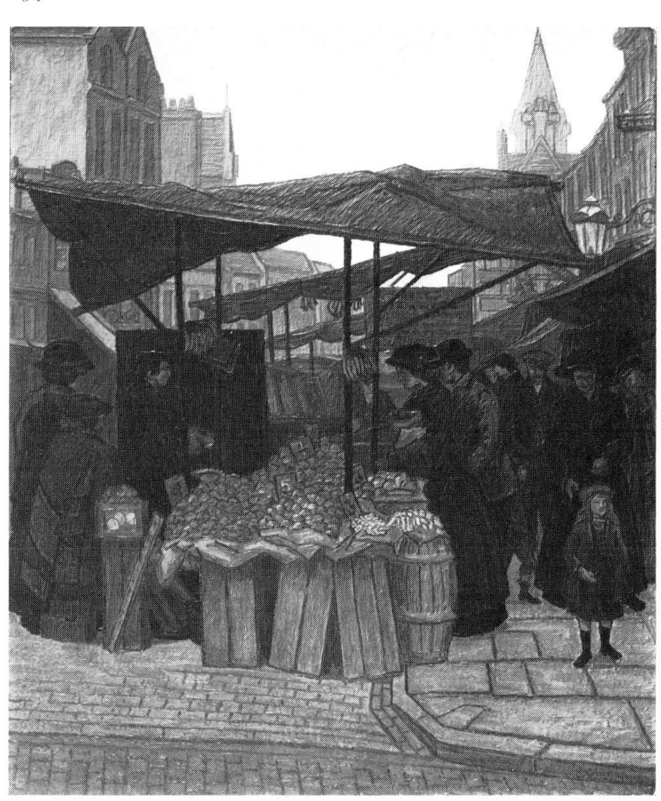

showings of the work of Gilman, Gore, Sickert, Bevan and Pissarro, who, together with Ginner [13], were the principal and characteristic exponents of the style which came to be associated with the group. This was certainly at best a 'Post-Impressionist' style. Among the younger men the colours used were often enriched far beyond the possibly naturalistic as intensification of hue took precedence over tonal organization – Gilman [14] and Ginner in particular came to paint at times like English Fauves, though the true influences were Van Gogh and Gauguin; there was a tendency, recalling Gauguin's 'cloisonnism', to enclose areas of dense impasto by means of a strong outline, particularly in the work of Bevan and in some of Gore's paintings such as *The Balcony at the Alhambra* of 1911; and there was an occasional Cézannesque organization of forms across the picture surface into highlighted planes and shadowed backgrounds, particularly in Gore's work of 1913–14. Sickert had already, by the time of the first Camden Town Group exhibition, begun to turn from the dense, heavily-worked surfaces of the *Camden Town Murder* paintings back to a lighter technique more consistent with his work before 1906. By the time of the last group exhibition his period of major influence over the younger painters was at an end, although he had almost another thirty years of work before him. The typical and most successful exponents of 'Camden Town' painting were Gore and Gilman.

Apart from the benefits they were also able to draw from late-nineteenth-century French painting, what distinguished the better painters of the Camden Town Group was their selection and interpretation of subjects. Camden Town, then a comparatively depressed area of mostly lower-middle-class housing, had provided motifs for Sickert, and the paintings of the other members of the nuclear group displayed a generally compatible range of unaugust sites and unsmartened persons. Gore's 1912 painting of *Harold Gilman's House, Letchworth* [15] with its bright reds and greens and muted yellows, showed just how much could be done to render vivid but not sensational a motif which was positively Cézannesque in its ordinariness. In his bed-sitter interiors of the years 1910–17 Gilman similarly made rich and vivid paintings out of everyday subjects.

By their unsentimental treatment of figures, interiors, and urban and suburban landscapes these painters accorded due respect to the most widely distributable (if still comparatively uncelebrated) interests of late-nineteenth-century English painting: a concern to come to terms with the furniture of a social world which a literary mythology did not any longer seem appropriately to embroider; a respect for the appearance of otherwise uncelebrated people; and an aspiration faithfully to record the conditions and surroundings in which unglamorous lives were lived. In the twentieth

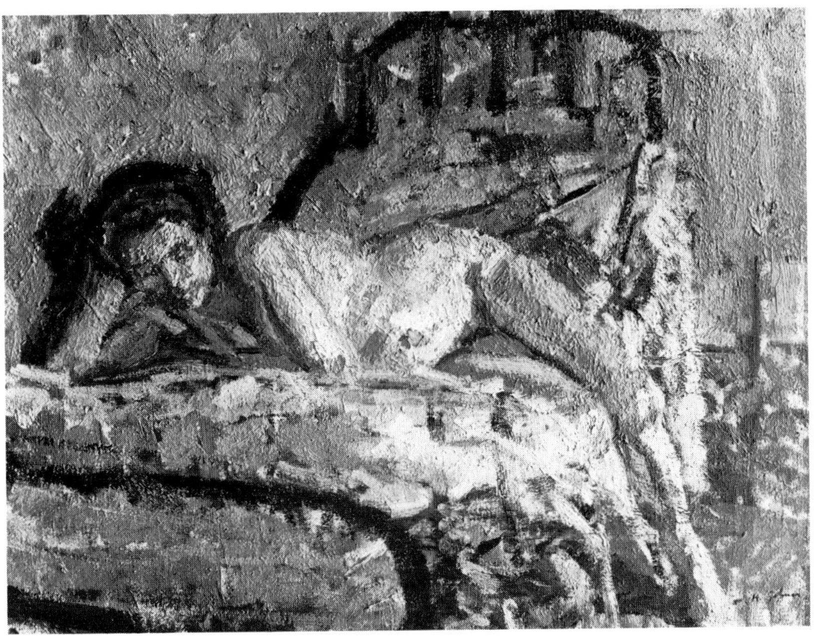

14. Harold Gilman: *The Model, Reclining Nude, c.* 1910–11. Oil on canvas, 18 × 24 in.

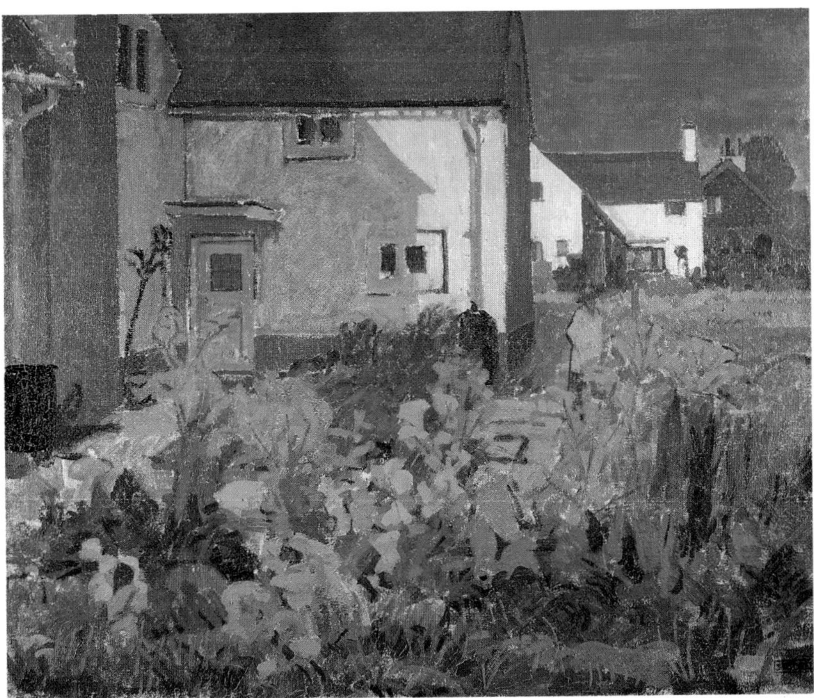

15. Spencer Gore: *Harold Gilman's House, Letchworth,* 1912. Oil on canvas, 25 × 30 in.

century at least, such concerns have usually been pursued in painting, if at all, at the expense of 'modernity' and sophistication of style. At their best the more representative painters of the Camden Town Group offered exceptions to this rule. The most widely esteemed and rewarded artists of the time were skilled men who painted portraits glamorizing the wealthy, as did Sargent, John Lavery and William Orpen, or who painted genre scenes sentimentalizing the poor, as did Alfred Munnings. Augustus John squandered much of his considerable talent doing both these things. During this period Sickert and the younger painters of the Camden Town Group stood for virtues central to the practice of art as a social activity, and for all their bright colours and studied forms it was this, rather than the mere pursuit of modernist style, that distinguished and dignified their work [16].

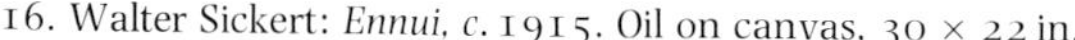

16. Walter Sickert: *Ennui*, *c.* 1915. Oil on canvas, 30 × 22 in.

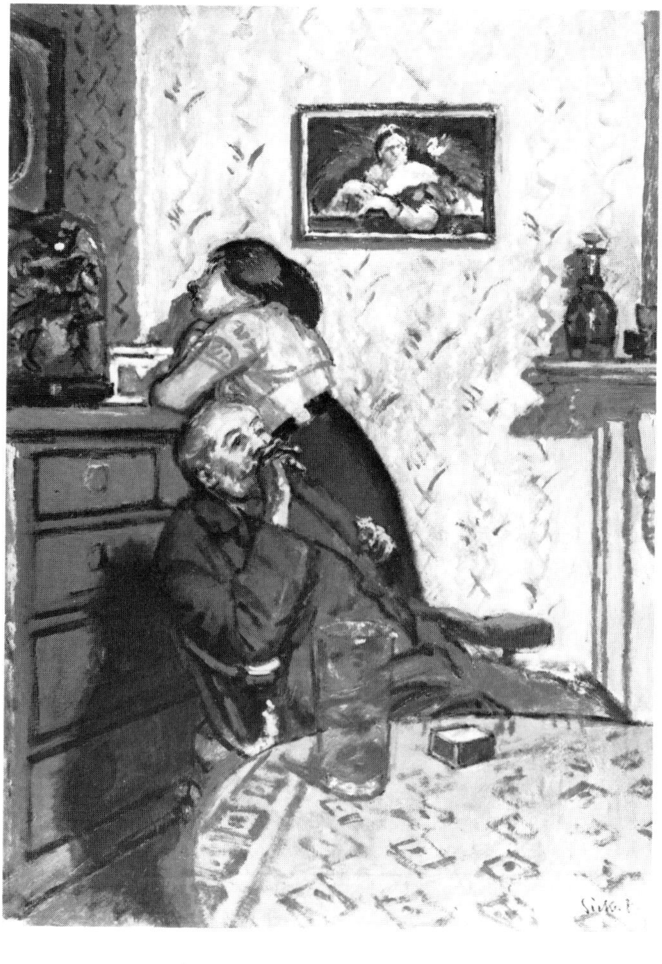

The outbreak of war in 1914, and the death of Gore from pneumonia in the same year, dispersed one of this century's very few successful, modern, realist movements. Ginner and Gilman exhibited as 'Neo-Realists' in the Goupil Gallery Salon and in the AAA exhibition of 1913, and in a two-man exhibition at the Goupil Gallery in April 1914, but Ginner was not really a strong painter and Gilman was to die of influenza in 1919. In 1915 the principle of Camden Town painting was perpetuated when Bevan, Gilman and Ginner were joined by John Nash in the formation of the Cumberland Market Group, but this alliance was subsidiary to the larger London Group, an amalgamation of Camden Town and Vorticist forces under Gilman's presidency, in which all four were involved and which had held its first exhibition the previous year. Within the London Group, which has survived to this day, one can find lingering traces of the characteristics of Camden Town painting ranging over a long period, but not generally such as do much service to the memory of Sickert, Gore or Gilman.

Ginner's article on 'Neo-Realism', first published in January 1914[28] and used as a foreword to the catalogue of the 'Neo-Realist' exhibition, expresses the aspirations of the best of Camden Town painting between the meeting of Sickert and Gore and the death of Gilman.

> It is a common opinion of the day, especially in Paris (even Paris can make mistakes at times), that Decoration is the unique aim of Art. Neo-Realism has another aim of equal importance . . . It must interpret that which, to us who are of this earth, ought to lie nearest to our hearts, i.e. life in all its aspects, moods and developments.
>
> Realism, loving life, loving its age, interprets its epoch by extracting from it the very essence of all it contains of great or weak, of beautiful or of sordid, according to the individual temperament.

The works which best fulfil these aspirations were those painted by Sickert between 1903 and 1910 and by Gilman in the last half-dozen years of his life. Gilman's work in particular offered a strong example of the possibility of coincidence of what have since been characterized as incompatible interests in the practice of modern art: decorative vividness on the one hand and critical interpretation of socially vivid subjects on the other. Very few painters in any country during this century have managed to reconcile these interests without recourse to a certain schematicness and informality of style, and/or to a kind of 'literary' symbolism (cf., for example, the painting of Max Beckmann, and of Picasso during the 1930s). Almost alone of those who achieved such a reconciliation, Gilman managed to embody a quality of solidity and monumentality in his compositions without evoking a sense of privileged allusion to some culture outside the

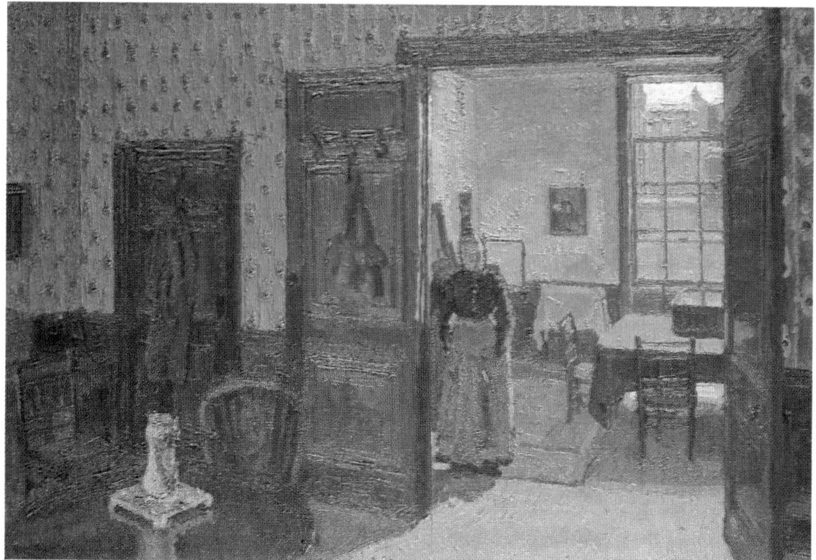

17. Harold Gilman: *Interior with Mrs Mounter*, 1916–17. Oil on canvas, 20 × 30 in.

world of reference of the subject itself [17, 18]. He was perhaps the only English painter of his generation to have profited from the observation that the quality of monumentality in some works of the Post-Impressionists – Cézanne, Gauguin, Seurat and Van Gogh – was in part produced by a kind

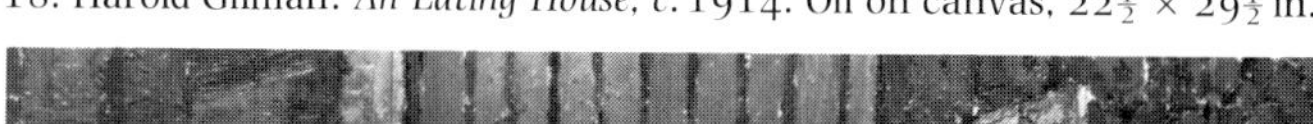

18. Harold Gilman: *An Eating House*, *c*. 1914. Oil on canvas, $22\frac{1}{2} \times 29\frac{1}{2}$ in.

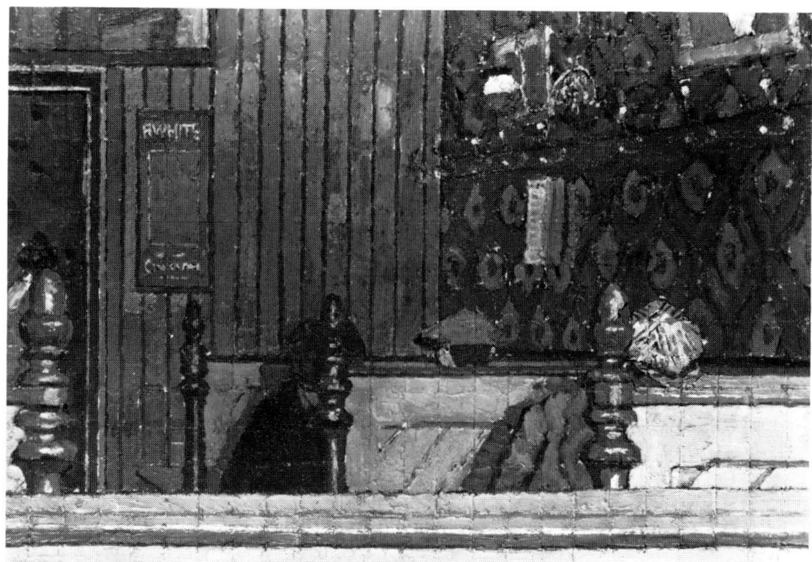

of traditional and social engagement with the subjects of their paintings, and not merely by a radical preoccupation with technique. (Ginner described Van Gogh as 'the most intense of modern Realists' in his 'Neo-Realism' article.)

Gilman's concern for intensity of colour on the painted surface did not distract him from his sense of the need to offer a defensible reconstruction of what he had seen and remembered. In his later works, the fidelity of his reconstitution was in great part a function of technical rigour. His procedure eliminated the possibility of fudging, getting it half-right, achieving elegance at the expense of description. Although the concept of systematicness in preparation was consistent both with the technical practice of Sickert and with what was taught at the Slade when Gilman was a student, no other English painter at the time did as much as he to devalue those bravura technical practices and mannerisms which were conventionally allowed to abbreviate the procedures of description.

> Good craftsmanship must be the natural result of a strong, forcible, and deliberate self-expression ... Neo-Realism by its very ideals finds itself opposed to the slap-dash, careless and slick painting which has been and is still so much in vogue.[29]

Though his independent drawings, particularly those of seascapes, were reminiscent of reed-pen drawings by Van Gogh, Gilman's preparatory studies for paintings had features in common with the drawings of a technical illustrator. The painting of *Leeds Market* now in the Tate Gallery may serve as an example of his practice [19]. It is clear from a preparatory drawing (also in the Tate) that in looking at the complicated roof structure he was concerned to represent it not so much 'expressively' as accurately, where the criteria of accuracy were such as might have been assented to by an engineer. This implies a better-than-merely-aesthetic concept of the significance of detail in representation; i.e., a concept grounded in some sense of criteria of efficiency in practices other than those of the modernist painter. On the other hand, in his representation of a barrel in the foreground, Gilman used bright pinkish-orange lettering against a bluish-green background – a contrast of complementary colours typical of 'Post-Impressionist' preoccupations with the supposed autonomy of decorative effects.[30] What he had seen may actually have furnished some genetic cause for this contrast, but the intensification of the colour is perceived essentially as a means to the enrichment of the painted surface itself.

Intensification of colour in a painting is normally pursued at the expense of topographical detail; i.e. it entails formalization. But Gilman seems to have achieved a high degree of intensification of colour without loss of clarity in composition and without the kind of arbitrariness of formalization

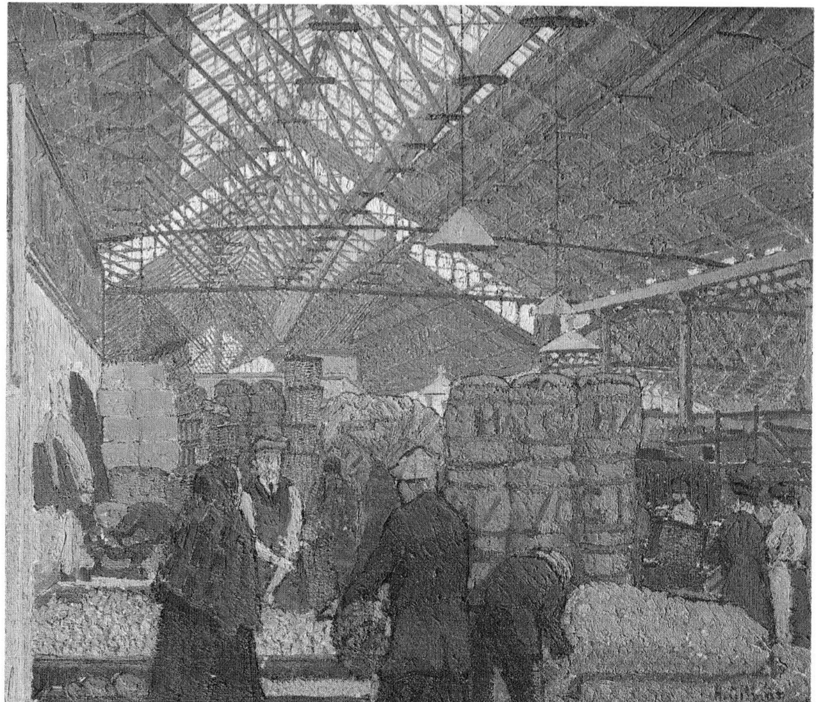

19. Harold Gilman: *Leeds Market, c.* 1914. Oil on canvas, 20 × 24 in.

which characterizes so much of modern art (for example the transforming of human figures into 'mechanical' puppets). Despite the richness of colour in the scene they occupy, the figures in his painting of Leeds Market are plausibly represented as individuals engaged on activities proper to their time and place.

The conventions of modernist practice have normally worked to single out certain aspects in a subject at the expense of others, and thus to provide a set of closures on 'extraneous' interests. Unlike the great majority of his contemporaries, Gilman seems to have approached the making of a painting as a dialectical activity, in which it was appropriate that there should be some adjustment and extension of technical interests and competences according to the possibly various aspects and interests proper to a given subject. The finished painting was the occasion of coincidence of these interests: a well-formed decorative object, serving critically to order an open but not arbitrary set of possibilities for the representation of the visible world.

'I consider his death', Wyndham Lewis wrote in 1919, 'a flat contradiction to every feeling that one had about his destiny.'[31]

3

'POST-IMPRESSIONISM' AND THE 'NEW MOVEMENT'

I

'On or about December 1910 human character changed,' according to Virginia Woolf.[1] From 8 November 1910 till 15 January 1911 the Grafton Galleries in London were the scene of the first of two major exhibitions principally organized by the critic Roger Fry, with the assistance of Clive Bell. The two had met earlier in the year and had found common ground in their enthusiasm for recent French art. Under the title 'Manet and the Post-Impressionists' the first exhibition provided a survey of late-nineteenth- and early-twentieth-century French painting unequalled in London to this day. There were two hundred and twenty-eight items in the catalogue, of which only nine were Manets. His work was already known and respected in England, and his comparatively uncontroversial name was probably used in part to provide the new movement with a respectable base. His inclusion also served, however, to highlight the exclusion of the Impressionists from a place in the history which was being established. The catalogue listed twenty-one works by Cézanne, twenty-two by Van Gogh and forty-six by Gauguin. There was also a considerable selection of work by painters associated with Fauvism, including nine paintings of Vlaminck's Cézannesque phase and three paintings each by Matisse, André Derain and Othon Friesz. Among the works on paper were twelve by Matisse and seven by Picasso. Matisse was also represented by eight sculptures.

Gauguin was already comparatively well known and popular in informed circles in England; the mythology surrounding the name of Van Gogh had prepared sufficient ground for the conditional acceptance of his paintings as the work of an inspired madman; and works by Cézanne had been included in exhibitions of 1898, 1906 and 1908 in London without arousing any great controversy. Considered as interesting, if odd, foreign painters, Gauguin and Van Gogh were unlikely to stimulate furious argument, and as for Cézanne, until Fry's curiosity was aroused by the 1906 showing he was almost universally regarded in England as an incompetent Impressionist.[2] (Even among the Camden Town painters it was not until well after 1910 that his influence made itself felt.) But at the Grafton Galleries these painters, and particularly Cézanne, were presented as the founding fathers of a new movement, *the* New Movement, of which Matisse and Picasso were to be regarded as the present torchbearers.

At the most superficial level, the effect of the exhibition was to bring the British public and the British art world abruptly up to date with the state of art in France,[3] but the outrage which the exhibition caused among members of the public and of the art world alike can only be explained in terms of the material it offered for a more fundamental revision of ideas: it was not merely a question now of what was going on in art, but of what criteria were to be considered appropriate in the modern period for identifying an endeavour as a work of art in the first place. This was the first exhibition in England – the first of many – at which a substantial number among the visitors were confronted not merely with a display of what they regarded as bad art, but with a selection which included much which they were unprepared to class as art at all. The period of provincial modernism in British art was thus launched with a vengeance.

'The period in which we find ourselves ... begins with the maturity of Cézanne (about 1885),' Bell wrote in 1913.[4] The Modern Movement was thus established as essentially a Post-Impressionist movement, and there is the ghost of a suggestion that the maturity of Cézanne established the *terminus post quem* for an historic epoch and not merely for a period in the history of art. The later paintings of Monet, which it would not now be controversial to class among the major works of twentieth-century art, were excluded from the Modernist canon: 'polychromatic charts of desolating dullness', Bell called them.[5] Years later he wrote, 'In 1911 ... to many of us Post-Impressionism meant anti-Impressionism';[6] the 'New Movement' was thus set up, in line with the new logic of development under Modernism, at the expense of a previous movement with which many who saw themselves as occupying positions at the centre of the English vanguard had only recently made themselves comfortable.

Reactions to the exhibition were mixed and largely extreme. There was a predictably sceptical response from the moderate liberal factions, but the more entrenched artists, critics and members of the public were stimulated to such vehement accusations of impudence and obscenity as men and women of established views customarily reserve for those moments of crisis when their picture of the world is threatened. Various speakers and writers found evidence of 'horror', 'madness', 'infection', 'sickness of the soul', 'putrescence', 'pornography', 'anarchy' and 'evil'.[7] The Chelsea Arts Club staged an exhibition of pastiches under the title 'Septule and the Racinists', at which works by Gauguin, Cézanne (one of his paintings of bathers) and Picasso (a Cézannesque portrait of 1910) were singled out for ridicule.

The increasing conservatism of the majority within the New English Art Club was expressed in the response of many of its senior members, who now found themselves caught earlier than they might have expected in the process of translation by which avant-gardists become 'reactionaries'. (Fry himself had resigned from the jury of the New English in 1908 in disappointment at what he regarded as a generally unreceptive attitude on the part of his colleagues towards the work of the Barbizon and Impressionist painters.) Enthusiasm for the work of Cézanne lay at the root of Fry's and of Bell's identification of the New Movement as a whole, and of the senior artists represented in the first Post-Impressionist exhibition it was Cézanne who stuck in the craw of the moderate middle generation of painters in England. They could not see him as other than an unskilful painter. Were they not themselves working to instil in their students precisely those virtues of fluent draughtsmanship, that grasp of the analysis of sophisticated forms, in which Cézanne's work was so palpably deficient? At some point after the exhibition, Henry Tonks, then teacher of drawing at the Slade School and an NEAC member, painted a caricature on the theme of *The Unknown God. Roger Fry preaching the New Faith and Clive Bell ringing the Bell* [20]. Fry is portrayed lecturing upon a dead cat to an unsympathetic audience among whom may be recognized D. S. MacColl, then Director of the Tate Gallery and a supporter of the NEAC, together with NEAC members Sickert, Steer and Sargent. Bell proclaims 'Cezannah, Cezannah'.[8] The presence of Sickert and Steer among the incredulous spectators in this tableau offers evidence of the gulf which Fry's exhibition had caused to open – or to seem to open – between the moderate and the extreme moderns.

That a painter like Sickert should have been characterized as a reactionary in relationship to a notion of progress according to which such 'Post-Impressionists' as Vlaminck were seen as comparatively advanced, should serve as a corrective to over-simplification in considering the issues at stake in the controversy over Post-Impressionism. The picture is confused for us, as it must have been for many of the participants, by the fact that the seeds of this controversy were sown in the earlier division between Academy and progressives when painters like Steer and Sickert had been

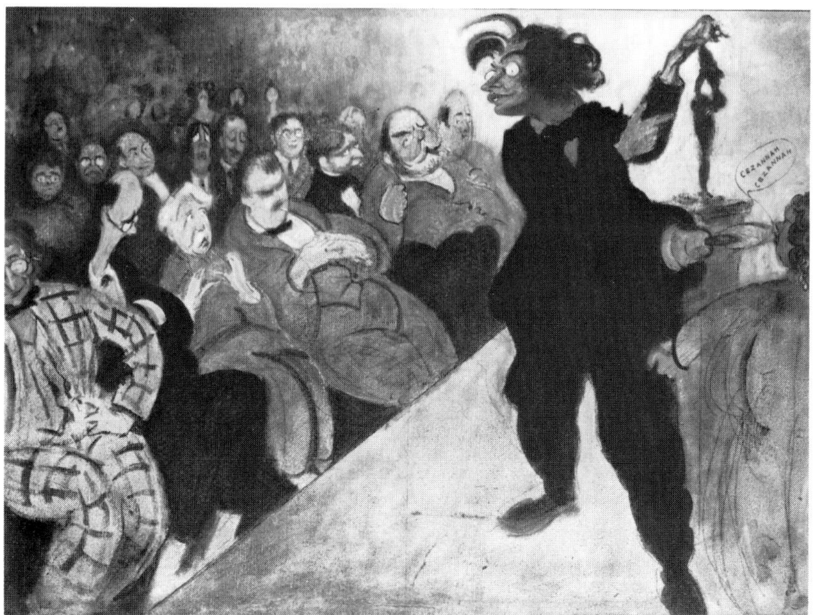

20. Henry Tonks: *The Unknown God. Roger Fry preaching the New Faith and Clive Bell ringing the Bell*, c. 1912. Oil on canvas, 16 × 21½ in.

numbered among the latter. It is important to observe that the issues at stake in the years 1910–12 are not expressible simply in terms of a conflict between 'progressives' and 'reactionaries'; the significant argument was between those like Fry and Bell who saw progress in art as involving the assertion of the autonomy of aesthetic experience, and those like Sickert who felt that art needed to be underwritten by the security of its reference to a world of 'gross material facts'. (Of course it was a necessary item of the former's thesis that the latter were reactionaries, but it need not be an item of ours unless we subscribe to a Modernist notion of progress.) It is significant that, by 1913, Clive Bell had a lot more to say for Whistler, whom he saw as an isolated champion of art's independence in the 'spent dip' of Victorian England,[9] than did Sickert, who had by then come to see his former mentor as limited by his adoption of an approach to painting's technology which was very much a function of belief in the technical autonomy of art.[10] For such as Sickert, opposition to the Academy did not necessarily entail, had obviously never entailed, assent to arguments such as Fry and Bell were attempting to articulate in defence of their belief in the separateness of 'art' from 'life'.

In fact, obscured as they may have been by the sense of a need to take sides, there were many points of compatibility between Sickert's preferences and those of Fry and Bell. Perhaps the most significant of these was their mutual disinclination to accept as a guide to future practice so apparently informal an art as that of hard-core Impressionism. But where Sickert, devoted to Degas in a way he was not to Monet, saw formality in art as evidence of professionalism and sophistication, Fry's and Bell's concern to establish links between the art of the Post-Impressionists and that of children, 'Primitives' and 'Byzantines' suggested that they were identifying the capacity to create form in terms of quite different criteria.

The fiercest arguments were thus those which centred not so much upon the works themselves as upon the aesthetic criteria employed to distinguish them. How was the 'aesthetic response' to be separated out from other responses? By what was it provoked? How were values to be recognized and established? How was art itself to be recognized? The answers which Fry and his supporters offered to such questions, some tentative, some assertive, suggested a drastic revision of the codes of practice for the professions of art, and no opposition was more vociferous than that provided by the more established figures among the ranks of the already accredited professionals. Much of the hostility to Cézanne's work expressed by the older and middle generations of painters and critics, comparatively unsusceptible as they were to conversion through contagion of enthusiasm, was aroused not so much by the paintings themselves as by the nature of the claims made for them. D. S. MacColl wrote in 1912 of 'A Year of Post-Impressionism' following the first of Fry's exhibitions,[11] and with some justice remarked on the incompatibility of the various interpretations of Cézanne's art advanced by the French painter's most ardent supporters. In a two-part article published in the *Burlington Magazine* under Fry's sponsorship in 1910, the French painter Maurice Denis had proclaimed Cézanne a 'classic', while the anonymous author (Desmond MacCarthy) of the introduction to the catalogue of 'Manet and the Post-Impressionists' implied that a decline in the status of the depicted object allowed greater scope for the expression of individual temperament. 'In no school', wrote MacCarthy, 'does individual temperament count for more. In fact, it is the boast of those who believe in this school, that its methods enable the individuality of the artist to find completer self-expression in his work than is possible to those who have committed themselves to representing objects more literally.' 'Personal feeling, then,' MacColl concluded, 'is the note of the movement, and the "Post-Impressionists" therefore are not classic at all, but extreme Romantics.'

MacColl's response was typical of those critics of the exhibition who felt that much which they held still to be of value was in danger of being supplanted as the result of an Unjustifiable and Fruitless Pursuit of Personal

Freedom. In reaction against the sentimentality and laxity of much 'imaginative' painting in the later nineteenth century, men like Sickert and MacColl were accustomed to view with some scepticism any notion of art based upon a belief in the priority of imagination and the sacrosanctity of temperament. On this issue at least the defenders of Post-Impressionism appeared, for all their involvement in the latest French art, to be asserting common cause with the Whistler of the 'Ten O'Clock Lecture', and Sickert for one was entitled to feel that that was a cause which had already been successfully undermined.

Sickert, MacColl and their more enlightened contemporaries admired the direct and ordered statement of an uncontrived, but not unsophisticated, relationship between painter and subject, and they responded to advances in the technology of painting which worked to intensify or to criticize the expression of this relationship. They could not accept a view of painting as essentially the expression of temperament. It was largely for these reasons that they admired Manet (in his less stagey works), Degas, Pissarro and the early Monet, and it was largely for the same reasons that they were resistant to the claims made by Fry and Bell on behalf of the art of Cézanne, Matisse and Picasso. A revolution in favour of the imagination, they felt, would lead inevitably to bad government.

Sickert himself surveyed the first Post-Impressionist exhibition for the *Fortnightly Review.*[12] He praised Fry for his enterprise, was concerned to point out to those alarmed by the exhibition that much of the work shown was already familiar to the cognoscenti, and wrote a forceful defence of Gauguin's claim to a place in the National Gallery (perhaps a symptom of Gore's influence upon him); but he effectively damned Cézanne with faint praise and made it quite clear that no man of sense need feel obliged to take Matisse or Picasso seriously. The terms in which he questioned the value of Picasso's work are of some significance: 'Why a nude child is carrying a bunch of flowers in front of grey vacancy, it were, perhaps an old-fashioned question to ask. I understand the tip has gone round that pictures need have no sense.' For those in a position to defend the notion of the significance of realistic subject-matter in painting, there were perhaps good reasons to reject the Picasso of the 'blue' and 'pink' periods, at least as he was represented by his supporters in England; nor, in the context of his pre-Cubist work, was it altogether absurd to see him, as Sickert did, as a follower of Whistler.

There can be no doubt that Sickert spoke for the most liberal among his contemporaries, but, as I have suggested, his influence and prestige among younger painters was from this time to decrease, or, at least, he was not to exert any significant influence after 1910 upon those who were not already of his circle. It was upon the issue of Post-Impressionism that the generations divided, and the first of Fry's exhibitions drove a great wedge between them. This was particularly true of the membership of the NEAC and, as has been suggested, the formation of the Camden Town Group was in part due to the distinctiveness of the younger painters' interests.

The nuclear members of the Fitzroy Street group were already acquainted with much of what was shown in the first of Fry's exhibitions, though the opportunity to see a considerable selection of Post-Impressionist paintings certainly acted as a stimulus to the younger members. For them as for Sickert, however, Cézanne's work was hard to assimilate. It was not until the last year of his life that Gore showed much evidence of having learned from him, and Ginner and Gilman remained more interested in Van Gogh. But for those less well informed than the Fitzroy Street painters about recent French art, and for artists of a slightly younger generation, the exhibition was an occasion for commitment to a newly fashionable cause, to the New Movement: Post-Impressionism. For a few years after 1910, many of the more ambitious younger painters looked to Fry for a lead. From this time until his death in 1934 his influence upon the development of art, and more directly upon its consumption, interpretation and criticism, was to be widespread and distinctive.

Among the 'English Post-Impressionists', or at least among those who remained loyal to the spirit of Post-Impressionism, there were not to be any artists of great importance. But the controversies of the period are of decided relevance for the development of the concept of modern art in England. In particular the terms in which art was promoted and interpreted are of significance for the subsequent history of English art. The issues involved are therefore discussed in this chapter largely in the context of Fry's and Bell's writings.

Roger Fry was born in 1866 into a close-knit Quaker family. The Pre-Raphaelites and Whistler were considered the advanced painters in England during the time when he was forming a taste for art. He studied Natural Sciences at Cambridge from 1885 to 1888 and graduated with first-class honours. Although he then turned to painting, at which he was never to become better than a good amateur, his training in the sciences and his comparatively advanced age distinguished him from those with whom his name is most often associated. In 1910 Clive Bell was twenty-nine and his wife Vanessa was thirty-one; the painter Duncan Grant was twenty-three. Fry was nearer to Sickert's generation than to theirs, and he had already by 1910 made a substantial reputation for himself as a critic and connoisseur. He had published books and articles on the art of the Italian Renaissance, and in 1903 had helped to re-establish the *Burlington Magazine*. He had been Curator of Painting at the Metropolitan Museum of Art in New York from 1905 to 1910 (then under the presidency of the millionaire Pierpont Morgan), and in 1905 had been offered and had had to decline the Directorship of the National Gallery in London. During the years between 1891 and 1910 he had travelled extensively and had acquainted himself at first hand with the art of a remarkable range of cultures and periods. He had been seen to be learned, discriminating and clear-headed. His espousal of the work of Cézanne and his promotion at the age of forty-four of the idea of a modern movement with Cézanne as its founding father was taken by his critics, and indeed by the majority of his associates at the time, as an inexplicable and ill-judged gamble with a highly successful career.

Obviously Fry's conversion to recent French painting was no matter of youthful enthusiasm. It was in fact the result of careful consideration, entirely consistent, as he saw it, with his taste for and education in earlier art. He saw the art of the Impressionists, to which he had been exposed while studying painting in Paris during the early 1890s, as the climax of 'the tendency to approximate the forms of art more and more exactly to the representation of the totality of appearance'.[13] Though he understood the importance of the Impressionists, he remained unconvinced by the theoretical justifications of their work, and he found their paintings too informal (i.e. not 'intellectual' enough) for his taste. His commitment to the Modern Movement dates effectively from 1906, when he came to see Cézanne's painting not, as he had expected it to be, as an incompetent or 'extreme' version of Impressionism, but as its antithesis, a rediscovery of those 'principles of structural design and harmony'[14] which he saw as underlying the best of earlier art. He saw in Cézanne a 'great advance in intellectual content' over Impressionism, and a 'finer, more scrupulous aesthetic sense'.[15]

For the first Post-Impressionist exhibition at the Grafton Galleries, Fry's selection from Cézanne's paintings emphasized his earlier, more expressionistic work. It is important to recognize that Fry's initial enthusiasm for Cézanne was due largely to a taste for the expressive qualities of his work. Cézanne's painting must have seemed radically distinct from the work of contemporary Edwardian painters such as Sargent, for whom Fry had always nurtured a fastidious distaste. Cézanne's painting is hardworking, vigorous, unallusive, 'timeless'; Sargent's in comparison facile, elegant, circumstantial, worldly. The expressiveness of Cézanne's work seemed comparatively uncompromised, more 'innocent', but also, paradoxically, more considered.

Fry devoted considerable thought to the art of 'primitive' cultures and of children (which were not then as now seen as unconnected), and found in their work the kind of formal strength which he felt was lacking in so much professional contemporary art. He thus became one of the earliest and most forceful English exponents of the view, so influential in twentieth-century aesthetics and art criticism, that sophistication in the illustrative functions of art leads, at least in the modern period, to loss of formal strength and of expressiveness. It was not that Fry wanted a thoughtless or unreflective art. In the conclusion of an article on *The Art of the Bushmen*, published in 1910, he spelled out what he saw as the alternatives facing the modern artist: 'The artist of today has . . . to some extent a choice before him of whether he will *think* form like the early artists of European races or merely *see* it . . .'[16] Children are comparatively free from the facility or need to produce resemblances according to criteria of representational accuracy. Fry believed that the artist who retains the capacity to 'think' form brings to its realization the same expressive vigour as characterizes the child's pictures. It was this capacity which he saw as distinguishing the Post-Impressionists from the Impressionists; and it was by such an interpretation of the significance of the former's work that he was able to render compatible the concepts of thoughtfulness and expressiveness. The 'aesthetic' or 'imaginative' life was a thoughtful life, and was seen by Fry as contrasted to the 'instinctive' life. What he meant by the latter is perhaps explained by his characterization of millionaires as 'the lords of the instinctive life'.[17]

For Fry, as for Clive Bell, the plastic virtues of Cézanne's work, thus represented as the embodiments of disinterested thought, served as a powerful critique of those who, in their terms, had prostituted art and pandered beauty to the 'plutocrats'.[18] Bell, in particular, who suggested a correlation between lack of 'formal significance' in art and 'spiritual famine' in society, and who believed that art had been in gradual decline since the days of Giotto, saw Cézanne as 'the Christopher Columbus of a new continent of form',[19] the man who had provided the example and inspiration to other artists to free themselves from that taste for the literary, the anecdotal and the imitative, which he saw as symptomatic of defective sensibility in the artist and of debased tastes in his public. The terms of Bell's condemnation of the art of Victorian England are those of a petulant snob, self-deceived in his advocacy of a liberal morality. He writes contemptuously of 'the artisan who tried to create illusions' and warns that 'we are not yet clear of the Victorian slough. The spent dip stinks on into the dawn'.[20] In his reaction against the lax painting of the nineteenth century Bell was on common ground with the more progressive members of the New English Art Club and with the painters of the Camden Town Group, but in his attempt to formulate a consistent view of art as a whole he propounded an all-embracing dogma which excluded much of what they saw reason to value. All 'literary', 'anecdotal', or 'illustrative' art was anathematized. In his book *Art*, a long tract disguised as a thesis, a tradition was concocted which withheld recognition from all forebears but those whose work was considered free from taint. With a few exceptions, casually established, the art of five hundred years was dropped from the canon. *Art* was to become a very influential book. It is in the context of such fervent assertions of the new creed that one should assess Sickert's obstinate defence of the illustrative traditions of art, from Michelangelo to Sir Edward Poynter.

Bell saw the art of the modern movement in terms implying spiritual renaissance, and faith in Cézanne as a tenet of the 'new morality'. *The New Renaissance* was the intended title of the book upon which he was working when he first met Fry early in 1910, the surviving portion of which was published as *Art* in 1914.[21] Years later, in the context of an account of that first meeting, Bell wrote, 'It was a moment at which everyone felt excitement in the air . . . certainly there was a stir: in Paris and London at all events there was a sense of things coming right' – in Munich too presumably, where the Russian painter Wassily Kandinsky was forecasting a coming 'epoch of great spirituality'.[22] '. . . In 1910', Bell continued, 'only statesmen dreamed of war, and quite a number of wide-awake people imagined the good times were just around the corner.'[23]

Fry propounded his own views on Post-Impressionism in a lecture delivered during the course of the 1910 exhibition. He was always the most persuasive of speakers and writers, and MacColl, in the article previously quoted, accorded his views due respect. Fry expressed the aim of the Post-Impressionists as 'the discovery of the visual language of the imagination', and implied that such a language would need to be free from dependence upon the actual appearance of things in the world.[24] Fry's use of the term 'imagination' is central to his expositions of art as a whole, and it deserves some investigation at this point. 'An Essay in Aesthetics', which he published in 1909, provides a clear outline of his philosophy of art at the time he was engaged upon the organization of 'Manet and the Post-Impressionists'.[25]

At the beginning of this essay Fry asserts a distinction between what he called the 'actual' and the 'imaginative' life in terms of the latter's independence from 'responsive action'. Art is seen as the chief organ of the imaginative life and thus as free from association with action. 'Art appreciates emotion in and for itself', whereas 'morality . . . appreciates emotion by the standard of resultant action'. 'Beauty' is the term we apply to objects which reflect a sense of 'purposeful order and variety' in the imaginative life; this sense is provoked by the 'emotional elements of design': rhythm of line, mass, space, light and shade, colour, and inclination of planes. The artist disposes these elements 'according to the emotions he wishes to arouse' (this is, I think, what Fry has in mind when he uses the term 'expression'); as a result of the autonomy of the artist's imaginative life, the 'emotional elements' are seen as having a high degree of independence of function in relation to 'natural forms'. 'We may, then,' concludes Fry, 'dispose once for all with the idea of likeness to Nature, of correctness or incorrectness as a test, and consider only whether the emotional elements inherent in natural form are adequately discovered . . .' It must have seemed at the time like a short step from this point to acceptance of the possibility of a wholly non-figurative art, and Fry was to take this step within the next three years.[26]

It is perhaps more obvious now than it was at the time that Fry's concept of the autonomy of the 'imaginative life' was only viable so long as the sense of 'imagination' was highly privileged; so long, for instance, as its reference was restricted to aspects of consciousness free from such promptings as those of practical need, desire, instinct and fantasy (if there be such aspects). In Fry's writing of the period under review it is clear that its reference was so restricted. In the 'Essay in Aesthetics' he employed 'imagination' and 'imaginative life' as terms synonymous with 'clear disinterested contemplation', 'disinterested intensity of contemplation', freedom from 'necessary external conditions', 'greater clearness of perception', 'greater purity and freedom of emotion', and 'clarified sense perception'. Even in 1909 this was perhaps not an interpretation of the concept of an imaginative life which he could justifiably take so much for granted among his readers, but the tools which the behavioural sciences provide for a critique of Fry's position were not then as ready to hand as they are now.[27]

In the central section of the 'Essay in Aesthetics' Fry's determination to get his aesthetics out from under the weight of nineteenth-century morality is instanced in criticism of John Ruskin. Fry is concerned above all to suggest not merely, as was Ruskin's antagonist Whistler, the autonomy of the imaginative life which art is supposed to serve, but its superior reality to 'mortal life':

> . . . I think the artist might if he chose take a mystical attitude, and declare that the fullness and completeness of the imaginative life he leads may correspond to an existence more real and more important than any that we know of in mortal life . . . It might even be that from this point of view we should rather justify actual life by its relation to the imaginative, justify nature by its likeness to art. I mean this, that since the imaginative life comes in the course of time to represent more or less what mankind feels to be the completest expression of its own nature, the freest use of its innate capacities, the actual life may be explained and justified by its approximation here and there, however partially and inadequately, to that freer and fuller life.

The 'freer and fuller life' of the imagination is represented, as we have seen, as one 'free from necessary external conditions' and thus as enabling 'greater purity ... of emotion'. Fry's belief in the superior reality of art is expressed in accents not uncommon among the 'upper middle classes' in England: those of a strong analytic intelligence employed in the service of a sensibility too fastidious not to be highly selective in the face of experience. It is hard to escape the twin conclusions that the world of art as delineated by Fry and Bell was one in which the intellectual was to be freed from the necessity to act upon his emotions; and that one of the functions which art fulfilled for them, as for many subsequent subscribers to the Modernist thesis, was to provide an imaginary immunity or escape from the determinations and obligations of social life. Certainly, the values for 'aesthetic experience' which Fry and Bell asserted were formulated and promulgated in contexts of discourse which excluded the possibility of their modification by the interests of those not privy to such discourse, and as certainly 'aesthetic experience' was seen by them as accessible only to a minority.

> ... the artist of the new movement is moving into a sphere more and more remote from that of the ordinary man. In proportion as art becomes purer the number of people to whom it appeals gets less. It cuts out all the romantic overtones of life which are the usual bait by which men are induced to accept a work of art. It appeals only to the aesthetic sensibility, and that in most men is comparatively weak.
> (Fry, 'Art and Life', 1917)[28]
>
> In saying that the mass of mankind will never be capable of making delicate aesthetic judgments, I have said no more than the obvious truth.
> (Bell, *Art*, 1914)

According to this self-certifying concept of aesthetics, it was a function of art both that it should express the intuitions of a minority, and that it should be immune to social experience. We are thus in a sense back, albeit at a different stage in its evolution, with the world which William Morris had surveyed. The condition which Morris had lamented was accepted as inevitable, was perhaps enjoyed by Fry and Bell. Morris had felt that if art could survive only as a minority interest it should not survive at all. Fry and Bell, who saw their position secure among the members of this minority, were concerned above all with the survival of art. In contexts where 'aesthetic experience' and 'social experience' were hard to reconcile, they accepted without question the ineffability of the former. Their aesthetics subsumed ethics. In his essay of 1909 Fry ridiculed Ruskin's view that 'the imaginative life subserves morality'; five years later, Bell, always the less sophisticated, wrote, 'Once we have judged a thing a work of art, we have judged it ethically of the first importance, and put it beyond the reach of the moralist.'[29] This, then, is the apotheosis of the aesthetic movement to which Whistler had contributed, the final rejection of the idea advanced by Ruskin and Morris that art should bear a special responsibility in social life. In a chapter on 'Art and Society', Bell suggested that the masses might dance and sing for their aesthetic pleasures.[30] Fourteen years later, referring back to the pre-war period in the dedication of his book on *Civilization*, he wrote to his sister-in-law, 'You remember, Virginia, we were mostly socialists in those days. We were concerned for the fate of humanity.'

1910, the year when Fry and Bell met and affirmed their mutual interest in recent French art, the year when 'quite a number of wide-awake people imagined the good times were just around the corner', saw also the breaking of a strike by Welsh miners at Tonypandy by troops acting under the orders of the Home Secretary, Winston Churchill. Plainly the miners were not among the wide-awake.

One should not, of course, dismiss what might in retrospect look like areopagite simple-mindedness as a mere function of Bell's extreme aestheticism. During the period between the end of the nineteenth century and the outbreak of war in 1914, many intelligent men accepted readily and perhaps with relief any system of ethics or of aesthetics which appeared to permit some independence for the life of the 'spirit' from the vexed and conscience-stricken world of the modern political economist. In his chapter on 'Art and Ethics', Bell acknowledged indebtedness to the *Principia Ethica* of the Cambridge philosopher G. E. Moore. This book, first published in 1903, was taken by Bell, and several other members of the Bloomsbury coterie to which he belonged, as a source of justification of what is now often seen as intellectual and social élitism. In his chapter on 'The Ideal', Moore had established a concept of value in terms which the young art lovers, in reaction against the nineteenth-century moral world of their parents, must have found irresistible. One passage in particular deserves quoting at length, since it was to condition and to rationalize the manners of a highly influential minority.

> By far the most valuable things, which we know or can imagine, are certain states of consciousness, which may be roughly described as the pleasures of human intercourse and the enjoyment of beautiful objects. No one, probably, who has asked himself the question, has ever doubted that personal affection and the appreciation of what is beautiful in Art or Nature, are good in themselves; nor, if we consider strictly what things are worth having *purely for their own sakes*, does it appear probable that any one will think that anything else has *nearly* so great a value as the things which are included under these two heads. I have myself urged

... that the mere existence of what is beautiful does appear to have *some* intrinsic value; but I regard it as indubitable ... that such mere existence of what is beautiful has value, so small as to be negligible, in comparison with that which attaches to the *consciousness* of beauty. This simple truth may, indeed, be said to be universally recognised. What has *not* been recognised is that it is the ultimate and fundamental truth of Moral Philosophy. That it is only for the sake of these things – in order that as much of them as possible may at some time exist – that any one can be justified in performing any public or private duty; that they are the *raison d'être* of virtue; that it is they – these complex wholes *themselves*, and not any constituent or characteristic of them – that form the rational ultimate end of human action and the sole criterion of social progress: these appear to be truths which have been generally overlooked.[31]

Taken at face value and in isolation, as it largely was within the Bloomsbury set,[32] this could be used as a mandate to the practitioner or lover of art to abstain from consideration of social questions in the pursuit of 'good states of mind'.

When you treat a picture as a work of art [Bell concluded] ... you have assigned it to a class of objects so powerful and direct as means to spiritual exaltation that all minor merits are inconsiderable. Paradoxical as it may seem, the only relevant qualities in a work of art, judged as art, are artistic qualities: judged as a means to good, no other qualities are worth considering; for there are no qualities of greater moral value than artistic qualities, since there is no greater means to good than art.[33]

Bell acknowledged that the influence of Moore's *Principia Ethica* 'on some of us was immense', though he labelled Fry as 'definitely anti-Moorist'. Bell himself felt that he and his friends were 'freed by Moore from the spell of an ugly doctrine in which we had been reared: he delivered us from Utilitarianism'.[34] G. E. Moore is not, of course, to be held responsible for Bell's use of his work as authorization. The weak link which Bell forged between Moore's ideas and his own was in identifying works of art with Moore's 'beautiful objects' and thus seeing them as ineffable means to 'good states of mind'. For Bell 'works of art' were singled out as such in terms of his own aesthetic and non-logical predilections, whereas by 'beautiful objects' Moore seems to have intended to specify a much wider and looser category.

To a certain extent Fry was the victim of his association with Bell. His was always a more supple and questioning intelligence than the younger man's. Over and over again one finds Fry's sophisticated deliberations stripped of their qualifying elements and rendered into bald assertions by Bell. But in areas where their influence was to be most strongly felt, and particularly during the decade 1910–20, there were important items of attitude and belief in common between the two men. They both held that aesthetic appreciation was a faculty with which only a minority were endowed; they both saw Cézanne as the virtual originator of the New Movement; they both emphasized that strength of expression was a characteristic alike of 'primitive' art (including the 'art' of children) and of the best art of the modern movement;[35] and they were both concerned to assert that not only was nothing of value lost in the decline of art's traditional illustrative or iconic functions, but further that the 'aesthetic experience' offered grew strong in inverse proportion to the priority accorded to illustrative or associative elements. There is a strong vein of special pleading in the last of these points. It is not hard to understand how such a thesis could be developed and hardened, as it was to be by later theorists, into the doctrine 'the more abstract the better'.

How one does one's singling out determines what he singles out. At the most superficial level, the emphasis which Fry and Bell came increasingly to place before all else upon the formal characteristics of paintings and sculpture led them to approve and encourage paintings with simplified forms and strongly accented 'decorative' designs [21]. The attention which

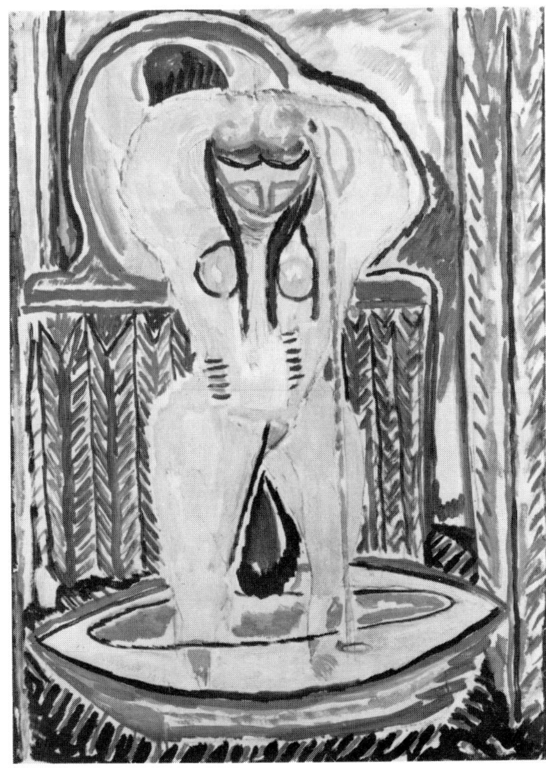

21. Duncan Grant: *The Tub*, 1912. Watercolour and tempera on board, 30 × 22 in.

they drew upon works in which a high priority could be seen to be placed upon form, as opposed, say, to iconography, resulted in the promotion in England of a number of painters of simplified, blockish still lifes, figures and landscapes recalling the work of Jean Marchand (a second-rate French painter, but one whom Fry admired) or of André Derain in his cubo-classicist manner. Many of Fry's own paintings of the period look like rough-hewn pastiches of Cézanne [22]. 'Mr Fry appears to think', observed D. S. MacColl, 'that the residual element of reality, which renders painting "classic", is the expression of solidity, and that solidity is most fully expressed by the elimination of light and shade and the addition of a thick contour.'[36]

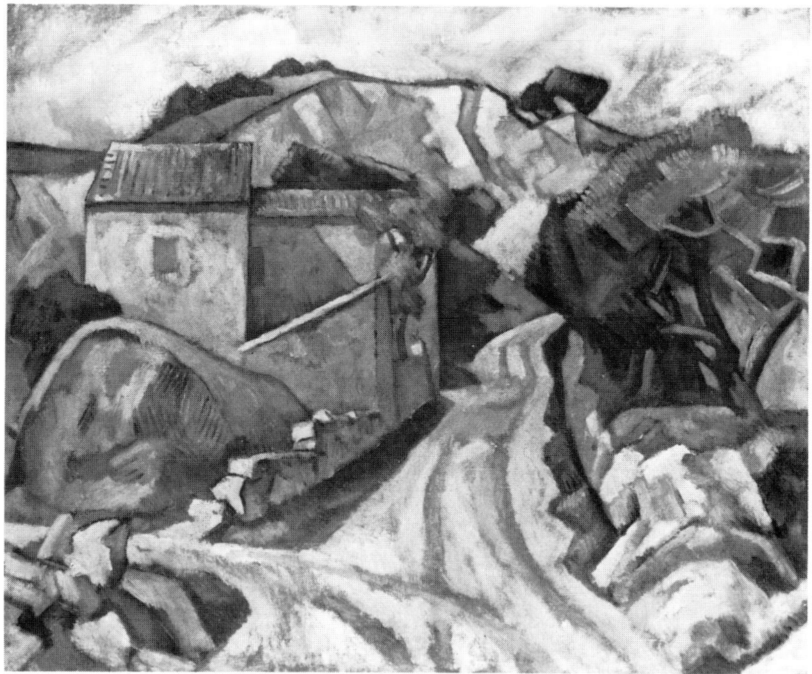

22. Roger Fry: *White Road with Farm*, c. 1912. Oil on canvas, $25\frac{1}{2} \times 31\frac{3}{4}$ in.

It is easy enough thus to caricature the Bloomsbury critics' influence upon the actual appearance of paintings produced by English artists; but there were more crucial, long-range consequences of the debates over Post-Impressionism and of the criticism and aesthetics of Fry and Bell. In particular, their identification of the English modern movement in terms of a move towards progressive autonomy for art, their denigration of art's traditional representational techniques, their elevation of the status of formal design per se, and their belief in the possibility of an art to which we need bring 'nothing but a sense of form and colour and a knowledge of three-dimensional space'[37] encouraged many artists and spectators over a very long period to value 'integrity' above epistemology, 'abstraction' above interpretation, and taste above understanding.

MacColl, at the conclusion of his 'Year of Post-Impressionism', wrote an eloquent and prophetic lament for the passing of what he had known as art.

> ... as much as possible every element of contingency must be excluded, all those features that made Plato distrust the art of painting because they render the idea a shifting thing. For this reason perspective will be minimised, for this reason changing light and shadow, the miracle of atmosphere, the decomposition of reflected lights; in composition the studied confusion of the picturesque, in expression all transitory emotion will be banished for severe symmetry and solemn calm. The illusion of the passing world will be reduced to its lowest term of abstraction, and for this reason sculpture, in what is obviously not flesh, will be preferred to painting. Detail and accessory will be as rigorously dealt with; such incident and detail as is admitted will be admitted reluctantly only because it is forced upon the artist to enhance significance. And symbolic realities thus admitted will wear some mark of strangeness, as by the faint tradition of religion people still 'dress for church'.

II

While newspaper critics and Academicians may have wished to dismiss the Post-Impressionist exhibition and its organizers, the language of their diatribes must even at the time have seemed strident and defensive; evidently they no longer spoke with the authority they had commanded a few years earlier. The *succès de scandale* of 'Manet and the Post-Impressionists' had by 1912 become a *succès d'estime* within a significant proportion of the profession. No exhibition at the Grafton Galleries had ever been better attended and virtually all the lower-priced works had found buyers. The gap between conservatives and avant-gardists was seen to widen, to the disadvantage of the former's prestige. When Sickert joined the Royal Academy in 1915 it was perhaps not because he had moved any further to the 'right', but because he recognized how far out of his own reach the 'left' had moved. Fry's advocacy of the New Movement was crucially influential. As no one else could have done, he mustered support from among those who, though they may not have been able to swallow Cézanne, let alone Matisse or Picasso, were unwilling to identify themselves with the conservative factions. In 1911 he was offered the directorship of the Tate Gallery, which was far from being an avant-garde institution. He declined this offer, but when the directors of the Grafton Galleries suggested he should take control of their programmes for the autumn months he agreed, seeing this as an opportunity to show 'non-academic' English art alongside contemporary French work. He was also commissioned by the Borough Polytechnic in London to decorate the students' dining room, and collaborated on the project with Duncan Grant, Frederick Etchells, Bernard Adeney, Albert Rutherston and Max Gill. During the summer of the next year he organized an exhibition of 'Quelques Indépendants Anglais' at the Galerie Barbazanges in Paris. He thus attracted around him a circle of mostly younger artists who responded to his views and his taste and for whose work he was able to secure attention and exposure. These were to be the English Post-Impressionists.

In October 1912 the 'Second Post-Impressionist Exhibition of English, French and Russian Artists' opened at the Grafton Galleries [23] with Fry once again as the prime mover. Fifty-two artists were chosen from three countries. Fry himself selected the French contribution, Clive Bell the English, and Boris von Anrep a comparatively unexciting Russian section.

23. Vanessa Bell(?) (formerly attributed to Roger Fry): *A Room at the Second Post-Impressionist Exhibition*, 1912. Oil on panel, $20\frac{1}{4} \times 24\frac{3}{4}$ in.

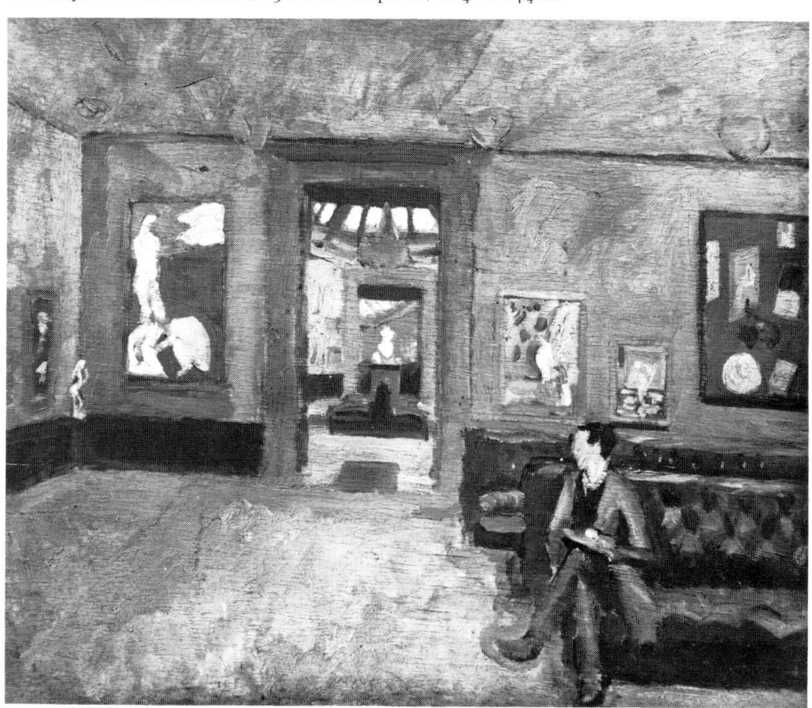

(Kandinsky, whose work had been shown at the Allied Artists Association exhibitions in 1909, 1911 and 1912, was a surprising omission.) Fry's introduction to the catalogue made clear that the previous exhibition had presented the 'Old Masters of the new movement', and that this movement was now to be surveyed in terms of its current adherents. Cézanne, whom Fry described as 'the great originator of the whole idea', was represented by five comparatively late oils and six watercolours. Pride of place was taken by Matisse, represented by nineteen paintings, including such major works as the *Portrait of Marguerite, Le Luxe, The Red Studio* and *La Danse*, by eight sculptures, including *La Serpentine* and four versions of the *Bust of Marguerite*, and by more than fifteen works on paper. Picasso, with thirteen paintings, including a Cubist *Tête d'Homme*, and three drawings, was accorded a similar prominence. Fry's introduction to the French section[38] made clear that these two were to be regarded as the major contemporaries: 'Between these two extremes', he wrote, 'we may find ranged almost all the remaining artists.' Among the other French artists included were Derain (six works), Vlaminck (nine), L'Hote (twelve), Van Dongen (four), Bonnard (three), Herbin (eleven) and a host of less considerable practitioners of Cubist and Fauve styles.

Fry defended the artists against predictable charges of incapacity and insincerity and made clear that their aim was not to 'exhibit their skill or to proclaim their knowledge'.

> They do not seek to imitate form, but to create form; not to imitate life, but to find an equivalent for life. By that I mean that they wish to make images which by the clearness of their logical structure, and by their closely-knit unity of texture, shall appeal to our disinterested and contemplative imagination with something of the same vividness as the things of actual life appeal to our practical activities. In fact, they aim not at illusion, but at reality.

Fry saw Picasso's recent work as representing the 'logical extreme of such a method ... a purely abstract language of form – a visual music'. The description would have been more appropriate to Kandinsky's latest work than it was to Picasso's, which was never at that time as far from the depiction of the 'things of actual life' as Fry seems to have thought. Neither Fry nor Bell ever really understood Cubism, and those few English artists who were later to see through the confusion between Cubism and abstract art were not to be among those supported by either critic.

Fry's strongest positive response was reserved for Matisse, whose work he saw as possessing 'to an extraordinary degree that decorative unity of design which distinguishes all the artists of this school'. Design as the unifying and essential characteristic of the work of art was seen by Fry as the means to establishing its plastic independence from 'the practical responses to sensations of ordinary life, thereby setting free a pure and as it were disembodied functioning of the spirit'. He saw this independence from 'associated ideas' as a characteristic of 'classic' art, the embodiment of 'a positive and disinterestedly passionate state of mind', and declared that 'this classic concentration of feeling' constituted the French artists' true claim to serious recognition. The sense and language of this essay are in places remarkably close to those of such recent and contemporary formulations of expressionist aesthetics in Europe as Matisse's 'Notes of a Painter' and Kandinsky's *Concerning the Spiritual in Art*.[39]

Bell introduced the English contingent at the second Post-Impressionist exhibition in terms of a similar emphasis upon 'plastic design', and it was in this context that he first identified 'significant form' as the basis of aesthetic experience. This phrase was to become a clarion call for the New Movement in England, particularly after the publication of Bell's *Art*, where the doctrine of 'significant form' was propounded at length.[40] In claiming victory for the new avant garde and the new aesthetics, Bell also employed the analogy with music which Fry had used and which was so central a feature of Kandinsky's treatise.

> Happily, there is no need to be defensive. The battle is won. We all agree, now, that any form in which an artist can express himself is legitimate, and the more sensitive perceive that there are things worth expressing that could never have been expressed in traditional forms. We have ceased to ask, 'What does this picture represent?' and ask instead, 'What does it make us feel?' We expect a work of plastic art to have more in common with a piece of music than with a coloured photograph ... These English artists are of the movement because, in choice of subject, they recognise no authority but the truth that is in them; in choice of form, none but the need of expressing it. That is Post-Impressionism.

Bell's assertion of victory was apparently justified, however absurd the platform may now seem. Even MacColl had had to admit, on returning to London three months after the first Post-Impressionist exhibition, that he found '... the new religion established, the old gods being bundled without concern into the lumber room, and the ardent weathercocks of the press pointing steadily for the moment into the paulo-post-futurum.'[41] Although there were still expressions of outrage from conservatives and Academicians, many who had been astonished by the first Post-Impressionist exhibition came to the second to learn, in particular about Cubism and Fauvism, and there were many conversions, particularly among the students at the Slade. From the date of the opening of the first exhibition the tutors at the Slade found themselves fighting an unsuccessful rearguard action against Post-Impressionism. Paul Nash, who studied at the school during the years in question, later described the atmosphere there during that period.

The Slade was then seething under the influence of Post-Impressionism. Roger Fry had brought about the second exhibition of modern continental art in London [Nash is here confusing the effects of the two exhibitions; he had left the Slade by the time the second opened], and now all the cats were out of the bag ... It seemed, literally, to bring about a national upheaval ... All this had a disturbing effect at the Slade. The professors did not like it at all. The students were by no means a docile crowd and the virus of the new art was working in them uncomfortably. Suppose they all began to draw like Matisse? Eventually, Tonks made one of his speeches and appealed, in so many words, to our sporting instincts. He could not, he pointed out, prevent our visiting the Grafton Galleries; he could only warn us and say how very much better pleased he would be if we did not risk contamination but stayed away.[42]

It was not altogether surprising that the mentors at the Slade should have felt a solemn responsibility to protect their students from the full effects of Post-Impressionism. If art had been recently reborn with Cézanne, if aesthetic sensibility was either innate or absent, and if, as Bell asserted, 'Art ... is not to be taught',[43] what price the notion of an education in art, either for the practitioner or for his audience? But they had no alternative concept of modern practice to offer these students that was half so definitely formulated as that of Fry and Bell, and of the more talented students of the 'Post-Impressionist years' almost all were in one way or another decisively affected, while several were drawn into the social world of the Bloomsbury group. The battlefield was after all well confined. University College, of which the Slade School is a part, is situated in the heart of Bloomsbury, between Fitzroy Square and Gordon Square, at that time the homes respectively of Virginia Stephen (later Woolf) and of her sister and her brother-in-law, Vanessa and Clive Bell. And until 1914 Fry lectured at the Slade.

Among the students at the Slade in the crucial years 1911–12 were a gang calling themselves the 'Neo-Primitives',[44] a term which suggests a Bloomsbury-derived view of modern practice. The group was dominated by Mark Gertler, who had been at the Slade since 1908, where he was regarded as the best draughtsman since Augustus John; among the other members were Christopher Nevinson, Edward Wadsworth and Stanley Spencer [24]. Also at the Slade at this time, besides Paul Nash, whose attendances were sporadic, and his friend Ben Nicholson, who was even less

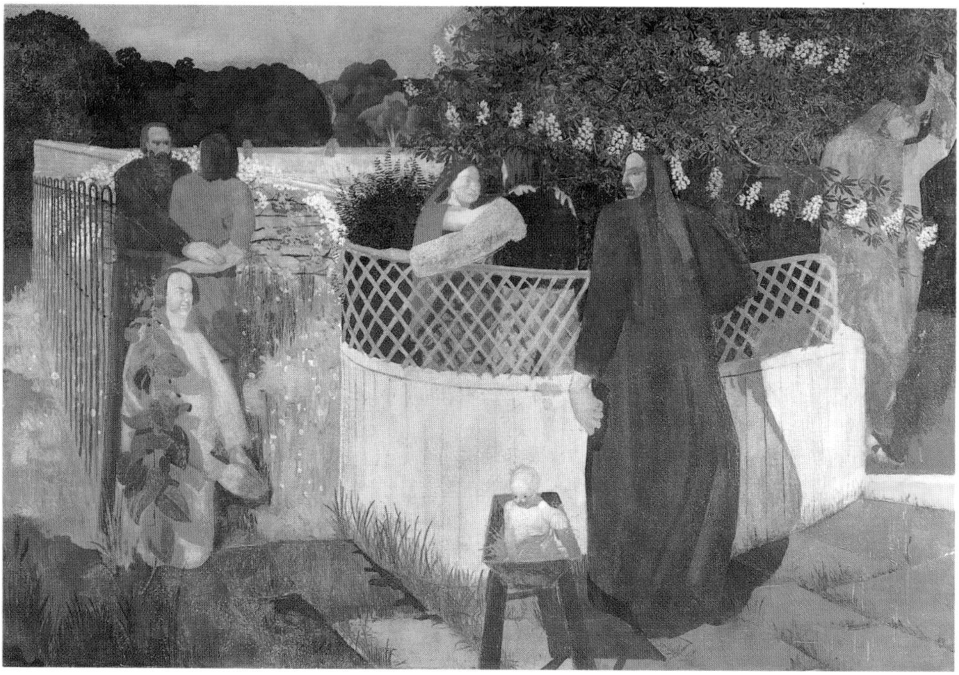

24. Stanley Spencer: *The Nativity*, 1912. Oil on panel, 40 × 60 in.

attracted to the college, were David Bomberg, a former pupil of Sickert's at the Westminster School of Art, and William Roberts. This must have been as heterogeneous a generation of students, in terms of origin, class and previous experience, as had ever been assembled together in an English art school. Nevinson was the son of a journalist, Nash the son of a judge, Nicholson of the painter William Nicholson; Bomberg and Gertler were both from Polish-Jewish families living in the East End of London; Stanley Spencer came from Cookham-on-Thames; Roberts had been apprenticed as a commercial artist in London; Wadsworth, a wealthy Yorkshireman, had studied engineering in Munich in 1906–7.[45] It was to a very large extent from among this group that the new recruits to the modern movement were to be drawn. However hard the older painters may have tried to resist the idea, during the years 1910–12 the terms of reference for a concept of modern art were comprehensively revised for a whole generation of younger artists.

Bloomsbury kept its eye on the Slade. Stanley Spencer had won the Slade Summer painting competition, and three small works of his were selected by Bell for inclusion in the second Post-Impressionist exhibition. Other

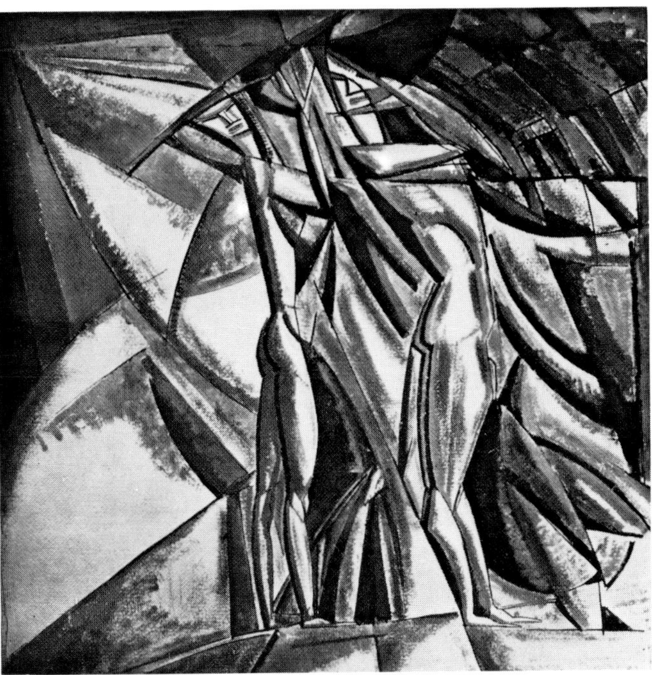

25. Wyndham Lewis: *Creation*, 1912. Whereabouts unknown (exhibited in the second Post-Impressionist exhibition, 1912)

exhibitors in the English section were the stone-carver Eric Gill, Spencer Gore, the sole representative of the Camden Town nucleus, Percy Wyndham Lewis, whose *Creation* [25] and *Timon of Athens* drawings [31] must have looked very adventurous and 'abstract' in company with the other English works, and Frederick Etchells, whose painting at the time showed mild Cubist influence. Two works by Edward Wadsworth were included during the extended period of the exhibition in January 1913.

Also included were a group of painters identifiable as members of the Bloomsbury coterie. Besides Fry himself there were two of his collaborators on the Borough Polytechnic murals, Bernard Adeney and Duncan Grant, together with Vanessa Bell, Boris von Anrep and Henry Lamb, represented in the exhibition by a head of Grant's cousin, Lytton Strachey, whose full-length portrait he was to paint two years later [26]. By the time of the 1912 exhibition those associated with Bloomsbury were already a closely knit group. In 1905 Vanessa Bell (or Stephen as she then was) had started a discussion group which she called the Friday Club. Clive Bell was involved, as was Henry Lamb. Fry addressed the club in February 1910 soon after his first meeting with Clive Bell, and shortly after this it was reconstituted as an

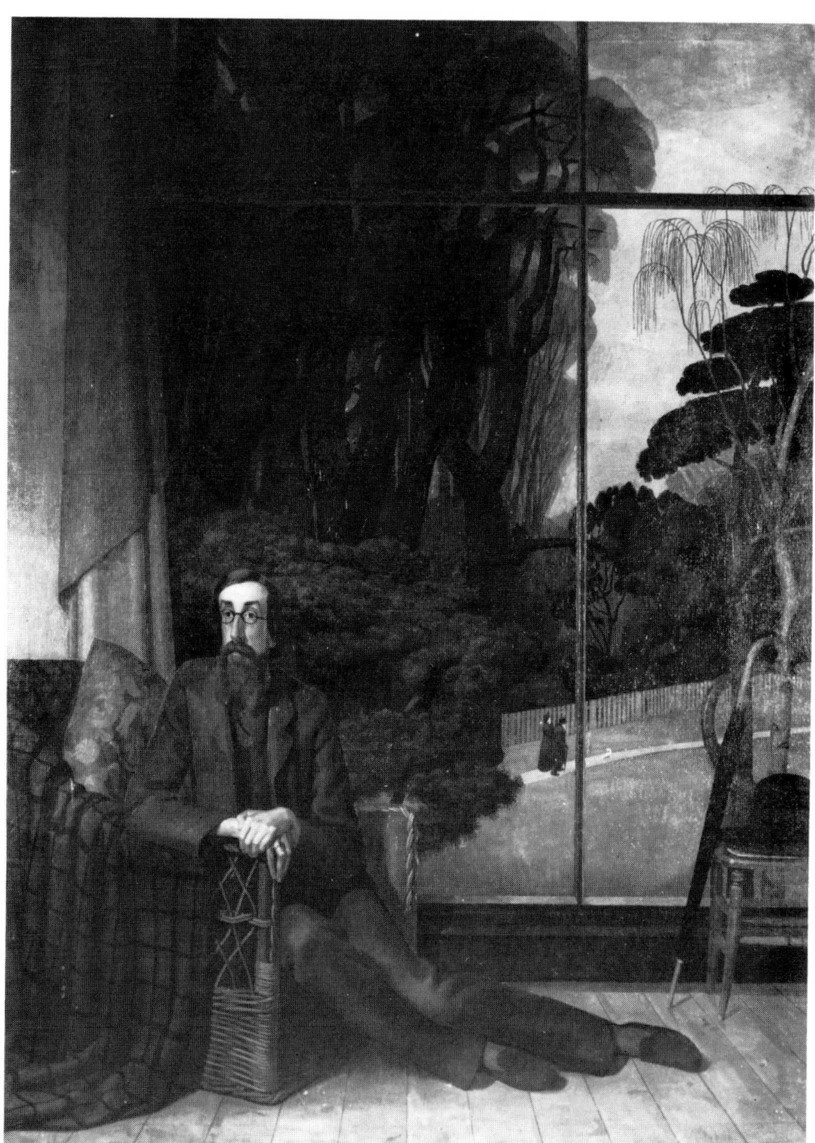

26. Henry Lamb: *Portrait of Lytton Strachey*, 1914. Oil on canvas, 96¼ × 70¼ in.

exhibiting society based on the Alpine Gallery. The Bells had met Duncan Grant in Paris, shortly after their marriage in 1907, and he had quickly become a close friend. He exhibited with the Friday Club in June 1910. After the first Post-Impressionist exhibition, younger artists from the Slade were attracted into the Alpine Gallery. Gertler, then still a student, exhibited with the club in 1911, Nevinson and Wadsworth in 1912 and Bomberg in 1913.

Fry had a one-man show at the Alpine Gallery in January 1912, and in March 1913 the Grafton Group was formed by Fry, Vanessa Bell and Grant.

None of the 'inner circle' of Bloomsbury were really very competent painters, though Vanessa Bell and Grant produced much of their most technically progressive work during the few years either side of 1912, buoyed on the high tide of Post-Impressionism. Grant had spent a considerable time in Paris and was strongly influenced by Matisse, whom he had met at Clamart in 1909. His best work was lyrical and modest, displaying that balance between lightness and dryness of touch and between harmony and intensity of colour which characterizes much of the best English painting between the assimilation of Impressionism and the onset of Cubist influence; but the most ambitious painting he contributed to the second Post-Impressionist exhibition, the *Queen of Sheba* [27], displayed already those failings which were to proliferate in his later work: an inability to make 'invented' figures and forms seem plausible in pastoral or decorative compositions, or to express, in a relaxed world of Matisse-like interiors, that degree of acceptance and organization of sensual experience

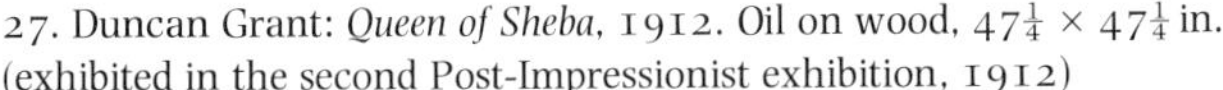
27. Duncan Grant: *Queen of Sheba*, 1912. Oil on wood, $47\frac{1}{4} \times 47\frac{1}{4}$ in. (exhibited in the second Post-Impressionist exhibition, 1912)

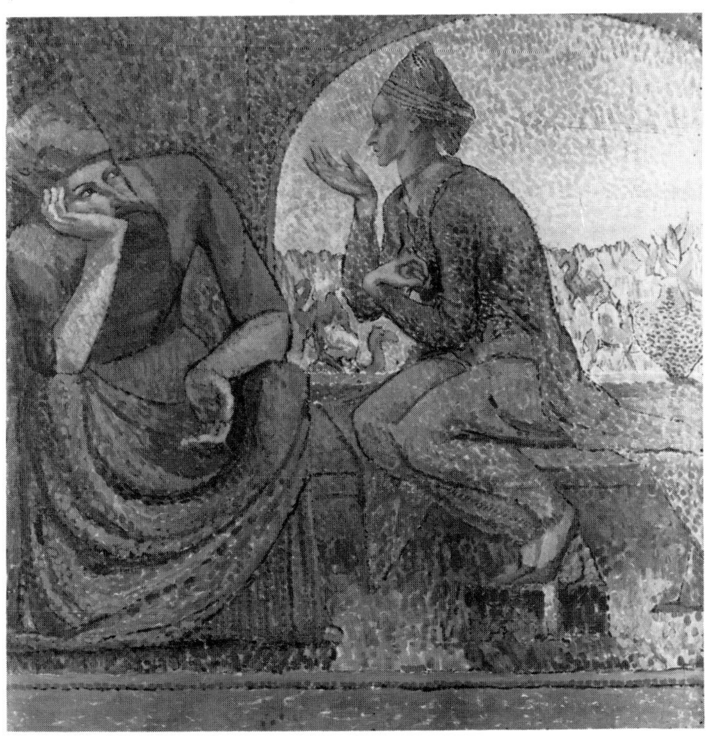

which is the strength of Matisse's work. Ezra Pound's caricature of the 'Post-Impressionist' still life might have been written before a work by Grant:

> Green arsenic smeared on an egg-white cloth.
> Crushed strawberries! Come let us feast our eyes!

Many of Grant's most successful works were portraits.

Similar virtues and similar failings are discernible in the work of Vanessa Bell. Both painters showed a willingness to 'experiment' up to a degree [28], and both produced attractive paintings with considerable saturation of

28. Vanessa Bell: *Triple Alliance*, 1915–16. Oil and collage on canvas, 33 × 25 in.

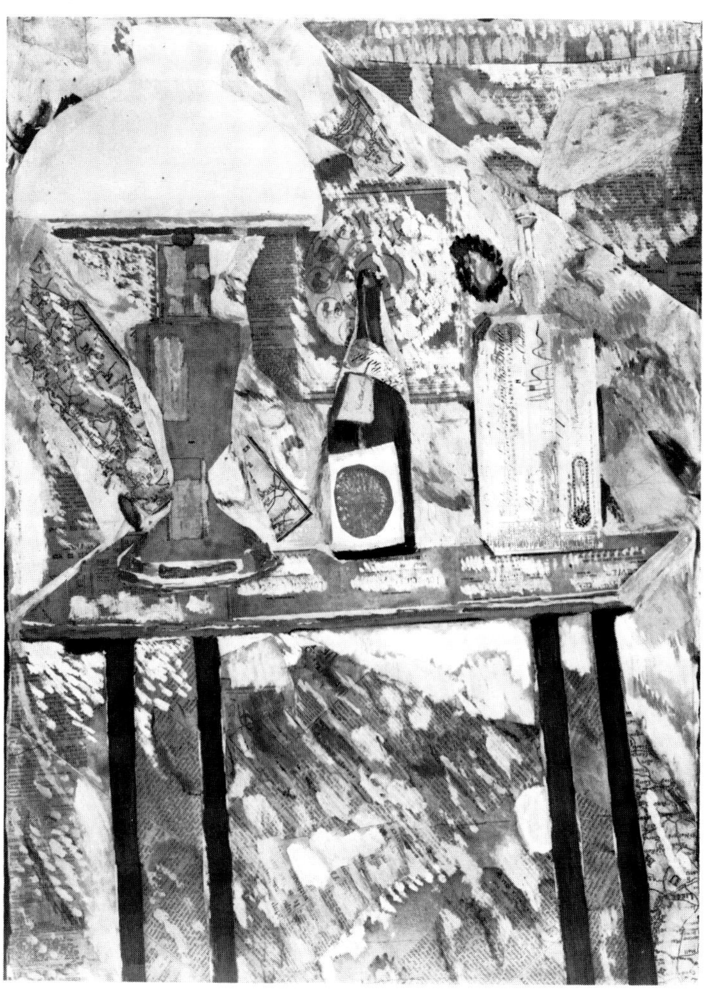

colour; there were even tentative 'experiments' with abstract design in the years *c.* 1914–16. Late in 1914, Grant produced a long abstract collage, intended to be viewed through a small rectangular aperture as it unwound to the music of Bach. A painting of *c.* 1914 by Vanessa Bell has rectangular forms 'floating' on a monochrome yellow field. Both works, which are now in the Tate Gallery, look thin and amateurish. Neither was able to learn much from Cubism and neither was even at best able to produce anything to instantiate the concept of 'decorative' painting which had not already been surpassed by Matisse. Matisse was after all unique in his capacity to charge forms of painting based on a hedonist aesthetics with just those sensations of actual life which Fry and Bell had ruled out of court in the formulation of their own theories. His influence was never to be very beneficial among those who responded too strongly to the superficial appearance of his paintings; it tended to encourage the application of a still-life sensibility to all subjects alike. It was perhaps with something like this in mind that Gilman and Ginner took their stand in 1914 for a 'Neo-Realist' approach to 'life in all its aspects, moods and developments', against what they saw as the 'common opinion of the day' that 'Decoration is the unique aim of art'.[46]

Of course for Fry the word 'decoration' had a richness and range of meaning which cannot have been apparent to all those who heard him use it. 'Decoration' for him signified that aspect of plastic art which bore witness, by means of embodied form and achieved unity of design, to the uncompromised functioning of the 'spirit'. If design or decoration thus understood was the expression of spirit, then better design must testify to a greater spiritual health. Although there is significantly no equivalent here for Ruskin's or Morris's passionate involvement in political economy, there are points of compatibility with the theories of the earlier critics.[47] Like them, Fry wished to see artists employed as designers determining the style of the man-made environment (or at least of the characteristic features of the middle-class interior), and like them he instigated a project by means of which he hoped somehow to influence matters in the right direction. Writing on 'Art and Socialism' in 1912, Fry turned from the 'abstractly creative artist' to consider the 'applied arts'.

> Now, in the present commercial State, at a time when such handiwork as is not admirably fitted to some purely utilitarian purpose has become inanely fatuous and grotesque, the artist in this sense [i.e. as 'prophet and priest'] has undoubtedly become of supreme importance as a protestant, as one who proclaims that art is a reasonable function, and one that proceeds by a nice adjustment of means to ends. But if we suppose a state in which all the ordinary objects of daily life – our chairs

and tables, our carpets and pottery – expressed something of this reasonableness instead of a crazy and vapid fantasy, the artist as a pure creator might become, not indeed of less importance – rather more – but a less acute necessity to our general living than he is today. Something of the sanity and purposefulness of his attitude might conceivably become infused into the work of the ordinary craftsman, something, too, of his creative energy and delight in work.

There is the suggestion here of an intuition on Fry's part that the high and isolated status which he among others claimed for the fine artist in the modern age might be defensible only in the context of what he would in the end have to recognize as indefensible socio-political circumstances. The insight is not pursued – Fry still places the aesthetic cart resolutely before the economic horse – but the latter is at least there. In writing thus about the role of the artist in the applied arts, he came closer than in any of his other writings to a position commensurable with William Morris's.

The practical consequence of Fry's speculations about the applied arts and the function of design was the opening in July 1913 of Omega Workshops Ltd in Fitzroy Square. Fry's co-directors were Grant and Vanessa Bell. The object was to encourage the production of well-designed household accoutrements. Artists were paid thirty shillings per week for part-time work designing furniture, textiles and items of pottery which were to be marketed as Omega products. Although the workshops remained in operation until 1919, Omega's main claim to art-historical importance is that for a few months in 1913 it provided a point of focus for a wide cross-section of the new English avant garde. Fry was assiduous in his recruitment, and there were few among the more talented younger artists who did not work in Fitzroy Square, for however brief a period. Among those involved at one time or another, besides the directors themselves, were Wyndham Lewis, Edward Wadsworth [29], Frederick Etchells, William Roberts, Paul Nash, the young sculptor Henri Gaudier-Brzeska, Henri Doucet, a young French painter, and Cuthbert Hamilton, a contemporary of Lewis at the Slade. If there was an identifiable Omega style, however, it was attributable to the group already closest to Fry. Omega was very much a Bloomsbury enterprise. Vanessa Bell's textiles, Grant's painted screens and Fry's pottery were among the more representative products of the workshop.

As a means of countering the influence of the manufacturing and retailing resources employed in the fast-growing English interior-decorating industry, the establishment of the Omega Workshops was a somewhat quixotic enterprise. The market for Post-Impressionist furniture was a limited one in England at around the time of the First World War and

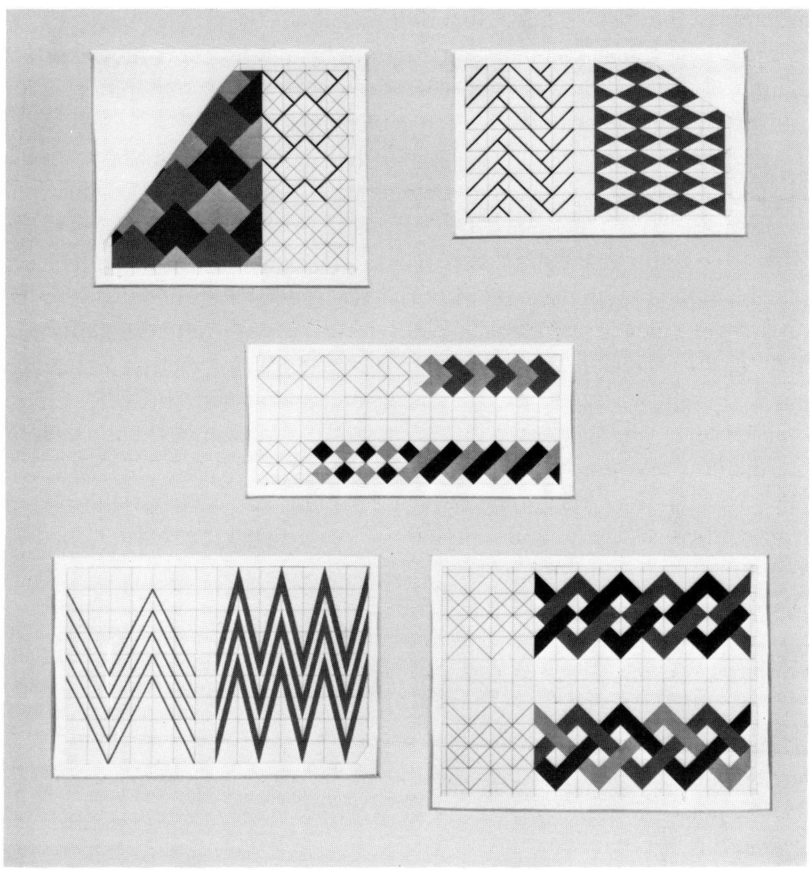

29. Edward Wadsworth: *Five Designs for the Omega Workshops*, 1913. Gouache and pencil on squared paper, centre design 3 × 6.9 in.

the products were comparatively expensive. Fry's late contribution to the Arts and Crafts movement, upon which Ruskin and Morris had in their day placed considerable faith, foundered upon the same rocks as had theirs: in an age of mechanized production, where wage levels are established within industry, the production of the hand-craftsman cannot be competitive in price, involving as it must do many more man-hours than its factory-made equivalent; it must therefore remain a luxury item within that development of capitalism in which price levels are determined by the cost of industrial labour. Omega Workshops Ltd sold mainly to those members of the liberal upper-middle classes already identifiable as friends and amateurs of the New Movement.[48]

A few commissions were however secured for Post-Impressionist schemes of interior decoration, and it was the most prestigious of these – for a room at the Ideal Home Exhibition – that led to the inevitable schism between the Bloomsbury nucleus around Fry and those younger artists who associated with Wyndham Lewis. Lewis accused Fry of appropriating on behalf of Omega a commission which had originally been offered to Lewis, Fry and Spencer Gore. He inflamed the issue by circulating a 'Round Robin' defaming Fry, and in October 1913 led a walkout from the workshops.[49] He was joined by Etchells, Hamilton and Wadsworth. In March 1914 the Rebel Art Centre was established in Great Ormond Street. The idea and the funds came from Kate Lechmere, a friend of Lewis's. He was a prime mover, and Etchells, Wadsworth, Nevinson and Hamilton were among the early participants. Where Bloomsbury saw Matisse as the best guide to the future of art, the secessionists were on the whole more impressed by Picasso and by Cubism and its derivatives. For Lewis in particular the concept of an avant-garde art entailed the embodiment of ideas rather than the renewal of decoration, in so far as these were contrastives. A new and energetic faction was thus established in opposition to the 'new orthodoxy' of Post-Impressionism.

4

CUBISM, FUTURISM, VORTICISM

December 1910, the month in which, according to Virginia Woolf, human character changed, saw also a change of government, or at least the return of an old one. In an election called during a period of constitutional crisis, the Liberals and Conservatives each gained 272 seats, and with the support of Irish and Labour members Asquith remained in office. But this was to be the last Liberal ministry of the century. The period from December 1910 until the spring of 1915 saw the decline of the Liberal party as a major force in British political life (although the ideology of liberalism-plus-utilitarianism remained rampant in British culture).

Pace the optimism of Clive Bell, it is against a background of political change and instability that we should assess the opposition to Post-Impressionism of those who saw the movement as 'the exact analogue of the Anarchist movements in the political world'.[1] When, in 1910, Frank Rutter published a defence of Post-Impressionism under the title 'Revolution in Art', he was using a term which was not then as casually employed as it is today, nor had it been often used in discussions of art. By 1914 social revolution in some form was seen by some intellectuals as a real possibility (albeit not by leaders of the working class). It is also in the context of this possibility that one should consider the work of those artists and writers who were eager for change – eager enough, some of them, to embrace the notion of change for its own sake.

During periods of rapid change, the radicals of one day become the liberals of the next, and by 1913 Fry was to lose his position in the leadership of the vanguard. The first Post-Impressionist exhibition was after all extreme only according to what was considered modern in England. The developments covered in this chapter are characterized by the same lack of coherence as governed political life at the time: factions grouped and split; conflicts of interest were made clear as never before; there was intrigue, bitterness, militancy and a proliferation of polemic.

Among those English artists in the immediate pre-war years whose work expressed an illiberal impatience for change Percy Wyndham Lewis was the leading figure. He was born in 1882 of an American father and an English mother. From 1898 to 1901 he studied at the Slade, where he was contemporary with Harold Gilman, though six years younger. Augustus John left the Slade in the year Lewis first attended, Spencer Gore a year later, in 1899. In 1910 Gilman was thirty-four, Gore and John thirty-two and Lewis twenty-eight. When Lewis left the Slade after three years' study he was still only nineteen. He spent most of the next seven years in Europe, often in John's company, visiting Madrid, Munich and Holland, and living for considerable periods of time in Paris. After his return to England in 1908 he continued to visit Paris at least once each year. Such experience was precocious in an English artist at the time, and Lewis was always to be in a sense a man caught between generations. He remained on good terms with Gore, John and Gilman, but his work, as it developed, was not easily seen as compatible with theirs.

No work of significance survives from Lewis's years abroad, and his earliest known extant oil painting was executed late in 1914 or early in 1915.[2] There is no record of any painting before 1911, and he may not have done much of consequence before that date. The study of his pre-war development is the study of works on paper. At the time of his return to England he was at least as much concerned with writing as with the visual arts, and he published his first stories in London in 1909. The few drawings datable to 1909–10 reveal little but an apparent interest in the creation of emphatic 'modern primitive' human types, as if he were establishing the dramatis personae for a particularly energetic piece of theatre. Such characters do in fact appear first in Lewis's early short stories. He was later to write that these had been composed from the materials discarded in the process of making paintings, the leftovers of his experience once it had been purged, in accord with Modernist concepts of practice in painting, of 'everything that smacked of literature';[3] but there was obviously more interchange between the two forms of his output than Lewis was in a position to acknowledge. In much of his work both as an artist and as a writer satirical modes are combined with expressionistic means. Such a combination was without significant precedent in recent English art, though there were precedents in literature, Dickens and Dostoievsky among them. A sense of interest in character and mood is discernible in all but Lewis's most abstract work. In 1902 he had seen and admired Goya's work in Spain, and had plainly not restricted himself, as had so many of his contemporaries, to a study of his technique. He had also no doubt been exposed while in Holland and in Germany to the works of the Art Nouveau and Symbolist styles in northern Europe, strong influences in the development of German Expressionist art at the time when he was abroad. Among Lewis's drawings of 1910–12 there are many which resemble some contemporary German work and which are unlike anything else.

The influence of Cubism on Lewis's art shows in a few surviving works of 1911. No painter in England made any significant use of Cubism earlier than this, although Picasso's *Demoiselles d'Avignon*, the first painting to which the term 'Cubist' can reasonably be applied, had been largely painted in 1907. Many of Picasso's earliest Cubist paintings had been based on highly expressive, 'sculptural' treatments of the human figure, but by 1909 the Cubism of both Picasso and Braque had become essentially a still-life mode. Lewis preferred the earlier, more expressionistic phase, and in his own drawings he turned the influence of Cubism to essentially expressive ends. If he ever painted or drew a still life it has not survived. With the exception of a handful of virtually abstract works of 1914–15, everything of interest that he produced was predicated upon a concept of the human figure as the embodiment of energy.

In *Smiling Woman ascending a Stair* of 1911–12 [30],[4] the earliest large work by Lewis which survives, complex three-dimensional forms are flattened into complexes of line, angle and plane, and the palette is restricted to the range of browns and greys employed by Braque and Picasso in their Cubist works of 1909–11. Depth is suggested not by the rounded modelling of contours or by the relationship of transparent to opaque areas, but by the insistence of edges and the implied directional force of lines. In terms of both subject-matter (a figure in motion) and treatment (lines 'energizing' the picture surface) there is compatibility here with the contemporary work of the Italian Futurist painters; like the Futurists, Lewis crossed the bounds of orthodoxy as established among the French Cubist painters in their interpretations of still-life and seated-model themes. But no painting comparable to Lewis's was shown by the Italians Boccioni, Severini or Carrà even in Paris before February 1912. Lewis may have been aware of Futurist paintings on comparable themes, but there can be no questioning the originality of his work of this period. The sense of irony, so pervasive a quality in all he produced, was entirely foreign to the spirit of the Futurist enterprise.

In numerous small drawings of 1912 Lewis pursued themes involving the integration of dynamic figures with virtually abstract backgrounds. In

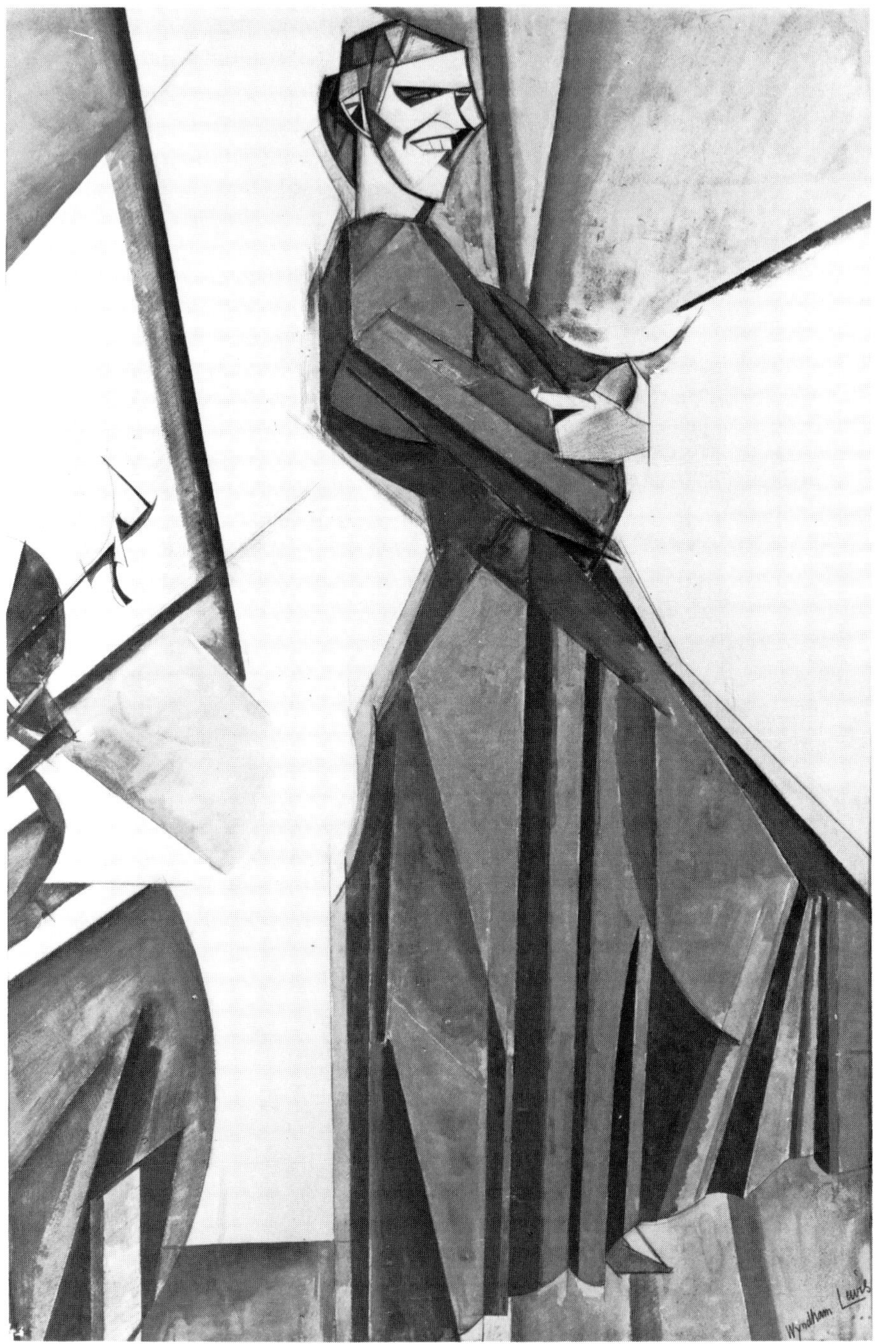

30. Wyndham Lewis: *Smiling Woman ascending a Stair*, 1911–12. Charcoal and gouache on paper, $37\frac{1}{4} \times 25\frac{1}{2}$ in.

the construction of the figures characteristics of the movements of machines are evoked as if as metaphors for qualities in human action. (Metaphor is of course usually characterized as a literary device. Its use in such contexts was a characteristic of the art and polemics of 'futurist' modernism – men's muscles 'interpreted' as pistons etc.) The tendency in Lewis's drawings is towards the energizing of the whole picture space by a rhythm established in delineating the figures, so that the total design becomes as it were an embodiment of human action or interaction, 'rationalized' according to the metaphor of mechanization, free from context, unspecific as to purpose and thus 'abstract'. The picture is a picture of a world invigorated and transformed by human action envisaged as an 'abstract' force.

The culmination of this development came with works such as those shown in the second Post-Impressionist exhibition, which included the lost drawing *Creation* [25] and some drawings for a portfolio on the theme of *Timon of Athens* [31]. Lewis's paintings of this period are all lost or destroyed.

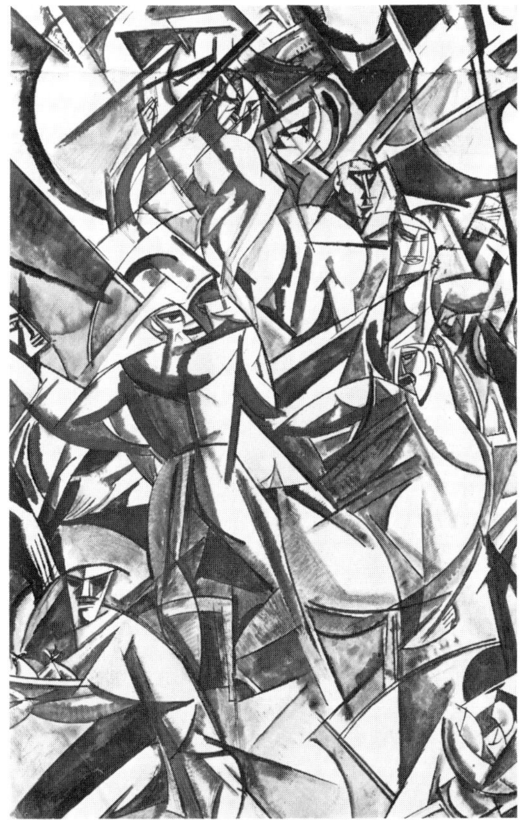

31. Wyndham Lewis: *The Creditors* (Design for Timon of Athens), 1912–13. Ink, wash, and watercolour on paper, $16\frac{1}{2} \times 10\frac{3}{4}$ in.

The most ambitious of which there is record was *Kermesse,*[5] a Cubist-influenced figure composition almost nine feet square, which made a considerable impression upon Clive Bell among others.[6] Lewis also painted some near-abstract decorative panels for Madame Strindberg's London nightclub, the Cave of the Golden Calf. *Kermesse* also hung for a while at the Cave, where it must have been seen, together with Lewis's decorations, by the many other artists who visited what Ezra Pound called 'the only nightclub poor artists could get into'. For those younger artists at the Slade who were interested in the latest developments in Paris, and who had not yet been to see for themselves, Lewis's work must already by 1912 have seemed very much more outlandish, and thus more exciting, than that of any other English painter.

The Cave of the Golden Calf, with its 'English Artists' Cabaret', typified the developing cosmopolitanism and bohemianism of London in the few years immediately before the outbreak of war. The brochure listed W. B. Yeats, Ezra Pound, August Strindberg, Frank Wedekind and Frederick Delius among 'the authors and composers under whose banners we range ourselves'. Besides Lewis, Spencer Gore and Charles Ginner contributed painted decorations and Eric Gill made the Golden Calf itself. There were also some brightly painted carvings by Jacob Epstein.

Epstein was born in America in 1880 of Polish-Jewish parents, but had taken British nationality two years after his arrival in England in 1905. He had studied sculpture in Paris in 1902–5, working hard to acquire technical skills at a time when Auguste Rodin was the established modern master and Aristide Maillol in the process of making his reputation. The Rumanian Constantin Brancusi is often credited with the transformation of the modern practice of sculpture over the next ten years. This change is associated with his elevation of the status of carving as a way of working. But it was not until 1904 that Brancusi enrolled as a student in Paris, and at that time the practice of sculpture was still seen as essentially a matter of mastery over modelling techniques. Epstein worked at both procedures. His early practice of carving was encouraged by an individual preference for the sculpture of early cultures. In the museums of Paris and later in the British Museum he studied not the widely approved works of the classical periods, but the 'less sophisticated' sculpture of pre-classical cultures in Egypt, Assyria and Greece.[7]

Epstein's first major commission after his arrival in England was for a series of carved stone figures to be mounted on the façade of the new British Medical Association building in the Strand. He chose to represent different stages in the life of man by means of over-life-sized nude figures, and when the first of these were unveiled in situ in 1908 there was outcry in the press on the grounds that the works were obscene. Senior liberal artists and

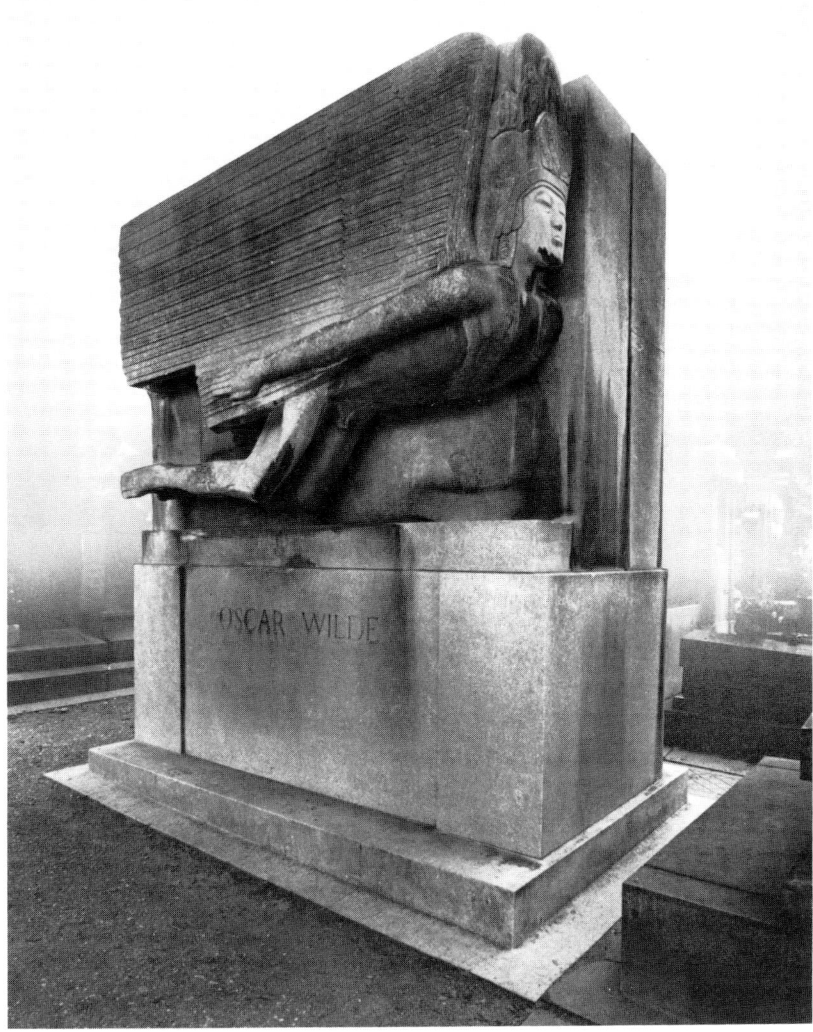

32. Jacob Epstein: *Tomb of Oscar Wilde*, 1911. Hopton Wood stone

authorities came to Epstein's defence and for the time being the statues were reprieved. Epstein thus found himself the subject of controversy at an early stage in his career. As he later wrote, 'London had become sculpture conscious.'[8]

Four years after the completion of the Strand statues, when Epstein went to Paris to install his monument for the tomb of Oscar Wilde in the Pere Lachaise cemetery [32], he found his work once again the subject of heated argument and establishment disapproval. In defending the Strand statues the Slade Professor of Fine Arts at Oxford had praised the unconventional 'Pre-Pheidian' style of the figures. For Wilde's tomb, direct carved in high relief from a single block of Hopton Wood stone, Epstein adopted a style which, though underwritten by his own museum studies and in particular by the Assyrian winged bulls in the British Museum, must have seemed harsher still and more 'primitive' to the vast majority of the cultured, whose tastes had been formed in study and celebration of the classical traditions of Greece and Rome and of Renaissance and post-Renaissance Europe. The 'sexual explicitness' of the figures in the Strand and of the winged angel on the Wilde tomb, amounting after all to no more than an absence of fig leaves, was considered indecent by many who would not have seen any cause to object to the representation of genitals on a neo-classical statue. In 1912 a majority still conceived of art as a matter of humanistic idealization, and of ideal forms as those which might be seen to involve reference to classical and Renaissance precedents. Here, as in the controversy over Post-Impressionism, the artist was seen to be working according to new and different interests. The increasing vehemence of the more advanced artists and critics in their rejection of classical, 'humanist' precedents was characteristic of the new expressionistic wave of modernism which swept across Europe in the half-dozen years before the outbreak of war. Writing in defence of Epstein late in 1913 the philosopher-critic T. E. Hulme asserted that it was 'the business of every honest man at the present moment to clean the world of these sloppy dregs of the Renaissance'.[9]

The smaller works which Epstein carved in 1913 of course attracted less public attention than his monumental commissions, but they were both more remarkable and more interesting as sculpture. In particular such works as the *Female Figure in Flenite* [33] suggested a high degree of confidence on Epstein's part in the expressive distortion of the human figure and in the strength of his response both to tribal sculpture and to the formal vigour of early Cubist painting. Among the painters in Paris there were some whose work had been influenced by their appreciation of African sculpture in the years 1905–10, but sculpture was then changing at a slower pace; Epstein's work showed the benefit of a sophisticated enthusiasm for tribal art certainly no later than did Brancusi's. He stayed in Paris from the autumn of 1912 until the spring of 1913 and came to know Brancusi during this time; he also met Picasso; but he was closest of all to the sculptor and painter Amadeo Modigliani, whom he saw 'for a period of six months daily'[10] and whose enthusiasm for African and other so-called primitive art was less reserved at that time than was Brancusi's.

When he returned to England Epstein moved to an isolated house on the south coast. It was here that his most individual works were produced. By

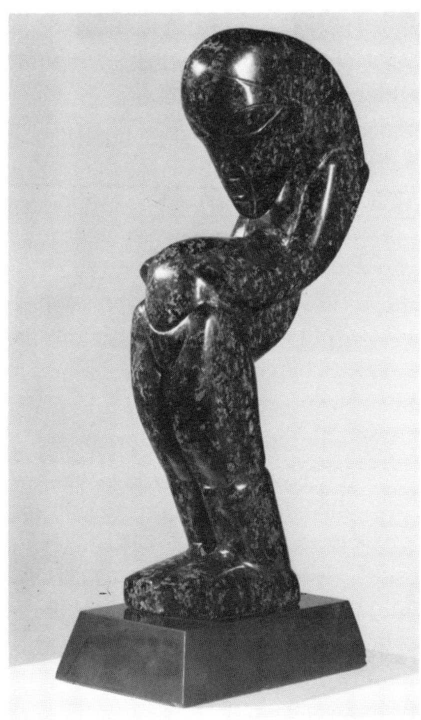

33. Jacob Epstein:
Female Figure in Flenite, 1913.
Serpentine stone,
$18 \times 3\frac{3}{4} \times 4\frac{3}{4}$ in.

early in 1913 his evident originality, his assimilation of archaic and tribal influences, and his knowledge of current work in Paris assured him of a position at the forefront of developments in sculpture in England parallel to Lewis's in painting. The two men were acquaintances rather than close friends, but there was considerable compatibility in the direction of their work over the next two years, particularly in so far as it was guided by their antipathies. Both men were concerned to oppose the interpretation of sensuality embodied in classical and Renaissance formal types, and both sought means to express a 'primeval' but modern vigour in their work.

In thus seeking to establish freedom from the governing tradition of five hundred years, Lewis and Epstein were on common ground with many of the protagonists of Post-Impressionism. Among the younger artists and their supporters in the years immediately before the war, distaste for the art of the Renaissance was virtually an item of faith. (It was one of the points that distinguished them from those older, more liberal figures Fry and Sickert.) As Clive Bell wrote much later, 'We were absurdly unjust to the Greeks and the Italians'.[11] In 1914 David Bomberg asserted his hatred of 'the Fat Man of the Renaissance',[12] and Gaudier-Brzeska wrote of the 'Solid Excrements in the quattro e cinque cento'.[13] In the same year T. E. Hulme promised a series of articles to be called 'Break-Up of the Renaissance',[14] dealing with the relation between a 'new constructive geometric art' and 'a certain general changed outlook' which he saw in terms of a gathering 'anti-humanistic reaction' in the modern period. The sense of a need for change, for the establishment of new criteria independent of the values of a liberal culture, mirrored some of the pressures for change within society as a whole. And as Bell suggested, the members of the artistic community mostly saw themselves as radicals of one persuasion or another.

The brief period from the opening of 'Manet and the Post-Impressionists' until the secession of Lewis and his allies from the Omega Workshops was one of considerable unity among the various heterogeneous candidates for membership of the avant garde. In the pre-war years there was a good deal of overlap between the social lives of artists and writers. They met each other often in certain cafés and at certain regular gatherings in private houses. The Cave of the Golden Calf was open from mid-1912 to February 1914, and there were various salons. The writer Ford Madox Hueffer (later Ford) kept virtual open house at the time he was editor of the *New Review*, in which work by Lewis and Ezra Pound was published. T. E. Hulme played host weekly in Frith Street. Hulme's at homes were very widely attended. As an early, albeit unprolific Imagist poet and a philosopher interested in art, his concerns touched those of a wide range of people. His visitors included his fellow Imagists Ezra Pound, Richard Aldington, Hilda Doolittle and F. S. Flint, Rupert Brooke, Rebecca West and D. H. Lawrence among other writers, A. R. Orage, editor of *The New Age* (a left-wing magazine widely read among the avant garde), the patron Edward Marsh, and a wide range of artists including Lewis, Epstein, Nevinson, Gaudier, Gore, Ginner, Gilman and Bevan, besides 'politicians of all sorts, from Conservatives to *New Age* Socialists, Fabians, Irish yaps, American bums, and labour leaders . . .'[15] Of the cafés, the Café Royal was among the most widely patronized. A catholic spirit prevailed. The Saturday at homes in Fitzroy Street had established an important early precedent, and the Camden Town Group was certainly intended to be widely representative. When the formation of the Grafton Group was being considered early in 1912 Wyndham Lewis and Etchells were among those Fry invited to a discussion at the Bells' house,[16] and the list of those involved during the first three months of operation at the Omega Workshops testified to a still greater catholicity.

During the three years from November 1910 to October 1913 those who felt they belonged with the progressive minority were drawn together, as were the various radical factions in political life, by the sense of a need for fellowship against the roused forces of reaction. The first Post-Impressionist exhibition provided a flag to rally round. Between late 1910 and autumn

1913 no young modern artist in England minded being called a Post-Impressionist. The new sense of community among them was celebrated by the formation of the Camden Town Group in May 1911, with Lewis and Grant as members alongside Gore and Gilman and John; and the last enterprise which that same community undertook before its final division into evidently incompatible factions was the formation of the London Group just two and a half years later.

The initiative for the formation of the London Group came from Fitzroy Street and Camden Town. In the autumn of 1913 a meeting took place in Sickert's studio to discuss a wider association which would include some younger artists such as those whose work was now showing the influence of Cubism. In Brighton in December 1913 there was an exhibition held under the auspices of the Camden Town Group of paintings and drawings by 'English Post-Impressionists, Cubists and Others', and the fully constituted London Group exhibited as such for the first time in March 1914 at the Goupil Gallery in London. Among the founder members and the participants at the 1914 exhibition were to be found the great majority of all the progressive artists in England then aged between twenty and forty. Camden Town and Cumberland Market were represented by Walter Bayes, Robert Bevan, Malcolm Drummond, Harold Gilman (who was elected President), Charles Ginner, Spencer Gore, J. B. Manson and John Nash; the secessionists from Omega were all involved, together with David Bomberg, C. R. W. Nevinson and William Roberts of the younger generation from the Slade. Paul Nash joined in time for the first exhibition. Epstein and Gaudier-Brzeska represented the modern movement in sculpture. (Probably as the result of a growing sense of alienation from the work of these younger men, and following a quarrel with Gilman, Sickert remained outside the group until 1916, by which time the twice-yearly exhibitions had become comparatively uncontroversial.)

Of all the different factors which composed the pre-war avant garde, Bloomsbury alone was not well represented in the formation of the London Group. Duncan Grant and Henry Lamb were listed but did not exhibit during the early years. Lewis's very public quarrel with Fry had broken out just before the group was formed, and it was to have a long aftermath. Bloomsbury closed its ranks, and many of those not included among them became aggressive in their opposition. Fry was not widely popular among the younger artists, and for a while non-membership of the Bloomsbury coterie became the principal unifying factor among a loose community.

But the new avant-garde alliance was itself precarious and short-lived. At the Brighton exhibition Lewis, Etchells, Hamilton, Wadsworth, Nevinson, Bomberg and Epstein exhibited in a segregated 'Cubist Room', and there was a separate introduction to the catalogue in which Lewis was at pains to distinguish the work of himself and his friends. The Ideal Home affair had provided him with an occasion upon which he could make his claim for leadership of a distinct faction in a sufficiently public context and in a sufficiently dramatic manner. In the Cubist Room at the Brighton exhibition the art of this faction was identified in terms designed to persuade that this, not Post-Impressionism, was the representative modern style.

Once it appeared that the modernist sensibility might prevail, as the critics found their writings attended to and the artists found their work discussed and reproduced in the press to an extent unequalled before or since, once there was a suggestion that things really might change in some quite dramatic way, then, of course, there was bound to be competition within the avant garde. Any picture is in a sense the picture of a world. While there was felt to be a need for strong opposition to the 'reactionaries' there was common ground between all who offered alternatives to the prevailing sensibility; but once that sensibility had been successfully undermined, the alternatives became competing alternatives and the different paintings were seen to be pictures of incompatible new worlds, serving different interests and embodying irreconcilable views of reality.

In accelerating the inevitable disunification of the pre-war avant garde, the influence of Italian Futurism was decisive. Filippo Tommaso Marinetti, poet, performer and propagandist-in-chief of the Futurist movement, acted as a powerful catalyst. On his first visit to England in April 1910 he had come principally as the leader of an avant-garde literary movement, but a 'Manifesto of Futurist Painting' had appeared in Milan two months before that, and by 1912 the movement was attracting considerable attention from artists and art critics. In March of that year Marinetti returned to London together with the painters Boccioni, Carrà and Russolo on the occasion of the opening of a touring exhibition of Futurist paintings at the Sackville Gallery. A fourth painter, Severini, came later in the year and the following spring was given a one-man show at the Marlborough Gallery (at that time a considerable distinction for a young artist). According to the *Daily Mirror* the Futurist exhibition was seen by 40,000 people.[17] Modern art had been established as good copy for the popular press by the first of Fry's exhibitions, and this was another *succès de scandale*. The writing of manifestos played an important part in the Futurist way of life, and three were reprinted in English translation in the catalogue to the Sackville Gallery. Among the younger artists they were evidently widely read.[18]

The 'Initial Manifesto of Futurism', written by Marinetti in February 1909 and first published in the magazine *Poesia*, had announced in extravagant rhetoric an aesthetic based on 'the love of danger, the habit of energy and boldness'; motor cars, liners, locomotives and aeroplanes, crowds, factories and revolutions were celebrated in violent opposition to a culture of museums, libraries and academies. This was the most forceful expression of the new iconoclasm, the vaunted rejection of epistemia in the name of 'progress', which characterized the expressionist, radical stream of the modern movement. 'We wish', wrote Marinetti, 'to glorify War – the only health-giver of the world – militarism, patriotism, the destructive arm of the Anarchist, the beautiful ideas that kill, the contempt for woman ... Art can be nought but violence, cruelty and injustice.'

The 'Technical Manifesto of Futurist Painting', which followed a year later, was signed by the artists Boccioni, Carrà, Russolo, Balla and Severini. They saw modern science as 'victorious' and believed that its 'vivifying current' must 'soon deliver painting from academic tradition'. 'Who', they asked, 'can still believe in the opacity of bodies?' Their concept of art owed much to the work of the French philosopher Henri Bergson (by whom Lewis had also been impressed) and to his poetic if irrational idea of a life force or vital impulse seeking freedom in the face of the resistance of matter.[19] Bergson conceived of time, in so far as we experience it, as 'duration', and of reality as a perpetual coming-to-be rather than as accomplished existence. As Bertrand Russell observed caustically, 'The modern world calls for such a philosophy.'[20] The radical modernists of the world of art found it very much to their taste. In virtual paraphrase of Bergson, the Futurist painters declared, 'The gesture which we would reproduce on canvas shall no longer be a fixed *moment* in universal dynamism. It shall simply be the dynamic sensation itself made eternal. Indeed, all things move, all things run, all things are rapidly changing.' They asserted 'that all subjects previously used must be swept aside in order to express our whirling life of steel, of pride, of fever and of speed', and 'that movement and light destroy the materiality of bodies'. Where the English philosophy of the time tended, as did Fry, to value disinterested contemplation, Bergson compared life to a cavalry charge and the whole of humanity to an 'immense galloping army' (Russell). The work of the Italian Futurists abounds in cavalry charges, riots, scenes of traffic and passage, and suggestions of 'interpenetration', 'simultaneity', 'synthesis' and 'dynamism'. Their work was aggressive, dramatic and 'modern'. It looked like Cubism in motion.

Perhaps to justify their exclusion from the second Post-Impressionist exhibition, Fry wrote with some justice that 'the Italian Futurists have succeeded in developing a whole system of aesthetics out of a misapprehension of some of Picasso's recondite and difficult works'. It is not hard to imagine how Bergson's poetic philosophizing, combined with half-understood and journalistic renderings of recent major revisions in the theoria of the physical sciences, might have appeared dramatically to interpret the still lifes of the Cubist painters – to those, at least, who sought an art which would express their own impatience for change.

In 'The Exhibitors to the Public', the third of the texts printed in the Sackville Gallery catalogue, the Futurist painters declared themselves 'absolutely opposed' to the art of the Post-Impressionists and the Cubists of France, and asked, 'Is it not, indeed, a return to the Academy to declare that the subject in painting is of perfectly insignificant value?' They asserted that 'there can be no modern painting without the starting point of an absolutely modern sensation', and declared that their own paintings were Futurist 'because they are the result of absolutely futurist conceptions, ethical, aesthetic, political and social'. Between Post-Impressionism and Futurism the lines of demarcation were thus clearly drawn, and drawn in such a manner as to make clear that the respective adherents were divided not merely by preference in matters of style, but by ideological difference. For the Post-Impressionists, as represented in England, art was autonomous with respect to social life; for the Futurists, modern art was to be the very expression of modern social and political consciousness and of a blind faith in progress achieved by means of technological development as they had internalized and idealized it.

In the month of the secession from Omega a 'Post-Impressionist and Futurist Exhibition', organized by Frank Rutter at the Doré Gallery, recognized the need for separate classifications. Among the works shown were Epstein's third *Marble Doves*, Lewis's *Kermesse*, Cubist-influenced drawings of heads by Frederick Etchells, and paintings by Edward Wadsworth and C. R. W. Nevinson, titled *L'Omnibus* and *The Departure of the Train de Luxe* respectively, which were based on typically Futurist themes and clearly heavily dependent on Futurist models.[21] Wadsworth's work was soon to be purged of its 'automobilist' tendencies by the influence of Lewis, but Nevinson had become a true convert. He had met Severini in London in the summer of 1912 and had obviously been impressed by his work. He had travelled to Paris with him, and had returned to England in the spring of 1913 as a confirmed disciple of Italian Futurism [34].

The apparently widening gulf between the English Post-Impressionists and those who now responded to the idea of a more militantly modernist art was perhaps as much as anything a gulf between men of very different backgrounds. The intimates of the Bloomsbury circle were members of the cultured English upper-middle classes who had mostly been privately educated; they flirted with radicalism in their art, their politics and their emotional relationships and were perhaps sometimes uncomfortable in their dealings with their servants; but they were not given to radical action.

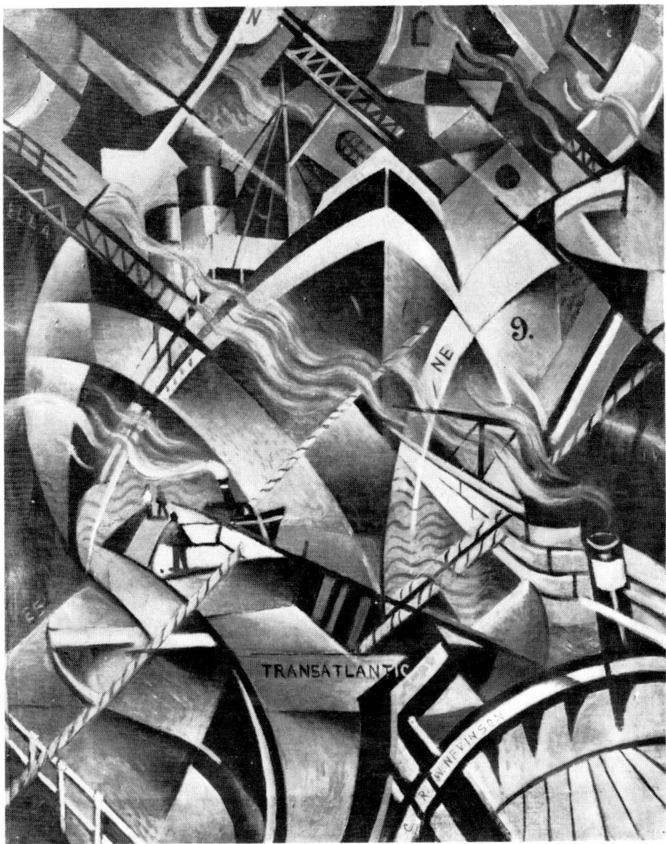

34. Richard Nevinson: *The Arrival*, 1913–14. Oil on canvas, 30 × 25 in.

The 'rebel' artists on the other hand were on the whole men who had less to lose and whose politics, in so far as they were identifiable, ranged over the spectrum from 'radical' militant left to 'radical' militarist right and back again. A typical instance of the interests of these artists and their supporters is T. E. Hulme's enthusiasm for the work of the French syndicalist Georges Sorel who, according to Hulme, 'Given the classical attitude, tries to prove that its present manifestation may be hoped for in working-class violence.'[22] Whatever the rebel artists were they were not typical liberals. Those of them who had attended the Slade had mostly been scholars rather than gentlemen; many had been to grammar schools; Bomberg and Roberts had commenced apprenticeships. Few of them had been born into the southern middle classes. They were mostly the children of working men, shopkeepers, foreigners or the nouveau riche. Bomberg was born in Birmingham, the son of an immigrant leather-worker. Etchells was the son of an engineer from Newcastle, Wadsworth of a mill-owner from Cleckheaton in Yorkshire. Gaudier was the son of a French carpenter and in the spring of 1914 was working and living in an earth-floored space under a railway bridge in Putney. Epstein was born in America and, like Bomberg, was a Polish Jew by origin. Lewis had been educated at Rugby, and was half American, but had bohemian inclinations and a cosmopolitan experience. For each of these men the concept of a rebel art involved a degree of truth to different forms of experience from those which were sought and valued in Bloomsbury. (Nevinson's almost complete dependence upon the influence of Italian Futurism in the pre-war years was perhaps a measure of the extent to which he was obliged to take such experience at second hand.)

Where Bloomsbury took pride in its considerable homosexual membership, the Futurists and the English rebels struck attitudes of aggressive heterosexuality. Bloomsbury was on the whole pacifist, and when conscription was introduced many of its denizens took to the country; among the rebels, on the other hand, there were some eager and early volunteers and several uncomplaining conscripts. Where the Post-Impressionists celebrated the rejuvenation of a lyrical and decorative tradition, these others, who had not the southern English gentleman's habit of shrinking from the consequences of industrialization, painted images of dynamic activity in an industrialized world. Two different and irreconcilable interpretations of culture were here brought face to face.

It was thus inevitable that there should at some point have been a withdrawal from the Bloomsbury-dominated Omega Workshops, and the rebel artists' response to Futurist critiques of 'passéism' was a spur to disassociation. During the month after the break with Fry, Lewis, Etchells, Hamilton and Wadsworth joined with Nevinson in organizing a dinner to honour Marinetti, thus adding emphasis to the realignment of forces.

This was the high point of Futurist influence in London. During the month of November 1913 Marinetti gave five of his lecture-performances, described by a member of one audience as '... a full and roaring and foaming flood of indubitable half-truths'.[23] Lewis plainly admired Marinetti, whom he described as 'the intellectual Cromwell of our time',[24] and he learned much from the Italian in the way of techniques for dramatizing and publicizing polemic. Although in his introduction to the Cubist Room at the Brighton exhibition he had made clear that so far as painting was concerned Futurism was a term of reference to the Italian painters alone, he introduced the work of himself and his 'colleagues' on that occasion in terms of a view of the painter's relationship to the modern world which, though less stridently expressed, was entirely compatible with that established by the Futurists.

... a man who passes his days amid the rigid lines of houses, a plague of cheap ornamentation, noisy street locomotion, the Bedlam of the press, will evidently possess a different habit of vision to a man living amongst the lines of a landscape ...

All revolutionary painting today has in common the rigid reflection of steel and stone in the spirit of the artist; that desire for stability as though a machine were being built to fly or kill with.[25]

The development of Lewis's own work in 1913 was towards the formalization of rhythm and the hardening of planes and lines. Tonal contrasts became stronger to the point where modelling was almost wholly excluded. In the most abstract works of this period (from which little survives) the particular energetic characteristics of the figures were subsumed into an 'architectural' organization of the picture surface as a whole. The Tate Gallery's *Composition* [35], probably executed late in 1913, is a good example of this phase.

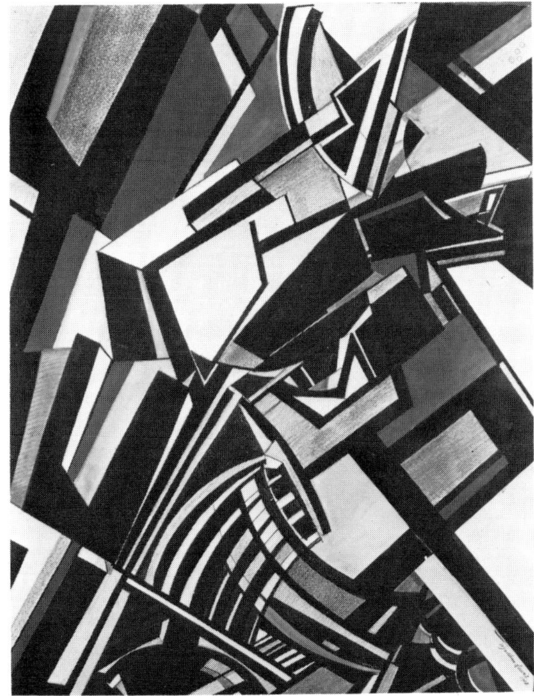

35. Wyndham Lewis: *Composition*, 1913. Watercolour, pen and pencil on paper, $13\frac{1}{2} \times 10\frac{1}{2}$ in.

In the Cubist Room at Brighton beside the works of Lewis and his 'colleagues' were hung some drawings by Epstein, whom Lewis praised as 'the only great sculptor at present working in England', and a painting by the independent David Bomberg, probably his *Vision of Ezekiel* of 1913. Lewis found the form and subject-matter of Bomberg's work academic, but the 'structure of the criss-cross pattern new and exciting'. Bomberg had visited Paris in the early summer of 1913 and had met Picasso, Derain and Modigliani among others, but his art had shown the effect of a precocious response to Cubism the previous year while he was only twenty-two years old and still a student at the Slade. The works with which he attracted attention in 1913–14 did not however owe much to French Cubism in its more sophisticated forms, though they were certainly regarded as 'Cubist' paintings in England at the time.

The Vision of Ezekiel was the first of a group of perplexing and ambitious works by Bomberg. Two more, *Ju-Jitsu* and *In the Hold*, were completed in time for the London Group exhibition in March 1914, and a fourth, *The Mud Bath*, was shown in a one-man exhibition at the Chenil Gallery in July of the same year. (All four paintings are now in the Tate Gallery.) *The Mud Bath* [36] measures approximately five by nine feet, *In the Hold* [37] approximately six and a half by eight and a half. Not many avant-garde works of this size were painted anywhere during the years 1910–14. The nature of the artist's ambition was also declared in his choice for each of the four paintings of a complex multi-figure, multi-level composition. These subjects were studied through successive drawings by means of which the structure became progressively more formal and the references to organic forms more

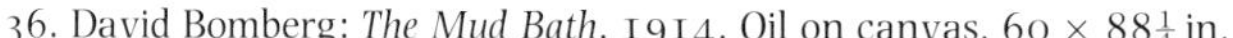
36. David Bomberg: *The Mud Bath*, 1914. Oil on canvas, 60 × 88¼ in.

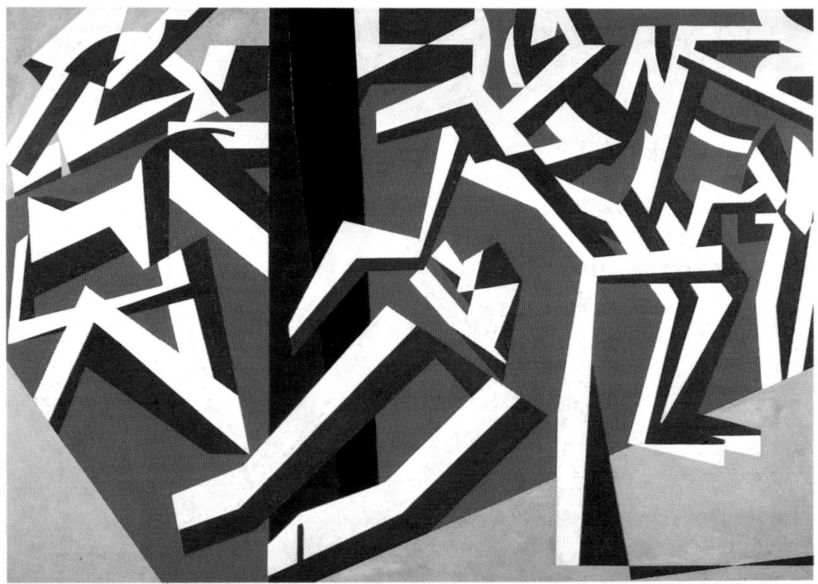

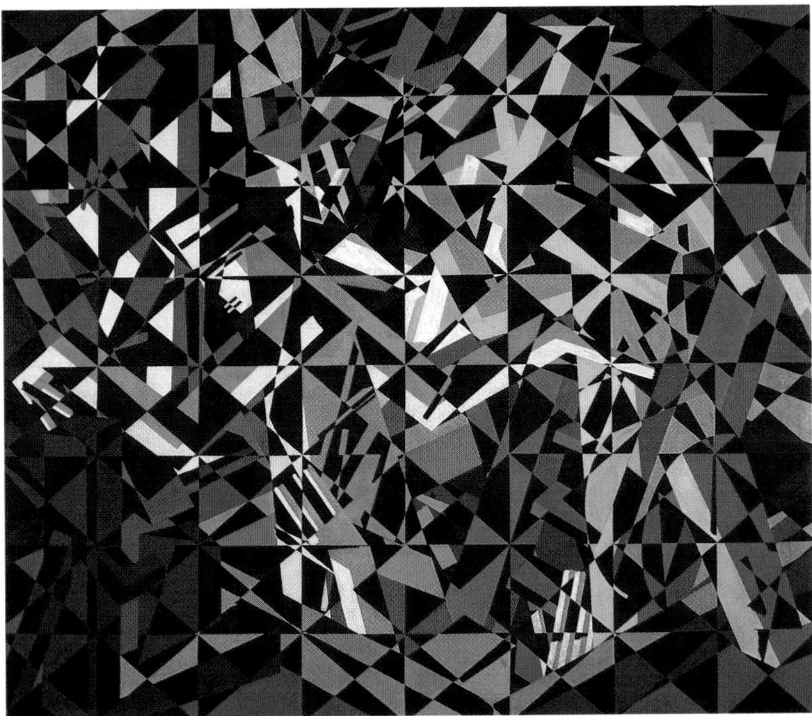

37. David Bomberg: *In the Hold*, 1913–14. Oil on canvas, $77\frac{1}{4} \times 91$ in.

obscure. His drawings and paintings were highly disciplined and quite free from the quality of barely contained energy which seems to enliven Lewis's work of the same period. Figures are stripped of all particularizing characteristics until they become little more than material for the manipulation of formal complexes. In *Ju-Jitsu* and *In the Hold*, predominantly straight-edged configurations based on the study of groups of figures become complicated, barely readable patterns of flat colour following the superimposition of lattices of straight lines running horizontally, vertically and diagonally from edge to edge and corner to corner. The origin of this procedure lay in the practice of squaring-up drawings for transfer of compositions to canvas, a technique associated with traditional practice in representational art, but the dramatic colouring-in of the resulting interstices produces a flickering 'abstract' surface. This achievement of virtually abstract images by means of a rigorous and almost academic practice results in the embodiment of a strange bloodless formality.

The introduction which Bomberg wrote for the catalogue of his one-man exhibition reads like a crude paraphrase of Bloomsbury aesthetics, with Futurist interjections.

I APPEAL to a *Sense of Form*. In some of the work . . . I completely abandon *Naturalism* and Tradition. I am *searching for an Intenser* expression. In other work . . . where I use Naturalistic Form, I have *stripped it of all* irrelevant matter.

I look upon *Nature*, while I live in a *steel city*. Where decoration happens, it is accidental. My object is the *construction of Pure Form*. I reject everything in painting that is not Pure Form . . .

Before Bell's *Art* was published Bomberg painted and drew as if to illustrate its central thesis. *The Mud Bath* is 'significant form' par excellence, a scenario divested of the emotions of everyday life, reductive, stark and 'primitive'; not so much the embodiment of a particular visual experience as a construction in its own right, particularized as a 'drama' of colour and shape. The modelling of figures is so reduced that the division between light and shade becomes merely a hard edge between two saturated colours. The effect is to establish an extreme contrast between the fictional depth of the space which Bomberg's marionettes inhabit and the flatness and facticity of the painted surface upon which figures and ground are interlocked. At the time no other painter in England or elsewhere had used bright, flat colour as dramatically as this in large figure-based compositions, or had proceeded so far in stripping the represented human form of its organic and particularizing qualities.

When Fry came to review the first London Group exhibition he expressed interest and admiration for Bomberg's work, but he admitted that it did not touch or please him.[26] But when T. E. Hulme surveyed the same exhibition for *The New Age* early in 1914 he discussed *In the Hold* in some detail and communicated his intellectual fascination with the work by means of a rigorous formal investigation.[27] Later in the same year he wrote a long review of Bomberg's Chenil Gallery exhibition. In the course of a consideration of the nature of form in the latter essay Hulme exposed the weak link in the aesthetic theories of Fry and Bell.

There is no such thing as a specific *aesthetic* emotion, a peculiar kind of emotion produced by *form* alone, only of interest to aesthetes. I think it could be shown that the emotions produced by abstract form, are the ordinary everyday human emotions – they are produced in a different way, that is all.[28]

Hulme was militantly anti-Bloomsbury and anti-Fry and became a forceful spokesman for an alternative concept of modernism during a short but decisive period. Though not an original thinker, he thought about things which most Englishmen did not, and thus became this country's most articulate and forceful propagandist for continental and particularly

German ideas on aesthetics and on abstraction in art as they had developed over the turn of the century. (Fry had always been fastidiously indifferent to German culture as a whole.) In considering the concept of modern art in England before and after the First World War it is hard to overestimate the importance of the ideas for which Hulme was a spokesman, and we should therefore consider them at this point.

The first strong influence on Hulme was the anti-rationalist philosophy of Bergson, by which the Italian Futurists were concurrently so deeply affected. Between 1909 and 1912 Hulme wrote often on the French philosopher's work, defending and recommending it to the readers of *The New Age*, and in 1913 he published a translation of his *Introduction to Metaphysics*.[29] (The fact that Hulme was writing poetry himself at this time may have predisposed him towards Bergson's metaphor-ridden writings.) Hulme published writings on art only between December 1913 and July 1914, at a time when he was deeply under the influence of work by recent and contemporary German aestheticians, in particular Theodor Lipps, whom he called 'the greatest writer on aesthetics', and Wilhelm Worringer. In 1908 Worringer had published his highly influential book *Abstraction and Empathy*.[30] In the winter of 1912–13 Hulme heard him lecture and talked with him in Berlin. This contact with Worringer gave Hulme access to the results of those recent wide-ranging speculations in aesthetics upon which Worringer himself had drawn.

The study of aesthetics in Germany at the turn of the century was under the influence of psychology to an extent which rendered it virtually a different subject from that studied in England. (Worringer's book was subtitled 'a contribution to the psychology of style'.) While the concept of the autonomy of art itself was recognized, following the writings of Hildebrand and Fiedler, subsequent German aestheticians emphasized the importance of the 'behaviour of the contemplating subject' (i.e. the spectator) in the study of aesthetic response to art. In particular Lipps's version of 'empathy' (*Einfühlung*) embodied a view of aesthetic enjoyment as 'objectified self-enjoyment', which was plainly not compatible with the concept of 'disinterested contemplation' as formulated by Fry in his 'Essay in Aesthetics'. In the writings of Alois Riegl an alternative was advanced to the materialist view that the origins and forms of art are decided by function, materials and technique. Riegl suggested that the history of art is not the history of ability but the history of 'artistic volition', and that materialistic factors merely inhibit the artist's 'will to form'. If the will to form is the decisive factor, then those styles in art in which naturalism is subordinate, such as the Byzantine and early medieval, are to be regarded not as incompetent (the prevailing nineteenth-century view), but as somehow differently directed.[31]

As a complementary alternative to the 'urge to empathy', Worringer posited an 'urge to abstraction' to explain aesthetic response to those non-naturalistic forms of art which Lipps had seen as frustrating to the spectator's attempts at 'self-activation'. According to Worringer's theory the artistic volition would pursue different ends among different peoples at different times.

> Whereas the precondition for the urge to empathy is a happy pantheistic relationship of confidence between man and the phenomena of the external world, the urge to abstraction is the outcome of a greater inner unrest inspired in man by the phenomena of the outside world; in a religious respect it corresponds to a strongly transcendental tinge to all notions. We might describe this state as an immense spiritual dread of space.[32]

Abstraction was seen as less materialistic and more spiritual, a symptom of the strengthening of the 'world-instinct', the fulfilment of 'an urge to seek deliverance from the fortuitousness of humanity as a whole, from the seeming arbitrariness of organic existence in general, in the contemplation of something necessary and irrefragable. Life as such is felt to be a disturbance of aesthetic enjoyment.'[33] Abstraction was seen by Worringer as an island of stability in a Bergsonian world of flux.

Here then, from the apparently authoritative pen of an academic German art historian, was what seemed like a theoretical justification of non-representational art; it was indeed taken almost as an exhortation to abstraction by certain artists in pre-war Europe.[34] If ever there was a period of 'inner unrest' inspired by external events, then this was surely it; and surely now was the time to turn away from those 'organic' forms characteristic of classic and Renaissance art and dear to the 'materialists' of the nineteenth century. No matter that Worringer's thesis was supported by tendentious and empty evidence; he seemed confident enough in his reference to a wide body of psychological, historical and archaeological fact and authority, and anyway the hypothesis was attractive.

In January 1914, Hulme delivered a lecture on 'Modern Art and its Philosophy'[35] which was largely a paraphrase of recent German writing. He opened with the basic assertion of what I have called 'Radical' Modernism (to distinguish it from the 'Traditional' Modernism of Fry, who was concerned to establish continuity), 'that the new art differs not in degree but in kind from the art we are accustomed to, and that there is a danger that the understanding of the new may be hindered by a way of looking on art which is only appropriate to the art that has preceded it.' He characterized the 'new' art as 'geometric' rather than 'vital' or 'organic'; i.e. as a product of the 'urge to abstraction' rather than the 'urge to empathy'; and he suggested that 'the re-emergence of geometrical art may be the precursor of the re-emergence of the corresponding attitude towards the world, and so of the break up of the Renaissance humanistic attitude.' He attributed the modern tendency towards flatness and stylization in art to 'the endeavour to get away from the [Bergsonian] flux of existence'.

Where Hulme, the aspiring theorist of modern art, went beyond Worringer, the academic art historian, was in his deliberate and, he believed, logical development of the hypotheses of German psychological aesthetics into an apologia for the work of his contemporaries. He pointed to the awakening of interest in archaic and non-naturalistic art and to the 'actual creation of a new geometrical art' which he saw as the only aspect of contemporary art 'containing the possibility of development'. He made clear that he was speaking neither of Futurism, which he saw as 'the deification of flux', nor of Post-Impressionism, nor of Cubism as represented by its early theorists Gleizes and Metzinger,[36] but of something nearer to hand. The significant new art, he believed, was characterized by 'a desire for austerity and bareness, a striving towards structure and away from the messiness and confusion of nature and natural things'. Hulme suggested that the 'association with machinery will probably be found the differentiating quality of the new art'. 'It has nothing whatever to do with the superficial notion that one must beautify machinery. It is not a question of dealing with machinery in the spirit, and with the methods of existing art, but of the creation of a new art having an organisation, and governed by principles, which are exemplified unintentionally, as it were, in machinery.'

This then, in Hulme's view, was to be the art of the brave new world to come. As with brave new worlds in general, it was the creation of an essentially late-romantic, pessimist, anti-rational and reactionary imagination; the manic in flight from the organic. The combination of a Bergsonian philosophy of 'élan vital' with the German concept of will to form, a belief in the efficiency of 'will', a faith in modern science and in the consequences of industrialization, and a naive enthusiasm for technological developments to come, these were the characteristics of the Radical Modernist ideology to which Hulme subscribed. However loudly they may have proclaimed revolution, the adherents of Radical Modernism – expressionists of the 'will to abstraction' – were on the whole in the grip of a technolatrous Utopianism rather than of any view of progress based on the Marxist concept of class struggle.

In support of his prognosis Hulme cited the work of Lewis, in which the human figure is perceived in terms of 'a few abstract mechanical relations'. He also referred to the drawings of Epstein. Epstein had been the subject of his first essay in art criticism in December 1913, and Hulme was working on a book on the sculptor's work when he was killed in action in 1917. The two men were close friends, and Epstein undoubtedly served Hulme as a source both of stimulus to speculation and of validating instances for his theories. The *Rock Drill* [38], Epstein's major work of the pre-war period and of his career as a whole, embodied the sensibility of Radical Modernism more dramatically than any other sculpture, English or continental, then or

38. Jacob Epstein: *Rock Drill*, 1913–14. Plaster and ready-made drill, height *c.* 120 in. Dismantled

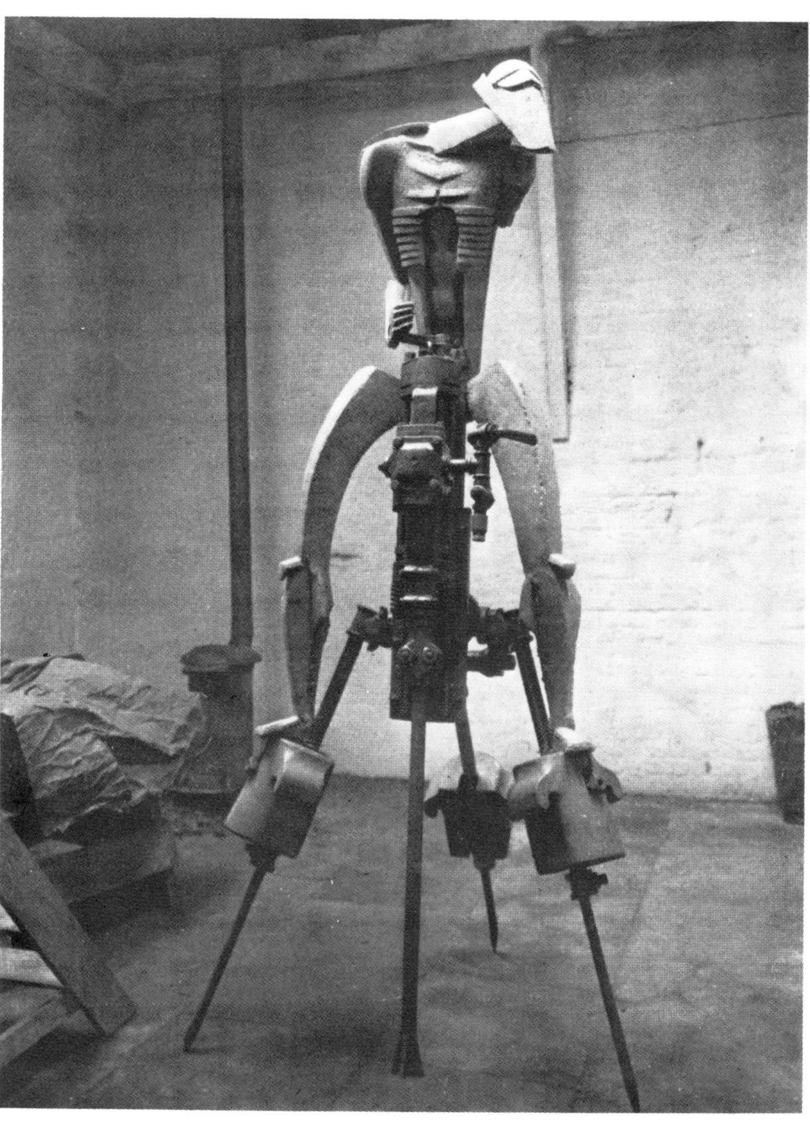

since; the aggressiveness, the 'primitivism', the abstraction, the anti-humanism, the celebration of energy, the use of mechanistic metaphors for human functions, the fundamental pessimism, all are to be found in this exceptional work. In retrospect Epstein described its origination and its demise.

It was in the experimental pre-war days of 1913 that I was fired to do the rock drill, and my ardour for machinery (short-lived) expended itself upon the purchase of an actual drill, second-hand, and upon this I made and mounted a machine-like robot, visored, menacing, and carrying within itself its progeny, protectively ensconced. Here is the armed, sinister figure of to-day and to-morrow. No humanity, only the terrible Frankenstein's monster we have made ourselves into ... Later I lost my interest in machinery and discarded the drill. I cast in metal only the upper part of the figure.[37]

The assemblage of real drill and plaster figure, altogether some ten feet high, was virtually complete by the end of 1913.[38] It was exhibited in March 1915 in a London Group exhibition at the Goupil Gallery. A year later Epstein exhibited the bronze cast of the torso, minus most of its right arm, which is all that is now left of the *Rock Drill* [39]. The sculpture cannot

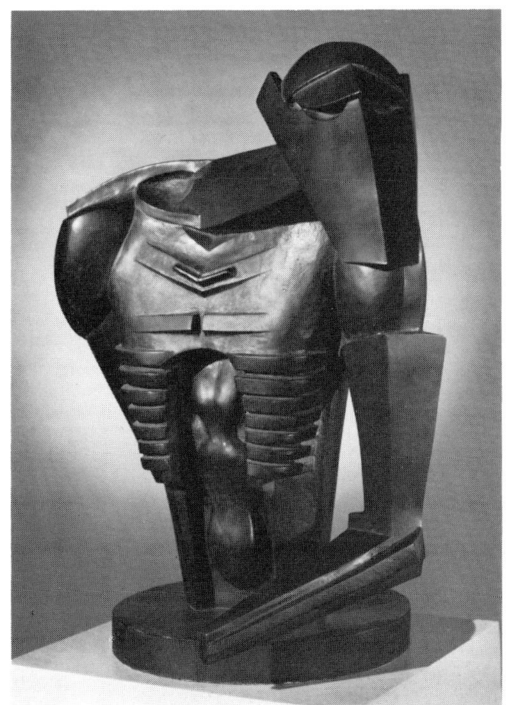

39. Jacob Epstein: *Rock Drill*, 1916. Bronze cast, $27\frac{3}{4} \times 23 \times 17\frac{1}{2}$ in.

have been attractive, but it was surely powerful enough to have made an impression on younger sculptors for most of the rest of this century. Whatever reason he had for thus emasculating his work, with hindsight it seems as if Epstein must have suffered loss of confidence with respect to an entire approach to life. He was perhaps encouraged to reassess the work by the coming of war and by the subsequent realization of those militarist fantasies which had so busied the Radical Modernist imagination, in England as in Italy.

For all the Futurists' show of opposition to Cubism, between mid-1913 and mid-1914 the distinction between the new orthodoxy and the new radical avant garde in England was seen by the members of the latter in terms of a line drawn between Post-Impressionism (including Matisse and the Fauvists) on the one hand and Cubism and Futurism on the other. The Rebel Art Centre was founded in March 1914 (the month in which Bell's *Art* was published) at premises in Great Ormond Street, with Lewis as a director and his friend Kate Lechmere as the source of funds. The legal registration was in the name of 'Cubist Art Centre Ltd'. The Omega secessionists were all involved, and the intention was plainly to establish a rival to 'Mr Fry's curtain and pincushion factory in Fitzroy Square',[39] which would serve as the focus of a wider range of activities and purvey a more modern style. The Futurist decorative designs of the Rebel Art Centre were to render obsolete the Post-Impressionist style of Omega in such all-important items as 'the painting of screens, fans, lampshades, scarves'. (Futurism was now a popular success and Lewis was by no means above capitalizing on this. Among other decorative works which he undertook at this time were some 'futurist' panels for the Countess of Drogheda's dining room.) The teaching of modern art was another function announced in the Rebel Art Centre prospectus, and the guiding principles were to be those of Cubism, Futurism and Expressionism. Expressionism, a term of reference above all to German art, was here a significant replacement for Post-Impressionism, the established term of reference to French art and its English derivatives.

The Rebel Art Centre attracted considerable publicity in its early days, but little work was done there, attendances were meagre in the extreme, and though Pound and Marinetti lectured as scheduled, many of the more ambitious plans remained unrealized.[40] The whole enterprise lasted a mere four months. But Marinetti, who must have been encouraged by the following that Futurism was attracting in bourgeois London society and among English artists, seems to have seen in the Centre and its supporters a potential Futurist colony in London. In June, while a large exhibition of Italian Futurist painting and sculpture was showing at the Doré Gallery, he and Nevinson published a Futurist-style 'Manifesto of Vital English Art', as from the address of the Rebel Art Centre. The signatories attacked the 'passéism' of English art and its 'absorption towards a purely decorative sense', gave the now customary 'Hurrahs' for 'motors', 'speed', etc., and finished by naming the 'great Futurist painters or pioneers and advance forces of vital English art – Atkinson, Bomberg, Epstein, Etchells, Hamilton, Nevinson, Roberts, Wadsworth, Wyndham Lewis'.[41]

Lewis, who was never a man easily subject to the process of colonization or complaisant of the spokesmanship of others, took the opportunity, as he had at the Omega Workshops eight months before, to publicize the existence of a distinct faction in English art. Then the rebels had dissociated themselves from Post-Impressionism; now they dissociated themselves from Futurism. A letter was sent from the Rebel Art Centre denying Marinetti and Nevinson any right to speak for the English artists and declaring that their use of the Centre's address was 'unauthorized'. The letter was signed by Richard Aldington, Bomberg, Etchells, Pound, Wadsworth, Lawrence Atkinson, Gaudier-Brzeska, Hamilton, Roberts and Lewis.[42] Bomberg characteristically asserted his independence from the Centre. Epstein, living outside London, did not sign the letter, but he and Hulme joined Lewis, Gaudier, Etchells and Wadsworth in disrupting a lecture by Marinetti and Nevinson at the Doré Gallery during the same month.

The inclusion among the dissenting signatories of the poets Aldington and Pound, and of Gaudier who had also not been named, was significant of a new alignment. Pound had admired work by Gaudier shown at the Allied Artists Association in 1913, and the two men had become close friends soon after their first meeting. Gaudier's large *Hieratic Head of Ezra Pound* was a tribute to the poet's role as an energizing influence. Pound's attention had been drawn to Lewis's work by Epstein at approximately the same time, and by the late spring of 1914 there had developed between the French sculptor, the American poet and the English painter a certain common understanding about what they wished for from the arts. At the close of 1913 Lewis and Nevinson had been planning the publication of a new magazine, no doubt influenced by the success of *Lacerba* as an organ of publicity for the Futurists. By February 1914 Nevinson had become discouraged and Lewis became the sole prospective editor. The project hung fire for a while, but in the late spring of 1914, with the emergence of a coherent and sufficiently substantial English faction, neither Post-Impressionist nor Futurist, composed of both writers and artists, there was good reason for proceeding. With Lewis, Pound and Gaudier as the prime movers, and with Wadsworth providing considerable assistance, the publication was hurriedly completed. In July 1914 the first copies of *Blast* appeared in London. (In the same month Austria-Hungary went to war with Serbia, and on the fourth of August the British government declared war on Germany.)

Blast was not an influential publication. How could it be? There was no time. It was to be an *ave atque vale* to the very pre-war radicalism which it was designed to promote and to celebrate. But it staked its claim to a place in history with a remarkable éclat. In 'Cinders', his posthumously published 'sketch of a new Weltanschauung',[43] Hulme wrote that 'through all the ages, the conversation of ten men sitting together is what holds the world together'. *Blast*, the 'Review of the Great English Vortex', struck out as if to establish itself as the occasion of such a conversation. Pound had first used the image of a vortex to describe the pre-war milieu of artists and writers in London,[44] and the term was adopted by Lewis to signify the still place 'at the heart of the whirlpool ... where all energy is concentrated'.[45] At the last moment of preparation for *Blast* the term was adopted to establish an image for the new movement, and those moderns who were now neither 'Post-

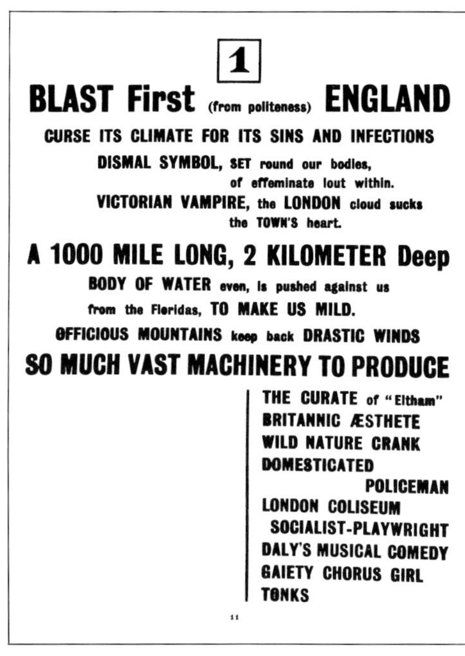

1

BLAST First (from politeness) ENGLAND

CURSE ITS CLIMATE FOR ITS SINS AND INFECTIONS

DISMAL SYMBOL, SET round our bodies,
of effeminate lout within.

VICTORIAN VAMPIRE, the LONDON cloud sucks
the TOWN'S heart.

A 1000 MILE LONG, 2 KILOMETER Deep

BODY OF WATER even, is pushed against us
from the Floridas, TO MAKE US MILD.

OFFICIOUS MOUNTAINS keep back DRASTIC WINDS

SO MUCH VAST MACHINERY TO PRODUCE

THE CURATE of "Eltham"
BRITANNIC ÆSTHETE
WILD NATURE CRANK
DOMESTICATED
POLICEMAN
LONDON COLISEUM
SOCIALIST-PLAYWRIGHT
DALY'S MUSICAL COMEDY
GAIETY CHORUS GIRL
TONKS

11

40. Page from *Blast* No. 1.

Impressionists' nor 'Futurists' identified themselves as 'Vorticists'. The magazine opened with a two-part manifesto in bold sans-serif type, partly organized in Futurist-style asymmetrical typography [40].[46] The signatories were Richard Aldington, Malcolm Arbuthnot, Lawrence Atkinson, Gaudier-Brzeska, Jessica Dismorr, Cuthbert Hamilton, Ezra Pound, William Roberts, Helen Saunders, Edward Wadsworth and Wyndham Lewis.

There can be no doubt that Lewis was anxious both to attract acolytes and to present to the public the appearance of a substantial and unified membership. The list of signatories therefore includes the names of several who, while they may have been sympathetic to the cause, were not significant as contributors. The Imagist poet Aldington was included as a friend of Pound's. Arbuthnot was an experimental photographer whom Lewis had met early in 1914. Atkinson was a music teacher and self-taught artist of forty-one who had joined the Rebel Art Centre soon after its opening and who passed through a Vorticist phase before devoting himself to sculpture in the twenties. The dating of his work is uncertain, but he produced a number of near-abstract compositions on paper which combine a typically Vorticist interlocking of forms with an uncharacteristic elegance of overall arrangement and tone [41]. Jessica Dismorr, twenty-nine years

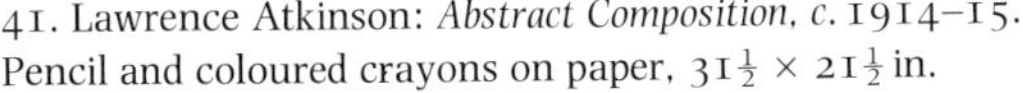
41. Lawrence Atkinson: *Abstract Composition*, *c.* 1914–15.
Pencil and coloured crayons on paper, $31\frac{1}{2} \times 21\frac{1}{2}$ in.

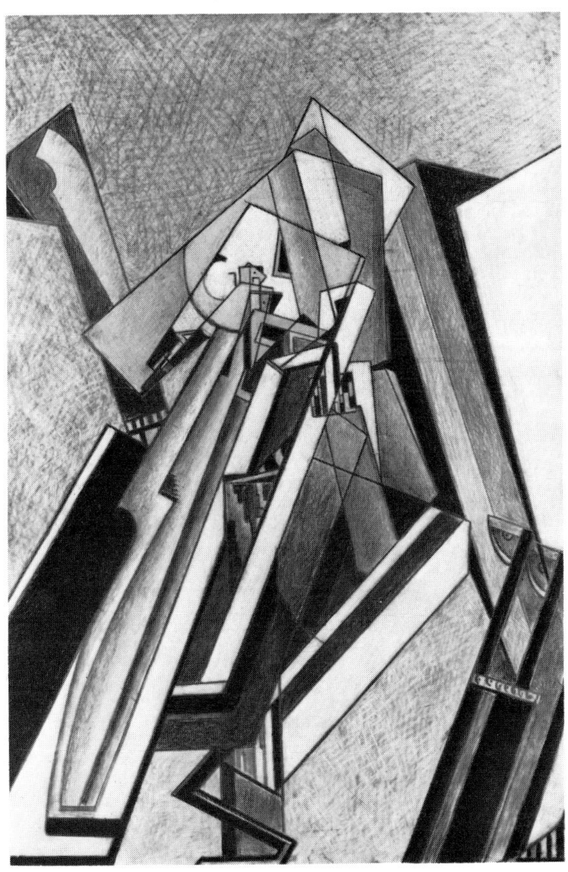

old in 1914, had studied art in Paris, where she had gained first-hand experience of the principles of Cubist and Fauve painting. Like her friend and contemporary Helen Saunders, who had studied briefly at the Slade, she produced near-abstract work while under the influence of Lewis in 1914–16. Hamilton had been with Lewis since the secession from Omega, and his work must obviously have been compatible, but nothing significant of his survives from this period and later examples are not particularly distinguished. William Roberts, at nineteen, was very much the youngest of

42. William Roberts: *The Toe Dancer*, 1914. Ink and gouache on paper, $28\frac{1}{4} \times 21\frac{1}{4}$ in.

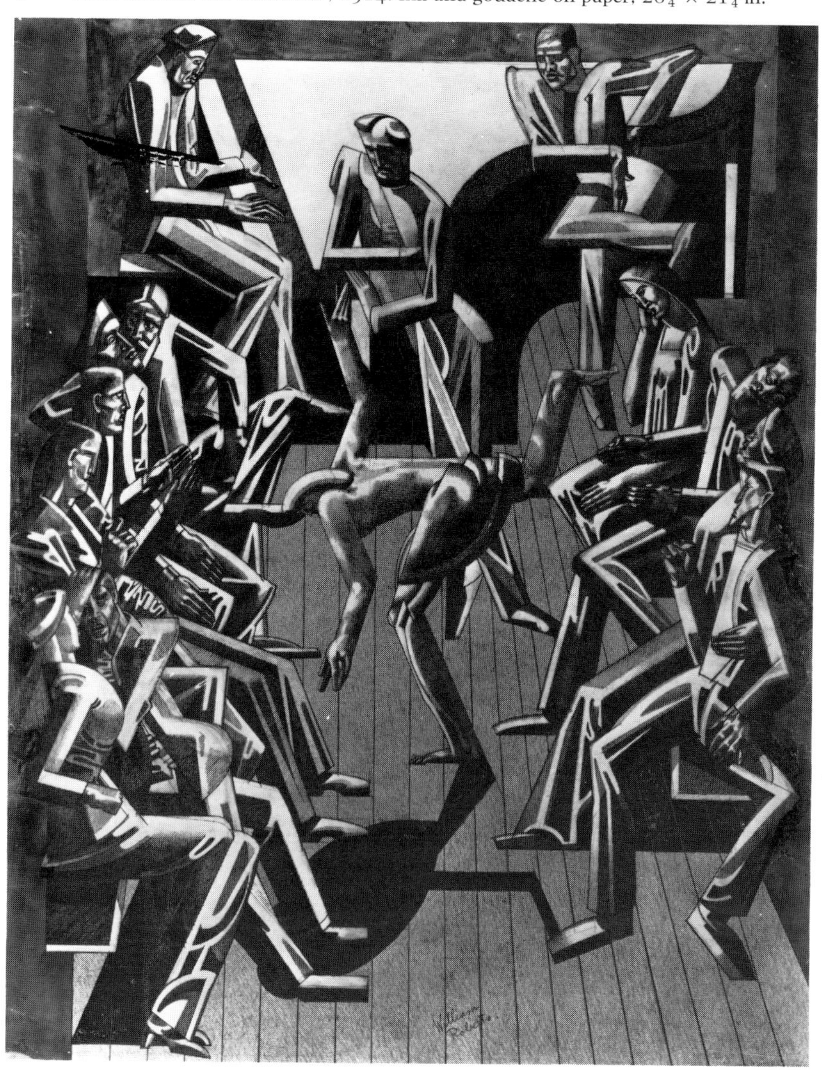

the group. In the winter of 1913–14, after leaving the Slade and following a visit to France and Italy, he had produced some highly formalized figure studies under the influence of his friend Bomberg. As a promising and precocious 'Cubist' he had been drawn away from Omega and into Lewis's circle early in 1914. *The Toe Dancer* [42], a complex figure composition with clear-cut, mechanized forms, shows him still at the end of that year close to Bomberg and possibly under the influence of Hulme's concept of modern art, but not decisively affected by Lewis.[47]

Lewis, Wadsworth and Gaudier were the artists who gave Vorticism its identity in 1914. Gaudier was then only twenty-three and not as free from the influence of Epstein as he would undoubtedly have become had he lived through the war. Much of his work of the previous year, though highly original in many respects, had been based on the expressive exploitation of naturalistic forms and conventional animal and figure subjects. But in his

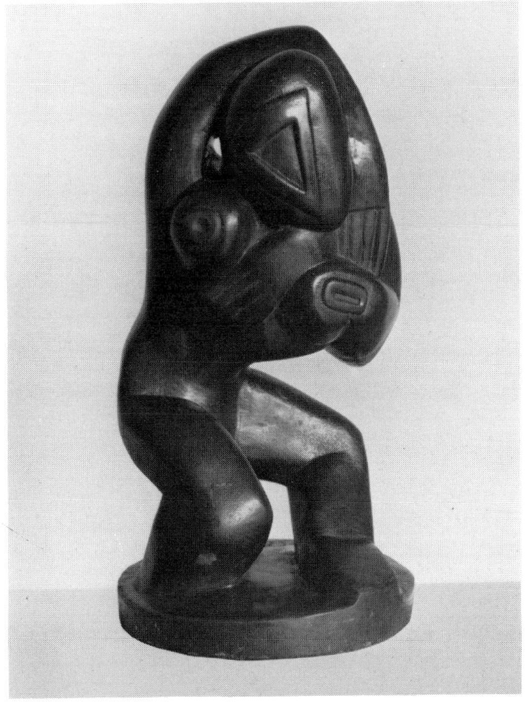

43. Henri Gaudier-Brzeska: *Red Stone Dancer*, c. 1913. Red Mansfield stone, 17 × 9 × 9 in.

Red Stone Dancer probably finished late in 1913 [43] he combined naturalistic with abstract elements and organic rhythm with extreme compression of form such as might be found in certain types of primitive Oceanic sculpture. The concentration of energy by means of the inter-volving of forms is a characteristic of Gaudier's subsequent work which

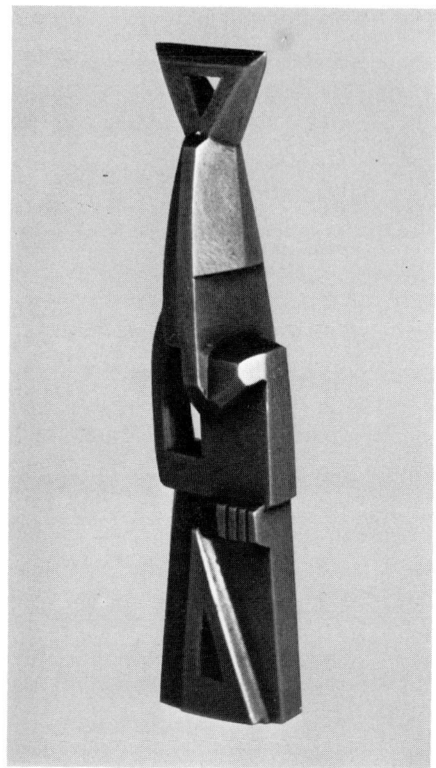

44 *(left)*. Henri Gaudier-Brzeska: *Ornement Torpille*, 1914. Cut brass, 7 × 2 × 1½ in.

45 *(below)*. Henri Gaudier-Brzeska: *Bird swallowing a Fish*, 1914. Carved plaster, height 12½ in.

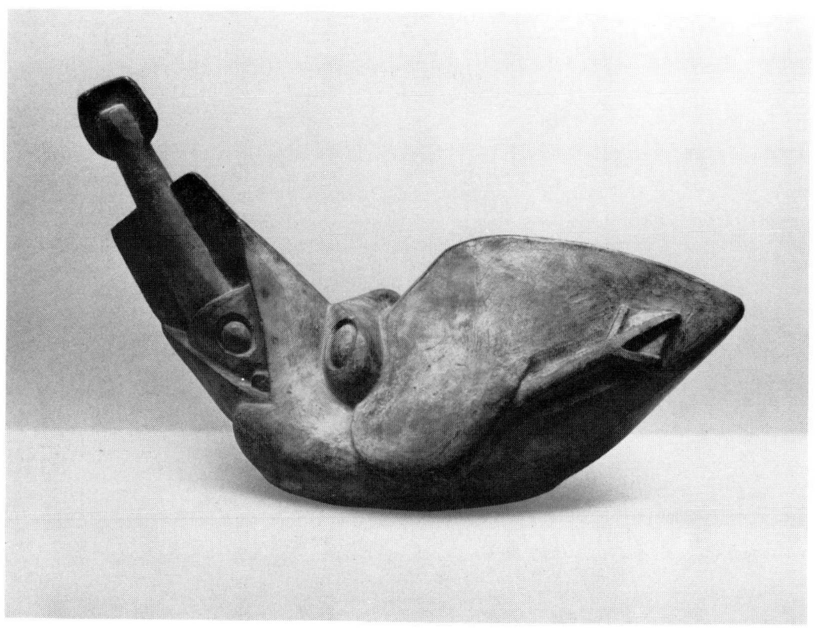

justifies his role as a Vorticist despite his continuing interest in animal subjects. In 1914, generally unable to afford the casting of vulnerable plaster sculptures into bronze, he made several small works cut and filed from brass in which the durability of the material and the ardour of the procedure combine to produce a quality of machine-like starkness. One of the most remarkable of these, *Ornement Torpille* [44], was owned by Hulme, whose theories it must have seemed to justify. *Bird swallowing a Fish* [45] was one of the few works in plaster which were cast during Gaudier's lifetime, originally into gunmetal. An image of naturalistic origin, made by means of a metaphor of mechanical action to embody a 'modern' aggression, this of all Gaudier's works best illustrates his contribution to the repertoire of Radical Modernism.

Gaudier contributed a manifesto on the 'Vortex' of sculpture to *Blast* no. 1 in which he celebrated 'sculptural energy', 'intensity', 'destruction', 'fecundity' and the will, and expressed his passionate enthusiasm for the art of Egypt, Africa, Oceania, South America and the paleolithic era, but his real and substantial talent was perhaps not likely to have been fulfilled in terms of the interests embodied in *Bird swallowing a Fish* and the brass carvings. Among his most successful works were two marble carvings of 1913–14, *Crouching Figure* [46] and *Maternity*, which could not by any stretch of the

46. Henri Gaudier-Brzeska: *Crouching Figure*, 1913–14. Marble, $8\frac{3}{4} \times 12 \times 4$ in.

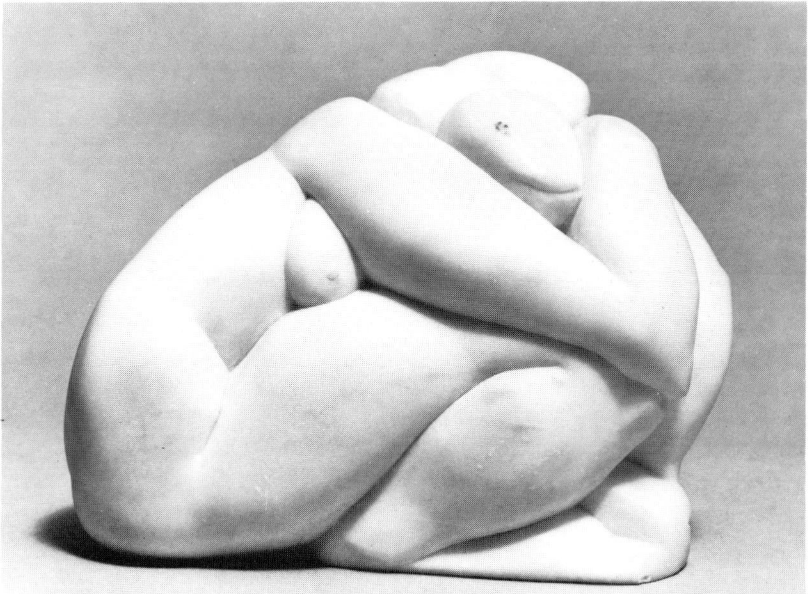

imagination be described as either anti-humanist or geometrical. For the second issue of *Blast* he was to have contributed an essay on 'the Need for Organic Forms in Sculpture'.[48]

Wadsworth was Lewis's most loyal disciple at the time of the publication of *Blast*. In mid-1913 he had painted some taut landscapes in watercolour [47] which showed an intelligent understanding of the relationship between Cézanne's late watercolours and Picasso's Cubist work of 1909–10, and he put the same sophisticated understanding of modern formal structure to work under the influence of Futurism and subsequently of Lewis to produce a series of dynamic abstract paintings in 1913–15 [48]. Virtually all these are now lost, but a number of woodcuts survive from the years 1914–18 to bear witness to his early ability to derive strong, simplified compositions from a sympathetic preoccupation with urban motifs and industrial landscapes. Of all the Vorticists his was perhaps the most realistic and least romantic interpretation of modern subjects; for him more than for any of the others the response to an industrialized world was

47. Edward Wadsworth: *Trees beside a River*, 1913. Watercolour on paper, $10\frac{1}{4} \times 13\frac{1}{4}$ in.

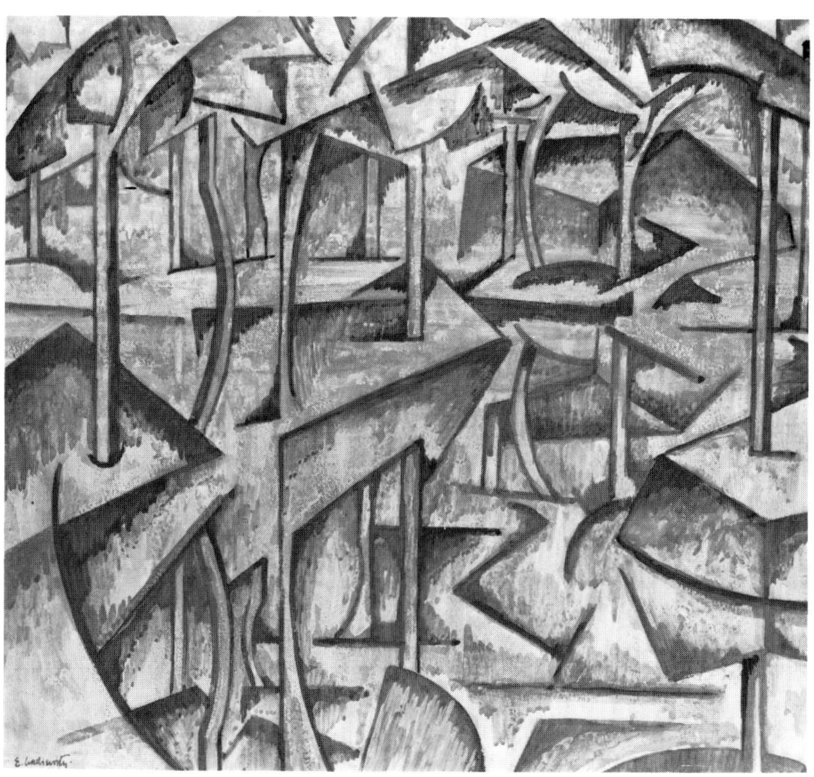

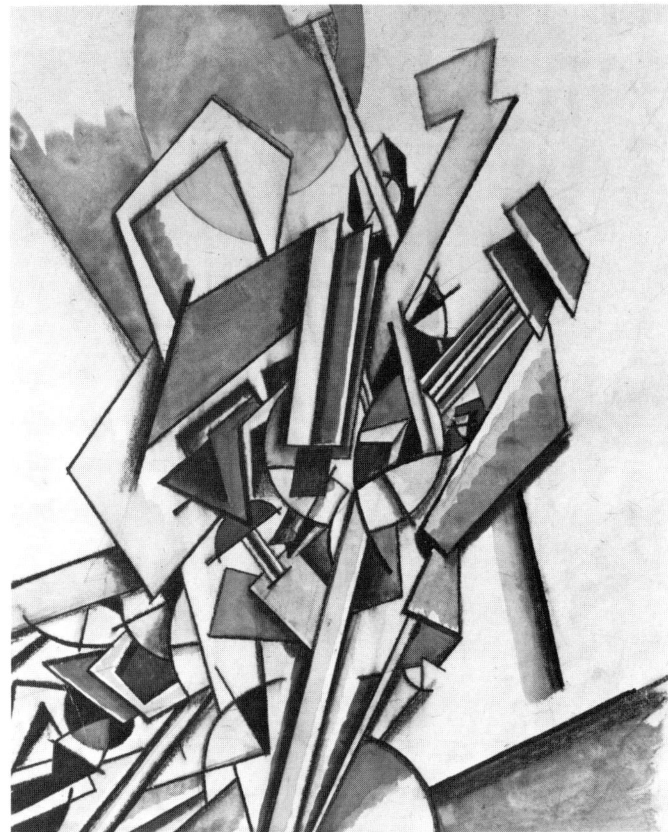

48. Edward Wadsworth: *Study for a Vorticist Painting*, *c*. 1914. Ink, chalk, watercolour, and gouache on paper, 13 × 10½ in.

unforced and innate. Wadsworth's very few surviving paintings of 1915 [49] show him relying heavily on the influence of Lewis, but unable to embody in his own work that restless energy which serves in the older man's work to compel recognition of a more profound and more profoundly troubled intelligence.

In the *Blast* manifesto the extent of industrialization in England was glorified in terms perhaps suggested by knowledge of the fact that the Italians were late-comers on the scene. Machinery was glorified as 'the greatest Earth-medium'. Though the authors were careful to disassociate themselves from Futurism ('the latest form of Impressionism') and from Marinetti's 'automobilist' romanticism, and though their own celebrations of modern science and technology were less tiresomely hysterical, the manifesto ran along Futurist lines at many points, not least in its expressions of nationalism. But elsewhere in *Blast* there is detectable, as a

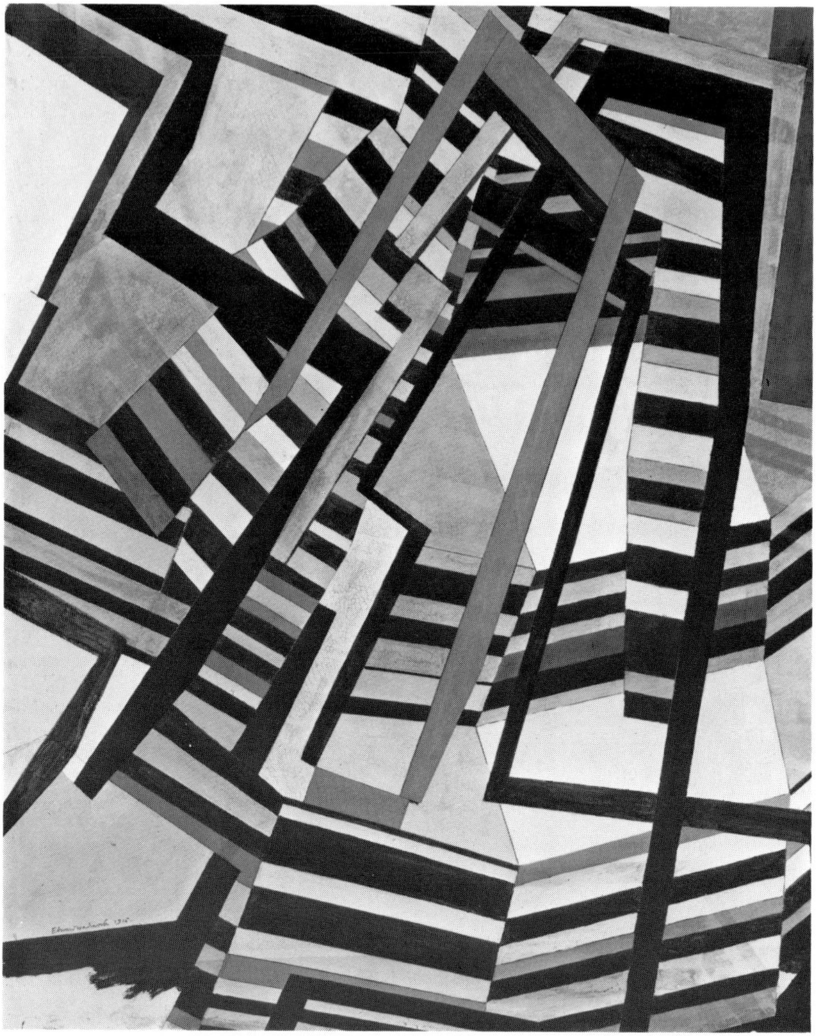

49. Edward Wadsworth: *Enclosure*, 1915. Gouache, collage, and pencil on paper laid on board, $20\frac{1}{2} \times 18$ in.

saving grace, that quality of reflexive irony, of intelligent if quixotic self-consciousness, which was stimulated in the friendship between Lewis and Pound.

> We start from opposite statements of a chosen world. Set up violent structure of adolescent clearness between two extremes ... Mercenaries were always the best troops ... The artist of the modern age is a savage.

Under the headings 'Blast' and 'Bless' the editors divided English characteristics, English culture and English institutions into sections for anathematization or approval.[49] They castigated pacifists, mystics, earnest socialists, hostile critics and conservative figures in religious, theatrical, and literary circles. Elgar, Galsworthy, Sidney Webb and Rabindranath Tagore were among the blasted. The inclusion of Bergson in the company of the damned was symptomatic of the ideological break with Futurism. Blessings were given to the strong, the militant, and the brave, to friends and fellow avant-gardists, to popular heroes and to sympathetic critics. The list included several suffragettes, aviators, music-hall artists and boxers, Sir Edward Carson the Ulster Unionist, Marat's assassin Charlotte Corday, Oliver Cromwell, James Joyce and Madame Strindberg.[50]

Blast was determinedly anti-Victorian and anti-picturesque, opposed to crankiness, sentimentality and 'democratic romanticism'. It was in favour of energy, 'bareness and hardness', and violence. 'There is one Truth, ourselves, and everything is permitted,' Lewis wrote. The mechanical and the geometric were upheld against the organic and the naturalistic, energy against sensibility, will against morality, in the assertion of an ideology compatible with Hulme's[51] and with the German tradition in aesthetics. Vorticism has traditionally been characterized as a kind of provincial Cubism, but until well into the 1920s 'Cubism' in England tended to be seen in terms of the early 'sculptural' phase of its development; Vorticism was in fact essentially an Expressionist movement, at least as it was represented in *Blast*. As if to emphasize this point the magazine included a 'review' by Wadsworth entitled 'Inner Necessity' which was largely composed of translations from Kandinsky's *Concerning the Spiritual in Art*, the confused but highly influential enchiridion of anti-rational, expressionist aesthetics as applied to the concept of a wholly non-representational art.

Illustrations in *Blast* were of works by Wadsworth, Lewis, Etchells, Roberts, Epstein, Gaudier, Hamilton and Spencer Gore, the last included together with a dignified obituary by Lewis in tribute to friendship rather than to compatibility. As if to discharge social obligations in the contemporary literary world, Lewis included writings by Ford Madox Hueffer and Rebecca West, and there were several poems by Ezra Pound which were perhaps more Imagist than Vorticist. In order to redress the overall balance of the literary contents, which he felt rightly were lagging somewhat behind the quality of the art, Lewis included a piece of his own literary work, *The Enemy of the Stars*, a 'Vorticist drama' written in a violently expressionist 'free prose' style quite unprecedented in England. In extending the spirit of avant-gardism into the use of language this stole the wind even from Pound's sails. The dramatis personae were figures straight from Lewis's own drawings of 1912–13, those embodiments of energy and of heroic invulnerability which so preoccupied his imagination throughout his life: 'Enormous youngsters, bursting everywhere through heavy tight clothes, laboured in by dull explosive muscles, full of fiery dust and sinewy energetic air, not sap.'[52] (Do they sound familiar? They reappear in other contexts, as ideal Aryan youths or as heroes of Soviet agriculture.)

Blast was above all Lewis's vehicle and his creation. His voice speaks through the manifesto; the criticisms in his 'Vortices and Notes' are sharper and the insights more profound than those of the other contributors. He, I feel sure, was principally responsible for the celebration of the 'Individual' and of 'the art of Individuals' which is the chief function of the first section of the manifesto. He attempted, both in his drawings and in his writings, to establish for the modern artist the image of a self-sufficient, radical super-ego, impervious to the erosion of independence and individuality which the forces of socialization effect upon the circumstanced lesser man. '"Life"', he wrote, 'is a hospital for the weak and incompetent ... Nature is a blessed retreat, in art, for those artists whose imagination is mean and feeble, whose vocation and instinct are unrobust.' The artist was to keep himself strong and pure for Art, seen by Lewis as 'non-life'. Hulme wrote in 'Cinders' of 'the floating heroic world' of man's attempts at self-assertion, and he described our attempts to impose unity upon the plurality of the world in terms of 'a kind of manufactured chess-board laid on a cinder-heap'. Both men embraced a pessimistic 'realism' connected to a romantic anti-rational tradition of philosophy. It was an authoritarian, not a democratic romanticism, and its vivid expression in the works of Lewis and of Hulme at the moment of terminal catastrophe in the liberal world should serve to remind us how powerful and how magnetic an alternative the concept of authoritarianism has been to the current of socialism in the culture and politics of Europe in the twentieth century.[53]

Lewis, I think, had an intuition even before the outbreak of war that the drift of his culture was away from him, and that there was a strong element of pathos in the Vorticist stand against the indifference of history. 'Our Vortex will not hear', he wrote, 'of anything but its disastrous polished dance.' Late in 1914 or early in 1915, while principally occupied in the writing of his first novel *Tarr*, Lewis made a number of tense and remarkable drawings using pencil, ink, watercolour, crayon and gouache [50].[54] They are less dynamic than his earlier works; there are analogies with the forms of modern architecture, but mostly such as suggest the style of glass-walled New York skyscrapers not yet built at the time. They pursue abstraction further than the energetic forms and rhythms of the earlier drawings, in the direction of a new 'classic' ordering of the world.

At the date of writing there are two oil paintings extant from this period of Lewis's work. The most impressive of these, *The Crowd* (now in the Tate

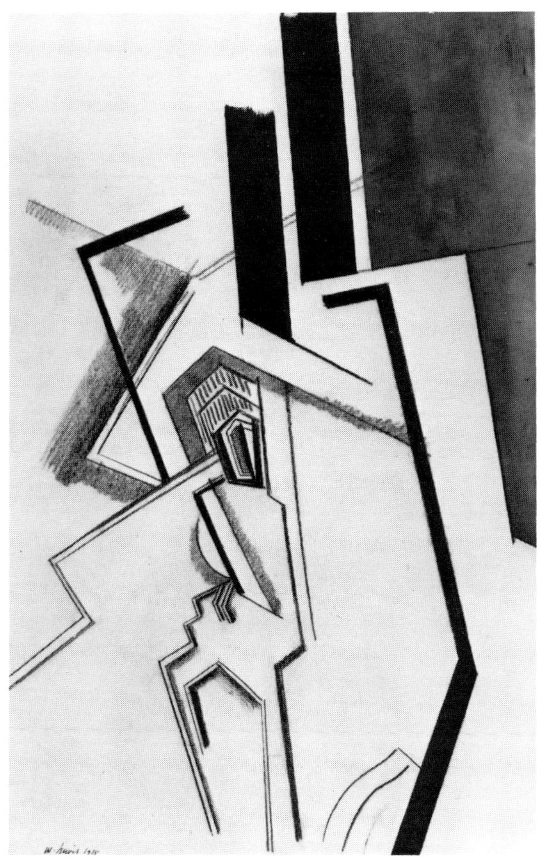

50. Wyndham Lewis: *Composition in Blue*, 1915. Ink, crayon, and watercolour on paper, $18\frac{1}{2} \times 12$ in.

Gallery) [51], shows antlike figures, mostly stylized beyond even those of Bomberg's paintings, struggling and massing in a world of high, rectilinear, abstract shapes suggestive of the same new-age architecture as the drawings. The colours are reds, yellows, oranges and browns, with white interstices. Two of the figures carry red flags, and the painting has often been referred to as 'Revolution'.[55] But it is unlikely that it was intended as a celebration of the possibility of socialist uprising. Vorticism was not so much the harbinger of a new order as a symptom of the terminal disease of the old. For those who took part, both those who went in eager anticipation, like Nevinson, and those, like Paul Nash, who went in trepidation, the war was to provide a lesson in art and in history. As Lewis wrote in retrospect, 'The brave new world was a mirage – a snare and a delusion.'[56] There was indeed nothing very brave or very new about the modern world which the Futurists and the Vorticists had welcomed in. Not revolution but war was its celebration.

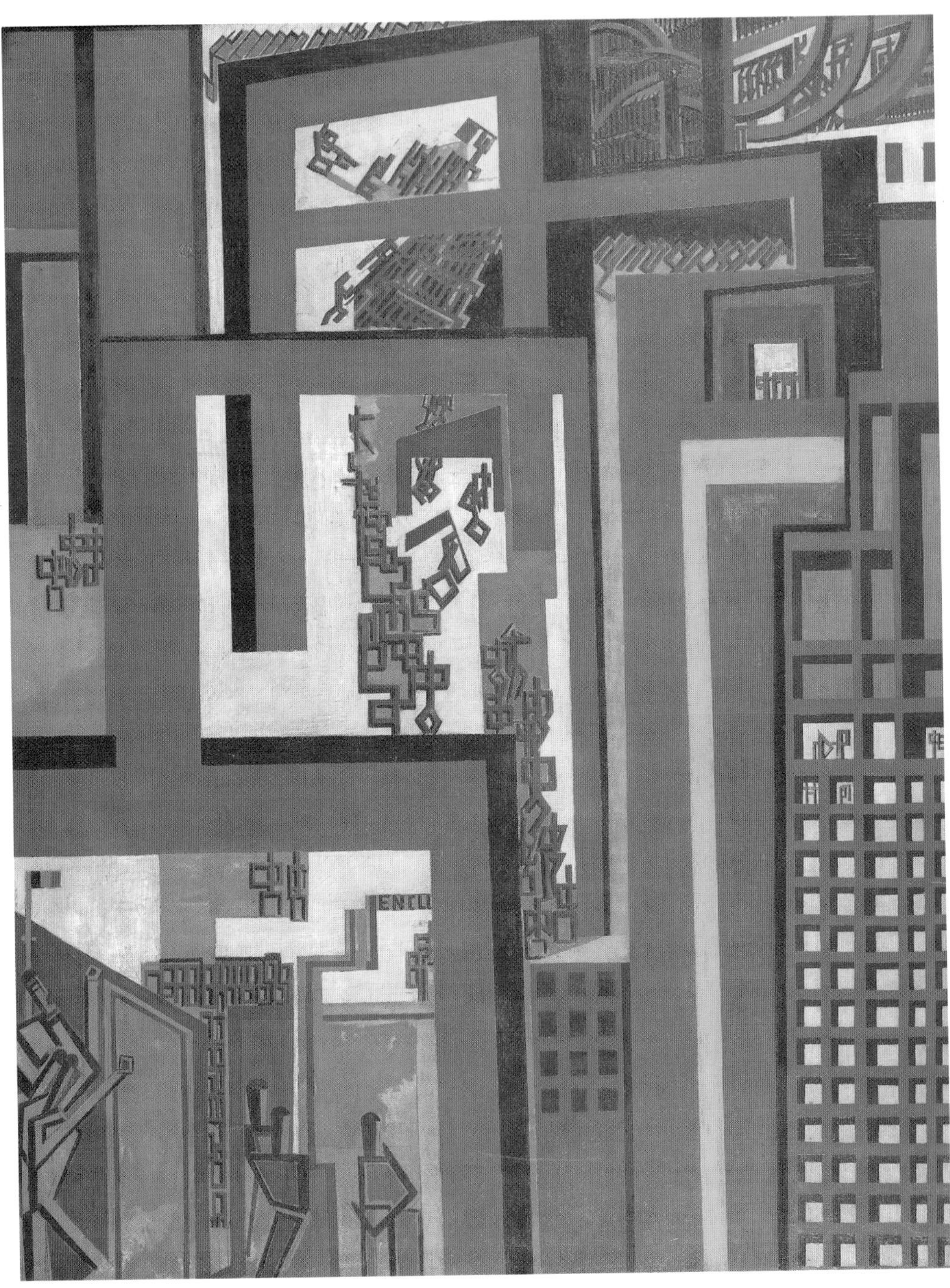

51. Wyndham Lewis: *The Crowd*, 1914–15. Oil and pencil on canvas, 79 × 60½ in.

5

THE GREAT WAR

Vorticist paintings were exhibited at the London Group in March 1915 and at the Allied Artists Association shortly after. In June the first and only Vorticist exhibition in England took place at the Doré Galleries. The members of the group on this occasion were listed as Dismorr, Etchells, Gaudier-Brzeska, Lewis, Roberts, Saunders and Wadsworth. Bernard Adeney, Lawrence Atkinson, Bomberg, Grant, Nevinson and Jacob Kramer accepted invitations to exhibit as independents. The Vorticist core of the show must have established an impression of considerable unity, with Lewis and Wadsworth as the principal exponents of the style, and must have represented a degree of practical achievement in painting which it is not now easy to assess. Of forty-nine works exhibited by the members of the group, thirty-eight were unaccountable for at the time of the Arts Council's survey of the movement sixty years later.[1] The work that now survives from the movement as a whole is mostly small in scale. In order to do justice to the ambitions of the Vorticists it is necessary to record that the major losses have been paintings of considerable size. Wadsworth's *Combat*, shown in the Doré Galleries' exhibition, measured six by eight feet;[2] Lewis's *Plan of War*, reproduced in the first issue of *Blast* [52], was eight-and-a-half feet high. Lewis also undertook two decorative schemes for 'Vorticist interiors', neither of which has survived.[3]

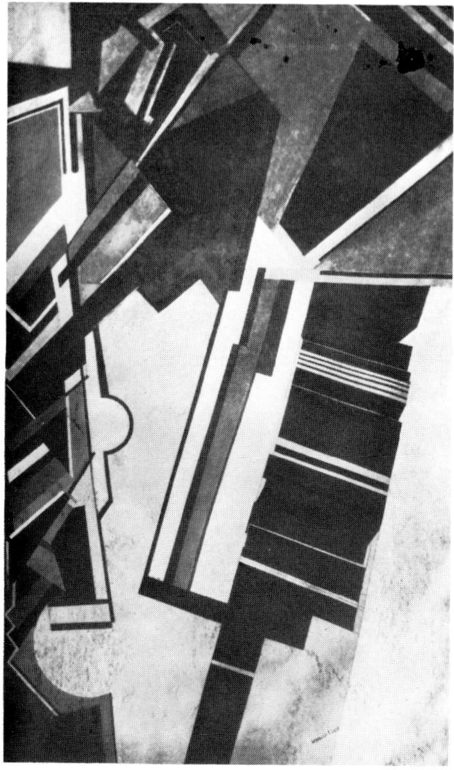

52. Wyndham Lewis:
Plan of War, 1913–14.
Oil on canvas, $100\frac{1}{2} \times 56\frac{1}{2}$ in.
Lost (reproduced from *Blast* No. 1)

Vorticism was defined by Lewis in the introduction to the group exhibition as:

> (a) *Activity* as opposed to the tasteful *Passivity* of Picasso; (b) SIGNIFICANCE as opposed to the dull or anecdotal character to which the Naturalist is condemned; (c) ESSENTIAL MOVEMENT and ACTIVITY (such as the energy of a mind) as opposed to the imitative cinematography, the fuss and hysterics of the Futurists.[4]

Otherwise the introduction added little to the rhetoric of *Blast* 1; the public were however referred to the forthcoming *Blast* 2 for 'a full and detailed exposition' of the Vorticists' ideas.

But *Blast* 2, which appeared in July 1915, was dominated by the contributions of Lewis to an even greater extent than its predecessor had been, and Lewis's interests were already ranging beyond those which could be expressed in explanation of Vorticist painting. His surviving works of late 1914–15 were as I have suggested not organized, as his works of the previous three years had been, in such a fashion as to express a contained and dynamic energy, but were composed according to structural principles analogous to those of modern architecture. During the later part of 1914 he had suffered a serious illness which had removed him from the social life of the London art world, and much of his remaining energy since the publication of *Blast* 1 had been taken up by the writing of his novel, *Tarr*. The place vacated in the avant-garde triumvirate by Gaudier's death was filled by T. S. Eliot, who contributed poems to *Blast* 2 and who was to be a lifelong friend of both Lewis and Pound. The balance between art and literature was thus shifting in favour of the latter, although Lewis never saw them as antinomic within his own practice.[5]

In the second issue of *Blast* the assertiveness of the earlier manifestos was moderated by the current of Lewis's speculations about the nature of art and of the relationship between art and culture in general. His principal contribution was a long 'Review of Contemporary Art'[6] in which he attempted to clear some ground for Vorticism by means of critical operations upon the growths of Cubism (as represented by Picasso), Futurism and Expressionism (as represented by Kandinsky). While acknowledging the achievements of Cubism, he criticized Picasso for the languor and tastefulness of his recent work, notably his collages; he applauded the vivacity of the Futurists but ridiculed their involvement with 'the crowd'; and while he credited Kandinsky as 'the only PURELY abstract painter in Europe', he disparaged his 'aetherialism' and his claim to total avoidance of representation. In the later part of the essay Lewis developed his own views on the nature of the modern artist's activity. What emerged in the space he had opened up for himself by his criticism of the European modern movements was a concept of art more widespread in its application than any such concept would have needed to be to underwrite the achievements of Vorticism alone. What was involved was a general critique of culture free from many of those closures characteristic of modernist writing about art.

> If the material world were not empirical and matter simply for science, but were organised as in the imagination, we should live as though we were dreaming. Art's business is to show how, then, life would be: but not as Flaubert, for instance writes, to be a repose and 'd'agir à la façon de la Nature', in giving sleep as well as dream.
>
> The Imagination, not to be a ghost, but to have the vividness and warmth of life, and the atmosphere of a dream, uses, where best inspired, the pigment and material of nature . . .
>
> The finest artists – and this is what Art means – are those men who are so trained and sensitized that they have a perpetually renewed power of DOING WHAT NATURE DOES, only doing it with all the beauty of accident, without the certain futility that accident implies.

The view represented here of the relationship between the imagination and the material world is significantly different and perhaps explicitly antagonistic to that expressed by Fry. We may identify in the contrast between these two views, and between the concepts of art to which they contribute, a conflict which has been fundamental to most major controversies in the criticism of modern art. It hinges on disagreement as to the nature and extent of art's representativeness. Lewis himself hinted at the nature of the contrast between his views and Fry's when in 1939 he reprinted his 'Review of Contemporary Art' under the title 'Art Subject to the Laws of Life' and prefaced it with an attack on Fry 'who was all for the amateur, all for the eternal child'.[7] The functions of the Imagination, as Fry conceived them, serve man's ability to dissociate himself from the material world and to transcend the contingent circumstances of his life. For Lewis, on the other hand, 'Imagination' was an aspect of activity, reflecting man's involvement in the material world and in the circumstances of his life.

Fry, the Traditional Modernist, saw creativity as innate and art as self-justifying, an activity sustained by its function as a means of perpetuating that sense of values which could be seen to be embodied in the tradition. According to this view the need to find means of expressing those values in terms appropriate to the circumstances of contemporary life is always likely to lead to significant technical problems for the artist, but the need is incidental nonetheless. The child and the primitive are not disqualified by any lack of sophistication in their understanding of the world they inhabit (although people who lack sophistication may be). By contrast Lewis, the Radical Modernist, conceived of artistic creation as wilful activity. He saw the essential function of art as the expression of value in modern life and in modern terms, and plainly considered that this would often necessitate militant opposition to the values embodied in those traditional forms which defined and thus limited the artist's resources of expression. The creative man, according to this view, is qualified as such by the force of his insights into contemporary life.

Within this latter view there was a further conflict, between on the one hand the urge to employ abstract forms as a means of effecting a radical break with tradition, and on the other the need to be able to establish 'truth to life' by means of such reference to particulars as was generally ruled out by the use of non-representational forms. This dilemma has been a feature of radical modernism throughout the century, but it has its roots in the first two decades of the century when non-representationalism was a major issue. It has never been satisfactorily resolved, and Lewis was among those first caught on its horns. (The development in his work of 1914–15 away from subjects based on human figures towards the exploitation of a range of generalized 'architectural' forms might be seen as an attempt to deal with this dilemma.)

Like so many of his friends and contemporaries Lewis was a very much less profound thinker when he was working to identify himself as a radical than when he was working to embody and to justify his speculations on the general nature of art and culture in his time. That history should hitherto have credited him more for his performance of the former function than of the latter is a token of the enduring precedence given in the twentieth century to a mythical value for modernism over historically bounded values relevant to the assessment of sense.

Lewis was a complicated and intelligent man, though as a propagandist for Vorticism in particular and for radical modernist art in general he often spoke and wrote as one with the mentality of a misanthropic demagogue. There were those, Paul Nash among them, who saw the war at its outset as the 'vindication of Vorticism'[8], but such a view could only have been defended in the most trivial of conversations. *Blast* 2 was published as a 'War Number'. In Lewis's 'War Notes' and in his essay on 'Artists and the War' his pessimism, his misanthropy and his morbid interest in the imagery of machinery ring out in phrases which echo like those launched from decorated platforms into empty halls: 'Murder and destruction is man's fundamental occupation'; men are primitives in the 'iron jungle' of the modern metropolis; the machine reflects man's basic, violent nature; art must reflect the 'forms of modern life'. Were his audience therefore to understand that the material for the most intense study of essential human nature was to be found in war and its machinery, and that it was only in mechanical and geometrical forms that the results of such study could adequately be expressed? Had the dubious concept of the necessity of an abstract art perhaps been pushed too far? Could the Vorticists' claims for the representativeness of their art still be sustained? Did anyone much care in 1915?

The iconoclastic radicalism and reflexive irony of *Blast* 1 were missing from *Blast* 2, and the essentially reactionary features of Vorticist ideology were thus more clearly displayed. An occasional note of jingoistic patriotism was struck in the reduced list of 'blasted' and 'blessed', and there appears in the blasting of Messrs 'Backbeitfeld', 'Hiccupstein' and 'Stormberg' the first evidence of that anti-semitism which was to become a neurotic feature of Ezra Pound's bathetic activities as a commentator on economics during the 1930s. As an American non-combatant stranded in London during the war, Pound worked to propagandize Vorticism and to extend its reach. He published a memoir of Gaudier-Brzeska in 1916[9] and despatched seventy-five Vorticist works (including forty-five by Lewis) for an exhibition at the Penguin Club in New York in the winter of 1916–17, which achieved little but the extension of the list of lost Vorticist works. Pound left London for good in 1919. A portrait by Lewis for which he sat twenty years later bore witness to the survival of their friendship. Thirty years after the publication of *Blast* 1 Pound signed another manifesto, in company with a group of Italian writers, which testified to the survival of his interest in authoritarian intellectual vitality: 'The live thought of the epoch', it began, 'is permeated by the fascist spirit.'[10]

Vorticism was overtaken by history. As Lewis admitted in the editorial to *Blast* 2, '*BLAST* finds itself surrounded by a multitude of other Blasts of all sizes and descriptions.' 'The War has stopped Art dead' he complained at the end of 1915.[11] And yet the War was the occasion of the first major exercise in this country in state patronage of modern art. Virtually every professional artist of any demonstrable competence who was prepared to put on uniform was offered employment as an official war artist sooner or later, either by the Ministry of Information or by the Canadian War Records Office under a scheme designed to provide a Canadian War Memorial.[12] Supporters of the new movements were among the advisers to the authorities of the Ministry of Information, and the choice of artists for the Canadian scheme was delegated to P. G. Konody, who had been among those blessed in *Blast* 1. Remarkably enough no artist seems to have been disqualified from initial consideration for either scheme on account of the radicalism of his style, though the express purpose of the Ministry's commissions was 'to preserve a pictorial record as complete as possible of the various sites and stages of the war',[13] rather than to encourage art for its own sake. It was the intention that priority should be accorded to eye-witness over imaginative reconstruction. The Ministry of Information was not concerned, as the artists themselves may have been, with imaginary lines of demarcation drawn between the modern functions of the artist and the photographer, with problems of redundancy in representational art in mind. The collection of over five thousand paintings, drawings, prints and sculptures now housed in the Imperial War Museum in London represents the fruits of the British scheme as supplemented by the museum's own acquisitions. It provides a quite remarkable record of the war in a wide range of styles, from the professional realism of Charles Pears's paintings of the war at sea to the unsophisticated Post-Impressionism of Henry Lamb's and Stanley Spencer's Macedonian tableaux.

If the principles of Radical Modernism in general and of Vorticism in particular are not well represented in this or in the Canadian collection (housed in the National Gallery of Canada, Ottawa), it is not so much because the radical artists were deprived of opportunities to produce war-based work as because their art did not equip them to work well to a brief which stressed the importance of documentary record. In one way or another the war imposed its requirements upon the artists, and the most successful were those whose art was most thoroughly modified by the experience.

The French army and the British Expeditionary Force of regular soldiers had taken the first brunt of battle in France from the outbreak of war until the end of 1914, when the stalemate on the Western Front allowed time for reorganization and replenishment of forces. It was at this time that volunteers were called for. Conscription was not introduced until January 1916, when it was rendered necessary by the appalling carnage of the previous year.

Gaudier-Brzeska was at the front as an infantryman with the French army by September 1914. He was killed in action in June the next year, at the age of twenty-four.

T. E. Hulme 'entered the army immediately and enthusiastically when war was declared',[14] was sent to the trenches in France as an infantryman and returned wounded in the spring of 1915. He went back to France a year later as an officer in the artillery, still 'in favour of this war', but 'without an ounce of bellicosity left'.[15] He was killed in September 1917 at the age of thirty-four, in a bombardment which also killed the sergeant of Lewis's gun a mere few hundred yards down the line.

Nevinson volunteered as a Red Cross ambulance driver in 1914, at a time when ill-health prevented enlistment for active service, and he was sent to France with the rank of private. He was back in London for a period early in 1915, was transferred to the Royal Army Medical Corps and was invalided out of the war early in 1916.

Wadsworth served with the Royal Naval Volunteer Reserve from 1914 to 1917, when he was invalided out. During 1917–18 he worked on schemes for dazzle camouflage for ships.

Paul Nash volunteered in August 1914 as a private in the Artists' Rifles, where he met the poet Edward Thomas. He spent the next two and a half years in England but was sent to the Ypres Salient in February 1917 following his commission as a lieutenant in the Hampshire Regiment. He was repatriated three months later after an accidental injury, and returned to the front for a short time in the autumn as an official war artist.

Bomberg joined the Royal Engineers as a sapper in 1915, was transferred to the King's Royal Rifles and was in active service in France in 1916. Late in 1917 he was transferred to a Canadian regiment as a war artist.

Lewis joined the army in 1915 and served in France as a lieutenant in the Royal Artillery until his attachment to the Canadian Corps HQ as a war artist late in 1917.

Stanley Spencer joined the RAMC in the summer of 1915, was sent a year later to Macedonia and returned to England in 1918.

Roberts joined the Royal Field Artillery as a gunner in March 1916 and was sent to France that summer. He was made an official war artist in 1918.

Epstein served in the Artists' Rifles from 1917–18 after being refused employment as a war artist. He had a German-sounding name, was Jewish and a sculptor. (Unless the *Rock Drill* be counted, the war produced no sculpture of significance to this study.)

The war came at a crucial period in the careers of each of these men, and to greater or lesser degrees it affected the development of their work. For Hulme the war became an interest which supplanted his interest in art. That energy and enthusiasm which he had employed in defending Epstein against his critics he now directed in a fevered defence of this war against the arguments of Bertrand Russell, who was concerned to establish that whatever their outcome such conflicts could not accord with the non-logical (i.e. ethical) upshots of *Principia Ethica*.[16] In passionate assertions of the dangers of German hegemony Hulme's self-image as a serving officer took priority over his romantic authoritarianism. Action in such a cause was a fulfilment of the more sensible aspects of his philosophy (or, we

53. Richard Nevinson: *Returning to the Trenches*, 1915–16. Oil on canvas, 20 × 30 in.

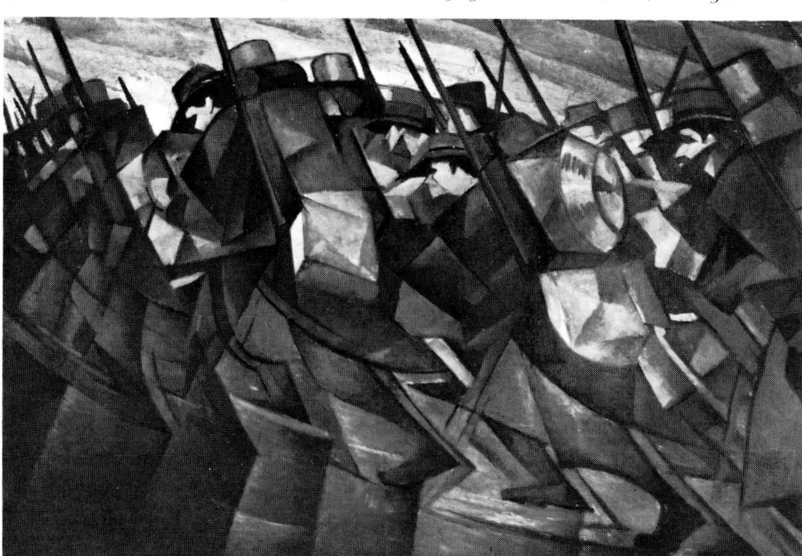

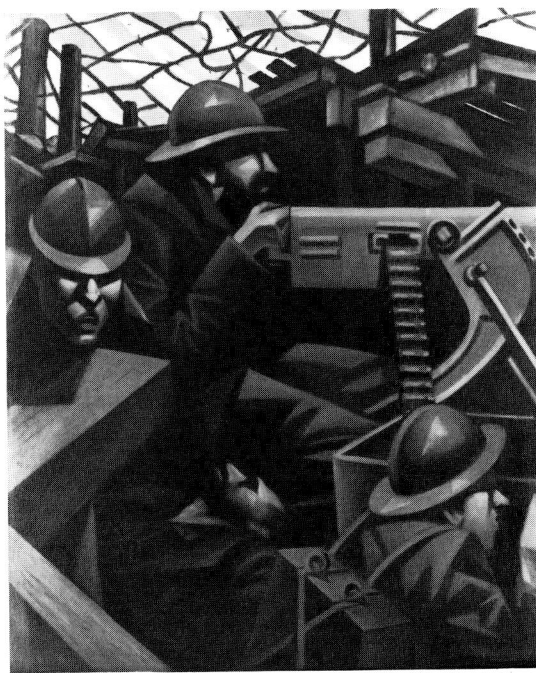

54. Richard Nevinson: *La Mitrailleuse*, 1915. Oil on canvas, 24 × 20 in.

might say, having something to do offered an alternative to romantic authoritarianism).

For the Futurist Nevinson also the war seemed at first to offer fulfilment of a kind. 'This war', he said early in 1915, 'will be a violent incentive to Futurism, for we believe there is no beauty except in strife, no masterpiece without aggressiveness.'[17] He was the first of the painters to enter wartime France and was the first of the younger artists to exhibit war work [53].[18] In the autumn of 1916 he held an exhibition of paintings of military subjects at the Goupil Gallery. His moderate brand of post-Cubist modernism, as instanced in works of 1915–16, was essentially a matter of rendering rounded surfaces by means of facets [54]; he thus established crystalline pattern in place of graduation, and flat linear rhythms in place of modulation into depth. For such appropriate subjects as groups of soldiers in uniform this technique served well enough to convey an impression of 'modern life' in terms of what was immediately identifiable and acceptable as 'modern style'. His exhibition was a great success and shortly after he was appointed an official war artist, the first of the moderns to be so employed.

Experience of war seems however, as it impressed itself upon him, to have forced Nevinson gradually to abandon his borrowed formalization in favour of a style which, if it was more traditional, was also traditionally associated with description rather than rhetoric. He was not, after all, an original painter, but he was a good reporter. In the depiction of those subjects by which his deeper feelings were touched he resorted to such conventional techniques as would serve him to convey actual rather than received experience. The requirements of veracity which he seems in the end to have seen as entailed by his official role no doubt also served to discourage his waning Futurist inclinations. The more impressive of his war works are scenes not of energy and aggression but of pathos and emptiness. In sombre paintings of dead soldiers and devastated landscapes he struck a balance between drama and documentation which none of the Vorticists could match.

For *Harvest of Battle*, a large commission from the Ministry of Information completed in 1919 [55], Nevinson resorted to a more thoroughly naturalistic style than he or any of his fellow modernists had employed since their earliest student days. There is an element of melodrama to the painting which it would have needed a far stronger artist wholly to exclude, but the work is convincing as a vehicle for personal observation and memory and for personal feeling, in a way that Nevinson's earlier, more modernist paintings are not. Though he was to remain a competent painter he was never to produce more interesting work than he did from 1915 to 1919. Having abandoned his Futurist image, he worked on after the war in a comparatively conventional style, now undistinguished by the interest of his war subjects, until his death in 1946.

For Hulme, the journalist-philosopher become man of action, and for Nevinson, the Futurist disciple become journalist-painter, the war provided more solutions than it raised problems. But for most of the others the experience of war was deeply disruptive in one way or another. Gaudier expressed the Vorticist's dilemma in a passage from the conclusion of his 'Vortex Gaudier-Brzeska', written in the trenches and published above an announcement of his death in *Blast* 2.

> I have made an experiment. Two days ago I pinched from an enemy a mauser rifle. Its unwieldy shape swamped me with a powerful IMAGE of brutality.
>
> I was in doubt for a long time whether it pleased or displeased me.
>
> I found that I did not like it.
>
> I broke the butt off and with my knife I carved in it a design, through which I tried to express a gentler order of feeling, which I preferred.
>
> BUT I WILL EMPHASIZE that MY DESIGN *got its effect* (just as the gun had) FROM A VERY SIMPLE COMPOSITION OF LINES AND PLANES.

The conflict which this quotation serves to symbolize – a conflict between concern for formal autonomy on the one hand and for the evocative

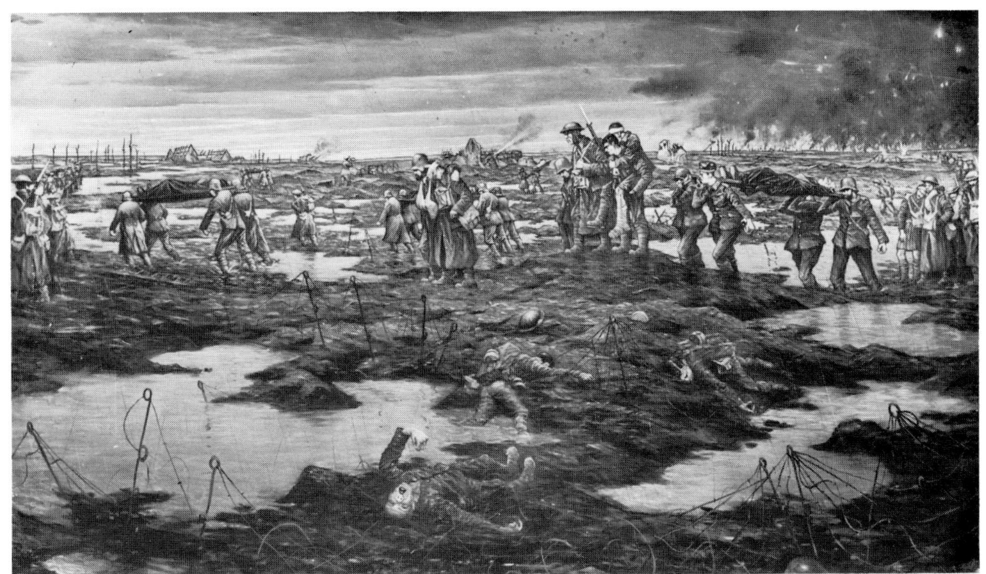

55. Richard Nevinson: *Harvest of Battle*, 1919. Oil on canvas, 72 × 125 in.

qualities of imagery on the other – was perhaps strongest for Gaudier himself and for Lewis. They had committed themselves more deeply to the concept of Vorticism than had the other artists, they had been more aggressive in their celebrations of the ideals of a 'modern' life, and they were perhaps moved by insights of greater critical power. In contexts of actual experience of the kinds of aggression and energy which characterize modern industrial war, the virtues of aggression and energy which the Vorticists had upheld as appropriate to life in the modern industrial world must suddenly have assumed quite different values. Those mechanized, 'abstract' forms which they had celebrated had now in real life taken on a range of associations with which they could not unreservedly identify.

Vorticism was after all an abstraction, and the evidence of twentieth-century art as a whole is that first-hand experience of war discourages the technical pursuit of such abstractions (if not of other similar ones). Lewis was moved by the death of Gaudier,[19] and his work faltered as the circumstances of modern war impressed themselves upon the culture at which his blasts had been aimed. 'You would think, to listen to them,' he wrote almost plaintively, 'that the splendid war army of England was fighting to reinstate the tradition of Sir Frederick Leighton, to sweep away the unorthodox splendours of the Russian Ballet, or revive a faded Kiplingesque jingoism.'[20] The art critic of the *Daily Telegraph* seemed to bear him out in reviewing an exhibition of modern English art in June 1916.

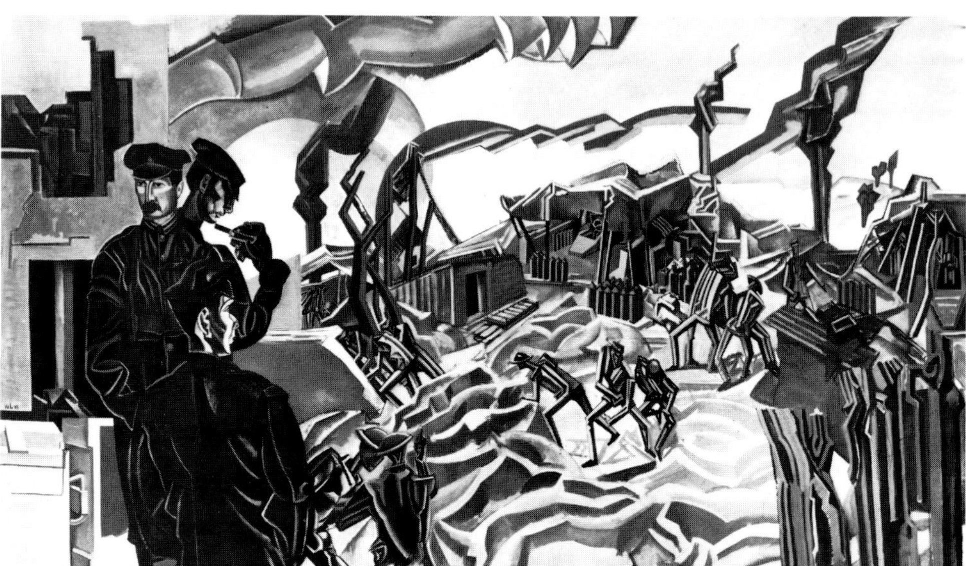

56. Wyndham Lewis: *A Battery Shelled*, 1919. Oil on canvas, 72 × 125 in.

'Less than ever', he wrote, 'do we feel inclined to look on with equanimity at these pranks . . . by which in piping times of peace it was possible to be mildly interested – or at least amused.'[21]

Nevinson had adopted his Futurist style easily enough and he abandoned it as easily under the pressures of the war. But Lewis could not respond so readily to the same pressures. He had in a sense foreseen what would happen. 'The War will take Marinetti's occupation of platform-boomer away,' he wrote in *Blast* 2. 'The War has for the moment exhausted interest in booming and banging.'[22] Lewis's own occupation had of course gone as well. He was a well practised bombardier, but his art during the years 1916–19 suffered from his inability to reconcile the surviving energies of a Vorticist style with the data of that laconic observation which seemed to be the most he could salvage of his pre-war arrogance and individualism. He found himself unable to celebrate the palpable destructiveness of mechanical war, and he was not the man to seek means of embodying its pathos. Where his drawings of 1912–14 were alive with tension, the works of 1916–19 look stiff and awkward. In the uniforms of the Royal Artillery his muscled heroes lose their invulnerability.

Lewis received two commissions for large war paintings, one from the Canadian War Memorials committee,[23] and one from the Ministry of Information. *A Battery Shelled* [56], completed in 1919 and now in the Imperial War Museum, is the stronger of these, and the nearest any of the pre-war radicals came to successful use of a radical formal vocabulary in a substantial subject-painting on a war theme. But even here the contrivances are so evident as to deprive the work of any real immediacy. It is a modern painting, but only 'stylistically' so; that is to say the formalizations of men, landscape, explosions and smoke appear as mannerisms unsecured by any sense of critical power in the artist's response to the subject. (This view seems to be supported by the comparatively naturalistic treatment of the figures at the left of the painting.)

In his introduction to 'Guns',[24] an exhibition of war works [57] at the Goupil Gallery in February 1919 (the first one-man show he had been offered), Lewis struck an uncharacteristically modest, almost defensive note. He asserted that the pre-war 'experiments' had been 'a logical development of much of the solidest art in this very various world', and drew attention to the work of Uccello, Goya, Van Gogh and Velazquez. 'This show', he wrote, '... pretends nothing, in extent: I make only the claim for it in kind that it attempts to give a personal and immediate expression of a tragic event. Experimentation is waived: I have tried to do with the pencil and brush what story-tellers like Tchekov or Stendhal did in their books.'

The other pre-war radicals fared little better. Edward Wadsworth had exhibited at least one thoroughly non-representational painting in the Vorticist exhibition, his *Enclosure* of 1915. Apart from the small woodcuts

57. Wyndham Lewis: *The No. 2*, 1918. Pen and ink, watercolour, and pencil, $21\frac{1}{2} \times 29\frac{1}{2}$ in.

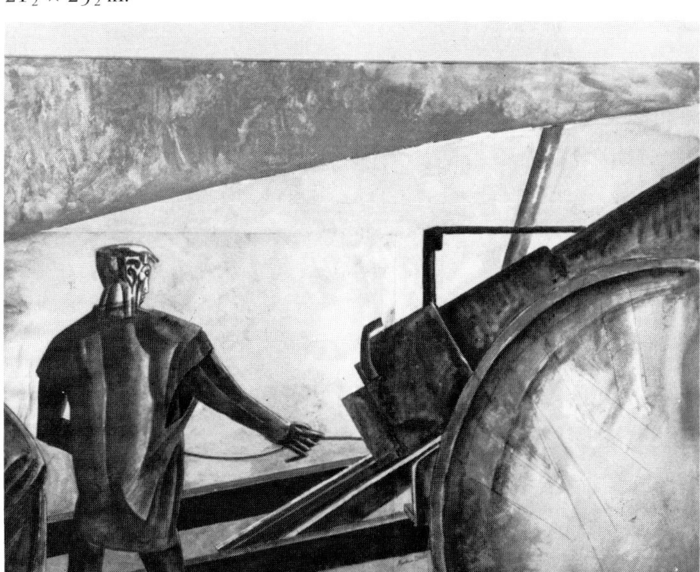

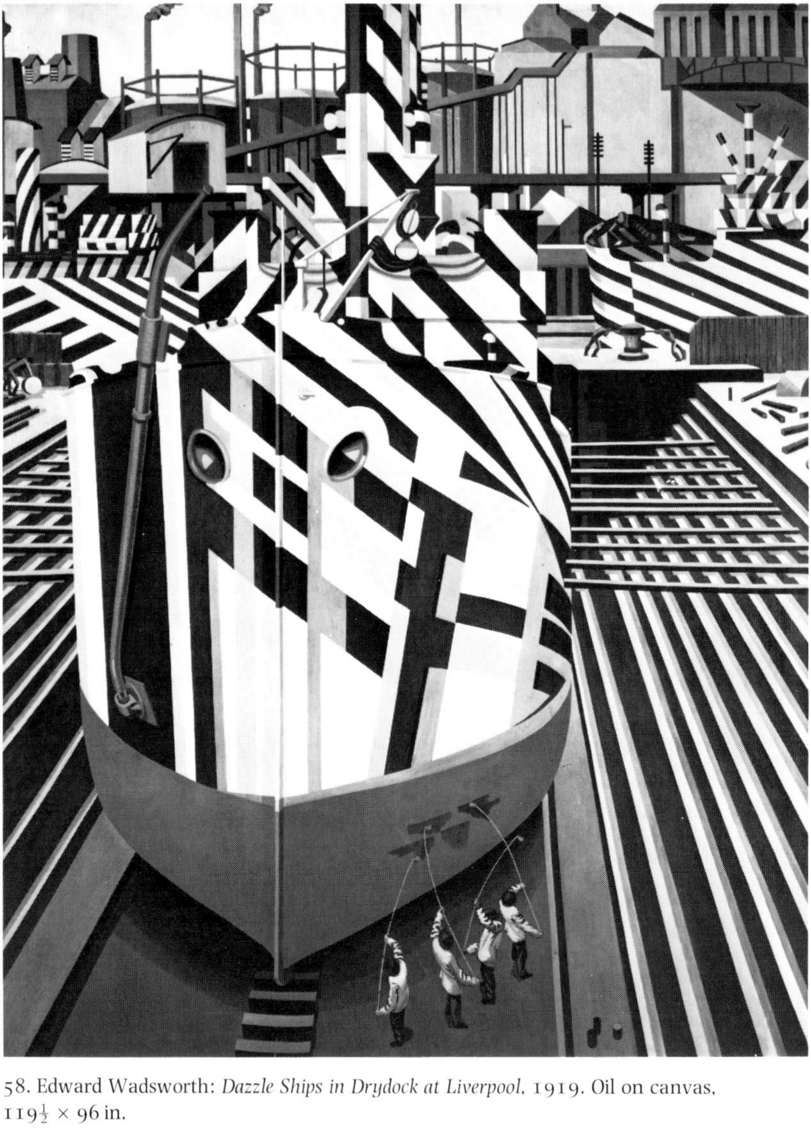

58. Edward Wadsworth: *Dazzle Ships in Drydock at Liverpool*, 1919. Oil on canvas, $119\frac{1}{2} \times 96$ in.

in which he continued to display a talent for the graphic simplification of complex industrial and urban subjects, his next extant datable work was the ten-by-eight-foot *Dazzle Ships in Drydock at Liverpool* [58] commissioned under the Canadian War Memorials scheme and finished in 1919. It displays the qualities of mechanical precision in draughtsmanship and competence in the organization of unmodulated surfaces which characterize all Wadsworth's mature work, but it reveals few 'Vorticist' elements which cannot be accounted for by the nature of the subject-matter. Wadsworth had responded enthusiastically to Lewis's example in formulating an energetic abstract style, but once removed from the older man's sphere of influence he returned to doing what he did best, distinguishing realistic subjects by means of a heightened definition of planes and edges. As did so many of his contemporaries he relied heavily on those comparatively traditional technical abilities in drawing and composition which had been fostered during his student days at the Slade. His work was none the worse for this.

Neither Bomberg nor Roberts produced much of any significance during the war. Both were given commissions for large works for the Canadian War Memorial, and Roberts also painted a six-by-ten-foot picture for the Ministry of Information, but these were not successful works.

Roberts's paintings[25] suffered to a great extent from the deficiencies which marred Lewis's. The influence of Vorticism and of Bomberg was reduced to a tentative polarization of tone and colour, a segmentation of the more complicated forms, and a mild angular stylization of the figures. The paintings thus become unspecific in treatment of the given subjects without any compensating gain in formal interest. His most successful works from the period of the war are small drawings in which comparatively informal and anecdotal subjects are energized by a tense and mildly mechanistic drawing style [59].

59. William Roberts: *The Gas Chamber*, 1918. Pen, ink, pencil, and watercolour on paper, $12\frac{1}{2} \times 20$ in.

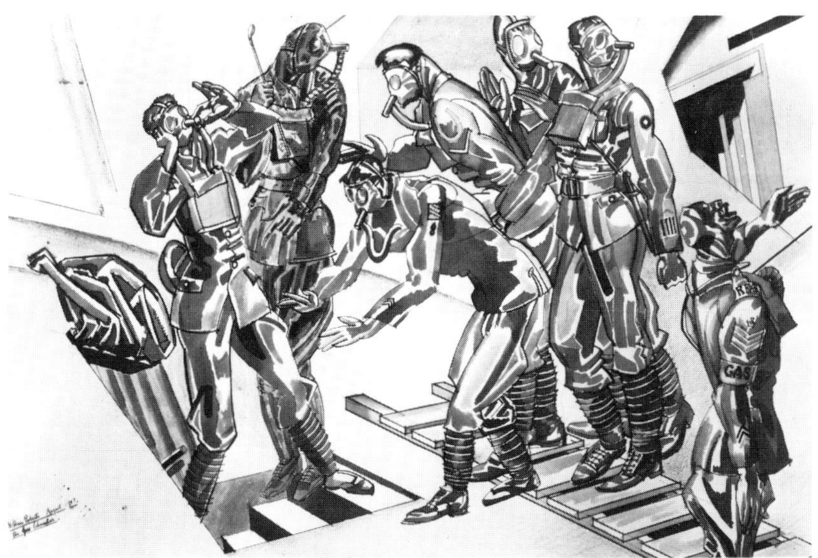

Despite warnings that 'Cubist' work would be inadmissible, Bomberg's first project on the given theme of a Canadian tunnelling company at work was for a composition following the style of his major pre-war paintings. His designs were rejected, and he produced a second version more in accord with the interests of his employers. The episode seems to have been deeply discouraging.[26] He was soon to abandon the attempt to pursue his earlier interests from the point at which they had been interrupted, and he was not to participate again in the social milieu of advanced art in England until after the Second World War.

The adjustment of 'Cubist' and 'Vorticist' style according to the limits imposed by (mostly justified) assumptions about the requirements of public bodies thus generally produced results which were unsatisfactory from both points of view. In the larger commissions the artists seem generally to have been unable to find ways of earning the money they sorely needed without involving themselves in what they must have seen as compromises. Such results are perhaps not best accounted for in terms of a conflict between enlightened freedom-loving artists on the one hand and oppressive public patronage on the other. Lewis's concept of a context of maximum freedom for artistic expression was for instance certainly not compatible with the concept of a utilitarian or liberal maximum freedom.[27] We should rather see these unsuccessful paintings as evidence of the difficulty of reconciling two different sets of interests rooted in different forms of social practice. The issue was plainly not so simple that it could have been resolved either, as it has been in some modern cultures, by coercing the artists, or, as the 'artistic' might wish to have it, by replacing the officials. No talk of the priority of aesthetic experience or of the sacrosanctity of temperament could secure for the radical painters the right to work as they wished on public commissions, nor was there much the officials could have offered to interest these painters in roles as everyman's representatives.

The Vorticists were in a sense caught out by a lack of depth in their understanding of the modern age which they claimed to represent. Not that the wartime achievements of the more established artists offered much to celebrate; Augustus John, for instance, whose interests were plainly not aroused by the war in any way, painted some quite appalling pictures of military subjects and military personnel.[28] The more successful paintings of the war years were produced by those who were best equipped to record actual and particular circumstances and to formalize, in so far as formalization was appropriate, with strict regard to those circumstances. None of the representative Camden Town painters was in action during the war, but the distinguishing feature of Camden Town painting – the particularizing of realistic subjects by means of in-

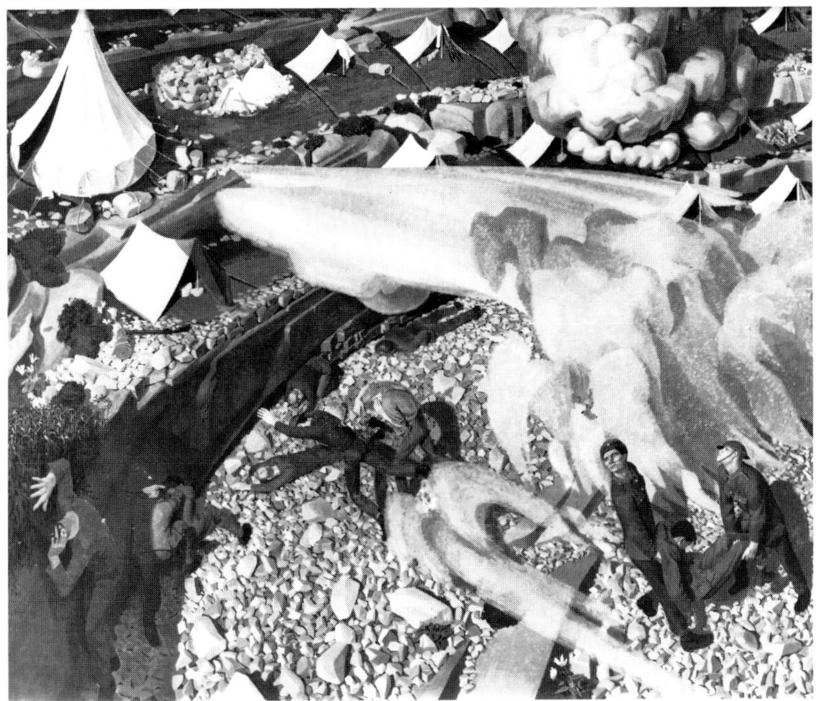

60. Henry Lamb: *Irish Troops in the Judaean Hills surprised by a Turkish Bombardment*, 1919. Oil on canvas, 72 × 86 in.

tensification, rather than wilful distortion, of characteristics of form and colour – was a feature also of the majority of the most convincing English paintings on war-related themes. Many of Nevinson's war works of 1916–19 suggest Camden Town rather than Futurist influence;[29] Walter Bayes, a founder member of the Camden Town Group, painted a large study of civilians sheltering in the London Underground which looks as if it should have a respectable place in the history of 'Socialist Realist' painting; Henry Lamb, whose *Irish Troops in the Judaean Hills* [60] is among the most successful of the Post-Impressionist paintings in the Imperial War Museum, was also a member of the Camden Town Group, if not a very active one; Gilman's large picture of *Halifax Harbour* [61], another Canadian commission, earned the express admiration of Lewis;[30] and John Nash, of the Cumberland Market Group, painted a couple of substantial oils which achieved a degree of documentary realism without any evident sense of compromise [62].[31]

Where the radical modernists were forced by the actual experience of war to adopt more naturalistic styles, those younger artists whose work was already steeped in naturalism were generally prompted by the subjects of

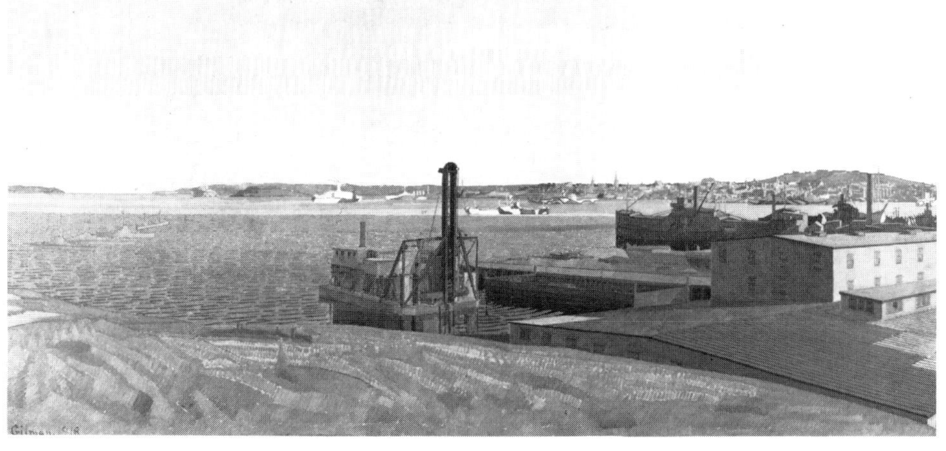

61. Harold Gilman: *Halifax Harbour at Sunset*, 1918. Oil on canvas, 77 × 132 in.

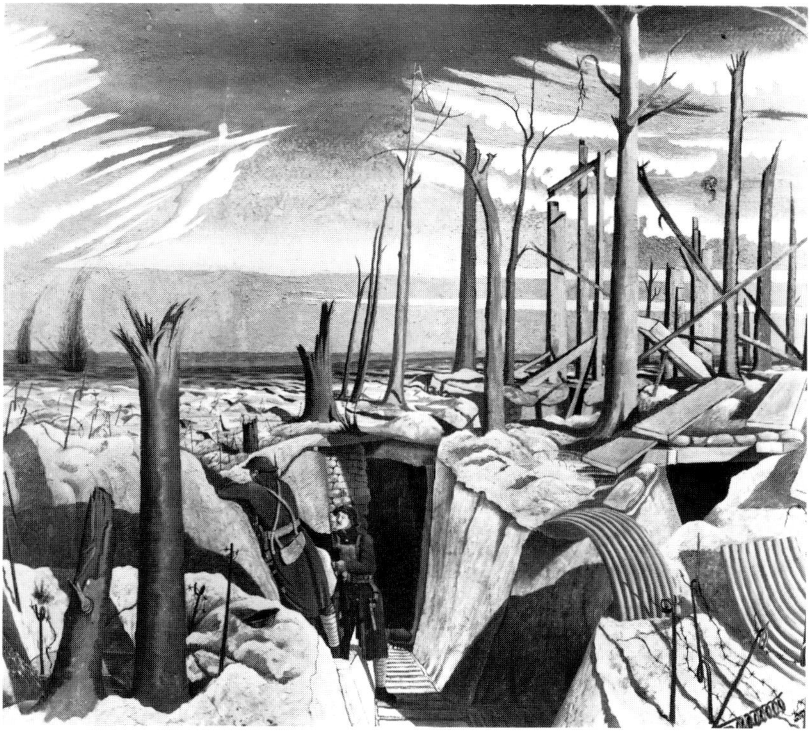

62. John Nash: *Oppy Wood*, 1919. Oil on canvas, 72 × 84 in.

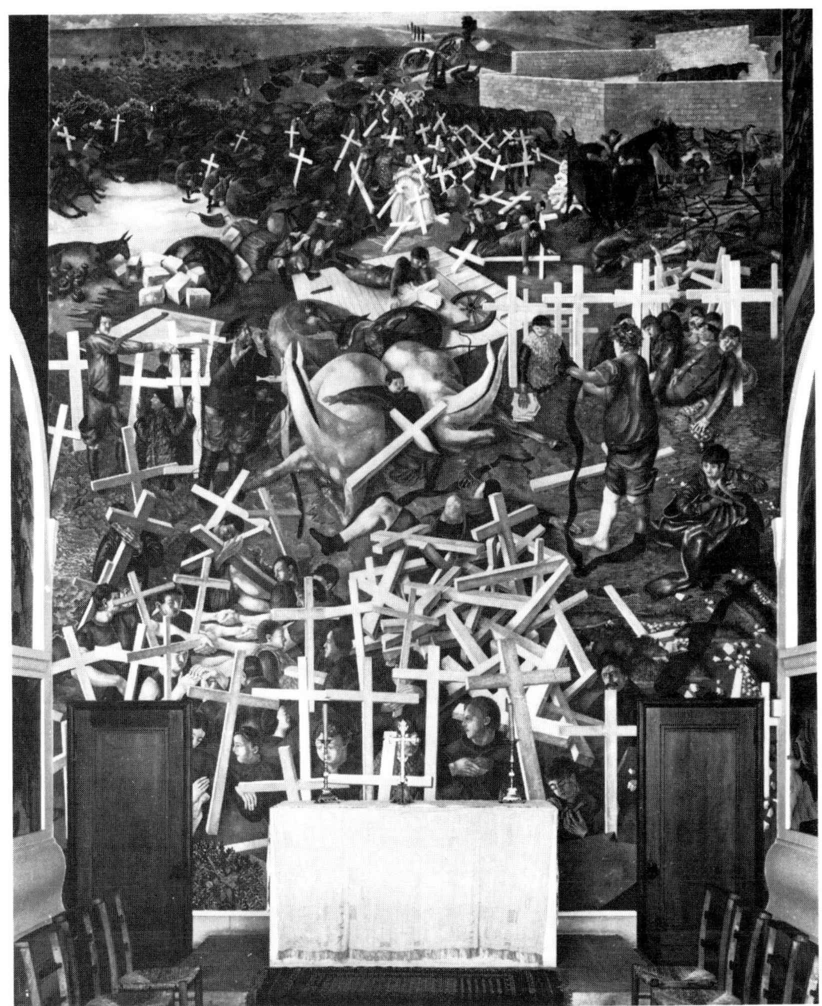

63. Stanley Spencer: *Resurrection, Macedonia*, 1928–9. Oil on canvas (Burghclere Chapel)

war to extend the emotional range of their work as they might never otherwise have done. Stanley Spencer for instance, one of the pre-war Slade generation whose early work had been heavily dependent on late Pre-Raphaelite sources and mannerisms, found himself projected into a world more compelling to the extension of understanding than that upon which his cloistered imagination had been inclined to feed. Besides a large work now in the Imperial War Museum,[32] the studies and memories with which he returned from the war provided the material for an entire decorative scheme, realized between 1926 and 1932 in the Sandham Memorial Chapel at Burghclere in Hampshire [63], largely from drawings begun in

1923. Although the reiterated items of an individualistic, homespun Christian symbolism here as elsewhere tend to expose the lack of sophistication which limits all Spencer's work, his scenes of army life in Macedonia evidently serve a highly idiosyncratic observation and a vivid recollection of actual events, and they thus catch a quality which we miss in the works of many more intelligent artists.

Of all the artists who recorded the war, the most successful was in fact the one who of all the younger modernists had shown least interest in recent European developments, who was still in 1914 more concerned with Dante Gabriel Rossetti than with Cézanne, let alone Picasso or Matisse. Paul Nash was an immature twenty-seven when he was sent to France early in 1917. He had never painted in oils. His first drawings of 1910–13 [64] had been

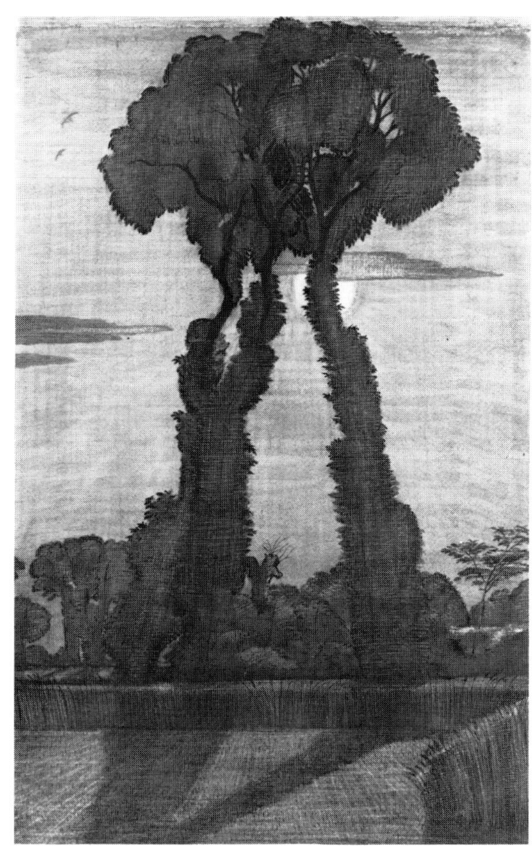

64. Paul Nash: *The Three in the Night*, 1913. Watercolour, ink, and chalk on paper, $20\frac{3}{4} \times 13\frac{1}{2}$ in.

produced largely under the influence of a romantic enthusiasm for the art of William Blake, Samuel Palmer, and the Pre-Raphaelites and of an ambition to write romantic poetry.[33] In pen and watercolour drawings of the subsequent three years he had developed an individual style which, though adequate to express an affection and an acute eye for the less dramatic qualities of the southern English landscape, promised little as a means to considerable modern art. Though he had studied briefly at the Slade in 1910–11 and had worked at Omega in 1913, he had not joined any of the modernist cliques. During the first years of the war he trained lightly and worked on his drawings and watercolours. While his contemporary Nevinson was painting the scenes of war, Nash drew trees.

When he went to war early in 1917, it was in terms of his involvement with the details of landscape that Nash explored the meaning of what he was faced with. There can be no doubt that he learned a great deal from the experience of war. From a front line trench at St Éloi he wrote back to his wife, 'This has been the most interesting week of my life,' and 'My inner excitement and exultation was so great that I have lived in a cloud of thought these last days.' He wrote of 'these wonderful trenches at night, at dawn, at sundown,'[34] and chafed with frustration and impatience when sent down from the line to attend a course.

> Shall I ever lose the picture they have made in my mind. Imagine a wide landscape flat and scantily wooded and what trees remain blasted and torn, naked and scarred and riddled. The ground for miles around furrowed into trenches, pitted with yawning holes in which the water lies still and cold or heaped with mounds of earth, tangles of rusty wire, tin plates, stakes, sandbags and all the refuse of war. In the distance runs a stream where the stringy poplars and alders lean about dejectedly, while farther a slope rises to a scarred bluff the foot of which is scattered with headless trees standing white and withered, hopeless, without any leaves, done, dead. As shells fall in the bluff, huge spouts of black, brown and orange mould burst into the air amid a volume of white smoke, flinging wide incredible debris, while the crack and roar of the explosion reverberates in the valley ... The earth rises in a complicated eruption of smoke, and bits begin to fall for yards wide splashing into the pools, flinging up the water, rattling on the iron sheets, spattering us and the ground nearby. As night falls the monstrous land takes on a strange aspect. The sun sinks in a clear evening and smoke hangs in narrow bars of violet and dark. In the clear light the shapes of the trench stand massy and cold, the mud gleams whitely, the sandbags have a hard rocky look, the works of men look a freak of nature, rather, the landscape is so distorted from its own gentle forms, nothing seems to bear the imprint of God's hand, the whole might be a terrific creation of some malign fiend working a crooked will on the innocent countryside. Twilight quivers above, shrinking into night, and a perfect crescent moon sails uncannily below pale stars. As the dark gathers, the horizon brightens and again vanishes as the Very lights rise and fall, shedding their weird greenish glare over the land ...[35]

Each of the various tableaux here evoked has its counterpart in the pen, watercolour and pastel drawings Nash sent back from the front [65]. It is interesting to compare Hulme's account of life as an enlisted man, written two years earlier.

> In reality there is nothing picturesque about it. It's the most miserable existence you can conceive of. I feel utterly depressed at the idea of having to do this for 48 hours every 4 days. It's simply hopeless. The boredom and discomfort of it exasperate you to the breaking point.
>
> It's curious to think of the ground between the trenches, a bank which is practically never seen by anyone in the daylight, as it is only safe to move through it at dark. It's full of dead things, dead animals here and there, dead unburied animals, skeletons of horses destroyed by shell fire. It's curious to think of it later on in the war, when it will again be seen in daylight.[36]

Nash was in France for a mere three months and spent a total of no more than three weeks in the front line during a period of comparative inactivity and good weather. Yet during that time the quality of his response to the scenery of war was sufficient to transform him from a greenery-yallery illustrator with literary inclinations into an individual modern artist in whose work the elements of Post-Impressionist style appear not as mere stylistic attachments but as the necessary means to the expression of the significance of what he saw.

His war work divides into two groups. The first is composed of the drawings and watercolours (some twenty in number) exhibited in June 1917 at the Goupil Gallery under the collective title 'Drawings made in the Ypres Salient'. A few of these were finished off after his repatriation, but essentially they represented the immediate responses of a serving officer (and, of course, once 'commissioned' as 'artists', the war artists *were* officers). Half the works were sold and the show attracted considerable favourable comment.[37] The second and much larger group of works, on paper and on canvas, resulted from Nash's brief but very busy tour of the battlefields of Flanders following his appointment as an official war artist in the autumn of 1917. Many of these were shown under the general heading 'Void of War' in a one-man exhibition at the Leicester Galleries in May 1918.

In the earlier group an essentially traditional technique, derived largely from Nash's study of watercolours and drawings by Palmer, Blake, Rossetti and Edward Lear, is used to express the fascination of a literary romantic with landscapes which add a new and unexpected source of reference to the concept of the picturesque. The technique is the graphic equivalent of the descriptive language in the letters to his wife. It is as if Nash were at first

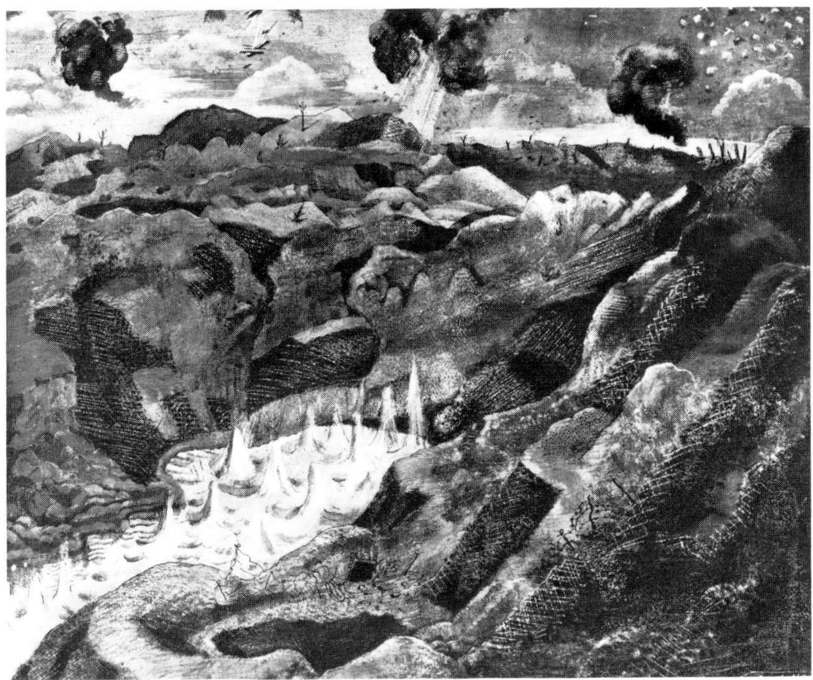

65. Paul Nash: *The Landscape – Hill 60*, 1917–18. Pencil, pen, and watercolour on paper, $15\frac{1}{2} \times 19\frac{1}{2}$ in.

striving to cope with the unprecedented in terms of a vocabulary with which he felt secure. The conflicts generated by the use of traditional means of observation upon subjects for which there was no precedent in the history of art enliven these small and conscientious works with a sense of truth to experience unmatched in any more unreservedly modernist accounts of similar scenes, but there was a limit to what could be expressed by means of techniques evolved in the study of picturesque detail. By the time Nash returned to Europe in late October, having had time to absorb the experience of the previous spring, he had gained a new confidence and had broadened the base of his sympathies. He worked hard, conscious of the significance of his new role and of the new range of responsibilities it entailed, and in the space of about a month produced a large number of works on paper, which served both to order his immediate responses and to provide sufficient additional material to occupy him in the production of more considered work during the eighteen months following his return to England. Expected to work from General Headquarters, he insisted on operating around the front-line trenches.[38] He was thus not merely an observer of the aftermath of war, but a witness of its progress across the landscape.

In these later works his earlier style was transformed not by the aping of a modern manner but by the adoption of those processes of formalization which came with the conviction of a broader purpose. Even in the smaller, more immediate works produced in Flanders, often at considerable speed,[39] anecdotal and textural details are purged except where they serve a general effect. Earlier he had allowed his fascination with detail and drama in the landscapes of war to lead him into familiar, romantic ways of visualizing and of representing. Now the strength of his own aroused feelings at scenes of utter devastation and at the outrage to life and to nature forced him into new, more appropriate and more disciplined resources of expression [66]. It needs to be said that his concept of 'life' was still a concept of 'natural' life, and his concept of outrage still of outrage to nature conceived in a pastoral fashion.

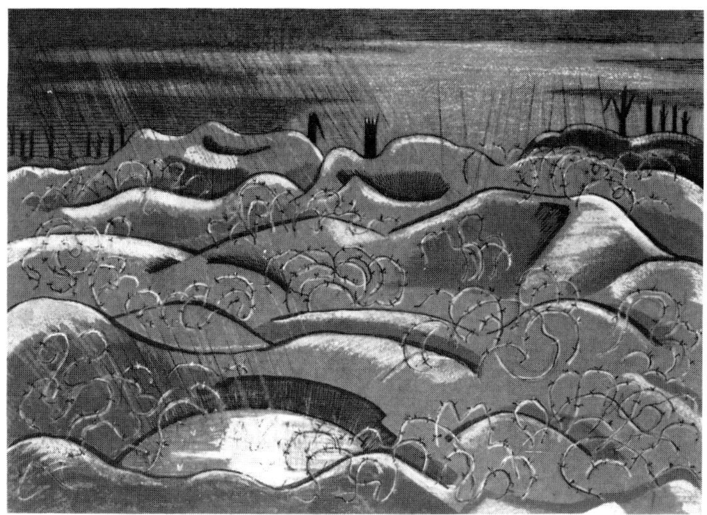

66. Paul Nash: *Landscape – Year of our Lord 1917*, 1917–18. Chalk and ink on paper, $10\frac{1}{4} \times 14\frac{1}{4}$ in.

In the middle of November he wrote from the battlefield of Passchendaele. His earlier enthusiasm at the scenery of war had given way to a deep disgust for which his vision of landscape was now a means of expression. (The expressive force of his art was all the stronger for his recognition of the limits upon the narrative power of pictures.)

I have just returned, last night, from a visit to Brigade Headquarters up the line, and I shall not forget it as long as I live. I have seen the most frightful nightmare of a country more conceived by Dante or Poe than by nature, unspeakable, utterly indescribable. In the fifteen drawings I have made I may give you some idea of its horror, but only being in it and of it can ever make you sensible of its dreadful nature and of what our men in France have to face. We all have a vague notion of the terrors of a battle, and can conjure up with the aid of some of the more inspired war correspondents and the pictures in the *Daily Mirror* some vision of a battlefield; but no pen or drawing can convey this country – the normal setting of the battles taking place day and night, month after month. Evil and the incarnate fiend alone can be master of this war, and no glimmer of God's hand is seen anywhere. Sunset and sunrise are blasphemous, they are mockeries to man, only the black rain out of the bruised and swollen clouds all through the bitter black of night is fit atmosphere in such a land. The rain drives on, the stinking mud becomes more evilly yellow, the shell holes fill up with green-white water, the roads and tracks are covered in inches of slime, the black dying trees ooze and sweat and the shells never cease. They alone plunge overhead, tearing away the rotting tree stumps, breaking the plank roads, striking down horses and mules, annihilating, maiming, maddening, they plunge into the grave which is this land; one huge grave, and cast up on it the poor dead. It is unspeakable, godless, hopeless. I am no longer an artist interested and curious, I am a messenger who will bring back word from the men who are fighting to those who want the war to go on for ever. Feeble, inarticulate, will be my message, but it will have a bitter truth, and may it burn their lousy souls.[40]

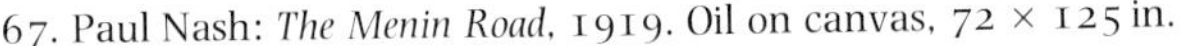

67. Paul Nash: *The Menin Road*, 1919. Oil on canvas, 72 × 125 in.

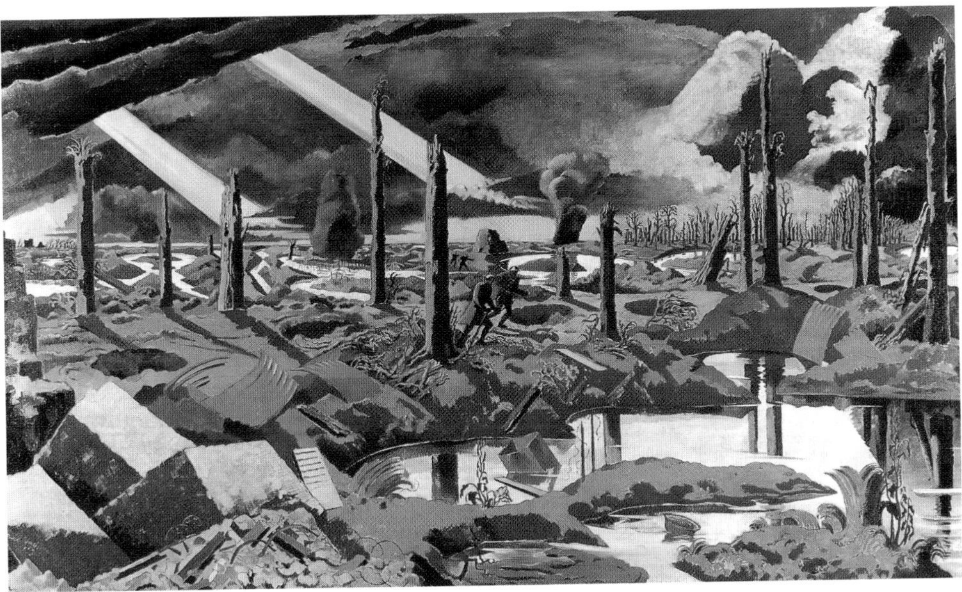

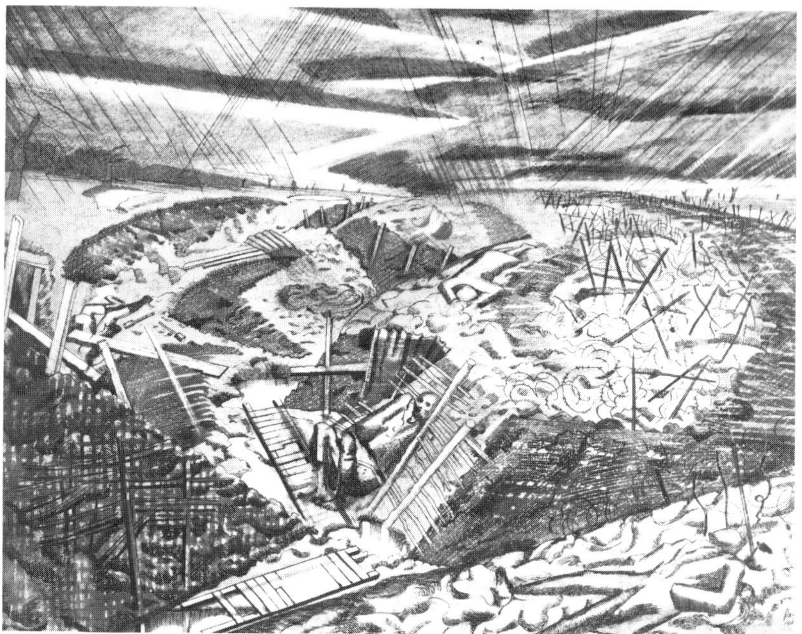

68. Paul Nash: *After the Battle*, 1918. Pen and watercolour on paper, $18\frac{1}{4} \times 23\frac{1}{2}$ in.

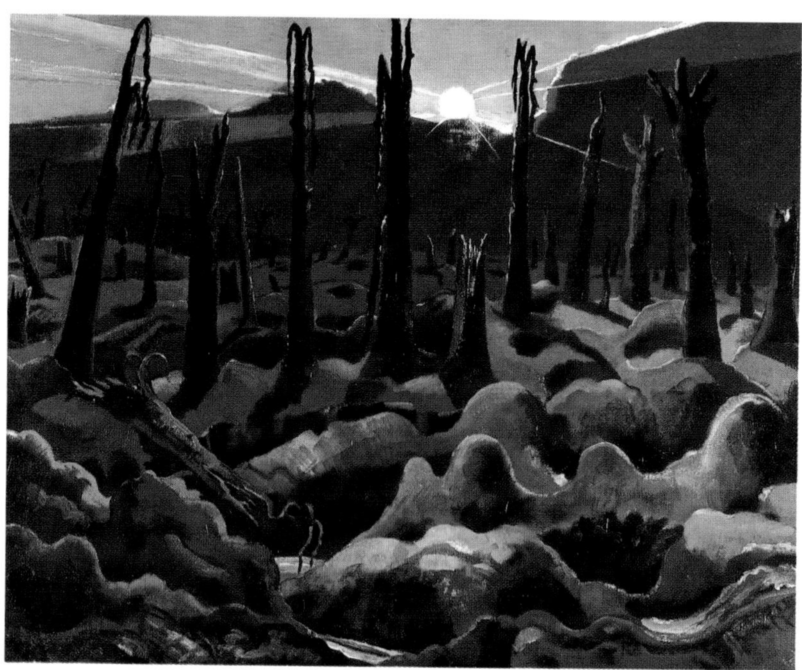

69. Paul Nash: *We are Making a New World*, 1919. Oil on canvas, 28×36 in.

Returning home, he polished up his watercolours and pastel sketches and produced several more studied compositions from the many drawings he had made. He began for the first time to work in oils at around the time he received a commission from the Ministry of Information for the large painting of the *Menin Road* which now hangs in the Imperial War Museum [67]. In this, in *After the Battle* [68], *The Mule Track*, *We are Making a New World* [69], *Landscape – Year of our Lord 1917* [66][41] and many other works on canvas and on paper he tried to do what he had said he would do. These works of late 1917–19 show occasional traces of mild Vorticist influence and of Nash's respect for Nevinson's early war paintings, but neither Vorticism nor the works of Nevinson were decisive for him, and he never altogether severed his connections with the English landscape-painting traditions of the nineteenth century. His was the most impressive and original body of work on war themes produced by any artist involved in the First World War. Although as vehicles for the expression of feeling in the face of particular scenes and particular events they stand outside the main channels of development in modern painting, some of them are among the most remarkable achievements of twentieth-century art in this country.

PART TWO

BETWEEN THE WARS

6

HIATUS 1919–1924

The majority of the radical English artists had been in the armed forces. The majority of those associated with Bloomsbury were pacifists and conscientious objectors and had not. After the introduction of conscription Clive Bell had found employment together with many others on the farm at Garsington Manor, home of the pacifist Member of Parliament Philip Morrell and of his wife Lady Ottoline. Duncan Grant had been exempted from military service on the condition that he too took up agricultural work. Bloomsbury had not been disbanded by war to the same extent as the Vorticists, nor had it been subject to the decimation of talent which had virtually destroyed all hope for the development of potential in the art of Camden Town. Of the three principal constituent factions within the pre-war avant garde the adherents of Post-Impressionism were thus best placed after the war. The conditions of social life may have been drastically changed by 1919, but the friendships and connections within the Bloomsbury set had predictably remained largely intact, and most of its members had been able to continue work to some extent at least. In December 1920 Fry published a collection of twenty-five essays under the title *Vision and Design*, which served to underline his status as an authority on the art of a wide range of cultures, past and present. Bell had started to write regularly as an art critic early in 1919 and he published his own collection in March 1922 as *Since Cézanne.*[1]

The controversies generated during the pre-war period provided the terms for the majority of subsequent discussions and divisions on art and aesthetics until the end of the 1920s, but the energies and opportunities were not now so equally distributed. What may be taken as an opening salvo in the post-war battle was fired by Bell in an article written early in 1920, appropriately enough on his return from a visit to Paris. He condemned the war work recently shown at Burlington House on the grounds that the artists were 'not expressing what they feel for something that has moved them as artists, but, rather, what they think about something that has horrified them as men. Their pictures depart, not from a visual sensation, but from a moral conviction. So, naturally enough, what they produce is mere "arty" anecdote.'[2] 'Critics should . . . make it clear', he wrote elsewhere in the same essay, 'that to talk of modern English painting as though it were the rival of modern French is silly. In old racing days . . . it used to be held that French form was about seven pounds below English: the winner of the Derby, that is to say, could generally give the best French colt about that weight and a beating. In painting, English form is normally a stone below French. At any given moment the best painter in England is unlikely to be better than a first-rate man in the French second class.' He finished with a bark at Lewis's heels.

Let us admire . . . the admirable, though somewhat negative, qualities in the work of Mr Lewis – the absence of vulgarity and false sentiment, the sobriety of colour, the painstaking search for design – without forgetting that in the Salon d'Automne or the Salon des Indépendants a picture by him would neither merit nor obtain from the most generous critic more than a passing word of perfunctory encouragement; for in Paris there are perhaps five hundred men and women – drawn from the four quarters of the earth – all trying to do what Mr Lewis tries to do, and doing it better.

Bell's exaggeration was offensive, but it was, in a sense, a defensible hyperbole, and in response Lewis could muster none of his earlier fire. '. . . conditions are 10 times worse here than in France,' he wrote. 'There is only one way of meeting this state of affairs, which it would be unwise to regard as anything but permanent. That is, to supplement exhibiting here very largely with exhibitions and practice abroad; and generally for the painter living mainly here to regard himself as a European first, and to paint and think for that wider audience.'[3] This was all very well, but as the French largely shared Bell's opinion, opportunities to exhibit abroad were rare indeed during the 1920s. It was not until the early 1930s that a handful of English artists were able to establish contact with the European avant garde on anything like equal terms, and Lewis was not to be of their company.

At the close of the war, purchasing power in England had dropped to one third of what it had been in 1914. The election of 1918 had produced a landslide victory for David Lloyd George's Conservative-dominated Liberal–Conservative coalition. As a result of the wartime split in the Liberal ranks, the Labour Party, with a mere fifty-nine seats, was now the official opposition, but although short-lived Labour governments were elected in 1924 and 1929, the Conservatives were effectively to dominate British politics for the rest of the decade and most of the next. A brief post-war boom in 1919 was followed by rapid inflation and by the inevitable slump.[4] In 1921 over two million men were unemployed. 'Structural unemployment' was to be a consequence if not a feature of Tory economic and social policy for the rest of the decade. Apart from the economic consequences of the war there was a price to be paid in terms of the after-effects upon the imagination of those poisons by means of which populations had been motivated to make war upon each other. 'It seems likely that public life at all levels suffered a deterioration of standards and a decline of taste.'[5] With the resources of expression that were available to them in the early twenties there did not seem to be much that English artists could do to make their work strongly felt either as means to dissent or as means to assert independent values.

The dominant artistic culture of the decade was a literary one. The year 1922 saw the publication of James Joyce's *Ulysses* and of Eliot's *Waste Land*, and it is in terms of works such as these that typical expressions of concern and experiments in form have been identified for the early twenties. D. H. Lawrence, Virginia Woolf, E. M. Forster and Aldous Huxley all rose to prominence during this period. Each of these was well known in Bloomsbury but had no real points of contact with younger artists outside that milieu.

Once the last fees had been paid in respect of commissions for war paintings, the painters, like other demobilized servicemen, found that neither income nor employment was easily secured. Paul Nash wrote later of 'Struggles of a war artist without a war' and of 'New Life in a different world'.[6] Lewis was supported throughout the twenties largely by the generosity of friends, Wadsworth among them. David Bomberg's principal energies in the years 1920–22 were taken up with his attempts to make a living from poultry farming. Bomberg's career during the twenties developed according to a pattern which was to be typical for those members of his generation who had won a reputation for advanced work in the years before the war. In 1919 he produced a large series of figure studies which suggested an interest in such formalizations as he had pursued earlier. It was as if he were testing how far his intuitions in post-war circumstances could be touched upon in a reactivated modernist style. But he produced no finished painting on this basis which matched his earlier work in quality or

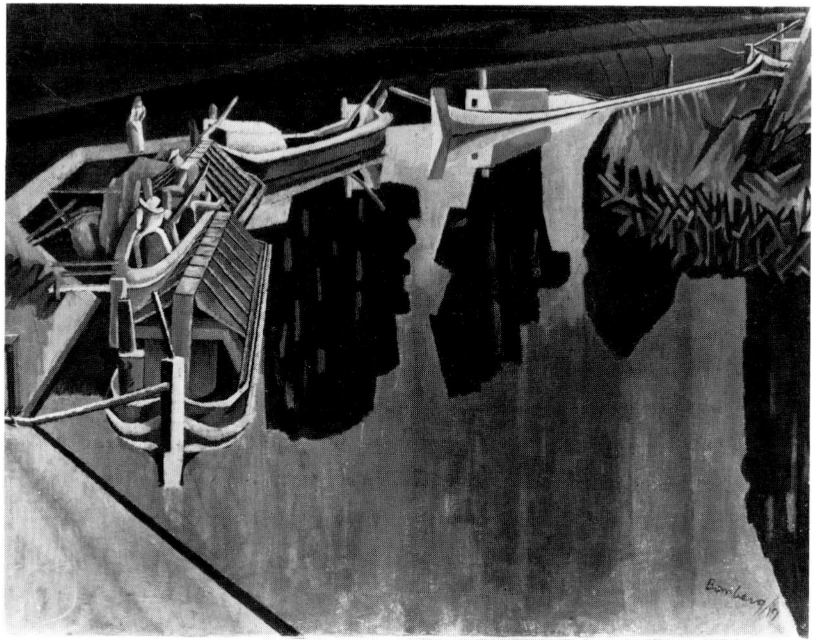

70. David Bomberg: *Barges*, 1919. Oil on canvas, 23½ × 30½ in.

inventiveness. The best of his early post-war works were comparatively modest [70]. During the twenties and thirties he generally pursued a much more naturalistic style characterized by fluid paint, strong colour, and looseness and complexity of surface. In 1923 he left England for Palestine, where he was to remain for four years. Apart from what he was paid for his war work, he had been unable to make any money from painting.

The twenties started badly for the majority of English artists, as for so many members of the population. For the next decade English art was consistently to be assessed against the standard of contemporary French work and consistently to be found wanting. So far as there was a market at all for contemporary art, the majority of the interested public liked bad British painting, and the enlightened few liked French painting. Fry's and Bell's admiration for French painting and sculpture was sufficiently whole-hearted as to be expressed in exaltation of those artists who were prepared to submit slavishly to French influence above those who, however unresponsive to continental art, were in some way original. These two wielded considerable power among dealers and collectors, and the part they played in promoting the hegemony of French culture was deeply resented during the twenties by the majority of English artists who were not of their immediate circle.

The remaining English Post-Impressionists however were loyally supported. 'Today,' wrote Bell in February 1920,

> when the Carfax Gallery opens its doors ... and invites the cultivated public to look at the paintings of Duncan Grant, that public will have the chance of discovering what has for some time been known to alert critics here and abroad – that at last we have in England a painter whom Europe may have to take seriously. Nothing of the sort has happened since the time of Constable; so naturally one is excited.[7]

Bloomsbury as a whole was very loyal to Grant. As late as 1965 Clive Bell's son could write of the twenties as 'the epoch of Duncan Grant's ascendancy in British painting'.[8] To Lewis, on the other hand, he was an invention of Fry's 'who could have received no attention in any country except England'.[9] Neither view deserves much support. Throughout his long career Grant [71] produced decorative works on untroubling themes. At worst his paintings are unrealistic, unoriginal and almost wholly devoid of vivid critical or interpretative qualities. At his rare best, and particularly before the early twenties when he reverted to techniques for modelling

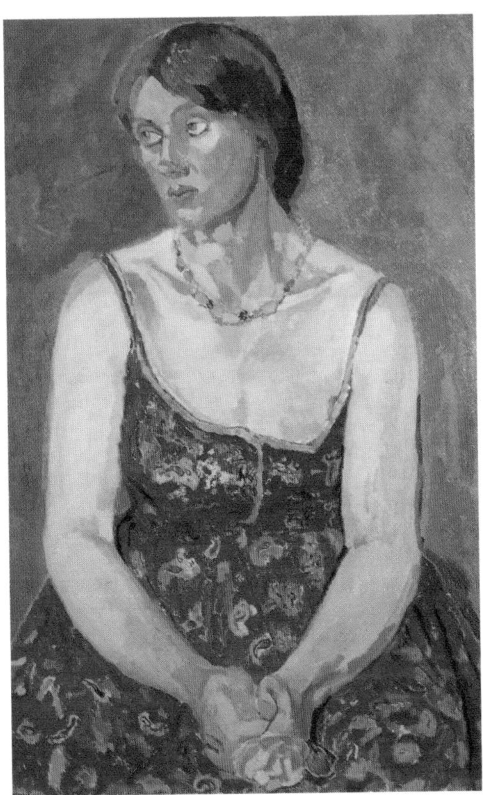

71. Duncan Grant: *Vanessa Bell*, 1918. Oil on canvas, 37 × 24 in.

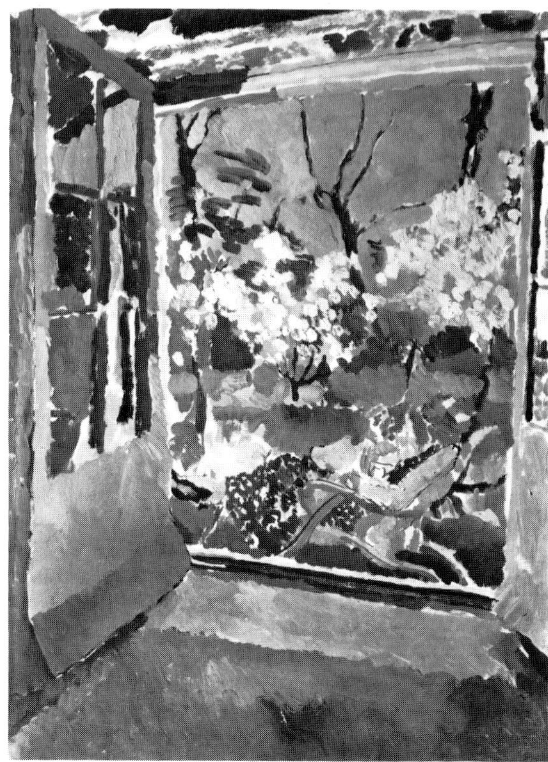

72. Duncan Grant: *Landscape through a French Window*, c. 1920. Oil on canvas, $30\frac{1}{2} \times 22\frac{1}{2}$ in.

form, he was capable of purveying a mood of relaxed, unprovocative hedonism in a distinctive range of fresh colours, casually applied [72]. Perhaps surprisingly in a painter so consistently supported by Fry and Bell, his paintings were never distinguished by any great originality in formal organization. After the closure of the Omega Workshops in 1919, he and Vanessa Bell continued to collaborate on projects for the decoration of interiors in a bright, 'Post-Impressionist' style. In so far as either made a significant contribution to the development of modern English art, it was made before 1920, and neither will therefore figure substantially in our account from this point on.

Mark Gertler was another of those who appeared to further the cause of English Post-Impressionism, and he was thus drawn into the Bloomsbury coterie during the war. In his *Merry-go-Round* [73], a large oil of 1916, he had produced one of the few remarkable pictures by a non-combatant on a war theme.[10] The painting shows men and women, most of the former in uniform, chasing each other round on stylized horses. The strength and simplification of the modelling and the exaggeration of the colour suggest affinities with the English Post-Impressionists, but the subject-matter and

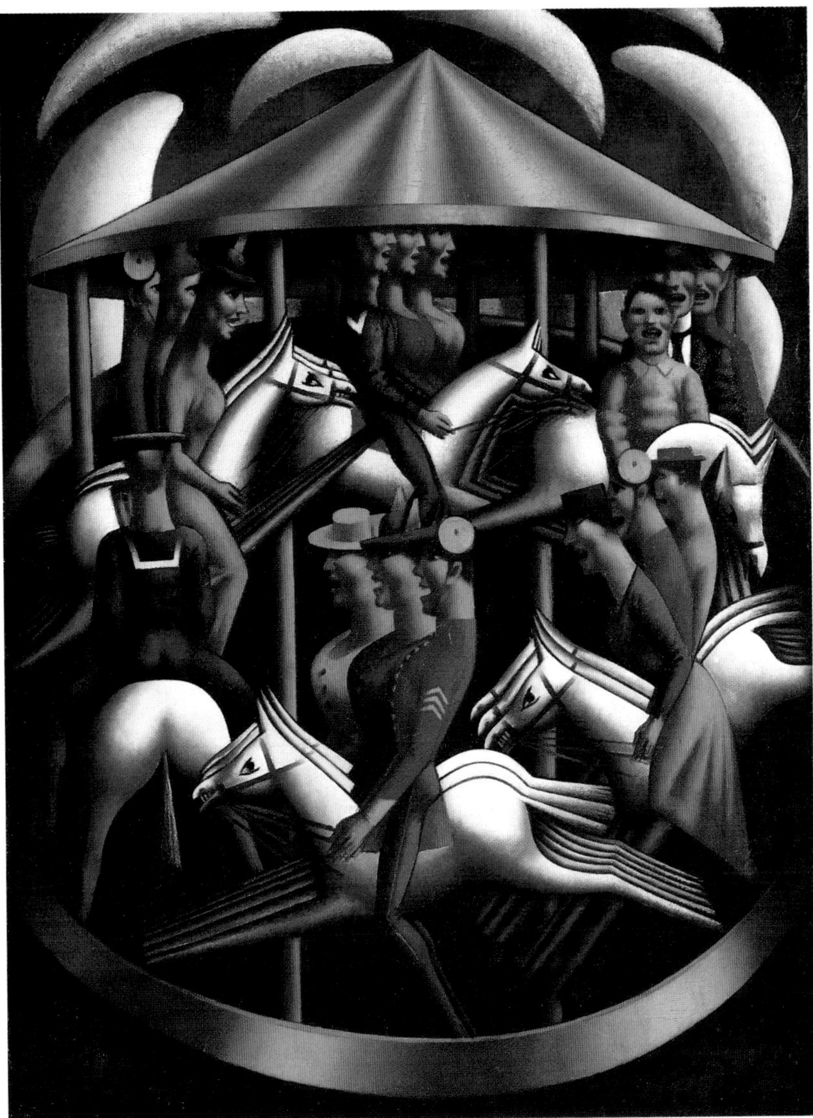

73. Mark Gertler: *The Merry-go-Round*, 1916. Oil on canvas, $74\frac{3}{4} \times 56$ in.

satirical treatment of the figures establish a mood more like that of Lewis's pre-Vorticist works. The painting was not typical however, and in his work of the early twenties Gertler concentrated on less troubling themes. He produced numerous still lifes and several paintings of heavy, roundly-modelled nudes in dusky warm interiors, which recall Renoir's late work

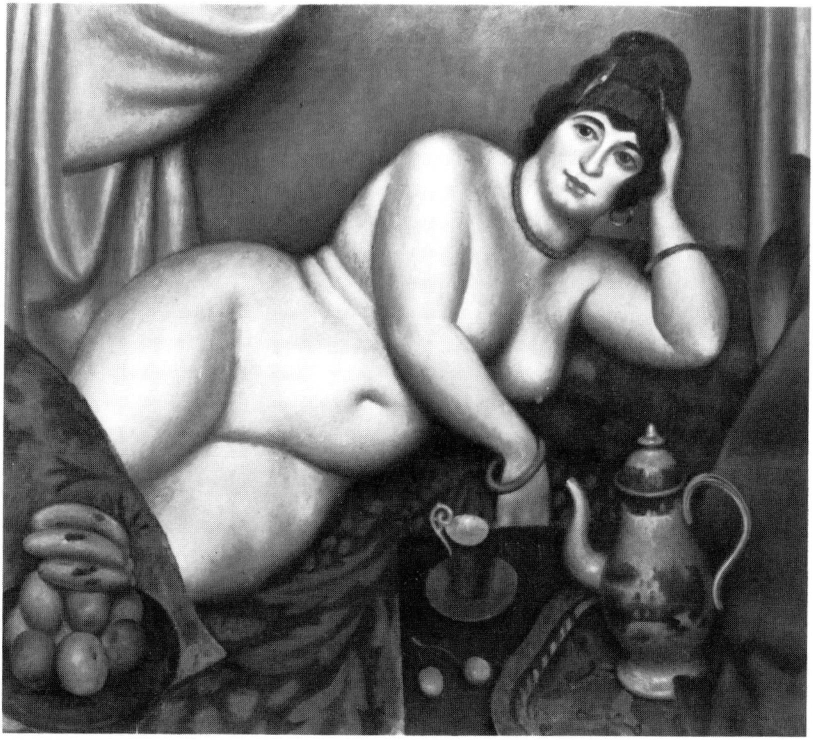

74. Mark Gertler: *Queen of Sheba*, 1922. Oil on canvas, $37 \times 42\frac{1}{2}$ in.

[74]. The very un-English quality of confident sensuality in these paintings was achieved in conditions of poverty and depression. Gertler killed himself in 1939.

Robust sensuality, particularly as embodied by the female nude, has not been a common characteristic in English painting, and those who attempt it thus tend to be or to become isolated figures. Gertler's Polish-Jewish origins account to a considerable extent for the distinctiveness of the mood established in his works. Matthew Smith, the only notable painter of the inter-war period whose work depended upon an unfraught involvement with richly sensuous subject-matter and colour, was born in Yorkshire, and, being ungregarious by nature and having had no outlandish origin or upbringing to excuse the manner of his work, was to be a comparatively solitary figure for the whole of his long working life. He had been a member of a largely undistinguished generation of students at the Slade, that which fell between the pioneering years of John, Gore, Gilman and Lewis and the later period when Gertler, Bomberg, Wadsworth and Nevinson were contemporaries. He had spent the years 1910–11 in Paris and had briefly attended a school run by Matisse. He thus gained an early first-hand experience of French art, particularly of Fauvist painting, and for a while he himself pursued a style characterized by the use of strong saturated colours and the avoidance of tonal modelling. After his return to London he was befriended by Epstein and subsequently by Sickert. The two *Fitzroy Street Nudes* [75] which he painted during the war have much in common with

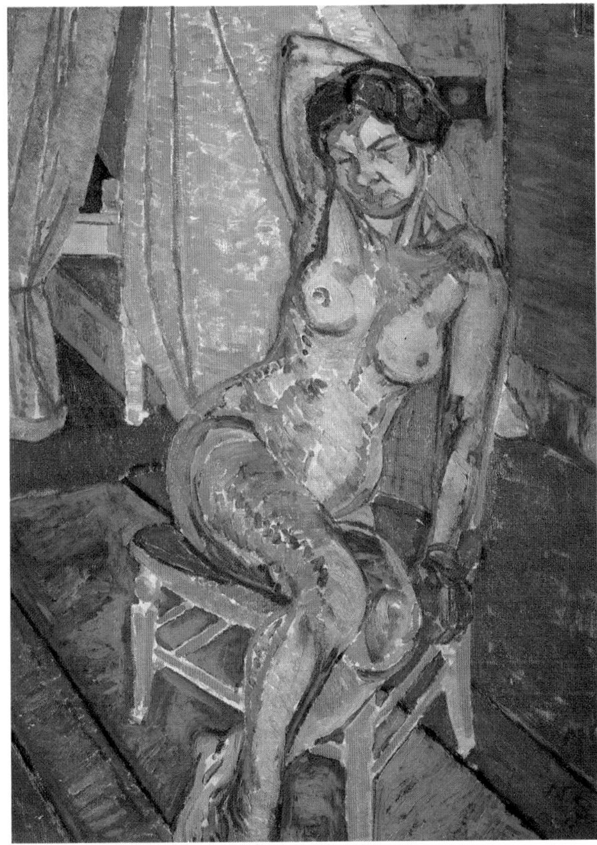

75. Matthew Smith: *Fitzroy Street Nude No. 2*, 1916. Oil on canvas, 40 × 30 in.

Camden Town painting at its boldest, although the extreme intensification of colour and the dramatic juxtaposition of complementaries, notably red and green in the Tate Gallery painting, bear witness to an understanding of recent French uses of colour for expressive purposes which was beyond that of any other English painter at the time. The *Fitzroy Street Nudes* were in fact too strong even for the London Group. When Sickert persuaded Smith to submit them for exhibition in 1916 they were rejected.

During the next three years Smith's career was interrupted by service in the war. With the exception of some striking landscapes produced in Cornwall in 1920 [76], his paintings were never again to be as challenging

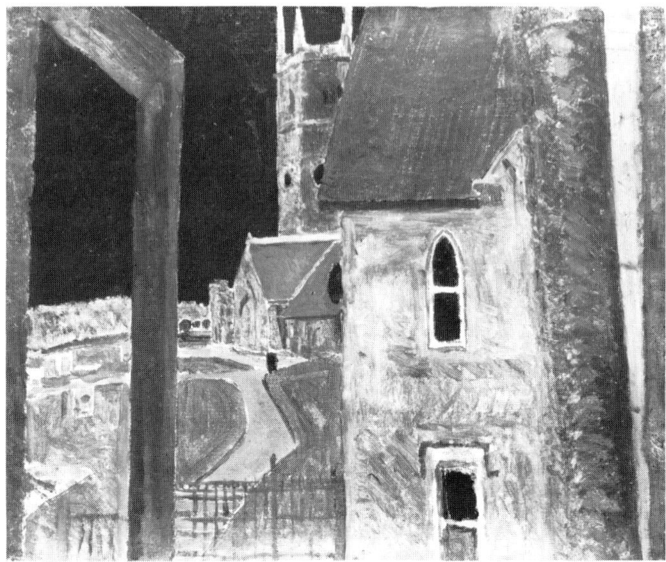

76. Matthew Smith: *Cornish Church*, 1920. Oil on canvas, 21 × 25½ in.

to contemporary taste in colour, nor were his subjects to be presented again with such lack of compromise; but he remained to the end of his life a singular figure. The consistently hedonistic nature of his subjects – nudes in interiors, warm-weather landscapes and still lifes of succulent fruit, patterned draperies and colourful ceramics – naturally encourages comparisons with Matisse, and it is thus easy to see his use of colour, upon which so much depends, as derived from the French painter's example. But Smith's brush was always a less critical instrument than Matisse's; the relationship between 'drawing' and 'colouring' functions is quite distinct in the two painters' works. Where Matisse strove consistently in his paintings to articulate a structure which would guarantee some independence for the role of colour in the accomplished decorative whole, Smith tended to use colour very much more descriptively, as a means to capture the richness of modulations of surface and illumination in the subject at hand. In his earlier work he had established some dramatic contrasts, but in his more typical work of the twenties the paint is generally applied in a fluid state, and one tint thus elides easily into another. The result is more immediately accessible and involves a less critical process of formalization either than his own earlier work or than Matisse's. To borrow terms from the critical vocabulary of Bloomsbury, Smith's paintings are 'anecdotal' where Matisse's are 'classic'. We are of course not used in English painting, particularly in English painting from the modern period, to find anecdote – the representation of particular visual elements from particular scenes –

selected and recounted on the basis of preference for rich colours and soft surfaces, and it is in offering us a precedent for selection on such terms that the originality of Smith's characteristic work seems to lie. After 1920 his painting generally lacks a cutting edge, but it is often very attractive [77].

Both Smith and Gertler showed with the London Group during the twenties. Gertler had been a member since 1915 and Smith was admitted in 1920. In 1917 Fry was elected to membership, and Vanessa Bell and Duncan Grant were among the Bloomsbury affiliates who joined in 1919. The English Post-Impressionists were thus strongly represented in the principal avant-garde exhibiting society at the beginning of the twenties, and throughout the decade the heightened colours and accentuated forms of their still lifes, landscapes and figure studies dominated the twice-yearly exhibitions.

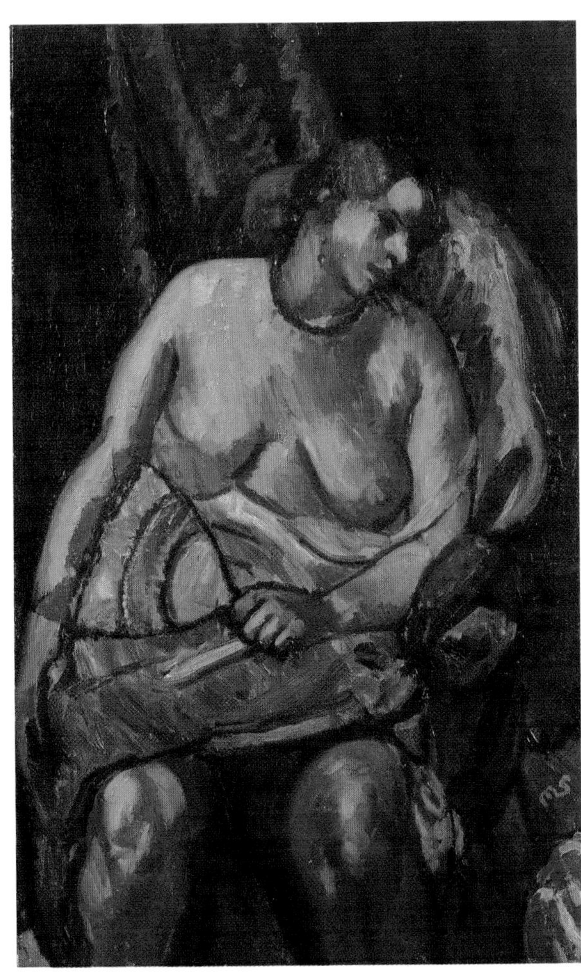

77. Matthew Smith: *Woman with a Fan*, 1925. Oil on canvas, $51\frac{1}{2} \times 32$ in.

Neither Lewis, Wadsworth nor Epstein had exhibited with the London Group since 1916; now in face of what they saw as a Bloomsbury takeover, many of the former radicals resigned. A dissenting nucleus once again grouped itself around Lewis, and once again secession provided the occasion for the formation of a new group. With a young American painter, Edward McKnight Kauffer, as the principal organizer, but with Lewis as the guiding spirit and propagandist, the X Group was formed. The members were Jessica Dismorr, Frank Dobson, Frederick Etchells, Charles Ginner, Cuthbert Hamilton, McKnight Kauffer, Lewis, William Roberts, John Turnbull and Edward Wadsworth.

The X Group was intended both to provide an alternative exhibiting facility to the London Group and to attest to the revival of the spirit of pre-war militancy. But the context was now utterly different. No one could now dream plausibly of 'good times just around the corner' or of 'manufacturing fresh eyes for people, and fresh souls to go with the eyes'.[11] Nor were any of these artists now working in styles consistent with the Vorticist hope (or fantasy) of radical re-education of consciousness. Rather the reverse. Despite the purported anti-humanism of the pre-war years, a spirit of something like classicism now prevailed in London as in contemporary

78. Edward Wadsworth: *The Cattewater, Plymouth Sound*, 1923. Tempera on panel, 25 × 35 in.

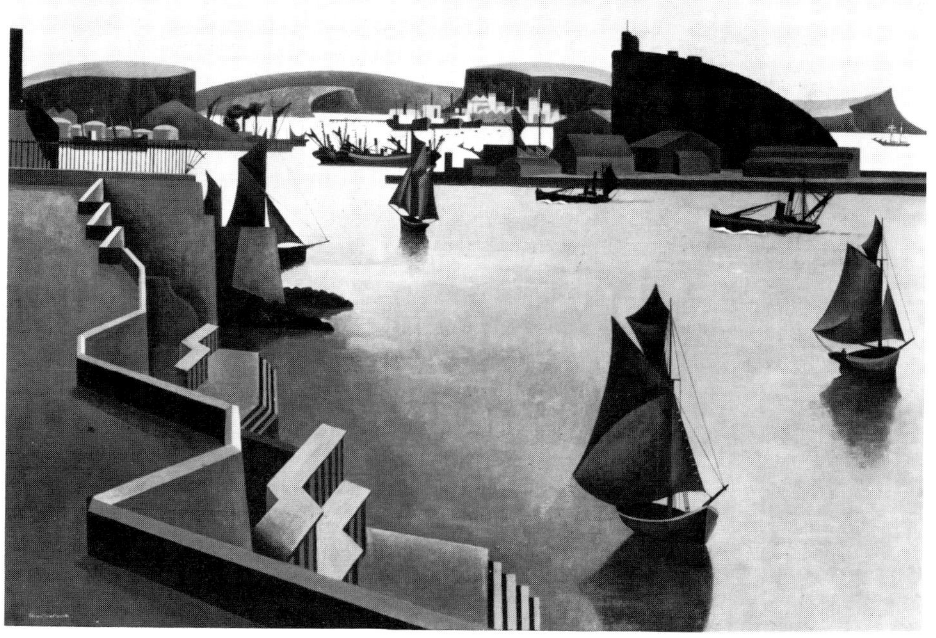

Paris. Clean lines, clear-cut forms and essentially stable compositions were features of the post-war work of all the ex-Vorticist members of the X Group. There was some interest in architecture. *The Caliph's Design*, a book which Lewis published in 1919, and which he later described as 'another *Blast*',[12] included an essay headed 'Architects! Where is your Vortex?' Etchells gave up painting for architecture at about this time.[13] Some of Wadsworth's paintings of the early twenties are compatible with the architectural style of Art Déco [78]. To replace the dynamic organizational principles which had characterized their Vorticist compositions in 1914 these artists now sought for means to embody qualities of order and stability, and in so far as they were concerned to reflect the sensibility of an industrialized world they referred now to the products rather than to the procedures of mechanization. This added little to the critical potential of their work, but it brought them closer in spirit to their fellow consumers in post-war society.

The X Group held one exhibition, at Heal's Mansard Gallery in March 1920, and then disbanded. There was nothing to hold them together. The mood of the twenties was one of isolation and retrenchment. No longer united by an avant-garde purpose, the former radicals were developing in their separate ways and in styles more conservative than would have

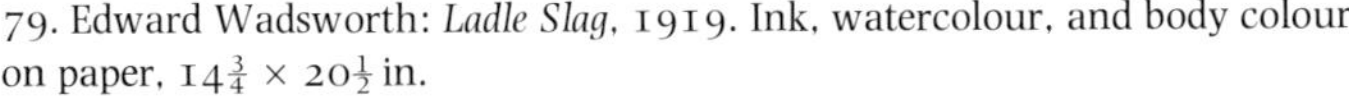

79. Edward Wadsworth: *Ladle Slag*, 1919. Ink, watercolour, and body colour on paper, $14\frac{3}{4} \times 20\frac{1}{2}$ in.

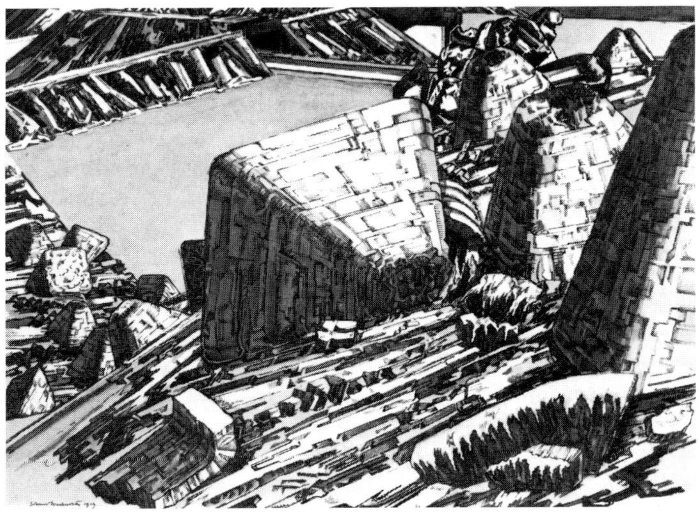

seemed worth pursuing before the war while there was still reason to submerge individuality in a common cause. In 1919 Wadsworth produced a series of paintings and drawings of the industrial landscapes of the Black Country [79].[14] Though these do not, as did his Vorticist works, reveal any

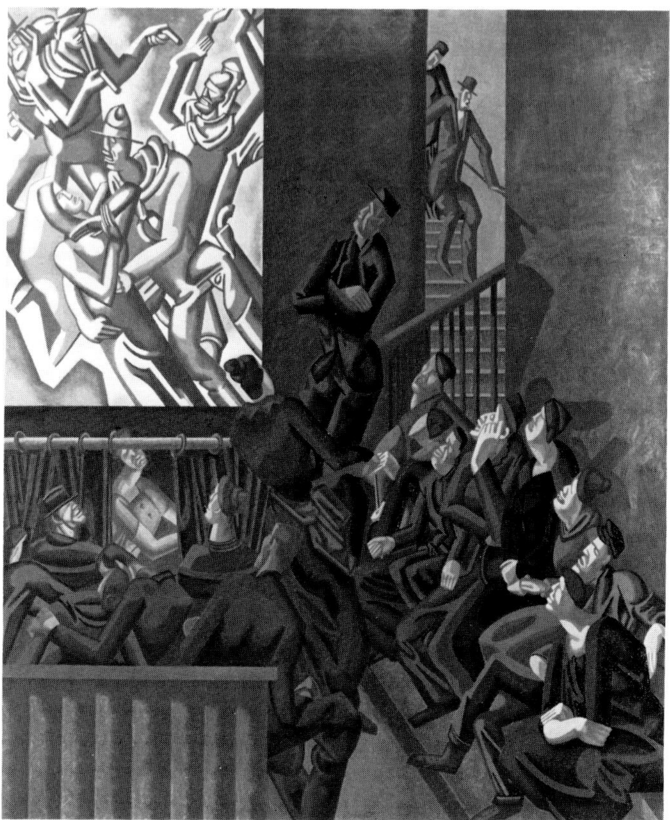

80. William Roberts: *The Cinema*, 1920. Oil on canvas, 36 × 30 in.

significant engagement with modernist theories concerning the embodiment of modern sensibility in non-naturalistic form, they are very much more original than anything he had produced while under the influence of Lewis, and they seem true to personal and particular experience of real circumstances in a way that his Vorticist works do not.

Like Wadsworth, William Roberts retreated from the 'extreme' position represented by his work of 1914–15. He continued to produce multi-figure compositions, usually on genre themes of urban recreation [80], but the 'post-Cubist' angularity of his style came increasingly to reflect a habit of formalization rather than a process of critical transformation. His style was gradually softened and relaxed during the twenties and his figures became more rounded, but otherwise he remained highly consistent to the end of his life. This meant, of course, that his work came to seem increasingly conservative and the interests which sustained it increasingly elusive. He began to exhibit at the Royal Academy in 1948 and continued to employ a style which had earlier appeared to serve 'Socialist' sympathies as a means to record such events as the Trooping of the Colour. A trace of irony in the formalizations and of acidity in the colour remain in his later works as reminders of the circumstances and the spirit in which that style was originally formed.

Charles Ginner's inclusion in the X Group suggests an attempt at the amalgamation of ex-Vorticist with ex-Camden Town talents, but ultimately his presence in such company could only emphasize how much had been lost through the deaths of Gore and Gilman and how much might have been achieved had they lived to find common ground with Lewis in the twenties. Though a competent and sensible painter, Ginner had never really been a radical.

Nor had Frank Dobson, the only sculptor included in the new group. He had been strongly impressed by Cézanne's work as represented in Fry's two Post-Impressionist exhibitions and had decided for sculpture only after his release from the army late in 1918. His earliest works, such as the *Concertina Man* [81], which was shown in the X Group exhibition,

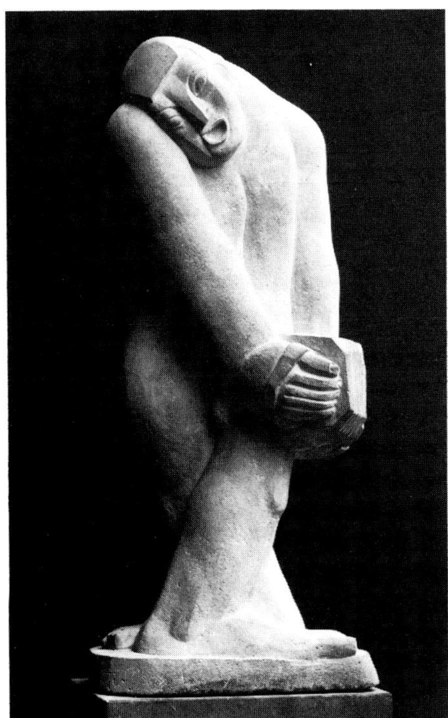

81. Frank Dobson: *The Concertina Man*, 1919. Portland stone, height 24 in. (exhibited in the X Group Exhibition, 1920)

suggested a degree of compatibility with post-Cubist painting, but he was in fact to find success with Fry and Bell during the early twenties as the most successful English exponent of that soft and broad-limbed classicism which they admired in the work of their favourite sculptor Aristide Maillol. (If neo-classicism was good enough for Paris, it was good enough for London.) For all the support he received in Bloomsbury, Dobson's participation in the X Group was a poor recompense for the loss of Gaudier and the apparent retrenchment of Epstein. Pleasant as his work often was, he could only have been promoted as a major figure in British sculpture by those unfamiliar with the work of either or hostile to the reputations of both. He joined the London Group in 1922 and was to be a prominent member throughout the decade.

The X Group was not, as the Vorticist group had been, an expression of compatibility and a product of friendship among inhabitants of one social and intellectual world. It was rather the outcome of something like a sense of duty. And perhaps it did serve to alert artists of a younger generation to the fact that modernism had some antecedent history in England.[15] But of all those who had taken part in the pre-war avant-garde movements, Lewis alone found such means to engage with post-war problems and disappointments as may be identified in terms of significant transformational functions in his work. He was soon to come to the conclusion that he was not a man for group activities.[16] In the X Group exhibition he showed seven self-portraits, and, as this perhaps suggests, he was now more inclined to introspection than he had been earlier. Reconsidering his former output in the light of subsequent experience, he set himself to relearn his profession according to a new interpretation of 'truth to life'. He worked at his drawing by 'practising tirelessly in work from models' [82].[17] The informal portraits

82. Wyndham Lewis: *Girl Reclining*, 1919. Black chalk on paper, 15 × 22 in.

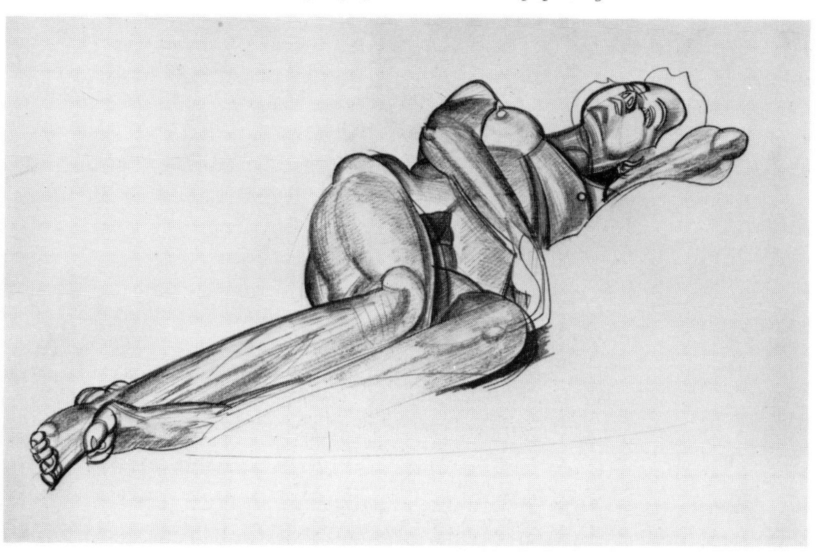

and tense nude studies which resulted are among the best English drawings of this century, though, except in so far as their influence may be detected in the drawings of Ben Nicholson, they have done little to 'advance' any modernist style.

Many of these drawings were exhibited together with some expressive paintings of figure subjects in a one-man exhibition which Lewis held at the Leicester Galleries in April 1921 under the title 'Tyros and Portraits'. The Tyro was described by Lewis as

> ... a new type of human animal like Harlequin or Punchinello – a new and sufficiently elastic form or 'mould' into which one can translate the satirical observations that are from time to time awakened by one's race ... The Tyro ... is raw and underdeveloped; his vitality is immense, but purposeless, and hence sometimes malignant. His keynote, however, is vacuity; he is an animated but artificial puppet, a 'novice' to real life.[18]

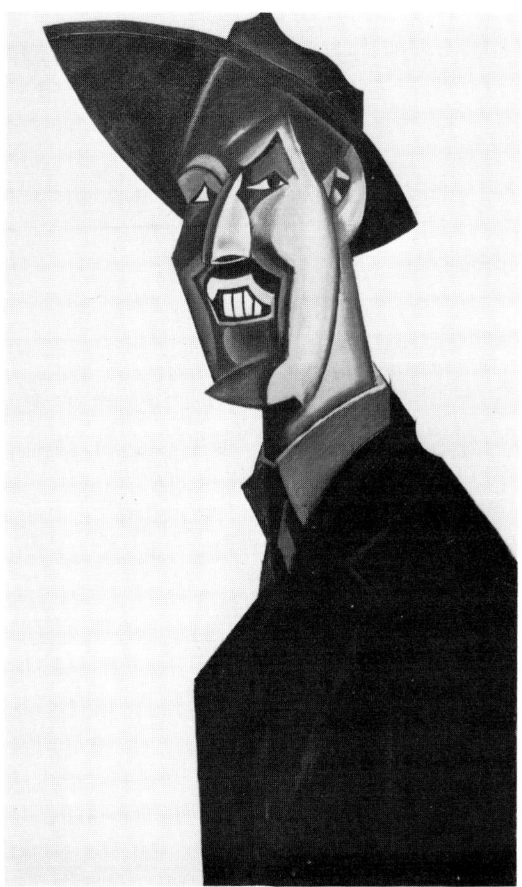

83. Wyndham Lewis: *Mr Wyndham Lewis as a Tyro*, 1920–21. Oil on canvas, 29 × $17\frac{1}{4}$ in.

The Tyros recall the energetic figures of Lewis's pre-Vorticist drawings and represent a revival of his interest in the possibility of satire in modern art. They are compelling symbols of the wastage of human hope and the frustration of purpose in the first quarter of the twentieth century, conveying no message to the aesthetician or the ideologue, unless it be such as might be expressed in a humourless sneer, and embodying no values but those of an indomitable and essentially 'uncreative' vitality [83].

In an introduction to the catalogue of his 1921 exhibition Lewis wrote of the new taboo of 'pure art' and suggested that 'My Tyros may help to frighten away this local bogey.'[19] But neither Roger Fry nor the theories for which he was a spokesman were to prove vulnerable to this army of 'grinners'. Lewis produced two issues of a magazine called *The Tyro*, of which he later wrote that they 'might be regarded as Blasts number 4 and 5',[20] but as he himself knew only too well, the context was not the same. The drift of English culture had been inexorably away from him since 1914. His most adventurous work proved now unsaleable, and he took to making portraits during the early twenties in order to bolster the slender income he derived from a small circle of friends and patrons. Where his sympathies were engaged with his subjects, as in the portrait of Edith Sitwell (painted mostly in 1923) [84],[21] he worked as well as he ever had, and certainly better than any other English portrait painter in this century, but in much of his work in this genre it is made clear how dull he could be when his critical faculties were relaxed or suppressed.

In the circumstances there was perhaps an element of rationalization in Lewis's replacement of a 'dogmatically anti-real'[22] by a determinedly anti-abstract attitude, but given the authoritarian aspects of his ideology his evolution was natural enough from radical modernist to radical conservative. Strong personalities of the latter type are not now as common in English as they are in American intellectual and political circles, and we have not tended to look to them for contributions to the vitality of modern culture. So far as the development of art was concerned Lewis was to be a virtual outcast from the early 1920s until the 1940s, a circumstance which he was still to attribute late in his life to the effects of his break with Fry in 1913.[23] He maintained, however, a considerable range of friendships in literary circles and he wrote copiously. Between 1920 and 1939 he produced twenty-three books. He was not to hold another exhibition until October 1932,[24] when he showed portrait drawings of 'Thirty Personalities', virtually all done during that summer.

As a central figure in the development of English art over a crucial fifteen-year period Lewis has featured largely in our study up to this point, both by virtue of the quality and originality of his work and in his role as a

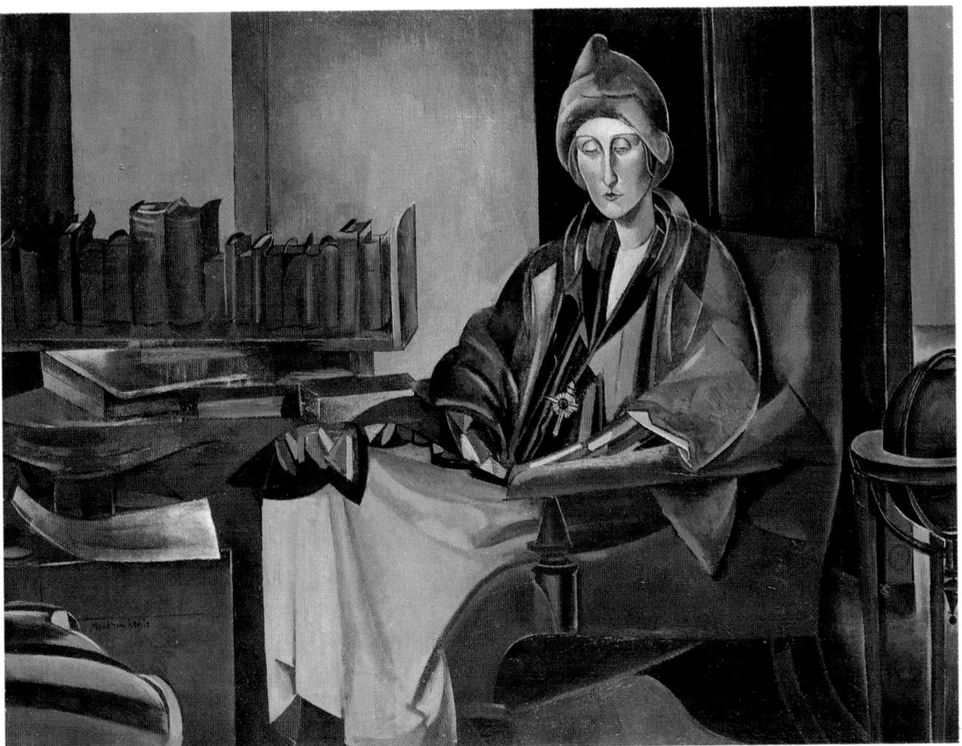

84. Wyndham Lewis: *Edith Sitwell*, 1923–35. Oil on canvas, 34 × 44in.

spokesman for the ideology and practice of radicalism in art. He presided over the rise of radical modernism in England and he watched his own fortunes fall with it. His later work will not occupy much space in the pages which follow. There is much to be learned, however, from the examination of his career as a whole, and many of the observations which were prompted by his earlier work are relevant to the general circumstances and tendencies of modern art in subsequent decades. In particular, as our history proceeds, we shall have further cause to consider the lack of fit between terms for discussing the idea of 'progress' in art and criteria for deciding the nature of 'realism'.

During the period between the wars younger artists with ambitions to be 'modern' were isolated from Lewis's earlier work by the break in continuity which the war years had made, and from his later work by its apparent conservatism. The influence of Vorticism upon those who had not been directly involved is identifiable only in terms of an occasional sharpening of line and shadow, and that only in the work of a handful of painters. Those most easily identified as 'talented' among the younger men, Paul Nash and

Ben Nicholson foremost among them, now shared with Lewis nothing so much as the conviction that art was no longer to be seen as a militant form of activity, that it was not now a matter of groups, programmes and manifestos, but a 'private' profession to be practised outside the busier contexts of social life, a quality to be refined and intensified. A happily institutionalized way of life, for the moment, appeared to be one which entailed restricted socialization and comparatively solitary activity.

The X Group had tried to recapture the spirit of pre-war avant-gardism, and it had failed. Such other groupings as were made tended to reflect an anxious liberalism. Nash and Nicholson may have found themselves in circumstances of some isolation, may up to a point even have welcomed this, but we should recognize that among younger English artists with ambitions to be 'modern', the true mainstream of provincialism flowed at this time through very much shallower channels. In his introduction to the X Group exhibition Lewis had suggested that its members were defending the ground gained by the Cubist, Expressionist and Vorticist movements against those who wished to put the armour off and to reinstate Pre-Raphaelitism. As an instance of such recidivation he cited a newly formed group 'naming itself the six and ten – something like that'. This was in fact the Seven & Five Society, which had been formed in 1919 and which held its first exhibition at Walker's Galleries in April 1920. The catalogue produced on this occasion contained a brief manifesto which is worth quoting in its entirety.

> The "SEVEN & FIVE" desire to explain that they are not a group formed to advertise a new "ism".
> They feel that the gladiators of the present warring sects are often concerned more with the incidental politics and temporary eddies of art than with its essential realities.
> A periodic explosion is essential in Art as in all other forms of organised activity, to blow away the crust of dead matter that time inevitably accumulates.
> The "SEVEN & FIVE" are grateful to the pioneers, but feel that there has been of late too much pioneering along too many lines in altogether too much of a hurry, and themselves desire the pursuit of their own calling rather than the confusion of conflict.
> The object of the "SEVEN & FIVE" is merely to express what they feel in terms that shall be intelligible, and not to demonstrate a theory nor to attack a tradition.
> Individual members have their own theories of Art, but as a group the "SEVEN & FIVE" has none.
> Each member is free to develop his own individuality: all that the group asks is that he shall do that, and not try to exploit someone else's.

Their desire is to group together men who do not attempt to achieve publicity by mere eccentricity of form or colour, but believe that to be sincere is not necessarily to be dull.

In this pathetic little document the prevailing mood of the early post-war years is vividly expressed. The reproving timorousness, the invoking of unspecified 'essential realities', the recall to order, the vaunting of a conservative concept of professionalism, the attaching of value to 'sincerity' in the absence of criteria for deciding truth, these are all characteristic features of a culture in recession. Pseudo-liberalism – the vaunting of principles of tolerance in the absence of theory – and laissez-faire within narrow limits characterize the mainstream art of the period between the wars.

The Seven & Five Society was an expedient alliance mostly composed of young ex-Servicemen reluctant to resume their education or to re-enter their professions at the point they had abandoned them. They regarded themselves as being 'in rebellion against academic art',[25] but at the time this need have involved little more than an interest in Impressionism. None of the original members of the Seven & Five are of particular concern to this study with the exception of Ivon Hitchens, a recent graduate of the Royal Academy Schools who was not party to the initial discussions but who joined in time for the opening exhibition,[26] in which he showed tempera paintings of downland scenes. The members represented no common cause, beyond such as might be understood from a reading of their manifesto, and were joined by nothing so much as a need to fill the hiatus in their professional lives and to share the costs of exhibiting. Typical titles of works included in the society's first show suggest neither a modern nor a cosmopolitan outlook: *An Orphan, To the Very Dregs, The Woodcutter's Cabin* and *Where Thrushes Sing*.

Yet for all its timidity, its provincialism and its conservatism – perhaps partly because these very qualities rendered it vulnerable to takeover – the Seven & Five was to become, under changed leadership and following a series of purges and recruitments, the principal platform for the only significant group movement in English painting during the 1920s. (A full list of members, exhibitors and exhibitions is given in the Appendix, p. 345.) Hitchens had been awoken to an interest in Cézanne by reading Clive Bell's *Art*, and in the third Seven & Five exhibition at Walker's Galleries late in 1922 he showed four works in which may be observed the effects of viewing the French painter through the eyes of Bloomsbury criticism. The result was a style in which landscape masses were arranged 'sculpturally' in order to present simple complexes of coherent, generalized forms to the eye [85]. The titles of two of these works, *Study of Essential Form* and *Study for a Three-*

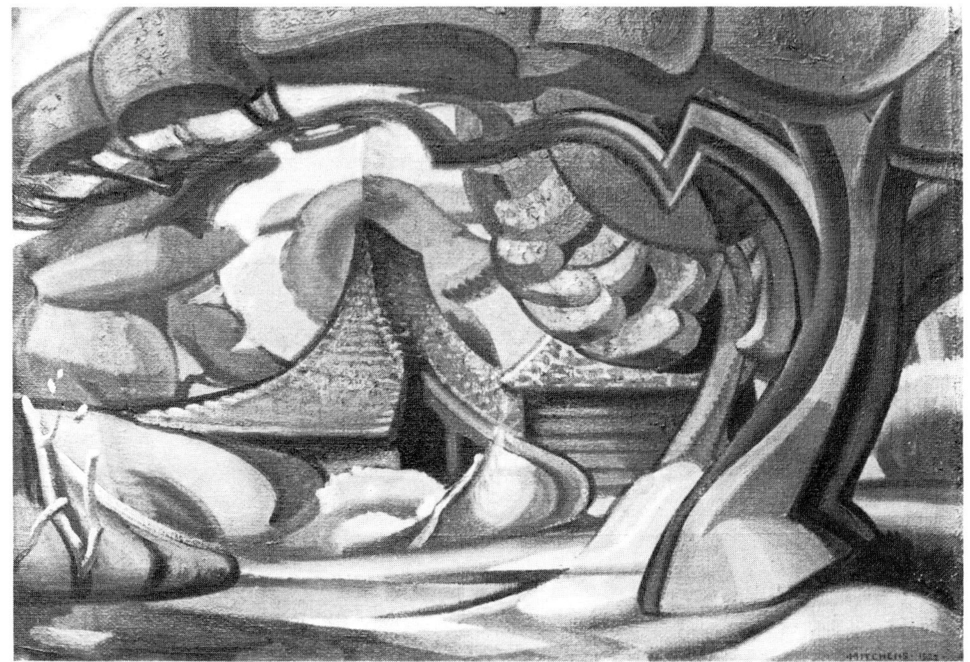

85. Ivon Hitchens: *The Curved Barn*, 1922. Oil on canvas, $25\frac{3}{4} \times 38\frac{1}{2}$ in. (exhibited, as 'The Barn', with the Seven & Five Society, 1922)

Dimensional Picture, characterize Hitchens's interests and betray his reading. In the early summer of the next year he visited Patersons Gallery to see an exhibition of paintings by Ben Nicholson, who had been making his own attempt to come to terms with the work of Cézanne. Hitchens liked the work and asked Nicholson to join the Seven & Five, to which he must have been welcomed as the son of William Nicholson, by then an established and successful painter. Nicholson was made a member in time to exhibit in the society's fifth exhibition at Patersons Gallery in December 1924. This date marks the end of his personal isolation from the activities of his contemporaries and the beginning of those developments which were to counter the isolationism of English art during the twenties.

7

STILL LIFE AND LANDSCAPE IN THE TWENTIES

The principal problem for the historian of English art of the twenties is that it is historically curiously rootless in contrast with the art of the pre-war and war years. For all the attention paid by novelists and historians of fashion to the activities of bright young things, the notable features of the history of the 1920s are features of a troubled economic and political history: a consistently high level of unemployment, a serious shortage of housing, the election of the first Labour Government in January 1924 and its fall ten months later, the General Strike of 1926, and the election of the second Labour Government in June 1929. That section of society from which the more modern painters of the 1920s were almost universally drawn can in no sense be said to have played a positive or significant part in this history, nor indeed did these painters, unlike some of their contemporaries in the field of literature, show in their art or their writings any awareness of the possibility that history might be made by those who neither made art nor talked about it.

The pre-war radicals had been preoccupied with a vision of the human figure in an industrial world and had embraced wholeheartedly the idea of a modern art expressing what they saw as 'modern rhythms', modern technology and modern ideology. By contrast, the most accomplished of the painters who rose to prominence during the 1920s, notably Paul Nash and Ben Nicholson, were concerned to employ the resources of modern art in the genres of still life and landscape; or perhaps we should rather say that the tendency of an exclusive interest in the technology of painting per se was that all possible subjects came to be interpreted either as still lifes or as landscapes. These genres had each at different times in the history of art served for the expression of modern ideas, but by the 1920s they were relatively 'neutralized' in so far as they were by then aesthetic categories before they were anything else. This means that they had become more appropriate for the expression of individual sensibility than for changing the currents of contemporary thought. The more advanced painters no longer felt themselves subject to pressures to justify formal innovation by reference to the *Weltanschauung*. Of all the pictures painted during the twenties there are very few, if any, which could have been considered remarkable by virtue of the artist's choice of subject; indeed, the subjects generally chosen were, in their very essence, historically uncontroversial, selected, as I've suggested, rather because they allowed for concentration upon painting in its strictly technical aspects than because they provided a source of vivid association. The history of English painting in the twenties is thus in essence a history of technical changes, or rather perhaps of the further development of a technical autonomy for painting. We will therefore be obliged, in this chapter, to pay more attention to the actual formal and technical characteristics of some representative paintings than has seemed appropriate up to this point. To allow such an emphasis is to impose a limitation, or rather to submit to the limitation which is endemic to the whole enterprise of Modernist art history: i.e. that a degree of self-certification is guaranteed for any work which that history can be seen to include.

Before the war it had seemed as if Nash, like Stanley Spencer, might help to extend the life-span of Pre-Raphaelitism well into the twentieth century, but after visiting his studio exhibition of drawings at 9 Fitzroy Street late in 1919 Nash's lifelong friend and correspondent Gordon Bottomley reproached him for succumbing to the fashion for 'triangles and general aerial geometry' and to 'the artistic internationalism that was springing up before the War'.[1] Nash's work was mild enough in comparison to the more militant formalizations of half-a-dozen years earlier, but we should not forget that at the beginning of the 1920s the majority of those who regarded themselves as practitioners or amateurs of mainstream painting and sculpture were still unaffected by French art beyond Impressionism. The need to acknowledge the quality and historical importance of French painting at the end of the nineteenth and the beginning of the twentieth centuries has tended to obscure the fact that many English artists who were neither irretrievably naive nor unremittingly reactionary still saw good reason in the twenties to draw upon a tradition in English art which had remained unbroken over this same period. Those, for instance, who responded most sympathetically and most intelligently to the art of the Pre-

Raphaelite Brotherhood – and Bottomley was certainly to be counted among these – saw it as evidence of the extent to which faithful observation and representation could serve imaginative lyrical or 'spiritual' subject-matter and 'transcendental' ends.

In actual practice, respect for such insular traditions among younger artists in the first third of the twentieth century too often entailed the indulgence of introspective obsession, at the expense both of the interests of realism and of vividness and facticity in the painted surface. A tendency to whimsicality was always the potential vitiating element in Nash's work, as in so much English painting of this century. His interests were often most successfully expressed in watercolour, a medium which readily serves for the expression of a view of the natural world as the source of poetical experience. He was not always able satisfactorily to reconcile his loyalty to the literary late-romanticism of the nineteenth century on the one hand and on the other his interest in the development of contemporary painting in a European context. He would sometimes undermine the formal qualities of his paintings by his attempts to use them as settings for operations better performed in verse or prose.

But although Nash was never to be so attracted to the ideology of Modernism as to lose sight of the possibility of an essentially romantic art, the experience of war had for the time being destroyed his interest in poetic

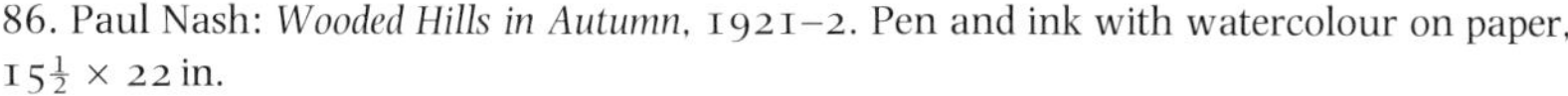

86. Paul Nash: *Wooded Hills in Autumn*, 1921–2. Pen and ink with watercolour on paper, $15\frac{1}{2} \times 22$ in.

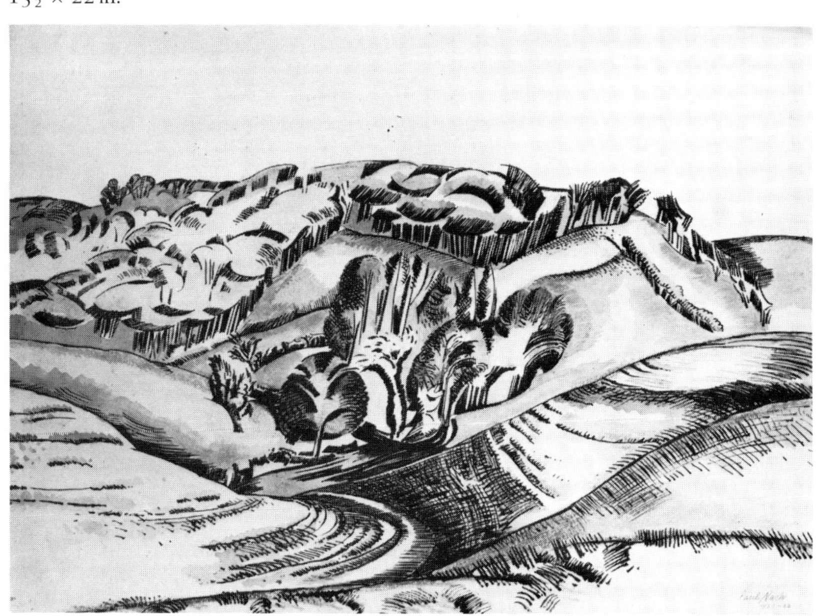

visions and had encouraged him to find robust means of attaching his work to the world of things and scenes. It cannot have been easy to come to terms with the remnants of English modernist influence in the circumstances of post-war isolation. If Nash developed a practical individual style earlier than any other painter of comparable age in the twenties, it was perhaps because his interest in landscape subjects established a context within which such influence was least likely to overwhelm more traditional limits [86].

In the autumn of 1921, after a couple of years during which he had tried his hand at theatrical design, wood engraving, teaching and art criticism, Nash suffered a severe breakdown, diagnosed as the product of 'war strain' aggravated by more recent troubles. On his release from hospital he rented a cottage on the south coast, at Dymchurch in Kent, and though he retained a pied-à-terre in London this was to be where the majority of his work was done over the next four years. Many of his most successful paintings were based on views along the division between sea and land. His style was still essentially naturalistic, however 'modern' it may now have seemed to Bottomley and others who had enjoyed the literary-imaginative qualities of his pre-war work and who now lamented their absence, but in the majority of the Dymchurch paintings, and in the Cézannesque landscapes he painted during the same years, Nash kept in check his tendency to dwell upon mood at the expense of pictorial structure. At best, as in *The Shore* of 1923 (Leeds City Art Gallery) [87], he used the 'naturally abstract' forms suggested by sea wall, steps and breakwaters as bases for his compositions, ordering them so as to establish a degree of abstraction appropriate to occasions of the meeting of sea, sky and land, yet without eliminating the particulars of substance and light by which such occasions are most vividly recalled.

Nash thus subdued for the moment his interest in literary-imaginative painting, but not his interest in insular traditions of response to landscape. During the nineteenth century the wealth of material yielded in the study of landscape had offered considerable compensation for the incipient literariness and the lack of sensuous appeal in so much of English painting. Nash's response to the desolation of trees and fields during the war appears both to have strengthened his attachment to the English landscape and to have awakened him to the possibility of complexity in his experience of it. In his Dymchurch paintings he seems to have explored the different modalities which this experience might be made to represent in terms of changes in light, weather and season. The influence of Cézanne, and in particular of his late watercolours, was also instrumental at this time in teaching Nash how to construct his paintings on the basis of formalizations upon landscape motifs. He painted no significant figure subject after 1914, and from the

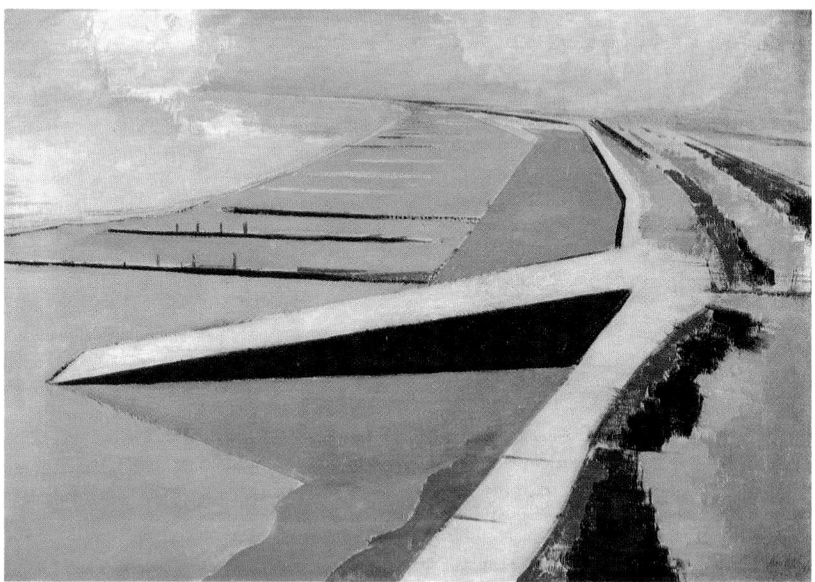

87. Paul Nash: *The Shore*, 1923. Oil on canvas, 24 × 36 in.

early twenties until his death in 1946 his most successful works were landscapes or were partially derived from landscape motifs.[2] In some of these he reconciled insular themes, evoking insular traditions, with European modernist styles pursued in so far as they might supplement rather than supplant those traditions. Too often in English art of the twenties, and especially in the work of those painters supported by Fry and Bell, European influences were used to suppress traditional native interests. On the whole, Nash was most successful when he was most obviously 'English'. He was never to become distinguished as one who added much to the technical resources of painting, but as an interpreter of the English landscape he has no equal in this century.

Paul Nash could so easily have been a mere provincial painter, and perhaps at any other period he would have seemed so. But during the post-war years, when English art as a whole was withdrawn and convalescent, he held an impressive balance between the exploitation of native interests and the exploration of those approaches to the technology of painting which derived from continental modernism.

In April 1925 Nash wrote to Bottomley, to the latter's dismay,

I am less & less concerned with picture-making & more & more interested by this elusive something which a painter pursues in painting, an engraver in engraving, a draughtsman in drawing or for that matter any artist in any art. My only side line – designing for the theatre – is not out of my course for I find in building scenes & making drawings from the models I learn more about tone & the 3 dimensional magic than in any other way but the theatre remains my only connection – as a painter – with literature – that is, my only conscious connection. I have still a certain amount of the literary stuff in my aesthetic system! But once one has begun to find the plastic values all other considerations seem irrelevant.[3]

Nash has generally been seen as representing the more 'literary' tendency in painting in England between the wars; that he of all people should have expressed such priorities is significant of the extent to which the concept of modern practice in art had come to entail a belief in the technical autonomy of pictorial form. Though Nash was no lover of Fry, 'plastic values' is a phrase straight from the Bloomsbury book.

In fact Nash continued to employ many devices in his art which were associated with those functions of scene-setting and story-telling which Modernist theory had tended to discredit and which modernist practice had tended to eliminate. Just what was at issue may be demonstrated by comparing Nash's paintings of the twenties with those of Ben Nicholson, who was always to be far more determined than Nash in his efforts to exclude 'literary' elements from his work, and who is thus more easily established in terms of Modernist valuations.

Nash and Nicholson had found common ground in their lack of enthusiasm for the Slade School during the years 1910–11. After the war they resumed their friendship, and in 1923 Nicholson paid a visit to Dymchurch. While there he painted a small seascape. Nash generally took an oblique view along the beach, emphasized distance and extension and played on contrasts between the formalities of the shoreline and the mobility of water [88]. He tended to evoke a spatial depth in his seascapes by allowing his colour to tail off into whiteness at the top of the canvas or paper.[4] Nicholson, on the other hand, faced straight out to sea and treated sea and shore alike [89], modifying the scale but not the direction of his brushmarks. He accepted the narrowness of tonal range offered by his subject as a means to integrate his painting within a range of colours which varies little between foreground (bottom edge) and furthest distance (top edge). He painted the breakwater as a near vertical intrusion into a composition dominated by horizontals. Expressed in terms of the conventional wisdom of Modernist criticism, the effect of such a device is to echo the framing edges of the support and thus further to 'flatten' the space of the painting. Nicholson did nothing to deny the opacity or to undermine the physical identity of his support; rather he emphasized the 'literal surface' of the board by coating it with a rough medium, and thereby

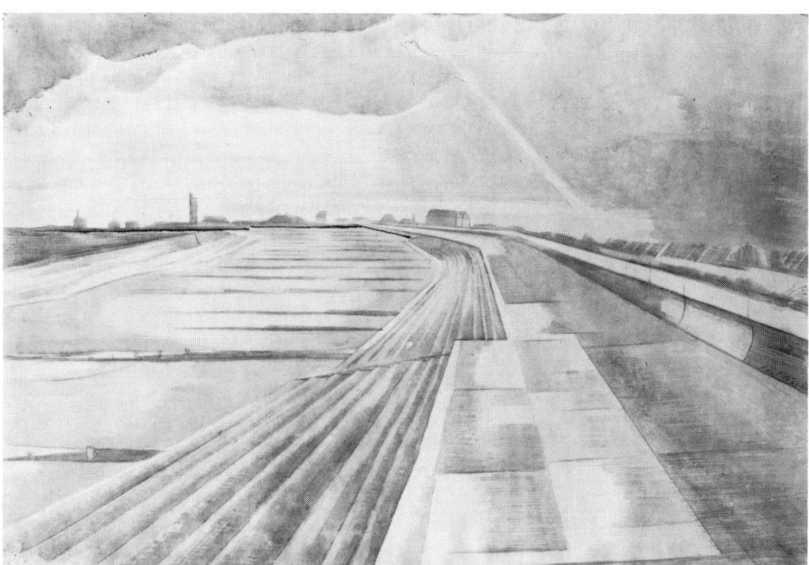

88. Paul Nash: *Dymchurch Wall*, 1923. Watercolour and pencil on paper, $14\frac{1}{2} \times 21\frac{1}{2}$ in.

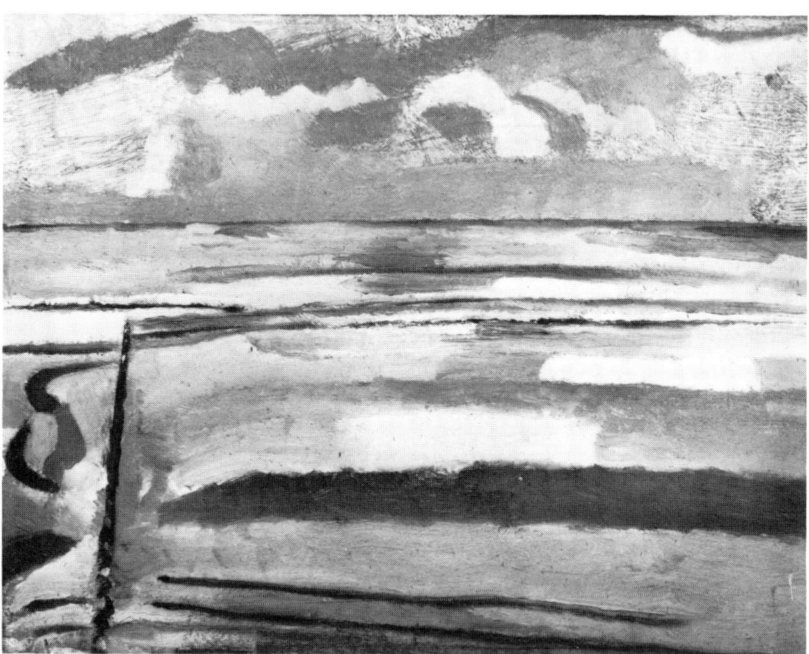

89. Ben Nicholson: *Dymchurch*, 1923. Oil on canvas stretched on board, $11\frac{1}{2} \times 15\frac{1}{4}$ in.

imposed upon himself the requirement that marks made in the priming stage be somehow incorporated as untransformed yet significant elements in the finished picture.

Nash and Nicholson might thus be seen as having taken alternative approaches to the problem of how to relate the world as we perceive it, three-dimensionally, to the flat surface of the painting. The works of these two may be used as instances of the two main avenues of development in English painting during the 1920s. Nash continued to establish the illusion of space in his work by essentially traditional means; that is to say he allowed a system of perspective, based on the acceptance of a single vanishing point, to govern his drawing and his composition. Within the ambience thus created he evoked particular moods by means of modulations in shading and colouring. Despite the absence of figures, there is always about his paintings something of the quality of a stage-set, an air charged, as it were, with a sense of anticipation or with the residue of a sequence of events. However lacking in anecdotal content his paintings of the twenties may in fact be, and however manifest may be the influence upon them of Cézanne and of Post-Impressionist theory in England, they still tend to invoke aspects of a persistent nineteenth-century tradition strongly associated with subject painting, and they tend to anticipate the reintroduction of subject painting in the 1930s, when many English artists, Nash foremost among them, responded to the influence of Surrealism. He thus provided a bridge between the English Romantic painting of the nineteenth century and the Romantic Revival which followed upon the heels of Surrealism in England in the later 1930s.

Nicholson on the other hand was concerned in his drawing and composition with the relationship of shapes as a function of the intensification of a surface, rather than with perspective as a means of subverting that surface. The space of the actual, three-dimensionally perceived world is evoked in his work not so much by illusion as by analogy; that is to say that the sense of depth is produced as a function of relationships in tone and colour and does not depend upon any 'tapering-off' towards the upper edge of the painting. There is no attempt to suggest a frame of anecdotal or emotive reference beyond the elements given in the painting itself, and it is to these alone that we look for the embodiment of significance and for the instantiation of relationship. To the extent that he had become emancipated from the Georgian social world graced by his father, where due respect was accorded to the reputation of Augustus John and to the memories of Velazquez, Manet and Whistler, Nicholson was innocent of interest in the traditional resources of English art. He responded strongly to the art of Cézanne and of the Cubist painters and he provided some basis for the development of abstract art in England in the 1930s.

Where Nash relied to a certain extent upon the spectator's ability to interpret, to associate and to fantasize, Nicholson made the (now discredited) demand that the spectator should come to his paintings as an 'innocent' (in the sense that Fry might have used such a term), capable of uncomplicated response to such 'dramatic' incidents as the sharp juxtaposition of two colours. The point may be illustrated by reference to one of the earliest paintings which can be seen as original and as characteristic of Nicholson's work. For three years after his marriage in 1920 to the painter Winifred Roberts he divided his time, when not travelling, between a studio in Chelsea and a villa in the Ticino in Switzerland, and it was during this period, often working side by side with his wife, that he seems really to have comitted himself to a career as a modern artist.

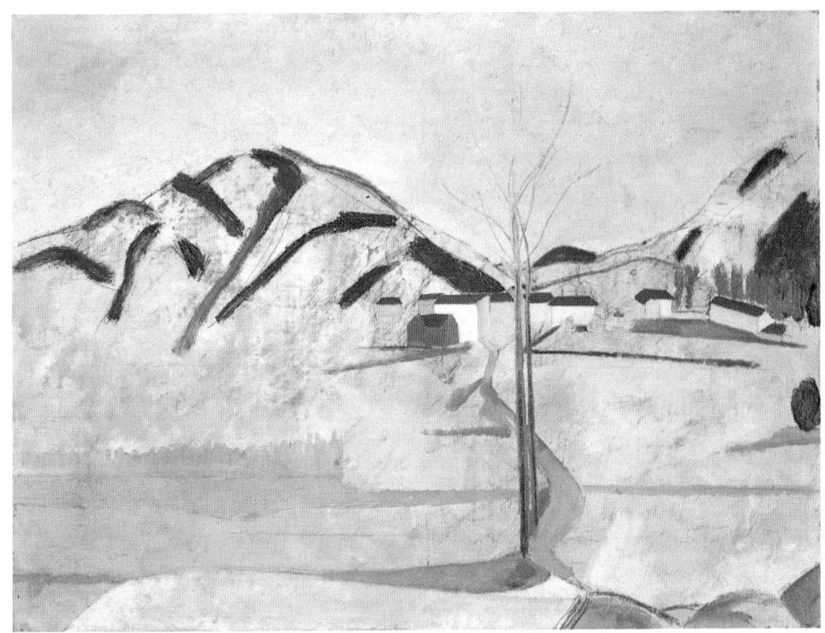

90. Ben Nicholson: *Cortivallo Lugano*, 1921–3. Oil and pencil on canvas, 18 × 24 in.

Cortivallo Lugano [90] was probably painted in the spring of 1923,[5] when Nicholson was aged twenty-nine and at the end of what was virtually his period of apprenticeship to modern painting. (During the same year Nash, Nevinson and Wadsworth were thirty-four, Bomberg thirty-two, and Roberts, whose involvement with the avant garde was then ten years old, twenty-eight.) The fresh, light tone and colour of this picture show the effects of an enthusiasm for the work of the Italian Primitives, while the choice of subject suggests some acquaintance with Cézanne's later landscapes; but at the heart of the composition Nicholson's more advanced technical interests are revealed. In the centre of the landscape a bright red house is outlined against the flat white wall of another further away. Along the edge which separates the one from the other, space appears to be generated, not because the imagination is drawn into the 'depths' of the picture as into the apex of a hollow cone, but because the red is perceived as closer and as more palpably the colour of an object, than the white; the two surfaces thus appear to 'separate' in space. In the foreground a vertical line of thin trees, pencilled directly into the paint, provides a point of reference in relation to which both houses become distant though not subordinate. The painting is sophisticated according to criteria different from those which we would be inclined to employ in regarding the work of Paul Nash, or of any other English painter of the time.

Nicholson had not been involved in any of the pre-war or wartime activities among the English avant garde and had been abroad for his health during the crucial years 1912–14. After the war he had been exposed to the influence of Wyndham Lewis and the X Group, which he later said had acted on him as an 'emetic',[6] but by the early twenties his tastes were much closer to those of Fry than of Lewis. During visits to Paris on the way to and from Switzerland in the years 1920–23 he divided his time between the Italian Primitives in the Louvre and the modern French works exhibited in the dealers' galleries; and over the same period he and his wife compiled a collection of photographs and reproductions covering works by Giotto, Uccello, Cézanne, Douanier Rousseau, Matisse, Derain, Braque and Picasso.[7] The preference for early ('pure') over later ('sophisticated') Renaissance work, the interest in the primitive Rousseau, and the taste in modern French art were all symptomatic of a view of art compatible with Fry's belief in the superior 'reality' of the life of forms in art to that life which a more strictly naturalistic art might evoke. There is a quality of fastidiousness about Nicholson's painting, an unwillingness or inability to embrace the grossness in the world at large of what Sickert had called 'gross material facts'. This might be interpreted as suggesting a limit on his view of the world similar to that which allowed Fry to identify the exercise of imagination in terms of 'pure disinterested contemplation'. Unlike many of his contemporaries who had attracted attention before the war, Nicholson had probably never considered the possibility of an art that was anything but asocial. It is as much to this as to the 'originality' of his work that Nicholson owes his status as the paradigm modernist painter in recent English art history.

Yet Nicholson was a more competent painter than any of the English Post-Impressionists (though, like so many who might have expected it, he never received any support from Fry or Bell). During the earlier 1920s what marked him out, more than anything else, was the evidence his work gave of a capacity technically to exploit the new type of pictorial space which underlay the development of French painting between Cézanne's mature works and the later Cubism of Braque and Picasso.

Among those less concerned than was Nash for the survival of insular traditions, it had been a consequence of the influence of French Post-Impressionism that consistent single-viewpoint perspective no longer seemed readily defensible in ambitious modern paintings. There is a substructure of perspective in Cézanne's landscapes, but it is continually subverted in the process by which individual motifs are delineated and are related to one another across the actual surface of the canvas. The English Post-Impressionists, and even the majority of the pre-war radicals, had tended to replace conventional procedures for ordering of composition by techniques for emphasizing the 'sculptural' qualities of individual forms. (This was the point of compatibility between the influence of the early 'expressionistic' Cézannes shown in the first Post-Impressionist exhibition in 1910 and the influence of contemporary teaching at the Slade, where the study of drawing was seen as the means to an understanding of 'structure'.) The result was typically to produce a kind of formal heftiness which effectively countered the more sophisticated influences of both English and French traditions, but which was compatible on the one hand with Fry's esteem for such second-rate French painters as Jean Marchand, and on the other with the Vorticists' interest in the expression of 'dynamic' force.

Nicholson's response to Cézanne was of a different kind. He understood that the relationship of separate marks across the surface could be adequate to establish a coherent illusion of things in space. He thus avoided any sense of the need for a new kind of 'sculptural' drawing in order to establish the significance of form. The 'conceptual priority' accorded to the acknowledgement of distinctive factive elements, operating as such upon the surface of his paintings, saved Nicholson's works from some of the dangers of formal 'crudity' involved in deciding priorities on the basis of a taste for the productions of children and of 'primitives'. The 'sleeves-rolled-up' interpretation of professionalism which his practice suggested served as some counter to the tendency towards 'amateurishness' which Lewis had so rightly seen as entailed in the preferences of Fry.

There is no significant evidence of the absorption of specifically Cubist influence in Nicholson's work until 1924, but he had been looking at recent and contemporary painting in Paris during the previous few years and was able to draw upon this first-hand experience for the whole of the decade. Much of the early interest in Cubism in England had been provoked by exposure to the very 'sculptural' paintings of 1907–09 (the phase often referred to as 'African Cubism') and had involved attempts to apply the style either as a means to energize what were essentially subject pictures (Lewis, Roberts, Bomberg) or as a means to provide an emphatic decorative framework for essentially lyrical compositions (Grant, Vanessa Bell). Nicholson responded most strongly to later phases in the work of Picasso and Braque, the so-called 'Analytic' or 'Hermetic Cubism' of *c.* 1909–12 and the 'Synthetic Cubism' which followed their introduction of collage techniques at the close of 1912.[8] Twenty-three years after the event Nicholson recalled a visit to Paris made in 1921 and a specific experience which he had plainly accorded a significant place in his autobiography:

> I remember suddenly coming on a cubist Picasso at the end of a small upstairs room at Paul Rosenberg's Gallery. It must have been a 1915 painting – it was what seemed to me then, completely abstract. And in the centre there was an absolutely miraculous green – very deep, very potent and absolutely real. In fact none of the actual events in one's life have been more real than that, and it still remains a standard by which I judge any reality in my own work . . .[9]

The influence of French Cubism was of fundamental importance for the subsequent development of modern art in England and elsewhere, and we must therefore digress in order to establish, in general terms, what was involved in the representative works of Picasso and Braque, the initiators and most important practitioners of Cubism. Particularly in the Analytic phase in 1910–12, where the 'fragmentation' of objects and surfaces is so pervasive as to skirt abstraction, and where conventional means of orientation are inadequate for the spectator, the Cubist painting exemplifies a new means of visualizing the relationships between pictured objects and between objects or object-clusters and background. The conventional reading of the picture-frame as a window on to something ceases to be consistent or credible. The spectator is confronted with the significance of his own role in reconstituting a picture of the world according to responses and conceptualizations evoked by individual signs, suggestions and codifications. The concept of painting-as-window suffered further defeat (through a kind of *reductio ad absurdum*) in 1912 when Braque and Picasso began to stick pieces of ready-coloured or printed paper over the paint-surface of their pictures and to evoke the presence of objects such as glasses by drawing them on top of these.

In sum, the art of the Cubists suggested the need to acknowledge new complications in the central issues of figurative painting: how relationships between elements are established within the picture; how such relationships represent or match relationships in the real world; and how the picture, as a 'map' of such relationships, itself relates to any relevant model of the world or body of ideas.

Braque's and Picasso's works of 1910–12 raise two issues which are of particular relevance to consideration of Nicholson's work from the mid-twenties onward. Firstly, there is the suggestion that a picture may justifiably be composed by abstracting from the specific situation visualized, or even by attempting to hypothesize a situation which is essentially 'unspecific' as to its picturesque elements: we are confronted with a formal notation for types of relationship between them, rather than, say, with a specific violin, of a definite colour, seen in a particular light and standing in a measurable relationship to a specific bottle or glass. The possibility that a painter might deal thus explicitly in formal tokens rather than in illustrative tokens, though it had been hinted at in Cézanne's work, was first fully explored in the work of the Cubists.

Secondly, it is implied in the works of Analytical and Synthetic Cubism that any mark made upon the surface, any shape outlined, or any element actually applied to that surface (such as a piece of newsprint) may 'function' either mimetically, as a means of reference to features of a three-dimensional world, or literally, as just that mark, shape or piece of paper having a certain value within the two-dimensional world of the picture, or as both at once. (In the previous history of painting it was an unshakable convention that two such functions or readings could not notionally coexist.) Marks upon the surface of a Cubist painting are not always underwritten either by evidence presented to the eye or by the activities of the imagination. This suggests a step forward in the development of technical autonomy for painting. There is a line which connects Whistler and Cubism, though of course the intellectual demands made of the Analytical Cubist were rather more acute than those made of the painter of Nocturnes. Contrary to the false antitheses of Modernist history, Nicholson's early exposure to a decidedly Whistlerian taste and paint-technology by no means disqualified him from appreciating the work of Braque and Picasso.

Nicholson destroyed many of the experimental works he painted during the early twenties. Of his surviving works two in particular, both painted in 1924, bear witness to his interest in principles of composition derived from Cubist painting. *Trout* [91] shows a table top, represented as if from above, upon which rectangular shapes, derived from the study of still-life objects, are disposed as if seen upright and almost in silhouette. At the top left a pattern of stripes (derived from a large painted jug)[10] serves both to establish the presence of an opaque form and to provide a background against which the other, more 'translucent' shapes seem to stand forward. A bright red rectangle at the top right provides a point of focus just where the composition might otherwise seem to tail off into indeterminate space beyond the edge of the table. The combination of or alternation between

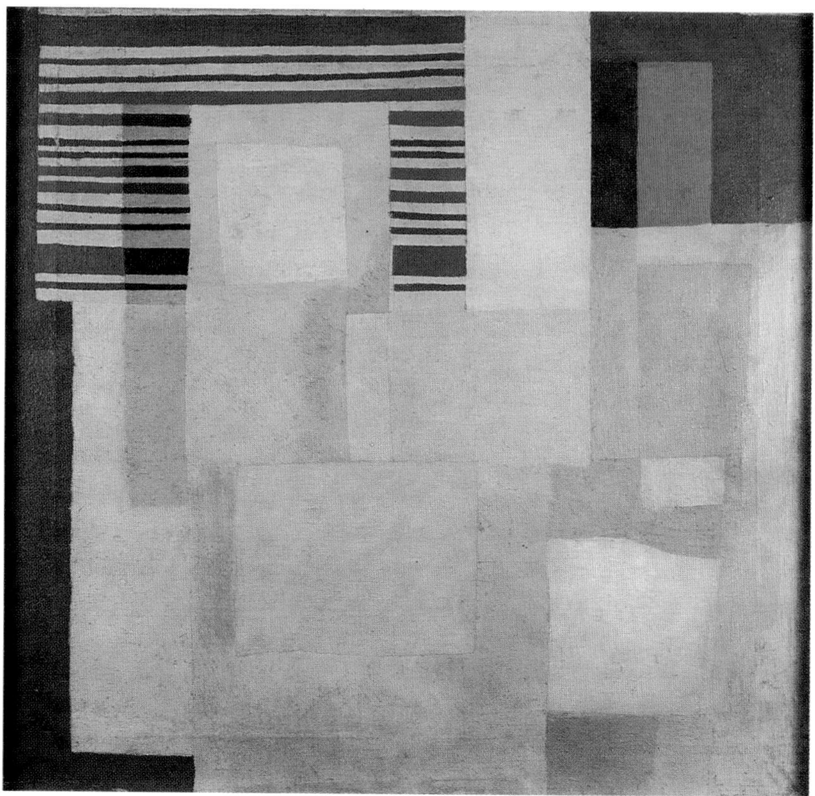

91. Ben Nicholson: *Trout*, 1924. Oil on canvas, 22 × 23 in.

'plan' and 'elevation' views upon a given subject was a device introduced into painting with Analytic Cubism; and the rendering of individual forms as independent flat surfaces, having autonomous functions within the painting, was a feature of Synthetic Cubism. These elements of Cubist practice were absorbed into Nicholson's work from 1924 onward.

The second of these experimental early paintings [92] was a completely non-figurative composition, organized into flat 'planes' according to principles derived from Synthetic Cubist practice, yet invested with a freshness and clarity of colour for which there was no precedent in relevant contexts within French art. (There is a probably accidental similarity to those experimental abstract paintings by Grant and Vanessa Bell which were essentially by-products of the interests of the Omega Workshops.) Nicholson here combined two aspects from previous Cubist art: on the one hand the 'transparent' quality of Braque's paintings of 1911–12, where forms and planes appear to interpenetrate in space, and on the other the formality of Picasso's work after 1913, where hard-edged areas of flat colour are used to suggest clear divisions between one 'level' and another, in virtual independence of other elements evoking the presence of objects in the same picture. Nicholson's *First Abstract Painting*[11] seems to purvey a quality of clear natural light without predicating the presence of particular objects. According to his own concept of the function of painting the 'state of existence' evoked is one which is determined but not material in character. It is perhaps in such terms that we should interpret Nicholson's concept of the superior 'reality' of the painting as an 'event' among other events in one's life; i.e. in terms of the attempt to invoke an imaginary freedom from the circumstances of material (and perhaps social) existence. (The notion of such a freedom was consistent with ideas expressed in such early propagandizing of non-figurative art as the writings of Malevich and Kandinsky.[12])

Although a sophisticated understanding of Cubism and a belief in the feasibility of non-representational art underlie all Nicholson's work from 1924 to the present day, the great majority of his output of the twenties was

92. Ben Nicholson: *First Abstract Painting*, 1924. Oil and pencil on canvas, $21\frac{3}{4} \times 24$ in. (probably exhibited, as 'Abstraction November', with the Seven & Five Society, 1924)

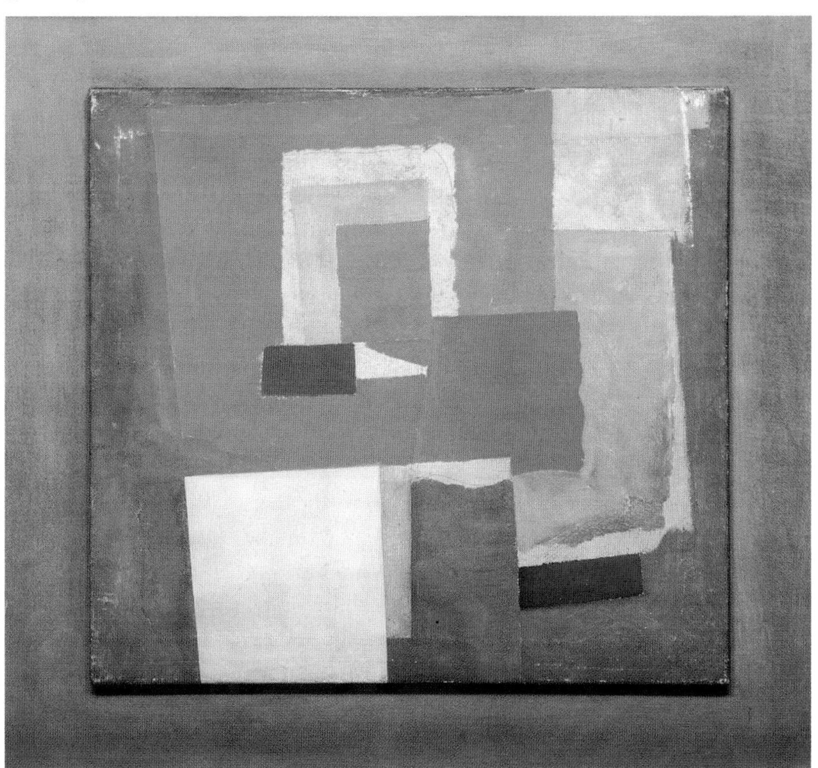

less obviously advanced, in terms of Modernist concepts of progress, than *Trout* or the *First Abstract Painting*. *Goblet and Pears* [93], probably painted a year or so later, is more representative of his production at the time. It is an apparently modest painting, but original and accomplished nonetheless.

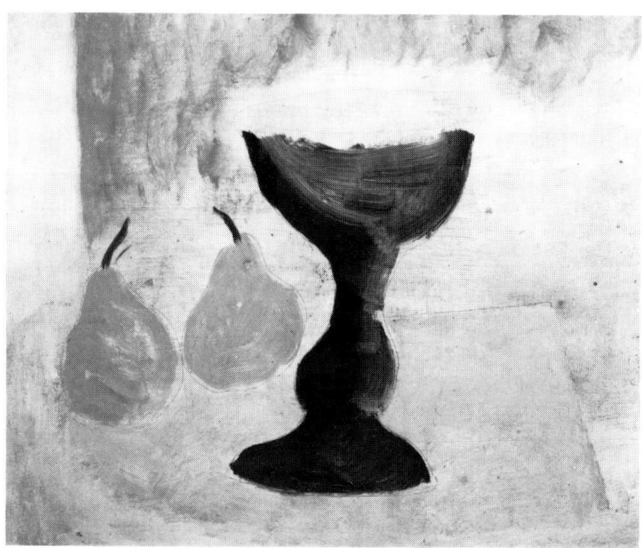

93. Ben Nicholson: *Goblet and Pears*, *c.* 1925. Oil and pencil on board, $14\frac{1}{2} \times 17\frac{1}{2}$ in.

The simplicity carried to a point which suggests naivety, the tendency to replace functions of modelling in the round with deft placing and considered use of silhouette, the balancing of strong with light tones, of firm with lightly established edges and of delicate drawing with emphatic paint handling, the 'poetic' economy in the disposition of shapes, and the unremitting good taste in the organization of tone; these are all characteristics of the majority of Nicholson's paintings during the twenties.

As in *Goblet and Pears*, there is a persistent tendency in Nicholson's works of *c.* 1925–32 for line to function descriptively with a degree of independence from painted and textured areas. This independence is most marked in the slightest of his paintings from this period, where an insistent decorative element, the curve of a handle or the filigree of a lettered sign, signifies a certain taste, as it might be in antique mugs or picturesque shopfronts, within which the difficult enterprise of picture-making has been contained and reduced to the status of a game or an elegant performance. The taste is exquisite enough – and it has undoubtedly been very pervasive in the milieu of Nicholson's admirers – but it nevertheless entails restriction of regard at best, and the indulgence of a privileged whimsy at worst. This tendency to indulge in 'tasteful' decoration, or to treat detail in an anecdotal fashion, has always been the strongest restriction upon the value of Nicholson's work.

On the other hand, the more the functions of drawing are assimilated into the procedures of construction, the less whimsical, on the whole, the paintings tend to be. From about 1926 onwards Nicholson's line has been characteristically crisp and precise, laid down on the paper as if representing were possibly an unproblematic activity. Where there is a degree of resistance from the material upon which he is working, the attendant danger of undue facility is overcome by the unpredictable nature of the incidents which occur on a richly textured surface.

By the time Nicholson first exhibited with the Seven & Five Society he had two individual exhibitions behind him,[13] and had sufficient reputation to be viewed by the other members as an important recruit. The society had already undergone considerable changes in membership (only five of the original members showed work in the 1924 exhibition), but with the marginal exception of Claude Flight, a late if not wholly convincing convert to Futurism, few of those recruited had been in a position to add much to the overall level of competence. There was, however, some evidence of interest in modern French art. At the third of the society's annual exhibitions in 1922 a group of five French painters had exhibited at Flight's invitation, and among them had been André l'Hote, a practitioner and theoretician of Cubism who had been among those represented in Fry's second Post-Impressionist exhibition ten years before. And Ivon Hitchens, who had been responsible for recruiting Flight, had recently become interested in the work of the Cubists, largely as the result of reading Fry and Bell, and had spent a summer in Paris. In the 1924 exhibition Hitchens showed four works painted on the continent, including a landscape of La Roche Guyon, where Braque had worked in 1909. In 1925 he held a one-man exhibition at the Mayor Gallery, showing landscapes and still lifes mostly painted in Cumberland, where he went during that summer to stay with the Nicholsons. Several of his works of this date, especially those showing flowers on windowsills, were very close in style to Winifred Nicholson's paintings on similar themes.

The Seven & Five was ripe for a purge. By 1926, two years after Nicholson joined, Hitchens was the only founder-member still exhibiting, and there had been considerable recruitment from among English artists with some interest in recent French painting. Early in 1926 Nicholson was elected as the first chairman. Winifred Nicholson and the ex-Vorticist Jessica Dismorr were among those who joined the society in that year, and of the eleven new members elected during the next five years seven were proposed by the

Nicholsons. (They were a sculptress, Betty Muntz, painters Christopher Wood and Cedric Morris in 1926, the potter William Staite Murray in 1927, David Jones, painter and poet, in 1928, and another painter, John Aldridge, in 1931.)

Sidney Hunt was another artist who joined in 1926, following a one-man show at the Mayor Gallery the previous autumn. His characteristic work at the time was a weak amalgam of Cubist and Art Déco styles. His borrowings bore more interesting fruit, however, in his editorship of the periodical *Ray* ('art miscellany'), of which there were two issues in 1926–7. Besides publishing his own work, Nicholson's and Flight's, Hunt reproduced and translated material culled from publications of the European modernist avant garde. At the time Hunt could indeed claim that his journal was, as its prospectus claimed, 'the only English periodical devoted exclusively to new art movements', but cosmopolitan contents, sans-serif type and eccentric layouts were not of themselves enough to establish the existence of a social base for these movements in England. In the context of the contemporary English art world, works such as Malevich's *Black Square*, reproduced on the first page spread of *Ray* 1, could only have been considered as outlandish or accidental, cut adrift from any cognate history. The editorial glosses were paraphrases of received modernist slogans.

> The black square, perilously near the zero point of art, is ... a signal and stimulus for new departures.

> New artists are coming through with the knowledge that we and all our works are only 'the nocturnal exhalations of a sinister fantasy'.

It was to be another five years at least before the characteristic tones of European modernist avant-gardism were to be heard in any well-rooted art discourse in England. As regards the Seven & Five, Nicholson's aim from the start had been to establish a group which would be both modern and international in outlook, and he achieved as much as was possible without threat to his own pre-eminence. But at no time during the twenties did the members constitute an avant garde; there was no such thing in English art at the time, which is to say that there was no concerted opposition to the modernist orthodoxy of Post-Impressionism. In the mid-1920s the Seven & Five was little more than an alternative to the London Group for those put off by the dominating Bloomsbury presence within that organization.[14] Fry and Bell were powerful figures during the twenties and they exercised a considerable influence over a wide range of dealers and patrons. Those artists they were not prepared to support were hard pressed to show and to sell work; in contrast, many of those whose work they approved were provided with a measure of financial security through the London Artists

Association, a scheme sponsored by the economist John Maynard Keynes among others whereby certain artists were guaranteed an annual income in return for the right to dispose of their work. The majority of those invited to join the LAA were already members of the London Group, and on the whole their work was very 'French'. The work shown in the Seven & Five exhibitions during the mid-twenties was not so different; it was perhaps a little less slavishly 'French', and more confidently naturalistic, but it was still broadly Post-Impressionist in style. The majority of the members in, say, 1926 would perhaps have regarded Van Gogh and Gauguin as undisputed masters, and Cézanne as an important though difficult painter, and they would have allowed the influence of Matisse to enrich their colours. They painted still lifes, landscapes and portraits of friends. Above all, they attempted to achieve 'freshness' of tone and colour and to instantiate a commitment to 'sincerity' in their approach to ideologically uncomplicated subjects.

The typical and leading representatives of the 'Seven & Five style' during the later 1920s were Ben and Winifred Nicholson and Christopher Wood. I have suggested that the impact of Cubism is discernible in all Nicholson's work after 1924, but it was not until 1932 that he was again to express as clear an interest as he had in *Trout* [91] and the *First Abstract Painting* [92] in the formal possibilities it suggested. The modernism of his art during these intermediate years lay rather in his exploration of qualities of facture and of touch – i.e. of aspects of a technology of painting which was effectively continuous with that of Whistler and of his own father – than in any great innovation in the interpretation of form or pictorial structure.

In Winifred Nicholson's case, the impact of Van Gogh, Gauguin and Matisse upon a sensibility educated under late-Pre-Raphaelite influences[15] resulted in brightly coloured naturalistic paintings of freshness and simple charm. It was in part the example of her uncomplicated treatment of coloured subjects in clear natural light that encouraged Ben Nicholson to lighten his own palette and to rely less on a tonal basis for his compositions.

Christopher Wood was welcomed into the Seven & Five early in 1927 as a painter with an unequalled range of contacts among continental artists. His recruitment marked the beginning of a brief but significant episode in English painting. The son of a Liverpool doctor, Wood had left England for Paris in 1921 at the age of twenty. More by virtue of his charm and boyish enthusiasm than of any proven talent as a painter, he had gained rapid access to a highly fashionable and cosmopolitan social world. He stayed initially with Alphonse Kahn, a wealthy collector whose modern acquisitions included works by Picasso and Matisse, and he was subsequently befriended by Antonio de Gandarillas, a Chilean diplomat with homes in

Paris and in London and with a range of friendships which included Picasso, Jean Cocteau, Igor Stravinsky and Serge Diaghilev, impresario of the Russian Ballet Company. Wood first met Picasso in the summer of 1923; Cocteau was to become a close friend during the next year, as was Moïse Kisling, a young Polish painter living in Paris. The less adventurous work of these three artists was variously reflected in Wood's painting during the years 1924–7, alongside echoes of the work of Augustus John, then still seen by many (Wood among them) as England's one authentic genius.[16]

No other young English artist of the twenties had anything like the same ease of access within the sophisticated French art world. If it seems surprising that Wood should have taken at least five years to produce any painting which demonstrated that he had seen enough to challenge his early admiration for John, we should remember firstly that he had had virtually no formal training in art before his arrival in Paris and that he was thus likely to view continental modern art as an unsophisticated and enthusiastic amateur, and secondly that Paris in the 1920s, like London, was altogether a quieter place than it had been before the war. It seemed as if a wave of neo-classicism had swept through European art in the wake of the war, and the established modern masters were all working in less obviously modernist styles than they had a decade earlier. Matisse was now based in Nice, where he painted figures in interiors in a decidely sensuous and apparently relaxed style. They are among his most beautiful paintings, but given the concept of a progressing modern art it was inevitable that they should have been regarded as implying a relaxation of his energies. Certainly those such as Duncan Grant who attempted to follow his example were cast hopelessly adrift. Picasso continued to produce decorative paintings in a late-Cubist vein throughout the twenties, but the most remarkable development in his art after the war was associated with the reintroduction of a form of naturalism and the pursuit of a roundly modelled neo-classical style. Braque, who had taken a long time to recover from the war, enriched the colour and texture of his paintings and turned his Cubism towards more obviously decorative ends. Derain, widely regarded as a major source of influence, was also working by this time in a deliberately conservative style. Clive Bell in Paris in 1919 had asked a painter-friend from the pre-war days about the coming generation of painters in Paris: 'Et les jeunes?' 'Nous sommes les jeunes,' had been the reply.[17]

The French art to which the more advanced English artists looked during the 1920s was the art of the pre-war years. Nicholson, working in comparative isolation and with some varied experience already behind him, was able to be stringent and selective in his view upon French art, but Wood, surrounded by the petits-maîtres of an École de Paris now largely resting on its laurels, felt the need to keep in touch with what was essentially a backward-looking art. Soft neo-classicism, pastoral lyricism and boudoir sensuality were features of the work of the main run of Parisian painters in the twenties: Marie Laurencin, Jules Pascin, Dunoyer de Segonzac, Kisling *et al.* It was really only once he had left Paris behind, geographically and emotionally, that Wood was able to develop an individual style.

For the greater part of the years 1921–5, and while he was not in Paris, Wood travelled with Gandarillas throughout Europe, the Balkans and North Africa, reading (he was particularly impressed by the letters of Van Gogh, which no doubt encouraged his tendency to idealize his own vocation), visiting museums, and working in sporadic bursts. (In letters to his mother written during a two-month stay in Taormina he mentioned some twenty separate paintings.) In or around 1923 he was introduced to the smoking of opium. Cocteau was one of the many who flirted with the drug during the 1920s. Its use had more serious consequences for Wood, who developed a dependence which became marked during the later twenties and which almost certainly was a contributory cause of his suicide in 1930. It has been said that in Paris in the 1920s one was either a wolf or a lamb; Picasso and Cocteau were among the leaders of the pack. Wood's relationship with the modern and cosmopolitan culture of Europe typifies that entered into by many an artistic young Englishman during the period between the wars. His work up to the time of his death is perhaps not sufficiently substantial to claim him a place among the major English painters of the period under review, but he remains one of its most poignant and most vivid figures.

Early in 1925 Wood spent some time at a school run by André l'Hote in Paris, and during the autumn of that year he was in London, passing a certain amount of his time in the company of Augustus John and of Frank Dobson, then president of the London Group. He sold several works and began to receive commissions for portraits, the one sure way to an income for a young painter at the time. There was even a commission, albeit abortive, for a décor for the Russian Ballet. Dobson selected some work for the London Group exhibition, and soon after Wood received a letter on behalf of the Seven & Five asking if he would like to join them.[18] The question of his membership seems to have been temporarily shelved, but he was in England again in 1926. He spent two months during the autumn in Cornwall and met the Nicholsons for the first time towards the end of that year. They showed each other recent work, and within a very short time a close friendship developed.[19] Wood joined the Seven & Five in time for the seventh exhibition in January 1927, and in April of that year he shared an exhibition with the Nicholsons at the Beaux-Arts Gallery. In March 1928 he stayed with them at Bankshead, their house in Cumberland. The model of artistic practice which the Nicholsons offered was plainly very different to those Wood had encountered in Paris.[20] There was a certain cultivated austerity in their style of living and at that time both were practising Christian Scientists.

The paintings of these three were often very close in subject and in treatment during the later 1920s, and there is a considerable similarity in Wood's and Nicholson's styles of drawing in 1928–30. For two and a half months in the summer and autumn of 1928 the Nicholsons and Wood were together in Cornwall, first at Feock and then at St Ives. In August 1928 Ben Nicholson and Wood first saw pictures by Alfred Wallis, a retired Cornish fisherman who had just begun to paint untaught, at the age of seventy, following the death of his wife. Nicholson later described this occasion:

> On the way back from Porthmeor Beach we passed an open door in Back Road West and through it saw some paintings of ships and houses on odd pieces of paper and cardboard nailed up all over the wall, with particularly large nails through the smaller ones. We knocked on the door and inside found Wallis, and the paintings we got from him then were among the first he made.[21]

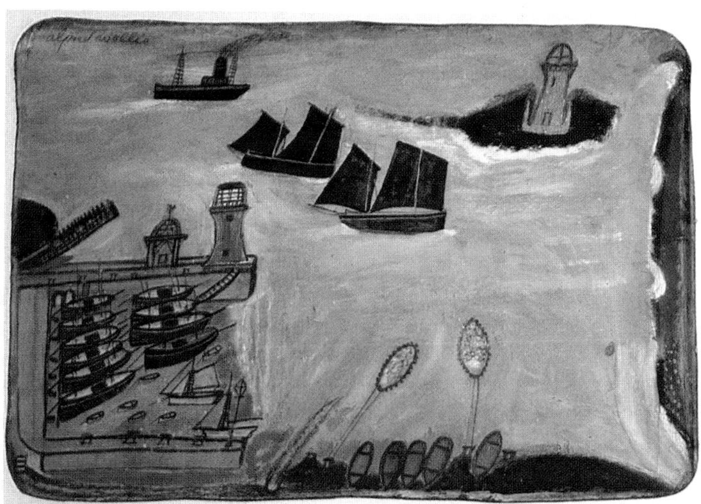

94. Alfred Wallis: *Three ships and lighthouse*. *c*. 1934–8.
Oil and pencil on board, $12\frac{1}{2} \times 18$ in.

Wallis painted mostly what he remembered: St Ives as it had been in his youth [94], sea voyages, sailing ships, lighthouses and wrecks, vividly recreated in ships' enamel paints on scraps of board or roughly cut-out card. Though Nicholson and Wood responded with equal enthusiasm to Wallis's paintings, different aspects of his work made themselves felt in their own. Wood, already encouraged by the example of the Nicholsons to consider technical alternatives to the mannerism of French painting of the twenties, found in Wallis's work a powerful antidote to the pursuit of a second-hand sophistication. After the Nicholsons had left he stayed on for a month in St Ives and visited Wallis daily.[22] His painting became more robust in shape and colour and he began to use enamels and glazes and generally to pursue a range of effects outside those available within normal oil-painting procedures. In the longer term, he was also perhaps encouraged by the strong 'naturally symbolic' nature of Wallis's work to develop a tendency in his own towards interpretativeness and fantasy in the treatment of observed or remembered subjects.[23]

Nicholson, on the other hand, seems to have been encouraged by Wallis's work to consider an extension to the range of objects which a painter might

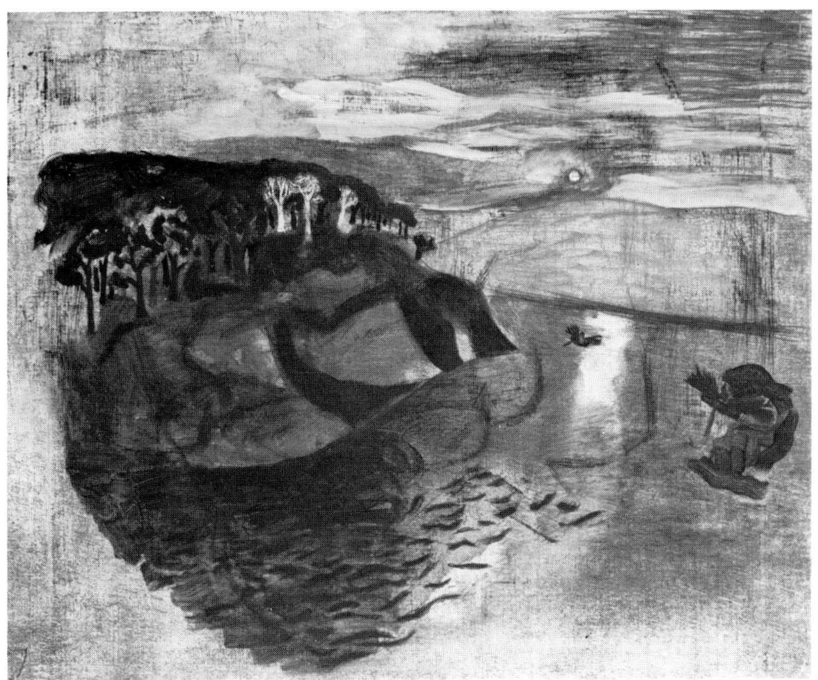

95. Ben Nicholson: *Pill Creek, Moonlight*, 1928/9. Oil, gesso, and pencil on canvas, $19\frac{1}{2} \times 24$ in.

produce. The more significant transformational effects of his enthusiasm for Wallis's pictures are to be detected in the early reliefs which he was to make between December 1933 and March 1934 [135], rather than in paintings with superficially comparable motifs produced before then [95]. The 'sincerity' and 'freshness' aimed at by the representative painters of the Seven & Five during the mid-twenties had often resulted in the production of somewhat 'childlike' pictures. In the tradition of Fry's and Bell's criticism, and of the pre-war reaction against sophistication, the concept of sincerity of approach was often interpreted by reference to standards inferred from the work of children, of 'primitives' such as the early Italian painters, and of naive artists such as Douanier Rousseau (whose work had been the subject of an exhibition at the Lefevre Gallery in 1926). There was a tendency during the mid-twenties to regard art as an activity requiring a form of artlessness. Nicholson had in fact painted uncomplicated subjects in a superficially naive manner before his visit to Cornwall (see for instance the landscape *Walton Wood Cottage no. 1*, exhibited at the Lefevre Gallery in July 1928), and was therefore no doubt already disposed to like Wallis's work.

'I suppose', Wyndham Lewis wrote in 1927, 'that there is no one who has not noticed . . . the prevalence of what now amounts to a cult of childhood, and of *the Child*. This irresponsible Peter Pannish psychology is the key to the Utopia of the "revolutionary" Rich . . . it is connected with the cult of the *primitive* and the savage . . .'[24] The cult of the primitive in the 1920s had many ramifications. It can be associated with that earlier, pre-war reaction against what was seen as the 'materialism' of the nineteenth century; it was consistent, in the shorter perspective, with the kinds of valuation placed by Bell, and to a lesser extent Fry, on the modern movement in art; and in a longer historical view it may be seen as a grotesque and attenuated reflection of the Romantic notion, for which the writings of Jean Jacques Rousseau are the locus classicus, that there is a vigour and an ethical value in innocence and that this is dissipated by technical sophistication. The cult of Innocence and of Naturalness has had a long and continuing history in modern English art and art education, where it has tended to militate against study of the epistemology of art. In so far as innocence is an ideological category, its promotion as a value in the practice of art is best regarded as a strategic resource and examined in terms of the ends pursued. It was common during the period between the wars for artists of considerable technical ability to be embarrassingly fey in statements about their work. (Nicholson was typical of this tendency and remained so until his death.) It is possible to discern a growing tendency among English artists of modernist persuasion to appear to require a form of simple-mindedness in the responses of their audience, as if they feared that a close examination of practical aspects might tell against the maintenance of some important mystique attached to the practice of art. This characteristic distinguishes between the art and writings of the younger artists after the war and those of the pre-war avant garde; Wyndham Lewis, for instance, might occasionally have written, and indeed painted, as if he were addressing an audience of men of lesser intelligence, but he was never one to conceal his own capabilities or to betray his sophistication in the name of an effete 'sensitivity'.

The Nicholsons and Wood showed works with Cornish subjects in the Seven & Five exhibition in March 1929 [96]. Two works by Wallis were also included. In Nicholson's paintings a richly romantic mood, evoked by specific impressions or memories of time and place, was balanced by the emphasis on explicit aspects of facture characteristic of all his work of the twenties and early thirties. The landscapes he painted between mid-1928 and 1930 form his major contribution to the genre [97].

By the time of his return from St Ives in November 1928, Christopher Wood had formed the style which he was to develop with great consistency over the next two years. Between July and September 1929 he painted in Brittany, at Dinard, Douarnenez and Tréboul, and he was in Cornwall again in the spring of 1929. In May 1930 he shared an exhibition with Ben Nicholson at the Bernheim Jeune Gallery in Paris,[25] and in June and July of that year he was once again in Tréboul, where he painted some forty pictures, his most successful and most individual works among them. In August 1930 he threw himself under a train at Salisbury station.

Wood's later works [98] share the principal characteristics of much of the best painting by younger English artists in the 1920s: a solid opaque paint surface, a means of application of the paint in which there is no attempt to subordinate the evidence of touch to the interests of modelling, texture treated as an aspect of the painted surface independent of texture in the subject, tonal modelling kept to a minimum, and saturation of colour short of garishness. What distinguishes Wood's better paintings from those of his contemporaries and near-contemporaries however is the presence of figures in his compositions and, in the paintings of his last year, the fugitive but persistent sense of emotional drama which attaches to them. Augustus John's gypsies, Picasso's saltimbanques and other echoes of the subject painting of the early twentieth century haunt Wood's paintings of 1930, yet without any diminution of the robustness of the facture [99]. The figures are not there as idealizations of a cultured style of living – as they are, for instance, in some contemporary paintings by Grant and Vanessa Bell – but as personalities evoking a strange independent existence of which the painting itself, in all its manifest facticity, can be seen as a mimesis.

His work of 1929–30 was in large part the product of the idiosyncrasies of his own history; its virtues were due as much to a certain lack of

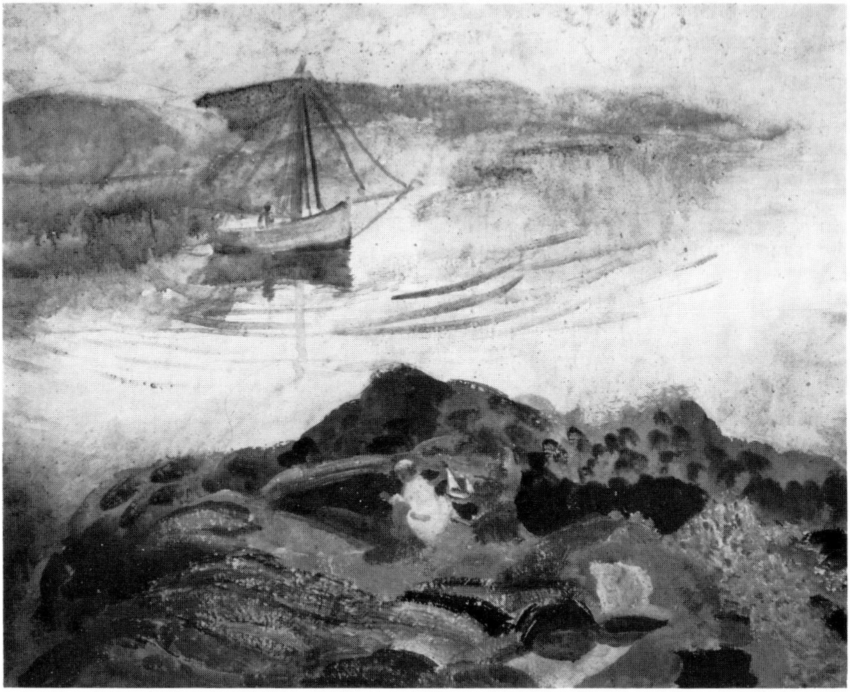

96. Winifred Nicholson: *Seascape with Dinghy*, *c.* 1928/30. Oil on canvas, $27\frac{1}{2} \times 34\frac{3}{4}$ in.

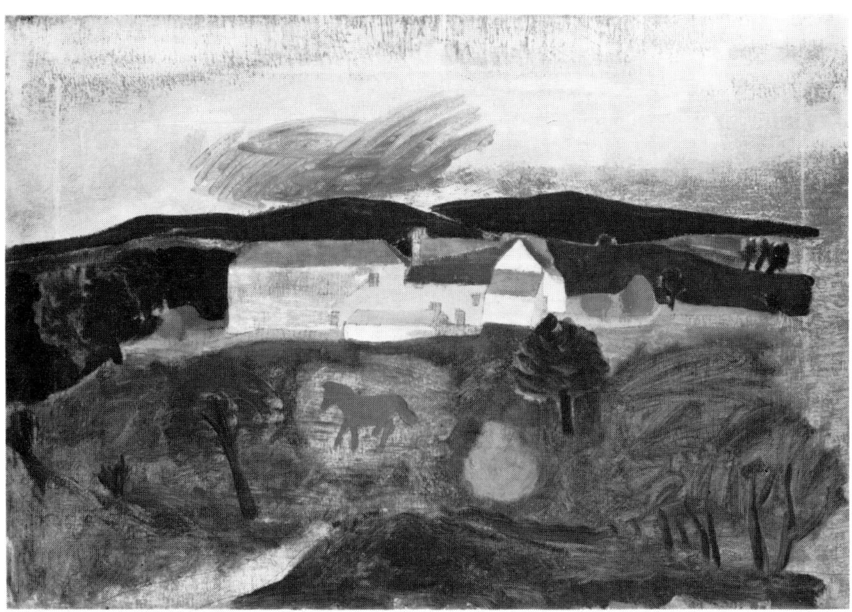

97. Ben Nicholson: *Birch Craig*, 1930. Oil on canvas, 24×36 in.

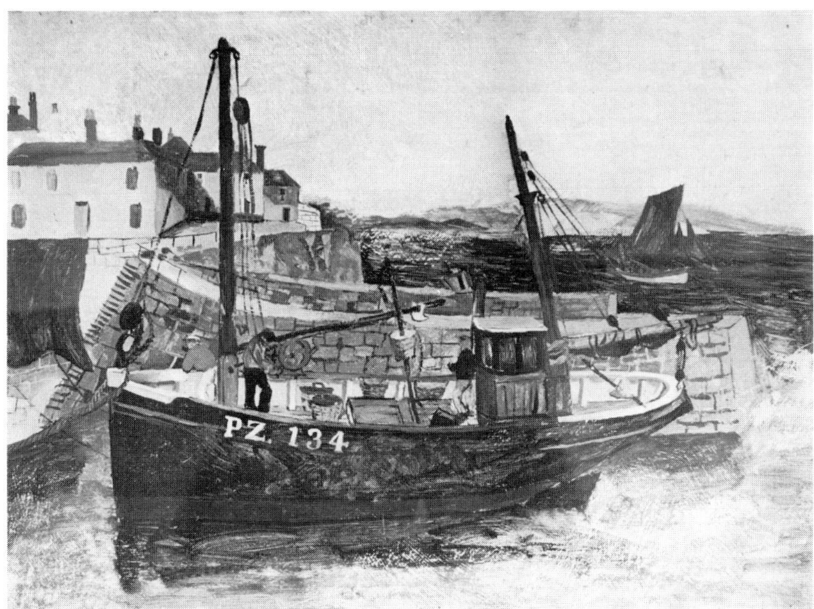

98. Christopher Wood: *PZ 134*, 1930. Oil on hardboard, 20 × 27 in.

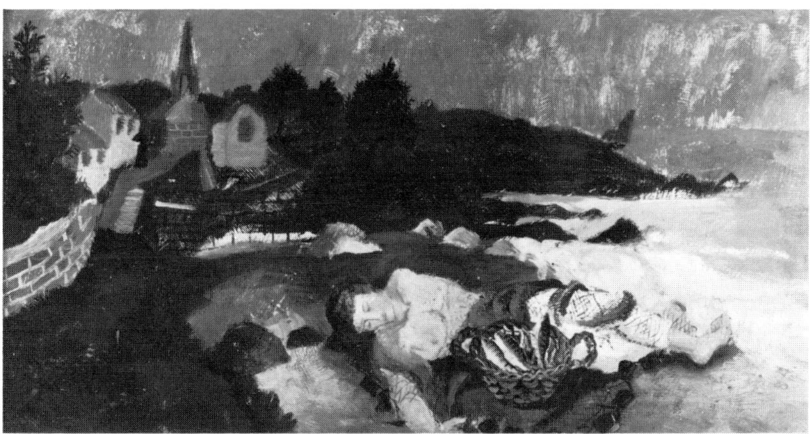

99. Christopher Wood: *Sleeping Fisherman, Ploaré, Brittany*, 1930. Oil on board, 15 × 28¾ in.

artfulness as to an achieved competence. It is not evident that he learned much directly from Picasso, however greatly he may have admired him, but he did absorb a great deal from lesser painters in Paris, Kisling and Pascin particularly, in whose work there remained a tenuous residue of that sense of mysterious interpersonal drama which had invested Picasso's blue and pink periods.

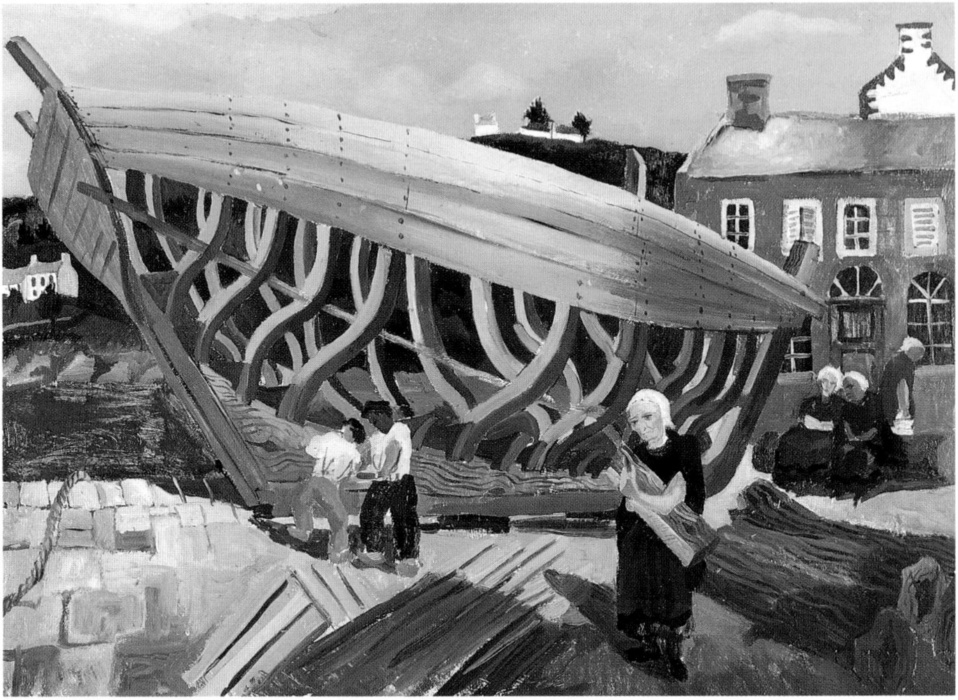

100. Christopher Wood: *Building the Boat, Tréboul*, 1930. Oil on board, 23 × 33 in.

Yet Wood was never possessed of the kind of quasi-modernist technical facility which seemed to come so easily to the petits-maîtres of the School of Paris. The tendency of his work was always towards a robustness of facture which bordered on the ham-fisted. The encounter with Wallis provided an 'ethical' justification for the technical exploitation of this quality. The result was a form of subject painting invested with a sense of poetic drama, yet devoid of those meretricious aspects of surface and treatment by means of which lesser French painters kept the material world at bay. In the history of English painting between the wars Wood's position was unique. The technical interests of advanced painting during this period virtually ruled out the appearance of people except as a complex form of still-life object or as disembodied tokens of a social world actually irrelevant to the purposes of the paintings themselves. On the continent the Surrealists treated human themes and subjects, but generally by means of deliberately disruptive pictorial strategies. In Wood's work alone in England the possibility was retained that a picture might somehow treat of the social and psychological lives of people without mediation either by an individualistic technical extravagance or by a covert reference to sophisticated insights from elsewhere.

There is idealization of course, an idealization of the lives of peasants and fishermen, but those types and images which might have provided others with grounds for the indulgence of sentimentality are transformed by Wood's technical interests into the means to embody a distinctive and individual pathos [100]. It is perhaps the sense of the possibility of a modern painting of human subjects that makes Wood's later works so intriguing, however unpromising his social circumstances and habits may in truth have been for the provision of appropriate subjects and for the development of appropriate insights.

Altogether twenty-one members showed in the Seven & Five exhibition of 1929. Of those who had shown in the first exhibition in 1920, only Ivon Hitchens had survived the changes of direction. By the late twenties he was showing brightly-coloured and freely painted pictures in which were variously discernible the influences of Cézanne's watercolours, of Kandinsky's paintings of the Murnau period, and of Matisse's works of the early 1920s. He experimented in the early 1930s with a means of organization of still-life subjects which owed something to Braque's decorative Cubism of the 1920s [101], and between 1935 and 1937 he painted a small number of abstract compositions of which the Tate Gallery's brightly-coloured *Coronation* is the principal example. The main line of development of his work, however, was to the time of his death in 1979 the exploitation of a relaxed, painterly version of modernism as a means to

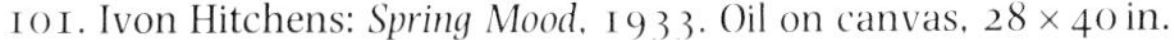

101. Ivon Hitchens: *Spring Mood*, 1933. Oil on canvas, 28 × 40 in.

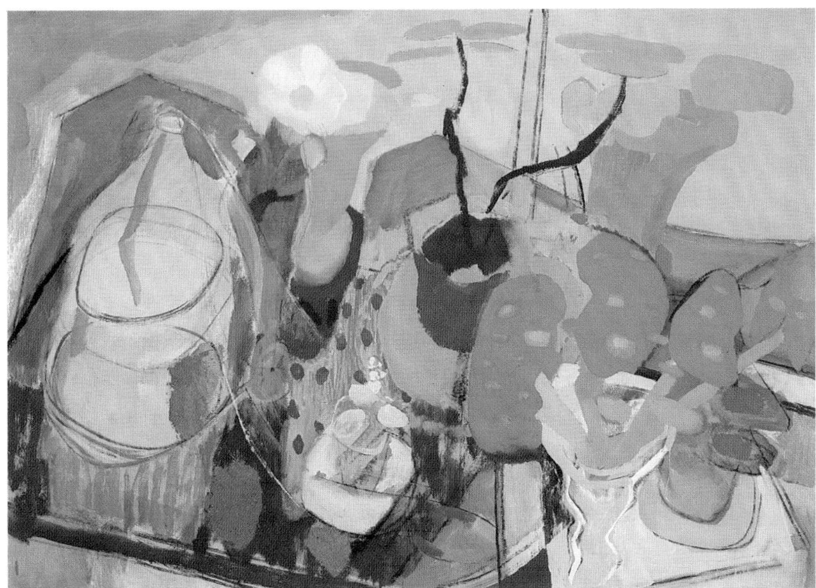

uncomplicated interpretation of lush still-life and landscape subjects.[26] It is possible to see his landscapes, in particular, as manneristic decorations, footnotes to a technical history which has its origins in Turner's works of the first decade of the nineteenth century.

Two more recent recruits to the Seven & Five showed work in 1929 which must then have seemed compatible with Hitchens's. Frances Hodgkins, born in New Zealand in 1869, had spent most of the years since 1901 in Europe and England. She had been in Paris from 1908 to 1912 and in St Ives during the war. Between 1927 and 1934 she was based in London. Although a painter of an older generation than the other members of the Seven & Five, she shared their interests and painted uncomplicated subjects in a fluid style which showed the effects of exposure to second-rate French painting of the twenties as well as to the work of Matisse [102]. She

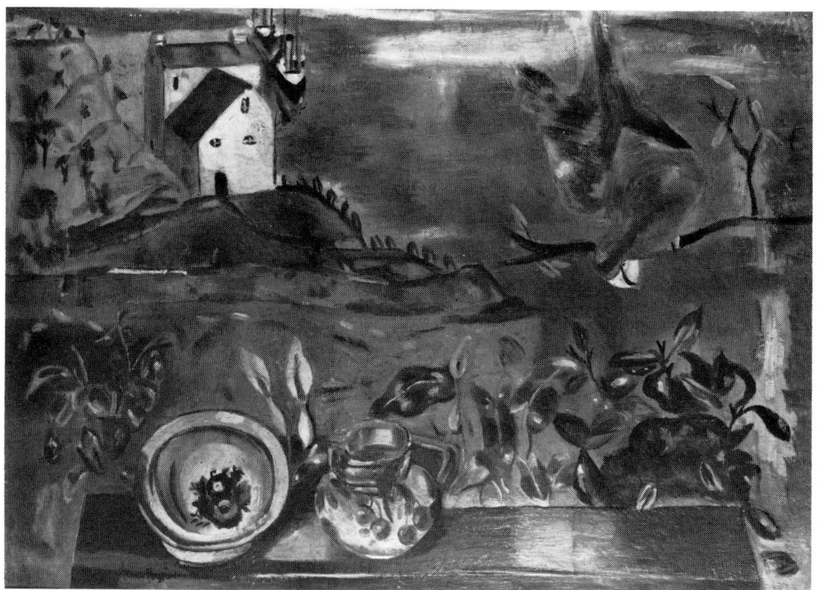

102. Frances Hodgkins: *Wings over Water*, 1934. Oil on canvas, 27 × 38 in. (exhibited with the Seven & Five Society, 1934)

exhibited with the Seven & Five until 1934, when the obvious divergence between Nicholson's interests and her own led to her resignation both from the society and from Unit One, another group in which they were at first both involved.

David Jones had joined the society in time for the 1928 exhibition. Born in 1895, he had studied at Camberwell School of Art, had served as a private on the Western Front during the war,[27] and had then returned to continue his study at Westminster School of Art under Walter Bayes. In 1921 he became a Catholic and left London to join the Guild of St Joseph and St Dominic, the community of 'craftsmen' founded by Eric Gill at Ditchling in Sussex. Here the ideology of 'the unity of all made things' engendered a curiously religiose attitude towards the production of art. Gill moved to Capel-y-Ffin in Wales in 1924 and Jones followed him there a year later, remaining until 1927. From then until a nervous breakdown interrupted his work in 1933 he produced a considerable number of watercolours, oils and book illustrations on themes typically invested with a strong and eclectic religious symbolism. Echoes of Celtic and Arthurian mythology and of Catholic iconography merge with reminiscences of the work of English nineteenth-century watercolourists, and specifically of William Blake, in compositions derived from actual still-life and landscape subjects. In the mid-twenties his work had much in common with the earlier watercolours

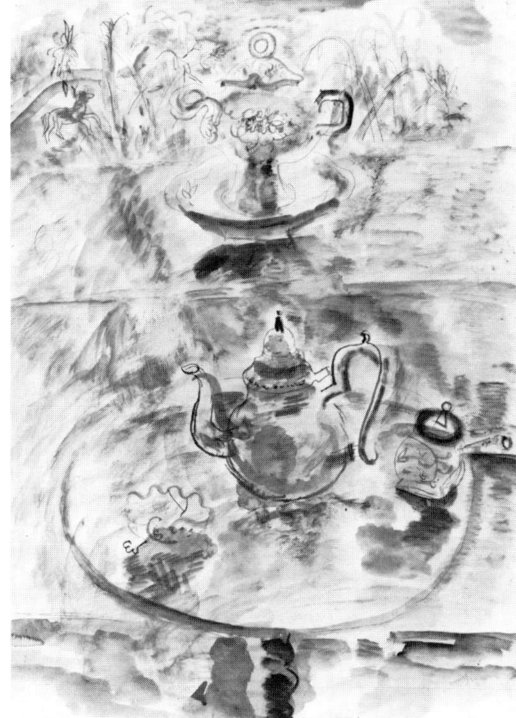

103. David Jones: *Hierarchy*, 1932. Watercolour on paper, 18 × 9½ in. (exhibited with the Seven & Five Society 1933)

and drawings of Paul Nash, but as his drawing became more practised he developed an individual calligraphic style, combining fine line drawing with loose washes of transparent colour in large watercolours packed with detail. The typical David Jones work of this period is a view through a curtained window into landscape, often with a detailed still life occupying the foreground [103].

In 1930 Jones and Hitchens shared an exhibition at Heal's Mansard Gallery. The tendency towards fluid treatment of naturalistic subjects which was the common element in their work and in Hodgkins's was continued and developed within the Seven & Five to a high point in 1932–4 and was the principal unifying feature in a group show of 'Objective Abstractions' at the Zwemmer Gallery in 1934 when Hitchens showed alongside a group of younger painters.[28] In the Seven & Five, Jones's work in particular provided some evidence of the continuing stimulus which could be derived from those insular traditions in which painting and drawing were at their closest to literature, and which were therefore liable to be considered as inconsistent with the development of modernist styles. The English art of the nineteenth century was in fact to be the subject of a revival of interest in the later 1930s; but the main dynamic within the Seven & Five was Nicholson's, and in relation to his interests, as they had developed by the beginning of the 1930s, those painters whose work typified the society's naturalistic style of the later twenties came increasingly to look like conservatives.

The majority of the other painters of the 1920s whose work offered a domesticated version of continental modernism exhibited with the London Group, where a more or less robust Post-Impressionism was the prevailing style. Paule Vézelay and Edward Wolfe (also a member of the Seven & Five from 1926 to 1931) were among the members for whom the influence of Matisse was decisive. Others who exhibited regularly with the group throughout the twenties included Paul and John Nash, Mark Gertler, Vanessa Bell, Duncan Grant, William Roberts and Walter Sickert. A retrospective exhibition in 1928 served to enhance the London Group's prestige, and over the next few years it attracted large entries to its annual exhibitions. But it remained broadly representative of middle-of-the-road interests. In so far as the continental influences which made themselves felt on the more advanced members were generally those of at least a decade earlier, its exhibitions may be taken as reflections of the comparative parochialism of the great majority of English art of the time.[29]

A majority of those who exhibited regularly with the London Group painted as if they wished they had been born in Paris. The better painters of the Seven & Five were those, like Nicholson, Wood and Jones, who were somehow attracted to native traditions or to explicitly native subjects, whatever may have been the degree of their interest in continental art. For all his apparent cosmopolitanism, Wood could never have been mistaken for a French painter, nor, for all his interest in Cubism, could Nicholson.

The same can be said of Paul Nash. It is a virtue in his work of the twenties that, while it is not negatively insular, it is nevertheless resolutely un-French. The finest of his landscapes of this decade – and they are among the best English art of the period – preserve an idiosyncratic independence between what might have seemed like incompatible sympathies: on the one hand a modest but intelligent interest in the technology of French modernist painting from *c.* 1880 to 1909, in which a significant dynamic was the tendency to formalize observed particulars, and on the other an abiding commitment to native traditions of respect for the particular character of particular places and scenes. Many of his most attractive pictures of the period are works on paper, in pencil and watercolour, in which unspectacular details of landscape are discreetly formalized without loss of those individual qualities in response to which they were initially singled out. The *Walnut Tree* is one of these [104], drawn in chalk and pencil during a visit to the Nicholsons at Bankshead in 1924.

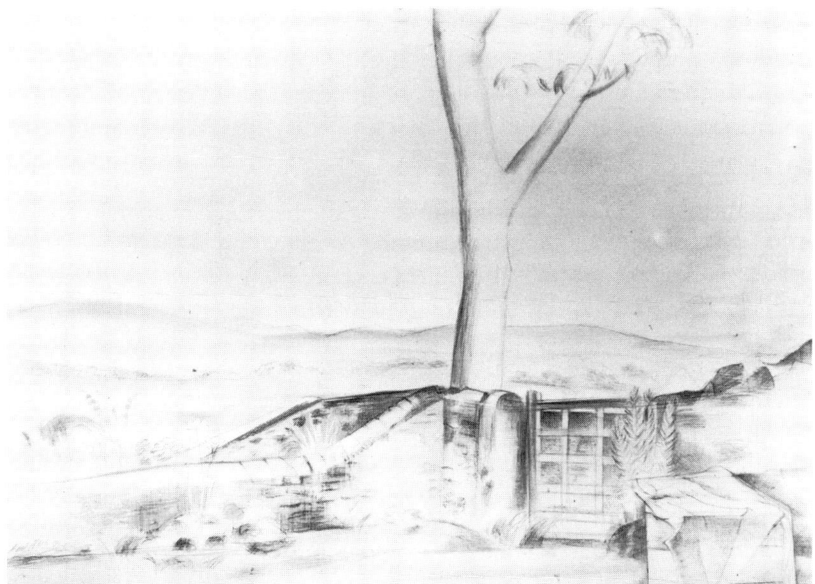

104. Paul Nash: *Walnut Tree*, 1924. Chalk and pencil on paper, $15\frac{1}{4} \times 21\frac{3}{4}$ in.

Nash produced a series of still lifes in 1927–9 in which he played off definite but often complex formal structures against emphatic oil-painting surfaces. The style of these works is essentially a developed English Post-Impressionism, with a comparatively modest tonal range. Their distinguishing characteristic is a preoccupation with framing and reflection. Where a typical Seven & Five member might treat the common subject of a still life in a window as an occasion for expressing technical interests in contrasted qualities of colour and light, Nash tended to construct his composition upon an armature of glazing bars or other linear features, and to dwell on differences of tone and contrasts of transparency and opacity among the facets into which the picture was thus divided. (See, for instance, *Cactus* of 1927–8, *Autumn Crocus* of 1928, *Dead Spring* of 1929.) The effect is as if Analytical Cubism had been married to the Metaphysical subject-painting of Giorgio de Chirico.

In fact, the origins of Nash's particular formal interests are at least partly to be found in a continuing interest in stage design and interior decor, but it is certainly true that when he first saw a substantial showing of de Chirico's work, at Tooth's Gallery in 1928, he was 'completely bowled over'.[30] He appears to have been confirmed in his own direction by this response, which led him rather to affirm elements already present in his work than to introduce new features. Some of his best paintings of the years 1929–30 are characterized by a range of autumnal tones and by pronounced but equivocal formal structures which recall Chirico's melancholy paintings of *c.* 1913–17, derived in part from images of the streets and piazzas of Turin. Chirico's own curious rationale might have served as a prescription for Nash's interpretation of the status of subject-matter as expressed in his paintings of the later twenties and early thirties.

Every serious work of art contains two different lonelinesses. The first might be called 'plastic loneliness', that is the beatitude of contemplation produced by ingenious construction and combination of forms, whether they be still lifes come alive or figures become still – the double life of a still life, not as a pictorial subject but in its supersensory aspect, so that even a supposedly living figure might be included. The second loneliness is that of lines and signals; it is a metaphysical loneliness for which no logical training exists, virtually or physically.[31]

For all the sense of ambiguity which Nash exploited in his paintings from 1927 onwards, his best works were in fact always derived from specific observed subjects. What was encouraged by his enthusiasm for de Chirico was an interest in the relevance of memory and association to the business of observation and formulation of subjects. The result was to emphasize Nash's innate tendency to deploy objects as points of reference for the recollection of emotional states. The death of his father in February 1929 affected him deeply, and it may be that the intensification of the 'metaphysical' aspects of his subjects was in part due to the speculations aroused by this event, speculations which might have been encouraged a year later by a first attack of the bronchial asthma which was in the end to lead to his own death.

The Tate Gallery's *Landscape at Iden* [105] was probably completed by Nash in the summer of 1929 during a period of respite in a 'grim disastrous year'.[32] The influence of de Chirico is manifest in the exaggeration of perspective and the emphasis upon inflected planes and cast shadows, but

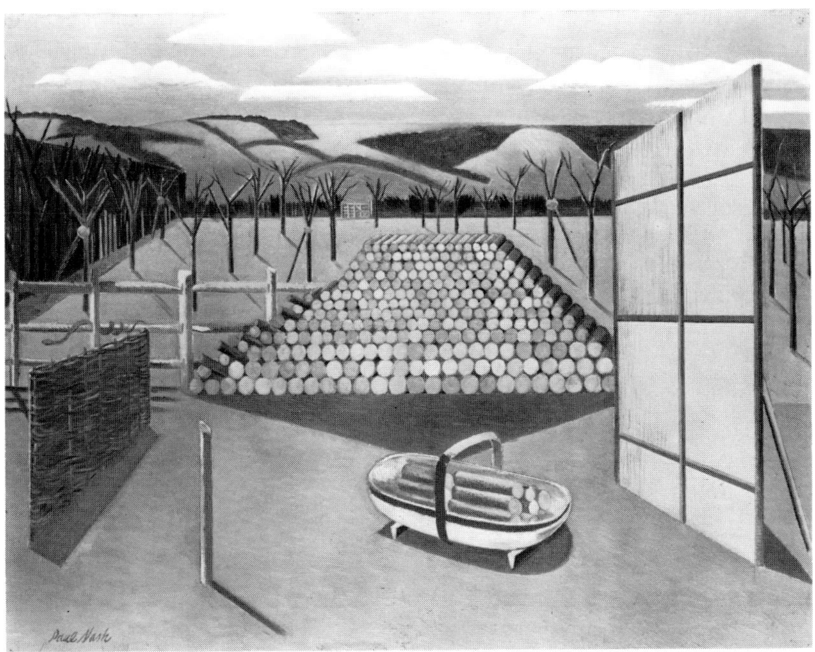

105. Paul Nash: *Landscape at Iden*, 1929. Oil on canvas, $27\frac{1}{2} \times 35\frac{3}{4}$ in.

the scene is none the less redolent of Nash's personal attachment to the English landscape and of his own tendency to formalize it in the pursuit of a definite pictorial structure. Like all the best of his works, while empty of any particular human presence, it conveys a strong sense of the possibility of reconstructing the state of mind of one present at such a place, at such a time. The manipulation of observed elements in pursuit of a particular range of associations is still more evident in *Northern Adventure* [121], another picture from the same year,[33] painted in London and showing the view from Nash's pied à terre, past a scaffold erected for advertising displays, into the forecourt of St Pancras Station. The window through which the view was seen has become detached and hangs at an angle in the top right-hand corner like an element in a Cubist collage. In his notes for *Outline*, Nash wrote of this period, 'Third exhibition at the Leicester Galleries, 1928. Making a name. Achievement and success. A new vision and a new style. The change begins. "Northern Adventure" and other adventures.'

Nash was not alone in his enthusiastic response to de Chirico. Although the Italian painter's most interesting work was done just before and during the First World War, he seems to have been seen by many English artists as representing the first significant continental departure of the post-war years. Christopher Wood had been interested in his work, which he saw in Paris during the mid-twenties, and Edward Wadsworth, who had also been living in France for much of the decade, painted a series of marine still lifes during the years 1926–9 which were strongly indebted to de Chirico both in mood and in technique [106].[34] By the early 1930s there was a small 'school' of English Metaphysical painters, which included Nash, Wads-

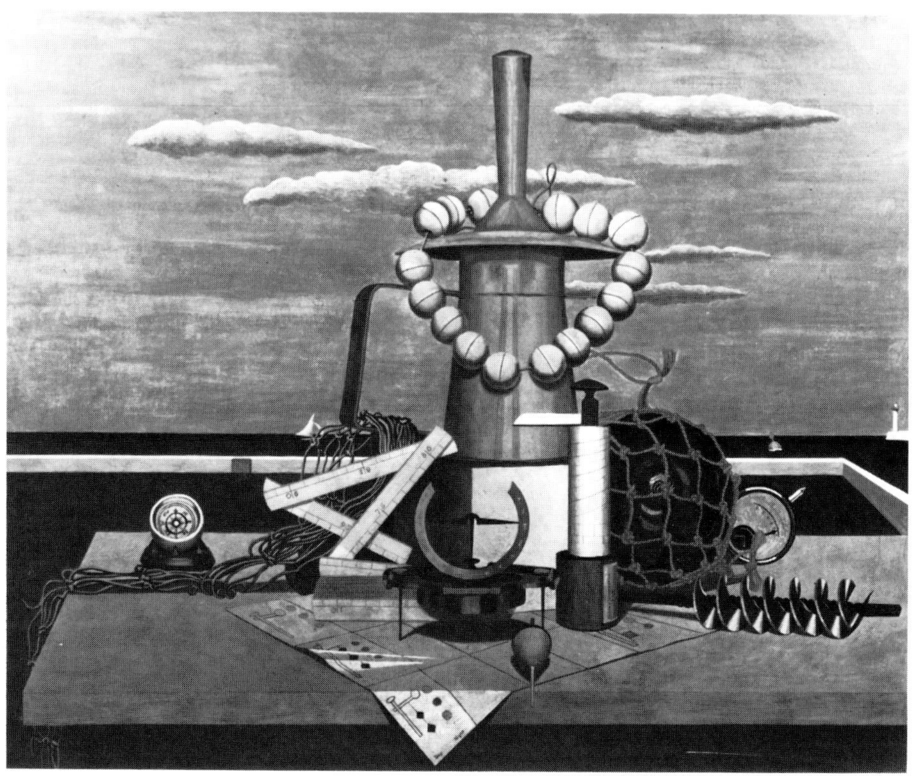

106. Edward Wadsworth: *Regalia*, 1928. Tempera on canvas laid on board, 30 × 36 in.

worth, John Armstrong and Tristram Hillier (another resident in France during the later 1920s). The work of the French painter Jean Lurcat, shown at the Lefevre Gallery in June 1930, offered an example of mediation between the 'literary-subject' painting of de Chirico and the formal qualities of Synthetic Cubism. Nash's painting *Opening*, of 1930–31 (originally titled *Opening Abstract*), is a work which illustrates the reconciliation of these different aspects of modernism.[35] By the time he painted it Nash was interested in those continental developments in which a basically Cubist style was pushed to the point of abstraction.

Such works demonstrate Nash's growing concern for the development of English art within the context of European modernism, but his deepest commitment was always to the English landscape. The painting which best represents the sum of his achievement up to the turn of the decade is one which could have been produced in no other country. *Wood on the Downs* [107], painted in the first half of 1930,[36] is an articulate and monumental treatment of a vivid but unsensational subject. In this fine work many of the

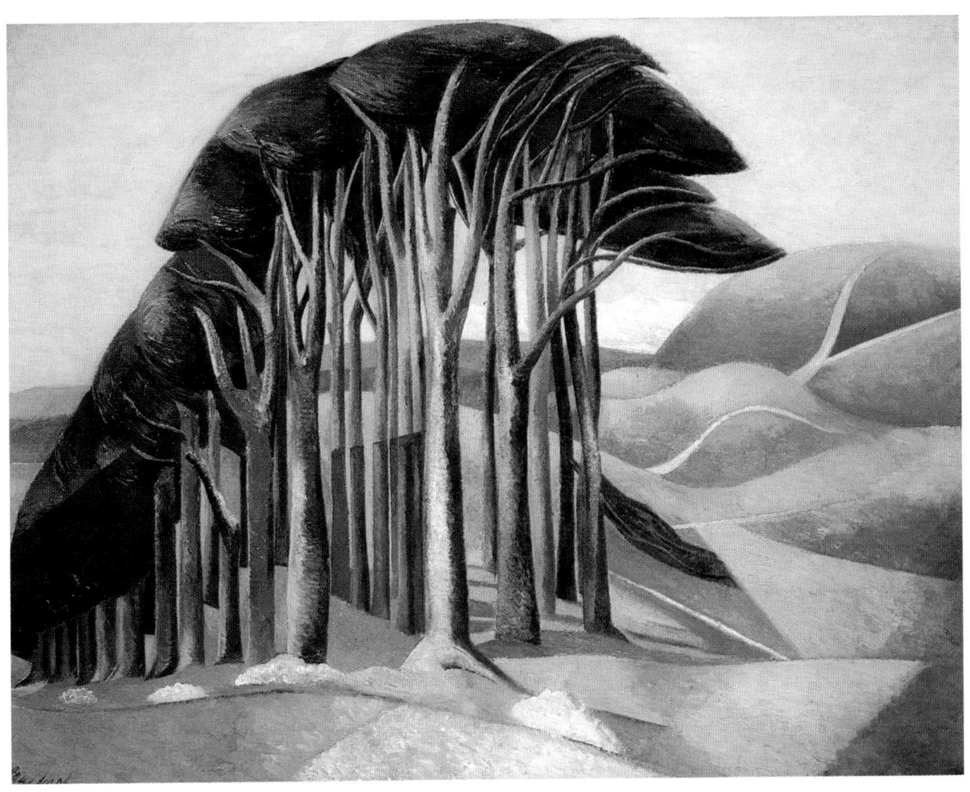

107. Paul Nash: *Wood on the Downs*, 1930. Oil on canvas, 28 × 36 in.

more fruitful technical concerns expressed in English painting in the first three decades of this century are recapitulated: the emphasis on a substantial paint surface which was a feature of the best work of the Camden Town Group; the concentration upon clear formal structure at the expense of anecdote which testified to a continuing recognition of the importance of Cézanne;[37] the search for vitality in pictorial form independent of representation of action; and the gradual naturalization of continental influence in the context of still-life and landscape themes appropriate to an English painter. With the most vivid of Nash's works of 1928–30, and of those produced by Nicholson and Wood during the same period, an unpromising decade may be seen as having closed on a note of distinct and independent achievement.

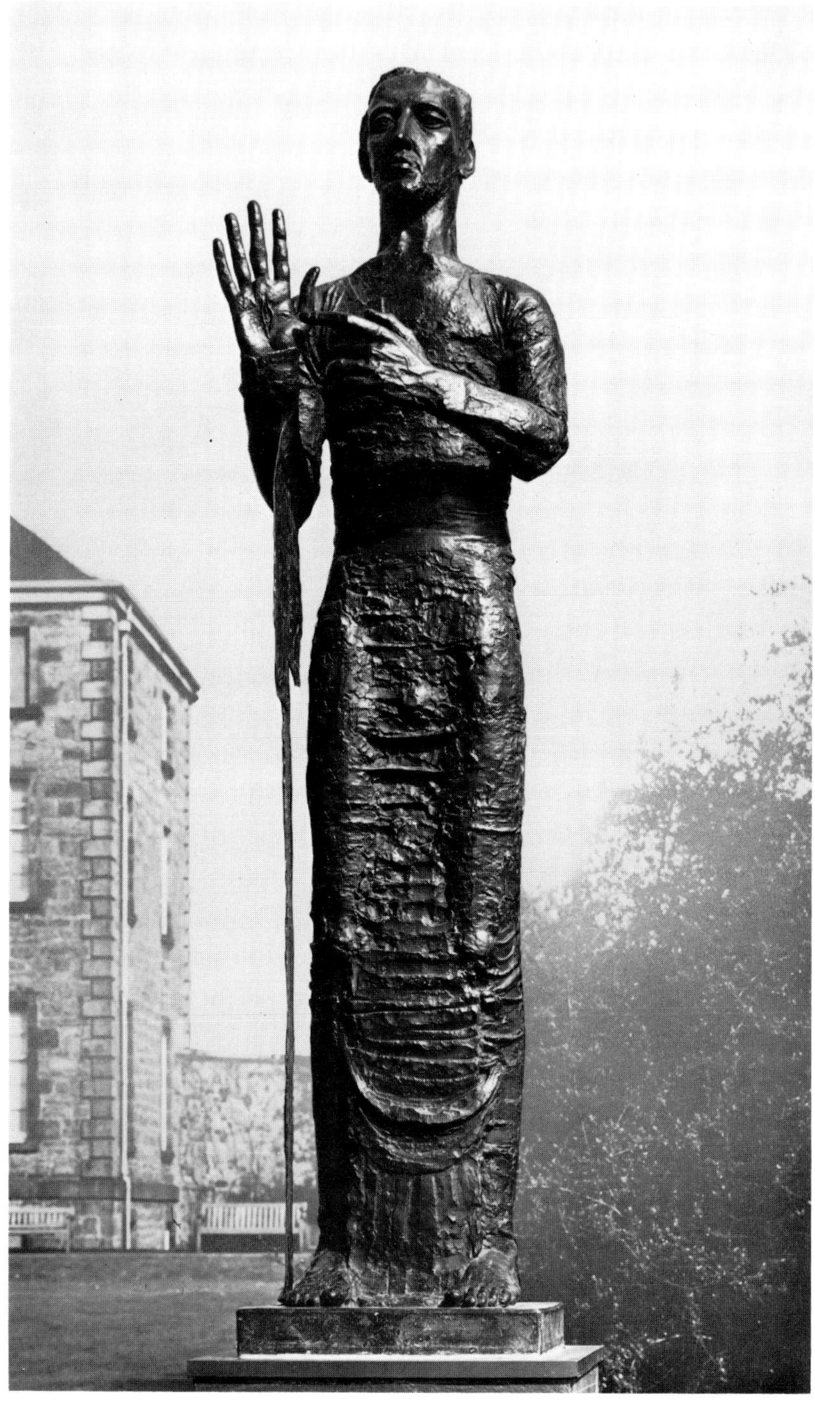

8

THE DEVELOPMENT OF MODERNISM IN SCULPTURE

So far as the art of sculpture is concerned, Epstein's position was unquestionable as the major surviving figure from the pre-war avant garde, although in fact the truncation of the *Rock Drill* [38, 39] seems to have marked a turning-point in his career. The most progressive of his pre-war works had all been carvings (the *Rock Drill*, though made in plaster and ultimately cast in bronze, shares the geometricizing tendency of the carvings and can thus be classified with them). However, Epstein had continued to make modelled sculpture, and the works he showed at the Leicester Galleries in February 1920, in his first post-war exhibition, were all bronzes made during the previous three years.[1] In his book *The Meaning of Modern Sculpture*, published in 1932, R. H. Wilenski suggested that Epstein had been strongly affirmed in his direct carved work by T. E. Hulme's theory of geometrical meaning in art, and that 'After Hulme's death Epstein advanced upon the line of least resistance and developed his amazing powers as a Romantic modeller.' It is certainly true that from this point on a technique for expressive modelling was the principal dynamic in Epstein's work, and that his occasional carvings – strange and ambitious though they mostly are – seem like exceptions to the development of that work. From 1916 until his death in 1959, the main emphasis of his activities was on portrait busts and studies from exotic models, with occasional works on religious themes.

108. *(opposite)*. Jacob Epstein: *Risen Christ*, 1919–20. Bronze, 86 × 21½ × 18½ in.

Despite what might seem like retrenchment from his earlier position, the notoriety which Epstein's major works continued to attract served to emphasize his role as the senior avant-garde sculptor, at least in the public eye, well into the 1930s. The major work in his 1920 exhibition was a standing bronze figure called the *Risen Christ* [108], over seven feet high. The head was modelled from one of Epstein's friends and the overall treatment was expressive of a highly emotive concern for a form of heightened realism, just where his audience was conditioned to expect formality. If the *Rock Drill* could be seen in retrospect as an omen of modern war, it was perhaps inevitable that the *Christ* should be interpreted as a proposal for atonement. In this case it was not the modernism of the work which gave strongest offence – after all there were other works in the exhibition, such as a *Bust of Lord Fisher*, to show how a precisely similar style and technique could be used for highly traditional purposes – it was rather the nature of the observations by which the subject was characterized. Contrary to the suggestions of crude pro-avant-garde versions of modern art history, the most violent controversies aroused by the English modern art of the early twentieth century were provoked not so much by the nature of formalizations in avant-garde styles as by the nature of the interpretation of recognizable subjects offered by comparatively 'realistic' works. In the eyes of an unsympathetic audience, more-or-less abstract works by English artists were likely to be seen as merely ridiculous apings of foreign styles rather than as immoral, blasphemous or bolshevik endeavours. And where the nature of the representation would otherwise have been beyond the comprehension of the uninitiated observer, a casually applied title would often be seized on as offering a stick with which to beat the artist. As Epstein later wryly observed, 'When once I named a work *Study* they were completely silent, waiting for some hint of my intention.'[2]

It was perhaps precisely because the subjects of his sculptures were usually so strongly asserted, and so vivid in terms of the mythology of a Christian culture, that Epstein was consistently made the object of outraged opinion in the years after the first war. Where the *Rock Drill* had attracted angrily dismissive notices at worst, the *Risen Christ*, which was technically a very much more conservative work, was received with no less a furore than had attended the Strand statues. The outcry was led by Father Bernard Vaughan writing in *The Graphic* (a mere three years, it should perhaps be remembered, after the Russian Revolution):

> ... if Mr Epstein's horror in bronze were to spring into life and appear in a room, I for one should fly from it in dread and disgust, lest perhaps he might pick my pockets, or worse, do some deed of violence in keeping with his Bolshevik appearance.[3]

There were many defenders, however, George Bernard Shaw among them, and all but the most hysterical of Epstein's detractors were obliged to acknowledge the technical virtuosity and the vividness of his portraits and studies from models (though the generously bare-breasted characters of the latter served to encourage the public's tendency to see all artists as sexual profligates). For the remainder of the period under review, and for the rest of Epstein's long working life, comparative financial and social success, earned by virtue of the esteem accorded to his portraits, was contrasted with occasional ridicule and vituperation provoked by the exhibition of his carvings. The controversies attendant upon the latter are carefully documented in his autobiography.[4] *Rima*, commissioned as a memorial to W. H. Hudson and installed on a site in Hyde Park in 1925; figures of *Night* and *Day*, carved for the Underground headquarters building in 1929; *Genesis* in 1931 [109]; *Ecce Homo* in 1935; *Consummatus Est* in 1937; *Adam*

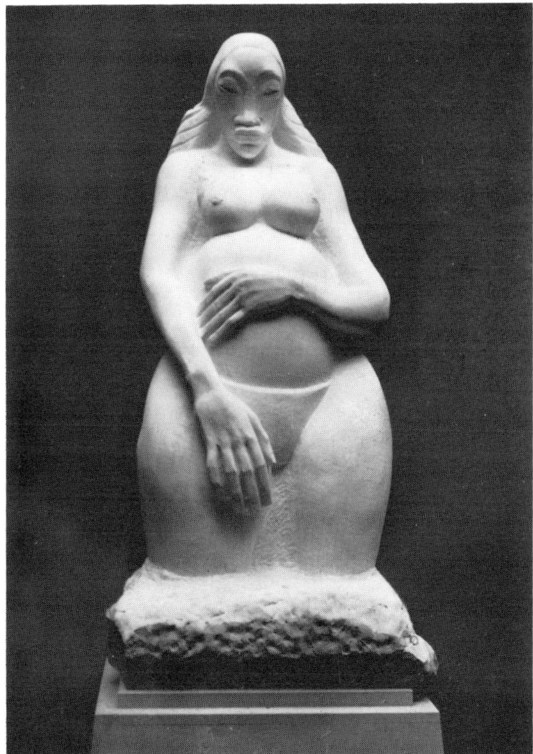

109. Jacob Epstein: *Genesis*, 1931. Seravessa marble, height $62\frac{1}{4}$ in.

in 1939; each of these was made the object of attention and argument in the popular press. (The long-term residence of *Ecce Homo* in a sideshow at Blackpool testifies to the persistence of 'vulgar curiosity' as a response to these works.)

Informed Modernist opinion on the relative merits of Epstein's carvings and bronzes was well represented in Wilenski's judgement: 'His contribution to *modern* sculpture consists entirely in his carvings. His bronzes, magnificent though they are, represent ... the climax of the Romantic sculpture of the nineteenth century.'[5] To say even this is perhaps to overemphasize the place of Epstein's post-1916 carvings in the history of modern sculpture. For all that they were identified with rampant and indefensible avant-gardism in the press, or asserted as paradigms of modernist practice by Epstein's defenders, none of these works was seen by the younger modernist sculptors of the post-war years as having much to offer them beyond what was implicit from his more adventurous works of the pre-war years; not, at least, as models of technical or formal innovation. In the modern period, public notoriety (i.e. strong valuation from 'outside' a practice) cannot always be taken as an indicator that avant-garde status is established within and in terms of that practice. At a time when the potential universality of the appeal of art was being promoted as a feature of liberal democratic beliefs, it was a symptom of the alienation of the values of the artist from the values of an unspecialized audience that while that audience still based its judgements, where it could, on a response to the treatment of subjects, the valuation of the artist and his co-initiates tended rather to be made in terms of degrees of technical innovation assessed apart from a concern with representation as such. In Modernist criticism the evocative aspects of representational subjects were seen as irrelevant to valuations of art as 'art'.

> The questions that eminent critics, writers, and dignitaries of divers churches discussed in public, while colonels, Socialists, and cultivated theosophical ladies wrangled over them at home, were: 'Has Mr Epstein done justice to the character of Christ?' and, 'What was His character?' Was Christ intelligent or was he something nobler, and what has Mr Epstein to say about it? ... Questions such as these ... were what the critics threw into the arena, and no one much blames the parsons and publicists for playing football with them. But the critics must have known that such questions were utterly irrelevant; that it mattered not a straw whether this statue, considered as a work of art, represented Jesus Christ or John Smith.
>
> This the critics knew; they knew that the appeal of a work of art is essentially permanent and universal ... About Mr Epstein's sculpture the important thing to discover is whether, and in what degree, it possesses these permanent and universal qualities ... (Clive Bell)[6]

So far as the development of sculpture was concerned, the devaluation of subject-matter within modernist practice and criticism, as evidenced in

Bell's writing and in the main run of criticism sympathetic to modern art for decades thereafter, entailed devaluation of those aspects of the technology of sculpture by means of which particular figurative detail and incident were conventionally recorded and represented. Generally speaking, sculpture that was modelled from pliant materials and then subsequently cast was seen as characterized by the skilful exploitation of just such 'anecdotal' features. In Paris, shortly before the war, the highly reductive carved sculpture of Constantin Brancusi had presented a decisive challenge to the pre-eminence, as exemplar of modern sculpture, of the modelled work of Auguste Rodin. By the end of the first war carving was well established as the modernist practice in sculpture.

Together with his close friend Modigliani, Epstein had played a considerable part alongside Brancusi in the radical transformation of the technology and the formal repertoire of sculpture before the war, yet in 1931 he was to declare that 'Rodin is without dispute the greatest master of modern times.'[7] It may have been that the interest in modelling so strongly affirmed in Epstein's early post-war work was what chiefly served to disqualify him as a mentor in the eyes of the members of a younger generation. For them a commitment to 'direct working' was now a means to assert interests distinct from those of the more conservative of their elders. The war had made for a hiatus in Epstein's activities and, as it did so decisively with Wyndham Lewis, in the dynamics of his relation with the continuing development of English art in general. At a time when Frank Dobson [110] was being promoted from Bloomsbury as the major figure of interest among sculptors in England (i.e. following his first one-man show of sculpture at the

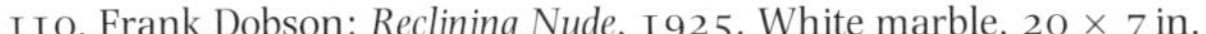
110. Frank Dobson: *Reclining Nude*, 1925. White marble, 20 × 7 in.

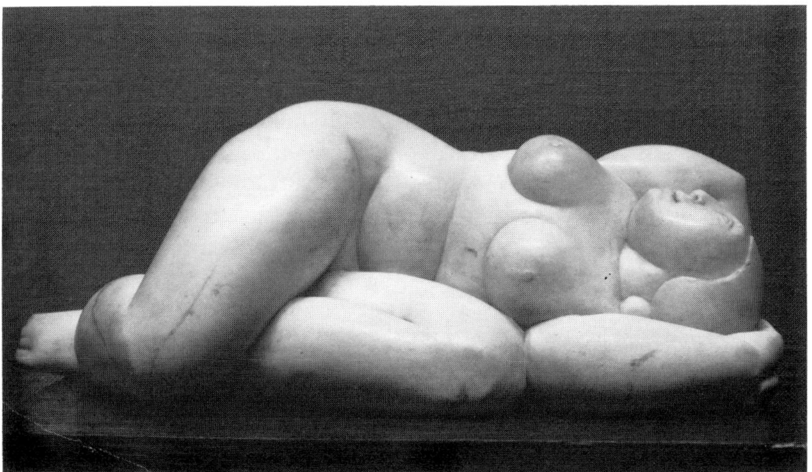

Leicester Galleries in 1921), Epstein must indeed have sorely missed the aggressive support of T. E. Hulme.

There were further reasons for the apparent discontinuity in the development of sculpture in England during the early twenties. The younger sculptors who were to rise to prominence by the end of the decade, Henry Moore and Barbara Hepworth, had both grown up in Yorkshire and were too young and too far removed from London to have had any first-hand experience of Epstein's works before 1920. A high proportion of those works were anyway now in America in the collection of John Quinn, along with so much of the output of the Vorticists, and were thus effectively lost to view and to immediate history. It is tempting to speculate on the difference that might have been made to the whole history of English sculpture in the modern period had those works been more accessible, and had the *Rock Drill* been cast in its entirety and set up where it might have been available for younger artists to view during the twenties. But the speculation is ultimately idle. Rather we should try to accept what can be deduced about the history of English sculpture on the basis of the knowledge that Epstein did choose to truncate the sculpture, and that the possibility that there might have been public recognition for a full cast is not consistent with what we know of the governing taste and interests of the post-war years. For all that it must surely have offered a strong counter-example to the view that the appeal of works of art resided essentially in formal as distinct from symbolic qualities, the sculpture was still likely to have been seen as anachronistic in a practice which was to become increasingly governed by claims for the autonomy and universality of 'sculptural experience'.

As it was, the two earliest monographs on Epstein, published in 1920 and 1925,[8] though they were well illustrated, naturally emphasized the modelled works with which the majority of his output was at that time consistent. Although the authors of the respective introductions were as laudatory as the sculptor might have wished, and although they made token acknowledgements of the historical importance of the pre-war carvings and the *Rock Drill*, neither could match the quality of engagement evident in the writings of Hulme.[9] Some very dull art books were published in the 1920s. Ezra Pound's assertive book on Gaudier-Brzeska, on the other hand, did much to keep the deceased sculptor's work and his epigrammatic writings in the minds of younger artists during the twenties. (There had been a memorial exhibition at the Leicester Galleries in 1918.) Henry Moore acquired a second-hand copy of Pound's book, probably in 1922, and his immediate interest in Gaudier's work was clearly reflected in many of his own sculptures during the formative years 1922–6;[10] specifically Moore's clay *Torso* of 1925–6 is virtually a free version of Gaudier's carved marble

Torso of 1913 (now in the Victoria and Albert Museum), which was illustrated in Pound's book, and Moore's marble *Dog* of 1922 is most unlikely to have been made independently of the example of Gaudier's many carvings on animal themes. More generally the contained rhythmic quality of Gaudier's carvings survives as an echo in many works of the twenties by Moore, Dobson and R. P. Bedford. The mechanistic imagery of the more typically Vorticist works, however, seems not to have been of practical interest to other sculptors in the twenties. The *Bird swallowing a Fish* [45] and the *Ornement Torpille* [44], like the *Rock Drill* [38, 39], represent a historical terminus.

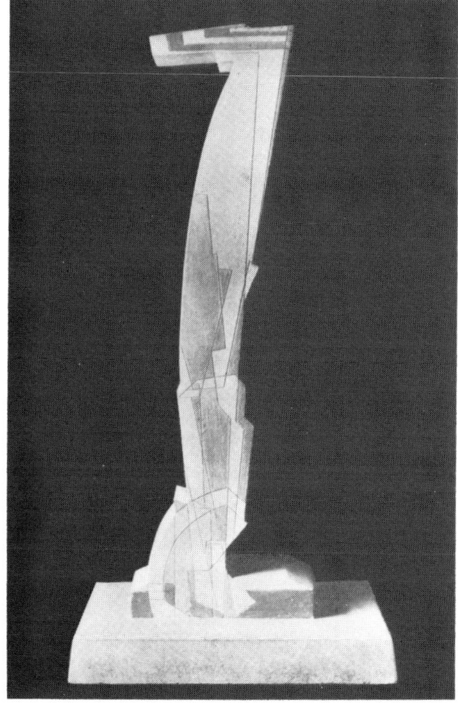

111. Lawrence Atkinson: *L'Oiseau*, c. 1920

Lawrence Atkinson, who had exhibited with the Vorticists, held an exhibition of abstract painting and sculpture at the Eldar Gallery in London in 1921, and a monograph published in 1922[11] was copiously illustrated with photographs of carved stone sculptures which look like free-standing versions of Vorticist drawings [111]. These do seem to represent some continuation of the pre-war mechanistic imagery into the sculpture of the post-war years, but they remained marginal to the mainstream of modernist activity and appear to have dropped out of sight and mind until recently, although Atkinson lived another ten years.

One other survivor from the pre-war avant garde continued to make sculptures during the period between the wars. Eric Gill's principal training was in the craft of lettering, and his initial interest in stone-carving was provoked as much by the cutting of inscriptions as by anything else. He had set up in business in 1904 as a master mason and had built up a small reputation for cutting inscriptions and tombstones and for lettering shop signs. His technique as a stone carver was learned largely at the Westminster Technical Institute rather than at a college of art and was developed in the business of earning his living. His first direct carvings of figures were made in 1910, in which year he met Epstein and formulated with him 'a great scheme of doing some colossal figures together (as a contribution to the world), a sort of twentieth-century Stonehenge'. They went so far as to negotiate for a site.[12]

Before he became a Catholic in 1912, Gill was an ardent Fabian, and his concept of sculpture reflected a kind of transcendental socialism (in so far as sculpture is capable of such a reflection). Following in the tradition graced by Ruskin and Morris of concern for the social consequences of mechanization and of the division of labour, he was militantly unwilling to accept the validity of distinctions between art and craft – or indeed any other, less specialized, form of labour.[13] In so far as Modernist theory and criticism presuppose such distinctions, Gill's was a genuinely radical position. In 1918 he produced a small book on *Sculpture*. Characteristically, he subtitled it 'An Essay on Stone-Cutting, with a Preface about God' and designed and printed it himself on hand-made paper.[14] (In the same year he carved a series of the Stations of the Cross for Westminster Cathedral, and two years later he exhibited six direct carvings at the Goupil Gallery.) Albeit with a certain pathos, his book captures the flavour of some of the more vivid interests of its period. It offers an English example of that bloodless, socialistic religiosity which was a strong component in the ideology of the European Modern Movement at the time of the founding of the Bauhaus in Germany, and which was reflected in the teaching instruction of the less practical members of the Bauhaus staff. It is nowadays hard to see handcraft as other than quaint, buttressed by regressive social practices and strange obsessions, but in the 1920s the history of the Arts and Crafts movement was still associated with dynamic and progressive forms of social and political criticism, rightly so to the extent that its adherents were aware that the degeneration of relations between design and manufacture was a function of the general division of labour. For Gill, the distinction between modelling and carving was a moral distinction, dependent upon a distinction between 'design', as the making of a model from which a finished work is derived, and 'craftsmanship', as the making of such works as 'owe part of their quality to the material of which they are made and of which the material inspires the workman and is freely accepted by him'.[15] This concept of 'truth to materials', inherited from the Arts and Crafts movement, was to be taken up as a slogan by younger sculptors such as Moore and Hepworth during the 1920s and 30s. It had its roots in a form of romantic materialism. Gill's promotion of the concept of inventive workmanship was founded on an idealization of all labour, for which the activity of the sculptor was the token. 'All men are artists . . .,' he wrote, 'for all men are concerned with Beauty'; and later, 'Sculpture is a matter of both workmanship and design. The combination in the same person of craftsman with designer must be revived. The revolution must come at the instance of the craftsman and not of the employer. The need is true religion and the subordination of the trader. Again: Laus Deo; vade Satanas.'

Gill was living at the time in Ditchling in Sussex, and in 1921 the small community of his family and friends was formalized into the Guild of St Joseph and St Dominic, described by him in that year as 'primarily a religious fraternity for those who make things with their hands'.[16] Gill's views on the unity of art and craft would not have permitted him to see himself as primarily a sculptor. His carvings do, however, deserve consideration alongside the best of English sculpture of the 1920s. They are paradoxical works. On the one hand they serve to recall how deeply rooted was the tradition of sculpture in England in ecclesiastical and funerary carving; on the other they celebrate the possibility of expression of a lay sensuality which is entirely without prurience. Gill's works are redolent of the history of sculpture, in so far as that history can be circumscribed by an interest in the technical resources of carving, yet they appear curiously naive, as if produced by one who believed that embodiment of meaning in stone could be an uncomplex achievement. In his most successful works, like the *Deposition* in black Hopton Wood stone of 1924 [112] and the *Girl* in Capel-y-Ffin stone of 1925 [113], the combination of an apparently casual profile with a careful working of the surface can be seen as the expression of a sense of the identity of given material with 'creative idea'. The ambitious *Mankind* of 1927–8 [114] is one of Gill's few sculptures of any size (it is eight feet high) which is conceived as free-standing and is modelled in the round. Its strange blend of 'classical' idealism with a kind of 'photographic' explicitness renders it curiously reminiscent of the style of the pin-up drawing as practised three decades later. As a candidate for a place in the history of modern English sculpture it must have suffered from comparison with the works of Moore, whose interest in the expressive possibilities of the human figure, as evident from his own works of the later twenties, was not really compatible with Gill's.

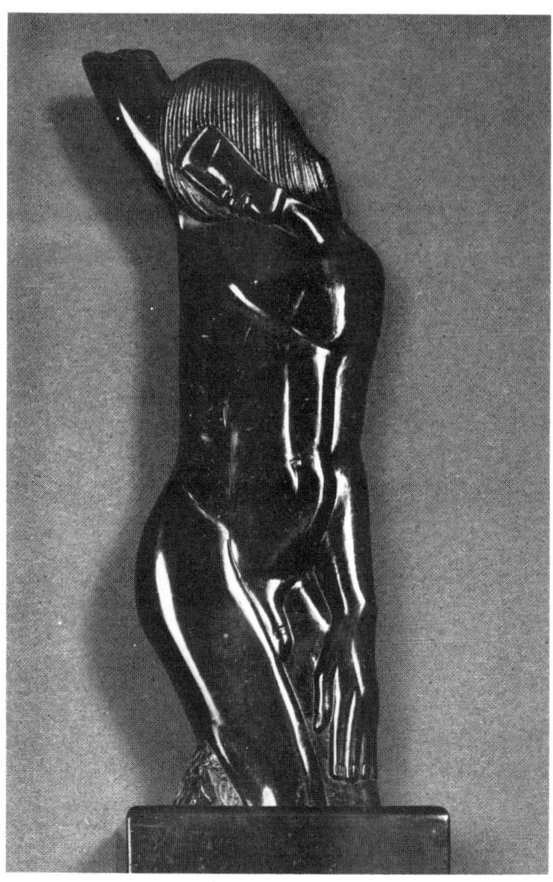

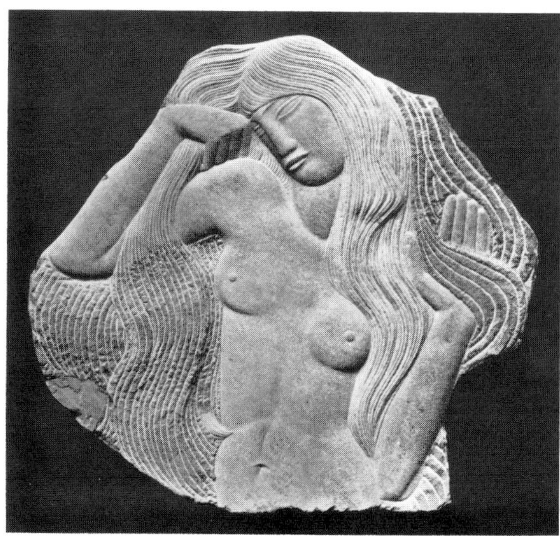

112 *(above)*. Eric Gill: *Deposition*, 1924. Black Hopton Wood stone, height 24 in.

113 *(left)*. Eric Gill: *Girl*, 1925. Capel-y-Ffin stone, height 36 in.

114 *(opposite)*. Eric Gill: *Mankind*, 1927–8. Hopton Wood stone, 95 × 24 × 18 in.

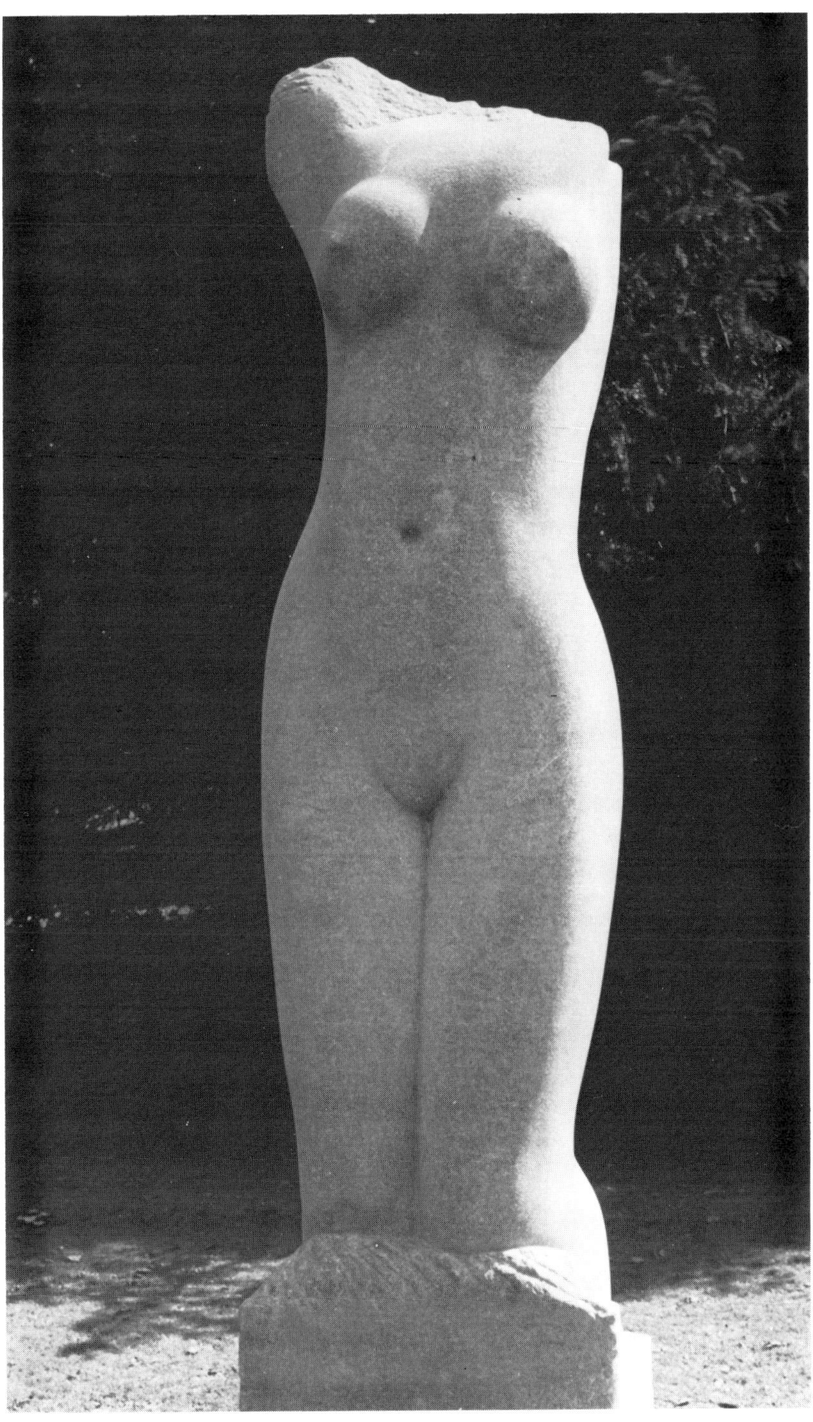

For all that his interests were at times difficult to reconcile with modernism, Gill's advocacy of carving was an expression of what was to be an important article of faith for younger sculptors during the twenties. He went so far as to affirm that it was from carving that sculpture took its definition:

> The cutting of stone is the type of the craft of the sculptor. The modelling of clay is for him merely the means of making preliminary sketches and great facility in it is not a necessity.

The elevation of the status of carving in the Modernist conception of sculpture was inextricably linked to the assertion of value in appropriate forms of activity. That is to say that in upholding carving as 'the type of the craft of the sculptor', Gill was seeking to establish the priority of that activity as a modern art activity, in face of the conventional view that carving was either a job to be delegated to assistants, who might be set to work to enlarge from the master's clay model, or it was a means to produce objects, such as decorative architectural features, which were unworthy of the designation 'sculpture'. As Gill observed, '. . . students are not trained in workshops to be stone-carvers, but in art schools to be modellers.' It was not that stone-carving was not taught at all at the time Gill was writing; the point is that it was not generally taught as a proper skill for one who wished to advance the art of sculpture as that art was conceived in the art schools. It was taught as a means of reproducing, not of originating. The class-character of the practice of carving was thus not such as to encourage its pursuit by modern-minded gentlemen, while those who had it in mind to earn their living by stone-cutting were likely to learn their craft, as Gill learned his, at a technical institute.

There were accomplished carvers among the regular exhibitors at the Royal Academy, but they were generally practitioners of highly conservative types of sculpture.[17] There were also men who knew how to carve on the staffs of those London art schools where sculpture was taught, but they were generally engaged as assistants and technical instructors rather than 'teachers'.[18] Gill's attempt theoretically to unify 'art' and 'craft' in the pursuit of a modern sculpture thus had radical implications: in that it entailed opposition to the mainstream view that carving was a conservative and subordinate activity, it suggested a revaluation in the prevailing division of labour.

Those principally responsible for the development of modern sculpture in England in the first third of the century were people who, by the nature of their previous social experience, were distinctly unrepresentative of the main body of those in a position to consider themselves as potential English sculptors. The anti-humanism and anti-classicism of the pre-war avant garde had been an expression, however indirect and mediated, of class interests distinct from those of the English literary bourgeoisie. Epstein was of Polish-Jewish origins and was twenty-five when he came to England. Gaudier was French by birth and came to London when he was twenty. Gill was something of an eccentric by nature and came to sculpture by way of architecture, lettering and wood engraving. The modern tradition in sculpture was a tradition of socially exceptional interests. After the war Henry Moore and Barbara Hepworth both benefited from newly established schemes to provide scholarships for study at the Royal College of Art. As the son of a Yorkshire coal-miner, Moore could not otherwise have hoped to train as a sculptor, and Hepworth's sex alone singled her out as a dramatic exception among students of sculpture at a time when the painting schools were full of young ladies. For each of these, factors in their class and cultural origins or their education militated against the adoption of a normal English view upon the social hierarchy of activities relevant to sculpture. Their unrepresentativeness was reflected in the comparatively unconventional nature of their technical interests.

A commitment to direct carving was one means to establish a modernist position in contradistinction to the conservative mainstream. A rejection of the classical style – as that style was exemplified in pompous or sentimental figure subjects of a vaguely 'Greek' disposition – was a further means of characterizing such a position; and an interest in ancient and 'primitive' art was a third. During the 1920s and early 30s modernist commitment in sculpture could thus generally be signified by means of pro-attitudes towards carving and towards 'primitive' and archaic art (which was generally also carved) and of anti-attitudes towards classicism and modelling. As Moore observed later, 'There was a period when I tried to avoid looking at Greek sculpture of any kind. And Renaissance. When I thought that the Greek and Renaissance were the enemy, and that one had to throw all that over and start again from the beginning of primitive art.'[19] In *The Meaning of Modern Sculpture* Wilenski provided a rationale for this attitude, among sculptors who had entered the practice in the early 1920s, which no doubt reflected what he had learned from the artists themselves:

> For the purpose of [their] creative work they began by assuming for the moment, that no one had ever made sculpture before and that it was their own task to discover the nature of the activity in which they were about to be engaged.
>
> They began, that is to say, at the beginning.
>
> . . . They began by asking themselves the question: 'What do we mean by sculpture?' . . . the accent in the question was on the 'we'.

(From a section on 'The Modern Sculptors' Creed'.)[20]

There is a compatibility here with the position of the more advanced painters. Of the same period in his own work Ben Nicholson wrote, 'One was wanting to get right back to the beginning and then take one step forward at a time on a firm basis . . .'[21] There is also continuity with the anti-classical and anti-humanist ideas of the pre-war avant garde, and in particular with the writings of Fry and Bell. Roger Fry published articles on 'Ancient American Art' and on 'Negro Sculpture' in 1918 and 1920 respectively. In 1919 there was a large exhibition of African and Oceanic art in Chelsea which occasioned an article from Clive Bell (reprinted in *Since Cézanne* in 1922), and Negro art was shown at the Goupil Gallery in 1921. Interest in 'primitive' sculpture flourished in England immediately after the war, and the effects of that interest were conditioned by the interpretations of the Bloomsbury writers.

In his article on Negro sculpture Fry asserted, of the works in a small show at the Chelsea Book Club, that 'some of these things are great sculpture – greater, I think, than anything we produced even in the Middle Ages. Certainly they have the special qualities of sculpture in a higher degree.' He went on to demonstrate what he meant by the 'special qualities of sculpture'.

> . . . the Negro scores heavily by his willingness to reduce the limbs to a succession of ovoid masses sometimes scarcely longer than they are broad. Generally speaking, one may say that his plastic sense leads him to give its utmost amplitude and relief to all the protuberant parts of the body, and to get thereby an extraordinarily emphatic and impressive sequence of planes. So far from clinging to two dimensions, as we tend to do, he actually underlines, as it were, the three-dimensionalness of his forms. It is in some such way, I suspect, that he manages to give to his forms their disconcerting vitality, the suggestion that they make of being not mere echoes of actual figures, but of possessing an inner life of their own.

For those with appropriate ambitions and with the ability to recognize it, here was a prescription for modernism in sculpture: the key qualities were 'three-dimensionalness' and immanent 'vitality'.

Fry's two articles were reprinted in *Vision and Design* in 1920. Soon after its first publication, this book was read with enthusiasm by Henry Moore, then a twenty-two-year-old student in Leeds. A grammar-school education and the profession of teaching were well-tested means of advancement from the industrial working class, and Moore, as the son of a father who believed in self-help, had trained as a teacher during the early years of the war. After military service from 1917 until early in 1919, he took advantage of an army grant to enter Leeds College of Art as a comparatively mature student, and from there won a scholarship to the Royal College of Art in London, where he embarked in 1921 upon a two-year course of study towards the award of a teacher's diploma, following this with a further year of advanced study in 1923–4. Moore himself has testified to the liberating effect which Fry's book had upon him:

Actually Roger Fry's Vision and Design was the most lucky discovery for me. I came on it by chance while looking for another book in the Leeds Reference Library. Fry in his essay on Negro sculpture stressed the 'three-dimensional realisation' that characterised African art and its 'truth to material'. More, Fry opened the way to other books and to the realisation of the British Museum. That was really the beginning.[22]

and later:

Once you'd read Roger Fry the whole thing was there. I went to the British Museum on Wednesday and Sunday afternoons and saw what I wanted to see.[23]

It appears from Moore's various (if mutually reinforcing) accounts of his own studentship that it seemed to him at the time as if the terms of reference for a concept of sculpture in the early 1920s were established not, as they were for the normal aspiring practitioner, by the determination of a specific antecedent practice and history, but by the distillation of some essentially 'sculptural' aspect from the whole of the world's art – the 'common world-language of form'.[24] Prevalent as they have become, and well buttressed as they were by writings such as those of Fry and Bell, and later of Wilenski and Herbert Read, claims of this kind need to be treated with some scepticism. It should be remembered, for instance, that Moore bought the time he spent foraging in the British Museum with a currency which was recognized even by the more conservative factions at the Royal College of Art: the kind of application to academic disciplines of modelling and of drawing from the cast and from life that was characteristic of one determined to make the most of opportunities for self-betterment.

... for a considerable while after my discovery of the British Museum there was a bitter struggle within me, on the one hand, between the need to follow my course at college in order to get a teacher's diploma and, on the other, the desire to work freely at what appealed most to me in sculpture. At one point I was seriously considering giving up college and working only in the direction that attracted me. But, thank goodness, I somehow came to the realisation that academic discipline is valuable. And my need to have a diploma, in order to earn a living, helped ... finally I hit on a sort of compromise arrangement: academic work during the term, and during the holidays a free rein to the interests I had developed in the British Museum.[25]

On the other hand, in so far as he was likely to feel socially disadvantaged in face of any genuine expression of interest in the classical tradition, modernist interests must have offered Moore a welcome and appropriate means of self-assertion.

It was not surprising that Moore should have felt torn between the demands of academic training and the heterogeneous attractions of the British Museum. By the years immediately after the first war the interests of mainstream and modernist practice in sculpture were so distinct as to be virtually irreconcilable. In painting there might be arguments over the ordering of priorities within the tradition of the art, but at least mainstream and modernist practitioners had more or less the same overall history in view. Modernist sculptors, however, were expressing interest in works which had never been seen as even potentially relevant to the mainstream history of sculpture, and which were thus not 'sculpture' at all for the majority. The conservative and classical traditions must have seemed all the more restricting as the enlarging Modernist concept of sculpture, articulated by Fry, asserted the relevance of the productions of a wide range of cultures, and as museums, exhibitions and publications made these available to view. In a section on 'The Modern Sculptors' Education', Wilenski emphasized the importance of the foundation of the museums in the nineteenth century and of increased facilities for travel and for publication. 'In the course of their studies the modern sculptors turned to the world's content of sculpture for assistance in their technical problems and for reinforcement of their morals by contact with other sculptors whose attitudes were similar to their own.' Among the cultures whose productions were studied by the modern sculptor, he listed Egyptian, Assyrian, Persian, Chinese, Japanese, Sumerian, Negro and Indian. Moore's own list was even longer.

The world has been producing sculpture for at least some thirty thousand years. Through modern developments of communication much of this we now know and the few sculptors of a hundred years or so of Greece no longer blot our eyes to the sculptural achievements of the rest of mankind. Paleolithic and Neolithic sculpture, Sumerian, Babylonian and Egyptian, Early Greek, Chinese, Etruscan, Indian, Mayan, Mexican and Peruvian, Romanesque, Byzantine and Gothic, Negro, South Sea Island and North American Indian sculpture; actual examples or photographs of all are available, giving us a world view of sculpture never previously possible.[26]

Much of this material had become available to view around the turn of the century, and it was largely as a result of this that the concept of sculpture changed so radically between 1900 and 1920. Buttressed as it was by a wide resource of literary reference and by a strong, if diminishing, sense of decorum, the classical tradition had up to then secured coherence of meaning and of style for the art of sculpture in England. As the authority of that tradition was undermined, there was a growing need for new means of establishing coherence in the activity, and for a new theoretical basis from which to defend claims to meaning for sculpture as a modernist practice. (It is clear from the ordering of Wilenski's book, in which the development of the Modernist conception of sculpture is vividly expressed, that the last vestiges of the authority of the classical tradition, or as he calls it the 'Greek prejudice', had had to be demystified and exorcised before the 'meaning of modern sculpture' could be established as it were in its place.) How was modern purpose now to be expressed for sculpture in face of the apparent diversity of its exemplars and interests?

The new unifying principle, as expressed in the statements of the sculptors themselves and in the writings of sympathetic critics, was that 'sculpture' was to be interpreted not as referring to a category of objects or to a set of techniques, but as identifying an innate category of experience – the response to 'significant form', as it were, wherever it might be found. Once this was established, as it was in avant-garde discourse by the early 1920s, then it was possible, by categorizing them as 'sculptural experiences', to assert the relevance to sculpture of a range of interests and memories which would have been ruled out as irrelevant in the traditional pursuit of the art; not just an interest in the products of cultures untouched by the classical tradition and by humanist ideals, but a devotion to the memory of the Yorkshire landscape or an interest in the shapes of stones and bones.

Previously, the echoes of a literary mythology had served to mediate between the human figure, as the central subject of sculpture, and other things in the world which might attract the sculptor's interest. The myth of Apollo and Daphne for instance, or the concept of a dryad, would implicitly legitimate any interpretation of the female form by reference to characteristics of trees. By the early 1920s, however, 'literary' had become a strongly pejorative term, customarily applied in denigration of art which evoked such associations. The very avoidance of titles with associations in classical mythology became a feature of early modernist sculpture which served to distinguish it from its near relatives in the work of those whose modernism was merely stylistic. The distinctness of Moore's and Hepworth's sculpture during the 1920s and early 1930s lay in their willingness, while still according the figure a determining place in the evolution of their sculpture, to subordinate the humanistic sensuality conventionally associated with representations of the figure to an interest in the appearance of other things, such as could previously have been considered relevant to the expressive purposes of sculpture only by virtue of the operation of a mediating myth. In

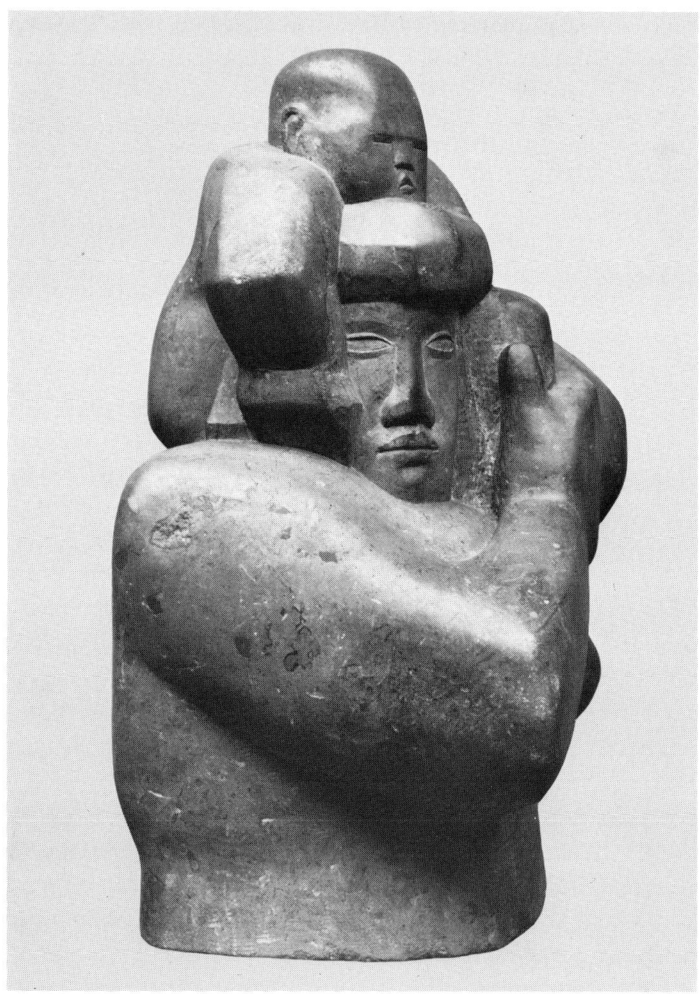

115. Henry Moore: *Mother and Child*, 1924–5. Hornton stone, height $22\frac{1}{2}$ in.

Moore's *Mother and Child* of 1924–5 [115], for instance, echoes of Epstein's pre-war work (the face from the tomb of Oscar Wilde [32]), of Michelangelo (the painted Doni tondo)[27] and of ancient South American sculpture combine in a composition which also embodies qualities of a kind associated with massive natural formations, recalling Gaudier's dictum that 'sculptural energy is the mountain'.[28] Rather than any literary occasion of metamorphosis, an expanded concept of sculpture itself – a concept which asserts the relevance of any 'strong experience of form' – is here what serves to mediate between the original figure subject and the various references embodied in the finished work.

For all that the proposition of the potential all-inclusiveness of sculpture as a category of experience has been well rehearsed since then, and might now be subject to some sceptical scrutiny, in the 1920s it was a radical and progressive idea. The assertion of the possible continuity and coherence of all sculpture, including the primitive, together with certain types of natural form, was a means by which those who felt ill at ease among sophisticates could achieve some sense of action against the domination of culture by a patrician, conservative, literary upper-middle class with highly specialized tastes. This assertion, rather than a simple commitment to carving, was the central plank in the avant-garde platform.

Gill offers an exception to support this rule. For all his great competence and sensitivity as a carver, and for all that his defence of carving was an expression of a kind of socialist idealism, he was not seen in the 1920s, and could not be seen now, as occupying a secure position in the vanguard of English sculpture. What moderated his modernism was precisely his adherence to a world of classical and biblical reference. His technique was advanced enough; his work was often formally adventurous; but despite his occasional mild eroticism his subjects were conservatively derived and conservatively interpreted. (His conversion to Catholicism no doubt played its part in this. The pantheism of modern sculpture has always been its weakest feature, inclining as it does towards an all-pervading sentimentality and a chronic disregard for history. But at least it has generally been a lay pantheism.)

In 1924 the professor of sculpture at the Royal College of Art resigned his post, and William Rothenstein, who had been principal since 1921 and who was favourably disposed towards Moore, offered him a part-time post as instructor. The Board of Education's representative had rejected Rothenstein's proposal that Epstein should be offered the professorship,[29] and Moore's appointment was designed initially to cover the hiatus while a compromise successor was found, but in effect the contract was for a term of seven years. Moore was expected to work two days per week for a salary of £240 per annum. Throughout the 1920s he was thus guaranteed a measure of financial security. Also in 1924, on the basis of his academic work, he was awarded a travelling scholarship for study in Italy. He took this up during the first six months of 1925, and the *Mother and Child* was completed after his return. There followed a three-year period of uneasy experimentation between the extremes of 'primitive' carving and 'academic' modelling while he attempted to reconcile the undeniable authority of Masaccio, Michelangelo and others with the modernist assertion of the quality of 'primitive' and non-humanist art, an assertion generally made, as we have seen, at the expense of regard for the classical tradition and the Renaissance. 'I couldn't seem to shake off the new impressions, or to make use of them without denying all I had devoutly believed in before.'[30] In 1928, however, he held his first one-man exhibition at the Warren Gallery, where Paul Nash had shown the year before, and received support in the form of sales of thirty drawings and several sculptures, among them the *Mother and Child* of 1924–5. Purchasers included Epstein, Augustus John and Henry Lamb.

It was in 1929 that Moore first achieved a substantial resolution of the contradiction between his various interests. The work in question was a *Reclining Figure* in brown Hornton stone [116] carved on a scale which was large for Moore at this date. Typically, the sculpture expressed a point of coincidence between an ancient and a modern influence. Of all the

116. Henry Moore: *Reclining Figure*, 1929. Brown Hornton stone, $33 \times 22\frac{1}{2} \times 15$ in. (exhibited in Unit One tour, 1934–5)

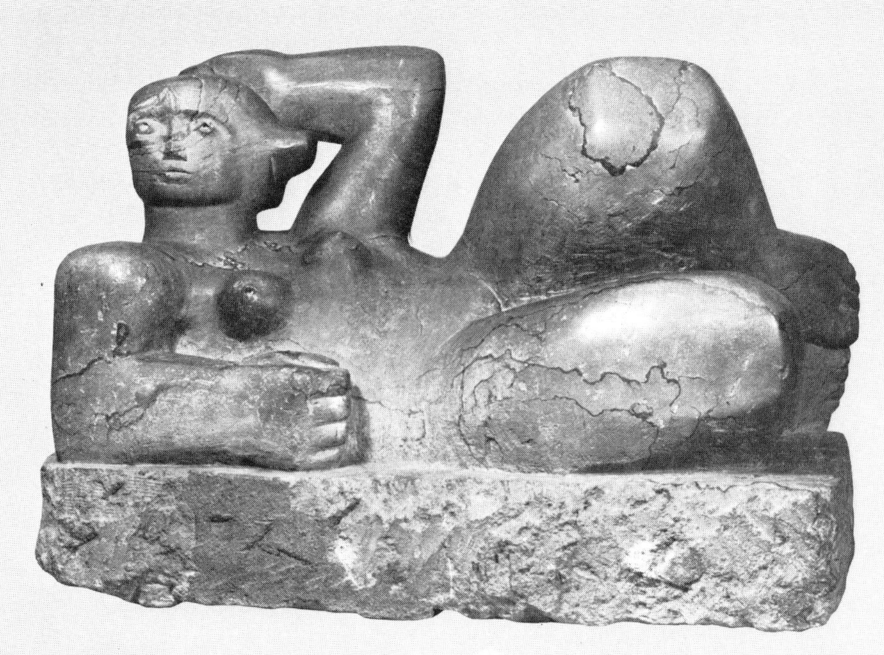

sculpture of the various cultures to which Moore had been exposed at the British Museum and on occasional visits to Paris from 1922 onwards, he had been most impressed by the early Mexican. The interest had perhaps served to establish his idiosyncrasy among those following the fashion for 'primitive' art. A specific point of departure for his *Reclining Figure* of 1929 was a photograph of a limestone carving of the rain god, Chacmool.[31] From this figure Moore derived both the device of turning the head at right angles to the shoulders, which permitted the sculpture to address the spectator, as it were, while presenting a view of the whole extended torso, and also perhaps the possibility of interpreting the figure in terms of a landscape of peaks and hollows. More generally, the theme of the reclining figure propped on one elbow was a type for ambitious figure sculpture from classical times onwards, by virtue both of its iconographical associations, which combined implications of contained energy and fluidity with passivity, and of technical interest in the complex and rhythmical forms which are presented by the human figure so posed.

There were also precedents within modern art for the exploration of this particular theme. It occurs in several of those of Picasso's works of 1918–23 in which heavy-limbed nudes are disposed in landscapes or on beaches (see, for instance, the *Trois Baigneuses*, Juan-les-Pins, of 1920, or more particularly *La Source* of 1921). In reconciling modernist practice and an interest in 'primitive' forms with a plastic, monumental classicism, Picasso's work of the early 1920s provided a strong precedent for a similar reconciliation in Moore's.[32] The sculptor Jacques Lipchitz, who had been in Paris since 1909, and whose work Moore must have been aware of by the end of the 1920s, had also recently (in 1928) made a large reclining figure in stone of the typically Cubist subject of *Woman and Guitar*. This offered a further precedent for recapitulation of a classic theme in a modern style, and Moore may have had Lipchitz's work specifically in mind at the time when he carved his *Reclining Figure* in Ancaster stone in 1930 (LH 94).[33] The influence of Synthetic Cubism is certainly apparent in several of Moore's works of 1927–9, notably the *Torso* in cast concrete (LH 37), the *Head and Shoulders* in Verde di Prato (LH 48) and the *Half-Figure* in cast concrete (LH 67) [117].

But of course the modernism of Moore's work was not generally as pronounced as that of either Picasso or Lipchitz at this time. In the 1929 *Reclining Figure* [116] the strongest secondary reference is to landscape. As with many of Moore's works of this period, the stone is comparatively roughly finished. (Several of the sculptures of the years 1926–34 were carved or cast in concrete, a material which combined relatively low cost with technical associations outside the field of antecedent fine art.) The

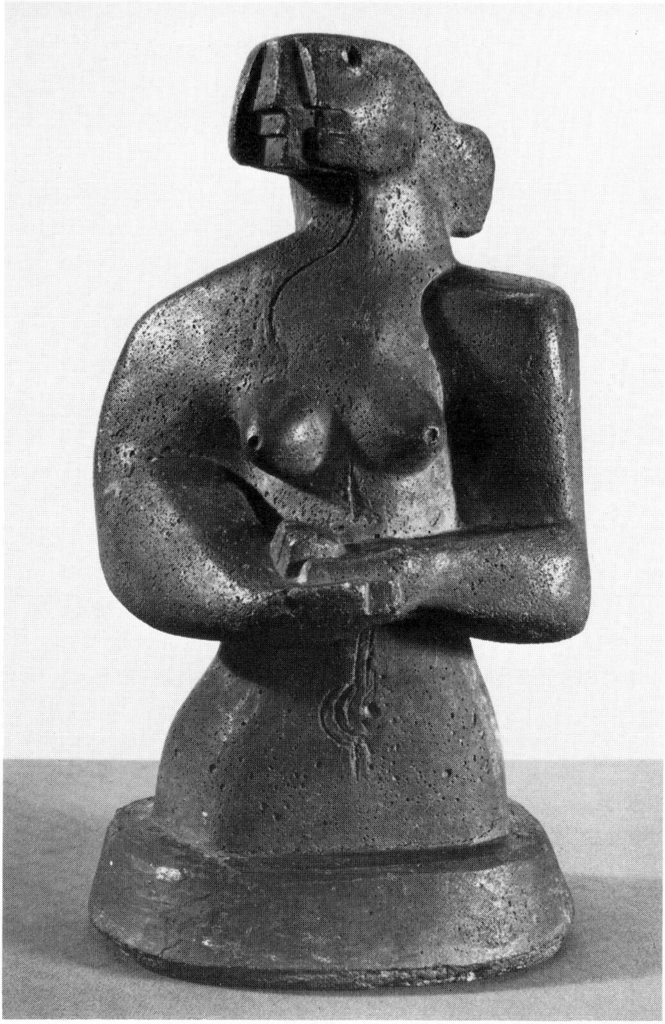

117. Henry Moore: *Half-figure*, 1929. Cast concrete, height $15\frac{1}{2}$ in.

Reclining Figure of 1929 was Moore's major contribution to the development of that moderate and vernacular modernism which characterizes the more advanced English sculpture of the 1920s and which reaches its point of maximum development in his work and in Hepworth's in the early 1930s. (The latest relevant works are Moore's *Mother and Child* [118], now in the Sainsbury Centre at the University of East Anglia, and *Reclining Figure* in carved concrete, now in the City Art Museum, St Louis, and Hepworth's *Kneeling Figure* in rosewood [119] now in the Wakefield City Art Gallery. All three were made in 1932.)

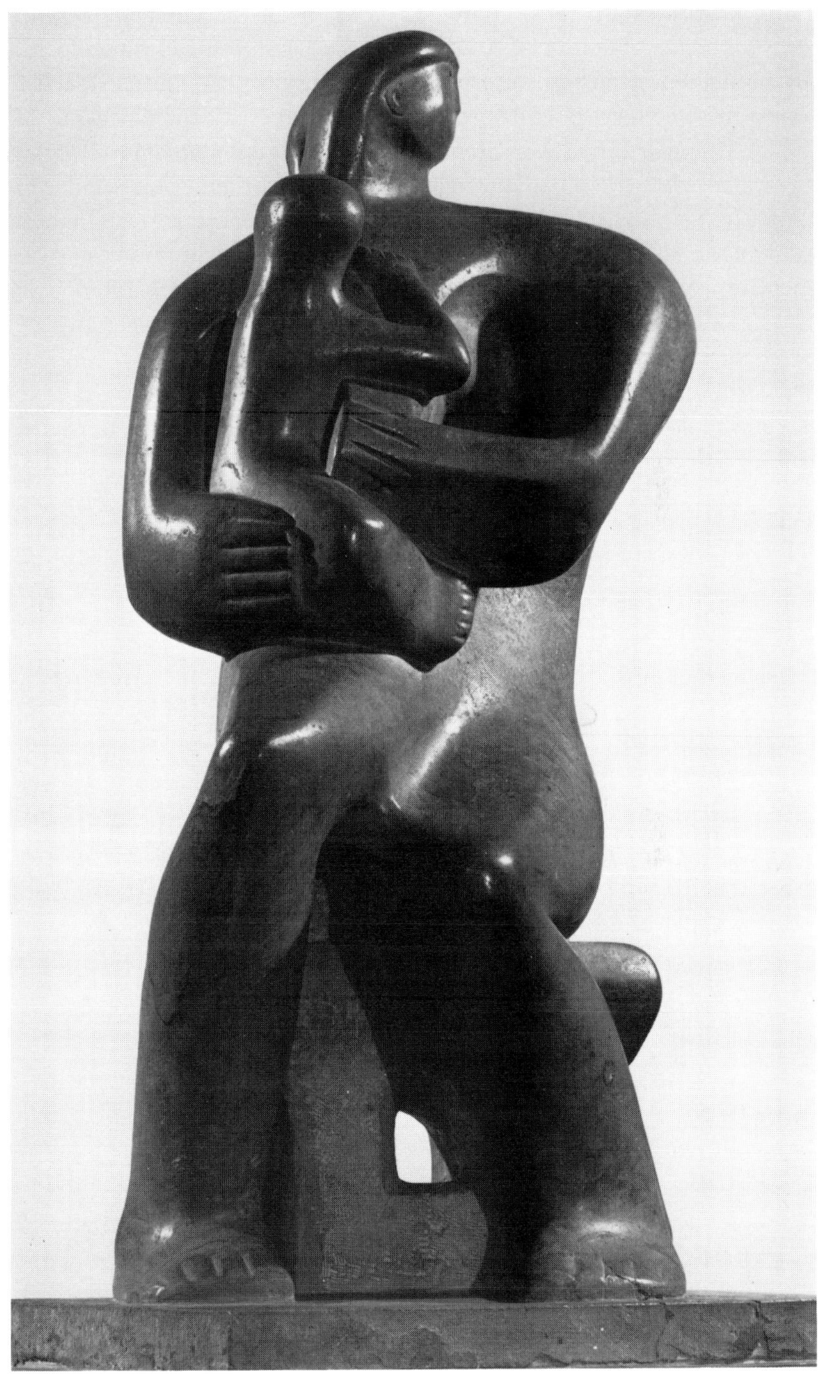

118. Henry Moore: *Mother and Child*, 1932. Green Hornton stone, height 35 in.

Like Moore, Hepworth had progressed by means of scholarships from Leeds to the Royal College of Art. She was five years younger than Moore, but the difference had been absorbed in his preliminary training as a teacher and in his war service, and they therefore arrived as contemporaries in London. Hepworth had won a one-year travelling scholarship to Italy in 1923, and while there had married John Skeaping, then Rome scholar in sculpture. She had stayed with him in Italy and had spent some time in study of the technique of marble carving under an Italian master-carver. They returned to England late in 1926 and held a joint exhibition of carvings in their studio in St John's Wood at the end of the next year. In June 1928 they shared an exhibition at the Beaux-Arts Gallery in London. Hepworth's earliest surviving works of any significance, two marble carvings of doves from 1927, clearly refer to Epstein's work on the same

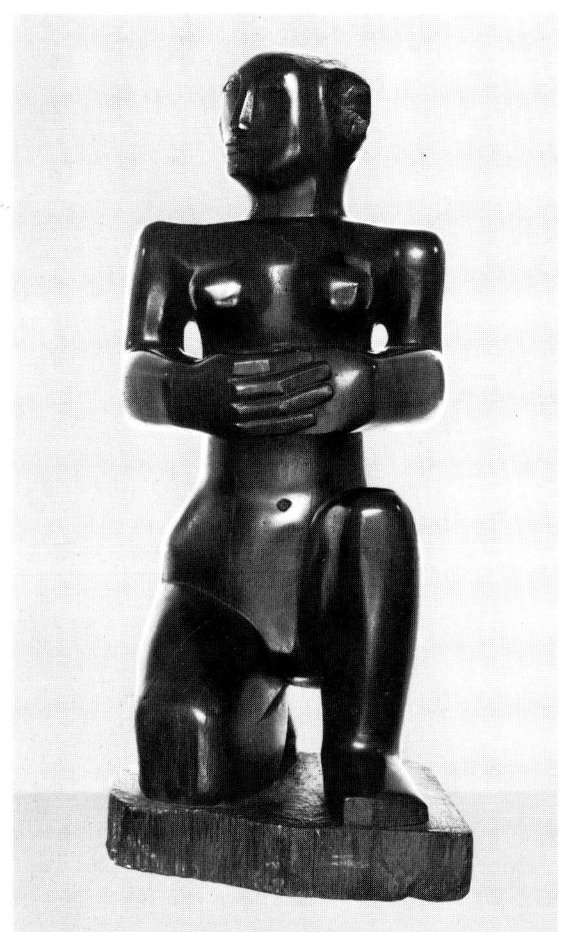

119. Barbara Hepworth: *Kneeling Figure*, 1932. Rosewood, height 27 in. (exhibited in the Unit One tour, 1934–5)

theme of fourteen years earlier. The majority of her extant works of the next four years are carvings on figure subjects. Generally these follow themes first explored by Moore, but where Moore tended to emphasize massiveness and surface texture in his material, Hepworth's inclination was to soften and refine. The torso with hands folded or clasped at waist level is a distinctive type common to both. The locus classicus for this particular theme is Mesopotamian sculpture of the third millennium B.C., and its appearance first in Moore's work and then in Hepworth's is certainly the result of the former's studies in the British Museum.[34] Typical examples from Moore's work, such as the two *Half-figures* in cast concrete of 1929 (LH 66 and 67) [117] or the *Half-figure* in veined alabaster of 1931 (LH 108), could be compared with Hepworth's *Figure in Sycamore* [120] (now in the Pier Gallery, Stromness) or the lost *Figure with folded Hands* in alabaster,

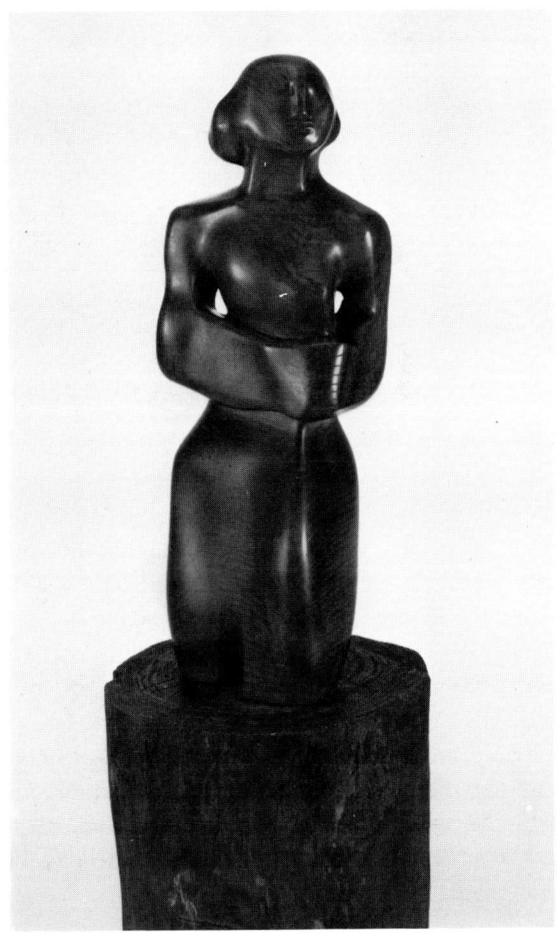

120. Barbara Hepworth: *Figure in Sycamore*, 1931. Height 25 in.

both of 1931. A further comparison might be made between Moore's *Head of a Woman* of 1926 and Hepworth's *Head* of 1930. The principal feature of the style these works display in common is an exploration of the potential formal expressiveness of the human figure, or rather of its analogues and resemblances. This is pursued in terms of a strong interest in particular in analogies with natural form, and a more tentative interest in the milder aspects of the liberties taken with the disposition and profile of human form and features by the Cubist painters (particularly Picasso) and sculptors (particularly Archipenko and Lipchitz).

This moderate vernacular modernism was in style entirely compatible with the most advanced of the painting being produced at the same time by members of the Seven & Five Society. Less competent or less adventurous versions of the type of sculpture which Moore and Hepworth were making in the later twenties were indeed produced at the same time by sculptors who had already shown with the society (Alan Durst, Kanty Cooper, Betty Muntz and Maurice Lambert). The younger sculptors' commitment to carving and their emphasis upon the formally generalizable aspects of the human body were consistent with the painters' interests in the facticity of the painted surface and the 'underlying structure' of still life and landscape themes. When Adrian Stokes came to review an exhibition of work by Ben Nicholson at the Lefevre Gallery in 1933, he emphasized the compatibility with sculpture:

> Mr Nicholson's canvases and panels serve him in the role of the carver's block. Just as the carver consults the stone for the reinforcement of his idea, so Mr Nicholson has started to paint when he prepares his canvases.[35]

In so far as degrees of modernism can be assessed in common between painting and sculpture, for instance in relation to the assimilation of continental influences, it might be said that the art of sculpture and the art of painting in England had reached equivalent points of development by the beginning of the 1930s. In April 1931 Hepworth saw and admired Nicholson's work shown at the Bloomsbury Gallery and she met him soon after. Late in 1931 Hepworth, Moore, Skeaping and Bedford joined the Seven & Five Society (Skeaping had exhibited by invitation in January of that year) and the principal advanced forces of modernist development thus came together. It was in the Seven & Five exhibition of February 1932, held at the Leicester Galleries, and in the subsequent formation of the group known as Unit One, that the identity of a new avant garde was first clearly established.

9

THE EARLY THIRTIES: UNIT ONE

During the 1920s, English artists who had been too young to be party to the modernism of the pre-war years had had gradually to learn for themselves how the terms of reference for art had been changed in those earlier developments. There were those who made their homes in France, but the contribution of these expatriates to the development of English art was not a significant one, nor were they likely to make much impression among the artists of diverse nationalities in Paris. Wood and Wadsworth benefited from the years they were able to spend abroad, and each was able to secure one exhibition in Paris,[1] but for all that they were exceptions in this respect, their identity as modern artists was largely secured in terms of the more limited context of English art. Socially and economically, the great majority of the younger English painters and sculptors were restricted to this insular context, where the sense of their comparative apprenticeship in relation to the major figures of continental modern art was regularly reinforced in the writings of the principal critics and in the priorities according to which dealers and collectors made their selections. As late as 1933, when Myfanwy Evans, then a young and sympathetic observer of the development of English art, visited the Lefevre Gallery to see Ivon Hitchens's one-man exhibition, she was told by the director, 'You don't want to look at that stuff ... Come up and see my Derains.'[2] While opportunities for English artists to show in Paris were exceptional and generally unrewarding, French artists were mostly assured of exposure in London.

But by the end of the decade, as we have seen, insular modernism had reached its peak in the work of Nash [121], Nicholson and Moore, and the situation began gradually to change. In 1930 Nash was forty-one, Nicholson thirty-six and Moore thirty-two. For these three in particular, the effects of several years of technical application and of measured assimilation of the transformations of European modernism were now manifest in their work. As Wyndham Lewis had suggested ten years before, this was the one

121. Paul Nash: *Northern Adventure*, 1929. Oil on canvas, 36 × 28 in. (exhibited in the Unit One tour, 1934–5)

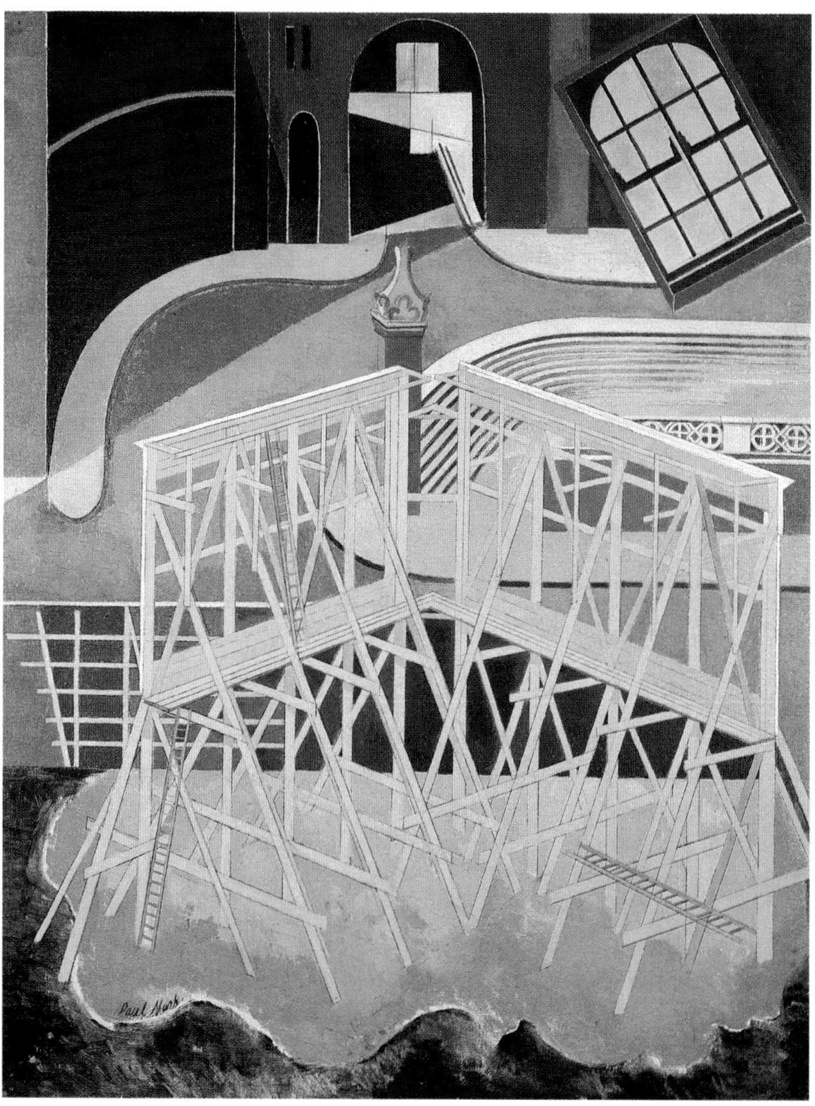

sure means to establish some international status for English art. It is a measure of the confidence which Nicholson, for instance, derived from his own new work that he felt able to establish some direct contact with major European artists on his trips abroad during the early thirties, rather than restricting himself, as he had tended to do during the twenties, to visits to museums and dealers' galleries. And where exhibitions of continental art of the previous twenty years had been avidly consumed in London during the years following the war, shows of more recent modern work were regarded now with some discrimination, as the more advanced English artists came to see themselves as engaged in potentially the same world of practice as the European modernists. Furthermore, those younger writers and collectors who were attracted by the group shows of the Seven & Five, and by the one-man shows of its members, now began to moderate the Bloomsbury hegemony by providing a measure of real, if modest, support. R. H. Wilenski, Herbert Read, Adrian Stokes, Geoffrey Grigson, H. S. Ede and Margaret Gardiner were among those who expressed their sense of community with the younger English artists in the early 1930s, either by writing about their work or by buying it or both.

As the new avant garde gathered strength and coherence it became clear that an interest in the post-Cubist European art of the post-war years was to be a feature serving to distinguish its members from adherents to a developed Post-Impressionism such as prevailed within the London Group. Not that the latter could be dismissed as representing a conservative establishment. For the vast majority in 1930, Post-Impressionism was still modern art. There was no collection of continental art on public view in London until the National Gallery of British Art at Millbank (now the Tate Gallery) opened its modern foreign gallery in 1926, and before the acquisition of the substantial Stoop bequest late in 1933 there was little in this collection that properly represented the twentieth century. During the years 1931–4, however, the interested English public was to be prepared for a new period of internationalism. The initiatives taken by Nash and Nicholson were of particular importance during this period of development of modernism in England.

In the spring of 1930 Nash travelled to the south of France with another younger painter, Edward Burra. They passed through Paris and at Léonce Rosenberg's gallery Nash saw for the first time a substantial collection of contemporary French art. His curiosity was aroused, particularly by the work of the Surrealists. (Although reproductions had been published in available French magazines, no explicitly Surrealist work was exhibited in London until the inclusion of work by Dali, Miró and Ernst in the Mayor Gallery's re-opening show in April 1933, ten years after the publication of

André Breton's first Surrealist Manifesto.) For all that he had been able to write of 'achievement and success' following his exhibition of 1928, Nash like many others found that sales of work were drastically reduced in the early thirties, and he turned to journalism as a means to supplement a declining income.[3] As a regular reviewer of exhibitions and publications he was thus encouraged to speculate on recent developments on the continent and in England. In December 1930 Nash published the first of a series of regular articles as art critic of the *Weekend Review*, and the following April he began also to write for *The Listener*, where he alternated with Herbert Read, at that time on the point of establishing himself as England's leading advocate of modern art. Nash was no polemicist, but during a period of transition in English art he wrote regularly and perceptively upon a wide range of issues relevant to that transition, occasionally anticipating possibilities which he was to assist in realizing, and always with a strong sense of the importance of considering English art in the context of the European Modern Movement as a whole. During the years 1931–3 he speculated often in public about the artist's relation to his own time and to the broader community. Such speculation is perhaps characteristic of the development of an avant garde. The *Weltanschauung* was back.

In his first review for *The Listener*, in discussing exhibitions of work by de Chirico and by various British painters, Nash signalled the close of the era of domination by French Post-Impressionism which had opened in 1910:

> During the last 20 years there have been four great influences on pictorial art – Henri Matisse, Pablo Picasso, Fernand Léger and Giorgio di Chirico ... Apples have had their day.[4]

In an article on 'Going Modern and being British'[5] he asked whether it was possible to do both, and made it clear that 'going modern' involved taking account of developments in European art since the war. In the course of his own investigation into the possibility of a new British modernism Nash wrote sympathetically about abstract art[6] and experimented briefly with non-representational compositions before deciding that abstraction was not for him. The most fully worked of these experimental paintings is the Tate Gallery's *Kinetic Feature* of 1931 [122], where a pattern of interlocking planes derived from a somewhat schematic reading of Cubism encloses an incongruous column which signals the persistence of the influence of de Chirico. If *Kinetic Feature* does little to advance Nash's status as a contributor to the development of non-representational art in England, it does at least serve to demonstrate the wide scope of his speculations and technical interests at a time when English artists and critics were again concerned to come to terms with major recent developments in Europe.

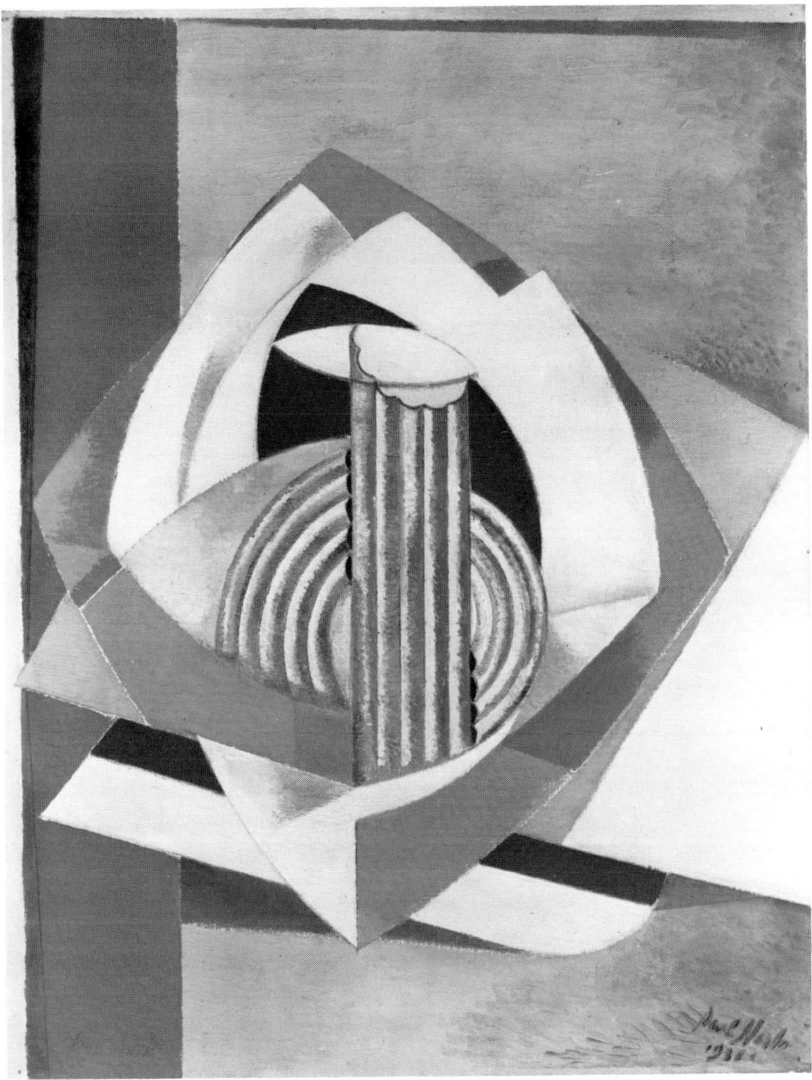

122. Paul Nash: *Kinetic Feature*, 1931. Oil on canvas, 26 × 20 in.

Nash exhibited *Kinetic Feature* in December 1931 in an exhibition at Tooth's Gallery of 'Recent Developments in British Painting'. The other exhibitors were Burra, J. W. Power, Wadsworth, Nicholson, John Bigge, John Armstrong, Moore and John Aldridge. Armstrong was working in a style which still owed much to Chirico's later work. Wadsworth's interest in Chirico had by 1931 given way to the influence of the French Purists Ozenfant and Léger. His paintings now looked flatter and were less

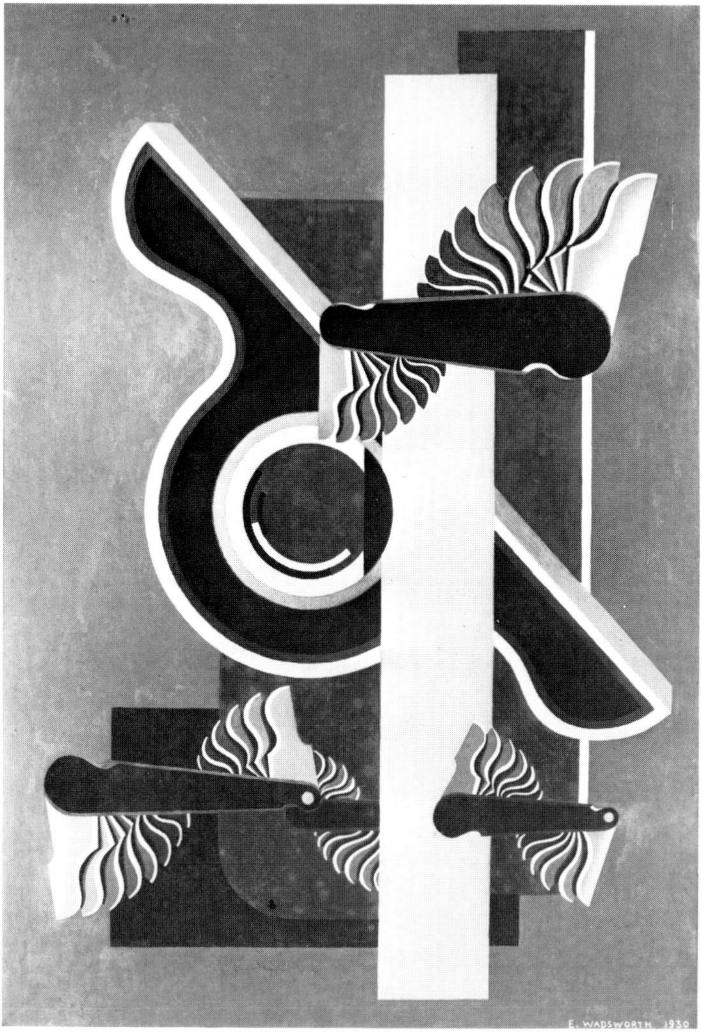

123. Edward Wadsworth: *Composition*, 1930. Tempera on panel, 35 × 25 in.

evocative, more rigorously formal [123]. In 1931 his work looked more like abstract painting than that of anyone else in England. Burra's work combined a satirical social reference weakly reminiscent of German New Realists such as George Grosz and Otto Dix with a tendency towards exaggeration of colour and dissolution of form of a kind found in the work of contemporary European Surrealists such as Miró, Ernst and Masson [124]. Aldridge was a persistent Post-Impressionist. With the inclusion of Moore and Nicholson, the range of work was plainly a wide one. Its strongest common element was the aspiration to cosmopolitanism.

By the end of 1931 Nash was preoccupied with the sense of a need for a broad modern movement in English art, design and architecture, and he seems to have been stimulated by the 'Recent Developments' exhibition to consider that the exhibitors were perhaps among the potential leaders of such a movement.[7] A few months later, in an article on 'The Artist in the

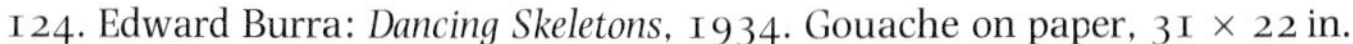

124. Edward Burra: *Dancing Skeletons*, 1934. Gouache on paper, 31 × 22 in.

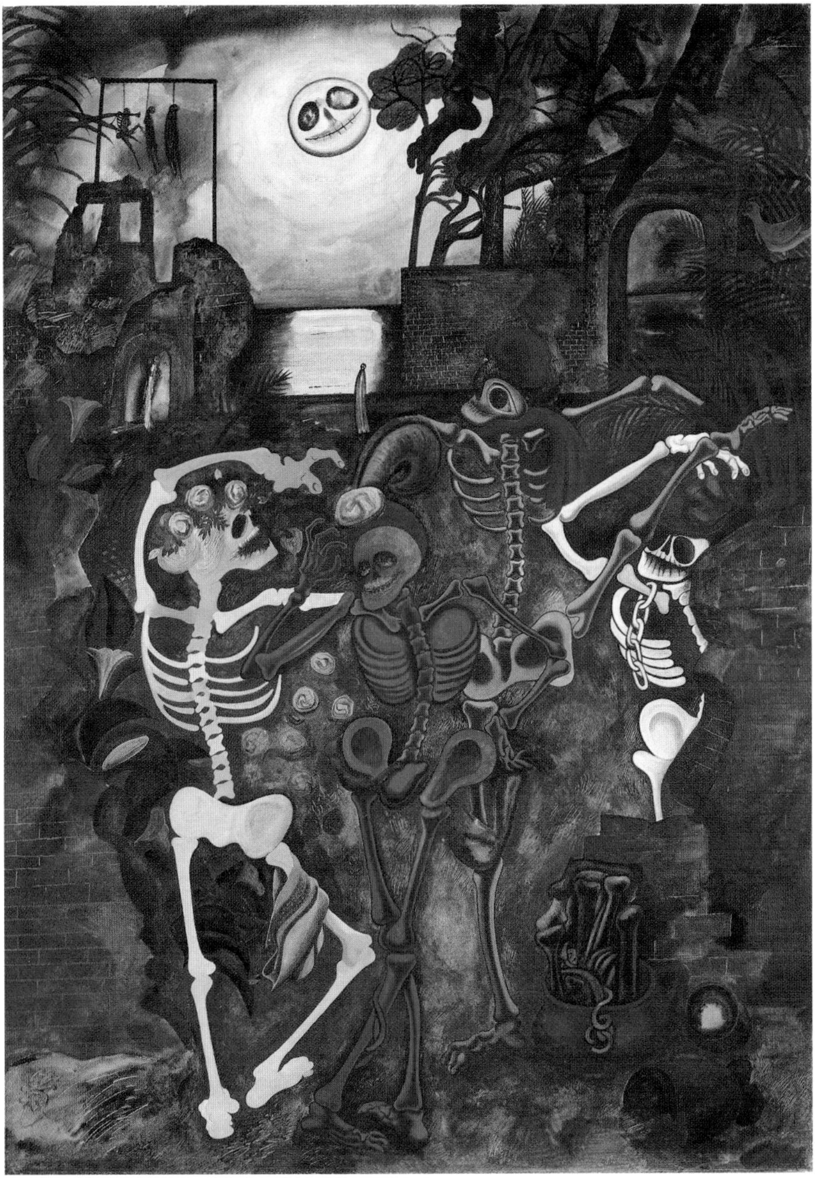

House',[8] he gave further evidence of what was in his mind: 'When the day comes for a more practical, sympathetic alliance between architect, painter, sculptor and decorator, we may see the acceleration of an important movement.' That Nash should have promoted such an alliance as desirable and possible was a reflection both of the range of his insular interests and acquaintances and also of his recent exposure to the ideas of the continental Modern Movement.

Despite the acute slump of 1929–32, which left $3\frac{3}{4}$ million people unemployed in England, the period since the war had seen a considerable overall rise in the standard of living of a majority of the population and particularly in the prosperity of the middle classes. The enlargement of the consumer market and the increase in production and distribution of standard commodities led to a converging of interests among those concerned with style. This interest was expressed in the rapid expansion during the later twenties and early thirties in the number of publications and organizations devoted to furtherance and exploitation of the relationship between art, design, architecture and industry.[9] The practical base of Modernist art criticism expanded accordingly.

The Modern Movement in design and architecture, though it had native origins in the work of such men as Morris, Ashbee and Mackintosh, was now largely seen as a continental movement, and, with the gradual waning of the insular mood of the twenties, artists who had spent the decade pursuing moderate modernist styles in comparative isolation were eager to find out what developments there had been in Europe since the war. An important feature of continental modernism during the twenties had been the propagandizing of unification of all the arts, under a universal aesthetic rationality, as the pursuit of a social ideal. There was a manifest contrast here with the reduced aspirations of contemporary English art. There had been no Weimar republic in England, and no English equivalent of the German Bauhaus where artists and designers might be brought together to work towards some putatively social, if utopian, end; there had been no revolutionary upheaval such as had led to the wholesale reorganization of the relations between art and design in Russia during the early 1920s; there had been no ideologically cohesive ensemble of artists and architects such as the Dutch De Stijl group appeared to be; and there was no figure among the English architects and designers who might play a dominant and stage-managing role such as had been assumed by Le Corbusier among the Purists in France. Those now interested in the so-called useful arts as a potential area of development of modern styles thus looked abroad to France, to Germany, to Scandinavia and to the Russian émigrés for ideas and for models of activity.[10]

The 1930s were not propitious years for the development of the Modern Movement's utopian idealism, and the revolutionary aspirations of that movement were thus pursued in England on a more modest scale and in more urbane tones. In the early years of the decade Nash, at whom no one could have levelled such accusations of Bolshevism as were applied by the Nazis to the teachers at the Bauhaus, became a model spokesman for this domesticated modernist idealism. A Society of Industrial Artists was formed in 1930, and in 1932 he was elected as its President and Chairman, a function he fulfilled for the next two years. If it seems surprising now that Nash should have been considered suited to such a role, we should bear in mind that the concept of an 'industrial artist' was not then interpreted in England as it is now, and that it was not backed up by the provision of a suitable training and education (a point which Herbert Read was to make forcibly in his book *Art and Industry*, published in 1934). Nash's work in the field of book illustration and in design for the stage and for textiles was alone sufficient to identify him as one concerned with the 'useful arts'. This concern was consistently expressed in his published writings during the early 1930s, at a time when the difficulty of selling paintings obliged him to turn his hand to the design of china, textiles, posters, etc.

During 1932, among his regular reviews of exhibitions, he published articles on 'Advertising and Contemporary Art', 'The Artist and Industry', 'Art and the English Press', 'Art and Photography', 'The Artist and the Community', 'The Artist in the House', 'Modern English Textiles', and on the opening of the Building Centre in September of that year. He also published a book of collected essays under the title *Room and Book*, and designed a glass bathroom for the dancer Tilly Losch.

In his article on 'The Artist and Industry', published in the *Weekend Review* on 24 September 1932, Nash declared that 'A marriage has been arranged – and will shortly take place.' He was referring to what was shortly to become Unit One. He had been acting upon his sense of a need for a new modern movement in England and aided by his work as a reviewer had identified various artists as potential members of an organized group. By the close of 1932 he had singled out Henry Moore, whose first two one-man exhibitions had established him among those interested in modern art as an ambitious and talented sculptor,[11] and the architect Wells Coates, an exhibitor at the opening of the Building Centre and a founder-member early in 1933 of the Modern Architectural Research (MARS) Group.[12] With these two and with Edward Wadsworth, who had established close contacts among the Purists, Nash discussed the formation and membership of a new avant-garde group. In a letter to Moore in January 1933[13] he suggested the title 'English Contemporary Group' and gave an account of his success in extracting promises from three leading galleries and a firm of publishers. 'All this goes to show that we shall not lack support once we combine and present a united front.' Apart from listing the artists who were finally to make up Unit One, Nash suggested Edward McKnight Kauffer 'as representing textile and other kinds of design', Frances Hodgkins, J. W. Power, William Roberts, and the sculptor Maurice Lambert (a member of the Seven & Five from 1928 to 1931). Ben Nicholson was an obvious candidate for inclusion and once brought into the discussions was bound to want to press the claims of those he could see as allies. His antipathy to forms of art with a strong illustrative or anecdotal aspect must undoubtedly have made it difficult for Nash to form as large a group as he might have wanted, and there were arguments and negotiations, but by early 1933 the composition and name of the group had been decided upon. The members were Moore and Hepworth (sculptors), Nash, Nicholson, Armstrong, Bigge, Burra, Hodgkins, Wadsworth (painters), and Wells Coates and Colin Lucas (architects). Frances Hodgkins resigned soon after and was replaced by Tristram Hillier, another painter.

In April 1933, after several years' closure, the Mayor Gallery had reopened in new premises in Cork Street designed and equipped by Brian O'Rourke. During the twenties the gallery had shown work by younger modern painters,[14] and now the style and interests of the gallery appeared to coincide with the broad aims of Nash's group. In the gallery's opening exhibition Wadsworth, Nicholson, Nash, Armstrong, Hillier, Bigge and Moore were shown alongside continental modern artists, including Braque, Léger, Herbin, Baumeister, Arp and a Surrealist contingent which included Dali, Miró and Ernst. Francis Bacon made a first London appearance in the same exhibition. In providing English artists with the first opportunity for at least a decade to press their own claims in London alongside those of major continental artists, the occasion marked the effective end of the period of isolation which had lasted since the war. In seeking a permanent base for Unit One, Nash had made preliminary overtures to Tooth, Lefevre and Zwemmer, but it was the Mayor Gallery that was settled upon. Soon after its opening the gallery was acting as showroom and office for the members of Unit One.[15]

Nash was an adroit publicist. In a correspondence in *The Times* he and Professor Tonks of the Slade were ranged on opposite sides of a controversy about 'the new type of professionalism in the arts', which Tonks felt was gaining ground at the expense of the study of Nature. The moment was right and the subject apposite. A letter announcing the formation of Unit One appeared above Nash's signature in the correspondence columns of *The Times* on 12 June 1933.[16] He cited the Pre-Raphaelite Brotherhood as a precedent for 'the formation of a group of artists with common sympathies', which, despite its naivety, 'changed the course of English painting to an incalculable degree'. He continued, perhaps with more fervour than truth:

> There is nothing naive about Unit One. It is composed, mainly, of artists of established reputations who are not very concerned as to how other English artists paint or make sculpture or build. But they have this in common with the Pre-Raphaelites; in the sense that those artists were a brotherhood, these are a unit: a solid combination standing by each other and defending their beliefs ... Unit One may be said to stand for the expression of a truly contemporary spirit, for that thing which is recognised as peculiarly of today in painting, sculpture and architecture.

Nash referred to English art's 'one crippling weakness – the lack of structural purpose', its sense of 'immunity from the responsibility of design'; Unit One was to offset this and to occupy itself with 'Design ... considered as a structural pursuit; imagination explored apart from literature or metaphysics.'

Nash's biographer, with twenty-two years' hindsight, wrote: 'Surely no artist has ever made a statement which so completely misrepresented his own deepest imaginative pursuit.'[17] We should, however, give Nash credit for making an active identification with what he thought should be the case.

Nash followed his letter to *The Times* with an article in *The Listener* in which he explained the aims of the new movement in terms of an implicit rejection of the Bloomsbury-inspired interests which had prevailed during the twenties.

> ... During the last five years a very definite change has taken place. The ingenious and agreeable exercises in formalised naturalism, 'Post-Cézannism' and 'Derainism' have ceased to be of the first interest; they no longer hold our attention. A desire to find again some adventure in art seems more and more cogent to our sculptors and painters and, now, to our architects. This seems to suggest, as well as any explanation, the meaning of 'the contemporary spirit'. It is the adventure, the research, the pursuit in modern life ... But the pursuit is not vaguely directed. It seems today to have two definite objects for the mind and hand of the artist. First, the pursuit of form; the expression of the structural purpose in search of beauty in formal interaction and relations apart from representation. This is typified by abstract art. Second the pursuit of the soul, the attempt to trace the 'psyche' in its devious flight, a psychological research on the part of the artist parallel to the experiments of the great analysts. This is represented by the movement known as Surréalisme.[18]

Nash here provides the first explicit recognition in England of that polarization within the avant garde which had been a feature of modernist development on the continent since at least the later twenties, and which was soon to contribute to the disintegration of Unit One. For the moment, however, it seemed that allegiance to modernism as a whole would be sufficient to establish coherence within the small avant garde in England. 'We regarded ourselves as the spearhead, as it were, of contemporary European painting and sculpture which, at that time, had scarcely penetrated to England' (Tristram Hillier[19]). At the time, this collective self-image was sufficient to provide a loose principle of unity (albeit there were several passengers).

There was also, in the years 1931–3, an apparent compatibility in the styles of work of the principal artists involved: Nicholson, Wadsworth, Hepworth, Nash and Moore. The transition in Nicholson's work from Cubism to abstract art [125, 134] was, as we shall further examine, effected under the influence of artists like Miró whose works were vaguely biomorphic and thus compatible with Surrealism. In Wadsworth's non-figurative works of 1932–3 [126] the mechanistic imagery of his still lifes and compositions of the preceding years gave way to a repertoire of hard-

125. Ben Nicholson: *Still Life*, 1933–5. Oil and gesso on board, $19\frac{1}{2} \times 23\frac{1}{2}$ in.

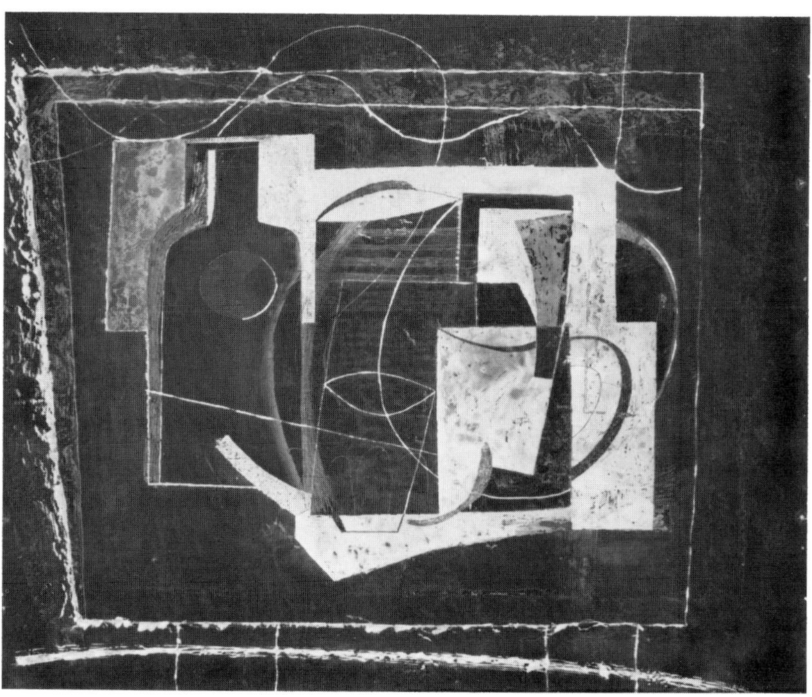

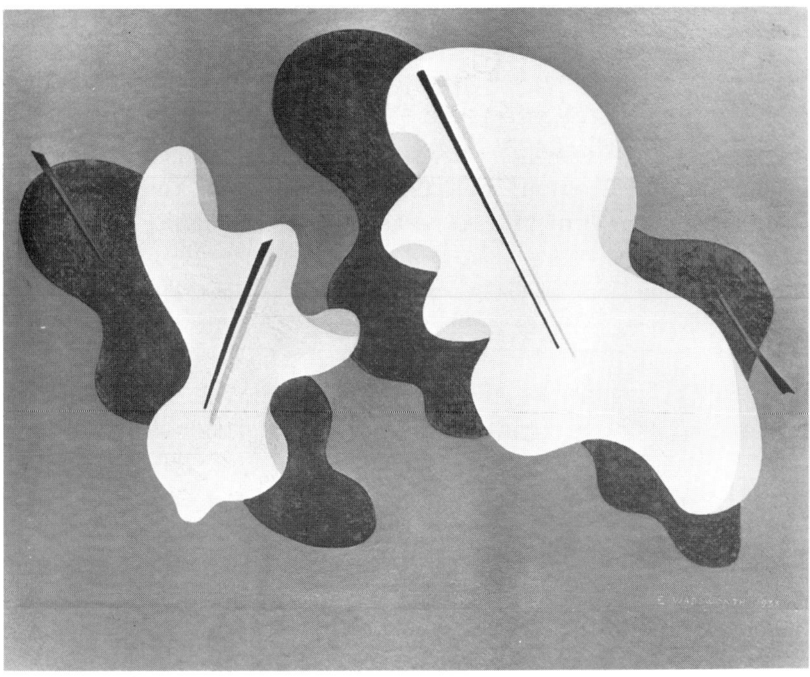

126. Edward Wadsworth: *Dux et Comes*, 1933. Tempera, $14\frac{3}{4} \times 20\frac{1}{2}$ in. (probably exhibited in the Unit One exhibition, Mayor Gallery, 1934)

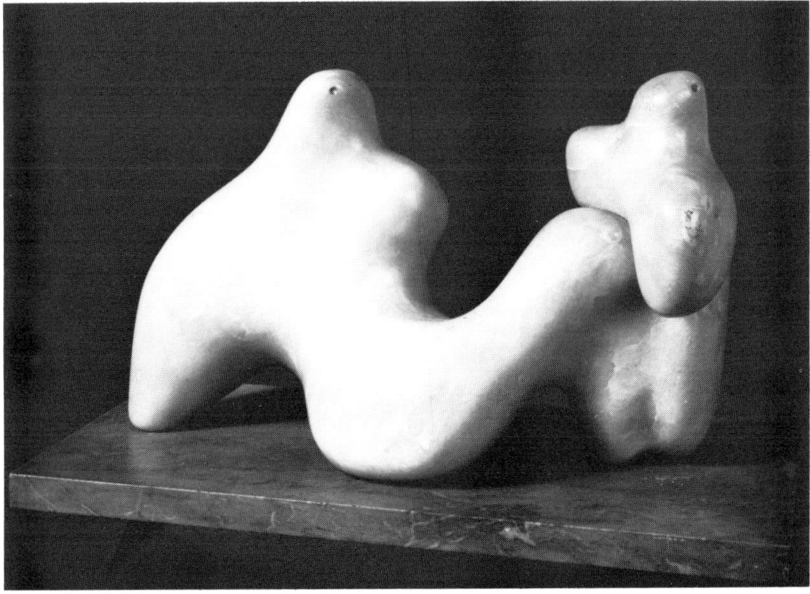

127. Barbara Hepworth: *Large and Small Form*, 1934. White alabaster, $10 \times 17\frac{1}{2} \times 9\frac{1}{2}$ in. (exhibited, as 'Birds and Rocks', in the Unit One exhibition, Mayor Gallery, 1934)

edged but fluid forms in dramatic relation which prefigured his return in 1934 to an interpretative figurative painting also compatible with certain aspects of Surrealism. Hepworth's characteristic sculptures of 1933–4, for all the self-conscious modernism of her published statements, were largely derived from 'mother-and-child' configurations and embodied the fluid and organic quality of natural forms [127]. Nash and Moore were the central figures in the identification of the new avant garde at this point, their work from 1931–3 apparently open to a range of influences wide enough to guarantee some point of contact with each of the other artists involved.

For Nash these years were not particularly productive so far as painting was concerned. Between December 1930 and July 1933, while he was living in Rye, much of his time was taken up with writing and designing. The majority of his surviving paintings from this period are watercolours and his principal completed project a series of illustrations for an edition of Sir Thomas Browne's *Urne Buriall and The Garden of Cyrus.*[20] His most persistent technical concern during this period was with the pictorial expression of 'structure' as perceived both in the man-made and in the natural world; but his formalities continued to be subverted by that abiding interest in the Metaphysical, in the imagery of dreaming, of memory and of afterlife, which was increasingly to determine the direction of his work.

128. Paul Nash: *Event on the Downs*, 1933. Oil on canvas, 20 × 24 in.

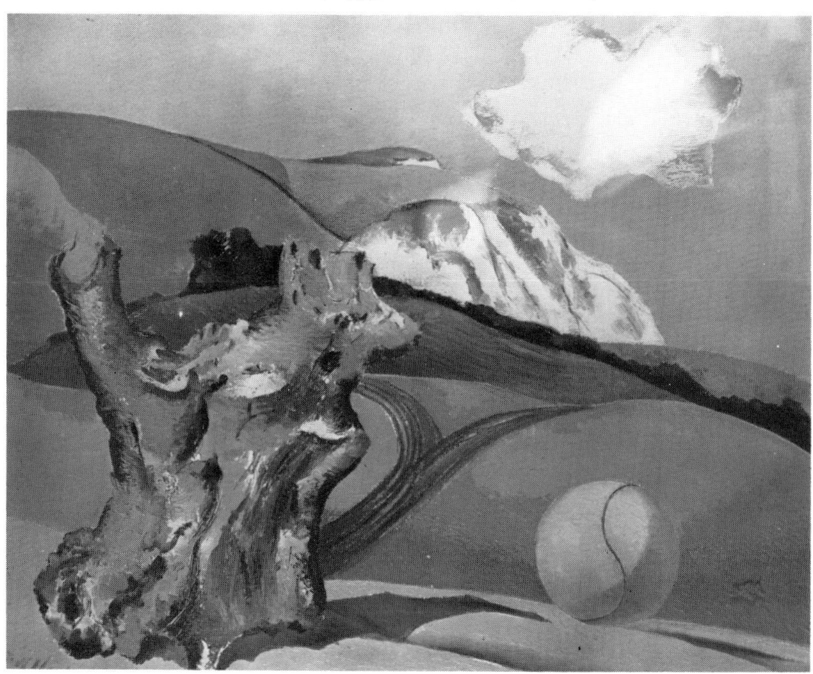

During the years in question his art thus displayed qualities compatible both with the concept of abstract pictorial form and with a view of the unconscious as an important source of imagery [128].

Moore's second one-man exhibition was held at the Leicester Galleries in April 1931. Epstein wrote an introduction for the catalogue in which he asserted that 'For the future of sculpture in England Henry Moore is vitally important.' Reactions to the show were clearly polarized. Moore was subjected to the standard accusations of Bolshevism and immorality and there were suggestions that a man who could make such things was not fit to have charge of students at the Royal College of Art. Pressure for Moore's dismissal was resisted until his contract ended in 1932, at which point he accepted an invitation to set up a new department of sculpture at Chelsea School of Art, where he was to continue teaching until the outbreak of war in 1939. In 1931 he acquired a cottage at Barfreston in Kent, where he worked during the vacations for the next three years. Despite the voices raised against his work, he was thus guaranteed a measure of continuing financial security and of varied facilities for working.[21]

Like Nash and Nicholson, Moore was by 1931 approaching the limits of development possible within the framework of a basically insular modern art. The works shown at his 1931 exhibition included a *Composition* carved early in the year in blue Hornton stone [129]. This sculpture marks an interest in the expressive distortion of the human form well beyond what was likely to be acceptable by anyone innocent of acquaintance with developments in European art since the end of the war. Specifically, Moore had been impressed by the potential for exploitation in sculpture of Picasso's more Surrealist paintings and drawings of the late twenties, for example *Figure by the Sea* of 7 April 1929 and the various drawings for a monument produced during 1928, at a time when Picasso himself was preoccupied with sculpture.[22] (During the thirties Moore was regularly to mine Picasso's work for suggestions for sculpture.) To many even of his sympathizers the *Composition* signified a departure not merely from a justifiable formal repertoire, but also from that comparatively decorous approach to the figure as subject which was characteristic of what I have called vernacular modernism. After all, the full impact of Surrealism was not to be felt in England for another five years.

From this point on, though he continued to draw upon the same basic range of formal types and of associations as had characterized his work of the 1920s, Moore's sculpture clearly expressed an awareness of those developments which had taken place in art in France since 1920. Much of what was of most interest to Moore was to be found in the art of painting, particularly that of Picasso, as instanced above, and of Miró, in whose

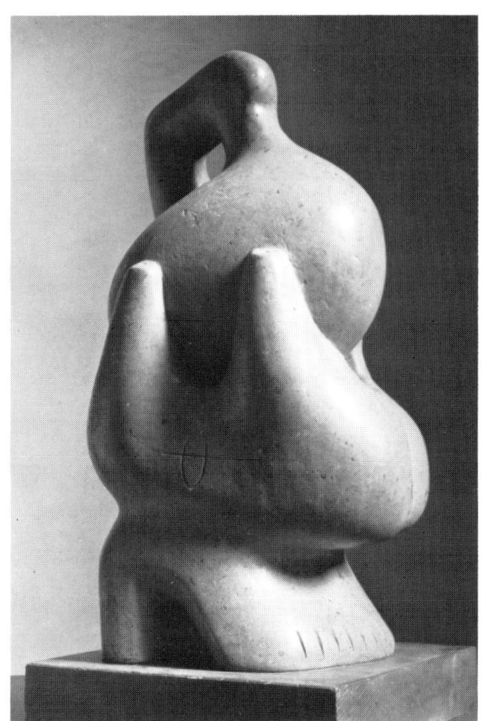

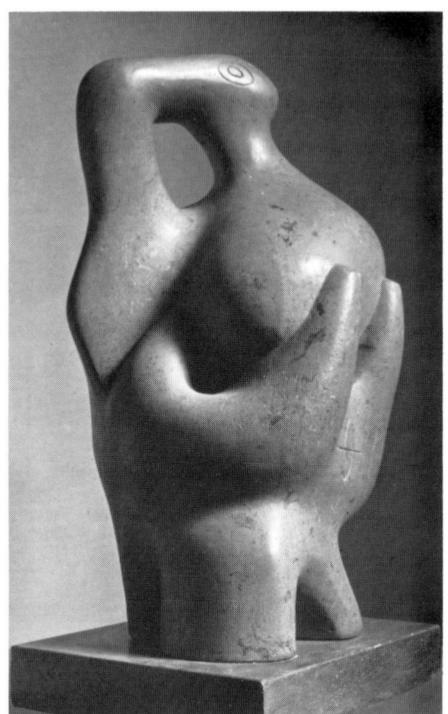

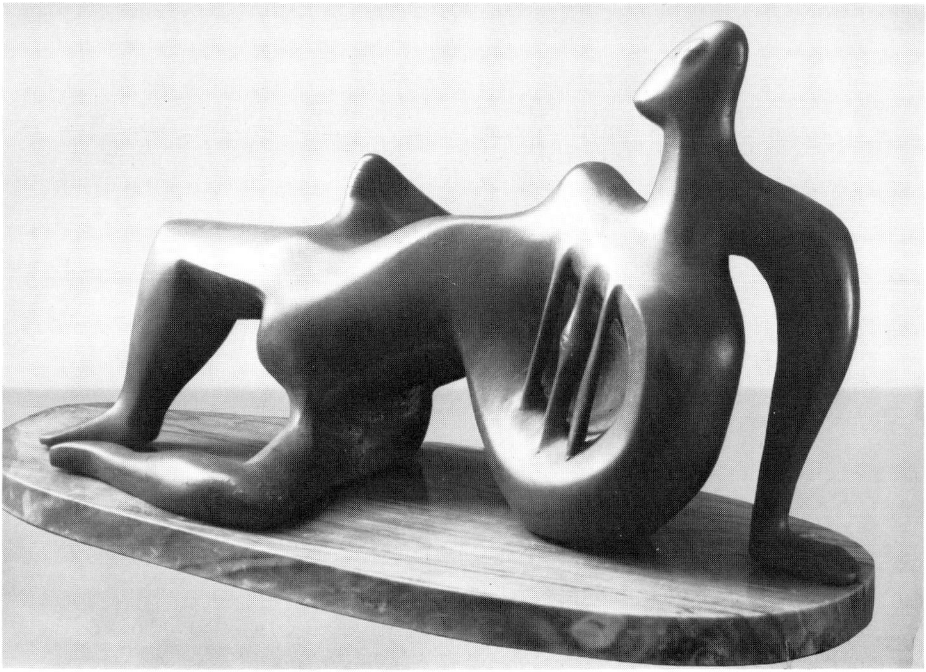

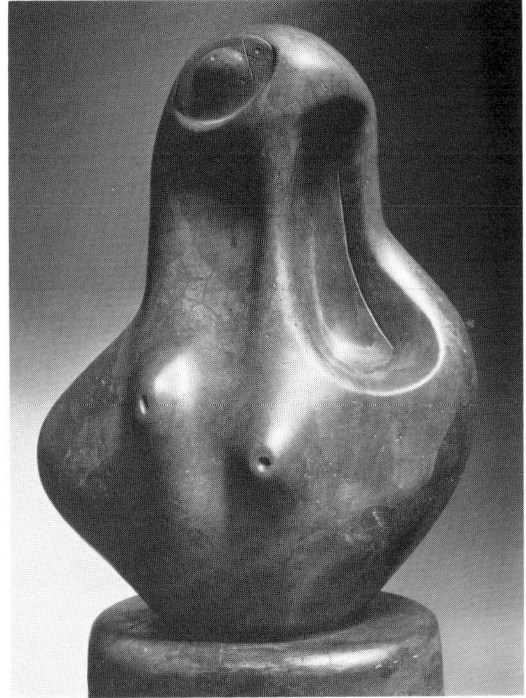

129 *(opposite, above)*. Henry Moore: *Composition*, 1931. Blue Hornton stone, height 19 in.

130 *(opposite, below)*. Henry Moore: *Reclining Figure*, 1931. Lead, height 17 in. (exhibited in the International Surrealist Exhibition, 1936)

131 *(right)*. Henry Moore: *Composition*, 1933. Concrete, height 23¼ in.

works of the 1920s highly abstracted shapes retain a strong sense of personality and of biological life. Brancusi had suggested the possibility of interest in what was thought of as a pure shape, for its own sake, and Arp's work had shown how much suggestion could be contained in a relatively simple shape so long as it could be seen as organic. The combination of these influences upon Moore, as he assimilated them, led to the investment of his compositions with the kind of psychological penumbra normally associated with figurative and evocative shapes in painting, where more is given in the way of context, and specifically associated with Miró's and Picasso's paintings of the 1920s. Extreme departures from literal anatomical accuracy, as in the lead *Reclining Figure* of 1931 [130], or extreme simplification, as in the *Composition* in carved concrete of 1933 [131], thus become the characteristic means of expression of that 'intense life of its own' which he sought for his sculpture. In a statement written for Unit One he defined his position in terms of a reconciliation of the 'abstract' and the 'human'.

All art is an abstraction to some degree (in sculpture the material alone forces one away from pure representation and towards abstraction).

Abstract qualities of design are essential to the value of the work, but to me of equal importance is the psychological, human element. If both abstract and human elements are welded together in a work, it must have a fuller, deeper meaning.

Of the minor artists involved in Unit One, Armstrong, Burra and Hillier seemed close to an illustrative form of Surrealism, while Bigge's work looked like a ham-fisted version of Wadsworth's. For Wadsworth, Nicholson, Hepworth, Nash and Moore, however, the moment at which proto-Surrealism and abstract art appeared as complementary aspects of a developing modernism was the point of maximum compatibility of aims and interests. It was as if these five artists had met, in 1931–3, at a crossroads from which different paths diverged, but where, for the moment, incipient abstraction and proto-Surrealism were stylistically indistinguishable and ideologically compatible. The time between the first discussions and the dissolution of Unit One – i.e. from the end of 1931 until late in 1934 – was the crucial period in the development of the second substantial phase of modernism in English art. During these three years the small avant garde sought in Unit One a common identity and a means of acting together.

The sense of theoretical coherence was enhanced by the participation of Herbert Read. On returning to London in April 1933, after two years as Professor of Fine Art in Edinburgh, Read was introduced into the group as a friend of Moore's (they had met five years earlier) and immediately became involved in their discussions.[23] He had already published several volumes of prose and verse and of literary criticism, including an essay on 'Psychoanalysis and the Critic' in 1925, and during the period in which Unit One was formed he published two influential books on art, *The Meaning of Art* in 1931[24] and *Art Now*[25] in 1933. His *Art and Industry* followed a year later. It would be hard to overestimate Read's importance as an advocate for European modernism and as a go-between in the relations between English artists and the continent. He had edited T. E. Hulme's *Speculations* in 1924,[26] and like the earlier supporter of radical modernism had looked to Germany as well as to France for his aesthetics. The fastidious formalist aesthetics of Fry had always differentiated against the expressionistic element in art; Read, by drawing attention to the symbolic features of art, to which he himself had been alerted by readings in the theory of psycho-analysis (and particularly the work of Carl Jung), and by stressing the function of form as a 'vehicle' for subjective content, was able to provide his contemporaries with a means of evaluating art which seemed capable of application equally to pure abstraction or to Surrealism.

Form, though it can be analysed into intellectual terms, balance, rhythm and harmony, is really intuitive in origin; it is not in the practice of artists an intellectual product. It is rather emotion directed and defined ... Frankly I do not know how we are to judge form except by the same instinct that creates it (*The Meaning of Art*).

The thing formed – and this is the key to the whole of the modern development in art – can be subjective as well as objective – can be the emergent sensibility of the artist himself (*Art Now*).

Read's stress on the essentially non-rational or pre-rational nature of the origins of art was an effective prescription for liberalism in response to the eccentricities of the modern artist (however thoroughly it may subsequently have been discredited by evidence that we 'learn' form from form). His approach to art was entirely appropriate to the expression of that congeries of interests which was gathered in Unit One in 1933, and from that year for the rest of the decade he was to be the principal spokesman, theorist and apologist for the avant garde, writing copiously, travelling frequently, and maintaining a wide range of contacts and correspondents in England and abroad.

It was Read who suggested that the members of Unit One should produce a book of statements and photographs,[27] and it was he who edited and introduced it. *Unit 1: The Modern Movement in English Architecture, Painting and Sculpture* was published by Cassells in April 1934. The volume was modelled in part on the cahiers of the Paris-based Abstraction-Création group (see the following chapter), with reproductions of artists' works accompanying their individual statements. Typography and layout were reminiscent of publications from the Bauhaus. Read's *Art and Industry*, published in the same year, was designed by Herbert Bayer, who had been a prominent figure at the Bauhaus, and was prefaced by acknowledgements to Walter Gropius, its founder and first director, 'who is the inspiration and leader of all who possess the new vision in industrial art', and to Laszlo Moholy-Nagy, an influential figure in Bauhaus teaching, 'who', according to Read, '... in his own book[28] gave me the necessary impetus to write this one'. With his interest in and knowledge of the European Modern Movement in architecture and design, Read no doubt helped to bridge the considerable gap between the architects of Unit One and the majority of the painters and sculptors.

Read's introduction to the *Unit 1* book emphasized that the need for modern artists to band together was to be seen in terms of the lack of a 'corporate existence in the state'. He made it clear that the Unit's aims were strategical and suggested that such an organization might come in the future to fulfil the functions of 'organization and formulation' previously fulfilled by the Academy. Unit One can thus be seen both as an attempt in the short term to alleviate current difficulties in exhibiting and selling modern work in England, and as a bid for cultural leadership and power for

Modernism in the long term. Modernism requires cosmopolitanism and the group was promoted by Read as the expression of a 'consciousness ... international in its extent ... a coherent movement of world-wide scope'.

As a means of securing publicity for modern art, Unit One was indeed remarkably successful. The group's activities were already well reported both in London and in the provincial press by the latter part of 1933,[29] and when the first (and only) London exhibition of the group's work opened at the Mayor Gallery in April 1934, coincident with the publication of the book, it was very widely reviewed. No show in London had aroused attention and controversy on such a scale since Fry's second Post-Impressionist exhibition in 1912, and it is important to recognize that where the earlier exhibition had been sensational largely by virtue of its presentation of recent continental art, the artists of Unit One were all English.

It is a measure both of the recent relaxation of hostility to modernism in art, and of the credibility which the participation of Nash and Read could secure, that a tour of the exhibition was arranged to follow its closure in London. Between May 1934 and April 1935 a representative selection (albeit one from which some of the artists had removed their more important or vulnerable work) was seen in Liverpool, Manchester, Hanley, Derby, Swansea and Belfast, on each occasion under the sponsorship of the local municipal authorities. At a time when public museums and galleries in London were highly conservative, it was not to be expected that the municipal galleries in the provinces would have done much to provide opportunities for exposure to modern styles of art. Unit One aroused controversy at each showing, was the subject of a sermon in Liverpool Cathedral,[30] of a heated correspondence in the *Liverpool Post and Mercury*,[31] and of a cartoon in *Ireland's Saturday Night*: 'That's not the Unit; that's the Limit.'[32] The reviewer for the *Irish News* noted that this was 'the first collection of modern art ever exhibited in Belfast'.[33]

Inevitably some reviewers were concerned to dismiss the exhibits and the activities of the exhibitors, with Nicholson's abstract compositions most often singled out for ridicule (by the time the show started its tour he was including at least one white relief in his contribution[34]), but on the whole the reception was surprisingly sympathetic and the characteristic response one of gratitude that an opportunity had been provided to see some 'modern art'. The level of debate was not high, however; certainly not as high as it had been during the earlier phase of avant-gardism. The early protagonists of modernism's second wave were not men who could match the considered eloquence of Fry or the vigorous rhetoric of Wyndham Lewis. Nor, following the pre-war rout of the conservatives, was there left one authoritative voice to speak in opposition. In reviewing the responses to the modernism of the early thirties one catches here and there the first evidence of that dulled compliance with the odd and alien which has come to typify the response to modern art of a public no longer confident of the power of common sense.

Among the more informed reviewers there were some who saw broad political implications in the group's avowed solidarity and detected '... a Soviet-like flavour, savouring of mass production, the collective man and the like'.[35] The reviewer of the *New English Weekly* was concerned to put such aspirations in their place: 'The new era cannot begin until the social structure is changed and it would be foolish to imagine that it can be changed by painting a couple of circles.'[36] Read himself expressed not dissimilar priorities in his introduction to the *Unit 1* book:

> Apart from the banal consideration that there are many types of art and no one standard of art, there is the very real fact that we live in an age of transition; an age in which the artist is to some extent divorced from his biological function. The artist, in the present unsatisfactory organisation of society, has no definite status or responsible function, and until the structure of society is mended, the position of the artist must be to some extent anomalous, and his practice inconsistent.

In fact, in so far as there was a genuine left wing in English art at the time, a faction attempting to render their production consistent with Socialist theory, it was represented not by Unit One but by a loose association largely composed of commercial artists and designers who gathered together to form the British section of the Artists International.[37] The initial idea had come from Clifford Rowe, a young illustrator for a London advertising agency who had spent eighteen months in Moscow in 1932–3. The formation of an English 'Artists International' was discussed in September 1933 at a meeting attended by Rowe, Pearl Binder (an illustrator whom he had met on his return journey from Russia), Mischa Black (an industrial designer), James Boswell and James Lucas (two illustrators and Communist Party members), James Fitton and James Holland. The association was named and formalized at a larger meeting soon after. Black was elected chairman and Betty Rea, a sculptor, secretary. Initial membership was thirty-two and besides those already named included an art historian, Francis Klingender, and an authority on folk music, A. L. Lloyd. A definition of aims was published in *International Literature* in April 1934.[38]

The recruiting base for the Artists International was the Central School of Art, where Fitton ran evening classes in lithography and where Boswell and Lucas were regular visitors. The facilities of the school were used for the production of pamphlets, cartoons, leaflets and posters in support of suitable causes. It is significant of the division of labour in English art practice that where Unit One recruited individuals who were primarily painters, sculptors or architects, the practical base of the membership of the Artists International lay rather in the so-called applied arts.

In October 1934 the AI staged an exhibition on 'The Social Theme'. Moore, Nash, Burra and Eric Gill were among those who gave their support. In line with a Leninist-cum-Stalinist view of the artist's function, the exhibition was essentially an exercise in propaganda. An accompanying manifesto made clear the gap that actually existed between a practice explicitly seeking consistency with historical materialism and the kind of vaguely 'socialistic' idealism which was seen as characteristic of Unit One.

> We must say plainly that the AI supports the Marxist position that the character of all art is the outcome of the character of the mode of material production of the period. Today, when the capitalist system and the socialists are fighting for world survival, we feel that the place of the artist is at the side of the working classes. In this class struggle, we use our experience as an expression and as a weapon making our first steps towards a new socialist art.[39]

We shall have cause to return to the Artists International in a subsequent chapter. Meanwhile, that such activities as those of the members of Unit One should have been capable of assimilation in the popular imagination into some vague picture of leftist activity can be seen as symptomatic of a polarization in English – and indeed European – politics during the early thirties, and of a general, if vague, identification of modern design and architecture with Socialism, if not with Bolshevism. The Labour Party had been destroyed as an effective independent force in Parliament when it fell in September 1931. England was ruled by a National Government for the rest of the 1930s, and during a period which saw massive unemployment, the formation of the British Union of Fascists (1932) and the establishment of Hitler as Chancellor of Germany (1933), 'leftism' came to be loosely associated with a wide range of attitudes or activities more easily and accurately characterized in terms of what they appeared to oppose than of what they proposed. A columnist in the *Daily Express*, writing of the Unit One exhibition in London as 'the most important spring art show', described Nicholson as the 'furthest left of the group',[40] and appears to have derived this judgement simply from the fact that Nicholson's work was by 1934 the most rigorously abstract, and thus the least obviously 'traditional', of all the exhibitors'.

The association of abstract art with the political left in particular, or with a 'changed way of life' in general, is of some broad historical interest. The mainstream of theory and criticism of art is now conditioned by the assumption that abstract art is defensible. At the outset of the 1930s in England no such assumption could be made, despite the claims which members of the earlier pre-war avant garde might have felt that they had established on the basis of their own non-figurative work.[41] We should break off here from consideration of Unit One to examine the development of abstract art in England during the 1930s in relation to the complex background of ideas, largely deriving from the European Modern Movement, from which that development is inseparable. Nicholson's work and activities are central to the promotion of abstract art in England during this period, and will therefore be considered in some detail.

10

'ABSTRACT' AND 'CONSTRUCTIVE' ART

There had been no Seven & Five exhibition in 1930, and the 1931 exhibition (the first of four to be held at the Leicester Galleries) had represented the high point of development of that 'poetic naturalism' which had been pursued among the better painters of the society during the twenties. Ben and Winifred Nicholson showed still lifes and landscapes from Cornwall and Cumberland and there was a substantial showing of work by Christopher Wood. As we have noted, the naturalistic style was to be continued and modified within the society during the early 1930s, but it had become clear by 1932 that Nicholson's work was beginning to develop in a different direction. In the Seven & Five exhibition in February of that year it must have been evident that there had been a reorientation. By this time Nicholson's interests and ambitions had become closer to those of Moore and Hepworth than of any of the longer-standing members of the Seven & Five.

What principally distinguished Nicholson from the other English painters of his generation at this time was still his continuing interest in and understanding of Cubist painting. Others like Nash and Wadsworth had assimilated aspects of Cubist style in such a manner as permanently to modify their work, but no other English painter exploited the technical aspects of Braque's and Picasso's work to the extent that Nicholson did. In the summer of 1932 Nicholson and Hepworth went together to Dieppe, where Braque was working. In November they exhibited together at Tooth's, by which time their work was evidently highly compatible. The next Easter they travelled to Avignon and Saint-Rémy. They returned via Paris and visited the studios of Arp and Brancusi. On the way back they visited Picasso at his studio in Boisgeloup.

I suggested earlier that an appreciation of Cubism underlies all Nicholson's work after 1924, but it should be stressed as a reservation to this that his work of the later twenties did not have Cubism as the principal dynamic. Now, however, what Nicholson saw in France seems to have confirmed him in his commitment to Cubism as the sine qua non for the development of an international modern art. Among the works he showed in the joint exhibition were several which bore witness to his ability to use a late-Cubist picture space and a late-Cubist repertoire of forms in paintings which nevertheless looked neither provincial nor slavishly derivative. *Au Chat Botté* [132], a comparatively large work of 1932, was painted on canvas following the visit to Dieppe. In the repertoire and disposition of forms it relates clearly to certain late-Cubist still lifes by Picasso (compare his *Still Life with Classical Head* of 1925), though in the articulation of the relationship between illusionistic space and painted surface it is closer to the earlier work of Braque. The quality of 'atmosphere', however – the degree to which the picture is organized as a means to embody an autobiographical

132. Ben Nicholson: *Au Chat Botté*, 1932. Oil and pencil on canvas, $36\frac{1}{4} \times 48$ in.

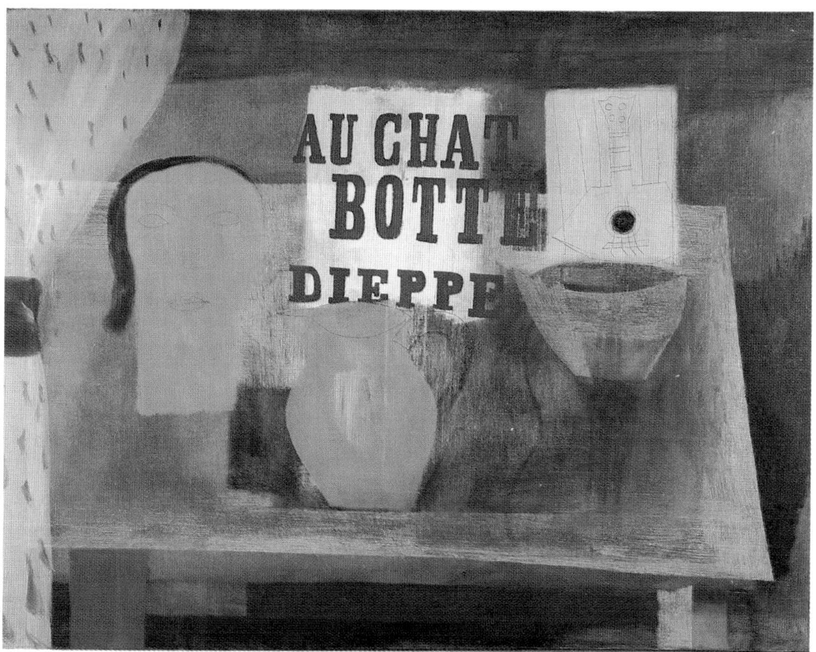

mood – distinguishes it from more orthodox Cubist paintings from which such 'narrative' elements were normally excluded.[1] (Indeed, in terms of a concept of 'orthodox' Cubist painting, they might be seen as anomalous.) It is a much more capable and more sophisticated painting than many to which contemporary English critics were inclined to defer because they were painted by Frenchmen. (The Bloomsbury writers had had a virtual monopoly on interpreting Cubism, though on the whole they misunderstood it. From this position they felt competent to put down artists such as Nicholson as imitators.)

In other works of the same and the subsequent year Nicholson experimented with the implications of a Cubist vocabulary and organization in compositions on boards prepared with a substantial gesso ground. In these paintings the Cubist tendency to codify subject-matter – i.e. to evoke the presence of whole objects or surfaces by the use of vivid fragments of colour or texture, significant details or snatches of lettering – is made compatible with a tendency, which had been encouraged in Nicholson by his response to Wallis's paintings, to emphasize the physical aspects of the medium and the factive aspects of the working procedure. In such paintings as *Auberge de la Sole Dieppoise* of 1932 or *Guitar* of 1933 [133] (both Tate Gallery) the transformation of substantial object (the piece of board) into sophisticated picture is achieved artfully and in full recognition of the resources of expression which Cubism made available to painting, but in Nicholson's work, unlike that of other late-comers to Cubism, the support – the piece of board or whatever – retains its appearance of substantiality to the end. In so far as mimesis is established in these pictures it is produced not by the creation of a consistent illusion but as a function of the spectator's competence in constituting whole scenes from details and fragments.

133. (*left*) Ben Nicholson:
Guitar, 1933.
Oil and gesso on board,
$34\frac{1}{2} \times 9\frac{1}{2}$ in.

134. (*right*) Ben Nicholson:
Composition in Black and White, 1933.
Oil on board, 45 × 22 in.

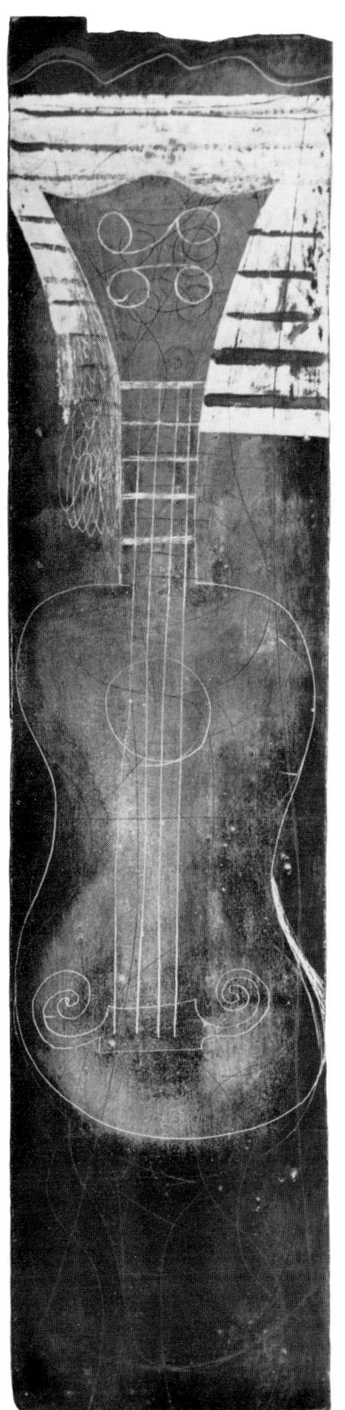

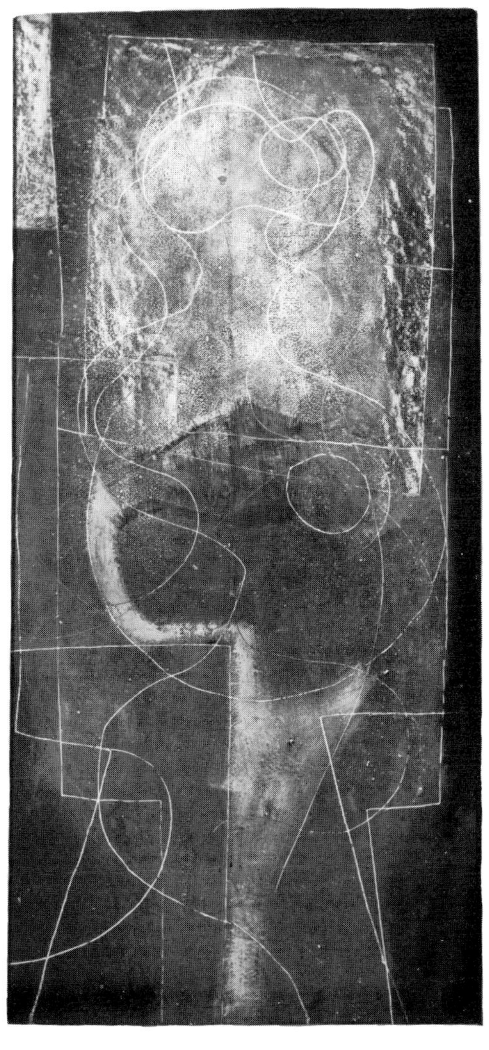

1932 was a particularly fruitful year for Nicholson, and the beginning of a period of rapid development in his art. In the later part of 1933 he returned to France, where he renewed and extended his contacts with European artists. It is not possible reliably to demarcate at all points between the art he and Hepworth saw and the artists they visited in 1932 and 1933 respectively:[2] Jean Hélion and the sculptor Giacometti were probably among those visited in 1933; it may also have been then that they first met Naum Gabo, who arrived in Paris from Berlin in 1932; and Nicholson first met Mondrian in Paris in 1933, though he did not visit his studio for the first time until the next year. The evidence of Nicholson's art, however, is that while the earlier visit confirmed him in his involvement with Cubism, he returned a year later justifiably confident of his practice in relation to that stage of modernism and eager to come to terms with subsequent developments. There is a rapid transition in his work of 1933 towards a form of abstract painting plainly influenced by developments in Paris in the later twenties. It is evident that he admired what he saw of the work of Miró, Arp and Calder. In particular he responded to those works of Miró of *c.* 1927 in which vivid and evocative abstract forms are freely disposed on washed grounds of soft, opaque colour. Of a painting by Miró seen in Paris at this time he wrote later, 'The first *free* painting that I saw, and it made a deep impression ...'[3] Technically the freedom was a freedom from means of organization of pictorial space dependent either upon a single-viewpoint perspective or on the 'shallow-box' space of Synthetic Cubism, which had come to replace it in those aspects of orthodox modernist practice which were not yet transformed by the effects of Surrealism [134].[4]

Arp had been a member of the Dada group in Zürich during the First World War, and was involved with the Surrealists during the twenties. His work was consistently abstract (or at least, when it was representational it was representational as it were by accident), though in so far as the shapes he formed in paintings, reliefs and sculptures were generally fluid and rounded (what T. E. Hulme would have called 'vital'), they were consistently suggestive of some form of organic 'life'. It is clear that Hepworth responded strongly to Arp's work, which immediately made itself felt as a strong influence in her own, and Nicholson must have been encouraged by her enthusiasm, if by nothing else, to consider the expressive potential of an art formed according to strategies in which traditional types of compositional rationality appeared to play little part.

Alexander Calder, though an American, had been working in Paris intermittently since 1926, and had fallen under the influence of Mondrian in 1930.[5] He had shown abstract wire sculptures in a one-man exhibition at the Galerie Percier in April 1931, and during the next year or two made a series of mobile sculptures which look like moving versions of Miró's paintings. Some of these were shown at the same gallery in 1932, when Nicholson probably saw them.

In assimilating these various influences, Nicholson experimented both with abstract shapes independent of the decorative sources which had provided motifs for his earlier experiments in abstract composition, and with bright saturated colours, particularly blues and reds, used independently of the suggestion of objects having those colours as properties. His typical works of 1933 (which, in their informality and occasionally robust capriciousness, are generally untypical of his output as a whole) show him in transition from a means of composition based on the shallow 'boxed' space of a late-Cubist still life, to a form of organization of pictorial space predicated on the idea that the 'reality' of the picture is a measure of the extent to which that space, or the forms within it in so far as they are seen as occupying a space, are left unspecific in their references to the world outside the picture. A significant feature of the development of the ideology of modern art since the later nineteenth century has been the entrenchment of the notion that the pursuit of autonomy for 'pictorial reality' is the pursuit of an important freedom. Recollecting this period years later Nicholson wrote, 'The particular value to me of the "Miró, Calder, Arp" contribution of the 1920s but exh. in Paris in the 1930s was a new *freedom*. Miró – freedom of ptg.; Calder – of mobiles; Arp – of free sculptural forms on a base: in fact a kind of liberation.'[6] (One might ask, 'Liberation for whom from what?')

The vaunting of principles of freedom in art was seen as important in the 1930s in a more than technical sense. In Russia the leadership had turned against abstract and experimental art during the early twenties. Of the radicals of the revolutionary years the majority of those who were not prepared to work as designers and teachers were exiles by 1925, Naum Gabo and his brother Antoine Pevsner among them. In Germany the Nazis were violently opposed to modernist styles, which they saw as significant of Bolshevism and as inimical to German nationalism. The Bauhaus became the object of persistent harassment and was finally closed by the police in March 1933. Paris had long been a gathering-place for modernist artists from many countries, and in the early thirties their ranks were swelled by those escaping from hostile régimes. Inevitably there were factions and divisions which reflected the divergence of individual ambitions, but on the principle of the need to defend a loose postulate of internationalism and modernism in art and architecture they were united. Within this avant garde it was generally held as an unquestionable assumption that, in the words of Herbert Read, '. . . the artist always has loyalties that transcend the political divisions of the society in which he lives'.[7]

In February 1931 the Association Abstraction-Création was founded in Paris 'pour l'organisation des manifestations d'art non figuratif' by a committee which included Arp, Gleizes, Hélion, Herbin, Kupka and Vantongerloo.[8] Over forty artists were represented in 1932 in the first of five annual publications; these included Arp, Calder, Robert Delaunay, Gabo, Hélion, Moholy-Nagy, Mondrian, Pevsner, Schwitters, Sophie Tauber-Arp, Van Doesburg, Vantongerloo and Wadsworth. At the invitation of Hélion, Nicholson and Hepworth joined the association in 1933 and both contributed to a 'permanent' exhibition which opened in Paris on 22 December of that year. Works by both were illustrated in the publications of 1933 and 1934. By 1935 the association had 416 'members or friends' of whom 209 came from Paris, 68 from Switzerland, 33 from America and 11 from Britain.[9] The association's avowed intention was that only artists whose entire output was abstract should be admitted as members. Few of those included actually fulfilled that requirement (how, indeed, might it actually be fulfilled?), but membership no doubt encouraged many, Nicholson and Hepworth among them, to see the practice of abstract art as an activity which might somehow be ideologically continuous with certain other commitments held in common among the members of a loose international community defined as such by shared commitment to the possibility of a non-figurative art. The cahier of 1933 appeared under the following editorial statement:

> Le Cahier 'Abstraction-Création' No. 2 parait au moment où, sous toutes les formes, sur tous les plans, dans quelques pays d'avantage qu'ailleurs, mais partout, la pensée libre est férocement combattue . . . Nous plaçons ce cahier No. 2 sous le signe d'une opposition totale à toute oppression, de quelqu'ordre qu'elle soit.[10]

The statements which Nicholson and Hepworth wrote for the *Unit 1* publication in 1934 reflected a Modernist idealism, a new-found conviction that the practice of abstract art was a function of an attitude to life characterized in terms of the pursuit of a universal 'right idea'.

> I feel that the conception itself, the quality of thought that is embodied must be abstract – an impersonal vision, individualised in the particular medium (Hepworth).
> What we are all searching for is the understanding and realisation of infinity – an idea which is complete, with no beginning and no end and therefore giving to all things for all time (Nicholson).

Nicholson also quoted the scientist Eddington in support of his own view of the universality of abstract art:

... not only the laws of nature, but space and time, and the material universe itself, are constructions of the human mind ... to an altogether unexpected extent the universe we live in is the creation of our minds. The nature of it is outside scientific investigation. If we are to know anything about that nature it must be through something like religious experience.

The implicit association which Nicholson here makes between a move into abstraction in art and a quasi-religious experience of nature is consistent with that tendency towards 'theosophical' idealism in modernist art which can be traced back, via the pseudo-philosophical self-justifications of Mondrian or Kandinsky or the romantic 'transcendental socialism' of the Bauhaus in its early days at Weimar, to the Symbolist movements in late-nineteenth-century France, and beyond. (The vaunted pursuit of 'innocence' and 'sincerity' among the painters of the Seven & Five during the 1920s can be accommodated within the margins of this development.)

The association of this broad historical tendency with the proclamation of a form of political freedom is the occasion of an abiding controversy which is reflected within the history of art. Two contrastive positions can be summarized thus: (1) the intuitions of the artist are by their very nature such as should be distributed to the point where they determine intellectual and social life; the artist is therefore propitiously an agent of historical change: 'A true, absolute order in human society could only be achieved if mankind were willing to base this order on lasting values. Obviously, then, the artistic factor would have to be accepted in every respect as the decisive one' (Kasimir Malevich).[11] This was the position to which Nicholson and Hepworth appeared to have gravitated by 1934. (2) Political and social existence determines the production of art or, at the very least, determines the meaning it can sustain at any given moment in history. In saying, in his introduction to *Unit 1*, that the position of the artist 'must be to some extent anomalous and his practice inconsistent' in an 'age of transition' and as the result of 'an unsatisfactory organisation of society', Herbert Read was characterizing the artist as one whose practice is determined by history and who, in his terms, is thus presumably not to be seen as an agent of historical change; though if this was his view it was not one he upheld with any consistency. Given a concept of the practice of art as inevitably 'inconsistent', it was perhaps easier for Read to keep an 'open mind' in his view upon contemporary developments than it was for such as Nicholson, who seems to have felt in the mid-thirties that, for those with a glimpse of the 'right idea', history was there for the making. We shall return later to discussion of the issues involved.

Nicholson was back in Paris by December 1933,[12] and it was then that he made his first work in relief [135]. It came about as the result of an unplanned if overdetermined incident, when a chip fell out of a gesso ground.[13] Nicholson exploited the accident and found himself carving in relief. A line now became not something drawn to suggest space or outline on the surface of a picture, but the meeting of two actual planes in real space. The literal depth of the surface served to keep the abstract image substantial.

During the next three months Nicholson produced a considerable number of abstract reliefs, painted in muted tones of brown and grey which emphasize the degree to which their development was coherent with an art largely determined by Cubism; on the other hand the reduction of his formal

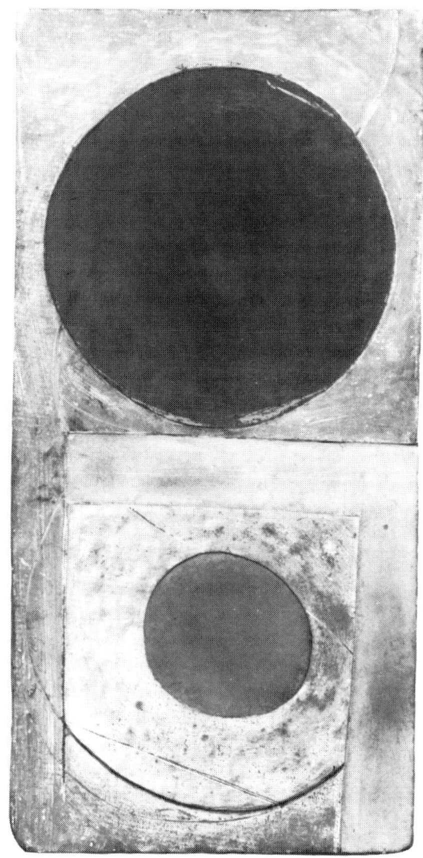

135. Ben Nicholson: *December 1933 (First Abstract Relief)*, 1933. Oil on board, $21\frac{1}{2} \times 10$ in. (exhibited, as 'Two Circles', in the Unit One exhibition, Mayor Gallery, 1934)

repertoire to circles and right-angles signifies a move in the direction of the more universalist varieties of abstract art. In his Cubist works of 1912–13, Braque had organized his compositions basically in terms of planes upon which specific objects or surfaces could be evoked and located in more or less specific positions by the application of detail or texture. The notion that the shapes of Nicholson's reliefs are to be seen as specific positions of continuous planes is consistent on the one hand with the intuition of this particular quality in Braque's work, and on the other with theoretical justifications of the more recent work of Mondrian, whom Nicholson was to visit for the first time in 1934[14] and whose rigorously abstract compositions were similarly proposed as specific and physical reflections of an ideal and 'metaphysical' resolution.

Nicholson's early reliefs have an insistently hand-made quality: lines and circles are drawn freehand and different surfaces are distinguished by different textures and by the application of different colours. By the time of

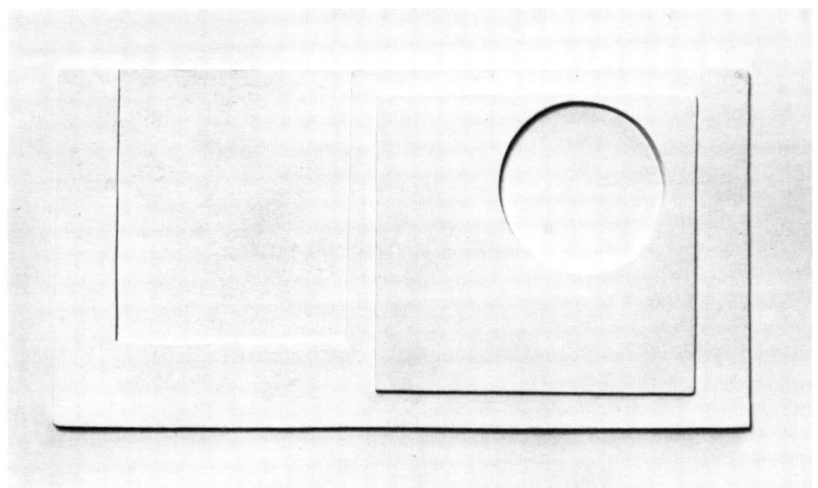

136. Ben Nicholson: *White Relief*, 1934. Oil on carved wood, $13\frac{3}{4} \times 24$ in.

the Seven & Five show of March 1934, however, he had begun to paint his reliefs an even white [136]. (Reviewing his *2 Circles*, exhibited on that occasion, the author of a notice in *The Studio* accused Nicholson of the kind of wilful extremism usually at that time considered the prerogative of the continental artist.) By the middle of the year he was using a ruler for the lines, and compasses for the circles of the majority of his reliefs.

In the wake of the Purism of the 1920s, no modern artist with international interests could have painted an even area of white, where that white was not to be interpreted as the local colour of some depicted object or surface, without some sense of the ideological context and implications of his action. Nicholson's decision to paint his reliefs white is nevertheless not to be seen simply as a means of establishing participation in the Modern Movement in design and architecture; one should perhaps rather interpret it in terms of an intuitive preference for and pursuit of an extreme clarity, where such clarity is associated, perhaps as a function of his involvement with the technology of representational painting, with qualities of light and atmosphere in particular places and at particular times.[15] The white reliefs are surely to be considered as much in relation to a tendency to topicalize as 'artistic' such memories as the snow and sunlight in the Ticino in the early twenties, or the light reflected from whitewashed cottages in St Ives in 1928, or the white-painted studios of Arp and Brancusi in 1932–3, as to the Modern Movement's stylistic preference for white buildings with slab-like walls. That is to say that the whiteness of the white reliefs should be perhaps taken as the distillation of a particular set of interests in the apperceptive world of painting, rather than as a reflection of an aspect of the history of design. On the other hand, of course, it should be said that this 'contrast' is a very tenuous one. The two halves of the pair, that is to say, are brought together in an aesthetics which entails belief in the universality of certain kinds of distinction, as the aesthetics of the Modern Movement certainly did. To be a consenting participant in that movement was inevitably to see white as somehow 'pure', and to see the 'harmonies' of a simple geometry as somehow reflecting a possible social harmony. As Nicholson progressively eliminated detail and emphasized the geometrical nature of his compositions, it was inevitable that his work should have been seen as compatible with the work of modern architects and designers as well as with the work of continental artists such as those who were fellow-members of the Association Abstraction-Création.

Between the spring of 1934 and the outbreak of war in 1939, while he continued to make figurative drawings and still-life paintings in a formalized Cubist style [125], Nicholson produced a considerable number of white reliefs, varying in size from a few square inches to around twenty square feet. (The Tate Gallery's relief of 1935 is typical of the larger examples [137].) In September 1935 Nicholson exhibited white reliefs at the Lefevre Gallery in what seems likely to have been the most internally coherent one-man exhibition by any modern British artist in the period between the wars. As a single and consistent body of work the white reliefs may be seen as the major contribution by an English artist to the European Modern Movement in the first half of the twentieth century.

With his abstract works of the mid-1930s, Nicholson thus established a position at the forefront of the avant garde in English painting, a position to

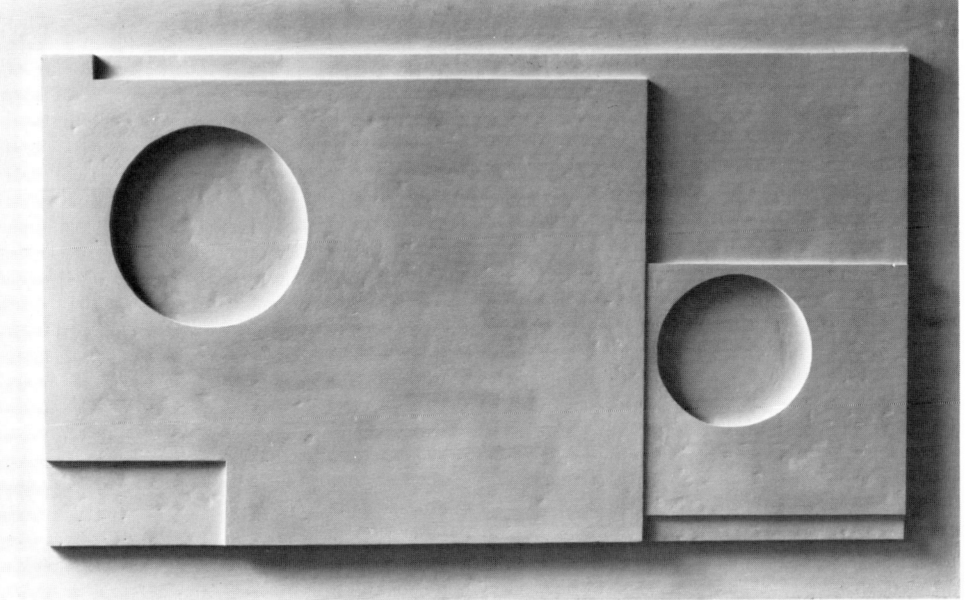

137. Ben Nicholson: *White Relief*, 1935. Oil on carved wood, 40 × $65\frac{1}{2}$ in.

which Nash might have seemed entitled a couple of years earlier. At this point the compatibility between Nicholson's work and Barbara Hepworth's was at its most marked, and the presentation of just such a united front as Unit One was in practice unable to maintain must have strengthened the impact of the work of each.

Since at least the beginning of 1932 the two artists had been working in close concert, and by the end of that year Nicholson was sharing the studio in Hampstead where Hepworth had worked since early in 1928. The presence of carver's tools and materials no doubt encouraged Nicholson in the development of his work into actual relief, while his example in turn seems to have provided Hepworth with the means to liberation from the domination of Moore's work, with which her own had so often up to then invited a comparison by which it was unlikely to gain. Of her first exposure to Nicholson's work in March 1930, she wrote later: 'The experience helped to release all my energies for an exploration of free sculptural form.'[16] The world which she conjured up in her statement in *Unit 1* was plainly one where Nicholson had had a hand in the interior decoration:

> Objects that we place near to each other, in their different aspects and relationships create new experience. A scarlet circle on the wall, a slender white bottle on a shelf near it, a bright blue box and lovely-shaped fishing floats . . .

In the joint exhibition which Nicholson and Hepworth held at Tooth's in 1932, Hepworth exhibited a *Pierced Form* carved in pink alabaster late in the previous year [138]. It was then given the title *Abstraction*, and in terms

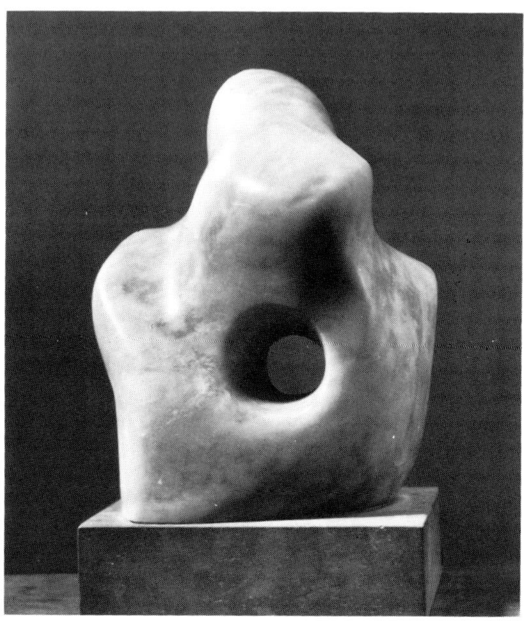

138. Barbara Hepworth: *Pierced Form*, 1931. Pink alabaster, height 10 in. (destroyed)

of the main run of English sculpture at the time must indeed have seemed like one, if only because the penetration of the stone where there was no evident suggestion of limbs must have seemed then to rob it of all those figurative associations with the human torso which are perhaps now easier to make. Although only ten inches high, the work was obviously an important one for Hepworth. She took a photo of it with her to show Picasso and Brancusi in March 1932 as evidence of her most 'experimental' work (it was probably the *Abstraction (alabaster)* listed in the catalogue of the 1933 Seven & Five Society exhibition), and she used two views of it to accompany her statement in the second *Abstraction-Création* cahier in the same year. In the statement itself she wrote of art in terms of a sense of its affinity with music, which is 'abstract art by definition', and concluded with the exhortation: 'In all the arts let us become pure spirits, not only liberators but necessarily and before all: liberated.' The nature of this liberation is further suggested elsewhere in the statement in a form which might be a simplified paraphrase of the quote from Eddington which Nicholson was to use in *Unit 1*: 'There is no reality except in ideas.' The freedom canvassed here, as in Nicholson's contemporary statements, is an impossible 'freedom' from the contingencies of the material world.

In fact, the majority of Hepworth's works of 1932–4 can be characterized either as variations on the vernacular modernist style of the later twenties (e.g. the *Kneeling Figure* in rosewood of 1932) or as explorations of her response to the particular works she saw in France in 1932 and 1933 and to modern European sculpture in general. The influence of Arp appears to have had a strong determining effect on the latter group of works, in which a more-or-less explicit mother-and-child theme prevails (e.g. *Mother and Child* of 1933 and 1934, and *Large and Small Form* of 1934 [127]). She later recalled the impression which her visit to Arp's studio had made and which she had considered as she and Nicholson travelled away in the train through the French countryside:

> ... seeing Jean Arp's work for the first time freed me of many inhibitions and this helped me to see the figure in landscape with new eyes ... thinking of the way Arp had fused landscape with the human form in so extraordinary a manner ... I began to imagine the earth rising and becoming human.[17]

If we are right about the extent to which memory of landscape and involvement in the making of sculpture were assimilated under an expanded concept of 'sculpture' during the 1920s, and given Hepworth's inclination to treat sculpture as essentially expressive of relationship, it is easy to see why Arp's works should have made so powerful an impression upon her if this was how she interpreted them.

In October 1934 triplets were born to Barbara Hepworth and Ben Nicholson. Her first work when she resumed in November, the *Two Forms with Sphere* [139], was distinctively different from her previous work, in that

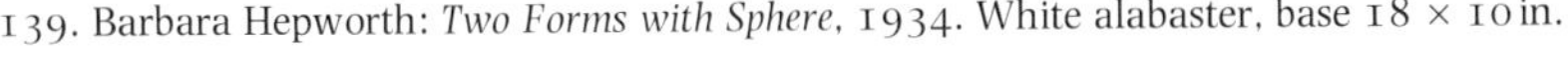

139. Barbara Hepworth: *Two Forms with Sphere*, 1934. White alabaster, base 18 × 10 in.

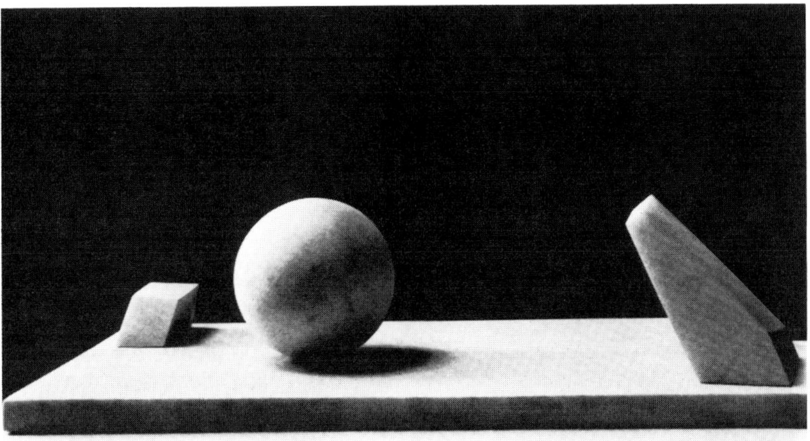

the forms were separated and were purged of those organic or 'biomorphic' features which had characterized the works of the previous two years. On the other hand, the work was consistent, in the degree of geometric simplification, with the concept of a wholly abstract sculpture which her *Abstraction-Création* statement had evoked. What remained of Arp's influence was the device of relating various forms on a flat surface, though this was mediated by a recent acquaintance with works by Giacometti (e.g. his carved wooden *Project for a Piazza* of 1930–31) in which more simply geometric forms were similarly deployed. Giacometti's works of the twenties and early thirties have been an important source of formal and technical ideas for English sculptors from the time they were made until the very recent past. For Hepworth, however, the predominant example became that of Brancusi, by whose studio she, like so many other visitors, had been deeply impressed. She later recalled 'the inspiration of the dedicated workshop'.[18] Where Moore's verdict was in the end that Brancusi, for all the importance of his contribution, had refined a single shape (the egg) 'to a degree almost too precious',[19] Hepworth seems to have taken 'the humanism, which seemed implicit to all the forms' she saw in Brancusi's studio, as a guarantee of the possibility of imputing a kind of 'universal' content to abstract and geometric shapes in sculpture.

The distinguishing feature of Hepworth's statements in *Abstraction-Création* and in *Unit 1* and, by implication from their observable characteristics, of her works after 1934, is that the implicit claims made in the twenties for the universality of 'sculpture' as a form of experience have been annexed to explicit claims made for the universality of 'abstract art' as a form of experience. In Hepworth's works of the mid-thirties, the more avant-garde features of English sculpture of the twenties were thus assimilated into the prevailing ideology of the European Modern Movement. It was a strange achievement, which serves perhaps to remind us how deep were the roots of the latter in the historical valuation of the (inevitably vernacular) Arts and Crafts movement as a source of progressive ideas.

For all the invocation of number in her *Abstraction-Création* statement, the forms of Hepworth's sculptures of the thirties are palpably hand-made and are in fact rarely subject to exhaustive description by reference to simple geometric forms. They are always, as it were, highly particularized. (The *Discs in Echelon* of 1935 [140], for instance, though they may look like perfect discs when seen side-on, are tear-shaped in vertical section.) In so far as they can be seen as representations however (and all art can come to be seen somehow as representation), Hepworth's abstract sculptures of the later thirties are typically proposed as features of a world conceived in terms of the idealization and the generalization of emotion and relationship:

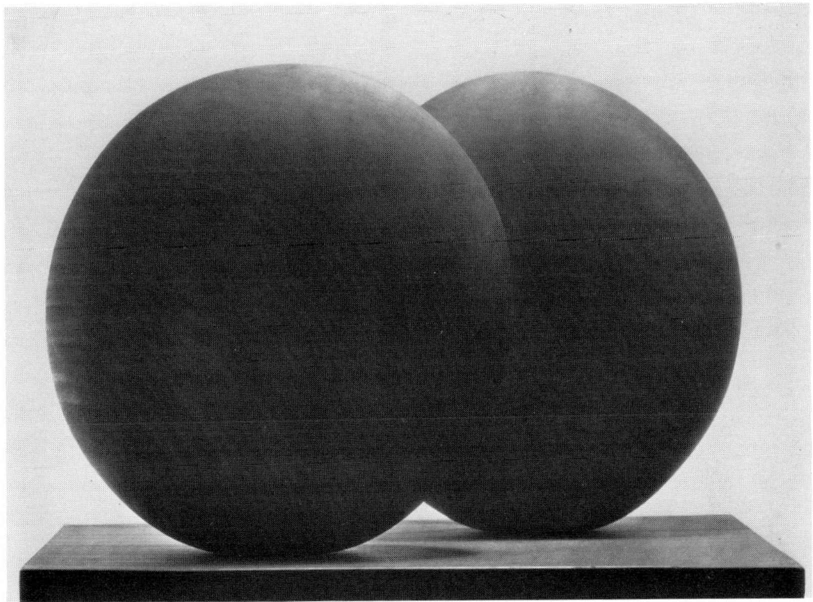

140. Barbara Hepworth: *Discs in Echelon*, 1935. Padouk wood, height $12\frac{1}{4}$ in. (exhibited with the Seven & Five Society, 1935)

'Carving is interrelated masses conveying an emotion.'[20] Of the particular innovatory quality of the *Two Forms with Sphere* [139] she later wrote:

> This formality initiated the exploration with which I have been preoccupied since then, and in which I hope to discover some absolute essence in sculptural terms giving the quality of human relationship.[21]

There is plainly room here for a high degree of sentimentality and, indeed, it is hard to avoid the conclusion that a form of sentimentality is what vitiates much of Hepworth's later work: the locating, in terms of pieces of sculpture, for instance, of the kinds of feelings about people which are really only defensibly introduced into discussion of works of art in the context of a carefully scrutinized analogy. But in the best of Hepworth's carvings of the 1930s – such as the *Discs in Echelon* and the white marble *Three Forms* of 1935, the *Two Forms*, also in white marble, of 1937, and the tulipwood *Forms in Echelon* of 1938 [141] – the final configurations are distinctive and remain memorable as products of a 'refined' aesthetic predilection.

In the overall view of Hepworth's work, and especially given the comparative interest of the works of 1934–9, we should bear in mind that from this, by far the most fruitful period of activity, little more than half her output survives. Among the works destroyed or damaged were, inevitably, some of her largest carvings, including the original versions of a series of

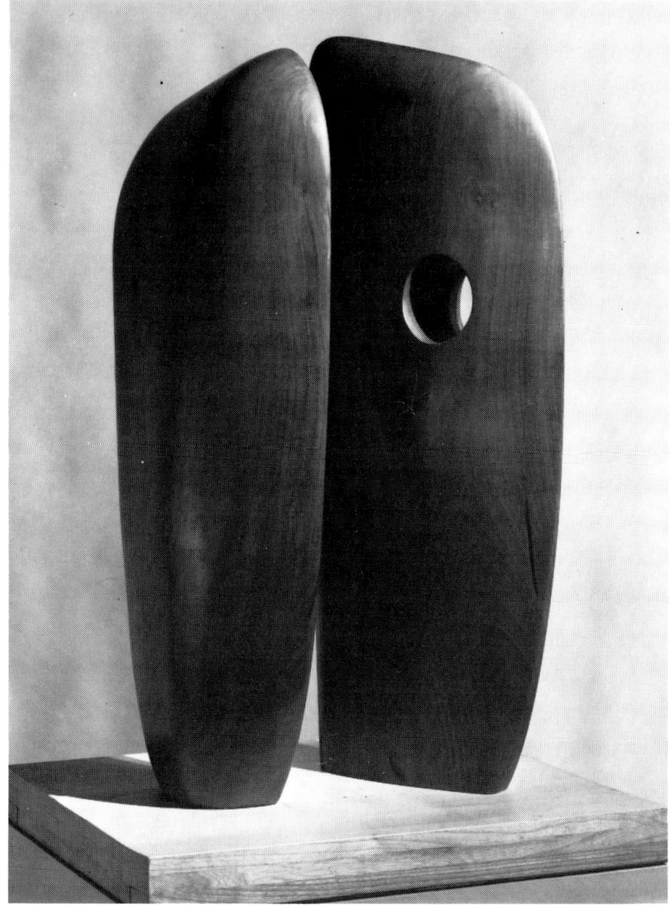

141. Barbara Hepworth: *Forms in Echelon*, 1938. Tulipwood, height 40 in.

single standing forms, made in 1937 and 1938, the tallest of which were some ten feet high. To assess these in terms of surviving bronze casts is to judge them as enterprises of a qualitatively different kind from what was initially envisaged and made.

The best of those works that remain reveal how a refined, if sometimes precious, technical interest in qualities of form and surface may be made the means of participation in a dream of future unity and harmony, founded on belief in the generalizability of intuition:

It is the sculptor's work fully to comprehend the world of space and form, to project his individual understanding of his own life and time as it is related universally in this particular plastic extension of thought, and to keep alive this special side of existence. A clear social solution can only be achieved when there is a full consciousness in the realm of thought and when every section constitutes an inherent part of the whole . . .

His conscious life is bent on discovering a solution to human difficulties by solving his own thought permanently, and in relation to his medium. If we had lived at a time when animals, fire worship, myth or religion were the deepest emotional aspects of life, sculpture would have taken the form, unconsciously, of a recognisable god; and the formal abstract relationships in the representation would have been the conscious way of revitalising these ideas; but now, these formal relationships have become our thought, our faith, waking or sleeping – they can be the solution to life and to living. This is no escapism, no ivory tower, no isolated pleasure in proportion and space – it is an unconscious manner of expressing our belief in a possible life. The language of colour and form is universal and not one for a special class (though this may have been in the past) – it is a thought which gives the same life, the same expansion, the same universal freedom to everyone.[22]

Nicholson's and Hepworth's commitment to abstract art took on the form of a zealous and missionary puritanism. 'Their imagination had been fired, not only by the idea of purity in individual works of painting or sculpture, but by the lofty beauty of a consistent abstract environment.'[23] At worst this involved the fetishization of 'purity' in life and interior decor, but at best their sense of common purpose was a real productive force. The consistency was plainly attractive to others, and by 1935 Nicholson and Hepworth were at the centre of an expanding group of 'abstract artists'. In the Seven & Five meeting of the previous year Nicholson had engineered a ruling that only non-representational works would be eligible for future shows – a significant indicator of his own sense of purpose in the year he made his first white relief. In October 1935 the society held what was considered at the time to be the first all-abstract exhibition in England – so considered with some justice in terms of the criteria then applicable.[24] The exhibitors were Francis Butterfield, Winifred Dacre, Barbara Hepworth, Ivon Hitchens, Eileen Holding, Arthur Jackson, Henry Moore, W. Staite Murray, Ben Nicholson, Roland Penrose and John Piper.[25] (See Appendix, p. 344.)

Francis Butterfield and Arthur Jackson (A. J. Hepworth, Barbara Hepworth's cousin, later to practise as an architect) were pupils of Nicholson and very evidently subject to his influence. Winifred Dacre was the name which Winifred Nicholson adopted during the time when she was living in Paris following her separation from her husband and while she painted experimental abstract oils and gouaches, in part under the instruction of the Swiss painter Hans Erni. William Staite Murray exhibited hand-made pots. John Piper, who had been making picturesque collages a

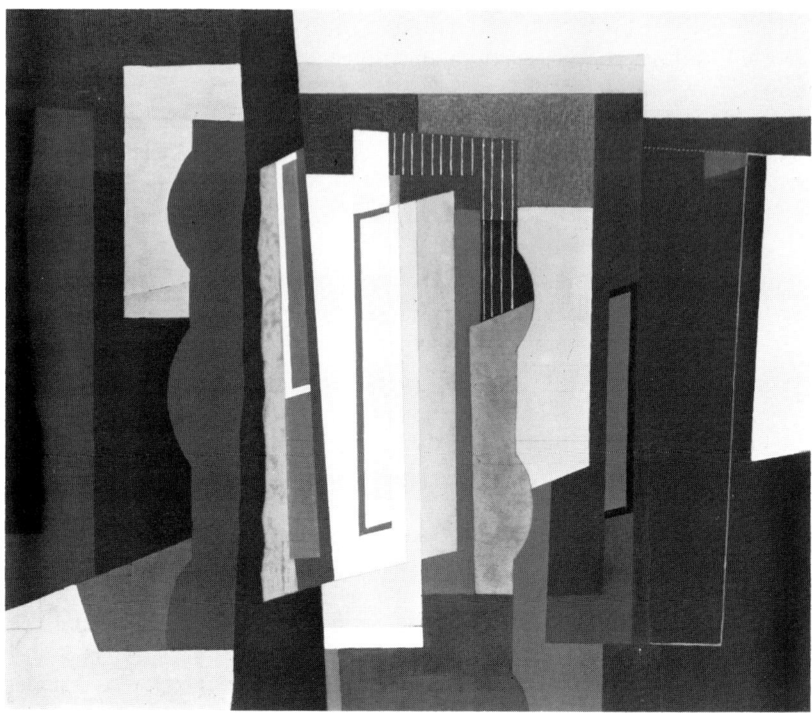

142. John Piper: *Abstract I*, 1935. Oil on a collage of canvas on plywood, 36 × 42 in.

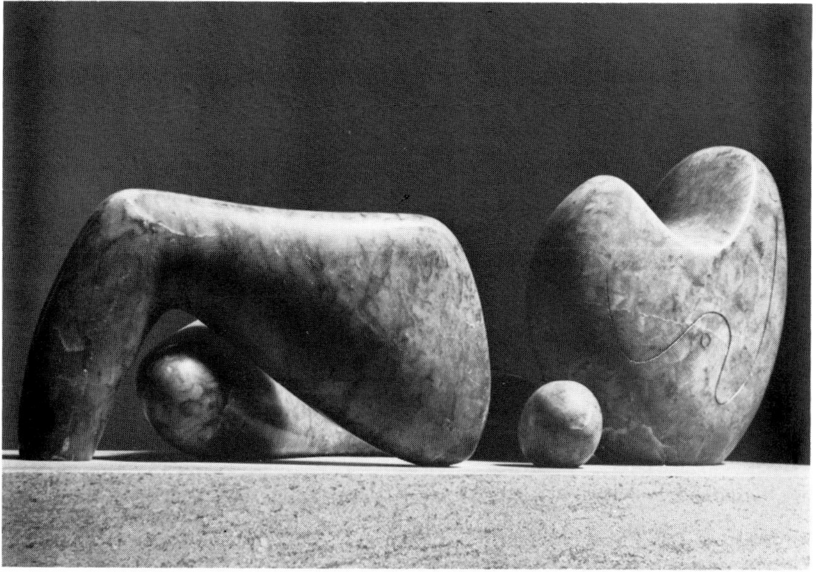

143. Henry Moore: *Four-piece Composition: Reclining Figure*, 1934. Cumberland alabaster, length 20 in. (exhibited with the Seven & Five Society, 1935)

year earlier, showed relief constructions and colourful abstract works [142] which synthesized elements from the formal repertoires of Picasso, Léger and Domela. His first wife, Eileen Holding, exhibited white-painted free-standing constructions. Ivon Hitchens showed works of a loose late-Cubist type which appeared to fulfil the criteria for inclusion, but which misrepresented his true interests. David Jones was listed as a member but did not exhibit and, had he not been ill, would undoubtedly have been unwilling to meet the requirement to produce non-figurative work.

Nicholson, Moore and Hepworth were clearly the dominating figures. The exhibition coincided with what was arguably the most fruitful moment in the careers of all three. Among the exhibits were Moore's *Four-piece Composition: Reclining Figure* [143], the original carved wood version of Hepworth's *Discs in Echelon* [140], and one of the most austere of Nicholson's white reliefs. Moore's sculpture was one of a series of small works in which he pushed the Mother-and-Child and Reclining-Figure themes to the point of maximum abstraction compatible with the retention of an appropriate sense of identity. These works reflect an interest in the carvings of Brancusi and more strongly perhaps a new interest in those early works of Giacometti in which a sense of psychological activity was evoked by virtually non-figurative forms. (A *Reclining Figure* and a *Reclining Woman Dreaming* which Giacometti made in plaster in 1929 may have served to confirm for Moore the extent to which a figure might be abstracted and still retain a quality of human presence.[26]) His two four-piece reclining figure compositions in particular are among Moore's most inventive and most evocative works. In a group of carvings of single forms of 1935–6 he was to pursue an interest in abstract form beyond the point at which references to the figure could easily be sustained [144]. He thus came to seem closer to the abstract artists than he really was in terms of his more representative interests.

However wide the margin may have been between the works of Nicholson, Moore and Hepworth and those of the least successful of the exhibitors at the Seven & Five, the exhibition as a whole must have seemed coherent in its vaunted modernism in a way that Unit One was not.[27] Where the 'modernism' of Hillier, Bigge and Armstrong, for instance, had been unconvinced and incompetent, the modernism of Piper, Jackson and Butterfield betrayed no worse than a seemingly resolute apprenticeship. Of the various tendencies apparent or latent in Unit One, 'abstraction' must thus, in the year 1935, have seemed to be dominant.

This was to be the last Seven & Five exhibition. Nicholson had earlier had plans to hold an international exhibition of abstract art under the society's auspices,[28] but as he himself was to observe later, with the Zwemmer

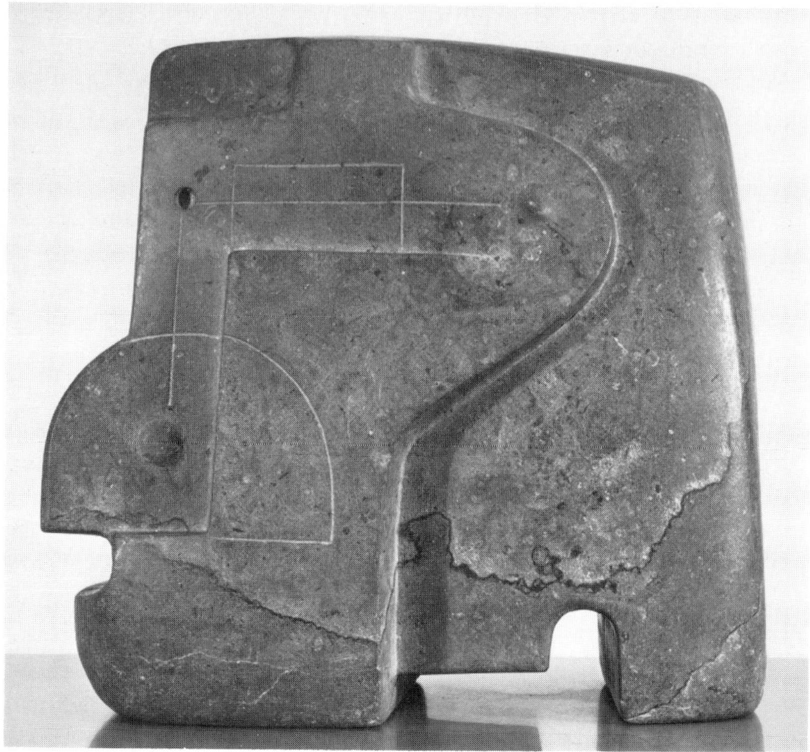

144. Henry Moore: *Square Form*, 1936. Green Hornton stone, $13\frac{3}{4} \times 12$ in.

exhibition the Seven & Five had achieved its object, 'and there was then no point in continuing further'.[29] The dynamic of the society had been the development of an avant garde within the limited context of an insular art. The stronger members were now in a position to have their work seen in the context of an international avant garde, and it was unlikely that they would continue to lend much support to a group which would never be able wholly to rid itself of the taint of its insular origins.

Under John Piper's secretaryship there was still talk of a further Seven & Five exhibition as late as January 1937,[30] but Nicholson's energies were by then engaged on other projects, and though the society was never formally disbanded, it was never to reassemble to any purpose. Nicholson's project for an international exhibition of recent abstract art was in fact fulfilled in the show 'Abstract and Concrete' organized by Nicolete Gray and shown in Oxford, Liverpool, London (at the Lefevre Gallery) and Cambridge between February and June 1936. The exhibitors were Calder, Domela, Erni, Gabo, Giacometti, Hélion, Hepworth, Holding, Jackson, Léger, Miró, Moholy-Nagy, Mondrian, Moore, Nicholson and Piper. The list reflects the composition of *Abstraction-Création* and of the remnants of the Seven & Five. (Wadsworth was a significant absentee. In 1934 he had suddenly abandoned his abstract style, a manner to which he was perhaps never more than formally committed, in favour of a return to the melancholy seaside themes which had preoccupied him in the twenties.)

That such a collection of recent European work could be assembled in England in 1936, and that English artists could now include their own work on equal terms, testifies to the nature of the connection established with the continental avant garde. That no London location for the show could be confirmed until the last moment serves, on the other hand, to demonstrate the limits of this cosmopolitanism.[31]

'Abstract and Concrete' was organized in co-operation with the journal *Axis*, which had commenced publication a year earlier as 'A Quarterly Review of "Abstract" Painting and Sculpture' under the editorship of Myfanwy Evans (later Myfanwy Piper). The fifth issue of the journal served as an illustrated accompaniment to the exhibition. On a visit to Paris at the end of 1933 Paul Nash had written to a friend to say that interest had been expressed in the 'petit mouvement' in England,[32] and the following autumn Hélion wrote to Winifred Nicholson, 'There is certainly a very strong movement growing in England and I hope that you will all stick together to provide it with a strong base. It should be time for you, as an English group, to start a magazine. There is never anything better to form a public.'[33] While staying in Paris during 1934, Myfanwy Evans visited Hélion at Nicholson's and Piper's recommendation and, as she later recalled, 'From the moment I entered his high, white studio, I was committed to action; talked into it by his eloquence in French and in English; conquered by his work and his words.'[34] Visiting Mondrian, Arp and Brancusi she felt 'the lyrical shock of their consistent surroundings' and the sense of 'private, active intensity in the midst of an indifferent world' that had recently impressed Nicholson and Hepworth, and was thus well prepared as a supporter of the development of abstract art in England. Hélion 'announced' that she should 'go back to England and start a magazine of Abstract Art comparable to *Abstraction-Création*'. On her return she set to work to obey his instructions, with John Piper acting as 'co-producer, lay-out man and cutter of the few colour blocks we were able to afford'.

The first of the eight issues of *Axis* appeared in January 1935, with contributions from Herbert Read, Geoffrey Grigson, Anatole Jakovski, Paul Nash and H. S. Ede, illustrated with a selection of works which clearly signalled its ideological connections with *Abstraction-Création*. Small though its circulation was to remain ('some sold in Cambridge, several by Zwemmer ... about 200 subscriptions at 2/6 each'), *Axis* immediately raised the level of critical discourse in England by providing, for the small minority of those concerned with modern art and its ancillary interests, an opportunity for speculation and for the expression of intellectual community. A few years earlier aspiring English writers could only have envied the kind of familiarity with which the European contributors to *Axis* discussed the works and ideas of the luminaries of the Modern Movement. But now these same writers could participate in the discourse secure in their confidence that the best of the English artists provided them with a base in appropriately vivid subjects of discussion.

The second issue contained two well illustrated articles on Nicholson's recent work, one by Read and one by the Swiss typographer Jan Tschichold. The third was devoted to contemporary sculpture, with articles on Brancusi, Moore, Hepworth and Calder. In the fourth there was due acknowledgement of the debt to Hélion, together with two articles on Piper and an intelligent review by J. M. Richards in which he considered Nicholson's show of reliefs at the Lefevre Gallery together with the Seven & Five exhibition at Zwemmer's. Richards was concerned to make the point that while 'Ben Nicholson's reliefs have an affinity with modern architecture . . . purely through a community of feeling and a similar concern for formal significance', the nature of the artist's concentration and curiosity is qualitatively distinct and needs to be maintained if abstract art is to be allowed 'to make its necessary contribution to the whole body of the contemporary aesthetic, such as the social responsibilities of the artist demand of him . . .' This was perhaps to be interpreted as saying that it was not enough for abstract art to be like mini-architecture. It had to be somehow like 'art'.

In his memoir 'A Nest of Gentle Artists',[35] Herbert Read gave an account of the development of a community of modern artists, designers, architects and sympathizers in Hampstead between 1932 and the outbreak of war in 1939. Moore, Nicholson, Hepworth and Cecil Stephenson (J. C. Stephenson) were all in occupation of studios in or near Parkhill Road when Read joined them in April 1933. Hélion was later to refer to this group of studios as 'that English Bateau-Lavoir'.[36] During the next year Walter Gropius, Marcel Breuer and Eric Mendelsohn came as refugees from Nazi Germany and were put up by Jack Pritchard in Lawn Road Flats, which Wells Coates had designed the previous year and where he himself was living. Laszlo Moholy-Nagy and Naum Gabo joined them there in 1935 and 1936 respectively. In 1936 Paul Nash moved to a house within easy walking distance across Parliament Hill. When Mondrian came to London in 1938, Nicholson and Hepworth found him a studio in Parkhill Road. Among their sympathizers living nearby during the thirties were H. S. Ede, then working at the Tate Gallery, Margaret Gardiner, Geoffrey Grigson, Roland Penrose and John Summerson.

This was the community which found expression in *Axis*. It was not, of course, to be expected that the critical discourse would be ideologically coherent, given the essential liberalism of its base and the latitude involved in prevailing interpretations of the meaning of 'abstract'. The very variety of *Axis*'s interests entailed a degree of dilution. For all that Myfanwy Evans might have felt that she had an 'absolute policy' at the outset, with hindsight it seems rather that *Axis* succeeded by steering a careful course between uncritical pluralism and mindless solidarity. The first editorial denigrated Surrealism as a 'literary pursuit' and suggested that the way ahead lay in the 'technical and emotional exploration of shapes left by the analysed object', but in the end the most emphatic editorial statement was one which, if taken seriously, was bound to betray any claims to theoretical significance made explicitly or implicitly within the pages of the magazine: 'There is nothing to be said about painting which is not utter nonsense except "I like this".' This statement could be said to imply: (a) that there are not practices in art which are historically more or less defensible than other practices; and/or (b) that there are not more or less valid critiques of those practices. Such a position was unlikely to provide much in the way of theoretical support for the more extreme varieties of abstract art then being practised. The point needs to be made that while Nicholson and Hepworth were uncompromising during the mid-thirties in their advocacy of abstract art and of the way of life it was believed to instantiate, and although their position seems to have been widely respected even among those who suffered from some of the consequences of their decisions, they had no supporters who were not also supporters of positions which Nicholson himself would at the time have considered irreconcilable. (Which is perhaps to say no more – or less – than that mutual incoherence is an inevitable feature of liberal valuations.)

Not that the tone of *Axis* was uniformly supportive. Reviewing the illustrations for the first issue, Geoffrey Grigson saw in them 'a small history of English ideas, English error and English performance', and offered a trenchant characterization of Nicholson's contemporary work:

> Too near to a surface object derived from art, instead of a portion of art. An image of infinity, ordered by saying 'no' rather than 'yes', which is without body enough to make the image perceptual. Admirable in technical qualities, in taste, in severe self-expurgation, but too much 'art itself', floating and disinfected.

In comparison, he summarized Moore's qualities in terms the purport of which is adequate comprehensively to characterize most of what the multitude of that sculptor's admirers have been able to offer to this day:

> Product of the multiform inventive artist, abstraction-surrealism nearly in control; of a constructor of images between the conscious and the unconscious and between what we perceive and what we project emotionally into the objects of our world; of the one English sculptor of large, imaginative power, of which he is almost master; the biomorphist producing viable work, with all the technique he requires.[37]

For all the hostility expressed to his work by academicians and conservative critics, among the members of the loose community of those interested in modern art during the thirties Moore antagonized no one. Praise for his work was consistent and virtually unqualified among the artists and critics sympathetic to modernism. The key to his success was the unrelenting pursuit of those idiosyncratic psychological interests which could be expressed in a set of evocative formal types, for which the term 'biomorphic' has become the standard description.

Grigson's esteem for Moore was clearly based on a high valuation for individuality and for 'imaginative power'. Though many of the artists themselves had forgotten him, Grigson had been in contact with Wyndham Lewis, and he took this occasion to rattle the skeleton in the cupboard: 'Moore and Wyndham Lewis are the only English artists of maturity in control of enough imaginative power to settle themselves between the new preraphaelites of *Minotaure* [i.e. the Surrealists][38] and the unconscious nihilists of extreme geometric abstraction.' He proceeded to recall with evident approval Lewis's own earlier assertion of the importance of individuality and of the priority of the artist's intuition:

> The important thing is that the individual should be born a painter. Once he is that, it appears to me that the latitude he may consider his is almost without limit. Such powerful specialised senses as he must have are not likely to be over-ridden by anything.[39]

What is revealed in the nature of such valuations for Moore's work, and in the assertion of the importance of individuality in the context of a discussion of abstract art, is that there was a considerable and deeply rooted anxiety that the implications of acceptance of abstract art somehow involved acceptance of the idea of collectivity and of an ill-defined socialism in which talent would be levelled down and life somehow impoverished. This anxiety has surfaced often in the criticism of art in the twentieth century. It has tended to divide those whose view of themselves as realists is underwritten by beliefs about the necessarily uncontrollable nature of human behaviour and human instincts, from those possessed by visions of a Utopia underwritten by belief in the possibility of a form of transcendental socialism of the spirit. The implications of different preoccupations and beliefs may not have been at all clear at the time – indeed they rarely are now – and most of the comparatively small section of those involved must have felt that the significant feature of their enterprises was that they were collectively working for the good of art, for the enlightenment of the unsympathetic majority, and for a better world for all. But as the decade proceeded the divisions were sometimes clear enough, as the following chapter will aim to demonstrate, to reveal serious underlying incompatibilities and more obviously overt absurdities.

So far as abstract art was concerned, the critical moment for assessment of its importance and its implications occurred in discussion of the nature of the relation between abstract art as art, on the one hand, and design as practical activity on the other. The crucial issue was: how and where were the intuitions of the abstract artist to be seen as distributed? The question was raised by Paul Nash in his contribution to the first issue of *Axis*. Under the title 'For but not with' he presented a typically well-mannered defence of his own interests and implied that the limit of his sympathy for the aims of abstract art was set by the fear of spiritual impoverishment:

> I discern among natural phenomena a thousand forms which might, with advantage, be dissolved in the crucible of abstract transfiguration; but the hard cold stone, the rasping grass, the intricate architecture of trees and waves, or the brittle sculpture of a dead leaf – I cannot translate altogether beyond their own image, without suffering in spirit.

In reminding his readers that abstract art had been 'practised now, in various forms all over the world, for 25 years', and was thus presumably not to be seen as controversial, he managed to strike a note of elder-statesmanship reminiscent of Sickert's admonitions to those alarmed by Post-Impressionism a quarter of a century earlier. In accounting for the interest in abstract art to which the formation of *Axis* testified, he quoted with approval a passage from *Art Now* in which Read transmitted the pseudo-explanation (by now apparently accorded the status of conventional wisdom) which Hulme had borrowed from Worringer: that the appearance of a 'geometric sensibility' is due to the need of the 'sensitive soul' for 'spiritual refuge' from the 'political, economic and spiritual chaos' of 'our outer world'. The mildly patronizing purport of his concluding remarks, again supported by a passage from Read, this time from *Art and Industry*, was that, just as the activities of the pure mathematician had their application in the practical sciences, so the field of applied design was the proper locus for the practice of the abstract artist.

The development of the practice of abstract art in Europe in the period between the wars gave rise to a plethora of speculations, justifications and critiques, which the circumstances of English art variously reflect. It is not easy either to disentangle the speculations one from the other or to identify their various structural assumptions. In so far as they raise substantive issues, these often have their causal origins in specific historical circumstances remote from those in which the speculations themselves are encountered. The implications of what it was possible for men to think and to learn in one set of circumstances are thus discussed apart from those circumstances, within the restricted conditions of discussion about art. Ripples from the Russian Revolution and its aftermath, from the Weimar Republic, from Nazi Germany and from the America of the Depression washed on the secluded beach of English art during the 1930s. It was during the later twenties and the thirties that determined attempts were made to rationalize and to entrench the intuitions of the earlier phases of European modernism. By the later thirties London had become the principal stage for the relevant activities, partly by sheer process of elimination as the intellectual émigrés moved westward, but also because the development of an English avant garde, and of an accompanying audience, however small, was taken to be a propitious sign. (Any prospect of commissions or of sales of work was bound to be attractive to the architects and artists of the European avant garde in the 1930s.[40])

The meeting of such various and developed historical themes at one place and time accounts in large measure for the diversity of texture in this period of English art history. On the other hand, it has to be said that discussion of these themes was largely contained in consideration of the relative merits of alternative artistic styles, in comparative ignorance of the historical themes which those styles had initially expressed. This was a general consequence of the lack of direct contact with the historical events in response to which these same styles had initially been developed. It was a price paid for the assertion of art's autonomy, and for the corresponding prevalence among modernist artists of a nonchalant attitude towards recent and contemporary history.

These were some of the underlying issues of dispute within the Modern Movement as a whole: could art somehow be self-determining, or was it determined by economic and political history? Was the construction of works of art a model for, or a mere reflection of processes of social (re)construction? Was abstract art merely a means to effect improvement in the appearance of man-made things, or was it a means to the expression of some sort of universal spiritual truth? Was it to be seen as a critical distillation of the faculty of design, or as philosophy without words but with universal application?

In the developed ideology of the Modern Movement, the two latter views were not antithetical. The character and condition of 'design', that is to say, were interpreted as visible evidence of the spiritual and moral state of man as a social being. The origins of the idea that the criticism of design had social, moral and political import lay in the English nineteenth century, specifically in the work of A. W. N. Pugin, John Ruskin and William Morris. (Following in this tradition Read spoke of the degradation of art in the modern period as a consequence of the expansion of capitalism.[41]) In so far as an idealized practice of 'design' can be divorced from a history of technology or of economics, the history of design in the early twentieth century is a history of the transformation of the idea that the condition of design is an index of the health of society into its false corollary: viz. that an improvement will be effected in man's spiritual and moral state if the things around him are well designed. In its extreme form this becomes the idea that under the concept of design, as a 'unity', is subsumed the totality of man's ordering and organizational faculties and activities, including those which involve the ordering of the lives of others. In this scheme, the 'aesthetic principle' is seen as a counter, rather than a complement, to the 'business principle'.

> ... our informing conception of the basic unity of all design in relation to life was in diametrical opposition to that of 'art for art's sake' and to the even more dangerous philosophy it sprang from: business as an end in itself (Walter Gropius quoted by Herbert Read).[42]

In further characterization of the nature of this informing conception, we might append another quotation from Gropius:

> ... the solution [i.e. to modern problems of production] depends on a change in the individual's attitude towards his work, not on the betterment of his outward circumstances, and the acceptance of this new principle is of decisive importance for new creative work.[43]

For all that Gropius may have seen himself as an opponent of the 'business principle', this is the language of management.

This aestheticization of politics gained a measure of credibility during the 1930s as a position of opposition to the politicization of aesthetics[44] by those who supported the Stalinist theory of Socialist Realism. Further, as was evidenced by the prefatory statement to *Abstraction-Création* no. 2, quoted above, the proponents of abstract-art-as-spiritual-health could claim a status as guardians of free thought by virtue of the monstrous nature of those whose voices were heard in opposition both to abstract art and to modernist design and architecture (which, committed as it was to the idea of a universal or 'international style', was naturally suspect in the eyes of nationalist organizations such as the Nazi party).

The concept of 'the basic unity of all design', and of abstract-art-as-good-design as the expression of that unity, was summarized by Read in his book *Art for Society*.

The claim of the abstract artist is that the forms he creates are of more than decorative significance in that they repeat in their appropriate materials and on their appropriate scale certain proportions and rhythms which are inherent in the structure of the universe, and which govern organic growth, including the growth of the human body. Attuned to these rhythms and proportions, the abstract artist can create microcosms which reflect the macrocosm – he can hold the world, if not in a grain of sand, then in a block of stone or a pattern of colours. He has no need of natural appearances – of the accidental forms created in the stress of the world's evolution – because he has access to the archetypal forms which underlie all the casual variations presented by the natural world.

The view that there were fundamental 'proportions and rhythms' inherent in all forms of life gained substance in the period between the wars from recent work in the natural sciences, particularly in botany. Wilenski, in *The Meaning of Modern Sculpture*, had asserted that 'We react with satisfaction to works of art which make us realise subconsciously that all human, animal and vegetable forms are manifestations of one life', and had reproduced plates from Blossfeldt's *Art Forms in Nature*, a study of 'formal principles in natural structure'. A 'Note on Biotechnics' by Karel Honzig was published in *Circle* in 1937, and d'Arcy Thompson's work on *Growth and Form* was widely consumed among the avant garde.[45]

In the development in England of the idea that (abstract) art expresses the fundamental constructive principles of life, a decisive role was played by the Russian émigré artist, Naum Gabo [145]. In the passage quoted above, Read echoes the rationale for the practice of abstract art which Gabo had been promoting consistently since 1920. In order to understand the significance of Gabo's theory of abstract art, and to assess his part in the activities of the English avant garde, we should briefly outline the circumstances in which his ideas were first formulated.

Though he had been in Scandinavia in 1914–17, Gabo returned to Russia in time to take part in the urgent and extensive discussions on 'technical questions, ideological problems, problems of the future destiny of art, general problems concerning art and life, and professional problems . . .'[46] which centred on the Vkhutemas ('higher workshops of artistic and technical education') in Moscow in the wake of the Revolution. In such discussions at moments of historical crisis, ideological material is often generated which it may take decades subsequently to examine and assimilate. According to Gabo's own account,

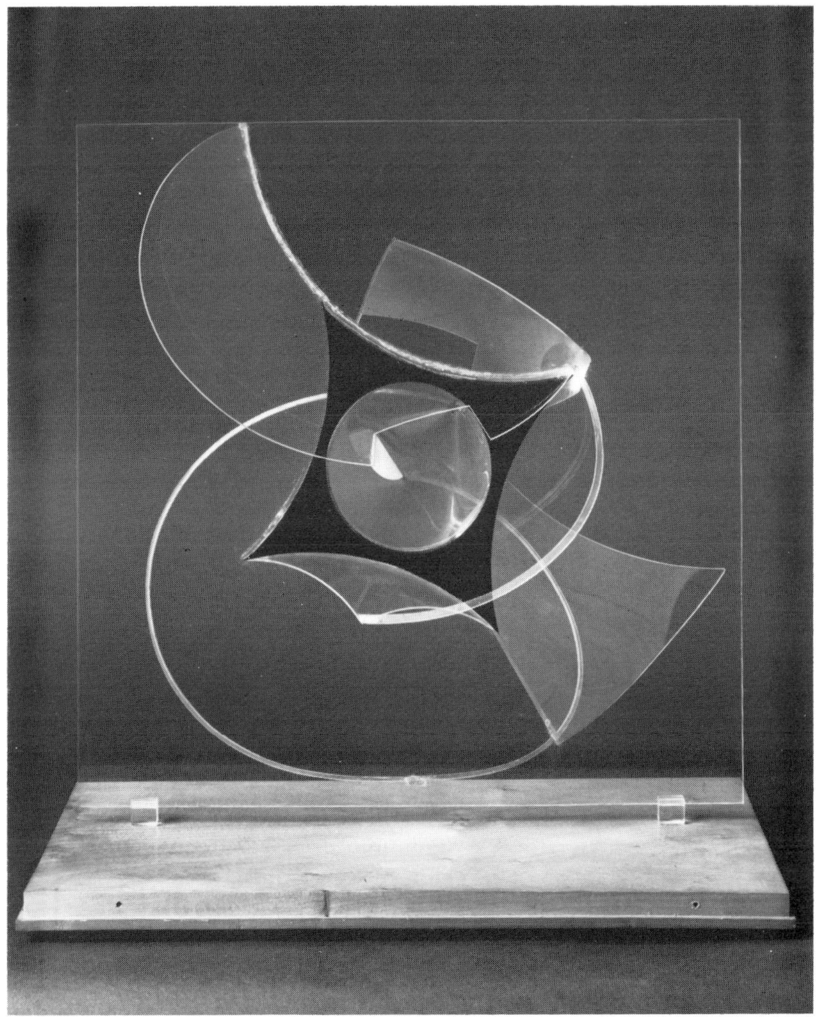

145. Naum Gabo: *Construction on a Plane*, 1937. Plastic, 19 × 19 in.

At the end of the third year two opposing ideologies had emerged, one group around Tatlin and the other around my brother Antoine Pevsner and myself. We had come to a point where these two groups could not be reconciled in their ideas ... the overwhelming majority of all the so-called abstract artists did not belong to any political party. We were politically neutral, but this group around Tatlin took a trend to join the communist party and based their ideology on Marxism ... The conflict in our ideologies, between Tatlin's group, who called themselves productivists, and our group only accelerated the open break and forced us to make a public declaration.[47]

Accordingly, in August 1920, Gabo and Pevsner flyposted five thousand copies of their 'Realistic Manifesto' around Moscow to coincide with an exhibition of their work on the Tverskoy Boulevard.

The manifesto proclaimed that 'The impasse into which art has come ... in the last twenty years must be broken', and made it clear that neither Futurism nor Cubism would serve for the future. They then asserted the 'fundamental principles of our work and our constructive technique' formed on the basis of the assumption that 'Space and time are the only forms on which life is built and hence art must be constructed'.[48] Following Kasimir Malevich, they upheld the idea that 'the value of art as an independent means of expression is integral to life'.[49]

The degree of autonomy to be accorded to art must have been the most vexed of all the issues raised in the discussions at the Vkhutemas. As we have seen, it is a question which recurs constantly during the whole period under review. It might be said that there is a deep paradox in the association of socialism with the pursuit of autonomy in and for an intensional activity such as the practice of art. In so far as the ideological complex of the Modern Movement could be said to have been generally socialist in character – as its conservative detractors at least believed it to be – it must be clear that the socialism involved was a 'socialism' which generally stopped well short of Marxism and of communism.

It was his stand against the autonomy of art that most distinguished Tatlin's position from Gabo's. Shortly after the publication of the Realistic Manifesto, a 'Programme of the Productivist Group' led by Tatlin was published to accompany an exhibition of work by Rodchenko and Stepanova. The first item of the group's programme is as follows: 'The sole premise is scientific communism, based on the theory of historical materialism.'[50] Among 'future tasks' were 'Proving by word and deed the incompatibility of artistic activity and intellectual production.' In 'the field of agitation' the group declared itself 'for ruthless war against art in general'. 'Down with art. Long live technic' was the first of its concluding slogans. The implication, for those trained as artists, was the acceptance of a role in party work which allowed for the employment of technical skills but not for the exploitation of 'individual intuition', in line, perhaps, with a proletcultish misunderstanding of Marx's dictum that 'In a communist society there are no painters, but at most men who, among other things, also paint.'

The standard argument against those, such as Gabo, who wished to preserve the social metaphysic grounded in and reciprocally grounding the autonomy of art, would have been that such men were merely seeking to defend their investment in bourgeois forms of activity and experience. From a Western point of view, however, Gabo was seen as a surviving participant in a revolutionary episode. In the early 1920s the climate in Russia had hardened against modernist individualism, or, it might be said, against any form of modernism in the fine arts. In 1922 Gabo had left Russia for good. His brother joined him in the West a year later.

Two uses of the concept of 'construction' in art thus need to be distinguished. For the Constructivists (or Productivists) around Tatlin, in search of a position consistent with the Party, art was to be seen as determined by material and economic forces and as constructive in so far as it entailed participation in social (re)construction in furtherance of communism. For Gabo, 'Constructive Art' was art which expressed a creative and dialectical principle independent of or subsuming the situational contingencies of political life. In an article on 'The Constructive Idea in Art' he asserted the clearly anti-Marxist and anti-materialist principle that man's a-historical 'creative genius' has priority in determining culture.

> The Constructive idea sees and values Art only as a creative act. By a creative act it means every material or spiritual work which is destined to stimulate or perfect the substance of material or spiritual life. Thus the creative genius of Mankind obtains the most important and singular place. In the light of the Constructive idea the creative mind of man has the last and decisive word in the definite constructivism of the whole of our culture.[51]

'The Constructive Idea in Art' was printed as a virtual editorial statement at the beginning of *Circle*, published in London late in 1937 as an 'International Survey of Constructive Art' under the joint editorship of Gabo, Ben Nicholson and the architect Leslie Martin.[52] Though Gabo had visited England in 1934, the idea of such a publication was probably first formulated in 1936, since it was on the occasion of the 'Abstract and Concrete' exhibition that the three editors really came to know each other.[53] During 1936, Nicholson and Hepworth, and Leslie and Sadie Martin compiled an anthology of photos and statements, with Winifred Nicholson helping with material gathered in Paris and with Gabo acting as an intermediary with members of the European Modern Movement.

> We wrote to certain artists throughout the world whom we knew were working in this direction and they sent photographs and articles. There were not all that many at the time and we knew every one of them.[54]

Gabo returned to England to get married in 1936 and stayed in the country until his departure for America in 1946. Although editorial responsibility was roughly divided into the three main technical categories of painting, sculpture or construction and architecture, Gabo's voice was plainly a strong one. He was a passionate and voluble advocate for his own view of art and of history, and that is the view which is expressed in *Circle*, in so far as it is possible to regard the publication as coherent.

Under four headings – 'Painting', 'Sculpture', 'Architecture' and 'Art and Life' – the editors of *Circle* aimed to gather together 'those forces which seem to us to be working in the same direction and for the same ideas', and to 'make clear a common basis and to demonstrate, not only the relationship of one work to the other but of this form of art to the whole social order' (from the Preface). The emergence of 'a new cultural unity' was proclaimed, with 'the constructive trend' as its 'common spirit'. Besides its editors, the contributors to *Circle* were Mondrian (on 'Plastic Art and Pure Plastic Art'), Winifred Dacre, Herbert Read (on 'The Faculty of Abstraction'), Le Corbusier (on 'The Quarrel with Realism'), Hepworth, Moore, J. D. Bernal (on 'Art and the Scientist'), J. M. Richards, Maxwell Fry (on 'Town Planning'; Fry was at the time working in partnership with Gropius), Marcel Breuer, Richard Neutra, Alberto Sartoris, Siegfried Giedion ('Construction and Aesthetics'), Walter Gropius ('Art Education and the State'), Léonide Massine ('Choreography'), Moholy-Nagy, Jan Tschichold ('The New Typography'), Karel Honzig, and Lewis Mumford. An appendix surveyed the work of the Congrès Internationaux d'Architecture Moderne. In the illustrated section on painting, Mondrian, Nicholson, Hélion and Moholy-Nagy were the most prominent; in sculpture Gabo, Pevsner, Hepworth, Moore and Brancusi. There was a carefully selected bibliography of compatible publications and a listing of relevant exhibitions plainly intended to emphasize the internationalism of the 'new cultural unity'. Besides 'Abstract and Concrete' the editors were able to draw attention to 'Thèse, Antithèse, Synthèse' held at the Kunsthalle, Luzern, in 1935, to the major exhibition 'Cubism and Abstract Art' at the Museum of Modern Art, New York, in 1936, and to 'Constructivism' at the Kunsthalle, Basel, in 1937. Reference was also made to an exhibition of 'Abstract Art in Contemporary Settings' at the showrooms of Duncan Miller Ltd in London in 1936, and to a substantial 'Abstract Section' in a large exhibition organized by the Artists International Association in London in 1937.

Circle was an ambitious, programmatic publication and at face value appeared to assert the success of a theoretically coherent international movement to which the English contingent had made a significant contribution. As such it can be taken as an expression of that 'sympathetic alliance' which Paul Nash had canvassed six years earlier when he was contemplating the formation of Unit One. Yet for all the appearance of consistency and rigour, *Circle*'s ideological base was essentially unsound, and for all that it may have appeared as a novelty in England, it was a late manifestation in the context of the history of the European Modern Movement as a whole. In a sense what *Circle* appeared to propose was that the spiritual and intellectual excitement of revolution is accessible to experience, through art, architecture and design, without the historical actuality; that ideas move mountains. It has become an implicit feature of the defence of modernism that art embodies a supervening reality which may be valued in such terms. But there always was and there always will be a deep contradiction involved in attempts to assert or secure some critical agency for the intuitions of the artist (and for design as an executive arm), while the principle of the autonomy of art is the creature of idealism. It is here suggested that the roots of this contradiction lay in responses to an earlier history, which was not principally English history, and in the desire for a moderation of socialism in practice which was incompatible with the ideals of socialism itself. Furthermore, the world which *Circle* hypothesized was largely the imaginative creation of the idealists of the 1910s and the early 1920s, and its realization had already been effectively ruled out by subsequent events in the political history of Europe. *Circle* was originally intended as an annual publication, but there seems to have been no move to publish a second compilation. In so far as the first was largely retrospective, it might have been difficult to find appropriate additional material.

In the late thirties, as it became increasingly clear that there were forms of abstract art which were incompatible with the kind of work published in *Circle*, 'Constructive' came to replace 'abstract' as a means of self-identification for those opposed to Surrealist influence. An exhibition of 'Constructive Art' was held at the London Gallery in 1937, with work by Calder, Dacre, Gabo, Giacometti, Hélion, Hepworth, Holding, Jackson, Moholy-Nagy, Moore, Nicholson, Piper and Stephenson [146], all of whom had had work illustrated in *Circle*. Two years later, in an exhibition of 'Living Art in England', held at the same gallery, Nicholson, Jackson and Stephenson were still showing as 'Constructivists' in company with Gabo and Mondrian (recently arrived in London) and with Alastair Morton, a new recruit to the cause. By then, however, the Surrealists far outnumbered all other categories, with Moore listed among their number. (Alternative designations were 'abstract' and 'independent'.)

The study of history has not, in the modern period, been considered a requirement in the education of artists, and Nicholson's commitment to, or understanding of, the ideological ramifications of the concept of Constructive Art was unlikely to have extended much beyond an intuitive sense that a 'right idea' was somehow involved, that 'the present constructive movement is a living force and that life gives birth to life' (a simple

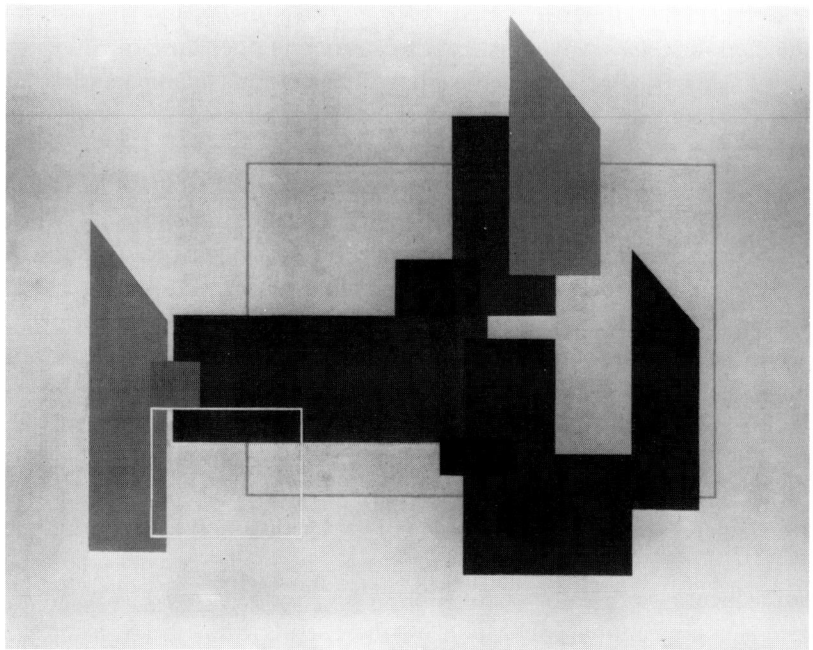

146. John Cecil Stephenson: *Painting*, 1937. Tempera on canvas, 28 × 36 in.

paraphrase of Gabo's position taken from Nicholson's statement in *Circle*). His art, however, as he purged it of those accidental features of surface which had been so marked before 1934, came to seem increasingly compatible with the works of the more 'absolutist' of the artists of the European Modern Movement, and in particular of Mondrian. Response to the highly 'purified' character of Mondrian's work became evident after Nicholson's second visit to his studio, in 1935.[55] In paintings produced alongside his white reliefs, from 1935 onwards for several years, Nicholson organized areas of unmodulated tone and colour in terms of a formal vocabulary reduced to rectilinear areas with the occasional appearance of a circle [147]. Although he could never have subscribed to Mondrian's essentially Symbolist approach to primary colour, he produced a number of paintings, between 1937 and 1940, in which saturated primary colours are used, as they were by the Dutch painter, without any sense of direct naturalistic reference. Echoing both the earlier optimism of Paul Nash and the idealism of *Circle*, Leslie Martin wrote in 1939:

> The important thing is this: that Nicholson, without sacrificing for a moment his integrity as an artist, has moved consistently and intuitively towards a position in which his art becomes part of a synthesis of modern design ... Once the barriers between the 'fine arts' and the

'practical arts' are broken down, then the artist can take his place as a workman in the formation of a new culture.[56]

But Nicholson's work never really moved very near to the barrier between the 'fine' and the 'practical' arts, in so far as consideration of the latter was seen as necessarily involving some reference to industrial manufacture, nor was it ever as free as Mondrian's and Gabo's from the sense of genesis in a world of particular landscape and still-life motifs. Echoes of Cubist forms of composition or of landscape configurations can be found in even his most rigorously 'geometric' works. In the Tate Gallery's large painting of 1937, for instance, the blocks of saturated colour are clustered within a containing rectangle which derives ultimately from the upraised table-top of the conventional Cubist still life. For all that many of Nicholson's reliefs of the later thirties [148] assume a monumental character in contrast to the earlier, more emphatically hand-made reliefs,

147. Ben Nicholson: *Painting*, 1935. Oil on canvas, 41¾ × 41¾ in.

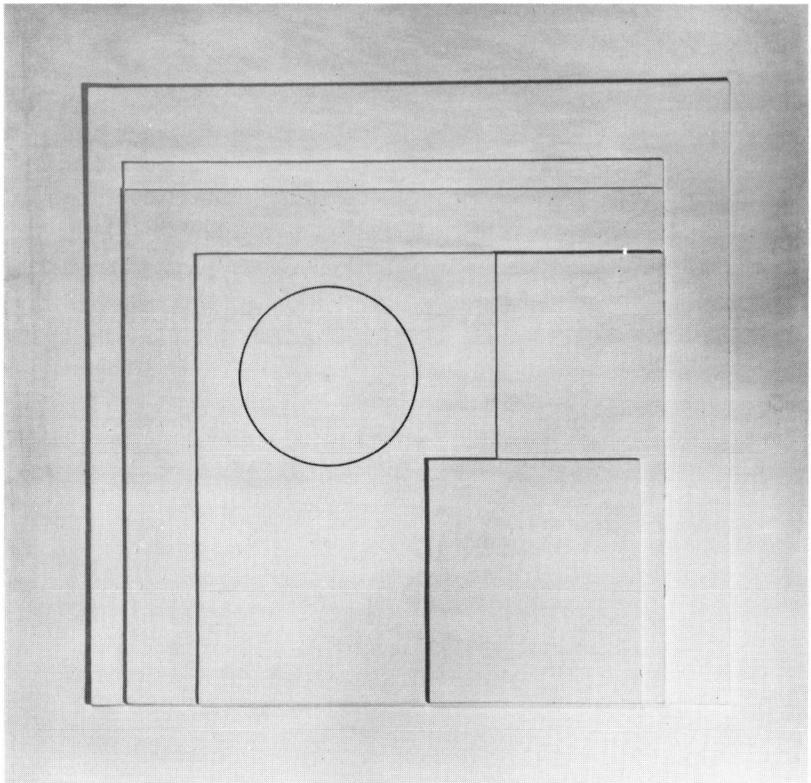

148. Ben Nicholson: *White Relief*, 1939. Oil on carved board, $30\frac{1}{2} \times 29$ in.

and although they could be interpreted at the time by reference to architectural forms, they are invested with an ultimately romantic quality more consistent with the mood of Nicholson's landscape paintings of the late twenties than with the actual monuments of the Modern Movement in architecture. This is perhaps to say that Nicholson's concept of nature has never been one which involved complete commitment to abstraction at the expense of particular experience and memory.

Nicholson's works are at their best when they are most substantial, in their factive aspect, however impalpable that to which they give expression or to which they directly or indirectly allude. It is as if the particular material identity of the successful finished work were something which Nicholson had to work for, against that fastidious formalizing in face of the material world, which was a strong feature both of English painting during the 1920s and of European abstract art at the same time and later, and of which Nicholson's own weakest work in both veins provides revealing illustration. This is the paradox of the white reliefs. They are the vivid outcome of both the strengths and the weaknesses of the preceding decade and a half of English art: assertively substantial in themselves, they evoke a world in which material identity is idealized almost out of existence. The residue of reference to the material world, and to forms of apperception appropriate to activity in that world, is in the end what saves them from appearing solely as formalizations. (A possible caution to this view is that the characteristic 'furniture' of Nicholson's world – the landscape of St Ives for instance – was itself subject to a kind of formalization, as it were in advance.)

In some of Nicholson's reliefs of the later 1930s, and indeed in the most interesting of his works from then until the time of writing, compositions organized from abstracted aspects of places and things retain some sense of identification – albeit often very fugitive – with the particular world of material identities in which they have their origin. For instance, in a painted relief of 1939 composed wholly of rectangles (now in the Pier Gallery, Stromness), the suggestion of a horizon between sea and sky, evoked by the meeting of a pale with a darker blue area near the top of the composition, is sufficient to stimulate an interpretation of the surrounding shapes not as, but by reference to, the kinds of colours and configurations and contrasts which occur in a view through a window out to sea. An olive green and a reddish brown thus evoke aspects of landscape, a patch of black a shadowed area near at hand contrasted with reflected light, and so on. The relief can thus be located, historically, in terms of a most persistent and fruitful theme in early-twentieth-century European painting: the view – often across a still life of some sort – from an interior to a brightly lit landscape or seascape; a scene by means of which the modulations of indoor and outdoor light are related. This theme was perhaps most vividly exploited by Picasso in late-Cubist paintings of *c.* 1920 and by Matisse in many of his most attractive works dating variously from the 1890s to the late 1940s. It was also, of course, a frequent theme in paintings by members of the Seven & Five in the late twenties and early thirties. Modes of abstract painting and sculpture have been generally dominant in the development of European art since the 1930s. In view of the consequent need to assess Nicholson's work of the thirties in the context of European abstract art within which it offers illustration of appropriate concerns, the painted relief may serve as an apt reminder of different but abiding interests.

The relief was almost certainly completed in Cornwall, and thus also betokens a change of interest which was anyway imposed upon both Nicholson and Hepworth. Shortly before the outbreak of war in September 1939, they left London in what was to become an evacuation. They stayed initially with Adrian Stokes in St Ives, where Nicholson responded

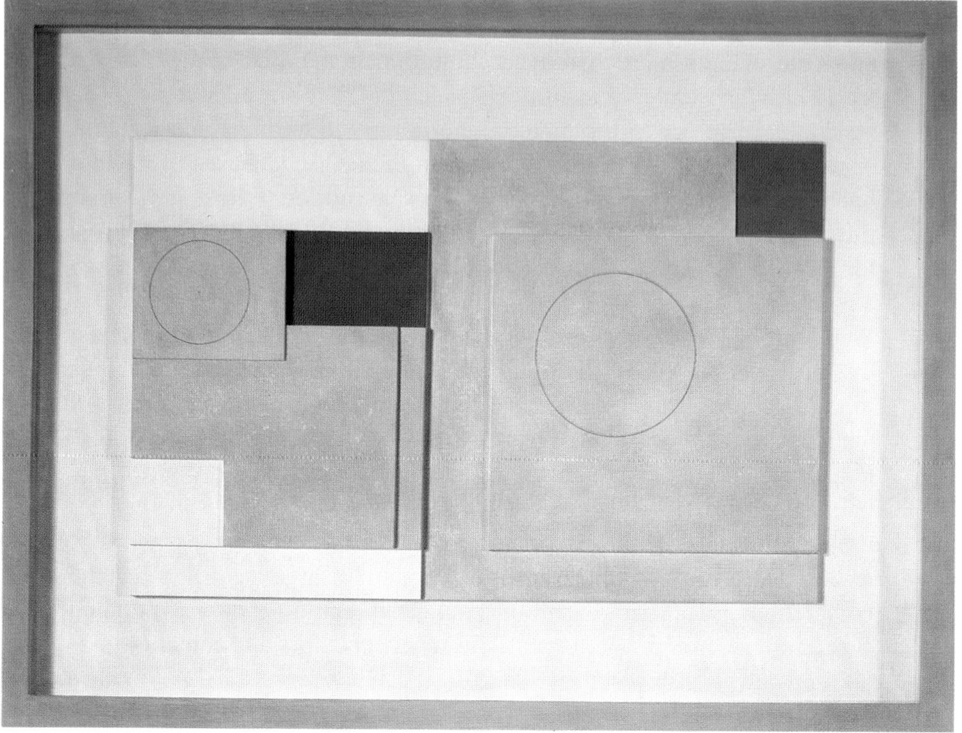

149. Ben Nicholson: *Painted Relief*, 1939. Oil and pencil on composition boards mounted on painted plywood. $32\frac{1}{2} \times 45$ in.

immediately to the difference in environment, reintroducing naturalistic colour and a degree of difference in texture to his reliefs [149]. His work was never again to be as rigorously abstract as it had been during the previous five years. In her turn Hepworth was able to take with her only one small work in string and plaster. It was to be two years before she was able to resume, and she was never to produce work of equal interest to the carvings of the later thirties.

Nicholson and Hepworth thus lost their position at the social centre of modern English art, and they were never to regain it. As it had become clear that the British government was morally unprepared to recognize the imminence of war, the majority of the European immigrants had continued their journey westward to America. Mondrian stayed in Hampstead until 1940, when a bomb damaged the house next door to his. Gabo alone stayed in England throughout the war, following his friends to St Ives. Myfanwy Piper was later to write of Nicholson and Hepworth in relation to their friends and contemporaries at the close of the thirties:

For Hepworth and Nicholson at least, art had crystallised into space and the history of art was in the future. For most of the rest, modern art, abstract art, with its life-lines to Cubism or primitive painting or sculpture or pre-history or Cézanne or Surrealism, was a means of dealing with the remnants of the object, of nature left to us; not a new world but the old world in new and shattered circumstances.[57]

Yet for all the development of Nicholson's work during the 1930s and for all that Hepworth was working at her best during the same period, their material circumstances did not ease. Nicholson's prices were if anything lower in 1938 than they had been in 1934, and throughout the decade the two artists remained largely dependent on the occasional purchases of works by friends. In Cornwall it was to be even harder. As Barbara Hepworth wrote later:

Everywhere there seemed to be abundant energy, and hope, and a developing interest in the fusion of all the arts to some great purpose. But just when we felt the warmth and strength of this new understanding it eluded us.[58]

11

THE LATER THIRTIES: SURREALISM, 'REALISM', ROMANTICISM

The increasing exclusiveness of Nicholson's and Hepworth's interests in relation to those of the other artist members had no doubt contributed largely to the break up of Unit One after the Mayor Gallery exhibition. But Paul Nash himself had been unable to maintain the extent of his early involvement much beyond the period of preparation for the London show and for the book. In January 1933 he had suffered a serious attack of bronchitis which left him with a chronic bronchial condition. In November he travelled to the south of France to avoid the English winter and he was abroad until the following June. He thus missed the Mayor Gallery exhibition entirely. Over the period of the Unit One tour the interests of the various members clearly diverged to the point of manifest incompatibility. If the Unit had ever been 'a solid combination standing by each other and defending their beliefs' it certainly was so no longer. Late in 1934 a ballot was organized whereby the members voted on each other, with a unanimous result in favour required to secure continued membership. This was no doubt a last resort to resolve, or perhaps to replace, disagreement. Predictably, Nash and Moore alone passed the test, and despite what seem to have been some half-hearted attempts to reorganize, Unit One was never properly reconstituted.[1] In truth, the interests of the more able members could no longer be served by so incoherent an alliance. In a letter to Conrad Aiken, written early in 1935, Nash composed a laconic *ave atque vale* to the new 'New Movement':

You can safely say there is a definite movement towards the practise of and experiment in abstract art – among the younger artists, which is more evident since the formation of Unit One which, with its change in composition, should become more than ever the central force and inspiration at the back of contemporary art in England – or some such balls![2]

In the Spring 1936 issue of *Axis*, the *Unit 1* book, which had been published at a price of 10/6*d*, was advertised for sale at 3/6*d*.

The direction of Paul Nash's own interests had been implicit in the individual statement he made for *Unit 1*, composed a crucial few months after his letter to *The Times* announcing the group's formation. He had visited Silbury Hill and the Avebury stones while staying at Marlborough in August 1933, and in the conclusion to his statement he gave expression to the decisive effect which they had made upon him; or rather, perhaps, to the sense of their appropriateness as symbolic indices for interests which he had been developing over the previous few years, even while he worked for the 'New Movement':

Last summer, I walked in a field near Avebury where two rough monoliths stand up, sixteen feet high, miraculously patterned with black and orange lichen, remnants of the avenue of stones which led to the Great Circle. A mile away, a green pyramid casts a gigantic shadow. In the hedge, at hand, the white trumpet of convolvulus turns from its spiral stem, following the sun. In my art I would solve such an equation.

Increasingly, the prehistory of England and the animism he attributed to objects found in the English landscape instilled his painting with analogical material for the expression of dramas of imaginative life. The *Landscape of the Megaliths* [150], shown in the Unit One exhibition in London, represents an early response to the experience of Avebury.[3] Though he had been busy enough, and though his interests had developed and changed considerably, the previous two years had been comparatively unproductive for Nash so far as painting was concerned. The English landscape now reasserted itself strongly in his work, while his tendency towards interpretative treatment of such subjects as that landscape offered was increasingly encouraged and diversified by contact with European Surrealism. From this point on, the development of the main body of his work was steady and consistent.

In April 1934, Nash wrote to Anthony Bertram:

I feel I am beginning now to find my way between the claims of 'Abstractions' and pure interpretation. As you know, I am far too interested in the character of landscape and natural forms generally – from a pastoral point of view – ever to abandon painting *after* Nature of

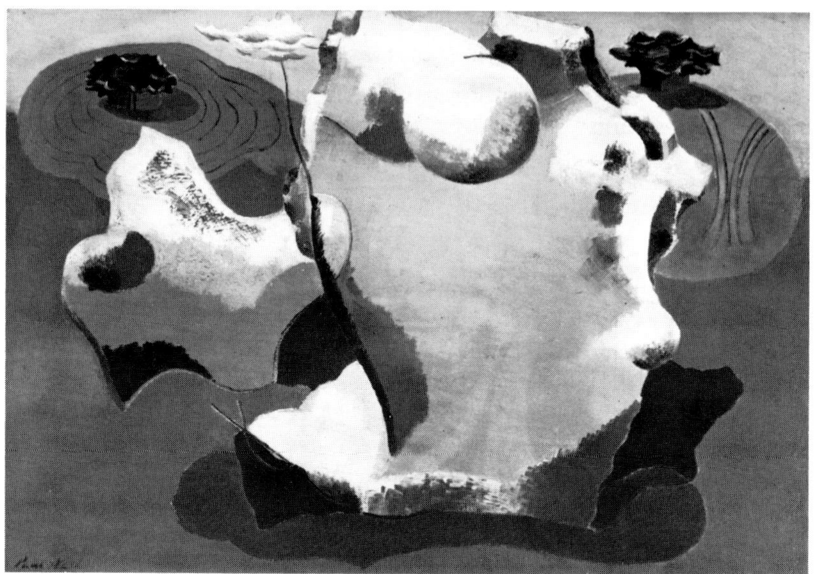

150. Paul Nash: *Landscape of the Megaliths*, 1933–4. Oil on canvas, $19\frac{3}{4} \times 28\frac{3}{4}$ in. (exhibited, as 'Landscape Composition', in the Unit One exhibition, Mayor Gallery, 1934, and in the International Surrealist Exhibition, 1936)

some kind or other. But I want a wider aspect, a different angle of vision as it were. This I am beginning to find through symbolism and in the power of association – not the rather freakish unlikely association of objects, so much as the *right* association as I feel it to be. It is only another step in the mystery of relationship. We are accustomed to seek forms which inter-relate, colours which are significant by juxtaposition. I desire to penetrate further – or if you like swing my net wider to include a relationship of spiritual personality – only I suppose I must find another word for spiritual, or be misunderstood.[4]

Nash wrote of painting *after* Nature, rather than *from* Nature. It is an important point that his major oil paintings of specific landscape themes were mostly done some time after the moment at which the relevant observation was made, often on the basis of drawings and watercolour sketches and increasingly, after 1931, with the aid of his own photographs.[5] In the transformation of a specific remembered scene into a composition of complex but well ordered relations, Nash allowed latitude for elements which were associative and evocative not merely of place, but also of personal or local or, increasingly after 1933, of 'mythic' history. A 'place' for Nash was thus not merely a picturesque scene; it was a congeries of interacting associations, fantasies and memories for which the arrangement of the finished picture was proposed as a suitable scenario. For him to paint a specific landscape or interior was to have seen it, often in retrospect, as the actual or potential occasion of a drama of moods and recollections. The sense of a need also to pursue formal interests of a kind which Clive Bell might have recognized often led him to simplify those very forms which were most instinct with idiosyncratic and evocative qualities. A strange balance is thus struck, as in de Chirico's work, between the mysterious and the monumental, as in the *Equivalents for the Megaliths* in the Tate Gallery [151].

Nash's visit of 1930 to the south of France in particular provided him with memories and with sketches which were not to be used as themes for finished oil paintings until several years later. *Harbour and Room* [152], dated 1932–6 by Nash himself, and *Voyages of the Moon*, largely completed in 1934, but slightly altered in 1937, are both based on earlier watercolours, dated 1931 and 1930 respectively, which themselves derive from scenes and details which had caught Nash's attention in a hotel in Toulon in 1930.[6] Particularly during the later twenties and early thirties, Nash tended to explore his more modernistic formal interests in drawings and watercolours rather than in oil paintings, perhaps because the latter represented a more considerable financial investment and were likely to receive a more sustained public scrutiny. This suggests a significant difference between Nash's practice and Nicholson's. Nicholson's interests were perhaps less diverse than Nash's, but they were always clearly

151. Paul Nash: *Equivalents for the Megaliths*, 1935. Oil on canvas, 18 × 26 in.

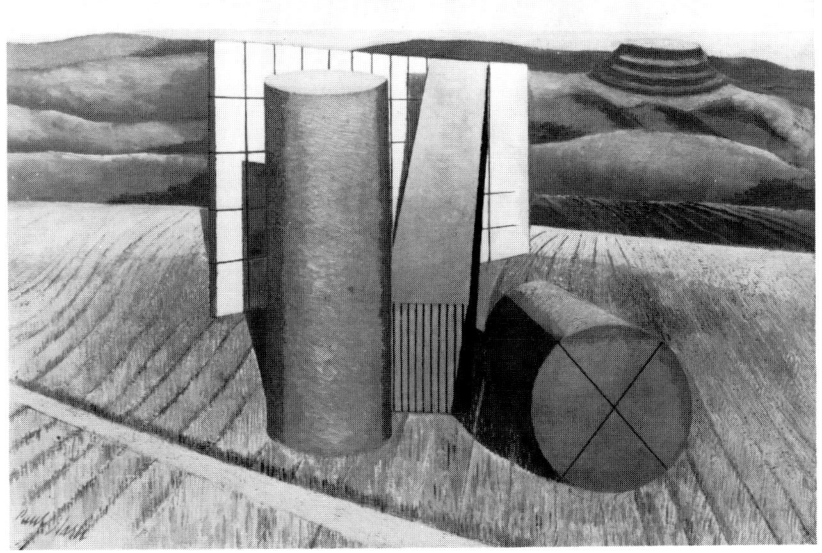

asserted in his work in their most developed form. By the mid-thirties, however, the example of European Surrealism had made it easier for Nash confidently to combine remembered elements into substantive compositions which departed significantly (if not always as far as at first appears) from conventional modes of representation based on the direct observation of integrated scenes. His painting thus came to seem more ambitious.

From 1933 onwards the works of the European Surrealists were featured in occasional exhibitions in London, with the Mayor Gallery taking the initiative. Apart from the Surrealist contingent in the re-opening exhibition of April 1933,[7] the gallery arranged one-man shows of the work of Ernst and Miró during the summer that followed. (Dali's first English one-man show was at the Lefevre Gallery in the following year.) 'As far as it can,' Geoffrey Grigson observed in reviewing the 'Art Now' exhibition in October 1933, 'the Mayor Gallery is doing the job which should be carried out by the Tate.'[8] In that April the Tate put on view the first work by Picasso to be purchased for a public collection in England: a small naturalistic flower painting of 1901. At about the same time, Moore, Nicholson and H. S. Ede launched an appeal to buy the more representative *Profile* of 1927, for presentation to a public gallery through the Contemporary Art Society. The appeal was abandoned at a total subscription of less than £7.[9]

The situation was improved in December 1933 when the Tate's modern French galleries were rehung to display the recently acquired Stoop bequest, with works by Degas, Matisse, Picasso, Modigliani, Van Gogh, Cézanne and Braque, but it was still the case that there was very little possibility of first-hand exposure in England to the continental art of the 1920s. Since the late 1920s, interested English artists had been looking at reproductions of Surrealist works in the various French periodicals available from Zwemmer's bookshop, but there was virtually no direct or sympathetic contact with fully-fledged Surrealism before 1933. Those English-language publications which had expressed an interest in Surrealism before 1934 were principally concerned with the literary aspects of the movement, or were published in Paris by expatriates and little circulated in England, or both.[10]

In the early 1930s, as we have seen, Nash was aware of the existence of a Surrealist movement, Moore was interested in Picasso's and Giacometti's Surrealist work, and Nicholson and Hepworth in Miró's and Arp's, but the more illustrative and anecdotal and technically stereotypical aspects of Surrealist art, as evidenced in the works of Dali, Ernst and Magritte, were unfamiliar or unattractive to English artists of any note until 1933 at the earliest.[11] And there was virtually no understanding of, or even acquaintance with, Surrealist theory.

The ground was not well prepared for the reception of Surrealism in England, nor for an understanding of its theoretical and political justifications. The twin tides of anti-rationalism which had flowed through the European avant gardes around the time of the First World War had not affected English art at the time or during the subsequent decade. On the one hand the direct influence of the earlier anti-materialist theories of Malevich, Kandinsky and Mondrian had been negligible, and by the time their work became the subject of informed interest, in the mid-1930s, the ideological and historical origins of those theories were lost to view among subsequent utopian rationalizations within which the paintings themselves had somehow become incorporated as objects of value. On the other hand England, virtually alone among the countries of Europe, had remained untouched by the ideas and activities of the Dadaists, insulated from them both by the isolating effects of the war itself and of its aftermath, and, perhaps, by a priggish distaste for irony and iconoclasm among those in a position to see themselves as informed about modern art.

Herbert Read was responsible more than any other writer for introducing the English public to modern art between the wars, but even he was ignorant about Dada and Surrealism in the early thirties. In 1933, in the original edition of *Art Now*, which included some informed discussion of Expressionism and abstract art, he devoted one short chapter (expanded and much revised three years later) to 'Subjective Idealism'.[12] In the context of a discussion of Picasso, he asserted that

> all links with the objective world are broken ... that love of the concrete which has characterised the art of Europe for centuries, and which has become inseparable from the very concept, is deliberately renounced. The painter instead turns all his perceptive faculties inwards, to the realm of his subjective fancies, his day dreams, his preconscious images. He replaces observation by intuition, analysis by synthesis, reality by 'symbolism'.

He devoted some three pages to 'Surréalisme' itself, in the course of which he dismissed 'Dada' as 'only a joke; or rather ... the gesture of men too bored with the tragedy of life to be anything but irreverent', appealed to his audience to 'at least make an attempt to understand the aim of artists so sincere and determined as Max Ernst, Joan Miró and André Masson', and avoided all reference to the political implications and affiliations of the Surrealist movement.

From 1934 onwards, however, as Nicholson and Hepworth and their allies and followers appeared increasingly to assert consistency and exclusiveness for the development of an abstract art, and as the works and writings of the continental Surrealists began to be exhibited and published in England, an interest in the evocative power of images and of relations between images, such as was expressed in Nash's statement in *Unit 1* and in his article in the first issue of *Axis*, came increasingly to characterize an antithetical position. A kind of variousness and unpredictability was increasingly exploited in English art as if in opposition to the idea of a universal harmony and its projected means of realization, unified design.

The European Surrealists had explored strategies for generating images of a kind normally ruled out by criteria of good conduct or of rationality in composition: collage as a means of making unlikely juxtapositions, frottage as a technique for generating suggestive pattern and texture, together with various other means of provoking 'chance' associations in pursuit of a critique of bourgeois rationality. Nash and Moore in particular were encouraged by the Surrealists' interest in the evocative power of 'found objects' to seek out such objects in the world as could be made to embody a sense of personality or to serve as the disguised sources of otherwise inexplicable compositional features. Nash recorded that after his visit to Avebury he became preoccupied with 'the problem of assembling and associating different objects in order to create that true irrational poise which is the solution of the personal equation'.[13] Moore wrote in 1937:

> Although it is the human figure which interests me most deeply, I have always paid great attention to natural form, such as bones, shells, and pebbles etc . . . There are universal shapes to which everybody is subconsciously conditioned and to which they can respond if their conscious control does not shut them off.[14]

Nash experimented with collage and with compositions of found elements between 1934 and 1937, and while Moore very rarely departed from conventional means of making sculpture, he did increasingly provoke incongruous responses to his figure-based sculptures after 1934, where he had earlier merely left them open to associations with aspects of landscape or of other 'natural' forms.

For those like Moore, Nash and Grigson whose support for abstract art was tempered by anxiety that an ideal harmony involved a degree of suppression or extinction of biological and psychological life, the influence of Surrealism served as a basis for introduction of the necessary 'humanizing' accidental and 'biological' element into the harmonious world of the planner. So much was clear, as we have seen, from Grigson's relative evaluations of Nicholson and Moore, and Nash's characterization of his own position in relation to abstract art. In a sense, the best of the 'pure' abstract art of the 1930s – a category in which Nicholson's and Hepworth's work is included or to which it can be related – seemed to express the interests of beings with no basic needs or pleasures. The 'accident' beloved of the Surrealists – whether this signified abnegation of certain kinds of control as a function of the means of application of paint, or unpredictability as a feature of response to the conjunction of incongruous images – was only trivially a 'random' occurrence instigated as an aspect of a technical strategy. More importantly, the celebration of 'accident' was an assertion of

152. Paul Nash: *Harbour and Room*, 1932–6. Oil on canvas, 36 × 28 in. (exhibited in the International Surrealist Exhibition, 1936)

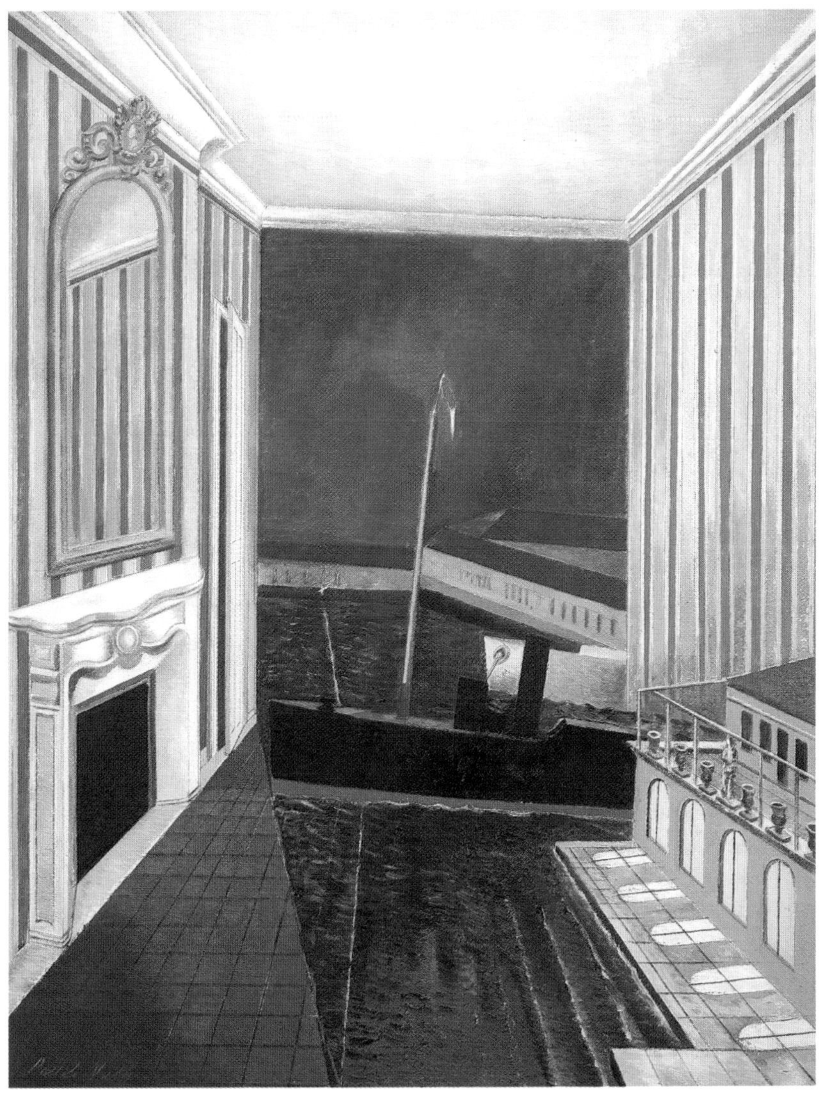

the need to see certain aspects of both private and social life as subject to control, planning and design only in the interests of oppression.

The advanced artists' interests came increasingly to be expressed in terms of antitheses. As we have seen, the avant garde promoted by Nash in 1933 as a coherent and unified movement had dissolved into factions within two years. By 1937 Moore could speak of 'the violent quarrel between the abstractionists and the surrealists'.[15] His own superficially ingenuous comment upon this quarrel was that he found it 'unnecessary', since 'All good art has contained both abstract and surrealist elements, just as it has contained both classic and romantic elements – order and surprise, intellect and imagination, conscious and unconscious.'[16] Certainly, in his own work of 1935–6, that reconciliation of 'abstract' with 'Surrealist' interests which had characterized the beginning of Unit One appeared to remain feasible as it did in no one else's. He was the only artist who continued regularly to show in exhibitions of abstract art while associating himself with Surrealism in England.

But whatever value there may have been in Moore's concept of the all-inclusiveness of good art, and in his own apparent ability to reconcile what were opposites for others, the development of an explicit interest in Surrealism in England generally marked a process of polarization within the ranks of the avant garde; first between the abstractionists (or 'Ben boys' as Paul Nash was wont to call them) and those who saw Surrealism as an alternative; and later between the advocates of Surrealism and those who proposed a form of Socialist Realism in the later thirties. The underlying issues are complex, and are not to be disentangled by a mere review of different styles of art. We should now therefore consider the spread of Surrealist ideas in England in relation to the competition of various interests and of different views on the function of art during the thirties.

Before 1935, informed interest in Surrealism in England, where it was more than a specialized interest in the work of individual artists, was largely shown in response to the literary aspects of the movement, and there was general ignorance about the political revolutionary claims of André Breton and others of the continental leaders. (Wyndham Lewis, as so often, was an exception. As early as 1927, in an issue of *The Enemy*, he referred to the Surrealists – pejoratively – as 'the intellectual wing ... of the communist party in Paris'.[17]) By early 1936, however, the position had changed dramatically. *Cahiers d'Art* no. x, of 1935, had published in French some excerpts from a purported 'English Manifesto of Surrealism'. This was the work of a nineteen-year-old English poet, David Gascoyne, who was then living in Paris in close contact with Breton, Eluard, Hugnet and others centrally involved in the movement. Gascoyne's declaration of principles was as follows:

(1) Complete agreement with the principles of surrealism as set forth by Breton.
(2) Complete adherence to the historical materialism of Marx, Engels and Lenin.
(3) Surrealism opens vast fields of action in England in poetry, the arts, philosophy.
(4) Complete and unrelenting opposition to fascism, war, imperialism, nationalism, humanism, liberalism, idealism, anarchic individualism, art for art's sake, religious fideism, and generally to any doctrine that would tend to justify the survival of capitalism.[18]

Although this 'manifesto' was the individual initiative of a writer, and seems to have passed unnoticed in England at the time (the more avid English consumers of *Cahiers d'Art*, such as Moore, were not great readers of French and were anyway more interested in the pictures than the text), Gascoyne's *Short Survey of Surrealism*, published as a book in London in November of the same year, received sufficient attention to justify retrospectively the claim that there were 'fields of action' to be opened up by Surrealism in England. Besides Surrealist poems, Gascoyne published sections from important theoretical texts, including Breton's first and second manifestos of 1924 and 1929, and illustrated a selection of works by relevant artists. Though the *Short Survey* was indeed no more than that, it was both informed and relatively representative.

Gascoyne left his readers in no doubt as to the nature of the movement and of its ambitions.

It is the avowed aim of the surrealist movement to reduce and finally to dispose altogether of the flagrant contradictions that exist between dream and waking life, the 'unreal' and the 'real', the unconscious and the conscious, and thus to make of what has hitherto been regarded as the special domain of poets, the acknowledged common property of all.

... only the imminence of proletarian revolution allows surrealism to hope that its aims will ultimately be fulfilled. The surrealist cause is the revolutionary cause ...

The terms of reference for the criticism of art appear to have changed quite dramatically in England during the years 1934–5. Perhaps because the political situation in Europe was now so clearly desperate – clearly so at least in the eyes of all whose minds were not closed by the need to believe that crisis could be avoided – it had suddenly come to seem that a modern art must be seen as somehow proposing a better-than-technical change.

'Revolutionary' became a strong positive valuation which critics of different loyalties competed in applying to the movements they supported. Gascoyne's concluding assertion was thus plainly open to challenge, particularly from those in the Artists International who had reason to regard themselves as the more-or-less official spokesmen for the radical left in art.

In March 1935, in response to Soviet policy that the Communist Party should form as many broad fronts as possible in opposition to Fascism, the Artists International had broadened its aims in order to attract all those concerned at the rise of Fascism, the suppression of (modernist) culture and the erosion of free speech. In line with this aim the name was changed to Artists International Association, and a large if nominal Advisory Council was established with a membership which included representatives of virtually every modern development of the previous three decades.[19] There was less emphasis upon propaganda and polemic and more upon debate and the 'raising of consciousness'. The membership increased considerably. In the same month that the *Short Survey of Surrealism* was published, the AIA sponsored the publication of a collection of essays under the title *Five on Revolutionary Art*.[20] As the author of the foreword asserted,

> Revolutionary art is at present an extremely controversial subject among those artists who are interested in the theory and history of their craft ... The future of art hangs on the future of civilisation. It is time the artists began to think what sort of future they want, and what they can do to get it.

In the opening essay, Read was there to arbitrate between the claims of the abstract artists and those of the Surrealists (about which he was by now better informed).

> ... within the general category of revolutionary art, we have two distinct movements, both professing to be modern, both *intentionally* revolutionary.
>
> The first of these has no very descriptive label, but it is essentially formalist ... It is sometimes called abstract, sometimes non-figurative, sometimes constructivist, sometimes geometric. It is most typically represented by painters like Mondrian, Hélion, Ben Nicholson, Moholy-Nagy; and by sculptors like Brancusi, Gabo and Barbara Hepworth.
>
> The second movement has a distinctive name – Surréalisme or Superrealism, and it is represented by painters like Max Ernst, Salvador Dali, Miró, Tanguy, and by a sculptor like Arp.
>
> The first movement is plastic, objective and ostensibly non-political. The second group is literary (even in paint), subjective, and actively Communist ...

> Superrealism is a negative art ... a destructive art; it follows that it has only a temporary role; it is the art of a transitional period. It may lead to a new romanticism, especially in literature, but that lies beyond its immediate function.
>
> But abstract art has a positive function. It keeps inviolate, until such time as society will once more be ready to make use of them, the universal qualities of art – those elements which survive all changes and revolutions ...
>
> The artists are waiting for their opportunity; abstract artists who are, in this time of transition, perfecting their formal sensibility, and who will be ready, when the time comes, to apply their talents to the great work of reconstruction.

Read's valuation of abstract art coincided with that idealization of the artist's and architect's progressive function which was to invest the publication of *Circle*. Though he wrote as a supporter of 'revolutionary art' the extent of his sympathy with Marxism – the prevailing theory of revolutionary politics – is to be measured by his belief that art is 'more marxist than the Marxians',[21] an assertion which might well have been made by Gabo. In so far as Read saw the main problem of existence as the reconciliation of reason and instinct, and works of art as the ideal occasions of such a reconciliation, his writing was bound to presuppose the positive and remedial value of art. It was as if belief in the necessarily progressive function of art made it possible for him to conceive of revolution in a highly privileged sense; i.e. as a form of voluntary change in the experience of individuals which was independent of the need for struggle between the classes of which those individuals were members.

On the other hand, for the three Marxist contributors to the AIA symposium, Francis Klingender, A. L. Lloyd and Alick West, who were concerned above all with the actual possibility of social change, and specifically with the possibility of defeat of the bourgeoisie by the working class, all modern art (or all 'modernistic' art) was to be viewed as potentially symptomatic of the development and decadence of the bourgeoisie. The problem was thus to see what, if anything, could defensibly be salvaged for the future. All three emphasized the 'negation of content' in modernist art, which they interpreted as a consequence of the flight from reality by the dominant class. In mitigation, they identified as saving graces firstly that modern art offered strong testimony to a need for concrete criticism and for a non-bogus sense of creativity, if only through its very lack of realistic content, and secondly that it provided examples of that 'formal sensibility and technical brilliance' which they saw as having been developed during a period of enforced individuality and specialization. Comparative poverty was a condition which many artists experienced in the 1930s, and real poverty was a condition which it must sometimes have been difficult for them not to observe. (In September 1932 between six and seven million people were dependent on the dole.) Klingender felt artists would come to find a sense of identity with the working class. 'Transposed with the vital energy of the new social content,' he wrote optimistically, 'the technical achievements of modern art will at last lead to an undreamed of enrichment of human experience.'

A. L. Lloyd's view of abstract art and Surrealism can be set against Read's.

> Artists who were taken for revolutionaries at the beginning of the century are, after thirty-five years' work, so far from resolving the problem left by the history of the nineteenth century of creating an art based, not on an abstract logic, but on dialectical materialism, that in most cases they have fallen to the other extreme, to the feudal limits of the bourgeoisie, by virtue of the smart modern forms of reaction ...
>
> The contemporary position ... is rather like this: On the one hand flourishes an abstract idealism concretising in form and colour, not the surface of objects represented, not even the symbol of states of mind, but, in so far as is possible, just the expression of the function of shape and colour ...
>
> On the other hand there are the surrealists, whose tendency is towards an idealised realism, often using ... a deliberately reactionary technique with a view to developing a three-dimensional corporeality of irrational dream states and phantasies ...
>
> It would be absolutely false to imagine that this extraordinary interior scission was some purely personal or aesthetic manifestation. This phenomenon, on the contrary, is characteristic of the whole bourgeois situation, in its departure from the freethought and materialism in which it was born, and its return to a quasi-mediaeval, metaphysical ideology which it had combated in the beginning.

The fifth contributor to *Five on Revolutionary Art* was Eric Gill, who appeared as author of a short article to the effect that 'All art is propaganda, for it is in fact impossible to do anything, to make anything which is not expressive of "value".' Gill equated Catholicism with a kind of ideal communism – or at least with opposition to the bourgeoisie ('the founders of the modern world, in which all things are merchandise, money is the ruling power and all things are made for the profit of investors') – and he was a supporter of the AIA, despite the express disapproval of his archbishop.[22]

The different views voiced in respect of the revolutionary status of art in the mid-thirties reflected argument on some substantial issues – a degree of recovery, as it were, of some of the 'lost' history of the ideological origins of modern art. It is a measure of the sudden improvement in the general level of critical discourse that such discussions took place at all. Klingender in particular was a scholar of distinction who did much to illuminate the history of art by means of an (occasionally vulgarized) historical materialist critique.[23]

Many of those who now contributed to the criticism of modern art, and to debate about its relationship with the possibility of social change, were men who had been educated in the traditions of a liberal bourgeois culture during the twenties, and had subsequently been provoked to review their own tastes and priorities as a result of the sudden spread of Marxist ideas. Where such ideas took hold, belief in the technical and moral autonomy of art was inevitably rendered insecure. As Marx and Engels replaced Fry and Bell on their bookshelves, many of those whose sense of the history of art had been governed by the criterion of 'significant form' now reconstructed that history in terms of a series of 'progressive' endeavours. Courbet replaced Cézanne as the typical heroic forebear of the modern artist, at least in the eyes of the avant-garde critics.

> The line of Daumier, Courbet, the early Van Gogh, Meunier and Dalou is that of the real art of the growing proletariat, while that of the bourgeoisie continues towards the abstraction of the twentieth century.[24]

The quotation is taken from an article by Anthony Blunt, published in the *Left Review*. The foundation of the *Left Review* by the Writers International in 1934 provided a forum both for the new generation of critics on the left, who aimed to survey contemporary art from a historical materialist position, and for many of the artist members of the AIA, who contributed cartoons and illustrations. James Holland was the art editor and James Boswell and James Fitton were regular contributors. The prevailing style of the artwork owed much to George Grosz, though there was no member of the AIA who could match the sharpness of the German artist's observation and attack or the quality of his draughtsmanship.

Blunt wrote regularly for the *Left Review*, and was typical of those university-educated young men who began to write about modern art in the mid-thirties with the assurance of a new-found interest in Marxism. He later described the prevalence of that interest among his contemporaries.

> ... quite suddenly, in the autumn term of 1933, Marxism hit Cambridge. ... I found that almost all my younger friends had become Marxists and joined the Communist Party; and Cambridge was literally transformed overnight ...

> The new ideas involved a complete reversal of everything that we had held before. Art for art's sake, Pure Form, went by the board totally. We believed, on the contrary, that art was a human activity, that works of art were created by men, that men were human beings, that human beings lived in society, and that society was influenced by social conditions, and ultimately by economic conditions. And this meant a reformulation not only of our theories but also our judgements on individual artists.[25]

Brief though this conversion may have been for many, the general standard of debate about art was undoubtedly improved in the mid-thirties as the spread of historical materialist ideas provided a strong counter to the privileged aesthetics which Fry and Bell had expounded. For some, an interest in Surrealism was the initial means of exposure to such ideas; for others, like Blunt, they were to be learned as aspects of an intellectual life enriched by the participation of European émigrés. It is important to recognize, however, that in so far as practising artists were active participants in public discussion in the mid and later thirties, they were mostly drawn from the ranks of the commercial artists, designers and illustrators who made up the majority of the early members of the AIA, rather than from the various factions of modernist painters and sculptors. The former had perhaps less cause for insecurity in face of Marxist critiques. So far as the modernist practice of fine art was concerned, there was little sympathy in England for the idea that art should be placed at the service of anyone, or indeed for the idea that it might need to be seen as determined by or expressive of a specific set of class interests.

On the other hand, when events challenged their broadly liberal sympathies, artists of every persuasion were united to a degree that the population as a whole was certainly not. Once its early phase of militant communism was terminated in the name of the broad front, the AIA served as a focal point for the expression of such sympathies. In November 1935, following Mussolini's invasion of Abyssinia, when the association organized an exhibition 'Against War and Fascism' in a house in Grosvenor Square, Augustus John, Henry Moore, Ben Nicholson, Barbara Hepworth, John Piper, Duncan Grant and Laszlo Moholy-Nagy were among those who contributed work. Copies of *Five on Revolutionary Art* were on sale. As the author of a notice in the *Left Review* noted wryly, 'From the Left wing of the R.A. to Unit One – those whom art politics have put asunder, an exhibition against War and Fascism has joined together.'[26] Similarly, the outbreak of the Spanish Civil War in July 1936 united the great majority of the modern artists as sympathizers with the Republican cause. A year later, Epstein, Moholy-Nagy, Moore, Gill, Grant, Vanessa Bell and Ben Nicholson were among those who gave works for an 'Artists Help Spain' exhibition and sale. In the spring of 1937 the AIA staged a 'First British Artists Congress' with an attendant exhibition of 'Artists for Peace, Democracy and Cultural Development', in an attempt at organizing 'progressive cultural opinion' in discussion of the 'Present Relation of the Artist to Society'.[27] Once again the platform was sufficiently broad and liberal to attract wide support. Around a thousand works were shown in the exhibition, in which abstract and Surrealist art was shown together with craft work and work from working men's societies. Two years later, in the catalogue for a massive exhibition held at the Whitechapel Art Gallery under the same slogan of unity 'for Peace, Democracy and Cultural Development', the association could claim 700 members. There were 112 exhibitors on this occasion, included among them virtually every English artist who could reasonably have been considered 'modern' at the time.

Such exhibitions attracted comparatively little attention, however, in relation to the interest generated by the International Surrealist Exhibition, which opened at the New Burlington Galleries on 11 June 1936. Gascoyne had concluded his *Short Survey* with a promise of things to come. During 1935 he and Roland Penrose, a wealthy collector and painter then living in Paris, had met and decided to form a Surrealist group in London. By the end of the year a nucleus of interested people was meeting in Hampstead, and from these a committee was formed to organize the Surrealist invasion. Its members were Hugh Sykes Davies, David Gascoyne, Humphrey Jennings, Edward McKnight Kauffer, Rupert Lee (chairman), Henry Moore, Paul Nash, Roland Penrose and Herbert Read. They were assisted by a French committee of André Breton, Paul Eluard, Georges Hugnet and Man Ray. Salvador Dali represented Spain and E. L. T. Mesens Belgium. The exhibition included over four hundred exhibits by some fifty-four artists drawn from fourteen nations. The major figures associated with the movement were all represented by considerable groups of works: Chirico, Dali, Ernst, Giacometti, Klee, Magritte, Masson, Miró, Paalen, Picasso, Man Ray and Tanguy; and there was a large contingent of English contributors. Many of these were no doubt persuaded of their own affiliation to the movement by little more than the opportunity to participate,[28] but there were by now several artists who had produced enough work in appropriate styles to appear as credible exhibitors in this context.

Moore and Nash were of course foremost among the latter. The inclusion of Moore's lead *Reclining Figure* of 1931 [130] must have demonstrated at least that he had taken more extreme liberties with the human figure than any other English artist since the first war. Nash showed four paintings: *Harbour and Room* [152], *Encounter in the Afternoon*, *Mansions of the Dead*

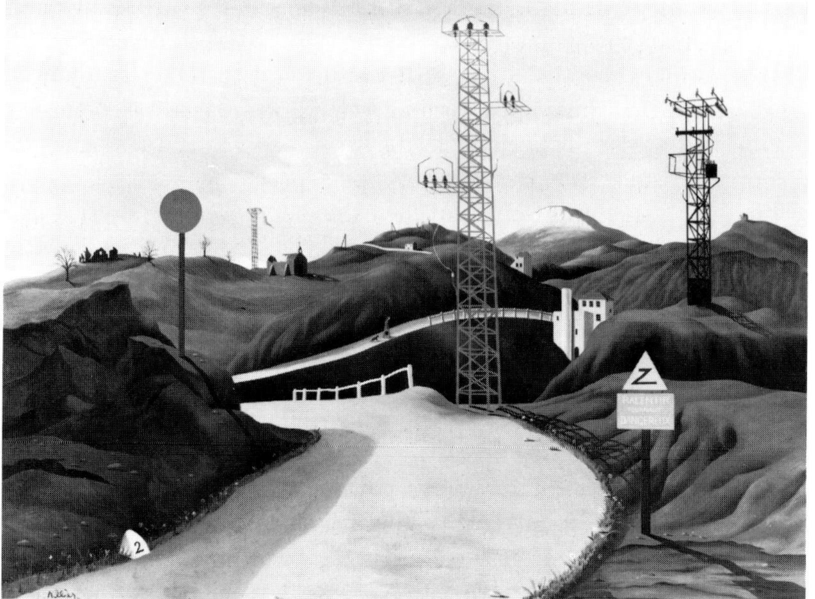

153. Tristram Hillier: *La Route des Alpes*, 1937. Tempera on canvas, $23\frac{1}{2} \times 31\frac{1}{2}$ in.

and *Landscape of the Megaliths* [150], together with five collages, two 'designed objects' and a 'found object interpreted'. Of the other former members of Unit One, Burra showed six oils and Bigge two. Hillier, who might well have been selected on the basis of his work of the early thirties, did not exhibit. In the next year, on his move to Vence in southern France, he virtually withdrew from participation in the modern movement and from that point pursued a style of 'heightened realism' in tempera paintings with sharply defined forms [153].

Penrose showed four oils and two constructions. His Surrealist work was not original but it was a competent emulation of continental models, with which he had a close acquaintance. Two of the other exhibitors, Humphrey Jennings and Julian Trevelyan, had met while students at Cambridge and had been involved in publication of the magazine *Experiment*, in which some early notice had been taken of Surrealist literature at the close of the 1920s.[29] Together with Tom Harrisson and Charles Madge, Jennings was soon to become involved in the formation of the Mass Observation Unit, an early endeavour to apply a form of casual social anthropology to the contemporary culture of Britain.

The print-maker Stanley Hayter was also substantially represented. As a long-time expatriate he played a more significant part in the history of French than of English art, but his Atelier 17 in Paris served for many younger English artists, Trevelyan among them, as a means of introduction to the European avant garde.[30]

John Banting and Eileen Agar were two other English exhibitors who had been producing work in a Surrealist vein for more than a brief period before the exhibition. Ceri Richards was a surprising absentee. At about this time he began producing relief constructions and paintings [154] strongly determined by the influence of Picasso and of Max Ernst and he made some interesting ink drawings which have strong points of resemblance (perhaps because they have a common source) with later work by the American-Armenian Arshile Gorky.

154. Ceri Richards: *The Female Contains all the Qualities*, 1937. Oil and mixed media on canvas, 42 × 35 in.

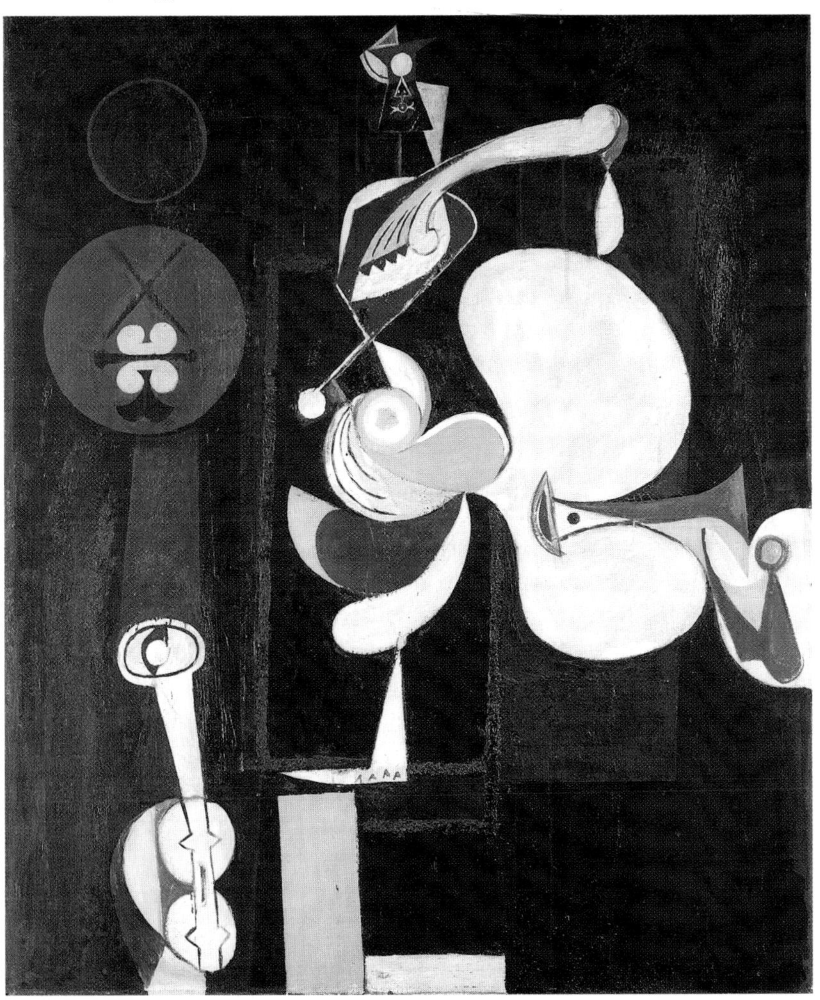

Read's reservations about Surrealism seem to have been subject to progressive modification as he found himself obliged to defend the movement to a hostile public. His introduction to the catalogue struck a note of challenge.

Do not judge this movement kindly. It is not just another amusing stunt. It is defiant – the desperate act of men too profoundly convinced of the rottenness of our civilisation to want to save a shred of its respectability.[31]

The Studio responded with a dismissive editorial: 'The quality of imagination is either feeble or vicious, sometimes both.'[32] The exhibition was visited by over 20,000 people and was widely, if on the whole unfavourably, reviewed. It was accompanied by lectures from Breton, Read, Eluard, Sykes Davies and Dali, some of which formed the basis for a book published later in the year under Read's editorship.[33] According to Read, this book was intended for that 'serious public of scientists, artists, philosophers and socialists' which the exhibition was supposed to have created, and 'in the confident hope of extending its membership'.

Considerable stress was laid by Read, Breton and Sykes Davies on the relevance to Surrealism of English Romantic literature, from the Gothick novels of the later eighteenth century to the Romantic poets.

In all the essentials of romanticism, Surrealism continues the earlier movement. But ... the advances made by Surrealism are now beyond question. It has continued the romantic impulse but it has developed, enlarged, co-ordinated and enriched it ... on an international scale and for the sake of all humanity (Sykes Davies).

At the time of the Spanish Civil War and the occupation of factories by workers in France (which he interpreted as the onset of revolution), Breton in particular was concerned to place the event of the International Surrealist Exhibition in the context of international politics, and to relate the aims of the movement to specific forms of political action. On the other hand he firmly rejected the doctrine of Socialist Realism and the interpretation of propaganda which was implicit in it.

... we expressly oppose the view that it is possible to create a work of art or even, properly considered, any useful work by expressing only the *manifest content* of an age. On the contrary, Surrealism proposes to express its *latent content*.

The key to this latent content, in Breton's view, was the 'fantastic', for

It is only at the approach of the fantastic, at a point where human reason loses its control, that the most profound emotion of the individual has the fullest opportunity to express itself; emotion unsuitable for projection in the framework of the real world and which has no other solution in its urgency than to rely on the eternal solicitations of symbols and myths.

It was precisely upon this issue that the Surrealists and their adherents in England were divided in their leftism from the nucleus of communists within the AIA and the *Left Review*. In a special supplement on Surrealism in the July 1936 issue of the *Left Review*, Read asserted that 'Reality transformed by the imagination' was 'the definition of art and the aim of Surrealism.' The movement was attacked by Blunt and West, on the other hand, on the grounds that it was essentially bourgeois and had 'no roots at all in the rising class'.[34] The proletariat, it was felt, needed neither mythology nor psychoanalysis; what it needed was support in the form either of critical action and ridicule against the ruling class or of affirmation of its own historic achievements.

The English artists (including theatrical and film producers) who today are consciously allying themselves to the working class are either adopting the activist manner of the continental early post-war phase (especially that of Grosz or the earliest Piscator productions), or else attempting in the light of later continental experience to create a new style – utilising all technical achievements of modern art – that will be able to express the basic content of the proletarian struggle in a fully convincing manner, appealing to the workers (Klingender).[35]

(The latter alternative was, of course, an incantation for a picture which has yet to be painted, a formula composed of Marxist paraphrase and pious hope. Many of the aspirations of the AIA members were kept alive by a roseate vision of the conditions of art – and life – in Stalinist Russia.)

On 23 June 1936 the AIA organized a debate at the Conway Hall in London on the social aspects of Surrealism. Over the next three years the 'social function' of the artist was to become the principal subject of public dispute among those interested in modern art. Nothing could have been more different from the critical discourse of the 1920s. By way of summary we might make a crude typification of the three principal points of view upon the subject and of the three relevant concepts of 'progressiveness': (1) the abstract and constructive artists on the whole idealized the artist as the typical designer of the forms of a new and harmonious world of which he was thus an important instigator; (2) the Surrealists saw the artist as the anarchic and unafraid guardian of the values of an 'uncensored' humanity and as an informed critic of the bourgeois world; while (3) the Marxists and would-be Social Realists saw the artist as the propagandist for and servant of proletarian revolution.

That it should have seemed possible to many participants and spectators to interpret the 'violent quarrel' between the abstract artists and the Surrealists as a mere function of the incompatibility of different technical or stylistic interests is a measure of the extent to which art's grip upon history had been loosened by the persistent concentration of artists and critics upon the assertion of an automatic moral autonomy for modernist art, and by the silencing, for one reason or by one eventuality or another, of those whose voices might have been raised in early opposition to this assertion. In fact the schism within the English modernists in the mid-thirties was a reflection of the opposition in Europe during the 1920s of two fundamentally irreconcilable concepts of radicalism in art: on the one hand the theoria of abstract art and of advanced design in the twenties generally proposed an ideal harmony as an implicit critique of the lack of 'spiritual satisfaction' and of 'progressive planning' in modern society; on the other, the theoria of Surrealism proposed irrationality and disorder as means of criticizing and subverting prevailing (bourgeois) concepts of reason and order. The antipathy between the 'extreme' advocate of abstract art and the 'extreme' advocate of Surrealism was a distant expression of the antagonism between different political philosophies: as it were between a highly idealized form of socialism-plus-planning without class-consciousness, and a highly idealized form of anarchy-plus-psychiatry with class-consciousness.[36] It is hard to imagine how the proponents of such fundamentally irreconcilable views, or even their distant and largely unconscious adherents, could act together to any very real purpose, were their ideological incompatibilities allowed to become explicit. The artists were driven apart, that is to say, not so much by the incompatibility of their technical interests as by the working-out of a historical logic of which they were perhaps largely unaware, and from which the purported forms of autonomy in art served to insulate them.

A concept of the social, technical and moral autonomy of art was what the adherents to abstract art and to Surrealism ultimately held in common, although in fact this autonomy was differently grounded for each. Though the positions of abstract artist and Surrealist were seen as antithetical within the restricted discourse of the contemporary English art world, and though we would assert that they were antithetical at a 'deep level', they were instantly reconciled, socially and tactically, in the face of any suggestion that art should submit to the dictates of a particular view of history, and that it should explicitly serve the interests of one class against those of another. What divided the Surrealists from the communists in England was not a dispute about the nature of proletarian culture within a class-based conception of culture, but rather what had divided Gabo from Tatlin: reluctance to surrender the notion that the artist's insights are 'special', and his activities necessarily privileged, whichever class is in power. It is either a cause or a consequence of such reluctance that the possibility of proletarian revolution is seen as entailing the likelihood of an impoverishment of the 'human spirit'. Commitment to the concept of revolutionary practice was, to say the least, marginal for abstract art, and should be viewed with some scepticism vis-à-vis Surrealism.

On the other hand, for the Historical Materialists, who were committed to the notion that the 'superstructural' activities of the artist are determined, like everyone else's, by basic economic and productive forces, any concept of 'progressive' function had to be related to a belief in the transforming potential of a whole class. Their problem, of course, was to find a contemporary art to support. The protagonists of Social Realism and of art-as-propaganda were bereft of technical history and of local precedent, and were so dependent upon German models as to be almost entirely inconsiderable in any view of the technical development of the fine arts in England. In so far as there was anything like an art expressing what Klingender called 'the basic content of the proletarian struggle' in England in the 1930s, it remains opaque to the scope of this study. Whoever it may have been produced for, 'art' was produced by the bourgeois, then as now.[37] What was notable about the large AIA exhibitions in the later thirties was not that they demonstrated alternatives, but that they provided the most liberal and permissive occasions for the exhibition of works of art across the whole technical and stylistic range of modern practice. The history of art was not credibly to be transformed into a history of 'progressive' endeavours (in a better-than-technical sense) independently of some form of social transformation. The art history of the 1930s is still principally a history of the art that was produced by accredited 'artists', and which enjoyed the support of the art-consuming bourgeoisie where appropriate standards of competence were maintained. (This is not, however, to reject the possibility of a democratized culture.)

Read's contribution to the Conway Hall debate was printed in the fourth issue of the *International Surrealist Bulletin*, published in London in September 1936.[38] He asserted that the Surrealist is 'naturally a Marxian socialist, and generally claims he is a more consistent communist than many who submit to all manner of compromise with the aesthetic culture and moral convention of capitalism.' But Read's concept of the artist was still such as to entail freedom from determination by those class interests which were actually seen by Marx as essential dynamics of revolution. The English Surrealists were indeed a social rather than a political group,[39] and their activities were easily enough incorporated into the contemporary art life of London.

There were some new recruits among the contributors to an exhibition of 'Surrealist Objects and Poems' which was opened at the London Gallery at midnight on 25 November 1937, and in April of the next year the group was provided with an organ of publicity and discussion with the founding of the *London Bulletin*. E. L. T. Mesens, then director of the London Gallery, edited the journal with assistance from Humphrey Jennings, Roland Penrose and others. As well as articles, reviews and poems, it carried notices and catalogues of exhibitions at the Mayor Gallery and Guggenheim Jeune as well as the London Gallery itself, at a time when all three were often showing Surrealist work. It was not exclusively devoted to Surrealist art; the second issue in May 1938 carried an article by Nash on John Piper, Ben Nicholson was featured in the eleventh and twelfth issues, and the fourteenth, in May 1939, was largely devoted to an 'Abstract and Concrete Art' exhibition at Guggenheim Jeune; overall, however, the *London Bulletin* served interests compatible with Surrealism. Breton, Eluard, Hugnet, Samuel Beckett and Henry Miller appeared as contributors alongside Read, Penrose, Nash, Jennings and Mesens.

The seventh issue, dated December 1938/January 1939, carried a translation of the manifesto 'Towards an Independent Revolutionary Art', signed by Breton and Diego Rivera but actually composed by Breton together with Leon Trotsky.[40] The manifesto announced the formation of an 'International Federation of Independent Revolutionary Art' (FIARI). The text had been sent from Paris, perhaps in the hope that the English Surrealists might form a branch of the federation. A group did meet at the London Gallery to discuss such a formation, but there was no agreement on the necessity for artistic activity to be integrated in accord with specific political aims or beliefs.[41] In the winter of 1939/40 another meeting was held with the aim of securing unity under a three-point programme, which involved adherence to the idea of proletarian revolution, acceptance of a ban on participation in other groups and submission to the requirement that members should not exhibit or publish except as Surrealists. Read, who had by this time adopted a peculiar anarchist philosophy, was expelled for his unwillingness to accept these conditions.[42]

By this time neither Nash nor Moore was any longer explicitly associated with the Surrealist group, and the movement, as such, was a spent force in England. In the 'Living Art in England' exhibition of early 1939, Nash exhibited as an 'independent'. Moore was still designated as a 'Surrealist', and certainly some of his most metaphorically expressive works are to be found among the smaller reclining figures of 1937–9. A small *Reclining Figure* in lead of late 1939 (LH 208), for instance, reveals a continuing interest in Picasso's more Surrealist works of the 1920s (see his drawing of a

Girl with Tambourine of 1925). But Moore was not one to accept a programme of any kind, and the label can have implied little more than his subscription to a set of stylistic and interpretational possibilities.

It should be said that despite the success of Surrealism as a subject of interest and debate in England in the later thirties, there were no truly Surrealist artists in England who were of any real significance to the history of the movement as a whole, or, indeed, to the history of English art. Those, like Jennings, Banting and Trevelyan, whose participation in the movement entailed some passing commitment to its political ideology, were not technically equipped to transform that commitment into a vivid art. On the other hand, those artists who were so equipped were comparatively indifferent to, or ignorant of, the problems involved in the concept of a revolutionary art. Nash and Moore lent their support to the movement, as they did to so many other endeavours, because they felt that it would advance the cause of art, but it is hard to imagine how they could have been very deeply committed to the ideas which gave that movement such coherence as it had.

Apart from his small collages and assembled objects, which were not very considerable works, the painting which most clearly illustrates Nash's interest in Surrealism is his *Landscape from a Dream* [155], begun in 1936

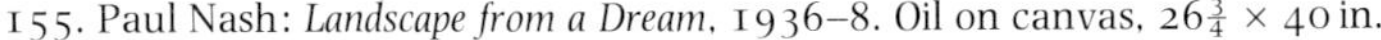

155. Paul Nash: *Landscape from a Dream*, 1936–8. Oil on canvas, $26\frac{3}{4} \times 40$ in.

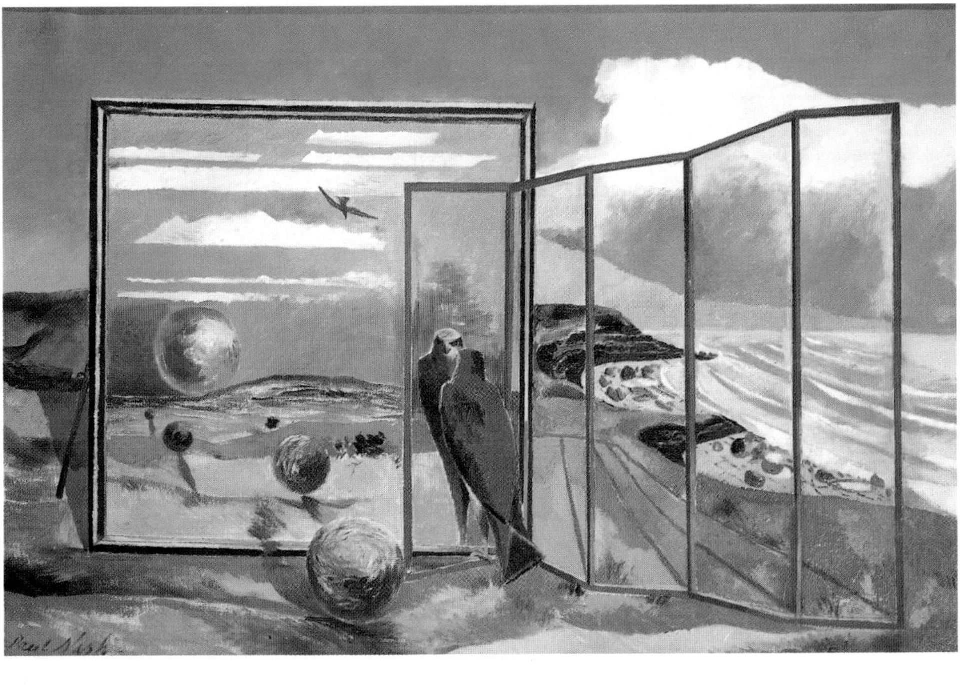

and finished not later than 1938.[43] Even here, though, his adherence to the tenets and characteristic technical practices of the movement is limited to a mildly incongruous juxtaposition of elements. On grassland above the shale cliffs of Dorset, a painted landscape is set up like a billboard beside the open framework of what looks like a folding screen. A hawk, standing on the grass, is reflected in the painting as if it were a mirror. Another bird hangs in the sky over the 'painted' landscape. A 'metamorphic' relation is established between the balls of grass in the 'real' and the 'painted' landscape and the enlarged sun setting in the latter. The warm evening light of the picture within the picture contrasts with the cooler and clearer light around it. The long reflections cast by the framework of the screen add poignancy to this contrast by encouraging the reading of the painted landscape as a mirror reflecting a 'real' sunset, somewhere, as it were, behind the spectator's back. As usually in Nash's painting, it is the arrangement of the composition, rather than the objects themselves, that is invented; and however unconventional that arrangement may be, what the painting ultimately embodies is an interest in the interpretation of the English landscape and in the expression of a melancholy and retrospective mood, rather than the uncovering of the subconscious, or the criticism of bourgeois rationality or whatever. The painting is formally but not 'ideologically' Surrealist, except in so far as the investigation of a kind of semantic paradox (picture or mirror?) was entailed by some of the Surrealists' technical interests. Comparison with Magritte is naturally invited, and Nash was certainly interested in his work for a while. The comparison is not one by which Magritte is likely to gain, however.

In terms of the development of art, the influence of Surrealism in England was most successfully assimilated into the modernist technology of painting where it was interpreted, as in Nash's work of the later thirties, as a means of updating and complicating a romantic interest in landscape subjects; where landscape, that is to say, was interpreted as the occasion and context of 'complicated' psychological experience, symbolically expressed.

As regards sculpture, the effect of the influence of Surrealism – which until the end of the thirties was very largely confined to the work of Moore – was to increase the range of variations which could defensibly be played on the formal themes presented by the human body, and thus also to increase the range of possible metaphorical associations which the subject could sustain. In Moore's case this led to the embodiment in his work of a combination of that 'pantheistic humanism' which had invested his output of the later twenties, with a sense of distinctive 'psychological identity' such as seemed sometimes to be expressed by Picasso's female figure subjects as a function of the distortions which he practised upon them. But just as Nash internalized devices for suggesting melancholy which had been developed in the work of de Chirico and Magritte, while avoiding the more explicit symbolism of the one and the underlying 'menace' of the other, so Moore borrowed from Picasso, from Giacometti and from Arp as much as would extend his formal range without seriously disturbing his preoccupation with an essentially lay-pantheist concept of 'natural' form.

In his introduction to the catalogue of the International Surrealist Exhibition, Read wrote, 'because our art and literature is the most romantic in the world, it is likely to become the most superrealistic'. In fact, for many artists in the later thirties an explicit Romanticism, or rather, at worst, a whimsical revivalism, came increasingly to supplant commitment to modernist developments. This was particularly true of some of the younger painters, John Piper foremost among them.

Axis acted as a sensitive barometer, marking the swift change of interests among the community of modern artists and their supporters. The fifth issue in the spring of 1936 had celebrated the first 'Abstract and Concrete' exhibition. The sixth appeared in the summer of the same year under the headline 'Abstraction? Surrealism?' and included an editorial in which Myfanwy Piper, while recognizing that 'The battle has been pitched

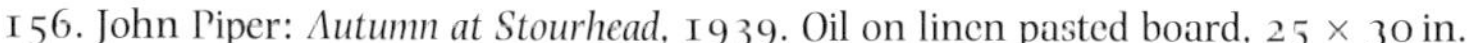

156. John Piper: *Autumn at Stourhead*, 1939. Oil on linen pasted board, 25 × 30 in.

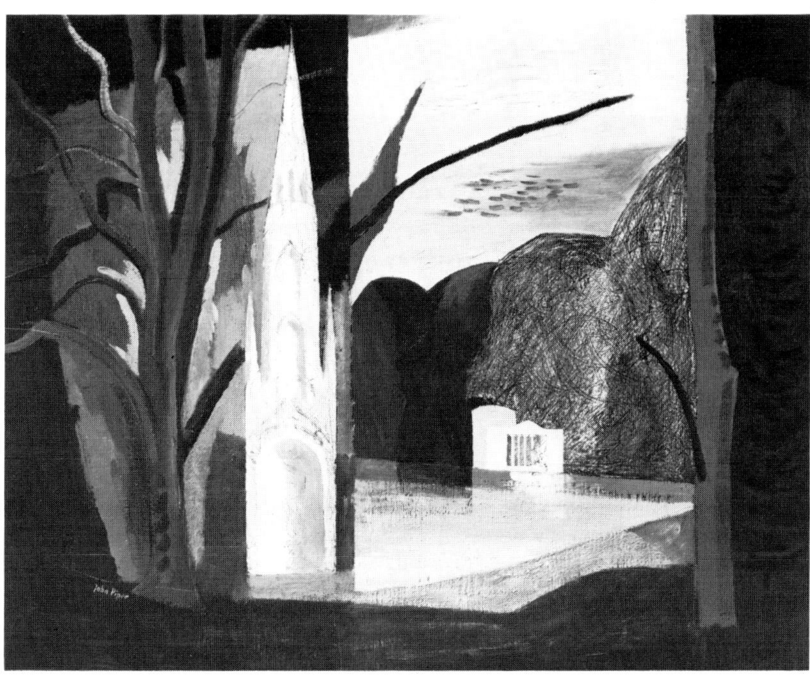

between abstract painting and sculpture and surrealist painting and sculpture,' asserted her right to admire either Ernst's work or Nicholson's work 'for itself – not as an act of faith or as a commitment to a line of behaviour.' In the seventh issue, that autumn, the leading article was a contentious piece by Geoffrey Grigson and John Piper, published under the title 'England's Climate'.

> Any Constable, any Blake, any Turner has something an abstract or a surrealist painting cannot have. Hence, partly, the artist's pique about them now, and his terror of the National Gallery. The point is fullness, completeness: the abstract qualities of all good painting together with the symbolism (at least) of life itself. Today both cannot go together. Abstraction and surrealism can choose, but they do not choose both. They can build, and be filled with an ambition for future life, but hardly can express a fullness of present life. Constructivism is building for the future – and so far an escape into the future. The Royal Academy a hesitation in the past . . . (Piper).
>
> About the time Christopher Wood killed himself it was becoming finally clear that good painting (e.g. Mantegna and Manet were good painters) was for the time being impossible. You must be drugged by the importance to yourself of your own time if you allege that there is any good painting now . . . Great art comes from great living; great living comes from our common humanity promising or filling out or still defining a high social shape to which each peculiar person can decently relate himself. I believe that men may have to wait a hundred years before such a shape is renewed (Grigson).

The article was illustrated with works by Constable, Christopher Wood, Fuseli and Samuel Palmer. Grigson's concluding statement has the ring of conservatism, but in so far as his critique of modernism followed from an assertion of the artist's lack of autonomy with respect to social life, it was not incompatible with the Marxist position.

The eighth issue of *Axis* appeared after a longer interval, in the early winter of 1937. The leading article, by John Piper, was on the aerial photography of prehistoric sites. The one article on an English artist was a celebration of Paul Nash by Myfanwy Piper, in which she described him as 'the contemporary heir of Cotman, Cox and Turner'. 'The contour of things past', she wrote, 'is given the aura of things present, so the reality *and* the romanticism of both is intensified. More than most other English painters Paul Nash has developed a personal idiom. He will neither proselytise nor be converted.' She claimed that in the contemporary situation the problem for the artist was to fight for his individuality against – and necessarily in consciousness of – the pressure to become part of a group or movement.

Nash's virtue, to her, was that he was 'a born, untroubled individualist'. Such an assessment of Nash was perhaps justifiable in terms of the specific quality of his work, but it could not really have been used as a basis upon which to defend the tendency towards insularity and technical conservatism which was becoming apparent in the work of many comparatively inconsiderable artists at the time. The eighth issue of *Axis* was the last. That small community to which it had given voice in 1935 had diverged and dispersed, the early sense of urgency now replaced by that form of dilettante posturing which so often signifies criticism in decline.

One further publication associated with the magazine appeared in 1937 under Myfanwy Piper's editorship. *The Painter's Object*[44] was a collection of essays by various artists which demonstrated nothing so much as the loss of coherence of the English avant garde in its relations with European art. On the one hand there was a substantial contribution from a heterogeneous selection of foreign artists: Léger, Hélion, Ozenfant, Kandinsky, Calder, Ernst, Picasso, de Chirico and Moholy-Nagy; on the other, the English painters who contributed were united by nothing so much as the insularity of their interests. Julian Trevelyan wrote about the imaginary cities which were the subject of his own modest Surrealist work, but the article was illustrated with a picturesque collage clearly related to Piper's topographical whimsies. Piper himself contributed an article on 'England's Early Sculptors' and another on the loss of the 'Valuable Object' which he supposed Cubism to have 'destroyed'. He concluded:

> It will be a good thing to get back to the tree in the field that everybody is working for. For it is certainly to be hoped that we shall get back to it as a fact, as a reality. As something more than an ideal.

As a *rappel à l'ordre* this was little more than a pious admonition prompted by anxiety. Piper's own work, which at least in 1934–6 had signalled a determined apprenticeship to some considerable continental models, became increasingly a matter of finding means to make the technical mannerisms of modern painting serve a fashionable interest in picturesque architectural detail or 'gothick' landscapes. In 1936 he contributed the first of many articles to the *Architectural Review*, and two years later he appeared as author of the *Shell Guide to Oxfordshire*.[45] Images of 'Pleasing Decay' (the title of one of his articles) and suggestions of vacant stage sets came to permeate his work [156].

Myfanwy Piper's introduction to *The Painter's Object* offered a kaleidoscopic picture of the kinds and topics of discourse then current in the art world; a picture which perhaps provides some contrasting reference for the change in interests which John Piper's activities revealed.

Left, right, black, red ... Hampstead, Bloomsbury, surrealist, abstract, social realist, Spain, Germany, Heaven, Hell, Paradise, Chaos, light, dark, round, square. 'Let me alone – you must be a member – have you got a ticket – have you given a picture – have you seen *The Worker* – do you realise – can you imagine – don't you see you're bound to be implicated – it's a matter of principle. Have you signed the petition – haven't you a picture more in keeping with our aims – *intellectual freedom*, FREEDOM, FREEDOM – we must be allowed, we can't be bound – you can't, you must fight – you *must*. That's not abstract, sir – that's not surrealist, sir – that's not – *not*. Anything will do – send it along – the committee will hang it – sit on it – no, not him, he'll want his friends in – it's a matter of *principle*.'

This passage helps, I think, to explain the growth of an insular and conservative tendency around 1937. I mean that this tendency seems at least in part to have been due to a reaction against the elaboration of political considerations in discourse about and around modern art, and that those responsible for this reaction were critics and artists like the Pipers, who experienced such an elaboration as a threat to their own professional self-images and to their essentially superficial view of artistic practice. A positive transformation of the concept of art could not possibly be in their interests.

Although there are points of contact and compatibility, the 'neo-picturesque' interests which Piper shared with such writers as Grigson and John Betjeman need to be distinguished from those of the 'neo-romantic' as manifest in the work of Nash and of Graham Sutherland in the later thirties. Where the former term signifies a certain antiquarian and sometimes ironic taste and curiosity, the latter, as a term of reference, is evoked rather by a sense that the expressive quality of Sutherland's and Nash's work bears some relation to what was expressed in the works of the earlier Romantic poets and painters. In this sense, 'neo-romanticism' was compatible with an attenuated Surrealism, whereas the 'neo-picturesque' involved a nostalgic reinstatement of just that Victorian bourgeois manner which the Surrealists had so often parodied.

Nash and Sutherland both contributed to *The Painter's Object*. Sutherland's essay, 'An English Stone Landmark', was an evocation of the kind of landscape which then provided the subjects for his paintings. Born in 1903, Sutherland had been principally an engraver, in a style clearly derived from the late-Romantic graphic art of the nineteenth century, and in particular from the work of Samuel Palmer, who had been the object of a revival of interest in the later twenties. He took up painting in 1931, and his development as a painter was spurred by a visit to Wales in 1934. Between

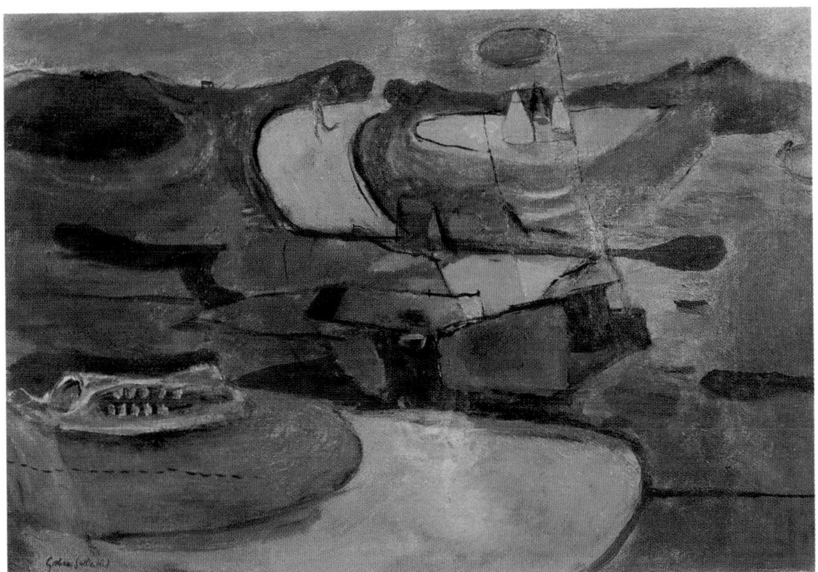

157. Graham Sutherland: *Welsh Landscape with Roads*, 1936. Oil on canvas, 24 × 36 in.

1935 and 1939 he regularly spent his holidays in Pembrokeshire. In his work of the later thirties he interpreted the forms and details of the Welsh landscape by reference to the 'visionary' paintings of Palmer and also to the precedents which Nash offered, especially in his watercolours, for the transformation of a landscape of 'natural' or prehistoric monuments into a 'melancholy' and expressive picture [157]. It is also clear that Sutherland was affected by those of Moore's drawings for sculpture in which forms amalgamated from figures and natural *objets trouvés* were tried out against evocative and highly textured backgrounds, suggestive of landscape. Two of Sutherland's paintings were selected for the International Surrealist Exhibition, but the effect of the movement upon him amounted to little more than a slight extension of the degree to which the forms of his landscapes were apparently left open to a kind of county-psychoanalytic reference or interpretation.

The most successful of Sutherland's works of the thirties were small gouaches, watercolours and pen and wash drawings. His etchings had mostly been small and highly textured and he retained until the end of his life a taste for the exploitation and magnification of detail. But his typical subjects were not really vivid enough for a larger scale. In his oil paintings the decorative texture of the painted surface too often reads rather as fussiness in the paint than as detail significant of meaning in the subject, for all the sense of underlying religious symbolism attached to trees, thorns or whatever. In paintings so strongly dependent on unreflective evocation, the consequence of such a failure adequately to establish the representational function of the painted surface is the expression of a kind of homeless hysteria.

Sutherland's romantic paintings naturally invite comparison with Nash's, and certainly, in so far as a cognate 'Romantic Revival' can be seen to commence in English art at the close of the thirties, Sutherland and Nash are its only interesting representatives among the painters. (In face of this statement one reservation needs to be made. Between about 1932 and 1938 Wyndham Lewis – the 'skeleton in the cupboard' – produced a few paintings on themes from a kind of mythical history, with schematic nude or strangely costumed figures in richly coloured and evocative settings. Technically they can be related to Synthetic Cubism and to certain aspects of Surrealism, with some clear references to William Blake, and they prefigure the second phase of romantic revivalism in the forties, when a group of young painters 'rediscovered' Lewis. His concept of 'super-nature' as an alternative to the 'super-real' was consistent both with his own earlier interests and with the idea of a return to an expressive form of painting based on the natural world.[46] The majority of these works were shown in a one-man exhibition at the Leicester Galleries in December 1937. They are clever paintings, as one would expect of Lewis, but technically careless and awkwardly rhetorical. In August 1939 he left for what was intended to be a few months' stay in America and Canada. He was not to return to England until the spring of 1945.)

Nash contributed two articles to *The Painter's Object*, 'The Nest of the Wild Stones' and 'Swanage, or Seaside Surrealism'. The first testified to the mild impact of the concept of unconscious association upon the imagination of an amateur naturalist, and the second to the amusement to be derived from applying a Surrealist iconography to a respectable English seaside resort. Both Nash and Sutherland had one-man shows in 1938,[47] and particularly as the influence of Surrealism became less explicit in Nash's work, and as the intensity of his colour increased, the two painters must have seemed to be clearly united by their interests.

But Nash was altogether a more considerable artist than Sutherland. He was a careful draughtsman, had, by the later thirties, a control of the watercolour medium which no other English artist with modern interests could match, and was always able to establish a strong, if largely traditional, formal structure for his more ambitious paintings. The finest of all his works, the rich and poetic landscapes which he painted from 1942 to 1944 based on views from Boars Hill near Oxford, lie outside the scope of this volume, though they represent the culmination of those developments in his work which we have been discussing. During the later thirties however, as he entered on this last phase, Nash's work showed a considerable increase in confidence and in vividness. The range and richness of his colour in particular increased considerably, and he was able, as Sutherland was not, to achieve substantial pictures from features of the observed and recollected English landscape. His concentration upon this landscape, and his tendency towards a melancholy introversion in his representation of it, was perhaps in part a response to the restrictions imposed on him by his asthmatic illness. In March 1938 he wrote to Bottomley:

> ... the damned disease is pretty crippling and has managed to rule out most pleasant adventures for the last five years – I mean anything like going out of England has been impossible.[48]

Nash exploited the picturesque in landscape wherever he could, for whatever symbolic and associative meaning it might be made to bear, drawing upon a wide field of personal reference in art, in literature and in autobiographical experience. Speculating on two fallen elms in a field, he found in one a fanciful resemblance to 'the horse in Blake's interpretation of the "sightless cousins of the air" ... Did it then crash to earth, fusing its image with the rigid tree?'[49] The other formed the subject of the painting *Monster Field* [158].

> The declining sun suffused the evening sky to a brickish red; beneath which the Malverns piled up intensely blue. A cornelian glow illumined the heavy summer green. The strange creature at hand seemed more ghastly, stained by this sweet tint. Something about its headlong purpose recalled Picasso. It was eminently bovine and yet scarcely male. Surely, *this* must be the cow of Guernica's bull. It seemed as mystical and as dire.

One should not, of course, make the mistake of interpreting Nash's painting exclusively in the spirit of his prose. As a writer he was given to whimsy and to an exaggerated fancifulness which was not always redeemed by irony, though he was by no means incapable of self-parody. In the best of his paintings, on the other hand, his technical interests and competence served to discipline his fancies. In an article on 'Unseen Landscapes' published in May 1938,[50] he expressed what he saw as the particular quality of his own current work, in implicit contrast to an interpretation based on Surrealist interests. Such landscapes, he wrote, were

> not part of the unseen in a psychic sense, nor are they part of the Unconscious. They belong to the world that lies, visibly, about us. They are unseen merely because they are not perceived.

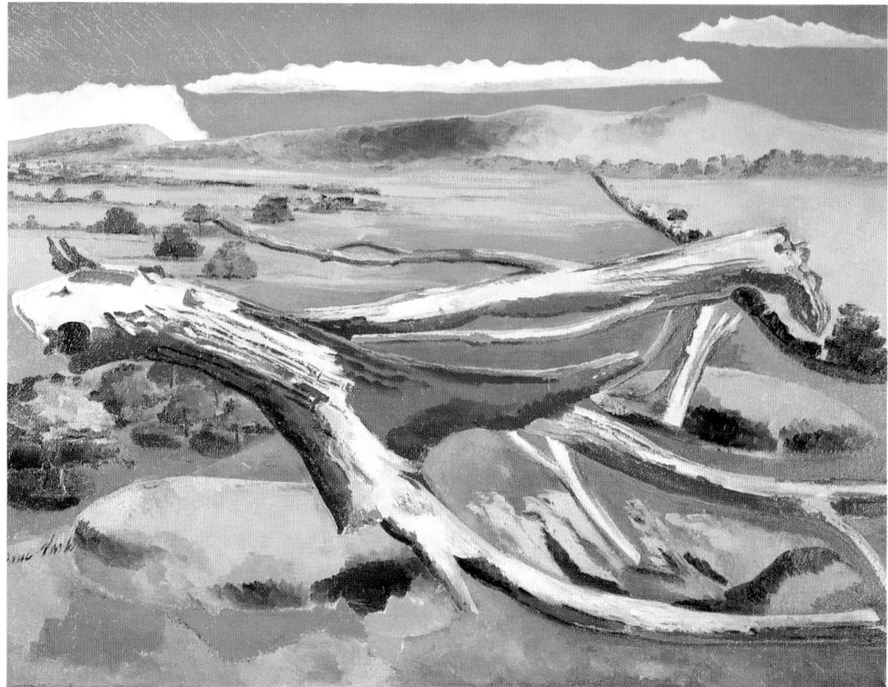

158. Paul Nash: *Monster Field*, 1939. Oil on canvas, $30\frac{1}{4} \times 40$ in.

In the end, it is indeed this that secures the sense of meaning of Nash's landscapes. They are rooted in the idiosyncratic observation of an actual, though not necessarily familiar, world. The technical means by which these observations are represented are such as to establish a degree of formality and decorum, but without ruling out an element of surprise and humour in juxtaposition and an occasional strategic ambiguity in detail. There was a strong underlying consistency to the development of Nash's work, but viewed overall it shows a certain technical variety and a wide range of mood. At his best he was a fine painter.

Henry Moore was also represented in *The Painter's Object*, and in his 'Notes on Sculpture'[51] he too reaffirmed his interest in the natural world as a source for his art. In his statement in *Unit 1* he had written:

> The human figure is what interests me most deeply, but I have found principles of form and rhythm from the study of natural objects such as pebbles, rocks, bones, trees, plants etc. ... There is in nature a limitless variety of shapes and rhythms ... from which the sculptor can enlarge his form-knowledge experience.

In 1934 he had bought a bungalow near Canterbury with enough ground around it to allow him to carve out-of-doors in an open landscape. He began work there in 1935, and described the resulting change of emphasis in his 'Notes on Sculpture'.

Recently I have been working in the country, where, carving in the open air, I find sculpture more natural than in a London studio, but it needs bigger dimensions. A large piece of stone or wood placed almost anywhere at random in a field, orchard or garden immediately looks right and inspiring.

The characteristic works of 1933–6 were comparatively small 'biomorphic' abstractions derived from busts or segmented reclining figures. The principal works of the later thirties, on the other hand, were large-scale one-piece reclining figures, in which the formal themes of the earlier versions of 1929–30 were recapitulated and reworked. Moore now developed the metaphorical and formal evocations of landscape and other 'natural' organic forms to a point where these began to determine the composition of the figures themselves. As the technical mannerisms of the Surrealists gained currency, he no doubt felt more confident in exploiting those associations which natural forms provoked.

Out of the millions of pebbles passed in walking along the shore, I choose out to see with excitement only those which fit in with my existing form-interest at the time. A different thing happens if I sit down and examine them one by one. I may then extend my form-experience more, by giving my mind time to become conditioned to a new shape.

There are universal shapes to which everybody is sub-consciously conditioned and to which they can respond if their conscious control does not shut them off.[52]

In the formulation of the earlier reclining figures, Moore had remained true to the basic configurations and normal disposition of the human body, even where he added to or distorted the elements of the figure as he did in the lead *Reclining Figure* of 1931 [130]. With the experience of the more abstract and exploratory works of 1932–5 behind him, however, he now carved his figures as if the human form were something to be recognized as the end product of selection from a whole range of metaphors. He wrote in 1937 of the condition of sculpture in the wake of Brancusi's reductive abstract works.

We can now begin to open out. To relate and combine together several forms of varied sizes, sections and directions into one organic whole ...

A hole can itself have as much shape-meaning as a solid mass.[53]

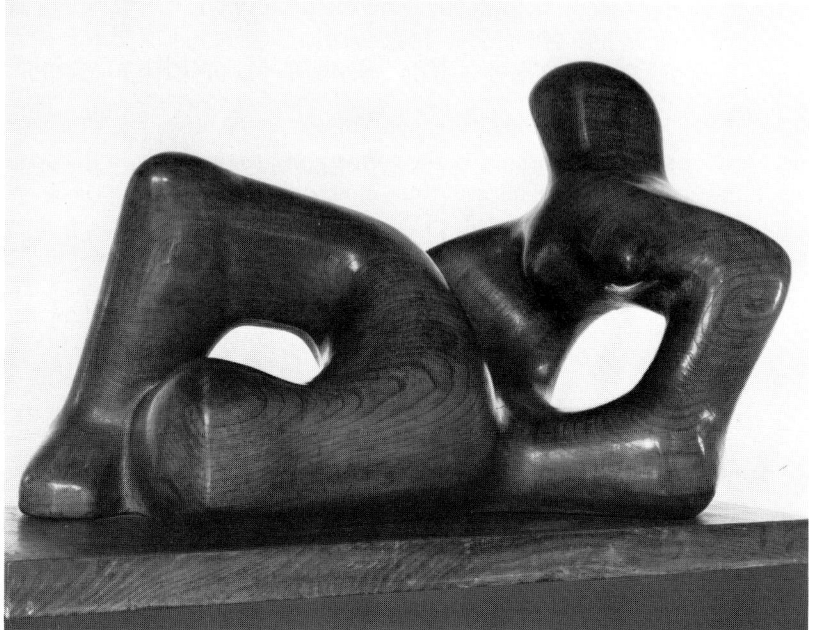

159. Henry Moore: *Reclining Figure*, 1936. Elm wood, length 42 in.

Between 1935 and 1939 Moore carved four large works on the theme of the reclining figure, three in elm wood [159, 160] and one, a 'recumbent figure', in Hornton stone [161].[54] The common feature in all four is that the torso is hollowed out beneath the breasts, as if the space formed between the crook of the supporting arm and the side of the trunk were enlarged at the expense of the solid torso. As a classical type, the nude reclining figure was conventionally male (a 'river God' as the type is known), and interest centred on the musculature of the torso. The translation of the pose into a female and passive type entailed finding some alternative means to detail the area between breasts and pubic mound. After all, it could hardly, with decorum, be treated as a series of transverse folds. In retrospect it is easy to see that what Moore achieved by hollowing out the torso was the excision of just that area in which, without an anachronistic detailing of surface, there could be least modulation and formal interest, and which, perhaps for that very reason, he had tended to contract in the earlier reclining figures. The positive effect of opening out the figure in this way was to render it more susceptible to treatment in 'rhythmic' terms, and to establish a smoother relationship between raised head and torso on the one hand and extended thighs and legs on the other. Each of the four figures was longer than the

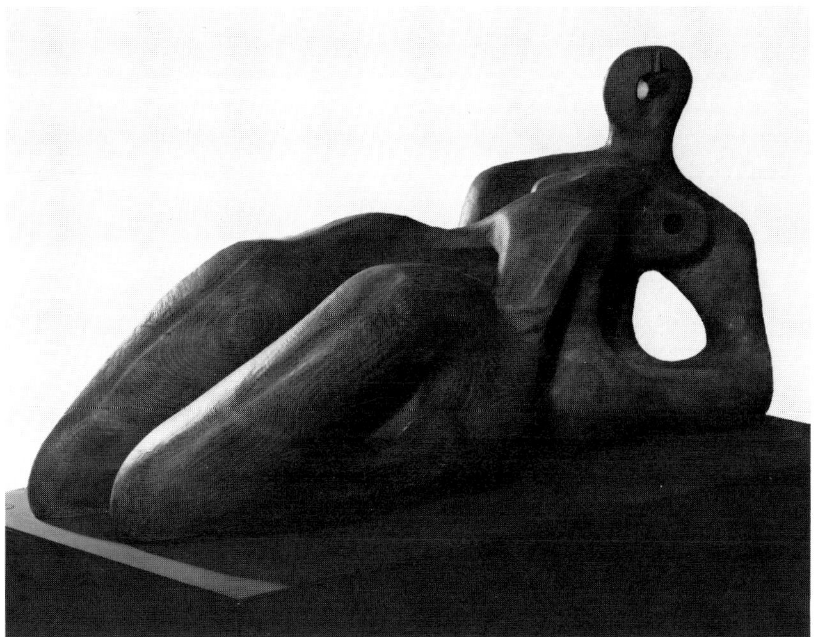

160. Henry Moore: *Reclining Figure*, 1939. Elm wood, 37 × 79 × 30 in.

last, as Moore exploited the possibility of a rhythmic analogy with natural form. In the 1939 work [160], which is 79 inches long, the forms are carved so as to appear as if shaped by the action of waves or wind, the strong grain of the wood exposed as if by just such a process of erosion.

From about 1936 on (and particularly between 1939 and 1942) the tendency of Moore's drawings, in which he explored a wide range of possibilities for sculpture and of analogical forms for human figures, was to contextualize the subject in terms of some kind of space, usually an open landscape. (The specific influence of continental Surrealism and of Picasso is often more explicit in these drawings than it is in the sculptures which relate to them.) Increasingly, a reference to some form of imaginary landscape seemed to become for Moore a means to establish psychological identity for the sculpture notionally placed within it.

The Hornton stone *Recumbent Figure* of 1938 [161], which is one of the most attractive of all Moore's works, was the first of his major sculptures to be designed as a free-standing element on a specific outdoor site, the terrace of a modern house overlooking the South Downs. It is perhaps because Moore took the particular location into account that a greater credibility seems to be established by this work than by many others for the concept of

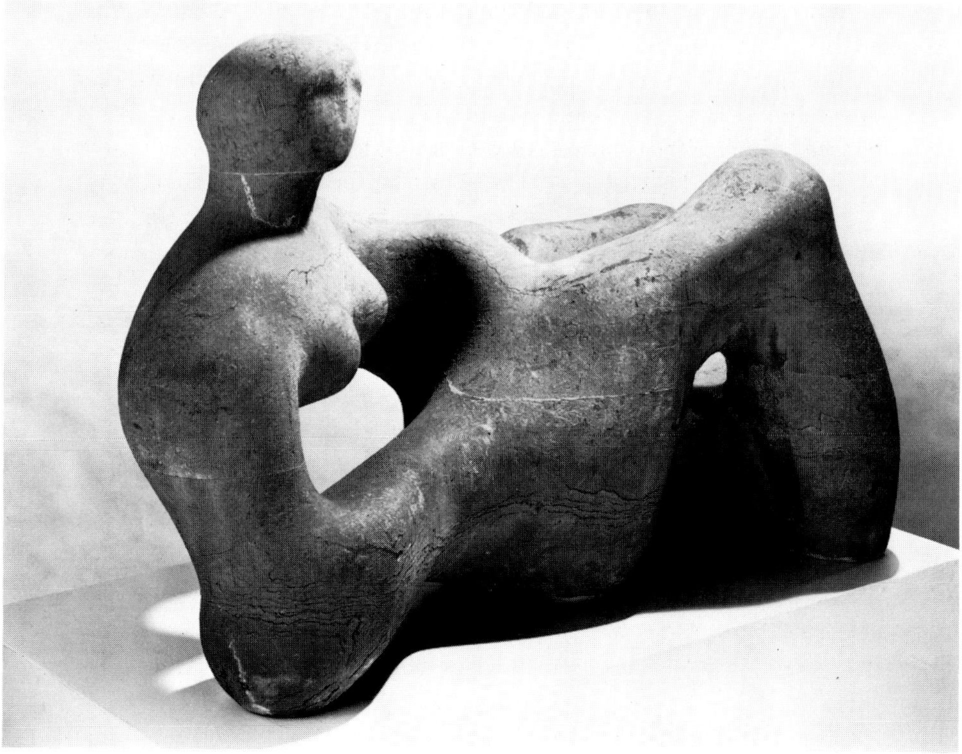

161. Henry Moore: *Recumbent Figure*, 1938. Green Hornton stone, $35 \times 52\frac{1}{4} \times 29$ in.

sculpture as an expression of unity and continuity between natural world and psychological content. Moore later recalled,

> I carved a reclining figure ... intending it to be a kind of focal point of all the horizontals, and it was then that I became aware of the necessity of giving outdoor sculpture a far-seeing gaze. My figure looked out across a great sweep of the Downs, and her gaze gathered in the horizon. The sculpture had no specific relationship to the architecture ... but it so to speak *enjoyed* being there, and I think it introduced a humanising element; it became a mediator between modern house and ageless land.[55]

Even in its present location in the Tate Gallery, the *Recumbent Figure* invites the imagination of landscape. Moore sought to present a 'human psychological content' in his work. If it is the case that such a content can defensibly be sought as a function of the mimetic aspect of sculpture, and if this content can be interpreted through some 'humanistic' sense of the unity of all natural and organic form, then this of all Moore's sculptures is the one that best makes that case.

As qualifications on the possibly laudatory aspect of this statement, there are two points to be made: (1) that during the period under review, while he successfully synthesized a very wide range of influences, Moore was not himself responsible for a single substantial technical advance which could be seen as such in the context of modern sculpture as a whole; and (2) that, by virtue of the very avuncularity of his modernism, and through his continued reliance on human and natural subjects, he did more than any other English artist to bring home to the uninitiated majority in this country how very far the specialized interests of modern artists had diverged from their own. On the one hand, at moments when there was a risk that his themes might appear 'unsocial', he allowed his meritocratic ambition in respect of an idealized public to contain his technical invention; on the other, what he embodied in the name of 'natural' and 'human' values was not such as the majority of that public was willing to identify as natural or human (unless persuaded by the authority of entrepreneurs that they should do so). This is perhaps to say that the inculcation of popular affection for an unmitigated modernist art is analytically not a realizable or defensible aim, so one might as well go ahead and pursue the strangenesses of specialization.

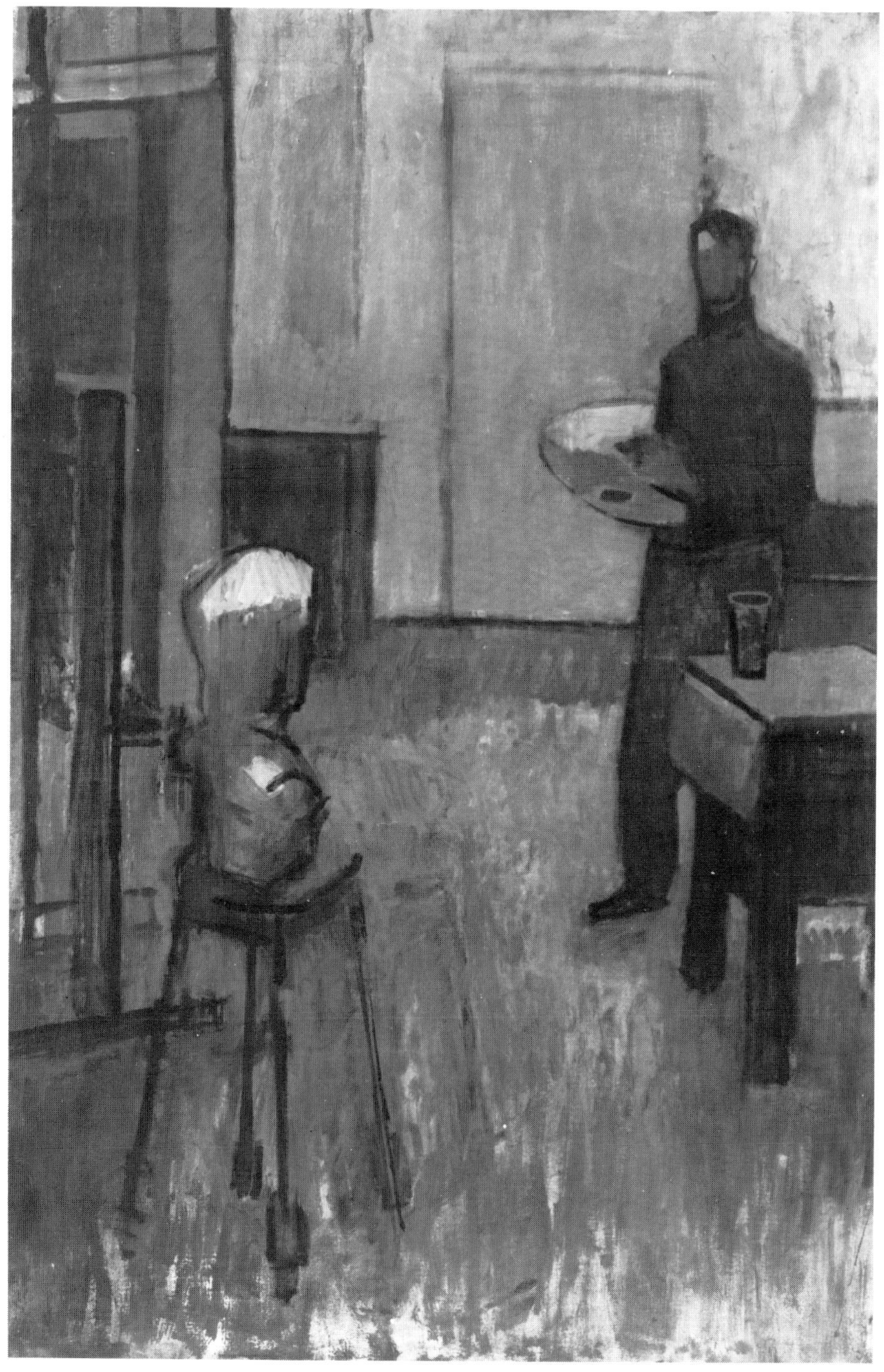

12

POSTSCRIPT: THE EUSTON ROAD SCHOOL

On 16 March 1938 a discussion was held between the Surrealists and the 'Realists'. Read, Penrose, Trevelyan, and Jennings appeared for the former, and Blunt, Alick West, Graham Bell and William Coldstream for the latter. The discussion was organized by Trevelyan on behalf of the AIA, and another AIA member, Robert Medley, took the chair. After the event, both sides claimed the victory. According to the *Left Review*, the 'Realists' 'carried the day ... by their humility and honesty ... Their aggressive opponents, the Surrealists, are betrayed by their very vociferation, the pretentious flourish of any pseudo-philosophical, pseudo-psychological, pseudo-literary pseudo-phraseology which has nothing to do with art, as people with a complete despair and sterility as regards the practice of art.'[1] According to Read, however, writing in the *London Bulletin*, 'No unprejudiced observer could describe the affair as anything but a rout.' The Realists, he asserted, were 'reduced to talking about the camera and Courbet'. He continued with a distant echo of Wyndham Lewis: 'Actually of course, our English Realists are not the tough guys they ought to be, but the effete and bastard offspring of the Bloomsbury school of needlework.'[2]

Blunt was by now a practised campaigner for the communist (i.e. vaguely Stalinist) left, and Read a familiar opponent whose views might be associated with Trotskyism, anarchism or liberalism or with various species of compromise between these. They had recently been ranged on different

162 *(opposite)*. William Coldstream: *Studio Interior*, 1932–3. Oil on canvas, 54 × 36 in.

sides of a controversy over Picasso's *Guernica*, which had been exhibited first at the New Burlington, and then at the Whitechapel Galleries,[3] and which Blunt had been 'horrified by ... from a theoretical point of view'.[4] The organization of the debate was no doubt an attempt to capitalize on this controversy. The two newcomers to the 'Realist' platform were both painters, and it was at these that Read's jibe was directed.

At the time of the debate Bell and Coldstream [162] were associated with the Euston Road School, which had been started a year earlier, though they had been friends since soon after Bell came to London from South Africa, in 1931. The school had been set up with some moral support from representatives of Bloomsbury – the names of Vanessa Bell and Duncan Grant appeared with those of Augustus John and John Nash as sponsors on an early prospectus[5] – and the majority of those who taught or visited at the school had been students at the Slade, where the long-standing connection with Bloomsbury was still maintained. In this final episode of the period under review, many of its most persistent strands come together.

Apart from Bell and Coldstream, the names generally associated with the Euston Road School are those of Claude Rogers, Victor Pasmore, Geoffrey Tibble and Rodrigo Moynihan. All six artists were born between 1907 and 1910. Coldstream, Rogers, Tibble and Moynihan were all at the Slade at various periods between the years 1925 and 1931. Pasmore studied part-time at the Central School between 1927 and 1931 and was not able to devote himself full-time to painting until 1938.[6] He met Rogers in 1933 through the Bloomsbury-controlled London Artists Association, of which Coldstream was also a member. At the time when the majority of these men were at the Slade, Cézanne was still seen as a controversial modern exemplar, there was a growing interest in the late work of Monet, and Picasso, Braque and Matisse were the objects of some enthusiasm. The hegemony of French painting was well established. Those who studied at the Slade seem to have shared an uncertainty, at the time they left, as to what to do with the training they had received. The early thirties cannot have been an easy period in which to decide what to do as a young painter, and each of them at some point experimented with abstract painting before turning away from it.

In April 1934, coincident with the Unit One exhibition, Bell, Tibble, Moynihan and Pasmore showed in the exhibition 'Objective Abstractions' at the Zwemmer Gallery, an event which has achieved a certain retrospective acclaim.[7] The other exhibitors were Ceri Richards, Thomas Carr and Ivon Hitchens. The presence of the last named serves as a reminder that there were precedents within the work of the Seven & Five Society for freely brushed paintings on comparatively informal themes, but it is clear that the exhibition was designed to strike an assertively modern note. The pictures were all listed under the simple title 'painting', and there was an introduction to the catalogue by Nicolete Gray, who also compiled a set of five questions to which each artist responded. From their answers to the questions and from what is known of the work they showed it is clear that the programmatic flavour of the enterprise expressed the interests of Bell, Tibble and Moynihan, and to a lesser extent Pasmore, rather than those of the other three exhibitors.[8] The last question, 'Do you consider your paintings "impressionist"?', can be taken as evidence that such a label would not necessarily have been seen by the majority of spectators as implying conservatism even in 1934, but it also signified the nature of the artists' current preoccupations. Tibble and Moynihan in particular had come strongly under the influence of a specific painting, Monet's *Rouen Cathedral*, then in the Tate Gallery.[9]

But the key question was the third: 'Have you a clear conception of the picture before you begin? Does it grow while working?' The question is incoherent, but Bell's, Moynihan's and Tibble's answers reveal a mutually consistent concept of practice.

Bell: 'No. Once the picture has been started, its growth is autonomous; that is to say, the additional marks are called into being by what is already on the surface of the canvas.'

Moynihan: 'No. The evolution is intimately bound up with the canvas and medium.'

Tibble: 'No. My pictures grow while working, guided entirely by my reaction to the picture at the time of painting.'

None of the paintings shown was either 'objective' in any strong sense or indeed 'abstract', but the point was that these three were attempting to establish the idea of a kind of painting which would be self-generating in the face of 'that scepticism of the true "eye" painter whose creative spirit must proceed by assuming nothing'.[10] The brush-strokes were to be seen as constituting an object, which was the picture, rather than reconstituting an object or scene, of which the picture was then to be seen as a representation. Where previous abstract art had been justified as the plastic expression of spiritual states or subjective feelings, their paintings were proposed as expressions of 'the visual attitude in painting, as opposed to the conceptual or idealistic', and as offering only 'answers to those questions which present or suggest themselves on the canvas'.[11]

An informal still life by Geoffrey Tibble, dated 1929 and now in the Tate Gallery, is one of the earliest works in which these interests are clearly

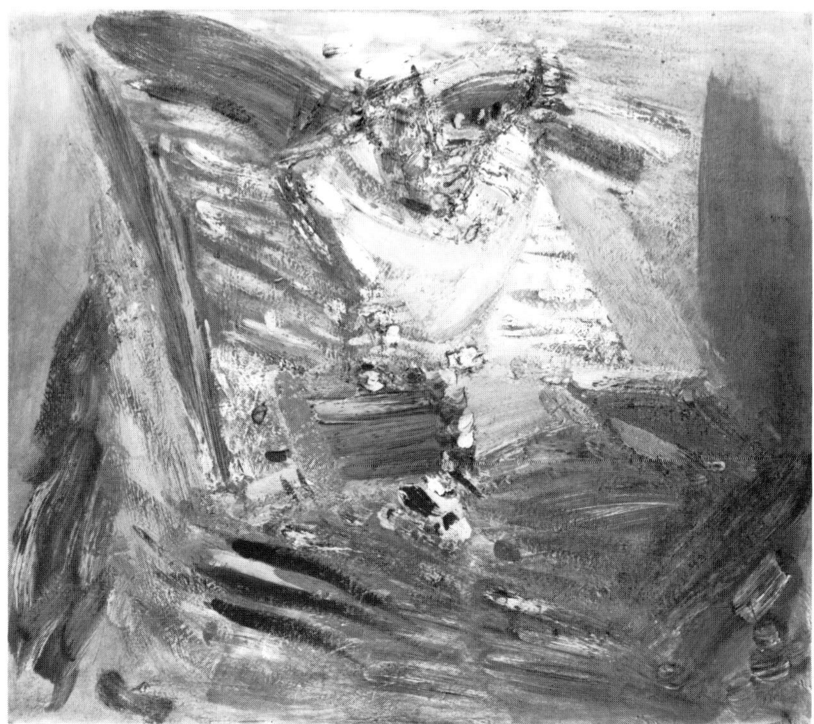

163. Rodrigo Moynihan: *Objective Abstraction*, 1934. Oil on canvas, 25 × 30 in.

expressed. Of the other paintings which have survived, however, those which best illustrate the aims of 'Objective Abstraction' are a series of paintings by Moynihan, now generally known by that title and dating from 1933 to '35 or '36 [163]. Reviewing the exhibition for the *New English Weekly*,[12] David Gascoyne (then only seventeen) wrote of the paintings which Moynihan exhibited,

> He has achieved some very curious effects; as though a Kandinsky had been using the bleary technique of a Monet with a range of pale dirty colours laid on very thickly ... the loose, free strokes crystallise into various tone groups which slowly begin to react upon each other beneath one's eyes ... One had thought that Impressionism could go no further than Monet; but now it seems it is being developed along a line of non-formal, i.e. non-geometrical, abstraction, an abstraction built purely from colour and light ...

With hindsight, though, one can establish some figurative cause for these paintings. For all that Moynihan may later have suggested that 'pure objective abstraction appeared in ... early 1933',[13] *Objective Abstraction No.*

1 of that year is clearly a still life on a table, and paintings of the next year bear a strong genetic relation to it, however transformed the subject may be by a treatment derived from the paint quality of Monet's and Turner's more encrusted works.

'Objective Abstraction' does not, in the end, seem to have been a fruitful development. Speaking to Moynihan many years later, Coldstream recalled:

> I was very much influenced by yourself and Geoffrey Tibble. Your pictures made a great impression on me ... not only the paintings but the programme you set yourselves, of trying to make a painting out of paint as it were; it seemed to me something on a reasonable basis, something on an intelligible basis, but I must say that struggling with it over quite a long period I never produced a result which really engaged my attention.[14]

Coldstream was to have shown in 'Objective Abstractions' but was presumably not satisfied that he had any compatible work that he could justify. Moynihan later asserted that the movement, if such it was, had floundered 'for lack of a context'.[15] It was perhaps not the time to attempt still further to extend the technical autonomy of painting, in face of mounting pressure to justify the function of art in relation to 'life', and to establish claims to 'progressiveness', to revolutionary status.

> I think the weakness, and why the style was rather short-lived, was that we throttled it by using such a restricted tonality and one kind of stroke and almost one size of canvas ...

> The doubts increased, all the time I felt cut off from something, some meaning that ought to lie somewhere, and, although the theoretical basis seemed right, one did have that cut-off feeling, and particularly at the time of the surrealist exhibition in 1936. Although I didn't like any of the paintings very much, they seemed to be connected to some sort of reality, however irrational (Moynihan).[16]

For all that it has been proclaimed as a precursor of Abstract Expressionism,[17] 'Objective Abstraction' was effectively a dead end. With no strong historical roots, it had nowhere to go. The cathedrals, as it were, failed to emerge from the morass of paint.

By 1936 Tibble and Moynihan had reverted to figurative styles. Pasmore had produced a few abstract paintings immediately after the Zwemmer Gallery exhibition, but he later destroyed them. By 1937 he had abandoned the informal, brightly coloured style, strongly indebted to Matisse and Bonnard, which had characterized his works of the early thirties, and was pursuing a kind of blurred 'realism', reminiscent of Degas and of Camden Town. Bell, also dissatisfied with what he had been doing, turned to journalism during the years 1934–7, while for the same period Coldstream worked in the GPO Film Unit run by John Grierson.

In 1937–8 he and Bell were together in Bolton for a while, along with Julian Trevelyan, in connection with Mass Observation. Coldstream painted a picture of backstreets under a pall of smoke [164] (now in the National Gallery of Canada at Ottawa) which typifies the 'realistic' style which he and Bell developed in common in the search for contact with a wider audience. 'The slump had made me aware of social problems,' he said at the time, 'and I became convinced that art ought to be directed towards a wider public. Whereas all ideas I had learned to be artistically revolutionary ran in the opposite direction. Public art must mean realism.'[18]

He later described his motives for briefly abandoning painting in terms of a desire 'to work in some medium which is by its nature more essentially of the present age, more easily accessible to a large number of people'.[19] A sense of the exclusiveness of modern art and its interests was what troubled many younger artists at the time. Few lived through the thirties with their concept of art essentially unchanged or with an unbroken sense of the value of the activity. Few felt able to concentrate upon their work in the way that those now senior artists Nicholson, Hepworth, Nash and Moore did. The

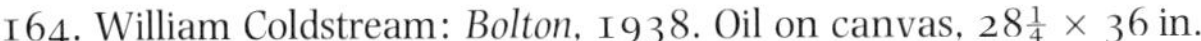

164. William Coldstream: *Bolton*, 1938. Oil on canvas, $28\frac{1}{4} \times 36$ in.

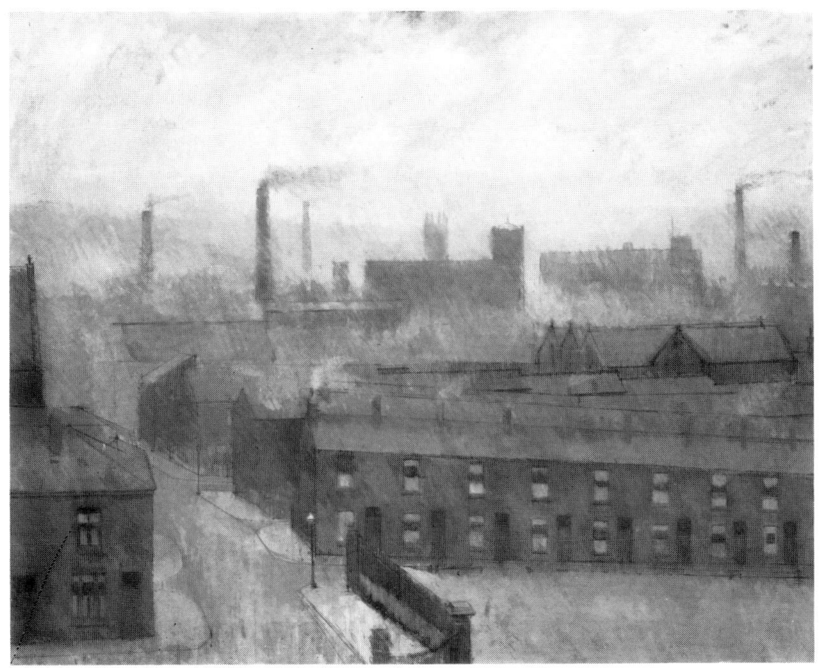

majority of them engaged in other activities, generally related by a broad concern for the condition of culture. They did so either to secure an income, or in search of a sense of purpose, or both.

In February and March 1937 Rogers and Pasmore showed together with Thomas Carr at the Storran Gallery. At the time Rogers was teaching in a school and Pasmore was working for the London County Council. Soon after, Rogers rented a studio at 12 Fitzroy Street, in order to set up an independent 'School of Painting and Drawing', and Pasmore, who was living nearby, joined him in the enterprise. Coldstream became associated soon after.[20] He did little direct teaching but he wielded a general influence. Bell followed, to become the principal spokesman within the group for a concept of 'realistic' craftsmanship. Tibble and Moynihan were occasional visitors, and Moynihan sometimes used the studios to work in. Another frequent visitor was William Townsend, who had been a member of the relevant generation at the Slade. As with so many art schools, formal and informal, the identification of what was taught and learned no doubt depends as much on reconstruction of the flavour of conversations in pubs and cafés as on description of technical idiosyncrasies.

During 1937 the school was moved to 316 Euston Road (thus following the earlier progression from Fitzroy Street to Camden Town). The name 'Euston Road School' was first applied by Raymond Mortimer in reviewing an exhibition of works by teachers and pupils arranged by Graham Bell at the Storran Gallery in 1938. The label was given in recognition of the debt to the Camden Town Group. It was appropriate and it stuck. According to Lawrence Gowing, who was an early pupil and one of the exhibitors at the Storran, the school 'opposed to the aesthetics of discrimination an aesthetic of verification'.[21] The idea seemed to be that the practice of art should entail fidelity of some sort to a world such as others might recognize, and that there was a form of craftsmanship appropriate to such a requirement. This was vague enough to cover some deep incompatibilities, for instance between the 'social realist' ambitions of Bell and Coldstream and the 'French' interests of Moynihan and Pasmore. A commitment to 'realism' was what the artists of the school seemed to have in common, but they would probably have found it hard to agree on a definition which would show that this was commitment to more than a slogan. Goya, Degas, Cézanne, Sickert, Bonnard, Picasso, Rivera, Orozco;[22] such interests were not easy to reconcile one with another, let alone with the concept of a 'realistic' practice of painting in England, except, perhaps, in terms of a concerted opposition to 'idealistic' abstract art.[23] There was, after all, no possibility of achieving a unity of theory and practice at the time, any more than we can will such a thing now.

In their search for contact with an audience, for a progressive function, the artists of the Euston Road School were reduced not so much to a kind of painting which 'the public' could appreciate and understand, as to a technical practice which no one could say was not painstaking and 'professional'. This was perhaps not entirely misguided. In a poll of visitors to the AIA's large exhibition at the Whitechapel Art Gallery in 1939, Coldstream's *Portrait of Inez Spender* (now in the Tate Gallery) attracted four times as many votes as the next most popular work.[24] There was no Federal Arts Project in England as there was in America, nor had the Arts Council yet been established, and the painting of portraits was still one means by which the painter could demonstrate a negotiable professionalism in the search for a role and an income.

In a confused pamphlet on *The Artist and his Public*, published in 1939 by the Bloomsbury-controlled Hogarth Press,[25] Graham Bell wrote of the 'damnable effect of there being no respect for the craft of painting as such' and of the lack of 'seriousness' in art under capitalism. 'To me', he wrote,

> the most significant artists living are Picasso, Rivera and Coldstream. I choose these ... because I think their attitude to painting, and the attitudes they have been compelled to make in the face of society, will have more influence on the future of painting than any others.

As a reservation on this piece of rampant if loyal parochialism, he added that 'to produce a great painter a whole class of Coldstreams is required'. He finished on a note which should now be familiar to readers of this book.

> Freedom for the exercise of the imagination, no matter what other bondage he has to endure, that is the essential condition for the rise of a great artist.

Claims for the importance of this area of English art seem to rest on a vague sense that the relation between the early informal 'abstractions' of Moynihan, Bell and Tibble and the later 'realist' style with which all three were associated is significant of some fundamental art-historical truth: that the critical nexus of painting is somehow defined by the rivalry of priorities, on the one hand for the 'autonomy' of the painted surface, and on the other for the 'objectivity' of subjects in the real (social) world. In the careers of those associated with the Euston Road School, it is supposed, this rivalry is vividly explored.[26]

Such claims will not stand up to much scrutiny. 'Experimental' works such as Moynihan's *Objective Abstractions* are noteworthy only if interest in the history of painting is restricted to concern for comparative novelty in technical aspects, where novelty is evaluated retrospectively in terms of subsequent developments. That the dynamic of painting in the 1940s and 50s can be identified by reference to 'informal' non-figurative paintings with loose brushwork is not alone sufficient to accord historical avant-garde status to so-called 'objective abstractions' of the early thirties, by Moynihan or anyone else, in which casualness in the interpretation of already informal themes (messy still lifes etc.) was pursued to the point where 'paint surface' has to be accorded a higher conceptual priority (is more 'evident') than 'subject-matter'.

For all the evocations of Monet and Turner, these paintings should rather be viewed in terms of a set of largely conventional technical interests, which have their English roots in the valuation of a late-nineteenth-century mannerism: the kind of meretricious bravura in the mediation between observed world and painted surface which was admired (though not by Sickert) in Whistler and Sargent and Augustus John, and which was itself a relatively trivial expression of the claims for vividness in the painted surface which were implicit in French painting from the mid-nineteenth century onwards. Such painting is at its best where the nature of the subject matter provides the strongest challenge to the autonomy of technique. Neither Monet nor Turner ever just 'painted with colour and light' or painted mere 'effects'. Moynihan's subjects, or Pasmore's, were rarely of interest in that they rarely provided challenges the solutions to which were not already well-rehearsed in the history of second-rate European painting.

Those painters who progressed from 'Objective Abstractions' to Euston Road 'realism' looked back to the turn of the century as if to an occasion of coincidence between the specialized technical interests of advanced painters and the demands on pictures made by a wide public, and then proceeded to act as if these interests could not now be reconciled and as if what was therefore required was a moral choice between them. Their choice was purportedly in favour of the wide public. The transformation of Objective Abstractionists into Euston Roaders was thus seen by those characteristically involved as exemplifying a purposive and democratic moral action.

This entailed a different idealization from that to which the 'constructive' abstract artists had been vulnerable, but it was an idealization none the less, and it was a consequence of a similarly privileged view of antecedent history. The underlying fallacy in both camps was that style, as a historical property of a 'realistic' art, could be willed into correspondence at a given moment with the dynamics of an enlightened sense of purpose.

The comparability of a *Reclining Nude* by Tibble [165] with the treatment of a similar subject by Harold Gilman, as illustrated on p. 39, provides a point of critical reference by means of which the technical interests of

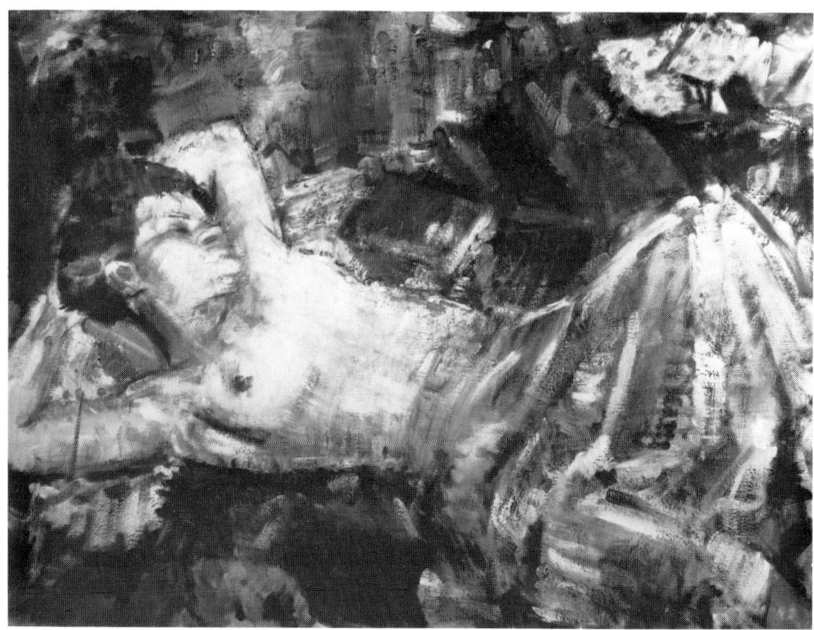

165. Geoffrey Tibble: *Reclining Woman*, 1938. Oil on canvas, 36 × 48 in.

Objective Abstraction might be related to the 'social' interests of Euston Road. The painters of Euston Road, that is to say, looked back to Camden Town, but without being able to envisage the reconciliation of what Gilman – and Sickert at his best – had reconciled. It is as if two mutually compatible and complementary aspects of the best Camden Town painting – the concern for a vivid surface and the concern for a vivid subject – had been abstracted by painters such as Tibble, Moynihan and Pasmore, and treated as means of characterizing antithetical positions. Where Gilman had employed a vivid painting style as the means to express an interest in other people and what they did and where they went, the painters of the Euston Road School acted as if the means to implement a concern for others was to avoid expressiveness in drawing and to abstain from that use of clear colour and thick paint which they had earlier been prompted to pursue as a sine qua non of modernist practice. As a consequence they produced a lot of very dull paintings.

The development from Objective Abstraction to Euston Road 'realism' should not be seen as implying any historically significant transformation or decision. Given the actual construction of the social world of artists and their audience, the idealized pursuit of a documentary and 'socially-relevant' realism and the assertion of autonomy for the technical development of painting and sculpture were not in the later thirties the antitheses they might have appeared to be, any more than they had been in Gilman's day. Rather, they marked the extreme points in the arc of a single pendulum, the opposite typical boundaries of an increasingly restricted world of decision. Between these apparent extremes the anxious modernist sought a virtuous practice, as if, in the moral and technical circumstances of his decision, any single position could in the end be better-than-arbitrarily fixed and valued in relation to any other, and as if a change of style could effect a change in the world or could transform one's moral relation to others.

The Euston Road School closed soon after the outbreak of war, at around the time when Sickert died. A significant number of those variously involved came to occupy senior and influential positions in the provision and administration of art education in England after the war[27] (Bell was killed in 1943). The fallacious belief that 'choice' of positions in the dialectic between technical autonomy and 'documentary' realism can be better-than-arbitrarily made, where it is not made venally, has been an endemic and crippling feature of that education, however ingeniously the circumstances of choice are camouflaged and the infinite variousness of possibilities proclaimed. Yet if there is one single lesson to be learned from the study of the first four decades of twentieth-century English art it is surely this: vividness in representation must entail the reconciliation of technical concerns for expressive form and surface on the one hand with the requirements of realistic description on the other (and such requirements are of course not to be satisfied by mere 'photographic' copying). The more the activity of art tends towards the pursuit of the one at the expense of the other, the smaller the value that is to be attached to either.

It is not enough, though, merely to have learned this. We should go on to seek answers to the question implied: what conditions are required that such a reconciliation may be achieved? The social value of the history of art as a means of inquiry is to be measured, I believe, in terms of the material it furnishes in pursuit of an answer to that question.

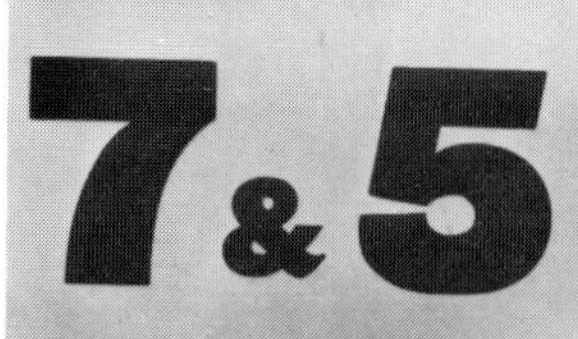

ZWEMMER GALLERY
26, LITCHFIELD STREET, W.C.2

OCTOBER 2nd to 22nd, 1935

1. FRANCIS BUTTERFIELD
2. WINIFRED DACRE
3. BARBARA HEPWORTH
4. IVON HITCHENS
5. ARTHUR JACKSON
6. DAVID JONES
7. HENRY MOORE
8. W. STAITE MURRAY
9. BEN NICHOLSON
10. JOHN PIPER

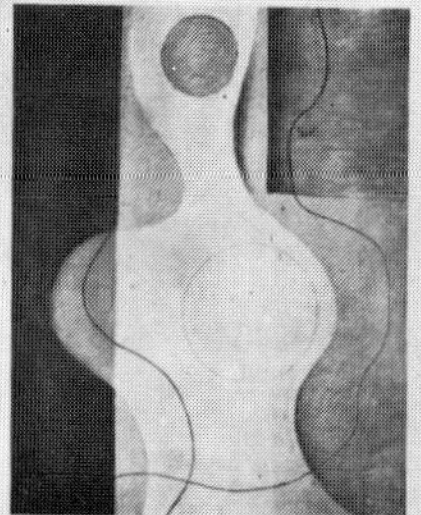
1.

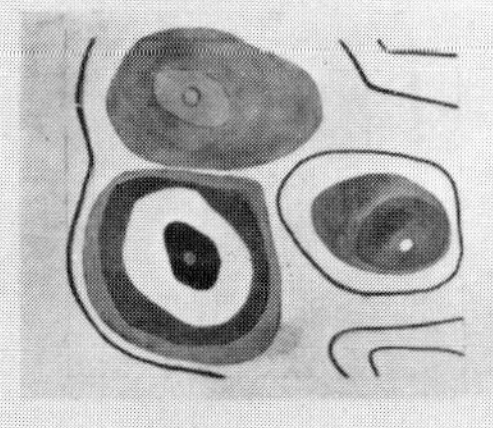
2.

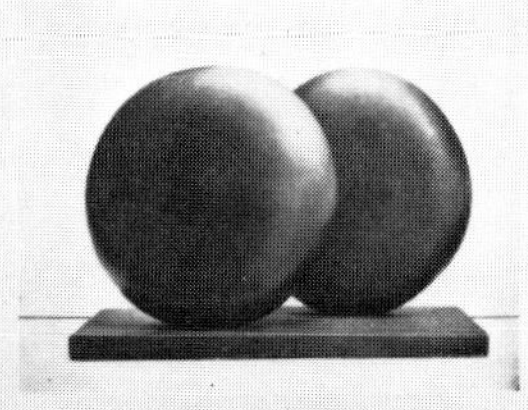
3.

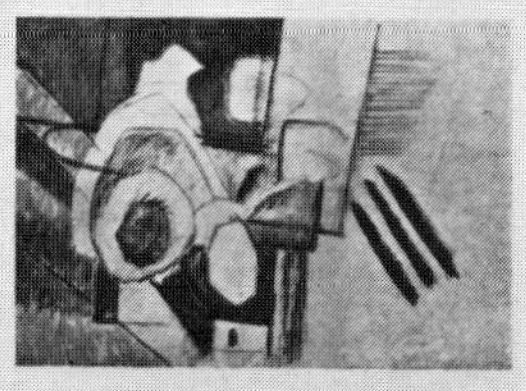
4.

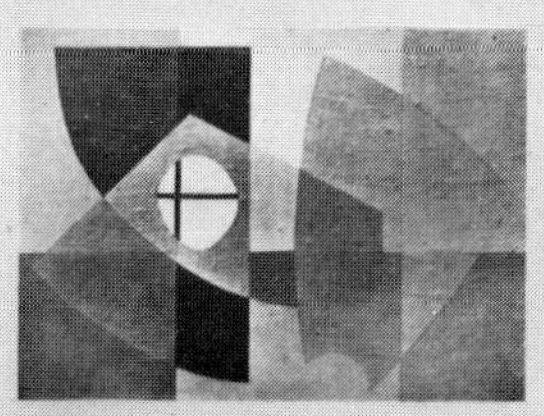
5.

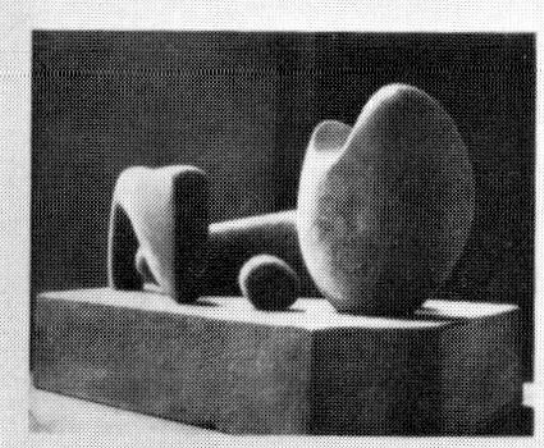
7.

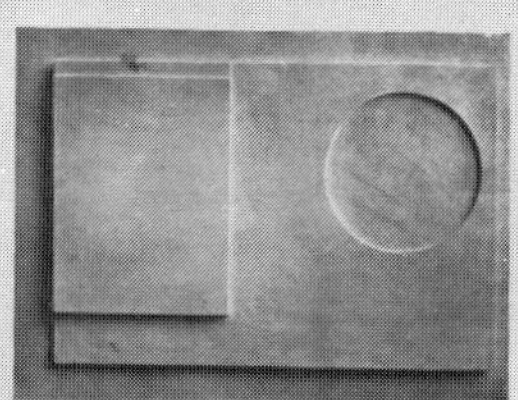
9.

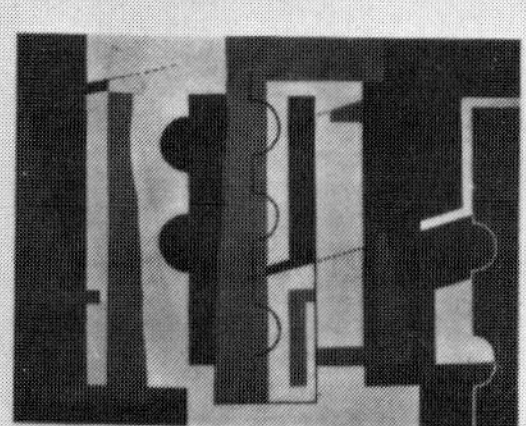
10.

APPENDIX:

THE SEVEN & FIVE SOCIETY

As an increasingly progressive exhibiting society for younger artists, the Seven & Five held a unique position during the period between the wars, complementing the larger and better documented London Group. The name was derived from an original intention that the membership should consist of seven painters and five sculptors, though eighteen artists showed in the first exhibition. The style used to designate the society changed from 'Seven & Five Society', to '7 & 5 Society' and finally, in 1935, to '7 & 5'.

The following table gives dates and locations of exhibitions and lists the members of the society and the names of other artists invited to show with them. The information has been extracted from catalogues and from the surviving records of the society, supplemented by the testimony of surviving members and by reference to contemporary reviews.

Original broadsheet for the last Seven & Five Society exhibition, October 1935

	WALKER'S Apr. 12–May 1, 1920	GIEVES June 1–30, 1921	WALKER'S Nov. 20–Dec. 9, 1922	PATERSONS Nov. 26–Dec. 22, 1923	PATERSONS Dec. 4–20, 1924	BEAUX-ARTS Jan. 6–23, 1926	BEAUX-ARTS Jan. 4–22, 1927	BEAUX-ARTS Feb. 14–Mar. 6, 1928	TOOTH Mar. 7–28, 1929	LEICESTER January, 1931	LEICESTER February, 1932	LEICESTER February, 1933	LEICESTER March, 1934	ZWEMMER Oct. 2–22, 1935
	1	2	3	4	5	6	7	8	9	10	11	12	13	14
E. L. Armitage	M†													
J. P. Barraclough	M†	M†	M†	M†										
H. A. Budd	M†													
G. C. Cowles	M†	M†												
L. S. Edmonds	M†													
E. S. Frith	M†	M†	M†	M†	M†	M								
C. U. Gill	M†													
R. R. Gill	M†	M†	M†											
H. E. Gooding	M†	M†	M†	M	M	M								
S. I. Hitchens	M†	M†	M†	M†	M†	M†	M†	M†	M†	M†	M†	M†	M†	M†
A. J. Oakley	M†	M†	M†	M†	M†	M								
J. D. Revel	M†													
G. C. L. Underwood	M†													
J. White	M†	M												
W. A. Wildman	M†													
H. S. Williamson	M†	M†	M†	M†										
G. R. Woolway	M†	M†	M	M	M†	M†	M†							
A. Howes	MS†	MS†	MS†	M†	M†	M†								
N. Janes		M†	M†	M†	M†	M†	M†	M†	M†	M				
P. H. Jowett		M†	M†	MS†	MS†	MS†	MS†	MS†	MS†	MS†	MS†	MS†	MS	
J. R. R. McCullough		M†	M†	M†	M†	M†	M†							
H. Morley		M†	M†	M										
M. Attenborough			M†	M†										
Claude Flight			M†	M†	M†	M†	M†	M†						
William Liley			M†	M†	M	M								
J. W. Power			M†	M										
André l'Hote			†											
Roger Bissière			†											
Simon Levy			†											
Walter le Wino			†											
Louis Latapie			†											
Alan I. Durst				M†	M†									
Lena Pillico				M†	M†	M†	M†							
B. Nicholson					M†	M†	M†	M†	M†	M†	M†	M†	M†	M†
Colin Sealy					M†	M†	M†							
Jessica Dismorr						M†	M†	M†	M	M				
Elizabeth Drury						M†	M†	M†	M†	M†	M†			
Evi Hone						M†	M†	M	M	M				
Sidney Hunt						M†	M†	M†	M†	M	M†			
Winifred Nicholson						M†	M†	M†	M†	M†	M†	M†	M†	M†
L. Pearson-Righetti						M†	M†	M	M†	M	M†			
Edward Wolfe						M†	M†	M†	M	M				
M. Jellett						†								
Constance Lane						†								
S. Fedorovitch						†	M†	M†	M†	M†	M	M†		
Edith Jenkinson						†								

	WALKER'S *Apr. 12–May 1, 1920* 1	GIEVES *June 1–30, 1921* 2	WALKER'S *Nov. 20–Dec. 9, 1922* 3	PATERSONS *Nov. 26–Dec. 22, 1923* 4	PATERSONS *Dec. 4–20, 1924* 5	BEAUX-ARTS *Jan. 6–23, 1926* 6	BEAUX-ARTS *Jan. 4–22, 1927* 7	BEAUX-ARTS *Feb. 14–Mar. 6, 1928* 8	TOOTH *Mar. 7–28, 1929* 9	LEICESTER *January, 1931* 10	LEICESTER *February, 1932* 11	LEICESTER *February, 1933* 12	LEICESTER *March, 1934* 13	ZWEMMER *Oct. 2–22, 1935* 14
Cedric Morris						†	M†	M†	M†	M†	M†			
Betty Muntz						†	M†	M†	M†					
R. G. S. Mackechnie							M†	M†	M					
Christopher Wood							M†	M†	M†	†	†			
Ruth Hermon							†							
Margaret Schofield							†							
Len Lye							†	M†	M†	M†	M	M†	M†	
J. W. Grant								†						
David Jones								M†	M†	M†	M†	M†	M	M
Maurice Lambert								M†	M	M				
W. Staite Murray								M†	M†	M†	M†	M†	M†	M†
George Lambourne								†						
Kathleen Murray								†						
Robert Medley								†						
Alison Debenham								†						
T. Masson Gibson								†						
A. G. du Plessis								†						
Frances Hodgkins									M†	M†	M†	M†	M†	
Odo Cross									†					
Winston McQuoid									†					
Alfred Walles (*sic*)									†					
Adrian Daintry									†					
Angus Davidson									†					
John Banting									†					
Kanty Cooper									†	†				
John Aldridge										M†	M†	M†	M†	
Basil Taylor										†				
F. Cole										†				
John Skeaping										†	M†			
Edward Bawden											M†	M†	M†	
R. P. Bedford											M†	M		
Barbara Hepworth											M†	M†	M‡	M†
Henry Moore											M†	M†	M‡	M†
Norah McGuiness												†		
Francis Butterfield													M†	M†
John Piper													M†	MS†
Arthur Jackson													†	M†
J. C. Stephenson													†	
Lewis Grahame													†	
Eileen Holding														‡
Roland Penrose														‡
Total Members 56	18	15	17	18	15	21	21	21	21	19	19	14	14	10
Total Exhibitors 87	18	14	21	14	13	23	25	25	23	17	18	15	15	11

M Member. ‡ Exhibited but no works listed in catalogue.

† Exhibitor. S Secretary.

NOTES

Introduction: The Turn of the Century

1. From a lecture on 'The Lesser Arts', delivered in 1878.
2. In letter 79 of *Fors Clavigera: Letters to the Workmen and Labourers of Great Britain*. The Grosvenor Gallery had opened recently under the direction of Sir Coutts Lindsay. In offering advice for the success of the project, Ruskin extolled the virtues of Burne-Jones's work. He concluded: 'Lastly, the mannerisms and errors of these pictures, whatever may be their extent, are never affected or indolent. The work is natural to the painter, however strange to us; and it is wrought with utmost conscience of care, however far, to his own or our desire, the result may yet be incomplete. Scarcely so much can be said for any other pictures of the modern schools: their eccentricities are almost always in some degree forced; and their imperfections gratuitously, if not impertinently, indulged. For Mr Whistler's own sake, no less than for the protection of the purchaser, Sir Coutts Lindsay ought not to have admitted works into the gallery in which the ill-educated conceit of the artist so nearly approached the aspect of wilful imposture.' Whistler took this as a blow at his livelihood, which in the long run it was.
3. See Whistler, *Whistler v. Ruskin. Art and Art Critics* (London 1878); also included in Whistler, *The Gentle Art of Making Enemies* (London and New York 1890).
4. Compare the above quotation with Maurice Denis' notorious slogan, from his 'Definition of Neo-Traditionism' of 1890: 'It is well to remember that a picture – before being a war horse, a nude woman, or some anecdote – is essentially a plane surface covered with colours assembled in a certain order.'

5. Apart from their considerable activities as writers and lecturers, both Morris and Ruskin attempted to establish model circumstances for artistic practice in the hope of effecting a reform both of contemporary design, and of the relevant conditions of labour. In 1861 Morris established the firm Morris, Marshall and Faulkner, Fine Art Workmen in Painting, Carving, Furniture, and the Metals. Ruskin established the St George's Guild in 1871. Neither was able to overcome the fact that in an age of industrial production, 'craftsmanship' is at worst an idealization and at best an expensive luxury.
6. From a letter of 1878, published in *The Gentle Art of Making Enemies, op. cit.*, pp. 127–8.
7. Four paintings by Monet were shown at the Royal Society of British Artists exhibition in 1887–8, an exhibition of twenty works was held at the Goupil Gallery in 1889, and some works were shown at the New English Art Club exhibitions of 1891 and 1893. Monet was in London with Whistler in the summer of 1887 and visited London again for the opening of the RBA show. He paid another visit in 1891.
8. 'Who gets the cars and the cocktails is a matter of complete indifference to anyone who cares for civilization and things of that sort. The trade-unionist is as good as the profiteer; and the profiteer is as good as the trade-unionist. Both are silly, vulgar, good-natured, sentimental, greedy and insensitive; and as both are very well pleased to be what they are neither is likely to become anything better.' This is from the conclusion to Clive Bell's *Civilization*, published in 1928 but, according to its dedication, the last part to be salvaged from a lengthy study of 'The New Renaissance' on which Bell was working in 1910, and of which *Art* was also an extract (see following note).
9. From *Art*, completed in November 1913, first published London, March 1914.
10. See, for instance, Bell's introduction to the second Post-Impressionist exhibition, quoted below, p. 64.
11. For a 'classic' exposition see Clement Greenberg, 'Modernist Painting', in *Forum Lectures*, Voice of America (Washington DC, 1960). 'The essence of Modernism lies, as I see it, in the use of the characteristic methods of a discipline to criticize the discipline itself – not in order to subvert it, but to entrench it more firmly in its area of competence ... "Purity" meant self-definition, and the enterprise of self-criticism in the arts became one of self-definition with a vengeance.'
12. From *Art, op. cit.*

From New English to Camden Town

1. See particularly his 'Ten O'Clock Lecture', first published as *Mr Whistler's 'Ten O'Clock'* (London 1885).
2. Alfred Thornton, *The Diary of an Art Student of the Nineties* (London 1938).
3. R. A. M. Stevenson, *The Art of Velazquez* (London 1895). The author was critic of the *Pall Mall Gazette* and a sympathizer with the NEAC. Writing on Velazquez's technique he asserted that 'Technique is art'.

4. 'Tonks was the Slade and the Slade was Tonks'; from Paul Nash, *Outline, an Autobiography* (London 1949).
5. In 'A Great Impressionist', a memoir of Degas published in the *Evening News*, 30 April 1927.
6. Wendy Baron, *Sickert* (London 1973). I am indebted to this study for many references and matters of fact and have generally accepted its authority in matters of chronology.
7. See Baron, *op. cit.*, p. 44. Sickert's essay was published as a contribution to a volume on *Jules Bastien-Lepage and his Art*. According to Dr Baron it was written in 1891.
8. According to Hubert Wellington, who was in Dieppe at the time. His reminiscences were broadcast as 'With Sickert at Dieppe', and were published in *The Listener*, 23 December 1954.
9. In an article of 1922 ('The Derby Day', *Burlington Magazine*, December 1922), Sickert bracketed Ford Madox Brown, John Leech and Charles Keene together with Mantegna, Michelangelo, Veronese, Canaletto and Hogarth in a discussion of 'illustrative' painting which in his opinion was undeservedly disparaged.
10. 'To come down to historical fact, I may as well say that it is my practice that was transformed from 1905 by the example of the development of Gore's talent'; from 'Whitechapel', *New Age*, 28 May 1914. See also 'A Perfect Modern', Sickert's obituary of Gore, published in *New Age*, 9 April 1914.
11. Baron cites two paintings of 1906 which imply close collaboration. She also asserts, with reason, that 'Sickert was directly responsible for taking Gore straight from his relatively conventional landscapc paintings into the studio, and there introduced him to the themes which establish the identity of Camden Town painting' (introduction to the catalogue of an exhibition, 'Camden Town Recalled', Fine Art Society, October–November 1976).
12. See 'Sargentolatry', *New Age*, 9 May 1910.
13. 'The Language of Art', *New Age*, 28 July 1910.
14. 'The No-Jury System; the Allied Artists Association', *Art News*, 14 July 1910.
15. In Wyndham Lewis and Louis F. Fergusson, *Harold Gilman* (London 1919).
16. 'The Language of Art', *op. cit.*
17. 'With Wisest Sorrow', *Daily Telegraph*, 1 April 1925. Quoted by Baron, *Sickert*, p. 12.
18. Charles Marriot, *Modern Movements in Painting* (Universal Art Series, London 1920).
19. *Walter Sickert: a Conversation* (Hogarth Press, London 1934).
20. Virginia Woolf was the dedicatee of Bell's *Civilization*. Bell's own view of Sickert's status was given in typical voice in *Since Cézanne*, published in 1922: 'Not much of English art is seen from Paris. We have but one living painter whose work is at all well known to the serious amateurs of that city and he is Sickert ... In the remoter parts of Europe as late as the beginning of the seventeenth century were to be found genuine and interesting artists working in the Gothic tradition: the existence of Sickert and Steer made us realize how far

from the centre is London still. On the Continent such conservatism would almost certainly be the outcome of stupidity or prejudice; but both Sickert and Steer have still something of their own to say about the world seen through an impressionist temperament.' The unjustified characterization of Sickert as a provincial and conservative Impressionist has stuck to this day.

21. As recounted by Baron, *op. cit.*, p. 109. According to Baron 'Sickert reported this in a letter to Miss Ethel Sands written during the 1914–18 War.' Although Sickert used the man accused and acquitted of the crime as a model for some of the Camden Town Murder compositions, his paintings on this theme are not identifiable as illustrations of the murder itself, which took place in 1907. Sickert seems to have used the title as if to point towards certain aspects of the subject matter. One painting in the series (Baron, cat. no. 269) has the alternative title *What shall we do for the Rent?*
22. From 'Idealism', *Art News*, 12 May 1910.
23. 'The New Life of Whistler', *Fortnightly Review*, December 1908.
24. 'Idealism', *op. cit.*
25. 'The New English and After', *New Age*, 2 June 1910.
26. See Charles Ginner, 'Harold Gilman', in *Art and Letters*, vol. 3, no. 3, 1919.
27. See Charles Ginner, 'The Camden Town Group', *The Studio*, November 1945.
28. In *New Age*; reprinted in *The Studio*, November 1945.
29. *Ibid.*
30. i.e., typical of 'Post-Impressionism' as interpreted as a 'New Movement' in England. Ginner, in his article, described Neo-Realism as 'the New Realism that is to oppose the headlong destructive flow of the New Academism, i.e. Post-Impressionism.' Ginner and Gilman were explicitly opposed to the concept of technical autonomy for painting.
31. Lewis and Fergusson, *op. cit.* (Note 15).

'Post-Impressionism' and the 'New Movement'

1. In 'Mr Bennett and Mrs Brown', the product of a talk on 'Character in Modern Fiction' which Virginia Woolf gave in May 1924. Her purpose was to stake the claims of and to characterize the 'Georgian novelists', such as E. M. Forster and D. H. Lawrence, as against the older generation of Arnold Bennett, John Galsworthy and H. G. Wells.
2. Fry wrote a favourable review of two early works by Cézanne shown in the International Society Exhibition of 1906. He also wrote to the *Burlington Magazine* in March 1908 in defence of Cézanne and Gauguin.
3. As former curator of painting at the Metropolitan Museum Fry must have been able to command the respect and co-operation of the Parisian dealers; the result was that such galleries and dealers as Bernheim Jeune, Druet, Vollard, Kahnweiler and Sagot were very free with loans of valuable work. They must also have encouraged Fry to show recent work by comparatively young painters.

4. In *Art*.
5. *Ibid.*
6. From the chapter on Sickert in *Old Friends: Personal Recollections* (London 1956).
7. For an extended account of the reactions to the first of Fry's Post-Impressionist exhibitions see the chapter 'The Post-Impressionists' in Ian Dunlop, *The Shock of the New* (London 1972). For a succinct if partisan account of both exhibitions see Benedict Nicholson, 'Post-Impressionism and Roger Fry', in *Burlington Magazine*, January 1951.
8. The painting was exhibited at the New English Art Club in 1923, but judging by the apparent ages of the dramatis personae must have been painted some time before this date.
9. See the chapter 'Alid ex Alio' in *Art*: 'Amongst Londoners of the "eighties" he is a bright figure, as much alone in his knowledge of what art is, as in his power of creating it.' Bell cited Ruskin as one in whose writing 'you will hardly find a sentence that gives ground for supposing that the writer has so much as guessed what art is'.
10. See Baron, *op. cit.*, pp. 132–3, where she instances a criticism of 'prima' painting made by Sickert in 1913.
11. Published in MacColl, *Confessions of a Keeper* (London 1931).
12. 'The Post-Impressionists', *Fortnightly Review*, January 1911.
13. From 'Art and Life', published in Fry, *Vision and Design* (London 1920), from notes of a lecture of 1917.
14. *Ibid.*
15. Letter to the *Burlington Magazine*, March 1908.
16. Originally published in the *Burlington Magazine*; reprinted in *Vision and Design*.
17. See 'Art and Socialism', originally published in *The Great State* (Harper 1912); reprinted with considerable alterations in *Vision and Design*. Fry was perhaps still smarting from the experience of working under Pierpont Morgan.
18. See the chapter on 'The Classical Renaissance and its Diseases' in Bell's *Art*.
19. *Art*.
20. *Ibid.*
21. 'Inspired by the first and second Post-Impressionist Exhibitions, I cut out of my *New Renaissance* a section and published it in the spring of 1914 under the simple and comprehensive title *Art*.' From the dedication to Bell's *Civilization*, published 1928.
22. At the conclusion of his *Über das Geistige in der Kunst* (Concerning the Spiritual in Art), written in 1910 and first published in Munich in 1912. The first English translation was published in 1914. Kandinsky was also on common ground with Bell in asserting modern man's 'sympathy and affinity with and ... comprehension of the work of primitives'.
23. From Bell's essay on Fry in *Old Friends, op. cit.* (Note 6).
24. As quoted by MacColl, *op. cit.* (Note 11).
25. 'An Essay in Aesthetics' was first published in the *New Quarterly* in 1909 and

was reprinted in *Vision and Design*. Bell described it as 'the most helpful contribution to the science ... made since the days of Kant' (in the Preface to *Art*).

26. See his introduction to the French Post-Impressionists at the second Grafton Galleries exhibition.
27. It is significant that the first notable sign of a change in the terms of reference for art criticism was to be Herbert Read's 'Psychoanalysis and the Critic', first published in 1925.
28. Though in justice to Fry, see below on 'Art and Socialism', pp. 71–2.
29. *Art*.
30. *Ibid*. '... after all, useful work must remain for the most part, mechanical; and if the useful workers want to express themselves as completely as possible, they must do so in their leisure. There are two kinds of formal expression open to all – dancing and singing.'
31. *Principia Ethica*, Cambridge edition, pp. 188–9.
32. A copious literature has been generated by, about and around the various groups and individuals eligible for consideration as members of the Bloomsbury set. Clive Bell was certainly a central figure, and his own account, given in a chapter of *Old Friends*, is sufficiently succinct to be easily précised. In 1899 Bell, Lytton Strachey, Saxon Sydney-Turner, Leonard Woolf and Thoby Stephen were freshmen together at Cambridge, where they formed a 'reading society'; after Cambridge they met often at the house in Gordon Square where Stephen lived with his sisters Vanessa and Virginia and his brother Adrian. In 1907 Bell and Vanessa Stephen were married, remaining in Gordon Square while Virginia and Adrian Stephen moved to Fitzroy Square. As members of the 'elder generation of Bloomsbury', Bell listed these together with Duncan Grant and the economist John Maynard Keynes, Roger Fry, H. T. J. Morton and Gerald Shove; he included Desmond and Molly MacCarthy and E. M. Forster as 'close friends'; the philosopher Bertrand Russell 'appeared to be a friend and was certainly an influence'. 'Younger associates' after the war included David Garnett, Francis Birrell, Raymond Mortimer, Ralph Partridge, Stephen Tomlin, Sebastien Sprott, F. L. Lucas and Frances Marshall. The biography of Virginia Woolf by her nephew Quentin Bell provides detailed and well-documented information about the various relationships within the group (two volumes, Hogarth Press, London 1972). See also the same author's *Bloomsbury* (London 1968).
33. From the chapter on 'Art and Ethics' in *Art*.
34. *Old Friends*, chapter on 'Bloomsbury'. Writing on Virginia Woolf in *Horizon*, June 1941, Duncan Grant described the effects of Moore on his friends: '"This is my Bible", was said by one, pointing to the *Principia Ethica* by G. E. Moore. This eminent philosopher was certainly the overwhelming influence on these young men. Conversations on the "Good" and the value of certain states of mind were a frequent subject of discussion ...'
35. 'The general effect of his [Matisse's] pictures is that of a return to primitive, even

perhaps of a return to barbaric, art' – from the introduction to 'Manet and the Post-Impressionists'; 'Most people who care much about art find that of the work which moves them most the greater part is what scholars call "Primitive"' – Bell, *Art*.

36. MacColl, *op. cit.*
37. Bell in *Art*.
38. 'The French Post-Impressionists', reprinted in *Vision and Design*.
39. 'Notes d'un peintre' was published in *La Grande Revue* (Paris) in December 1908. Fry met Matisse early in that year and it seems very likely that he would have familiarized himself with this important statement of the French painter's aesthetic. Fry's 'emotional elements of design' ('Essay in Aesthetics') might be the 'various elements' Matisse writes of in his definition of composition as 'the art of arranging in a decorative manner the various elements at the painter's disposal for the expression of his feelings'; and Fry's 'classic concentration of feeling' ('The French Post-Impressionists') echoes the 'state of condensation of sensations' which Matisse saw as constituting a picture. See also Kandinsky, *op. cit.*: '... mastery over form is not the end but, instead, the adapting of form to internal significance'.
40. 'For a discussion of aesthetics, it need be agreed only that forms arranged and combined according to certain unknown and mysterious laws do move us in a particular way, and that it is the business of an artist so to combine and arrange them that they shall move us. These moving combinations and arrangements I have called ... "Significant Form"' (*Art*).
41. MacColl, *op. cit.*
42. *Outline, an autobiography and other writings* (London 1949), pp. 92–3. Nash was admitted to the Slade in the autumn of 1910; he seems never to have been at ease there and did not attend after Christmas 1911.
43. *Art*.
44. See Nevinson's autobiography, *Paint and Prejudice* (London 1937).
45. Gertler, Nevinson, Wadsworth and Spencer were at the Slade from 1908 to 1912, Nash and Ben Nicholson for periods between autumn 1910 and Christmas 1911, Roberts from 1910 to 1913, and Bomberg, after two years at the Westminster School of Art, from 1911 to 1913. In those days curricula were rigidly formulated and were intended to be observed. The emphasis was upon drawing, and prizes were given for such projects as drawing and painting from the antique, painting a head, and painting subject pictures on approved themes. There was no universal system of grants such as applies today; students were either fee-payers, like Nash (who found he could ill afford it) and Nicholson, or scholars like Wadsworth, Bomberg, Gertler and Roberts.
46. Ginner, 'Neo-Realism', *op. cit.*
47. In 'Art and Socialism' Fry described Ruskin's address on the *Political Economy of Art* as 'a work which surprises by its prophetic foresight when we read it half a century later'.
48. An interesting and trenchant gloss on the relations between the Arts and Crafts

movement and later enterprises such as Fry's is given near the end of Eric Gill's *Autobiography* (London 1940), pp. 268–70.

49. For an extended and documented account of this affair, which has continued to arouse partisan passions into the second generation, see Quentin Bell and Stephen Chaplin, 'The Ideal Home Rumpus', *Apollo*, October 1964. For an alternative version see W. Michel, *Wyndham Lewis, Paintings and Drawings* (London 1971). See also William Roberts's amusing account in his pamphlet *Some Early Abstract and Cubist Work 1913–1920* (London 1957): 'This was not a dispute of two erudites over a subtle point of aesthetics, but a clash between rivals for the profits of the English interior-decorating market.'

Cubism, Futurism, Vorticism

1. E. Wake Cook, letter to the *Pall Mall Gazette*, 10 November 1910, quoted in William Wees, *Vorticism and the English Avant-Garde* (Toronto 1972). The critic of the *Morning Post* compared 'Manet and the Post-Impressionists' to the Gunpowder Plot.
2. The most extensive and up-to-date catalogue of Lewis's work is to be found in Walter Michel's *Wyndham Lewis: Paintings and Drawings* (London 1971).
3. From an essay published in *Beginnings*, ed. L. A. G. Strong (London 1935).
4. Evidence for the more likely dating of 1912 is given in the catalogue to the exhibition 'Vorticism and its Allies', Hayward Gallery 1974.
5. *Kermesse* was one of several works formerly in the collection of the American John Quinn which were dispersed following the sale of his estate in 1927 and which are now lost. The transfer of many works to America and the sharp decline of interest in works of this type and period following the war resulted in the destruction or loss of a very high proportion of the output of Lewis, Wadsworth, Nevinson, Epstein, Hamilton and Etchells from the period 1912–16. Decades later a revival of interest in this episode in English art, as expressed in the exhibitions of 'Abstract Art in England 1913–15' at the d'Offay Couper Gallery in 1969 and of 'Vorticism and its Allies' in 1974, was to result in the reintroduction of many works long out of currency and in the republication of early photographs of others. We are indebted to the researches of Anthony d'Offay and Richard Cork, the respective organizers of these exhibitions.
6. *Kermesse* was first shown at the AAA in July 1912. Bell reviewed the exhibition for *The Athenaeum* and wrote of the painting as 'pure formal composition' – high praise from him.
7. See *Epstein – An Autobiography* (London 1963), p. 12.
8. *Ibid.*, p. 23. Much of the comment and correspondence is reprinted in Epstein's autobiography. The *Evening Standard and St James' Gazette* in a front-page article objected that while this sort of thing was all very well in an art gallery, reserved for the eyes of the appreciative, 'to have art of the kind indicated, laid bare to the gaze of all classes, young and old, in perhaps the busiest thoroughfare of the Metropolis of the world ... is another matter.' In an obituary tribute written fifty

years after the controversy over the Strand statues, Henry Moore acknowledged a debt of gratitude to Epstein for the way in which he had withstood the first wave of opposition to modern sculpture (*Sunday Times*, 23 August 1959).

9. 'Mr Epstein and the Critics', *New Age*, 25 December 1913. Reprinted in S. Hynes, ed., *Further Speculations by T. E. Hulme* (Minnesota 1955).
10. Epstein, *op. cit.*, pp. 46–9.
11. 'How England met Modern Art', *Art News*, October 1950.
12. Statement in the catalogue of his one-man exhibition, Chenil Gallery, July 1914.
13. In *Blast* 1, June 1914.
14. In 'Modern Art I. The Grafton Group', *New Age*, 15 January 1914. Reprinted in Hynes, *op. cit.*
15. Nevinson, *Paint and Prejudice: an Autobiography* (London 1937). There are several first-hand accounts of Hulme's 'at homes', including one in Epstein, *op. cit.*, pp. 59–60.
16. Wees, *op. cit.*, pp. 56–7, refers to a letter from Fry to Lewis, now in the Lewis Collection, Cornell University.
17. This estimate was quoted by Boccioni in a letter to Vico Baer dated 15 March 1912. The degree of interest aroused by the catalogue is signified by Boccioni's mention, in a previous letter, that 17,000 copies had been printed for the Paris showing of the exhibition. Both letters are printed in *Futurism* by Joshua Taylor (Museum of Modern Art, New York 1961).
18. The 'Initial Manifesto of Futurism', 'Futurist Painting: Technical Manifesto' and 'The Exhibitors to the Public' are reprinted in Taylor, *op. cit.*, in the translations used for the Sackville Gallery catalogue.
19. For evidence of the Futurists' acquaintance with Bergson's writings see Taylor, *op. cit.*, pp. 12 and 119. See also B. Petrie, 'Boccioni and Bergson', *Burlington Magazine*, March 1974. Lewis had heard Bergson lecture, possibly before his return to England in 1908. As he later wrote, 'I began by embracing his evolutionary system' (Rose, ed., *Letters of Wyndham Lewis* (London 1965), letter of 1949).
20. *History of Western Philosophy* (London, 1961 ed.), p. 757.
21. Both paintings are now lost but were reproduced in *The Graphic*, 25 October 1913. Other English artists represented in the exhibition were Cuthbert Hamilton, Spencer Gore, Charles Ginner, Harold Gilman, Sickert, and Alfred Wolmark.
22. From Hulme's introduction to his own translation of Georges Sorel, *Reflections on Violence* (London 1916). Hulme's introduction is printed in *Speculations: Essays on Humanism and the Philosophy of Art* by T. E. Hulme, ed. Herbert Read (London 1924). Lewis had also read Sorel's work with interest.
23. Edward Marsh, quoted in Robert Ross, *The Georgian Revolt 1910–1922*, p. 37.
24. In the article 'A Man of the Week: Marinetti', *New Weekly*, 30 May 1914, quoted by Wees, *op. cit.*, p. 100.

25. 'The Cubist Room'. Lewis's introductory essay is reprinted in Michel, *op. cit.*, pp. 430–31.
26. 'Two Views of the London Group, I', *The Nation*, 14 March 1914.
27. 'Modern Art III. The London Group', *New Age*, 26 March 1914. Reprinted in Hynes, *op. cit.*
28. 'Modern Art IV. Mr David Bomberg's Show', *New Age*, 9 July 1914. Reprinted in Hynes, *op. cit.*
29. Hynes, *op. cit.*, contains a full bibliography of Hulme's writings.
30. Originally published as *Abstraktion und Einfühling* (Munich 1908).
31. Interest in early medieval and Gothic art was of course fostered in England in the nineteenth century, notably by Pugin, Ruskin and Morris, and the Pre-Raphaelite painters had advocated a return to what might have been regarded as a more 'spiritual' art, but in each case the motivation had been 'ethical'. Reigl and Worringer were concerned with 'feeling' rather than 'faith', and with the psychology rather than the social significance of style. This made their writings acceptable to those for whom Ruskin, Morris and the Pre-Raphaelites were features of an embarrassing past.
32. *Abstraction and Empathy*, translated by Michael Bullock (London 1963), p. 15.
33. *Ibid.*, p. 24.
34. Kandinsky knew Worringer in Munich at the time when his own work was developing towards abstraction. Many of the concepts in his *Concerning the Spiritual in Art* echo those of Worringer.
35. The lecture was delivered to the Quest Society in Kensington Town Hall. 'Modern Art and its Philosophy' is printed in *Speculations*.
36. *Du Cubisme* by Albert Gleizes and Jean Metzinger was first published in Paris in December 1912, and as *Cubism* in English translation in London during the next year. As the first published theoretical justification of Cubism, albeit one in which Picasso and Braque had had no part, the essay gained an immediate currency among interested artists and critics.
37. Epstein, *op. cit.*, p. 56.
38. Richard Cork refers to the draft of a letter from Bomberg to Roberts mentioning a visit to Epstein's studio, 'about December 1913', when the sculptor was in process of completing the work (catalogue to 'Vorticism and its Allies', Arts Council of Great Britain 1974, p. 73). Epstein, *loc. cit.*, refers to a visit by Gaudier and Pound in 1913 when the former was 'very enthusiastic' about the *Rock Drill*.
39. The phrase is Lewis's, from *Blast* 2, July 1915.
40. Besides the intended teaching programme under Lewis's professorship there were to be plays and dances and a lecture by 'some figure from the world of avant garde music, such as Schoenberg or Scriabin'.
41. 'Vital English Art' was published in full in the *Observer* on 7 June 1914 and was quoted in various other papers.
42. The repudiation was reported in various London papers and journals during the

week after the publication of the manifesto. The *Observer* of 14 June was one of those which carried the full text.

43. Printed in *Speculations*; the material from which *Cinders* was assembled by Herbert Read was written over a period of several years.
44. In a letter to William Carlos Williams, December 1913 (*Letters of Ezra Pound 1907–1941*, ed. Paige, London 1951, p. 65).
45. As reported by Violet Hunt in *I have this to say: the Story of my Flurried Years* (London 1925).
46. Precedents for the typographic style of *Blast*'s less conventional pages were set by the Futurists' 'parole in libertà', but there was also a deliberate 'vulgar' reference to the appearance of advertisements.
47. *The Toe Dancer* shows a performance at the home of the socialist Stewart Gray, where artists and political radicals were provided with quarters during the early months of the war. Epstein, Bomberg and Roberts were among the visitors.
48. Mentioned in Ezra Pound's *Gaudier Brzeska: a Memoir* (London 1916).
49. The device had been used a year earlier by the French poet and critic Apollinaire in a Futurist manifesto published in *Lacerba*: 'Merde' to some and 'Rose' to others. Fry was the only English recipient of a Rose.
50. An excellent glossary on those blasted and blessed is to be found as an appendix to Wees's *Vorticism and the English Avant Garde*. This study brings together material from a wide range of sources, and I have been much indebted to it.
51. Hulme, with whom Lewis had quarrelled, did not contribute to *Blast*, though Hynes, *op. cit.*, suggests that he had expected to produce an essay on Epstein's drawings.
52. Lewis was concerned to provide a modern iconography for the delineation of 'modern man'. The idea that man's nature is 'changed' by the change in his relations to the world effected by industrial and technological development is one which has achieved its typical expression in the more absurd writings of Marshall McLuhan, whom Lewis came to know in Toronto during the Second World War.
53. In November 1945 Ezra Pound was tried in Washington on charges of treason against the United States and of broadcasting propaganda on behalf of the Axis régime. He was subsequently incarcerated in a Federal government asylum for the insane, from which he was not released until 1958. In a publication of 1935 Pound had written of Mussolini, 'Take him as anything save the artist and you will get muddled with contradictions' (*Jefferson and/or Mussolini*, London 1935). Marinetti was a close associate of Mussolini and was to remain with him virtually to the end. In a note of 1939, written to preface the republication of his essay on 'The Art of the Great Race' from *Blast* 2, Lewis drew attention to his own 'forecast of the political revolutions that have swept the world': 'Every real individuality and excellence would welcome conditions where there would be hierarchy of power and vitality. The Best would then be Free. Under no other conditions is any true freedom at all possible.' Pound and Lewis, like many authors who supported Fascism between the wars, believed in the possibility of

an 'authoritarian democracy' and saw socialism as involving the levelling of all down to a mean at which the individual man of vitality (or artist) could not operate.

54. Twelve sheets from a sketchbook of this period were exhibited at the d'Offay Couper Gallery, London, in November 1969.
55. By Lewis among others. See his introduction to the catalogue of the exhibition 'Wyndham Lewis and Vorticism', Tate Gallery, 1956.
56. In 'The Skeleton in the Cupboard Speaks', *Wyndham Lewis the Artist from Blast to Burlington House* (London 1939).

The Great War

1. See Richard Cork's introduction to 'Vorticism and its Allies'.
2. The painting was listed in the catalogue of the Quinn collection in 1920. It was reproduced in a photograph in the *Daily Mirror* of 11 June 1915, together with Wadsworth's *Blackpool* and Etchells's *The Pigeon Juggler*, both now also lost.
3. These were a panel and some decorations for Ford Madox Hueffer's study and three panels for the Eiffel Tower Restaurant in London, the latter executed with the assistance of Helen Saunders. See Michel, *op. cit.*, pp. 335–6.
4. The introduction is reprinted in Michel, *op. cit.*, pp. 432–3.
5. See his article in L. A. G. Strong, ed., *Beginnings* (London 1935): 'When a painter is also a writer, whether good or ill should ensue, artistically upon this double birth ... depends upon how these partners are mutually balanced. With me, I am inclined to claim, the equilibrium was practically perfect ...'
6. Reprinted in Michel and Fox, eds., *Wyndham Lewis on Art* (London 1969).
7. In *Wyndham Lewis the Artist from Blast to Burlington House* (London 1939).
8. The phrase appears in *Outline*, p. 215.
9. Ezra Pound, *Gaudier Brzeska: a Memoir* (London 1916).
10. See Noel Stock, *The Life of Ezra Pound* (Penguin edition, Harmondsworth 1974), p. 515. The manifesto was published in February 1944 and was signed by four Italian writers as well as by Pound. Stock considers that 'it bears every mark of Pound's authorship'. See also the previous chapter, Note 53.
11. In a letter to Kate Lechmere; Rose, ed., *Letters of Wyndham Lewis*, p. 69.
12. The Canadian scheme was sponsored by Lord Beaverbrook. Besides paintings and drawings done during the war by artists attached to Canadian companies, various artists were paid to produce large finished oil paintings after the armistice. Those commissioned to produce works in the latter category included John, William Nicholson, Gilman, Ginner, Etchells, Lewis, Roberts, Bomberg, Wadsworth and Paul Nash. The first works produced under the Canadian scheme were exhibited at Burlington House in London in 1917 and the larger works were shown together two years later. The Ministry of Information scheme commenced in 1916 with the initial aim of providing a visual record of the war. Pictures were required essentially for reproduction in the service of propaganda and of information to the public. At the close of the war the idea

was advanced of commissioning a considerable number of large-sized pictures which would hang round the walls of a special memorial hall. Although an appropriate space has never been provided for them, the paintings themselves were produced. Of course many of them are without much merit, but taken as a whole the collection is remarkable; it includes one painting by Sargent of 90 × 240 in. (*Gassed*), several of 72 × 125 in. (by Colin Gill, Nevinson, Lewis, D. Y. Cameron, Roberts, Paul Nash, George Clausen, Ambrose McEvoy, John Lavery, Charles Sims, Walter Bayes and Darsie Japp), others of 72 × 86 in. (by John Nash, Henry Tonks, Gilbert and Stanley Spencer, Henry Lamb and John Dodgson), and several more large paintings of assorted sizes by various artists including Augustus John and Gilbert Rogers. All these are housed in the Imperial War Museum.

13. *A Concise Catalogue of Paintings, Drawings and Sculpture of the First World War 1914–18*, Imperial War Museum; introduction to the first edition, 1924.
14. Sam Hynes, introduction to Hynes, ed., *Further Speculations by T. E. Hulme*, p. xxv.
15. Hulme quoted in Hynes, *op. cit.*, p. xxviii.
16. Hulme's writings on the war were published under the pseudonym 'North Staffs' in *New Age* between November 1915 and March 1916, and in the *Cambridge Magazine* from January to March 1916. In one of the latter series, under the title 'The Kind of Rubbish We Oppose', Hulme criticized Russell's pacifism as expressed in a lecture he had attended, and at the conclusion of his article expressed the nature of the argument between them in such terms as are relevant to discussion of the issues at stake in contemporary controversies about art:

> The polemic is not one between *reason* and *impulse*. It is a polemic between two systems of value. You may win in this struggle if you clearly recognize the true character of the things at issue. Do not, however, falsely simplify matters by assuming that it is a struggle between the assailants and defenders of privilege. It is not Democracy against Privilege, but, rather,
>
> One ideology + Democracy
> against
> Another ideology + Democracy
>
> The character of the second ideology is such that it does not attach the same positive values to the abolition of minor privileges that the first does (abolition of restrictions on growth of personality, etc.). Nor does it make the same appeals to *ressentiment*. But I am now convinced that the abolition of such privileges is a necessary political measure in order that the clear character of this opposition may not be disguised.

It was by no means incidental that Hulme should have been associated, however briefly, with the radical modernists, and that Russell should have been, as Bell put it, a 'friend' of Bloomsbury. (Garsington Manor, the home of Lady Ottoline Morrell, was a refuge to many pacifists following the introduction of conscription during the war. Russell was among the visitors, together with

Mark Gertler, Clive Bell, Aldous Huxley, Lytton Strachey, and many other figures from the Bloomsbury coterie.)

Hulme's *Cambridge Magazine* articles, together with Russell's rejoinders, are reprinted in Hynes, *op. cit.*

17. As reported in the *Daily Express*, 25 February 1915; quoted in Wees, *op. cit.*, p. 118.
18. In a review of the London Group exhibition of March 1915, published in *Blast* 2, Lewis refers to paintings by Nevinson titled *Marching Soldiers* and *Searchlights*. The former was probably *Returning to the Trenches* [53], now in the National Gallery of Canada, Ottawa.
19. 'This little figure was so preternaturally *alive*, that I began my lesson then: a lesson of hatred for this soul-less machine, of big-wig money-government, and these masses of half-dead people, for whom personal extinction is such a tiny step, out of half-living into non-living, so what does it matter?' From Lewis, *Blasting and Bombardiering* (London 1937), pp. 114–15.
20. 'Artists and the War', *Blast* 2.
21. *Daily Telegraph*, 13 June 1916.
22. 'Marinetti's Occupation'.
23. *A Canadian Gun Pit*, 1918, 120 × 132 in., now in the National Gallery of Canada, Ottawa.
24. Reprinted in Michel, *op. cit.*, pp. 433–4.
25. *The First German Gas Attack at Ypres*, 1918, 120 × 144 in., National Gallery of Canada, Ottawa, and *A Shell Dump, France*, 1918–19, 72 × 125 in., Imperial War Museum.
26. For a fuller account see William Lipke, *David Bomberg: A Critical Study of his Life and Work* (London 1967).
27. See Chapter 4, Note 53.
28. See for instance his large *Fraternity* in the Imperial War Museum.
29. His painting of *The Food Queue* in the Imperial War Museum seems to owe a great deal to Robert Bevan's treatment of figures. It would have been natural for younger painters to look to Camden Town precedents when dealing with 'realistic' figure subjects.
30. 'If you are to seek for anything dramatic in his death, it is that his last picture (that of Halifax Harbour), on exhibition during his last illness, was in many ways the best he had done.' Lewis, from Lewis and Fergusson, *op. cit.* (London 1919). Lewis also referred to the painting as 'one of the two or three best' in the 1919 Canadian War Memorial exhibition (which included his own *A Canadian Gun Pit*). In his review of the London Group in *Blast* 2 Lewis had written: 'Among the Camden Town Group, I admire many qualities in Mr Gilman's and Mr Ginner's paintings. I still hope to find myself on common ground with these two painters one of these days.'
31. *Over the Top* and *Oppy Wood* [62] in the Imperial War Museum.
32. *Travoys arriving with Wounded at a Dressing-Station at Smol, Macedonia, September 1916*, 1919, 72 × 86 in.

33. See Nash's early letters to his friend and correspondent Gordon Bottomley in Abbott and Bertram, eds., *Poet and Painter: being the Correspondence between Gordon Bottomley and Paul Nash 1910–1946* (London 1955). These letters provide a vivid account of the development of the painter's interests over the course of his working life.
34. Letters of 4 and 6 April 1917, printed in *Outline*, pp. 193–4.
35. Letter of 6 April, *Outline*, pp. 196–8.
36. From 'Diary from the Trenches', compiled from letters to his aunt and printed in Hynes, *op. cit.*, p. 157.
37. See *Poet and Painter*, p. 85.
38. See *Outline*, p. 216.
39. 'Visit to Brigade HQ Zillebecke. The chance I have been waiting for. Sanctuary Wood at Dawn. Gheluvelt. The German pill-box. I escape from the Brigadier. Adventures in Passchendaele. I draw the German Front line. The Menin Road. The mule track. Sunrise at Inverness Copse. About noon I get back to HQ. I have made fourteen drawings. I fall asleep for hours.' From notes for the continuation of his autobiography, *Outline*, p. 216.
40. *Outline*, pp. 210–11. See Note 39.
41. The last of these is in the National Gallery of Canada, Ottawa, the others all in the Imperial War Museum. *After the Battle* was not shown during the war. It was probably not finished in time, but even if it had been it could not have been exhibited. Despite the express intention that artists should provide a documentary record of the war, the Ministry of Information censor prevented public exhibition of pictures which showed bodies of the dead. Nevinson included his *Paths of Glory*, a painting showing two dead soldiers entangled in barbed wire, in the selection for his Leicester Galleries exhibition in March 1918. It was not passed. Nevinson left it hanging, but covered it in brown paper with the word 'censored' written across. He was reprimanded for this gesture by the War Office. (See Robert Cumming's introduction to the catalogue of an exhibition of 'Artists at War, 1914–1918', Kettle's Yard, Cambridge, October–November 1974.)

Hiatus: 1919–1924

1. Both books were published in London. *Vision and Design* had achieved its fourth printing by 1925, *Since Cézanne* by 1928. In 1929 Bell's *Art* was in its ninth printing.
2. The self-certifying distinction between what men experience as 'men' and what they experience as 'artists' was, and remains, a conventional tactic of Modernist criticism.
3. Letter to John Quinn dated 14 June 1920. Published in Rose, ed., *Letters of Wyndham Lewis*.
4. At the end of 1919 a highly influential pamphlet on *The Economic Consequences*

of the Peace was published by John Maynard Keynes, whose friendships within the Bloomsbury circle survived the war.

5. David Thomson, *England in the Twentieth Century* (Harmondsworth 1965).
6. From 'Notes for the Continuation of his Autobiography' in *Outline*.
7. From 'Duncan Grant', published in *The Athenaeum*, 6 February 1920, reprinted in *Since Cézanne*.
8. Quentin Bell, from his introduction to N. Carrington, ed., *Selected Letters of Mark Gertler* (London 1965).
9. From a letter of 1947, Rose, *op. cit.*, p. 412.
10. The painting was much admired by D. H. Lawrence, who wrote to Gertler: '... it is the best *modern* picture I have seen: I think it is great and true. But it is horrible and terrifying.' N. Carrington, ed., *op. cit.*
11. Wyndham Lewis, from *Rude Assignment: a Narrative of my Career up-to-date* (London 1950), p. 125. He was describing the aims of *Blast*.
12. In a note written to introduce *The Caliph's Design* when he republished it as part of *Wyndham Lewis the Artist from Blast to Burlington House*.
13. His best-known work as an architect is the Crawford building in Holborn. He was also responsible for the English translation of Le Corbusier's *Vers une Architecture*.
14. These formed the substance of an extremely successful exhibition at the Leicester Galleries in January 1920. Twenty of them were illustrated in a publication by the Ovid Press later in the year, under the title *Black Country*. Arnold Bennett's introduction to the Leicester Galleries catalogue was reprinted as the text of the book. Wadsworth also exhibited a selection of these works as his contribution to the X Group show.
15. 'Wyndham Lewis & "X group" acted for me as an emetic': Ben Nicholson, in a letter to Ronald Alley, 27 July 1962.
16. 'I had tried the "group" game, in the art-racket: I had found it more trouble than it was worth. And in *The Caliph's Design* ... it was not as part of a rather bogus battalion, but as *a single spy*, that I was speaking.' From 'The Skeleton in the Cupboard Speaks', in *Wyndham Lewis the Artist*.
17. From Lewis's introduction to the catalogue of the exhibition 'Wyndham Lewis and Vorticism', Tate Gallery, 1956.
18. Quoted in the *Daily Express*, 11 April 1921, under the heading 'Dean Swift with a Brush – The Tyroist explains his art'. The report is printed in Michel, *Wyndham Lewis*, *op. cit.*
19. Reprinted in Michel, *op. cit.*, and in Michel and Fox, eds., *Wyndham Lewis on Art* (London 1969).
20. In 'The Skeleton in the Cupboard Speaks', *op. cit.*
21. 'Mrs Lewis remembers that the head was, to all intents and purposes, finished, the coat largely finished and the legs in position when the painting was abandoned. When Lewis took it up again in about 1935, he added the forearms and background, and slightly altered the coat' (Michel, *op. cit.*).

22. Lewis, introduction to the Tate Gallery catalogue, 1956.
23. In a letter to James Thrall Soby of 20 September 1947 (Rose, ed., *op. cit.*, p. 412), Lewis blamed Bloomsbury influence for his exclusion from the series 'Penguin Modern Painters' published under the general editorship of Kenneth Clark. The selection as actually published was in fact so arbitrary as to deprive this accusation of any force it might have had.
24. At the Lefevre Galleries. In a preface to the catalogue Lewis wrote of his drawings: 'Coming from the workshop of an extreme experimentalist, they may at first be regarded rather as a demonstration of traditional draughtsmanship. They are not that. I have always practised side by side the arts of experiment and arts of tradition ... There is no 'left' and no 'right' in the universe of art ... I move with a familiarity natural to me amongst eyeless and hairless abstractions. But I am also interested in human beings.' A portfolio of *Thirty Personalities and a Self-Portrait*, largely taken from the works in the exhibition, was published by Desmond Harmondsworth Ltd in 1932.
25. H. S. Williamson, letter to the author, 23 February 1965.
26. Ivon Hitchens, letter to the author, 5 February 1965.

Still Life and Landscape in the Twenties

1. In a letter of 12 December 1919 (*Poet and Painter*, p. 114). Bottomley's regret at what he saw as his friend's modernism should be interpreted in the context of his belief that Nash and his 'companions' were 'finding again the English secret, the English soul that the Pre-Raphaelites found and lost'.
2. A large oil with a reclining nude in front of a tree-fringed lake was shown as *The Lake* in Nash's one-man show at the Leicester Galleries in 1924; when he exhibited the painting three years later, however, the figure had been painted out and the picture retitled *Chestnut Waters*. The attempt to produce a substantial composition on such a theme probably reflects Nash's appreciation of Cézanne's series of *Baigneuses*, the principal modernist exemplars for ambitious paintings combining figures with landscape.
3. Letter of 22 April 1925 (*Poet and Painter*, p. 182).
4. *Winter Sea* (York City Art Gallery) is the strong exception among Nash's seascapes. It was begun in the spring of 1925 before he left Dymchurch, but was largely worked in 1937. It is a more complex and more impressive painting than any of the others on similar subjects.
5. The painting is signed and is dated 1921; there is another version of the subject, however, titled *Winter in Cortivallo*, which is dated 1923 and which looks in all other respects like a previous attempt. As many of Nicholson's early paintings were dated retrospectively it seems likely that *Cortivallo Lugano* was painted later than 1921. It was exhibited in Nicholson's first one-man show at Patersons Gallery in 1923. Winifred Nicholson described it, in conversation with the author, as the painting in which Ben Nicholson 'first struck oil'.
6. Letter to Ronald Alley, 27 July 1962.

7. The collection was still largely intact in Winifred Nicholson's studio at Bankshead, Cumberland, in 1965.
8. For elaboration upon these terms and upon the stylistic distinctions they imply see, e.g., John Golding, *Cubism: a History and an Analysis 1907–1914* (London 1959).
9. Quoted, from a letter of 3 January 1944, by John Summerson in his introduction to the monograph *Ben Nicholson* in the Penguin Modern Painters series (West Drayton 1948).
10. The jug itself was the subject of an oil painting which Nicholson produced in 1911; it had belonged to his father and still occupied a place in his studio at the time of writing. The consistency of his taste over some seven decades is reflected in the consistency of the repertoire of still-life forms in his paintings and drawings.
11. The painting is inscribed 'first abstract ptg BN' in an early hand and is dated '1924' in a later hand. The date seems plausible. The white square in the painting was worked on some time after 1924, perhaps in the 1930s, when Nicholson reworked many of his still lifes of the 1920s in the light of the experience of his white reliefs. This is probably the painting, *Abstraction November*, singled out for attack by P. G. Konody in a review of the Seven & Five exhibition of December 1924 as 'a dadaistic futility . . . a picture that consists merely of superimposed squares of flat tints and looks uncommonly like a sample sheet of paripan wall paints.'
12. See, for instance, Kasimir Malevich in *The Non-Objective World* (Munich 1927): 'Under Suprematism I understand the Supremacy of pure feeling in creative art. To the Suprematist the visual phenomena of the objective world are, in themselves, meaningless; the significant thing is feeling, as such, quite apart from the environment in which it is called forth.' The idealist category of 'feeling as such' is central to Modernist aesthetics.
13. At Patersons Gallery in 1923 and at the Adelphi Gallery in 1924.
14. 'One main interest in making the "7 & 5" a going concern was that "Bloomsbury" in the shape of the London Group dog's dinner controlled the only place where we could exhibit.' Ben Nicholson, letter to Ronald Alley, 1962.
15. Her grandfather, the Earl of Carlisle, had been a patron and acquaintance of William Morris and of various of the Pre-Raphaelite painters; he was also an amateur watercolourist, and it was he who first encouraged Winifred Nicholson to paint.
16. The principal source for information about Wood's movements and contacts is an unpublished correspondence with his mother, which was maintained on a very regular basis between 1921 and his death in 1930. I am obliged to the directors of the Redfern Gallery for making a copy of this correspondence available to me.
17. The incident is mentioned in the title essay of Bell's *Since Cézanne*.
18. As a friend of Nicholson's, Dobson probably acted as the intermediary in introducing Wood to the Seven & Five.

19. An unpublished memoir of Wood by Winifred Nicholson refers to the contacts between the three artists in the years 1926–30, quoting extensively from correspondence. The memoir, a copy of which is lodged in the Tate Gallery archives, was written soon after Wood's death.
20. 'The Bankshead life is the painters' life – here it is a mixture of atmospheres and influences which one unconsciously is fighting all the time'; from a letter to Winifred Nicholson written from Paris in the early summer of 1928. And from a letter to his mother (5 May 1928): 'I have profited a great deal from Bankshead and I know my painting is different and I hope in a different street to what it was ...'
21. 'Alfred Wallis', in *Horizon*, January 1943. Reprinted in Edwin Mullins, *Alfred Wallis* (London 1967).
22. Wood recorded this and acknowledged Wallis's influence on him in letters to Winifred Nicholson which are quoted in her memoir.
23. Shortly before his return from St Ives he wrote to his mother: 'It is a great moment in my life, I feel things are becoming really vital and the studentship has passed, my work is forming something quite personal and sure, unlike anybody else's, and I don't think anyone can paint the pictures I am doing' (letter of 28 October 1928).
24. From 'A Brief Account of the Child-Cult', in *Time and Western Man* (London 1927).
25. Wood sold most of the works included in the show, though at prices around half of what he might have expected to receive in London. Nicholson, who was unknown in Paris in 1930, sold nothing.
26. 'I can think of no paintings better suited to reconcile those who pride themselves on being "old-fashioned" with the changed viewpoint of the modern artist than Mr Ivon Hitchens. The reason for this is ... a certain loveliness in the colour of his paintings.' From a review of Hitchens's one-man show at Tooth's Galleries, by Herbert Furst, *Apollo*, January 1929. The judgement still holds good.
27. Jones's war experience formed the basis for a major literary work, *In Parenthesis*, published in 1937. It does not seem to have provided him with any material that he could use in his art before that date.
28. See the concluding chapter.
29. A retrospective survey of the membership of the London Group was published in the catalogue of a jubilee exhibition: 'London Group 1914–64: 50 Years of British Art' (Tate Gallery, London, 1964).
30. According to the testimony of Henry Moore, in conversation with the author.
31. Giorgio de Chirico, 'Sull' Arte Metafisica', 1919.
32. From a letter to Gordon Bottomley, 27 December 1929 (*Poet and Painter*, p. 194). 'Apart from personal loss I felt acutely the pathos of my father's death ... His going broke up our old home at Iver Heath ... Work has been going on with certain developments but there have been too many interruptions for a productive period.' *Landscape at Iden* has generally been dated 1928. The

confusion which led to this error is explained by Andrew Causey in his catalogue to the Paul Nash exhibition at the Tate Gallery, 1975.

33. Exhibited at the London Group in October 1929.
34. Wadsworth exhibited at Tooth's in May 1929, in the gallery where de Chirico's work had attracted considerable attention the year before. Naturally the critics were confident in identifying the source of influence.
35. See Causey, *op. cit.*, catalogue nos. 104 and 121. As so often in Nash's work, the composition was first established in an earlier drawing, dated 1927.
36. *Landscape at Iden* and *Wood on the Downs* are dated 1928 and 1929 respectively by Margot Eates in her monograph *Paul Nash 1889–1946* (London 1973). The conclusive evidence for the later dating of both paintings is summarized in Causey, *op. cit.* Regarding *Wood on the Downs*, Causey also quotes a letter from Nash to Rex Nankivell of the Redfern Gallery, 22 December 1931: 'The drawing for the painting was made there [i.e. Ivinghoe Downs] on the canvas and a separate drawing made with notes on the colours ... The sketch used to supplement the drawing was afterwards coloured and exhibited at Tooth's . . . It differs slightly from the painting which was of course developed quite separately and unnaturalistically nearly a year later according to plan. The painting is simply a synthesis of a scene and mood of nature at a particular time of year – March.'
37. Roger Fry's *Cézanne: A Study of his Development* was published in 1927.

The Development of Modernism in Sculpture

1. In the catalogue of works appended to *The Sculptor Speaks*, Epstein and Haskell (London 1931), there is a listing for *Venus* as 'commenced 1914' and as 'exhibited Leicester Galleries 1920'. Epstein produced two carved versions of *Venus*. The second and largest is an eight-foot-high figure in the style of the more innovatory of the pre-war works. Neither version was in fact shown at the Leicester Galleries in 1920. Epstein was probably confusing that exhibition with one in 1917.
2. In Epstein and Haskell, *op. cit.* The proliferation of the use of 'study', 'composition', etc., as titles for advanced work was a general symptom of the withdrawal from illustration and anecdote by advanced artists in the period between the wars.
3. *The Graphic*, 14 February 1920.
4. *Epstein: An Autobiography* (London 1963). See also Epstein and Haskell, *op. cit.*
5. *The Meaning of Modern Sculpture* (London 1932).
6. From 'Art in Art Criticism' in *Since Cézanne*. Bell took this opportunity to promote Maillol as 'the greatest living sculptor', in riposte to the critic of the *Nation* who had asserted that Epstein 'now stands for European sculpture as Rodin stood before him'.
7. In Epstein and Haskell, *op. cit.*
8. *Epstein* by Bernard van Dieren (the model for the head of the *Risen Christ*)

(London and New York 1920), and *Epstein*, with an introduction by Hubert Wellington, published in the Contemporary British Artists series (London 1925).

9. Epstein requested that Hulme's article of 1913 should be reprinted in 1931 as an appendix to *The Sculptor Speaks*, in implicit recognition of the fact that the quality of critical attention and of theoretical speculation achieved by Hulme had not been bettered in the intervening eighteen years.
10. Read (in *Henry Moore: A study of his Life and Work*, London 1965) reports that 'Henry ... picked up a second-hand copy in 1922 or 1923'. Moore himself testified in 1960 to his having found the book 'a great help and an excitement'. He felt that it 'was written with a freshness and insight', and that 'Gaudier speaks as a young sculptor discovering things' (Donald Hall, 'An Interview with Henry Moore', in *Horizon*, vol. 3 no. 2, New York, November 1960).
11. *The New Art*, 'a Study of the Principles of non-representational Art and their application in the work of Lawrence Atkinson', by Horace Shipp (London 1922). No dates are given for the many works illustrated, though *L'Oiseau* [111] is listed as having been awarded the Grand Prix at the Milan Exhibition of 1921. The turgid and confused prose of the book was unlikely to have won many converts to its subject; its publication may indeed have been partly responsible for the obscurity into which author and artist were immediately plunged.
12. From a letter to William Rothenstein, 25 September 1910 (W. Shewing, ed., *Letters of Eric Gill*, London 1947).
13. Ruskin may well have been recalled to people's minds immediately after the war by the celebration of the centenary of his birth with an exhibition at the Royal Academy in 1919. In the same year the foundation manifesto of the Weimar Bauhaus was published, with its criticism of '... class distinctions that raise an arrogant barrier between craftsman and artist'.
14. Published at Saint Dominic's Press, Ditchling, Sussex. The Ditchling community published a periodical called *The Game* during the 1920s, and Gill himself published various other works, including *Songs without Clothes* (1921), *Id quod visum placet* (1926), *Art and Love* (1927), and *Christianity and Art* and *Art and Prudence* (1928).
15. This and the following quotations are from Gill's *Sculpture*.
16. *The Game*, September 1921. At this time there were seven members of the community. David Jones first visited Ditchling in January 1921 and stayed for the best part of four years, though he was never formally a member.
17. In his *Sculpture of To-Day* (London 1921), Kineton Parkes listed several members of 'the devoted band of direct workers', including Gill and Ernest Cole, together with a number of more conservative figures.
18. It has been a characteristic feature of art education in England during the modern period that enterprising students have often learned more from competent technical assistants than from those 'artists' employed as 'teachers' in part on the strength of their subscription to the Modernist notion that art can't be taught. Thus Moore learned how to carve from an assistant at the Royal

College, Barry Hart, who was employed as an instructor in techniques of pointing and copying.

19. Donald Hall, *op. cit.* (Note 10).
20. Wilenski, *op. cit.* The English sculptors whose works were used to illustrate the book were R. P. Bedford, John Skeaping, Maurice Lambert, Henry Moore, Barbara Hepworth, Leon Underwood, Gaudier, and Epstein.
21. From a letter to the author, November 1966.
22. From a statement in *Partisan Review*, New York, March–April 1947.
23. From John and Vera Russell, 'Conversations with Henry Moore' in the *Sunday Times*, London, 17 and 24 December 1961.
24. The phrase is Moore's, from an article on 'Primitive Art' in *The Listener*, London, 24 August 1941. 'Through the workings of instinctive sculptural sensibility,' Moore writes, 'the same shapes and form relationships are used to express similar ideas at widely different places and periods in history.'
25. *Partisan Review, op. cit.* This was written soon after Moore had completed the somewhat traditional Northampton *Madonna and Child*. In later accounts of this period of his life he tended to place less emphasis upon his willing subjection to academic study.
26. Statement in the *Architectural Association Journal*, vol. XLV (London 1930). See also the article on 'Primitive Art' cited above, Note 24.
27. In his 'Essay in Aesthetics' of 1909, Fry had written of this work: '... when we look at Michelangelo's "Tondo" in the Uffizi, and find a group of figures so arranged that the planes have a sequence comparable in breadth and dignity to the mouldings of the earth mounting by clearly-felt gradations to an overtopping summit, innumerable instinctive reactions are brought into play.' John Russell (in his *Henry Moore*, Harmondsworth 1973) suggests that this passage might have provided Moore with 'one of the initial germs' of 'the notion of the human body as a metaphor for landscape'.
28. From Gaudier's manifesto printed in *Blast* 1 in June 1914, reprinted in Pound's book. Echoes of this slogan are to be found throughout Moore's published writings and interviews.
29. Gill and Dobson were also considered as candidates and were rejected. The professorship went in the end to Ernest Cole, whom Read in 1965 described as 'a safe compromise ... a product of the same effete Parisian tradition as Rothenstein himself', but whom Kineton Parkes in 1921 classed alongside Epstein and labelled as 'One of the English sculptors who has broken away from tradition, and is indeed the most rebellious of them all'. Retrospective views by Moore's admirers and confidants tend to overestimate the extent to which he was isolated in his modernist aspirations.
30. *Partisan Review, op. cit.* As a source of information about Moore's trip to Italy see also the letter to William Rothenstein published in John Rothenstein, *Modern English Painters: Lewis to Moore* (London 1956). The letter is there dated 12 March 1924, but it must actually have been written a year later, as Moore did not leave England until January 1925.

31. The sculpture, which was found at Chíchén Itzá in the Yucatan, is now in the Museo Nacional de Antropología in Mexico. It was produced during the Toltec-Maya culture, A.D. 900–1000.
32. 'Perhaps that's what makes Picasso's work often seem capricious: a conflict between an interest in the approach illustrated by archaic art and the art of primitive peoples and a respect for the Mediterranean tradition. At any rate, as I look back, I am very conscious of such a conflict throughout my own work, particularly since I went to Italy first in 1925 ...' (Moore in *Partisan Review, op. cit.*).
33. References are to the standard catalogue of Moore's work contained in *Henry Moore, Volume One: Sculpture and Drawings 1921–1948*, ed. David Sylvester, fourth (revised) edition (London 1957). Ascription of dates in this catalogue is occasionally open to scrutiny. The *Torso* (LH 37) in particular seems unlikely to have been made as early as 1926.
34. Moore's enthusiasm for Mesopotamian art was expressed in a review of Christian Zervos's *L'Art en Mésopotamie*, published in *The Listener*, 5 June 1935.
35. In *The Spectator*, London, 27 October 1933.

The Early Thirties: Unit One

1. Wadsworth showed at the Galerie Barbazanges in 1927. He was also accorded the unusual distinction of a foreign-language monograph on his work: *Wadsworth*, in Cahiers 13 Sélection, Chronique de la Vie Artistique (Antwerp 1933), with texts by Waldémar George, Michael Sevier and Ossip Zadkine.
2. Myfanwy Piper (formerly Myfanwy Evans), 'Back in the Thirties', in *Art and Literature*, no. 7, Winter 1965.
3. Causey (*op. cit.*) has extracted figures from Nash's notebooks in the Tate Gallery Archive to show that from sales of work in 1931–2 he earned almost exactly half of what he had earned in 1929–30. Causey also quotes a letter to Hilda Felce of 23 November 1931: 'Thank God I seem to be able to write, journalism is now my sole means of subsistence.'
4. 'Giorgio di Chirico', in *The Listener*, 29 April 1931.
5. *Weekend Review*, 12 March 1932.
6. See, for instance, his article 'Abstract Art' in *The Listener*, 17 August 1932. In support of the idea of an abstract art Nash quoted Fry's introduction to the second Post-Impressionist exhibition, and continued, 'Since those days painting has taken two routes: the broad main way of Post-Impressionism, and the narrower path of discovery towards a purely abstract language of form.' He identified 'three distinct schools of abstract painting'; the first was synonymous with Cubism, the second 'derives inspiration from natural form but resolves an abstract equivalent' (Wadsworth was offered as an example), and the third involved the production of 'purely abstract form without adventitious aid'. According to Nash, Picasso was 'the greatest of all abstract painters'.

7. In an article in *The Listener*, 5 July 1933, Nash recorded that 'It was upon the effect of this exhibition that the idea [of Unit One] was based.'
8. *The Listener*, 16 March 1932.
9. In the early thirties the *Architectural Review* began to support and to publish the work of the Modern Movement in architecture and design, and in 1930 *The Studio* published a special issue on *Modern Interiors* (by H. Hoffmann). In 1933 there was a large exhibition of 'British Industrial Art in relation to the Home' at Dorland Hall in London. 1934 saw the publication of several relevant books, including *Industrial Art Explained* by John Gloag, *Art and Industry* by Herbert Read, *The Modern House* by F. R. S. Yorke, and *Twentieth-Century Houses* by Raymond McGrath. The Royal Academy staged an exhibition of 'British Art in Industry' in 1935.
10. Significant events for the history of English design included the International Exhibition of Modern Decorative and Industrial Arts in Paris in 1925, and the Stockholm Exhibition in 1930 to which the Design and Industries Association arranged a visit. The Russian-born architect Berthold Lubetkin came to England via Paris in 1930 and formed the organization 'Tecton' with five former students from the Architectural Association.
11. Their paths had already crossed. In 1924 Nash had been appointed an assistant in the School of Design at the Royal College of Art, and both had held exhibitions at the Warren Gallery in the later twenties.
12. The Congrès Internationaux d'Architecture Moderne (CIAM), in which Le Corbusier was a dominant influence, met on board S.S. *Patras* in the Aegean in 1933. An invited English contingent formed itself into the Modern Architectural Research Society (MARS Group) under Coates's leadership. The group was well to the left of the norm in contemporary architectural practice. Its formation was announced by Coates in a letter to *The Listener*, published on 12 July 1933.
13. Letter dated 17 January.
14. Minutes of the Seven & Five for 1926 record a decision to approach the Mayor Gallery with a view to holding a show there.
15. Douglas Cooper, then working at the Mayor Gallery, acted as secretary to the group.
16. The full text of Nash's letter was published in the book *Unit 1*, ed. Herbert Read (London 1934).
17. Anthony Bertram, *Paul Nash* (London 1955).
18. *The Listener*, 5 July 1933.
19. From a letter to the author, 24 November 1966.
20. *Urne Buriall and The Garden of Cyrus* by Sir Thomas Browne, edited by John Carter with thirty drawings by Paul Nash (London 1932). Nash's drawings for the hand-coloured collotypes were made between the summer of 1931 and the spring of 1932, and he subsequently used several of them as bases for works in watercolour and in oil.

21. 'And it must rejoice every man, who joins in the public homage *now* rendered to his powers (and what man is to be found that more or less does not?) to hear, with respect to one so lavishly endowed by nature, that he has not been neglected by fortune; that he has never had the finer edge of his sensibilities dulled by the sad anxieties, the degrading fears, the miserable dependencies of debt; that he has been blessed with competency even when poorest; has had hope and cheerful prospects in reversion, through every stage of his life ...' Thomas de Quincey of William Wordsworth in *Tait's Edinburgh Magazine*, April 1839.
22. According to Read (*Henry Moore*, London 1965), Moore recalled acquiring a copy of a special issue of the journal *Documents*, published in 1930, in which Picasso's paintings, drawings and sculptures of 1927–9 were featured. In vol. 4 of *Cahiers d'Art*, a journal which Moore regularly consulted from the time of its first publication in 1927, Christian Zervos published an illustrated article on Picasso's projects for a monument, one of which, a sculpture of 1928, seems to have provided a clear precedent for some of the specific formal 'inventions' in Moore's *Composition*.
23. 'Read ... was always the "Eminence Grise" behind the whole outfit and the only one of us who had any sense of organisation' (Hillier, *loc. cit.*, Note 19).
24. *The Meaning of Art* was first broadcast as a series of lectures by the BBC.
25. The principal sections in the original edition were 'Background', 'From Science to Symbolism', 'Subjective Realism', 'Abstraction' and 'Subjective Idealism'.
26. In his introduction, Read echoed and affirmed Hulme's radical modernism: 'He knew very certainly that we were at the end of a way of thought that had prevailed for four hundred years; in this, and in his premonition of a more absolute philosophy of life, he had advanced the ideals of a new generation.'
27. Asserted in a letter to the author, 1 February 1967.
28. i.e. *Von Material zu Architektur*, published as a Bauhaus book in 1929, expanded and translated as *The New Vision* in 1938.
29. As early as 28 June 1933, the reviewer of the *Yorkshire Post* reported that 'Extraordinary interest is being taken in London in the foundation and fortunes of "Unit One" ...'. The *Yorkshire Post*'s own interest may have owed much to the fact that Read, Wadsworth, Moore and Hepworth were all born in the county.
30. As reported in the *Liverpool Post and Mercury* of 4 June 1934. 'You can see', the Dean is reported as saying, 'how all that you have noticed in the paintings is taking shape in buildings and gardens. The rhythm is already passing into the everyday activity.'
31. The correspondence was closed by the editor after nineteen letters had been printed.
32. 16 March 1935, in the series 'Barney's Blunders'.
33. *Irish News*, 11 March 1935.
34. The reviewer of the *News Chronicle* in Manchester, in the edition of 17 May 1934, noted that Nicholson 'produces "pictures" of three or more circles bored

into white plaster'. Inaccurate as this description was, it must have referred to one or more of Nicholson's carved and painted white reliefs.

35. *The Scotsman*, 28 October 1933.
36. *New English Weekly*, 3 May 1934.
37. The Artists International Association, as it came to be called, has recently been the subject of some interest and research, no doubt in response to the revival of 'Art for Society' as a topical issue in the later 1960s and the 70s. The best documented account is by Tony Rickaby, 'Artists' International', in *History Workshop*, Autumn 1978. See also Donald Drew Egbert, *Social Radicalism and the Arts: Western Europe* (New York 1970); Robert Radford, 'When Politics and Art seemed to coalesce', two-part article in *Art Monthly*, October–November 1978; and 'James Boswell (1906–71): Drawings, Illustrations and Paintings', catalogue of an exhibition at the Nottingham University Art Gallery, 1976.
38. 'The International unity of artists against Imperialist War, War on the Soviet Union, Fascism and Colonial Oppression.

    'It is intended to further these aims by the following practical measures:

    '1. The uniting of all artists, in Great Britain, sympathetic with these aims, into working units ready to execute posters, illustrations, cartoons, book-jackets, banners, tableaux, stage decorations, etc.

    '2. The spreading of propaganda by means of exhibitions, the press, lectures and meetings.

    '3. The maintaining of contacts with similar groups in 16 other countries.'

    (Quoted by Rickaby, *op. cit.*)
39. The manifesto was quoted in *The Studio*, December 1934.
40. *Daily Express*, 11 April 1934, in the column 'These Names Make News'.
41. '. . . my old friend Mr Read the critic . . . would rather have had nothing happen in 1914, so that when, by 1930 or thereabouts, 'abstraction' was ripe for discovery upon these shores, he could have weighed in without all these echoes of premature bombardment in his rear.' Wyndham Lewis in 'The Skeleton in the Cupboard Speaks' (1939). Lewis added, 'There is nothing being done in 1939 in England that was not done by us – Gaudier, Mr Wadsworth, and myself – in 1914.'

'Abstract' and 'Constructive' Art

1. Nicholson described the origin of this painting in an article, 'Notes on "Abstract" Art', published in *Horizon* in October 1941.

> About space-construction: I can explain one aspect of this by an early painting I made of a shop-window in Dieppe though, at the time, this was not made with any conscious idea of space but merely using the shop-window as a theme on which to base an imaginative idea. The name of the shop was 'Au Chat Botté', and this set going a train of thought connected with the fairy tales of my childhood and, being in French, and my French being a little mysterious, the words themselves had also an abstract quality –

> but what was important was that this name was printed in very lovely red lettering on the glass window – *giving one plane* – and in this window were reflections of what was behind me as I looked in – *giving a second plane* – while through the window objects on a table were performing a kind of ballet and forming the 'eye' or life-point of the painting – *giving a third plane.* These three planes and all their subsidiary planes were interchangeable so that you could not tell which was real and which unreal, what was reflected and what unreflected, and this created, as I see now, some kind of space or an imaginative world in which one could live.

2. There is some conflict between objective evidence and published testimony. Hepworth's own published accounts are unreliable as to dates.
3. From a letter quoted by John Summerson in his introduction to *Ben Nicholson* in the Penguin Modern Painters series (West Drayton 1948).
4. It is interesting to compare Clement Greenberg's view of the state of painting in America at around the same time:

> The first problem these young Americans [i.e. those later known as the 'Abstract Expressionists'] seemed to share was that of loosening up the relatively delimited illusion of shallow depth that the three master Cubists – Picasso, Braque, Léger – had adhered to since the closing out of Synthetic Cubism. If they were to be able to say what they had to say, they had also to loosen up that canon of rectilinear and curvilinear regularity in drawing and design which Cubism had imposed on almost all previous abstract art.
>
> ... Miró became a crucial factor at that time. His example and his procedures were still seen as opening a new way *inside* Late Cubism; contours still had to be faired and to be closely adjusted to the frame, but at least they no longer had to be wedged in place.

Excerpts from '"American-Type" Painting' and from 'The Late Thirties in New York', printed in Greenberg, *Art and Culture* (Boston 1965).

5. See *Calder: An Autobiography with Pictures* (London 1967), p. 113. Calder describes how his first visit to Mondrian's studio prompted the desire 'to paint and work in the abstract'.
6. Letter to the author, November 1966.
7. From the preface to Read's inappropriately titled *To Hell with Culture* (London 1962).
8. Abstraction-Création was by no means the first attempt to organize the interests of abstract art in France. An exhibition under the title 'Art d'Aujourd'hui' in 1925 had assembled work by Russian, Dutch, and other European artists together with Cubists and Surrealists from France. The group 'Cercle et Carré' was founded in 1930 by Joaquín Torres-Garcia and Michel Seuphor, and organized exhibitions of largely non-figurative art. And in the same year Theo Van Doesburg published a manifesto for what he hoped would be a new movement under the title 'Art Concret'.
9. These figures were published in the *Cahier Abstraction-Création* for 1935.

10. 'The second issue of "Abstraction-Création" appears at a time when, under all régimes, on all levels, in some countries more effectively than others, but everywhere, free thought is fiercely opposed ... We place this second issue under the banner of a total opposition to all oppression, of whatever kind it may be.'
11. From *The Non-Objective World*, first published as *Die Gegenstandslose Welt* in Munich in 1927 as number 11 of the Bauhaus books.
12. Winifred Nicholson, from whom Ben Nicholson was by then separated, had taken an apartment on the Quai d'Auteuil. Nicholson used to stay nearby and was thus able to visit his children.
13. Information from a letter to the author, November 1966.
14. Nicholson's account of this visit is quoted in Summerson, *op. cit.*, from a letter of 3 January 1944: '... The paintings were entirely new to me and I did not understand them on this first visit (and indeed only partially understood them on my second visit a year later) ...'
15. In a review of Nicholson's exhibition at the Lefevre Gallery in 1935, largely devoted to consideration of his carved reliefs, Paul Nash recorded that he had said, 'I find I judge paintings by the quality of light given off ... in my own work it is my only way of judging its achievement or progress' ('Ben Nicholson's Carved Reliefs', *Architectural Review*, October 1935).
16. From a statement published in *Barbara Hepworth: Carvings and Drawings*, with an introduction by Herbert Read (London 1952).
17. *Ibid.*
18. *Ibid.*
19. 'The Sculptor Speaks', *The Listener*, 18 August 1937.
20. Hepworth, *op. cit.*
21. *Ibid.*
22. From a statement by Hepworth published in *Circle: International Survey of Constructive Art* (London 1937). There is an interesting compatibility at points here with Barnett Newman's concept of an 'epistemology of intangibles'. (See his article on 'The Art of the South Seas', originally published in *Ambos Mundos*, June 1946; first published in English in *Studio International*, February 1970.)
23. Myfanwy Piper, 'Back in the Thirties', in *Art and Literature*, Winter 1965.
24. See for instance J. M. Richards's joint review of the Seven & Five show and of Nicholson's exhibition at the Lefevre Gallery. 'We can now be said to possess a school of abstract artists.' Richards described the Seven & Five as 'a group of artists working all with the same intentions' and as 'the only group now exhibiting one consistent point of view' ('London Shows', in *Axis* 4, November 1935).
25. Holding is not listed in the sheet printed as a catalogue for the exhibition (see the Appendix), nor in any of the minutes or records I have consulted, but her work was mentioned in Richards's review. See also below, Note 30. Penrose was also unlisted, but was praised by the reviewer of the *New English Weekly* for the 'original and personal plastic equations' which he showed as a guest exhibitor.

26. A selection of Giacometti's recent sculpture was illustrated in the journal *La Surréalisme au Service de la Révolution* in July 1930.
27. See Note 24.
28. 'Ben Nicholson tells me he has heard nothing about a Ben Nicholson abstract group – but would like to. The 7 & 5 Society, he says, has gone "abstract" and only works coming within a definition of that bewildering expression will be hung in the next exhibition. But in this exhibition all the most important foreign abstract artists will be represented by their *latest* work. This should be rather a swell show and very stimulating to the young idea in London' (Paul Nash, letter to Conrad Aiken, 31 January 1935).
29. Letter to Ronald Alley, undated but probably written in 1962.
30. On 12 January 1937, Moore wrote to Winifred Nicholson in Cumberland, 'I've heard nothing about a definite date of a 7 & 5 meeting – but I expect I shall when we go back to Hampstead in 2 or 3 days time – and I expect Eileen or John Piper (as secretary) will let you know about it . . .' Earlier, on 30 July 1936, Piper had written to Winifred Nicholson, 'It would be nice if we could fix a meeting of the 7 & 5 to take place so that you could come to it. I think it most important that it should go on, and there seems to be a great deal of enthusiasm (Eileen, Jackson, Staite Murray, Ivon, Henry Moore, all talk or write enthusiastically about it). Personally, I am for abolishing the non-figurative rule entirely – the only rule about *kind* of work should be "*bad* work excluded . . ." I should also like to invite Frances Hodgkins to rejoin.' While she and Ben Nicholson were still together, Winifred Nicholson had been one of the most energetic of the members. It seems likely that the demise of the society can be largely attributed to the combination of her physical isolation from London at the time with Nicholson's dogmatism and subsequent lack of interest.
31. The fifth issue of *Axis*, published in Spring 1936, carried a notice to the effect that 'The exhibition will probably be held in London in April.'
32. Undated letter to Ruth Clark. The Nashes left England in November and were in Nice by January, having stayed in Paris on the way.
33. Letter dated 7 September 1934. Hélion wrote of his disgust with 'most of the crowd that was in Abstraction-Création . . . They all believe that they are gods golden fishes.'
34. This and the following quotations, unless otherwise ascribed, from M. Piper, *op. cit.*
35. First published in *Apollo*, September 1962.
36. In M. de Sausmarez, ed., *Ben Nicholson* (a Studio International special publication, London 1969). The 'Bateau-Lavoir' was the tenement building in the Rue Ravignan in Paris where many of the Cubists and their associates lived in the early years of the movement. Hélion was in England in 1936.
37. Grigson, 'Comment on England', in *Axis* 1.
38. *Minotaure* was a lavishly illustrated French periodical published by Skira from June 1933 to October 1938 and edited by E. Tériade. The editorial committee included Breton, Duchamp and Eluard.

39. From 'Great Nature and the Specialised Sense', in *The Caliph's Design* (London 1919).
40. When Gabo came to England, Leslie Martin bought a small construction from him. It was the first work Gabo had sold since his departure from Russia in 1922.
41. See his book *Art and Society* (London 1937), composed in 1936 from lectures given at the University of Liverpool in 1935–6.
42. In *Art for Society*. The quotation is taken from Gropius's book *The New Architecture and the Bauhaus* (London 1935).
43. From *Idee und Aufbau des Staatlichen Bauhauses Weimar* ('The Theory and Organization of the Staatliche Bauhaus') (Munich 1923).
44. The formulation is Walter Benjamin's.
45. *Art Forms in Nature* was published in an English edition in two volumes in London in 1929 and 1931 respectively. *On Growth and Form* was first published in 1916 and a new edition was published in 1942.
46. 'Russia and Constructivism', an interview with Naum Gabo by Arbam Lassaw and Ilya Bolotowsky, published in *Gabo*, with introductory essays by Read and Martin (London 1957).
47. *Ibid.*
48. 'The Realistic Manifesto', from the translation published in *Gabo, op. cit.*
49. Gabo, from 'Russia and Constructivism', *op. cit.*
50. 'The Program of the Productivist Group', from a translation published in *Gabo, op. cit.* The translation was originally made for a Hungarian magazine, *Egyseg*, published in Vienna in 1922. According to Gabo the programme was published 'several months after the "Realistic Manifesto" as a reply to it'. He adds that 'Our differences with this group were much deeper and of longer standing than can be understood from these two documents alone.'
51. Cf. Malevich: 'A true absolute order in human society could only be achieved if mankind were willing to base this order on lasting values. Obviously, then, the artistic factor would have to be accepted in every respect as the decisive one.' From *The Non-Objective World, op. cit.* (Note 11).
52. First reprinted in a facsimile edition in 1971.
53. There is a conflict of evidence concerning the motives for publishing *Circle* and the date of its first proposal. According to Hepworth (*op. cit.*, Note 16) the idea was conceived in 1935 out of a sense of 'intellectual responsibility'. Gabo (in a statement published in de Sausmarez, ed., *Ben Nicholson*, 1969) testified that 'It was at the Nicolete Gray exhibition [i.e. 'Abstract & Concrete', which opened early in 1936] that I met Leslie Martin, Ben Nicholson and also Barbara Hepworth . . .' Ben Nicholson, in conversation with the author, asserted that the motive for the publication of *Circle* was to 'do something' in face of the success of the International Surrealist Exhibition, which opened in London in June 1936.
54. Gabo, *op. cit.* (Note 53).
55. See Note 14. See also 'Mondrian in London', reminiscences by Winifred Nicholson, Barbara Hepworth, Miriam Gabo, Herbert Read, Ben Nicholson and

Naum Gabo, with an introduction by the author, *Studio International*, December 1966.

56. 'Architecture and the Painter, with special reference to the work of Ben Nicholson', *Focus*, no. 3, 1939.
57. M. Piper, 'Back in the Thirties', *op. cit.*
58. Hepworth, *op. cit.* (1952).

The Later Thirties: Surrealism, 'Realism', Romanticism

1. The ballot was probably Nicholson's idea, since he had used the device to good effect as a 'democratic' procedure for purging the Seven & Five. An account of the ballot and its results is given in letters of Paul Nash, one to Henry Moore, written from Whitecliff near Swanage and thus datable to the time between October 1934 and January 1935 when he was staying there, and a second to Conrad Aiken, dated 31 January 1935. In the latter, Nash wrote: 'Only Henry Moore and myself received the unanimous vote. We quickly invited Wells Coates to join us and so saved our faces by presenting a base representing the 3 arts on which to build up again. So far nothing more has happened, because I have been exiled and I cannot persuade the others to proceed without a general discussion ...'
2. See previous note. Aiken had written to Nash for information about Unit One to be included in a 'London letter'.
3. Dated 1934 by Causey, *op. cit.* Between November 1933 and June 1934 Nash was abroad, and for much of this time he was either ill or travelling. If the painting was finished by the time of the Unit One exhibition in April 1934, it seems more likely that Nash painted it between his first visit to Avebury in August and his departure in November 1933. Some support for this view is provided by Margaret Nash's testimony that this was Nash's first painting of Avebury (as cited in Causey).
4. Quoted in Anthony Bertram, *Paul Nash: The Portrait of an Artist* (London 1955).
5. Nash was invited to Pittsburgh in the autumn of 1931, to serve on the jury for the Carnegie International Award. His wife gave him a camera to take on the trip.
6. See Causey, *op. cit.*, catalogue nos. 123, 129 and 148.
7. Mainstream response can be illustrated by P. G. Konody's review in *The Observer* of 23 April 1933: 'The works shown by Max Ernst, Francis Bacon and Paul Klee in what seems an intentional desire to outrage aesthetic conventions, can but be taken as practical jokes.'
8. In *The Bookman*, October 1933.
9. Announced in *The Listener*, 31 May 1933. The writer also observed that Picasso was at that time unrepresented in the Luxembourg, then the principal modern collection in Paris. Grigson gave news of the failure of the appeal in a letter to the *Weekend Review*, published on 29 June 1933.

10. For a comprehensive account of these see Paul C. Ray, *The Surrealist Movement in England* (Ithaca and London 1971). Relevant periodicals included the *Transatlantic Review*, founded in Paris in 1924 and really only concerned with the literary aspects of Surrealism, *transition*, published in Paris in English from 1927 until June 1930, revived as *Transition* in March 1932, and *Criterion*, the English literary journal edited by T. S. Eliot which made occasional unfavourable references to the activities of the European Surrealists. A special issue of *This Quarter* in September 1932 was devoted to discussion of Surrealist theory and translations of relevant texts. There had been reference to Masson, Arp and Ernst in Sidney Hunt's *Ray* ('art miscellany') in 1926–7, but not such as to arouse much attention.
11. In his own enthusiastic review of the Max Ernst exhibition at the Mayor Gallery, published in the *Weekend Review* of 17 June 1933, Nash noted that by the tenth day of the exhibition no notice had appeared.
12. In the revised edition the chapter on 'Subjective Realism' was retitled 'Expressionism', 'Abstraction' was retitled 'Towards Abstraction', and 'Subjective Idealism' was expanded into two chapters, 'Superrealism (1)' and 'Superrealism (2)'.
13. 'The Life of the Inanimate Object', *Country Life*, 1 May 1937.
14. 'The Sculptor Speaks', *op. cit.*
15. *Ibid.*
16. *Ibid.* This view of art as the reconciliation of such supposed antitheses echoes that of Herbert Read, first expressed in his 'Psychoanalysis and the Critic' in 1925, and maintained with some consistency. Cf. Read in 1962, recalling the mid-thirties: 'I tried to argue, and I still believe, that such dialectical oppositions [as those 'between the two extremes represented by the Circle group and the Surrealist group'] are good for the progress of art, and that the greatest artists (I always had Henry Moore in mind) are great precisely because they can resolve such oppositions' (*Apollo, op. cit.*).
17. *The Enemy*, September 1927. Lewis, whose reading was as cosmopolitan as anyone's, was attacking *transition*. Two years later, in 'A World Art and its Tradition' (*Drawing and Design*, February 1929), he was writing with apparent approval of 'such effective energetic knots as that formed by the association of Ernst, Milhaud, Tanguy etc.'. Such approval, however, should be understood in terms of his reservation that 'The function of an artist of the Left, at present, is to secure the equilibrium of the jelly-like Centre, I think – by his presence rather than his technical influence however.'
18. 'Fragments du premier manifeste anglais du Surréalisme'; this translation from Ray, *op. cit.*
19. Among its members were Vanessa Bell, Epstein, Eric Gill, Grant, Augustus John, McKnight Kauffer, Dame Laura Knight, David Low, Moore, Nash and Read.
20. B. Rea, ed., *Five on Revolutionary Art* (London 1935).
21. 'Surrealism – the Dialectics of Art', *Left Review*, 10 July 1936.

22. It was suggested that Gill risked bringing his Church into disrepute by his participation in what was seen as a communist organization. See *Letters of Eric Gill* (London 1947).
23. Apart from his articles in *Left Review* in 1935–6, and his work as a contributing editor to the American journal *Art Front*, Klingender's publications include the pamphlet *Marxism and Modern Art* (London 1943), which contained a critique of 'Roger Fry's Formalism', *Hogarth and English Caricature* (London 1944), *Art and the Industrial Revolution* (London 1947), his best known and most influential book, *Goya in the Democratic Tradition* (London 1948, from a manuscript of 1940), and the posthumously published *Animals in Art and Thought* (London and Cambridge, Mass., 1971).
24. Anthony Blunt, 'The Realism Quarrel', *Left Review*, April 1937.
25. Anthony Blunt, 'From Bloomsbury to Marxism', *Studio International*, November 1973.
26. Montague Slater, quoted in Radford, 'When politics and art seemed to coalesce', *Art Monthly*, October 1978.
27. AIA *Artists' News-Sheet*, January 1937. The ideological incoherence of the AIA at the time may be illustrated by the coincidence in this bulletin of claims for the association on the one hand that it was concerned to organize 'progressive cultural opinion' and on the other that 'We have members of all schools of aesthetic thought, and do not favour any particular aesthetic.'
28. 'They [i.e. Roland Penrose and Herbert Read] ... sought out native Surrealists (in England), and in their search they came and selected three paintings from my studio, and so, overnight, so to speak, I became a Surrealist ... They also visited Francis Bacon and decided he was not sufficiently surreal for inclusion' (Julian Trevelyan, *Indigo Days*, London 1957).
29. *Experiment* was a basically literary magazine edited in Cambridge by J. Bronowski, William Empson, Kathleen Raine and Humphrey Jennings. Trevelyan's article 'Dreams', originally published in *Experiment* and republished in *transition* in June 1930, was an early English evocation of a proto-Surrealist view of art: 'Aesthetic pleasure justifies itself in the fantasies of a dream-world ... Let us gladly shout, TO DREAM IS TO CREATE.' (Quoted in Ray, *op. cit.*)
30. Trevelyan, *Indigo Days*. Trevelyan went to Paris in 1931 and enrolled in Hayter's engraving school. Picasso, Masson, Miró, Calder, Kokoschka and Zadkine were among those who came to work at the Atelier while he was there.
31. In a cartoon in the *Left Review*, July 1936, James Boswell printed this paragraph from Read's introduction across a sketch of the fur-coated and double-breasted visitors to the exhibition.
32. *The Studio*, August 1936.
33. *Surrealism*, edited with an introduction by Herbert Read and with contributions by André Breton, Hugh Sykes Davies, Paul Eluard and Georges Hugnet (London 1936).
34. Blunt, *Left Review*, April 1937.
35. From *Five on Revolutionary Art*.

36. If there was something like a middle-of-the-road position it was represented by Moore's work of the 1930s, which might be seen as the expressive equivalent of that leftish but essentially empirical liberalism in face of these political poles which is still at the time of writing the acceptable position for the modern man of culture.
37. Early in 1939 the AIA staged an exhibition of 'Art for the People' at the Whitechapel Art Gallery. The works on display were all by members. There were sections for 'Realists', 'Surrealists' and 'Abstract Artists'. The show was opened by an arbitrarily chosen 'man in the street' and attracted over 40,000 visitors.
38. Though dated July 1936. Three previous issues of the *Bulletin Internationale du Surréalisme* were published in 1935 in Prague, the Canary Islands and Brussels respectively.
39. Though they were not incapable of acting together on suitable political issues. A 'Declaration on Spain', calling on the English government to end its policy of non-intervention, was published by the 'Surrealist Group in England' in *Contemporary Poetry and Prose*, a magazine edited by Roger Roughton, a young Communist Party member. The signatories were Sykes Davies, Gascoyne, Jennings, Diana Brinton Lee, Rupert Lee, Moore, Nash, Penrose, Valentine Penrose, Read and Roughton.
40. In 1938 Breton went to Mexico to give occasional lectures on French art and poetry. He was introduced to Trotsky, then living in exile in Mexico, by the muralist Diego Rivera. The use of Rivera's name in place of Trotsky's was perhaps a concession to expectations that the artists to whom the manifesto was addressed might be sceptical of a plea for autonomy which carried the name of a known 'political' revolutionary. See Franklin Rosemont, *André Breton and the First Principles of Surrealism* (London 1978), and Breton's own account, 'Visit to Leon Trotsky'.
41. According to Conroy Maddox, who first exhibited with the English Surrealists early in 1939, the collapse of the English movement can be attributed to its failure to establish a coherent political position on this occasion. See Ray, *op. cit.*
42. See Ray, *op. cit.* Among those present at the meeting were Read, Penrose, Mesens, Jennings, Jacques Brunius, Ithell Colquhoun, Eileen Agar, Edith Rimmington, Hayter, A. C. Sewter, Dr Grace Pailthorpe, Reuben Mednikoff, John Banting, Gordon Onslow Ford and Charles Howard.
43. The painting was certainly in an advanced state by the end of 1936. See Causey, *op. cit.*, cat. no. 159. According to the testimony of Margaret Nash the painting was much admired by Breton.
44. M. Piper, ed., *The Painter's Object* (London 1937).
45. Paul Nash had written and illustrated the first version of the *Shell Guide to Dorset* in 1935.
46. The essay 'Super-Nature versus Super-Real', together with 'The Skeleton in the Cupboard Speaks', forms an introduction to Lewis's retrospective collection of his own writings on art, *Wyndham Lewis the Artist from Blast to Burlington*

House, published in 1939. In the former Lewis wrote, 'The *super-naturalist* would be aiming – in my case is aiming – at the opposite to the *super-realist*. The emphasis would be upon *nature*, not upon the *real*. With the super-naturalist it is from within nature that the change is effected, not from without. The "real", in the photographic sense, would never make its appearance at all. Art, as he understands it, involves a banishing of that kind of reality.' Lewis took the occasion to remind his audience of his own claim to a place in history: '...the movement of which Vorticism was a part was, as understood by me, a first step towards a reform in the European vision. It was a discipline preliminary to a complete abandonment of the naturalism we inherit from the Greeks.

'That discipline *I* have undergone ...'

47. Sutherland at Rosenberg and Heft, and Nash at the Leicester Galleries.
48. Letter of early March 1938 (*Poet and Painter*, p. 214).
49. This image was the basis for the painting *Monster Shore* (now in the Hamilton Art Gallery, Ontario). This and the following quotation are taken from the article 'Monster Field', published in the *Architectural Review*, September 1939, though originally intended for the *London Bulletin*. In 1946 Counterpoint Publications Oxford published a limited-edition booklet, *Monster Field: a discovery recorded by Paul Nash*, with a facsimile of the manuscript for the article, illustrated by the painting itself together with Nash's three original photographs of the trees and two watercolours based on them.
50. *Country Life*, 21 May 1938.
51. Despite the change of title this was a reprint of 'The Sculptor Speaks'.
52. 'Notes on Sculpture'.
53. *Ibid.*
54. The earliest of these, made in 1935–6, is now in the Albright Art Gallery, Buffalo. The other three are reproduced here.
55. 'Sculpture in the open air. A talk by Henry Moore on his sculpture and its placing in open-air sites. Edited by Robert Melville and specially recorded with accompanying illustrations, by the British Council' (London 1955). Published in Philip James, ed., *Henry Moore on Sculpture* (London 1966).

Postscript: The Euston Road School

1. Randall Swingler, 'What is the Artist's Job', in *Left Review*, April 1938.
2. Herbert Read, 'Discussion between Realists and Surrealists', *London Bulletin*, April 1938.
3. There were 3,000 visitors at the New Burlington and 12,000 at the Whitechapel. Some comparative measure for these figures is given by the 50,000 reported as having visited the 'complete retrospective' of Christopher Wood, held at the New Burlington Galleries in the same year.
4. Anthony Blunt, 'From Bloomsbury to Marxism', *op. cit.* He gave vent to his views in an article in the *Spectator* to which Read responded. Blunt felt at the

time that *Guernica* 'was merely an expression of his [Picasso's] private sensation of horror and was irrelevant to the revolutionary movement as a whole'. Blunt described the debate in retrospect as 'a splendid set to ... all carried out in the most friendly manner, because Read and I happened to be members of the same club and we used frequently to meet there by chance.' Public disputes were made up over lunch. Blunt subsequently made amends to *Guernica* by publishing a book on the painting: *Picasso's Guernica*, the Whidden Lectures for 1966 (London 1969).

5. See below, Note 20.
6. He was rescued from employment as a civil servant by the patronage of Kenneth Clark, then director of the National Gallery. Clark took considerable interest in the Euston Road School and the artists associated with it. He also supported Coldstream for a while at the time the latter left the GPO Film Unit.
7. Ronald Alley, in the catalogue of Victor Pasmore's retrospective exhibition at the Tate Gallery in 1965, refers to it as 'the historic *Objective Abstractions* exhibition'. Lawrence Gowing, in the catalogue of Moynihan's retrospective at the Royal Academy in 1978, writes of the exhibition: 'Nothing so like a real, anarchic avant-garde had generated itself in England since the war.'
8. Although his work had in fact much in common with theirs, at least in terms of its informal appearance and typical subject matter, Hitchens must have been surprised to find himself in such company. His participation in the show was the result of an acquaintanceship with the director of the gallery, Hubert Wellington.
9. According to Moynihan in a conversation with David Sylvester broadcast by the BBC on 12 May 1962. (Abridged version published in the catalogue of Moynihan's retrospective at the Royal Academy.)
10. Moynihan, unpublished statement of 1934, quoted by Gowing, *op. cit.*
11. *Ibid.*
12. 29 March 1934.
13. *Op. cit.* (Note 9).
14. 'A Nonconformist', William Coldstream interviewed by Rodrigo Moynihan, *Art and Literature*, Lausanne, Spring 1965.
15. As interviewed for 'British Art in the Thirties', a programme broadcast by the BBC in December 1965.
16. *Op. cit.* (Note 9).
17. e.g. by Alan Bowness in the catalogue to 'British Art and the Modern Movement 1930–40', Arts Council 1962: 'Objective Abstraction ... was a remarkable anticipation of post-war Abstract Expressionism.'
18. In R. S. Lambert, ed., *Art in England* (London 1938).
19. *Op. cit.* (Note 14).
20. The prospectus, which is undated, announced 'A new School/for a limited number of pupils of /Drawing and Painting/under the direction of/Claude Rogers/Victor Pasmore/William Coldstream.' Fees were thirty-six guineas a year or twelve guineas a term, with daily rates for part-time study. There was to

be 'an evening life class without tuition' once a week. A page of text described the intentions of the organizers.

This School is established solely for the study of Drawing and Painting.

To-day there is a tendency in the art schools to concentrate on the teaching of the applied arts, industrial and commercial design, and to relegate to a secondary position the study of free drawing and painting. It is becoming, therefore, increasingly difficult for those who wish to take up Drawing and Painting as ends in themselves to find a school where they will receive wholehearted encouragement in this subject only, and at the same time obtain direct contact with teachers who are themselves practising painters.

This school hopes to supply this want. The teachers will, from time to time, work with the students so that they may have the advantages of private tuition with the added stimulus of meeting and working with others whose interests are similar. Furthermore, the following painters have promised to visit and criticise, and occasionally themselves work in the school, namely: Vanessa Bell, Duncan Grant, Augustus John, and John Nash, and the studios will also be open to practising artists who wish to draw or paint from the model without instruction.

This direct contact and exchange of ideas between artists and students is important and is an advantage which hitherto students have been able to enjoy only through private acquaintanceship.

In teaching, particular emphasis will be laid on training the observation, since this is the faculty most open to training. No attempt, however, will be made to impose a style and students will be left with the maximum freedom of expression. Every effort will be made to develop the particular interests of each pupil, and students will be encouraged to paint original pictures in the studio from whatever source stimulates them.

Instruction will be given in drawing and painting from life: the head and figure, still-life and landscape, and in making and painting from drawings and designs. When possible opportunities will also be given for working on large scale paintings and decorations.

21. *Op. cit.* (Note 7).
22. As painters who worked on large-scale public projects in a post-revolutionary period, the Mexicans Rivera and Orozco were of interest to the would-be English realists, as they were to younger painters in New York during the Depression. '... we saw this movement [the Mexican school] as a great revolutionary movement leading away from the dead end of Abstract art and Surrealism towards a new realist, communal and monumental art ...' (Blunt, *op. cit.*, 1973).
23. 'The realism of the Euston Road was something the Surrealists disagreed with because it did not leave enough room for the imagination, but primarily the people we were most at loggerheads with were the geometrical abstract group' (Coldstream, in 'British Art in the Thirties', *op. cit.*, Note 15).
24. As reported in the *AIA Newsheet*, April 1939.
25. Brought out as number five in the series 'Hogarth Sixpenny Pamphlets'.

26. See for instance Gowing, *op. cit.*: 'When the artist whose insight at 23 Gascoyne described is recognised as the same Rodrigo Moynihan, whose work in the forty-odd years since has taken turn after turn as formidably clear-sighted and looks now in the seventies as impressive as ever, then one realises that the received history of these years . . . will have to be rewritten.'
27. Coldstream taught at Camberwell School of Arts after the war, before being appointed Professor at the Slade in 1949. In 1959 he was appointed Chairman of the National Advisory Council on Art Education, the body responsible (via the first 'Coldstream Report') for the restructuring of art education in the 1960s and for replacing the National Diploma in Design with the Diploma in Art and Design in 1963. Rogers taught part-time at Camberwell from 1945 to 1948 and was a lecturer at the Slade from 1948 to 1963. From 1961 to 1968 he was a member, together with Lawrence Gowing, of the National Council for Diplomas in Art and Design (the body set up under the recommendations of the 'Coldstream Report' to administer the Dip.AD), and chairman of its Fine Art Panel. From 1963 to 1972 he was Professor of Fine Art at Reading University. Pasmore was a visiting teacher at the Central School of Arts and Crafts in London from 1949 to 1953, and from 1954 to 1961 Master of Painting at Newcastle University (formerly King's College, Durham). Moynihan was Professor of Painting at the Royal College of Art from 1948 to 1957.

LIST OF ILLUSTRATIONS

1. James McNeill Whistler: *Nocturne in Black and Gold: The Falling Rocket*, *c*. 1874. Oil on panel, $23\frac{3}{4} \times 18\frac{3}{4}$ in: 60.3×46.6 cm. The Detroit Institute of Arts (Purchase; The Dexter M. Ferry Jr Fund)
2. John Singer Sargent: *Monet painting at the Edge of a Wood*, 1888. Oil on canvas, $21\frac{1}{4} \times 25\frac{1}{2}$ in: 53.9×64.7 cm. London, Tate Gallery
3. Philip Wilson Steer: *Walberswick, Children Paddling*, *c*. 1889–94. Oil on canvas, $25\frac{1}{4} \times 36\frac{3}{8}$ in: 64.2×92.4 cm. Cambridge, Fitzwilliam Museum
4. Augustus John: *The Blue Pool*, 1910. Oil on panel, $12\frac{1}{2} \times 19\frac{1}{2}$ in: 31.8×49.5 cm. Aberdeen Art Gallery and Museums
5. William Nicholson: *A Downland Scene*, 1910. Oil on canvas, 13×16 in: 33×40.5 cm. London, Marlborough Fine Art Ltd in 1981
6. Walter Sickert: *The Juvenile Lead*, *c*. 1907. Oil on canvas, 20×18 in: 51×45.8 cm. Southampton Art Gallery
7. Walter Sickert: *Mamma mia Poveretta*, 1903–4. Oil on canvas, $18\frac{1}{8} \times 15$ in: 46.1×38.2 cm. Manchester City Art Gallery
8. Walter Sickert: *Noctes Ambrosianae*, 1906. Oil on canvas, 25×30 in: 63.5×76.2 cm. Nottingham City Museum and Art Gallery (Photo: Layland Ross Ltd)
9. Spencer Gore: *Stage Sunrise, the Alhambra*, 1910. Oil on canvas, 16×20 in: 40.6×50.8 cm. London, Anthony d'Offay Gallery in 1981
10. Walter Sickert: *Portrait of Harold Gilman*, *c*. 1912. Oil on canvas, 24×18 in: 61×45.7 cm. London, Tate Gallery
11. Walter Sickert: *L'Affaire de Camden Town*, 1909. Oil on canvas, $23\frac{1}{2} \times 15\frac{1}{2}$ in: 59.7×39.4 cm. Private Collection (Photo: Royal Academy of Arts, London)

12. Spencer Gore: *Self-Portrait*, *c.* 1914. Oil on canvas, 16 × 12 in: 41 × 30.5 cm. London, National Portrait Gallery
13. Charles Ginner: *The Fruit Stall, King's Cross*, 1914. Oil on canvas, 25¾ × 20 in: 65.4 × 50.8 cm. London, Anthony d'Offay Gallery in 1981
14. Harold Gilman: *The Model, Reclining Nude*, *c.* 1910–11. Oil on canvas, 18 × 24 in: 45.7 × 61 cm. London, Arts Council of Great Britain
15. Spencer Gore: *Harold Gilman's House, Letchworth*, 1912. Oil on canvas, 25 × 30 in: 63.5 × 76.2 cm. Leicester Museum and Art Gallery
16. Walter Sickert: *Ennui*, *c.* 1915. Oil on canvas, 30 × 22 in: 76 × 56 cm. Oxford, Ashmolean Museum
17. Harold Gilman: *Interior with Mrs Mounter*, 1916–17. Oil on canvas, 20 × 30 in: 51 × 76 cm. Oxford, Ashmolean Museum
18. Harold Gilman: *An Eating House*, *c.* 1914. Oil on canvas, 22½ × 29½ in: 57 × 74.9 cm. Sheffield City Art Gallery
19. Harold Gilman: *Leeds Market*, *c.* 1914. Oil on canvas, 20 × 24 in: 50.8 × 61 cm. London, Tate Gallery
20. Henry Tonks: *The Unknown God. Roger Fry preaching the New Faith and Clive Bell ringing the Bell*, *c.* 1912. Oil on canvas, 16 × 21½ in: 40.6 × 54.6 cm. Private Collection
21. Duncan Grant: *The Tub*, 1912. Watercolour and tempera on board, 30 × 22 in: 76.2 × 55.9 cm. London, Tate Gallery
22. Roger Fry: *White Road with Farm*, *c.* 1912. Oil on canvas, 25½ × 31¾ in: 64.8 × 80.6 cm. Edinburgh, Scottish National Gallery of Modern Art (Photo: Tom Scott)
23. Vanessa Bell(?) (formerly attributed to Roger Fry): *A Room at the Second Post-Impressionist Exhibition*, 1912. Oil on panel, 20¼ × 24¾ in: 51.3 × 62.9 cm. Paris, Musée National d'Art Moderne
24. Stanley Spencer: *The Nativity*, 1912. Oil on panel, 40 × 60 in: 101.6 × 152.4 cm. London, University College
25. Wyndham Lewis: *Creation*, 1912. Whereabouts unknown (Photographed from the catalogue of the *Second Post-Impressionist Exhibition*, Grafton Galleries, 1912)
26. Henry Lamb: *Portrait of Lytton Strachey*, 1914. Oil on canvas, 96¼ × 70¼ in: 229.4 × 178.4 cm. London, Tate Gallery
27. Duncan Grant: *Queen of Sheba*, 1912. Oil on wood, 47¼ × 47¼ in: 120 × 120 cm. London, Tate Gallery
28. Vanessa Bell: *Triple Alliance*, 1915–16. Oil and collage on canvas, 33 × 25 in: 83.8 × 63.5 cm. University of Leeds, Westwood Hall
29. Edward Wadsworth: *Five Designs for the Omega Workshops*, 1913. Gouache and pencil on squared paper, centre design 3 × 6.9 in: 7.5 × 17.7 cm. London, British Council
30. Wyndham Lewis: *Smiling Woman ascending a Stair*, 1911–12. Charcoal and gouache on paper, 37¼ × 25½ in: 94.5 × 65 cm. Bradford, Vint Trust (Photo: Courtauld Institute)

31. Wyndham Lewis: *The Creditors* (Design for Timon of Athens), 1912–13. Ink, wash, and watercolour on paper, $16\frac{1}{2} \times 10\frac{3}{4}$ in: 42×27.5 cm. Hartford, Connecticut, Wadsworth Atheneum (The Ella Gallup Sumner and Mary Catlin Sumner Collection)
32. Jacob Epstein: *Tomb of Oscar Wilde*, 1911. Hopton Wood stone. Paris, Père Lachaise Cemetery (Photo: Étienne Hubert)
33. Jacob Epstein: *Female Figure in Flenite*, 1913. Serpentine stone, $18 \times 3\frac{3}{4} \times 4\frac{3}{4}$ in: $15.7 \times 9.5 \times 12$ cm. London, Tate Gallery
34. Richard Nevinson: *The Arrival*, 1913–14. Oil on canvas, 30×25 in: 76.2×63.5 cm. London, Tate Gallery
35. Wyndham Lewis: *Composition*, 1913. Watercolour, pen and pencil on paper, $13\frac{1}{2} \times 10\frac{1}{2}$ in: 34.3×26.7 cm. London, Tate Gallery
36. David Bomberg: *The Mud Bath*, 1914. Oil on canvas, $60 \times 88\frac{1}{4}$ in: 152.4×224.2 cm. London, Tate Gallery
37. David Bomberg: *In the Hold*, 1913–14. Oil on canvas, $77\frac{1}{4} \times 91$ in: 196.2×231.1 cm. London, Tate Gallery
38. Jacob Epstein: *Rock Drill*, 1913–14. Plaster and ready-made drill, height *c.* 120 in: 300 cm. Dismantled (Copyright-holder of photograph not known)
39. Jacob Epstein: *Rock Drill*, 1916. Bronze cast, $27\frac{3}{4} \times 23 \times 17\frac{1}{2}$ in: $70.5 \times 58.4 \times 44.5$ cm. London, Tate Gallery
40. Page from *Blast* No. 1. London, Victoria and Albert Museum (Photo: A. C. Cooper Ltd)
41. Lawrence Atkinson: *Abstract Composition*, *c.* 1914–15. Pencil and coloured crayons on paper, $31\frac{1}{2} \times 21\frac{1}{2}$ in: 80×54.5 cm. London, Anthony d'Offay Gallery in 1981
42. William Roberts: *The Toe Dancer*, 1914. Ink and gouache on paper, $28\frac{1}{4} \times 21\frac{1}{4}$ in: 71.8×54 cm. London, Victoria and Albert Museum
43. Henri Gaudier-Brzeska: *Red Stone Dancer*, *c.* 1913. Red Mansfield stone, $17 \times 9 \times 9$ in: $43.2 \times 22.9 \times 22.9$ cm. London, Tate Gallery
44. Henri Gaudier-Brzeska: *Ornement Torpille*, 1914. Cut brass, $7 \times 2 \times 1\frac{1}{2}$ in: $18 \times 5 \times 4$ cm. Collection: Grattan Freyer
45. Henri Gaudier-Brzeska: *Bird swallowing a Fish*, 1914. Carved plaster, height $12\frac{1}{2}$ in: 31.8 cm. University of Cambridge, Kettle's Yard Collection
46. Henri Gaudier-Brzeska: *Crouching Figure*, 1913–14. Marble, $8\frac{3}{4} \times 12 \times 4$ in: $22.2 \times 30.5 \times 10.2$ cm. Minneapolis, Walker Art Center
47. Edward Wadsworth: *Trees beside a River*, 1913. Watercolour on paper, $10\frac{1}{4} \times 13\frac{1}{4}$ in: 26×35 cm. Private Collection (Photo: Courtauld Institute)
48. Edward Wadsworth: *Study for a Vorticist Painting*, *c.* 1914. Ink, chalk, watercolour, and gouache on paper, $13 \times 10\frac{1}{2}$ in: 33×26.5 cm, London, Anthony d'Offay Gallery in 1981
49. Edward Wadsworth: *Enclosure*, 1915. Gouache, collage, and pencil on paper laid on board, $20\frac{1}{2} \times 18$ in: 52×45.7 cm. London, Anthony d'Offay Gallery in 1981
50. Wyndham Lewis: *Composition in Blue*, 1915. Ink, crayon, and watercolour on paper, $18\frac{1}{2} \times 12$ in: 47×30.5 cm. London, Anthony d'Offay Gallery in 1981

51. Wyndham Lewis: *The Crowd*, 1914–15. Oil and pencil on canvas, 79 × 60½ in: 200.7 × 153.7 cm. London, Tate Gallery
52. Wyndham Lewis: *Plan of War*, 1913–14. Oil on canvas, 100½ × 56½ in: 255 × 143 cm. Lost (reproduced from *Blast* No. 1) (Photo: A. C. Cooper Ltd)
53. Richard Nevinson: *Returning to the Trenches*, 1915–16. Oil on canvas, 20 × 30 in: 50.8 × 76.2 cm. Ottawa, The National Gallery of Canada (Gift of the Massey Foundation, 1946)
54. Richard Nevinson: *La Mitrailleuse*, 1915. Oil on canvas, 24 × 20 in: 61 × 50.8 cm. London, Tate Gallery
55. Richard Nevinson: *Harvest of Battle*, 1919. Oil on canvas, 72 × 125 in: 182.9 × 317.5 cm. London, Imperial War Museum
56. Wyndham Lewis: *A Battery Shelled*, 1919. Oil on canvas, 72 × 125 in: 182.9 × 317.5 cm. London, Imperial War Museum
57. Wyndham Lewis: *The No. 2*, 1918. Pen and ink, watercolour, and pencil, 21½ × 29½ in: 54.6 × 74.3 cm. Collection: H. Anson-Cartwright (Photo: courtesy Walter Michel)
58. Edward Wadsworth: *Dazzle Ships in Drydock at Liverpool*, 1919. Oil on canvas, 119½ × 96 in: 303.5 × 243.8 cm. Ottawa, The National Gallery of Canada
59. William Roberts: *The Gas Chamber*, 1918. Pen, ink, pencil, and watercolour on paper, 12½ × 20 in: 31.8 × 50.8 cm. London, Imperial War Museum
60. Henry Lamb: *Irish Troops in the Judaean Hills surprised by a Turkish Bombardment*, 1919. Oil on canvas, 72 × 86 in: 182.3 × 218.4 cm. London, Imperial War Museum
61. Harold Gilman: *Halifax Harbour at Sunset*, 1918. Oil on canvas, 77 × 132 in: 195.6 × 335.3 cm. Ottawa, The National Gallery of Canada
62. John Nash: *Oppy Wood*, 1919. Oil on canvas, 72 × 84 in: 182.9 × 213.4 cm. London, Imperial War Museum
63. Stanley Spencer: *Resurrection, Macedonia*, 1928–9. Oil on canvas. Burghclere Chapel (Photo: Jeremy Whitaker)
64. Paul Nash: *The Three in the Night*, 1913. Watercolour, ink, and chalk on paper, 20¾ × 13½ in: 52.7 × 34.3 cm. Private Collection (Photo: A. C. Cooper Ltd)
65. Paul Nash: *The Landscape – Hill 60*, 1917–18. Pencil, pen, and watercolour on paper, 15½ × 19½ in: 39.4 × 49.5 cm. London, Imperial War Museum
66. Paul Nash: *Landscape – Year of our Lord 1917*, 1917–18. Chalk and ink on paper, 10¼ × 14¼ in: 25.9 × 35.9 cm. Ottawa, The National Gallery of Canada
67. Paul Nash: *The Menin Road*, 1919. Oil on canvas, 72 × 125 in: 182.9 × 317.5 cm. London, Imperial War Museum
68. Paul Nash: *After the Battle*, 1918. Pen and watercolour on paper, 18¼ × 23½ in: 46.4 × 59.7 cm. London, Imperial War Museum
69. Paul Nash: *We are Making a New World*, 1919. Oil on canvas, 28 × 36 in: 71 × 91.4 cm. London, Imperial War Museum
70. David Bomberg: *Barges*, 1919. Oil on canvas, 23½ × 30½ in: 59.7 × 77.5 cm. London, Tate Gallery

71. Duncan Grant: *Vanessa Bell*, 1918. Oil on canvas, 37 × 24 in: 94 × 61 cm. London, National Portrait Gallery
72. Duncan Grant: *Landscape through a French Window*, *c.* 1920. Oil on canvas, $30\frac{1}{2} \times 22\frac{1}{2}$ in: 77.5 × 57.2 cm. Ireland, Private Collection (Photo: courtesy Agnew's)
73. Mark Gertler: *The Merry-go-Round*, 1916. Oil on canvas, $74\frac{3}{4} \times 56$ in: 189.9 × 142.2 cm. London, Tate Gallery
74. Mark Gertler: *Queen of Sheba*, 1922. Oil on canvas, $37 \times 42\frac{1}{2}$ in: 94 × 107.3 cm. London, Tate Gallery
75. Matthew Smith: *Fitzroy Street Nude No. 2*, 1916. Oil on canvas, 40 × 30 in: 101.5 × 76.2 cm. London, The British Council
76. Matthew Smith: *Cornish Church*, 1920. Oil on canvas, $21 \times 25\frac{1}{2}$ in: 53.3 × 64.8 cm. London, Tate Gallery
77. Matthew Smith: *Woman with a Fan*, 1925. Oil on canvas, $51\frac{1}{2} \times 32$ in: 130.8 × 81.3 cm. Liverpool, Walker Art Gallery
78. Edward Wadsworth: *The Cattewater, Plymouth Sound*, 1923. Tempera on panel, 25 × 35 in: 63.5 × 88.9 cm. Private Collection (Photo: A. C. Cooper Ltd)
79. Edward Wadsworth: *Ladle Slag*, 1919. Ink, watercolour, and body colour on paper, $14\frac{3}{4} \times 20\frac{1}{2}$ in: 37.5 × 51.2 cm. Manchester City Art Gallery
80. William Roberts: *The Cinema*, 1920. Oil on canvas, 36 × 30 in: 91.4 × 76.2 cm. London, Tate Gallery
81. Frank Dobson: *The Concertina Man*, 1919. Portland stone, height 24 in: 61 cm. Whereabouts unknown (Photo: courtesy Mrs Mary Dobson)
82. Wyndham Lewis: *Girl Reclining*, 1919. Black chalk on paper, 15 × 22 in: 38.1 × 55.9 cm. London, Tate Gallery
83. Wyndham Lewis: *Mr Wyndham Lewis as a Tyro*, 1920–21. Oil on canvas, $29 \times 17\frac{1}{4}$ in: 73.7 × 43.8 cm. City of Kingston upon Hull, Ferens Art Gallery
84. Wyndham Lewis: *Edith Sitwell*, 1923–35. Oil on canvas, 34 × 44 in: 86.4 × 111.8 cm. London, Tate Gallery
85. Ivon Hitchens: *The Curved Barn*, 1922. Oil on canvas, $25\frac{3}{4} \times 38\frac{1}{2}$ in: 65.5 × 98 cm. Collection of the Artist's Estate in 1981
86. Paul Nash: *Wooded Hills in Autumn*, 1921–2. Pen and ink with watercolour on paper, $15\frac{1}{2} \times 22$ in: 39.4 × 55.9 cm. University of Manchester, Whitworth Art Gallery
87. Paul Nash: *The Shore*, 1923. Oil on canvas, 24 × 36 in: 62.2 × 94 cm. Leeds City Art Gallery
88. Paul Nash: *Dymchurch Wall*, 1923. Watercolour and pencil on paper, $14\frac{1}{2} \times 21\frac{1}{2}$ in: 36.8 × 54.6 cm. Private Collection (Photo: Colnaghi's)
89. Ben Nicholson: *Dymchurch*, 1923. Oil on canvas stretched on board, $11\frac{1}{2} \times 15\frac{1}{4}$ in: 29 × 38.5 cm. Collection: Andrew Nicholson (Photo: A. C. Cooper Ltd)
90. Ben Nicholson: *Cortivallo Lugano*, 1921–3. Oil and pencil on canvas,

18 × 24 in: 43 × 60 cm. London, Tate Gallery

91. Ben Nicholson: *Trout*, 1924. Oil on canvas, 22 × 23 in: 56 × 58.5 cm. Private Collection

92. Ben Nicholson: *First Abstract Painting*, 1924. Oil and pencil on canvas, 21¾ × 24 in: 55 × 61 cm. London, Tate Gallery

93. Ben Nicholson: *Goblet and Pears*, *c.* 1925. Oil and pencil on board, 14½ × 17½ in: 37 × 44.5 cm. University of Cambridge, Kettle's Yard Collection Collection

94. Alfred Wallis: *Three ships and lighthouse*, *c.* 1934–8. Oil and pencil on board, 12½ × 18 in: 32 × 46.5 cm (irregular). Stromness, Orkney, The Pier Gallery

95. Ben Nicholson: *Pill Creek, Moonlight*, 1928/9. Oil, gesso, and pencil on canvas, 19½ × 24 in: 49.5 × 61 cm. Helen Sutherland Collection

96. Winifred Nicholson: *Seascape with Dinghy*, *c.* 1928/30. Oil on canvas, 27½ × 34¾ in: 69.5 × 88.5 cm. University of Cambridge, Kettle's Yard Collection

97. Ben Nicholson: *Birch Craig*, 1930. Oil on canvas, 24 × 36 in: 61 × 91 cm. Collection: Jake Nicholson (Photo: A. C. Cooper Ltd)

98. Christopher Wood: *PZ 134*, 1930. Oil on hardboard, 20 × 27 in: 50.5 × 68.5 cm. Eastbourne, Towner Art Gallery

99. Christopher Wood: *Sleeping Fisherman, Ploaré, Brittany*, 1930. Oil on board, 15 × 28¾ in: 38 × 73 cm. Newcastle upon Tyne, Laing Art Gallery, Tyne and Wear County Council Museums

100. Christopher Wood: *Building the Boat, Tréboul*, 1930. Oil on board, 23 × 33 in: 58.4 × 83.8 cm. University of Cambridge, Kettle's Yard Collection

101. Ivon Hitchens: *Spring Mood*, 1933. Oil on canvas, 28 × 40 in: 71 × 102 cm. Private Collection (Photo: Christie's Images)

102. Frances Hodgkins: *Wings over Water*, 1934. Oil on canvas, 27 × 38 in: 68.6 × 96.5 cm. Leeds, Temple Newsam Art Gallery

103. David Jones: *Hierarchy*, 1932. Watercolour on paper, 18 × 9½ in: 45.7 × 24.1 cm. Collection: Hon. Hubert Howard (Photo: J. R. Freeman Ltd)

104. Paul Nash: *Walnut Tree*, 1924. Chalk and pencil on paper, 15¼ × 21¾ in: 38.7 × 55.2 cm. Manchester City Art Gallery

105. Paul Nash: *Landscape at Iden*, 1929. Oil on canvas, 27½ × 35¾ in: 69.9 × 90.8 cm. London, Tate Gallery

106. Edward Wadsworth: *Regalia*, 1928. Tempera on canvas laid on board, 30 × 36 in: 76.2 × 91.4 cm. Private Collection (Photo: courtesy Colnaghi's)

107. Paul Nash: *Wood on the Downs*, 1930. Oil on canvas, 28 × 36 in: 71.2 × 91.5 cm. Aberdeen Art Gallery and Museums

108. Jacob Epstein: *Risen Christ*, 1919–20. Bronze, 86 × 21½ × 18½ in: 218.5 × 54.5 × 47 cm. Edinburgh, Scottish National Gallery of Modern Art (Photo: Tom Scott)

109. Jacob Epstein: *Genesis*, 1931. Seravessa marble, height 62¼ in: 158.1 cm. London, Granada Television Ltd

110. Frank Dobson: *Reclining Nude*, 1925. White marble, 20 × 7 in: 50.8 × 17.8 cm. London, Courtauld Institute
111. Lawrence Atkinson: *L'Oiseau*, *c.* 1920. Whereabouts unknown (Photographed from H. Shipp, *The New Art*, London 1922)
112. Eric Gill: *Deposition*, 1924. Black Hopton Wood stone, height 24 in: 61 cm. Canterbury, The King's School (Photo: W. L. Entwistle)
113. Eric Gill: *Girl*, 1925. Capel-y-Ffin stone, height 36 in: 91.4 cm. Whereabouts unknown (Photographed from Joseph Thorp, *Eric Gill*, Jonathan Cape, London 1929)
114. Eric Gill: *Mankind*, 1927–8. Hopton Wood stone, 95 × 24 × 18 in: 241 × 61 × 45.7 cm. London, Tate Gallery
115. Henry Moore: *Mother and Child*, 1924–5. Hornton stone, height 22½ in: 57 cm. Manchester City Art Gallery
116. Henry Moore: *Reclining Figure*, 1929. Brown Hornton stone, 33 × 22½ × 15 in: 84 × 57 × 38 cm. Leeds City Art Gallery
117. Henry Moore: *Half-figure*, 1929. Cast concrete, height 15½ in: 39 cm. Norwich, University of East Anglia, Robert and Lisa Sainsbury Collection
118. Henry Moore: *Mother and Child*, 1932. Green Hornton stone, height 35 in: 89 cm. Norwich, University of East Anglia, Robert and Lisa Sainsbury Collection (Photo: courtesy of the artist)
119. Barbara Hepworth: *Kneeling Figure*, 1932. Rosewood, height 27 in: 68.6 cm. Wakefield City Art Gallery
120. Barbara Hepworth: *Figure in Sycamore*, 1931. Height 25 in: 63.5 cm. Stromness, Orkney, The Pier Gallery (Photo: Tate Gallery)
121. Paul Nash: *Northern Adventure*, 1929. Oil on canvas, 36 × 28 in: 91.5 × 71.2 cm. Aberdeen Art Gallery and Museums
122. Paul Nash: *Kinetic Feature*, 1931. Oil on canvas, 26 × 20 in: 66 × 50 cm. London, Tate Gallery
123. Edward Wadsworth: *Composition*, 1930. Tempera on panel, 35 × 25 in: 88.9 × 63.5 cm. Collection: Alex Hollweg
124. Edward Burra: *Dancing Skeletons*, 1934. Gouache on paper, 31 × 22 in: 78.7 × 55.9 cm. London, Tate Gallery
125. Ben Nicholson: *Still Life*, 1933–5. Oil and gesso on board, 19½ × 23½ in: 49.5 × 59.5 cm. Helen Sutherland Collection
126. Edward Wadsworth: *Dux et Comes*, 1933. Tempera, 14¾ × 20½ in: 37.5 × 52 cm. Private Collection (Photo: Marlborough Fine Art Ltd)
127. Barbara Hepworth: *Large and Small Form*, 1934. White alabaster, 10 × 17½ × 9½ in: 25 × 45 × 24 cm. Stromness, Orkney, The Pier Gallery
128. Paul Nash: *Event on the Downs*, 1933. Oil on canvas, 20 × 24 in: 50.8 × 61 cm. London, Department of the Environment
129. Henry Moore: *Composition*, 1931. Blue Hornton stone, height 19 in: 48.3 cm. Collection: Mary Moore (Photo: courtesy of the artist)
130. Henry Moore: *Reclining Figure*, 1931. Lead, height 17 in: 43 cm. Collection: Mr and Mrs Fred Zimmermann (Photo: courtesy of the artist)

131. Henry Moore: *Composition*, 1933. Concrete, height 23¼ in: 59 cm. London, The British Council
132. Ben Nicholson: *Au Chat Botté*, 1932. Oil and pencil on canvas, 36¼ × 48 in: 92.3 × 122 cm. Manchester City Art Gallery
133. Ben Nicholson: *Guitar*, 1933. Oil and gesso on board, 34½ × 9½ in: 88 × 24 cm. London, Tate Gallery
134. Ben Nicholson: *Composition in Black and White*, 1933. Oil on board, 45 × 22 in: 114 × 56 cm. Borough of Thamesdown, Swindon Permanent Art Collection Art Collection
135. Ben Nicholson: *December 1933 (First Abstract Relief)*, 1933. Oil on carved board, 21½ × 10 in: 54.5 × 25.5 cm. Private Collection (Photo: A. C. Cooper Ltd)
136. Ben Nicholson: *White Relief*, 1934. Oil on carved wood, 13¾ × 24 in: 35 × 61 cm. Private Collection (Photo: Courtauld Institute)
137. Ben Nicholson: *White Relief*, 1935. Oil on carved wood, 40 × 65½ in: 101.5 × 166 cm. London, Tate Gallery
138. Barbara Hepworth: *Pierced Form*, 1931. Pink alabaster, height 10 in: 25.4 cm. Destroyed (Photo: courtesy of the Barbara Hepworth Museum)
139. Barbara Hepworth: *Two Forms with Sphere*, 1934. White alabaster, base 18 × 10 in: 45.7 × 25.4 cm. Whereabouts unknown (Photograph from Alan Bowness, *Barbara Hepworth*, Lund-Humphries, London 1963)
140. Barbara Hepworth: *Discs in Echelon*, 1935. Padouk wood, height 12¼ in: 31.1 cm. New York, The Museum of Modern Art (Gift of W. B. Bennet)
141. Barbara Hepworth: *Forms in Echelon*, 1938. Tulipwood, height 40 in: 101.6 cm. London, Tate Gallery
142. John Piper: *Abstract I*, 1935. Oil on a collage of canvas on plywood, 36 × 42 in: 91.4 × 106.7 cm. London, Tate Gallery
143. Henry Moore: *Four-piece Composition: Reclining Figure*, 1934. Cumberland alabaster, length 20 in: 50.8 cm. London, Tate Gallery (Photo: courtesy of the artist)
144. Henry Moore: *Square Form*, 1936. Green Hornton stone, 13¾ × 12 in: 35 × 30.6 cm. Norwich, University of East Anglia, Robert and Lisa Sainsbury Collection
145. Naum Gabo: *Construction on a Plane*, 1937. Plastic, 19 × 19 in: 48 × 48 cm. Collection: Sir Leslie Martin (Photo: James Austin)
146. John Cecil Stephenson: *Painting*, 1937. Tempera on canvas, 28 × 36 in: 71.1 × 91.4 cm. London, Tate Gallery
147. Ben Nicholson: *Painting*, 1935. Oil on canvas, 41¾ × 41¾ in: 106 × 106 cm. Collection: Andrew Nicholson
148. Ben Nicholson: *White Relief*, 1939. Oil on carved board, 30½ × 29 in: 77.5 × 73.7 cm. Collection: Jake Nicholson (Photo: A. C. Cooper Ltd)
149. Ben Nicholson: *Painted Relief*, 1939. Oil and pencil on composition boards mounted on painted plywood, 32½ × 45 in: 82.6 × 114.3 cm. New York, Museum of Modern Art (Gift of H. S. Ede and the artist)

150. Paul Nash: *Landscape of the Megaliths*, 1933–4. Oil on canvas, 19¾ × 28¾ in: 50 × 73 cm. London, British Council

151. Paul Nash: *Equivalents for the Megaliths*, 1935. Oil on canvas, 18 × 26 in: 45.7 × 66 cm. London, Tate Gallery

152. Paul Nash: *Harbour and Room*, 1932–6. Oil on canvas, 36 × 28 in: 91.5 × 71 cm. London, Tate Gallery

153. Tristram Hillier: *La Route des Alpes*, 1937. Tempera on canvas, 23½ × 31½ in: 59.7 × 80.6 cm. London, Tate Gallery

154. Ceri Richards: *The Female Contains all the Qualities*, 1937. Oil and mixed media on canvas, 42 × 35 in: 106.7 × 88.9 cm. London, Tate Gallery

155. Paul Nash: *Landscape from a Dream*, 1936–8. Oil on canvas, 26¾ × 40 in: 67.9 × 101.6 cm. London, Tate Gallery

156. John Piper: *Autumn at Stourhead*, 1939. Oil on linen pasted board. 25 × 30 in: 63.3 × 76.2 cm. Manchester City Art Gallery

157. Graham Sutherland: *Welsh Landscape with Roads*, 1936. Oil on canvas, 24 × 36 in: 61 × 91.4 cm. London, Tate Gallery

158. Paul Nash: *Monster Field*, 1939. Oil on canvas, 30¼ × 40 in: 76.8 × 101.6 cm. Durban Art Gallery, South Africa

159. Henry Moore: *Reclining Figure*, 1936. Elm wood, length 42 in: 107 cm. Wakefield City Art Gallery

160. Henry Moore: *Reclining Figure*, 1939. Elm wood, 37 × 79 × 30 in: 94 × 200.7 × 76.2 cm. The Detroit Institute of Arts (Gift of the D. M. Ferry Jr Trustee Corporation)

161. Henry Moore: *Recumbent Figure*, 1938. Green Hornton stone, 35 × 52¼ × 29 in: 88.9 × 132.7 × 73.7 cm. London, Tate Gallery

162. William Coldstream: *Studio Interior*, 1932–3. Oil on canvas, 54 × 36 in: 137.2 × 91.5 cm. London, Tate Gallery

163. Rodrigo Moynihan: *Objective Abstraction*, 1934. Oil on canvas, 25 × 30 in: 63.5 × 76.2 cm. Collection of the artist in 1981 (Photo: A. C. Cooper Ltd)

164. William Coldstream: *Bolton*, 1938. Oil on canvas, 28¼ × 36 in: 71.8 × 91.4 cm. Ottawa, The National Gallery of Canada (Gift of the Massey Foundation, 1946)

165. Geoffrey Tibble: *Reclining Woman*, 1938. Oil on canvas, 36 × 48 in: 91.5 × 121.9 cm. City of Leicester Museum and Art Gallery

SELECTED BIBLIOGRAPHY

I. SOURCE MATERIAL

(including published documents, contemporary criticism, memoirs etc.)

A.I.A. *Artists International Association. The First Five Years 1933–38*. London 1938

A.I.A. *Activities since 1938*. London 1942

Ashcroft, T. *English Art and English Society*. London 1936

Bell, C. *Art*. London 1914

Bell, C. *Since Cézanne*. London 1922

Bell, C. *Old Friends: Personal Recollections*. London 1956

Bell, G. *The Artist and his Public*. London 1939

Blanche, J.-E. *Portraits of a Lifetime: The Late Victorian Era. The Edwardian Pageant 1870–1914*. London 1937

Blanche, J.-E. *More Portraits of a Lifetime 1918–1938*. London 1939

Breton, A. (trans. D. Gascoyne) *What is Surrealism?* London 1936

Casson, S. *Artists at Work*. London 1933

Caudwell, C. *Studies in a Dying Culture*. London 1938

Day Lewis, C. (ed.) *The Mind in Chains: Socialism and the Cultural Revolution*. London 1937

Epstein, J. *Let There Be Sculpture: An Autobiography*. London 1940. (Revised edition: *Epstein: An Autobiography*. London 1955)

Epstein, J., and Haskell, A. *The Sculptor Speaks: A Series of Conversations on Art*. London 1931

Evans, M. (ed.) *The Painter's Object*. London 1937

Fry, R. *Vision and Design*. London 1920

Fry, R. *Transformations*. London 1926

Fry, R. *Reflections on British Painting*. London 1934

Fry, R. (intro.; ed. D. Sutton) *Letters of Roger Fry*. 2 vols. London 1972

Gascoyne, D. *A Short Survey of Surrealism*. London 1935

Gertler, M. (ed. N. Carrington, intro. Q. Bell) *Selected Letters of Mark Gertler*. London 1965

Gill, E. *Sculpture: An Essay on Stonecutting with a Preface about God*. Ditchling 1918

Gill, E. *Art-Nonsense and other Essays*. London 1929

Gill, E. *Sculpture and the Living Model*. London 1932

Gill, E. *Beauty Looks After Herself*. London 1933

Gill, E. *Art and a Changing Civilization*. London 1934

Gill, E. *Autobiography*. London 1940

Gill, E. (ed. W. Shewing) *Letters of Eric Gill*. London 1947

Grigson, G. *The Crest on the Silver: An Autobiography*. London 1950

Grigson, G. (ed.) *The Arts Today*. London 1935

Hepworth, B. *A Pictorial Autobiography*. Bath 1970. (New edition Bradford-on-Avon 1978)

Hillier, T. *Leda and the Goose: An Autobiography*. London 1954

Hulme, T. (ed. H. Read) *Speculations: Essays on Humanism and the Philosophy of Art*. London 1924

Hulme, T. (ed. S. Hynes) *Further Speculations by T. E. Hulme*. Minneapolis, Minnesota, 1955

John, A. *Chiaroscuro: Fragments of an Autobiography*. London 1952

Jones, D. *Epoch and Artist*. London 1959

Klingender, F. *Marxism and Modern Art*. London 1943

Lambert, R. (ed.) *Art in England*. London 1938

Lewis, P. Wyndham. *The Caliph's Design*. London 1919

Lewis, P. Wyndham. *Time and Western Man*. London 1927

Lewis, P. Wyndham. *Men without Art*. London 1934

Lewis, P. Wyndham. *Blasting and Bombardiering*. London 1937

Lewis, P. Wyndham. *Wyndham Lewis the Artist from Blast to Burlington House*. London 1939

Lewis, P. Wyndham. *Rude Assignment: A Narrative of My Career Up-to-date*. London 1950

Lewis, P. Wyndham (ed. W. Rose) *Letters of Wyndham Lewis*. London 1962

Lewis, P. Wyndham (eds. W. Michel and C. Fox) *Wyndham Lewis on Art*. London 1969

Lewis, P. Wyndham, and Fergusson, L. *Harold Gilman: An Appreciation*. London 1919

MacColl, D. *Confessions of a Keeper*. London 1931

Marriott, C. *Modern Movements in Painting*. London 1920

Martin, J., Nicholson, B., and Gabo, N. (eds.) *Circle: International Survey of Constructive Art*. London 1937

Moore, G. *Principia Ethica*. Cambridge 1903

Moore, H. (ed. P. James) *Henry Moore on Sculpture*. London 1966

Nash, P. *Room and Book*. London 1932
Nash, P. *Monster Field: A Discovery recorded by Paul Nash*. Oxford 1946
Nash, P. *Outline: An Autobiography and Other Writings*. London 1949
Nash, P. (ed. M. Nash) *Fertile Image*. London 1951
Nash, P., and Bottomley, G. (eds. C. Abbott and A. Bertram) *Poet and Painter: being the Correspondence between Gordon Bottomley and Paul Nash 1910–1946*. London 1955.
Nevinson, C. *Paint and Prejudice: An Autobiography*. London 1937
Parkes, K. *Sculpture of To-Day*. London 1921
Pevsner, N. *An Inquiry into Industrial Arts in England*. Cambridge 1937
Pound, E. *Gaudier Brzeska: a Memoir*. London 1916
Pound, E. (ed. D. Paige) *Letters of Ezra Pound 1907–1941*. London 1951
Rea, B. (ed.) *Five on Revolutionary Art*. London 1935
Read, H. *Reason and Romanticism*. London 1926
Read, H. *The Meaning of Art*. London 1931
Read, H. *Art Now*. London 1933
Read, H. *Art and Industry*. London 1934
Read, H. *Art and Society*. London 1937
Read, H. (ed.) *Unit 1: The Modern Movement in English Painting, Sculpture and Architecture*. London 1934
Roberts, W. *Some Early Abstract and Cubist Work 1913–1920*. London 1957
Rothenstein, W. *Since Fifty: Men and Memories 1922–38*. London 1939
Rutter, F. *Revolution in Art: An Introduction to the Study of Cézanne, Gauguin, Van Gogh and Other Modern Painters*. London 1910
Rutter, F. *Evolution in Modern Art: A Study of Modern Painting 1870–1925*. London 1926
Rutter, F. *Since I Was Twenty-Five*. London 1927
Rutter, F. *Art in My Time*. London 1933
Sausmarez, M. de (ed.) *Ben Nicholson*. London 1969
Shipp, H. *The New Art: A Study of the Principles of Non-representational Art and their Application in the Work of Lawrence Atkinson*. London 1922
Sickert, W. (ed. O. Sitwell) *A Free House or the Artist as Craftsman: being the Writings of Walter Richard Sickert*. London 1947
Skeaping, J. *Drawn from Life*. London 1977
Stokes, A. *Colour and Form*. London 1937
Thornton, A. *Fifty Years of the New English Art Club 1886–1935*. London 1935
Thornton, A. *The Diary of an Art Student of the Nineties*. London 1935
Trevelyan, J. *Indigo Days*. London 1957
Wadsworth, E. (intro. A. Bennett) *Black Country*. London 1920
Wertheim, L. *Adventure in Art*. London 1947
Wilenski, R. *The Modern Movement in Art*. London 1927
Wilenski, R. *The Meaning of Modern Sculpture*. London 1932
Woolf, V. *Walter Sickert: A Conversation*. London 1934

II. FURTHER READING

(including historical surveys, commentaries, monographs, exhibition catalogues etc.)

Anthony d'Offay Gallery. *S. F. Gore 1878–1914*. Exhibition catalogue. London 1974

Arts Council of Great Britain, Welsh Committee. *British Art and the Modern Movement 1930–1940*. Exhibition catalogue. Cardiff 1962

Arts Council of Great Britain. *William Roberts ARA*. Exhibition catalogue. London 1965

Arts Council of Great Britain. *Decade 1890–1900; Decade 1910–20; Decade 1920–30*. Exhibition catalogues. London 1967, 1965, 1970

Arts Council of Great Britain. *Vorticism and its Allies*. Exhibition catalogue. London 1974

Arts Council of Great Britain. *Thirties: British Art and Design Before the War*. Exhibition catalogue. London 1979

Arts Council of Great Britain and University of Nottingham. *Vision and Design: The Life, Work and Influence of Roger Fry 1866–1934*. Exhibition catalogue. London 1966

Baron, W. *Sickert*. London 1973

Baron, W. *The Camden Town Group*. London 1979

Bell, C. *Victor Pasmore*. Harmondsworth 1945

Bell, Q. *Bloomsbury*. London 1968

Bertram, A. *Paul Nash: the Portrait of an Artist*. London 1955

Bowness, A. (ed.) *Ivon Hitchens*. London 1973

Browse, L. *William Nicholson*. London 1956

Browse, L. *Sickert*. London 1960

Buckle, R. *Jacob Epstein Sculptor*. London 1963

Camden Arts Centre. *Hampstead in the Thirties: A Committed Decade*. Exhibition catalogue. London 1974

Chamot, M. *Modern Painting in England*. London 1937

Colnaghi's. *Edward Wadsworth 1889–1949*. Exhibition catalogue. London 1974

Cork, R. *Vorticism and Abstract Art in the First Machine Age*. Vol. 1: *Origins and Development*. Vol. 2: *Synthesis and Decline*. London 1976

Dangerfield, G. *The Strange Death of Liberal England 1910–1914*. London 1935

d'Offay Couper Gallery. *Abstract Art in England 1913–15*. Exhibition catalogue. London 1969

Dunlop, I. *The Shock of the New*. London 1972

Earp, T. *Frank Dobson Sculptor*. London 1945

Eates, M. (ed.; with essays by Herbert Read, John Rothenstein, E. H. Ramsden and Philip James) *Paul Nash: Paintings, Drawings and Illustrations*. London 1948

Eates, M. *Paul Nash 1889–1946*. London 1973

Egbert, D. *Social Radicalism and the Arts; Western Europe: A Cultural History from the French Revolution to 1968*. New York 1970

Emmons, R. *The Life and Work of Walter Richard Sickert*. London 1941

Evans, M. *Frances Hodgkins*. Harmondsworth 1948

Farr, D. *English Art 1870–1940*. Oxford 1979

Fine Art Society Ltd. *Camden Town Recalled*. Exhibition catalogue. London 1976

Fishman, S. *The Interpretation of Art: Essays on the Art Criticism of John Ruskin, Walter Pater, Clive Bell, Roger Fry and Herbert Read*. Berkeley, Los Angeles, 1963

Gabo, N. (with introductory essays by Herbert Read and Leslie Martin) *Gabo: Constructions, Sculptures, Paintings, Drawings, Engravings*. London 1957

Hall, B. Fairfax. *Paintings and Drawings by Harold Gilman and Charles Ginner in the Collection of Edward le Bas*. London 1965

Halliday, F. *Matthew Smith*. London 1962

Handley Read, C. *The Art of Wyndham Lewis*. London 1951

Hendy, P. *Matthew Smith*. Harmondsworth 1944

Hepworth, B. (ed.; intro. H. Read) *Barbara Hepworth: Carvings and Drawings*. London 1952

Hodin, J. (with a catalogue by Alan Bowness) *Barbara Hepworth*. London 1961.

Imperial War Museum. *A Concise Catalogue of Paintings, Drawings and Sculpture of the First World War 1914–1918*. London 1924. (Second edition 1963)

Ironside, R. *David Jones*. Harmondsworth 1949

Jones, A. *The Life and Opinions of T. E. Hulme*. London 1960

Kettle's Yard. *Artists at War 1914–1918*. Exhibition catalogue. Cambridge 1974

Laughton, B. *Philip Wilson Steer 1860–1942*. Oxford 1971

Lipke, W. *David Bomberg: A Critical Study of his Life and Work*. London 1967

Marlborough Fine Arts Ltd. *Art in Britain 1930–40 Centred around Axis, Circle, Unit One*. Exhibition catalogue. London 1965

Meadmore, W. *Lucien Pissarro*. London 1962

Michel, W. *Wyndham Lewis: Paintings and Drawings*. With an essay by Hugh Kenner. London 1971

Mortimer, R. *Duncan Grant*. Harmondsworth 1944

Mullins, E. *Alfred Wallis: Cornish Primitive Painter*. London 1967

Newton, E. (with a souvenir by Max Jacob) *Christopher Wood: His Life and Work*. London 1959

Newton, E. (ed.) *Christopher Wood*. London 1938

Nichols, R. *William Nicholson*. Harmondsworth 1948

Nicholson, B. (intro. H. Read) *Ben Nicholson*. Vol. 1: *Paintings, Reliefs, Drawings 1911–1948*. London 1948. Vol. 2: *Work since 1947*. London 1956.

Nicholson, B. (intro. J. Russell) *Ben Nicholson: Drawings, Paintings and Reliefs 1911–1968*. London 1969

Portsmouth City Museum and Art Gallery. *Unit 1*. Exhibition catalogue. Portsmouth 1978

Raine, K. *Humphrey Jennings 1907–50: A Tribute*. London 1960

Ray, P. *The Surrealist Movement in England*. Ithaca and London 1971

Read, H. *A Coat of Many Colours*. London 1945

Read, H. *The Grass Roots of Art*. London 1947

Read, H. *The Philosophy of Modern Art*. London 1952

Read, H. *Henry Moore: A Study of his Life and Work*. London 1965

Read, H. (ed.) *Henry Moore*. Vol. 1: *Sculpture and Drawings 1921–1948*. London 1944. (Revised ed. D. Sylvester. London 1957)

Richards, J. *Edward Bawden*. Harmondsworth 1946

Roberts, W. *William Roberts: Paintings and Drawings 1909–1964*. London 1964

Rothenstein, E. *Stanley Spencer*. Oxford and London 1945

Rothenstein, J. *Modern English Painters*. 3 vols. London 1952–74

Royal Academy of Arts. *Rodrigo Moynihan: A Retrospective Exhibition*. Exhibition catalogue. London 1978

Russell, J. *Henry Moore*. Harmondsworth 1973.

Sackville-West, E. *Graham Sutherland*. Harmondsworth 1943

Shone, R. *Bloomsbury Portraits: Vanessa Bell, Duncan Grant and Their Circle*. Oxford 1976

Speaight, R. *The Life of Eric Gill*. London 1966

Spencer, G. *Stanley Spencer*. London 1961

Summerson, J. *Ben Nicholson*. Harmondsworth 1948

Sutton, D. *Walter Sickert: A Biography*. London 1976

Tate Gallery (eds. M. Chamot, D. Farr, and M. Butlin) *The Modern British Paintings, Drawings and Sculptures*. 2 vols. London 1964

Tate Gallery. *London Group 1914–64 Jubilee Exhibition: 50 Years of British Art*. Exhibition catalogue. London 1964

Tate Gallery. *Victor Pasmore*. Exhibition catalogue. London 1965

Tate Gallery. *Ben Nicholson*. Exhibition catalogue. London 1969

Tate Gallery. *Edward Burra*. Exhibition catalogue. London 1973

Tate Gallery. *Paul Nash*. Exhibition catalogue. London 1975

Thorp, J. *Eric Gill*. London 1929

Treece, H. (ed.) *Herbert Read: An Introduction to his Work by Various Hands*. London 1944

Wagner, G. *Wyndham Lewis: A Portrait of the Artist as the Enemy*. London 1951

Wees, W. *Vorticism and the English Avant-Garde*. Toronto 1974

West, A. *John Piper*. London 1979

Wildenstein and Co. *Duncan Grant and his World*. Exhibition catalogue. London 1964.

Woods, St J. *John Piper*. London 1955

Woolf, V. *Roger Fry: A Biography*. London 1940

ADDITIONAL BIBLIOGRAPHY, 1993

Arts Council of Great Britain *Thirties: British Art and Design before the War*. Exhibition catalogue. London 1979

Buck, L. (ed.) *The Surrealist Spirit in Britain*. Exhibition catalogue. London 1988

Carline, R. *Stanley Spencer at War*. London 1978

Causey, A. *Edward Burra*. Oxford 1985

Causey, A. *Paul Nash*. Oxford 1980

Collins, J. *The Omega Workshops*. London 1984

Compton, S. (ed.) *British Art in the Twentieth Century: The Modern Movement*. London and Munich 1986

Cork, R. *David Bomberg*. London and New Haven 1987

Gardiner, M. *Barbara Hepworth: A Memoir*. Edinburgh 1982

Falkenheim, J. *Roger Fry and the Beginnings of Formalist Criticism*. Ann Arbor 1980

Laughton, B. *The Euston Road School*. Aldershot 1986

Grigson, G. *Recollections: mainly of writers and artists*. London 1984

Harries, M. and S. *The War Artists: British Official War Art of the Twentieth Century*. London 1983

Lewison, J. *Ben Nicholson: The Years of Experiment 1919–1939*. Exhibition catalogue. Cambridge 1983

Lewison, J. *Ben Nicholson*. Exhibition catalogue. London 1993

Lewison, J. ed. *Circle: Constructive Art in Britain 1934–40*. Exhibition catalogue. Cambridge 1982

Morris, L. and Radford, R. *AIA. The Story of the Artists International Association*. Oxford 1983

Myers, J. *The Enemy: a Biography of Wyndham Lewis*. London 1980

Nairne, S. and Serota, N. (eds.) *British Sculpture in the Twentieth Century*. London 1981.

Nicholson, W. *Unknown Colour: Paintings, Letters and Writings by Winifred Nicholson*. London 1987

Spalding, F. *British Art since 1900*. London 1986

Spalding, F. *Roger Fry: Art and Life*. London 1980, California 1981

Spalding, F. *Vanessa Bell*. New York and London 1983

Tillyard, S. *The Impact of Modernism. The Visual Arts in Edwardian England*. California 1988

Watney, S. *The English Post-Impressionists*. London 1980

Yorke, M. *Eric Gill: Man of Flesh and Spirit*. London 1981

INDEX

AAA, *see* Allied Artists Association
'Abstract and Concrete' (exh. 1936), 274–5 & 376 n31, 285–6, 319, 377 n53
'Abstract and Concrete Art' (exh. 1939), 316
abstract art/abstraction: apparent disposition to in Fry's and C. Bell's writing, 55, 59; 'visual music', 63; D. Grant's and V. Bell's experiments with, 71; Worringer on, 96; Vorticism and, 104, 111–13, 373 n41; 'radical modernism' and, 118–19; B. Nicholson and, 181, 242, 250, 252–3, 259, 260–65 passim, 277, 287–92; P. Nash and, 234 & 370 n6, 295; Wadsworth and, 236; Moore and, 247–8, 273; Unit One and, 248, 273; association with leftism, 252, 261–2; Abstraction-Création, 260; Hepworth and, 265–71 passim; in Seven & Five, 271–3, 375 n24, 376 n28; 'Abstract and Concrete' exh., 274–5, 285; *Axis* and, 275–8, 319; and Surrealism as antithetical, 278–9, 299–302, 304–6, 313–15, 319–20; and design, 279–82; Gabo and, 282–5; *Circle*, 285–7; Read on, 304–5; Lloyd on, 306; Blunt on, 307; 'social function' of, 313–15; 'Objective Abstractions', 334–7, 341–2; Euston Road School opposed to, 339 & 384 nn22–3; organization of, in France, 374 n8; mentioned, 117, 202, 309, 322, 379 n12; *see also* autonomy, Constructive Art, 'purity', 'radical modernism', universality
'Abstract Art in Contemporary Settings' (exh.), 288
Abstract Expressionism, 337, 374 n4, 383 n17
Abstraction-Création, 249, 260 & 374 nn8–9 & 375 n10, 264, 266, 268, 275, 281, 376 n33
'abstraction, urge to', 95–7
Academy/academician, *see* Royal Academy
Adelphi Gallery; B. Nicholson exh. 1924, 183 & 365 n13
Adeney, Bernard, 62, 67, 115
Aesthetic Movement, 16–17, 57
African sculpture, 82, 107, 218–20
'Against War and Fascism' (exh.), 308
Agar, Eileen, 311, 381 n42
AI/AIA, *see* Artists International/Artists International Association
Aiken, Conrad, 294 & 378 nn1–2
Aldington, Richard, 84, 101–3
Aldridge, John, 184, 235–6, 347
Alley, Ronald, 383 n7
Allied Artists Association, 29–30 & 350 n14, 35, 41, 63, 101, 115, 355 n6
Alpine Gallery, 68–9
America/American art, 19, 80, 90, 156, 258, 260, 280, 285, 292, 311, 324, 340, 355 n5
anarchy/anarchism/anarchist, 47, 75 & 355 n1, 87, 303, 313–14, 316, 333, 383 n7
Apollinaire, Guillaume, 358 n49
Arbuthnot, Malcolm, 102–3
Archipenko, Alexander, 230
Architectural Association, 371 n10
Architectural Review, 321, 371 n9, 382 n49
architecture/architects, 112–13, 117, 157 & 363 n13, 217, 238–41 passim & 371 nn9–10, 12, 249, 259, 264, 271, 276, 280–81, 286–7, 290, 305, 321, 330
Armitage, J. L., 346
Armstrong, John, 106, 235, 240, 248, 273
Arp, Jean (or Hans), 240, 247, 254, 258–60, 264, 275, 298, 304, 319, 379 n10
'Art Concret', 374 n8
'Art d'Aujourd'hui' (exh.), 374 n8
Art Déco, 157
art education, 65, 190, 216 & 368 n18, 219, 282, 286–7, 339, 343, 354 n45, 383 n20, 385 n27

'art for art's sake', 17, 281, 303, 308; *see also* autonomy
Art Front, 380 n23
Art Nouveau, 77
'Art Now' (exh.), 298; *see also* Read
'Artists for Peace, Democracy and Cultural Development' (exh.), 309
Artists International/Artists International Association, 251–2 & 373 nn37–9, 286, 304–9 & 379 n19 & 380 n27, 313, 315, 333, 340 & 384 n24, 381 n37
Arts and Crafts Movement, 73, 212, 213, 268, 354 n48
Arts Council, 115, 340
Ashbee, C. R., 238
Asquith, H. H., 75
Assyrian art, 80, 82, 220
Atelier 17, 310–11 & 380 n30
Atkinson, Lawrence, 101–3, 115, 211 & 368 n11; *Abstract Composition*, 103, ill. 41; *L'Oiseau*, 211 & 368 n11, ill. 111
Attenborough, Mary, 346
autonomy, 60–61, 95; cultural, 14–17; for 'pictorial reality', 259; formal, 124; moral, 307, 314; of aesthetic experience, 48, 365 n12; of art, 146 & 362 n2, 280, 284, 287, 314, 381 n40; of decorative effects, 43; of 'growth' of a picture, 335; of 'imaginative life', 55; of painting, 337; of 'sculptural experience', 210; of technical development, 342; social, 18, 88, 314, 320; technical/of technique, 17, 48, 168, 172, 179, 307, 314, 341, 343, 351 n30; *see also* 'art for art's sake', C. Bell, 'freedom', liberalism (ideology of), 'purity'
Axis, 275–9, 292, 300, 319–21, 375 n24, 376 n31

Babylonian art, 220
Bach, J. S., 71
'Backbeitfeld', 119
Bacon, Francis, 240, 378 n7, 380 n28
Balla, Giacomo, 87
Bankshead, 188 & 366 n20, 199, 365 n7
Banting, John, 311, 317, 347, 381 n42
Barbazanges, Galerie; exhs: 'Quelques Indépendants Anglais', 62; Wadsworth 1927, 370 n1
Baron, Wendy, 26 & 350 nn6–7 & 351 n21 & 352 n10
Barraclough, J. P., 346
Bastien-Lepage, Jules, 20, 350 n7
Bateau-Lavoir, 276 & 376 n36
Bauhaus, 212 & 368 n13, 238–9, 249, 259, 261, 377 nn42–3
Baumeister, Willi, 240
Bawden, Edward, 347
Bayer, Herbert, 249
Bayes, Walter, 29, 85, 131, 196, 359 n12; *The Underworld*, 131
Beaux-Arts Gallery; exhs: B. and W. Nicholson and Wood 1927, 187; Hepworth and Skeaping 1928, 228; Seven & Five 1926–8, 346–7
Beaverbrook, Lord, 359 n12
Beckett, Samuel, 316
Beckmann, Max, 41
Bedford, R. P., 211, 230, 347, 369 n20
Bell, Clive: and autonomy, 17–18 & 348 nn8–10 & 12, 48, 146 & 362 n2; *Art*, 22, 46, 54 & 352 n21, 56–8 & 353 n30, 61 & 354 n37, 64, 94, 100, 165, 349 nn8–9, 352 nn9, 21, 35; and Post-Impressionism, 45–71 passim & 349 n10 & 352 n9; on Cézanne, 46–7, 53; and G. E. Moore, 57–8; 'significant form', 64, 354 n40; on Lewis's *Kermesse*, 80 & 355 n6; on Greek and Italian art, 83; wartime employment, 145; post-war writing and influence, 145–9 passim, 171, 183, 184–5, 190, 218; *Since Cézanne*, 145–6 & 362 n1, 218; on war artists, 146; on Lewis, 146; and Grant, 149–50; and Dobson, 159; in Paris 1919, 186; on Epstein's *Christ*, 208–9 & 367 n6; reaction against in thirties, 307–8; on Sickert, 350 n20; on Bloomsbury set, 353 n32; mentioned, 32, 75, 84, 176, 218, 219, 297, 352 n22, 360 n16
Bell, Graham, 333–5, 338–40, 343
Bell, Quentin, 149 & 363 n8, 353 n32, 355 n49
Bell, Vanessa, 51, 62, 65, 67–72 passim, 150, 178, 180, 191, 198, 308, 334, 353 n32, 379 n19, 383 n20; *A Room at the Second Post-Impressionist Exhibition*, 62, ill. 23; *Triple Alliance*, 70, ill. 28; 'Abstract Painting', 71
Benjamin, Walter, 377 n44
Bennett, Arnold, 351 n1, 363 n14
Bergson, Henri, 87, 95–7 passim, 111, 356 n19
Bernal, J. D., 286
Bernheim Jeune, Galerie, 351 n3; Wood and B. Nicholson exh. 1930, 191 & 366 n25
Bertram, Anthony, 241 & 371 n17, 295
Betjeman, John, 322
Bevan, Robert, 30, 35–6, 38, 41, 84–5
Bigge, John, 235, 240, 248, 273, 310
Binder, Pearl, 251
Birrell, Francis, 353 n32
Bissière, Roger, 346
Black, Mischa, 251
Blake, William, 134, 136, 197, 320, 324–5
Blanche, Jacques-Émil, 36
Blast, 101–2 & 358 n46, 107–12 & 358 nn49–51 & 53, 115–20, 124, 126, 157, 356 n13, 361 n18, 363 n11, 369 n28; page from *Blast* no.1, 102, ill. 40
Bloomsbury/Bloomsbury group/Bloomsbury set: Fitzroy Street, 29; V. Woolf and, 32, 57, 353 n32; and G. E. Moore, 57–8, 353 n34; and Post-Impressionism, 65–74 passim; recruits from Slade, 65–7; and Second Post-Impressionist Exhibition, 67; Friday Club, 67; Grafton Group, 69; Omega Workshops, 72–4; and London Group, 85, 156, 184 & 365 n14; class and cultural character of, 88, 90; Bomberg and, 93–4; Hulme and, 94; and war, 145, 360 n16; post-war influence of, 145–56 passim, 165, 172, 184, 218; Gertler and, 150; Dobson and, 160, 209; and London Artists Association, 184–5; moderation of hegemony of, in early thirties, 233, 241; monopoly on interpreting Cubism,

256; and Euston Road School, 333–4; membership and affiliations of, 353 n32; mentioned, 36, 60, 322, 382 n4; *see also* C. Bell, V. Bell, R. Fry, D. Grant, Omega Workshops, Post-Impressionism
Bloomsbury Gallery: Nicholson exh. 1931, 230
Blossfeldt, 282 & 377 n45
Blunt, Anthony, 307–8, 313, 333–4 & 382 n4
Boccioni, Umberto, 77, 86–7, 356 nn17 & 19
Bolshevism/Bolshevik, 206, 239, 245, 252, 259
Bomberg, David: at Slade, 66 & 354 n45, 152; and Friday Club, 68; on Renaissance, 83; and London Group, 84, 92; class, 89; at Brighton exhibition, 91–2; and Cubism, 92, 130, 178; Chenil Gallery exh., 92–4; Fry and Hulme on, 94; and 'Manifesto of Vital English Art', 101; and Vorticist exh., 115; war service, 121; as war artist, 129–30; post-war years, 147–8; mentioned, 105, 113, 175, 357 n38, 358 n47, 359 n12; *Vision of Ezekiel*, 92; *Ju-Jitsu*, 92–3; *In the Hold*, 92–4, ill. 37; *The Mud Bath*, 92, 94, ill. 36; *Barges*, 147–8, ill. 70
Bonnard, Pierre, 25, 26, 63, 337, 339
Borough Polytechnic, 62
Boswell, James, 251, 307, 380 n31
Bottomley, Gordon, 168–71 passim & 364 n1, 325, 362 n33, 366 n32
bourgeois/bourgeoisie, 217, 284, 300, 305–7 passim, 313–15 passim, 318, 322
Brancusi, Constantin, 80, 82, 209, 247, 254, 264, 266, 268, 273, 275, 276, 286, 304, 327
Braque, Georges, 77, 176–80 passim, 183, 186, 240, 254–5, 263, 298, 334, 357 n36, 374 n4
Breton, André, 234, 302–3 passim, 309, 312–13 & 380 n33, 316 & 381 n40, 376 n38, 381 n43
Breuer, Marcel, 276, 286
Brighton Exhibition, 85–6, 90–91
British Museum, 80, 82, 219–20, 225, 229
British Union of Fascists, 252
broad front, 304, 308
Bronowski, J., 380 n29
Brooke, Rupert, 84
Brown, Ford Madox, 13, 350 n9
Brown, Fred, 19, 21, 33
Browne, Sir Thomas, 244 & 371 n20
Brunius, Jacques, 381 n42
Budd, H. A., 346
Building Centre, 239
Burlington House, *see* Royal Academy
Burlington Magazine, 49, 51
Burne Jones, Sir Edward, 16, 348 n2
Burra, Edward, 233, 235–7, 240, 248, 252, 310; *Dancing Skeletons*, 237, ill. 124
Butterfield, Francis, 271, 273, 344, 347
Byzantine art, 49, 95, 220

Café Royal, 84
Cahiers d'Art, 302–3, 372 n22
Calder, Alexander, 255, 258–60 & 374 n5, 274, 276, 287, 321, 380 n30
Camberwell School of Art, 196, 385 n27
Cambridge/Cambridge University, 51, 274, 275, 307, 310 & 380 n29, 353 n32
Camden Town Group, 28, 35–41, 46, 51, 53, 67, 84–5, 130–31, 145, 153, 159, 203, 337, 339, 341–2, 350 n11
Cameron, D. Y., 359 n12
Canadian War Memorial, 120 & 359 n12, 126, 128–9
Canadian War Records Office, 120
Canaletto, 350 n9
Capel-y-Ffin, 197
capitalism/capitalist system, 252, 281, 303, 315, 340
Carfax Galleries; exhs: Camden Town Group 1911–13, 37–8; Grant 1920, 149
Carlisle, Earl of, 365 n15
Carolus-Duran, 20
Carr, Thomas, 334, 339
Carrà, Carlo, 77, 86–7
Carson, Sir Edward, 111
Cave of the Golden Calf, 80, 84
Central School of Art, 252, 334, 385 n27
Cézanne, Paul: and Post-Impressionism, 46–54 passim, 177; and English Post-Impressionists, 59–60, 65; and Second Post-Impressionist Exhibition, 63; Wadsworth and, 108; P. Nash and, 134, 170, 174, 203 & 367 n37, 241 & 364 n2; Dobson and, 159; Hitchens and, 165–6, 195; B. Nicholson and, 166, 174–7; Seven & Five and, 185; responses to in thirties, 241, 293, 307; Euston Road School and, 334, 339; mentioned, 23, 26, 32, 35, 36, 38, 42, 179, 298, 367 n37
'Cercle et Carré', 374 n8
Chamot, Mary, 22
Chelsea Arts Club; 'Septule and the Racinists' exh., 47
Chelsea Book Club; Negro Art exh., 218
Chelsea School of Art, 245
Chenil Gallery; Bomberg exh. 1914, 92–4, 356 n12
child art/childishness/children, 49, 52–3, 59, 118, 177, 190
Chinese art, 220
Churchill, Winston, 57
Circle: International Survey of Constructive Art, 282, 285–8 & 377 nn52–3, 305, 375 n22, 379 n16
Clark, Kenneth, 364 n23, 383 n6
class struggle, 97, 252, 305, 313–15
Clausen, George, 19, 359 n12
Coates, Wells, 239–40 & 371 n12, 276, 378 n1
Cobden, Richard, 25
Cocteau, Jean, 186–7
Coldstream, William, 332–4, 337–40 & 383 nn14 & 20 & 384 n23, 383 n6, 385 n27
Cole, Ernest, 368 n17, 369 n29
Cole, F., 347
collage, 178–9, 201, 271–2, 300, 310, 317, 321
Colquhoun, Ithell, 381 n42
Communism/Communist, 251, 283–5, 302, 304, 306–8, 313–15, 333, 381 n39; *see also* Marxism, revolution, 'revolution', Socialism
Congrès Internationaux d'Architecture Moderne (CIAM), 286, 371 n12
Conservative Party, 75, 147

Constable, John, 149, 320
Constructive Art, 285–7, 287, 304, 313–14, 341; *see also* Constructivism, N. Gabo
Constructivism/Constructivist, 285–6, 304, 320, 377 n46; *see also* Constructive Art, Productivism
Contemporary Art Society, 298
Contemporary Poetry and Prose, 381 n39
Conway Hall, 313, 315
Cooper, Douglas, 371 n15
Cooper, Kanty, 230, 347
Cornwall, 153, 187–92 passim, 196, 254, 291–3
Cotman, John Sell, 320
Courbet, Gustave, 16, 33, 307, 333
Cowles, G. C., 346
Cox, David, 320
Criterion, 379 n10
Cromwell, Oliver, 111
Cross, Odo, 347
Cubism/Cubist: and Second Post-Impressionist Exhibition, 63–4, 183; Vorticism and, 74, 104–5, 111; Lewis and, 77, 117, 324; Epstein and, 82; Brighton Exhibition, 85–6; and Futurism, 87–8; Bomberg and, 92; *Du Cubisme*, 97 & 357 n36; and Rebel Art Centre, 100; Wadsworth and, 108, 254; B. Nicholson and, 176–81, 185, 198, 254–9, 263, 289, 291; 'African', 177; 'Analytic', 178–80, 200; 'Synthetic' 178–80, 202, 225, 258 & 374 n4, 324; Hitchens and, 183, 195, 273; Nash and, 200–2, 254, 370 n6; Moore and, 225, 230; mentioned, 67, 69, 97, 164, 186, 284, 286, 293, 321, 365 n8, 374 n8, 376 n 36; *see also* Braque, Picasso
'Cubism and Abstract Art' (exh.), 286
'Cubist Art Centre Ltd', *see* Rebel Art Centre
Cubist Room, *see* Brighton Exhibition
Cumberland, 175, 183, 188, 254, 365 n7
Cumberland Market Group, 41, 85, 131

Dacre, Winifred, *see* Nicholson, Winifred
Dada/Dadaism/Dadaist, 258, 299, 365 n11
Daily Express, 252
Daily Mirror, 86, 139
Daily Telegraph, 125–6
Daintry, Adrian, 347
Dali, Salvador, 233, 240, 298, 304, 309, 312
Dalou, Aimé-Jules, 307
Daumier, Honoré, 307
Davidson, Angus 347
Davies, Hugh Sykes, 309, 312 & 380 n33, 381 n39
de Chirico, Giorgio, 200–2 & 367 n34, 234–5, 297, 309, 319, 321
de Gandarillas, Antonio 185–6, 187
de Quincey, Thomas, 372 n21
de Segonzac, Dunoyer, 187
De Stijl, 238
de Vlaminck, Maurice, 45, 47, 63
Debenham, Alison, 347
'Declaration on Spain', 381 n39
Degas, Edgar, 25 & 350 n5, 26, 31, 32, 35, 49, 50, 298, 337, 339
Delaunay, Robert, 260
Delius, Frederick, 80
Denis, Maurice, 49, 348 n4
Derain, André, 45, 60, 63, 92, 176, 186, 231, 241
Design and Industries Association (DIA), 371 n10
Diaghilev, Serge, 186
dialectical materialism, 306
Dickens, Charles, 76
Dieppe, 25, 26, 32, 36, 255, 350 n8, 373 n1
Diploma in Art and Design (Dip AD), 285 n27
Dismorr, Jessica, 102–4, 115, 156, 183, 346
Ditchling, 197, 213 & 368 n16, 368 n14
division of labour, 13, 212, 216, 252
Divisionism, 28, 29
Dix, Otto, 236
Dobson, Frank, 156, 159–60, 187 & 365 n18, 209–10, 211, 369 n29; *The Concertina Man*, 159, ill. 81; *Reclining Nude*, 209, ill. 110
Dodgson, John, 359 n12
d'Offay Couper Gallery; 'Abstract Art in England' (exh.), 355 n5, 359 n54
Domela, César, 273, 274
Doolittle, Hilda, 84
Doré Gallery; exhs.: 'Post-Impressionist and Futurist Exhibition', 88; Italian Futurist painting and sculpture, 100; lecture by Marinetti and Nevinson, 101; Vorticist exhibition, 115
Dorland Hall; 'British Industrial Art in relation to the Home' (exh.), 371 n9
Dostoievsky, Fyodor, 76
Doucet, Henri, 72
Drogheda, Countess of, 100
Druet, 351 n3
Drummond, Malcolm, 36, 85
Drury, Elizabeth, 346
du Plessis, A. G., 347
Duchamp, Marcel, 376 n38
Duncan Miller Ltd.; 'Abstract Art in Contemporary Settings' (exh.), 286
Durand Ruel, 35
Durst, Alan, 230, 346
Dymchurch, 170, 172–3, 364 n4

École de Paris, *see* School of Paris
Eddington, Sir Arthur, 261, 266
Ede, H. S., 233, 275, 277, 298
Edmonds, L. S., 346
Egyptian sculpture, 80, 107, 220
Einfühlung, *see* empathy
Eldar Gallery; Atkinson exh. 1921, 211
Elgar, Edward, 111
Eliot, T. S., 117, 147, 379 n10
Eluard, Paul, 302, 309, 312 & 380 n33, 316, 376 n38
empathy, 95–6
Empson, William, 380 n29
Enemy, The, 302 & 379 n17
Engels, Frederick, 303, 307
English Artists' Cabaret, 80
'English Contemporary Group', *see* Unit One
'English Manifesto of Surrealism', 302–3 & 379 n18
'English Post-Impressionists, Cubists and others', see Brighton Exhibition

Epstein, Jacob: early years, 80, 90; interest in tribal art, 82–3; and London group, 85, 91, 156; and 'Post-Impressionist and Futurist Exhibition', 88; Hulme on, 97–8; and 'Manifesto of Vital English Art', 101; influence on Gaudier-Brzeska, 105; and *Blast*, 111; war service, 122; and Smith, 153; Leicester Galleries exh. 1920, 205–7 & 367 nn1–2; on Rodin, 209; post-war influence, 210, 228–9; and Gill, 212; and Moore, 222, 224, 245; mentioned, 84, 160, 217, 355 n5, 358 n47, 369 nn20 & 29

Works: carvings for the Cave of the Golden Calf, 80; Strand Statues, 80–82 & 355 n8; tomb of Oscar Wilde, 81–2, 222, ill. 32; *Female Figure in Flenite*, 82–3, ill. 33; third *Marble Doves*, 88; *Rock Drill*, 98–100 & 357 n38, 122, 205–6, 210–11, ills. 38, 39; *Risen Christ*, 204, 206–8, ill. 108; *Bust of Lord Fisher*, 204; *Genesis*, 207, ill. 109; *Rima*, 207; *Night* and *Day*, 207; *Ecce Homo*, 207; *Consummatus Est*, 207; *Adam*, 207; *Venus*, 367 n1

Erni, Hans, 271, 274

Ernst, Max, 233, 236, 240, 298–9 passim & 378 n7 & 379 n11, 304, 309, 311, 320, 321, 379 nn10 & 17

Etchells, Frederick, 62, 67, 72, 74, 84, 85, 88–90 passim, 100, 111, 115, 156–7 & 363 n13, 355 n5, 359 nn2 & 12

Etruscan art, 220

Euston Road School, 334, 339–43 passim & 383 n20 & 385 n27, 383 n6

Evans, Myfanwy, *see* Piper, Myfanwy

'Exhibitors to the Public', 88

Experiment, 310 & 380 n29

Expressionism, 100, 111, 117, 164, 248, 299, 379 n12

Fabianism/Fabian, 84, 212

Fascism, 120, 239, 252, 303–4, 308, 358 n53

Fauvism/Fauvist, 38, 45, 63, 64, 100, 104, 153

Federal Arts Project, 340

Fedorovitch, Sophie, 346

Fergusson, Louis, 31 & 350 n15

FIARI, see International Federation of Independent Revolutionary Art

Fiedler, Conrad, 95

Fildes, Luke, 13

'First British Artists Congress', 309

First Surrealist Manifesto, 234, 303

Fitton, James, 251, 307

Fitzroy Street Group, 29–31, 35–6, 51, 84–5, 339

Five on Revolutionary Art, 304–8

Flight, Claude, 183, 184, 346

Flint, F. S., 84

Ford, Ford Madox, 84, 111, 359 n3

Ford, Gordon Onslow, 381 n42

Forster, E. M., 147, 351 n1, 353 n32

Fortnightly Review, 50

'freedom', 130, 164, 181, 258–61, 265–6, 276, 281, 322, 340, 358 n53; 'personal', 49–50

Friday Club, 67–8

Friesz, Othon, 45

Frith, E. S., 346

Fry, Maxwell, 286

Fry, Roger: 'Manet and the Post-Impressionists', 36, 45–51 & 351 n3, 52, 54–65 passim, 67, 69, 351 n3, 352 n7; and Cézanne, 46–7 & 351 n2, 52–3, 59–60, 63, 367 n37; and NEAC, 47; and 'aesthetic response', 49; early career, 51–2; as a painter, 51, 60, 67, 69; aesthetic theories, 52–6, 71, 248, 351 n25, 354 n39; 'The Art of the Bushmen', 53 & 352 n16; 'An Essay in Aesthetics', 54–6, 95 & 352 n25, 369 n27; on Ruskin, 55, 71 & 354 n47; 'Art and Life', 56 & 352 n13; influence, 59–61, 75–6, 148, 171, 176, 183–5 passim, 190, 218–20; and Second Post-Impressionist Exhibition, 62–5, 183; Introduction to the Second Post-Impressionist Exhibition, 63–4 & 354 n39, 370 n6; and Friday Club 67; exh. at Alpine Gallery, 69; and Grafton Group, 69; 'Art and Socialism', 71 & 362 n1, 352 n17; and Omega Workshops, 71–4, 90, 100; and Ideal Home affair, 74, 85, 162, 355 n49; and Renaissance, 83; on Futurism, 87; on Bomberg, 94; Hulme on, 94; and 'traditional modernism', 96, 118; Lewis's view of art contrasted, 118; *Vision and Design*, 145 & 362 n1, 218–19; and Grant, 149–50; and Dobson, 159; taste in French painting, 177; and modernist sculpture, 218–20; 'Ancient American Art', 218; 'Negro Sculpture', 218; reaction against in the thirties, 307–8; mentioned, 175, 250, 353, n32, 380 n23

Works: *White Road with Farm*, 60, ill. 22

Fuseli, Henry, 320

Futurism, 77, 86–91 & 356 nn17–19, 93, 97, 100–2, 109, 111, 116, 117, 123–4, 126, 131, 183, 284, 358 nn46 & 49

Gabo, Miriam, 377 n55

Gabo, Naum, 258, 259–60, 274, 276, 282–9 & 377 nn46 & 50 & 53 & 55, 292, 304–5, 314–15, 377 n40; *Construction on a Plane*, 283, ill. 145

Galerie . . ., *see under name*

Galsworthy, John, 111, 351 n1

Gardiner, Margaret, 233, 277

Garnett, David, 353 n32

Gascoyne, David, 302–4, 309, 336, 381 n39, 385 n26

Gaudier-Brzeska, Henri: at Omega Workshops, 72; on Renaissance, 83; and London Group, 85; and 'Manifesto of Vital English Art', 101; and Pound, 101; and *Blast*, 101–2, 111, 124; and Vorticism, 102, 105–8, 115; and Vorticist exh., 115; death of, 117, 121, 125 & 361 n19; memoir by Pound, 119, 210–11; and war, 121, 124–5; 'Vortex Gaudier-Brzeska', 124; influence, 210–11 & 368 n10, 223 & 369 n28; mentioned, 84, 217, 357 n38, 369 n20, 373 n41

Works: *Hieratic Head of Ezra Pound*, 101; *Red Stone Dancer*, 105, ill. 43; *Ornement Torpille*, 106–7, 211, ill. 44; *Bird Swallowing a Fish*, 106–7, 211, ill. 45; *Crouching Figure*, 107, ill. 46; *Maternity*, 107–8; *Torso*, 210–11

Gauguin, Paul, 25, 26, 35, 36, 38, 42, 45–7 passim, 50, 185
General Strike, 167
George, Waldémar, 370 n1
German Expressionism, 77
Gertler, Mark, 65–6 & 354 n45, 150–52, 198, 360 n16; *The Merry-go-Round*, 150–51 & 363 n10, ill. 73; *Queen of Sheba*, 152, ill. 74
Giacometti. Alberto, 258, 268, 273–4 & 376 n26, 287, 298, 309, 319; *Project for a Piazza*, 268; *Reclining Figure*, 273; *Reclining Woman Dreaming*, 273
Gibson, T. Masson, 347
Giedion, Siegfried, 286
Gieves Gallery; Seven & Five exh. 1921, 346–7
Gill, C. U., 346, 359 n12
Gill, Eric: at Second Post-Impressionist Exhibition, 67; and Jones, 197; *Sculpture*, 212; and carving, 212–16 & 368 n17; modernism of his work, 223; and AIA, 252, 308, 379 n19; on 'Revolutionary Art', 306 & 380 n22; mentioned, 354 n48, 369 n29
Works: *The Golden Calf*, 80; *Stations of the Cross*, 212; *Deposition*, 213–14, ill. 112; *Girl*, 213–14, ill. 113; *Mankind*, 213, 215, ill. 114
Gill, Max, 62
Gill, R. R., 346
Gilman, Harold: at Slade, 21, 43, 76, 152; and Fitzroy Street, 29; and NEAC, 35; and Camden Town Group, 35–6, 38; and Neo-Realism, 41, 71, 351 n30; and Cumberland Market Group, 41; and London Group, 41, 85; works *c.*1912–18, 41–4; war work, 131–2, 359 n12; and Euston Road School, 341–3; mentioned, 51, 84, 356 n21
Works: *The Model, Reclining Nude*, 39, 341–2, ill. 14; *Interior with Mrs Mounter*, 42, ill. 17; *An Eating House*, 42, ill. 18; *Leeds Market*, 43–4, ill. 19; *Halifax Harbour*, 131–2, ill. 61
Ginner, Charles, 30, 35–43 passim, 51, 71, 80, 84, 85, 156, 159, 351 n30, 356 n21, 359 n12; *The Fruit Stall, Kings Cross*, 37, ill. 13
Giotto, 53, 176
Gleizes, Albert, 97 & 357 n36, 260
Gloag, John, 371 n9
Gooding, H. E., 346
Gore, Spencer: at Slade, 21, 29, 76, 152; and Sickert, 26–8 & 350 nn10–11, 50; and Fitzroy Street, 29–30; and Post-Impressionism, 35; and Camden Town Group, 36, 38, 41, 85; and Cézanne, 51; at Second Post-Impressionist Exhibition, 67; and Ideal Home affair, 74; and Lewis, 76, 111; and London Group, 85; and *Blast*, 111; mentioned, 84, 159, 356 n21
Works: *Stage Sunrise, the Alhambra*, 28, ill. 9; *The Balcony at the Alhambra*, 38; *Harold Gilman's House, Letchworth*, 38–9, ill. 15; *Self-Portrait*, 36, ill. 12; decorations for the Cave of the Golden Calf, 80
Gorky, Arshile, 311
Gothic art, 220
Goupil Gallery; exhs: Whistler, 'Nocturnes, Marines and Chevalet Pieces' 1892, 16; 'London Impressionists' 1889, 25; Salon 1913, 41; Ginner and Gilman 1914, 41; first London Group 1914, 85; London Group 1915, 99; Nevinson, war work 1916, 123; Lewis, 'Guns' 1919, 127; P. Nash, 'Drawings made in the Ypres Salient' 1917, 136; Gill 1920, 212; 'Negro Art' 1921, 218; Monet 1889, 349 n7
Gowing, Lawrence, 339, 383 nn7 & 10, 385 nn26 & 27
Goya, 77, 127, 339
GPO Film Unit, 338, 383 n6
Grafton Galleries, 62; exhs: Impressionist paintings 1905, 35; 'Manet and the Post-Impressionists' 1910, 45–6, 52, 61, 65; 'Second Post-Impressionist Exhibition' 1912, 62, 65
Grafton Group, 69, 84
Grahame, Lewis, 347
Grant, Duncan, 36, 51, 62, 67–72, 85, 115, 145, 149–50, 178, 180, 186, 191, 198, 308, 334, 353 nn32 & 34, 379 n19, 383 n20
Works: *The Tub*, 59, ill. 21; *Queen of Sheba*, 69, ill. 27; 'Abstract Kinetic Collage Painting with Sound', 71; *Vanessa Bell*, 149, ill. 71; *Landscape through a French Window*, 150, ill. 72
Grant, J. W., 347
Graphic, The, 206
Gray, Nicolete, 274, 335, 377 n53
Gray, Stewart, 358 n47
Greek sculpture, 80, 217, 220, 221
Greenberg, Clement, 349 n11, 374 n4
Grierson, John, 338
Grigson, Geoffrey, 233, 275–8, 298, 300, 320, 322, 378 n9
Gropius, Walter, 249 & 372 n28, 276, 281, 286
Grosvenor Gallery; Whistler exh. 1877, 14 & 348 n2
Grosz, George, 236, 307, 313
Guernica, see Picasso
Guggenheim Jeune Gallery; 'Abstract and Concrete Art' exh. 1939, 316
Guild of St Joseph and St Dominic, 197, 213

Hamilton, Cuthbert, 72, 74, 85, 101–2, 104, 111, 156, 355 n5, 356 n21
Hampstead, 265, 276, 292, 309, 322
Hardy, Thomas, 30
Harrisson, Tom, 310
Hart, Barry, 368 n18
Hayter, Stanley, 310–11 & 380 n30, 381 n42
Hayward Gallery; 'Vorticism and its Allies' exh. 1974, 355 nn4 & 5
Heal's Mansard Gallery; X Group exh. 1920, 157; Jones and Hitchens exh. 1930, 198
Hélion, Jean, 258, 260, 274–6 & 376 nn 33 & 36, 286–7, 304, 321
Hepworth, A. J., *see* Jackson, Arthur
Hepworth, Barbara: and Epstein, 210, 228–9; and 'truth to materials', 212–13; as student, 217; and the figure, 221–2; 'vernacular modernism' *c.* 1927–32, 226–30; and B. Nicholson, 230, 245–58, 265; and Seven & Five, 230, 254, 269,

271, 344, 347; and Unit One, 240, 242–4 passim, 248, 294; work 1933–4, 244; visits to France 1932–3, 254–8; exh. at Tooth's Gallery 1932, 255; and Arp, 258, 267–8; and Abstraction-Création, 260–61, 266, 268; work and ideas in thirties, 265–71; and Brancusi, 268; and abstract art in England, 271–7 passim, 299–301 passim; and *Circle*, 285–6 & 377 n53; and 'Constructive Art', 287; move to Cornwall, 291–3; and AIA, 308; mentioned, 304, 338, 369 n20, 372 n29, 374 n2, 377 n55
Works: carvings of doves, 228; *Kneeling Figure* (rosewood), 226, 228, 267, ill. 119; *Figure with folded Hands* (alabaster), 229; *Head*, 230; *Large and Small Form* (white alabaster), 243, 267, ill. 127; *Pierced Form* (pink alabaster), 266, ill. 138; *Mother and Child* (1933, 1934), 267; *Two Forms with Sphere*, 267–9, ill. 139; *Discs in Echelon*, 268–9, 273, 344, ill. 140; *Three Forms* (white marble), 269; *Two Forms* (white marble), 269; *Forms in Echelon*, 269–70, ill. 141; standing forms, 269–70
Herbin, Auguste, 63, 240, 260
Hermon, Ruth, 347
'Hiccupstein', 119
Hildebrand, *see* von Hildebrand
Hillier, Tristram, 202, 240, 242, 248, 273, 310, 372 n23; *La Route des Alpes*, 310, ill. 153
historical materialism, 252, 284, 303, 307–8, 315
Hitchens, Ivon, 165–6, 183, 195–6 & 366 n26, 198, 271, 334, 344, 346, 376 n30, 383 n8
Works: *Study of Essential Form*, 176; *Study for a Three-Dimensional Picture*, 165–6; *The Curved Barn*, 166, ill. 85; *Spring Mood*, 195, ill. 101; *Coronation*, 195
Hitler, Adolf, 252
Hodgkins, Frances, 196, 240, 347, 376 n30
Hogarth Press, 340
Hogarth, William, 350 n9
Holding, Eileen, 271–4 passim & 375 n25, 287, 347, 376 n30
Holland, James, 251, 307
Hone, Evie, 346
Honzig, Karel, 282, 286
Howard, Charles, 381 n42
Howes, Alan, 346
Hudson, Nan, 29
Hudson, W. H., 207
Hueffer, Ford Madox, *see* Ford, Ford Madox
Hugnet, Georges, 302, 309, 316, 380 n33
Hulme, T. E: anti-humanism, 82, 83–4; at homes, 84 & 356 n15; and 'radical modernism', 89, 94–8, 111, 372 n26; on Bomberg, 94; 'Modern Art and its Philosophy', 96; disruption of Marinetti–Nevinson lecture, 101; 'Cinders', 102 & 358 n43, 112; and *Blast*, 111–12; and the war, 121–4 passim & 360 n16, 136; Epstein and, 205, 210 & 368 n9; Read and, 248 & 372 n26; mentioned, 105, 107, 258, 279, 356 n22, 357 n29
humanism/anti-humanism, 82, 97, 99, 108, 156, 216, 222, 224, 268, 303, 318, 330; *see also* Hulme, T. E.
Hunt, Sidney, 184, 346, 379 n10
Huxley, Aldous, 147, 360 n16

Ideal Home affair, 73–4 & 355 n49, 86
imagination/imaginative life, 19 & 349 n1, 53, 54–6 & 353 n27, 63, 112, 117–18, 176, 241, 278, 340
Imagism/Imagist, 84, 103, 111
Imperial War Museum, 120, 126, 131, 133, 141, 359 n12, 360 n13, 361 nn25 & 28–9 & 31, 362 n41
Impressionism, 16–17, 19–35 passim, 45–7 passim, 52, 53, 69, 165, 168, 336, 350 n5, 351 n20
impressionism, 22, 26, 109, 335
Indian art, 220
industrialization, 14, 90, 97, 108–9, 125, 157, 349 n5, 358 n52
'Initial Manifesto of Futurism', 86
Innes, J. D., 36
'International Exhibition of Modern Decorative and Industrial Art', 371 n10
International Federation of Independent Revolutionary Art (FIARI), 316
International Literature, 251
International Surrealist Exhibition, 247, 296, 301, 309–12, 319, 323, 337, 377 n53
Ireland's Saturday Night, 250 & 372 n32
Irish News, 250 & 372 n33
Italian Primitives, 175–6, 190

Jackson, Arthur, 271, 273–4, 287, 344, 347
Jakovski, Anatole, 275
Janes, Norman, 346
Japanese art, 220
Japp, Darsie, 359 n12
Jellett, M., 346
Jenkinson, Edith, 346
Jennings, Humphrey, 309–10 & 380 n29, 316–17, 333, 381 nn39 & 42
John, Augustus, 21, 22–4, 29, 36, 40, 65, 76, 85, 130 & 361 n28, 152, 174, 186–7, 191, 224, 308, 334, 341, 359 n12, 379 n19, 383 n20; *The Blue Pool*, 22, ill. 4; *Fraternity*, 361 n28
Jones, David, 184, 196–8 & 366 n27, 273, 344, 347, 368 n16; *Hierarchy*, 197, ill. 103
Jowett, P. H., 346
Joyce, James, 111, 147
Jung, Carl, 248

Kahn, Alphonse, 185
Kahnweiler, D. H., 351 n3
Kandinsky, Wassily, 54 & 352 n22, 62–3, 64, 111, 117, 181, 195, 261, 299, 321, 336, 354 n39, 357 n34
Kauffer, Edward McKnight, 156, 240, 309, 379 n19
Keene, Charles, 350 n9
Keynes, John Maynard, 185, 353 n32, 362 n4
Kisling, Moïse, 186–7, 193
Klee, Paul, 309, 378 n7

Klingender, Francis, 251, 305–7 & 380 n23, 313, 315
Knight, Dame Laura, 379 n19
Kokoschka, Oscar, 380 n30
Konody, P. G., 120, 365 n11, 378 n7
Kramer, Jacob, 115
Kunsthalle, Basel; 'Constructivism' exh. 1937, 286
Kunsthalle, Luzern; 'Thèse, Antithèse, Synthèse' exh. 1935, 286
Kupka, František, 260

Labour party, 75, 147, 167, 252
Lacerba, 101, 358 n49
Lamb, Henry, 29, 36, 67–8, 85, 120, 131, 224, 359 n12; *Portrait of Lytton Strachey*, 67, 68, ill. 26; *Irish Troops in the Judaean Hills*, 131, ill. 60
Lambert, Maurice, 230, 240, 347, 369 n20
landscape, 135–41 passim, 153–4, 157, 165, 167–75 passim, 185, 190–203 passim, 221, 225, 230, 254, 267, 289–91, 295–8 passim, 317–19, 322–7 passim, 329, 369 n27, 383 n20
Lane, Constance, 346
Latapie, Louis, 346
Laurencin, Marie, 187
Lavery, John, 19, 40, 359 n12
Lawrence, D. H., 84, 147, 351 n1, 363 n10
le Corbusier, 238, 286, 363 n13, 371 n12
le Wino, Walter, 346
Lear, Edward, 136
Lechmere, Kate, 74, 100
Lee, Diana Brinton, 381 n39
Lee, Rupert, 309, 381 n39
Leech, John, 350 n9
Leeds City Art Gallery, 170
Leeds College of Art, 219, 228
Lefevre Gallery, 240; exhs: Douanier Rousseau 1926, 190; B. Nicholson 1928, 190; B. Nicholson 1933, 230; Hitchens 1933, 231; B. Nicholson 1935, 264, 276, 375 nn15 & 24; 'Abstract and Concrete' 1936, 274; Dali 1935, 298; Lewis, 'Thirty Personalities' 1932, 162 & 364 n24
Left Review, 307–8, 313, 333, 380 nn23–4, 380 n31
Léger, Fernand, 234, 235, 240, 273, 274, 321, 374 n4
Legros, Alphonse, 20, 21
Leicester Galleries; exhs: Nash, 'Void of War' 1918, 136; Lewis, 'Tyros and Portraits' 1921, 161; Nash 1928, 201; Epstein 1920, 205 & 367 n1; Dobson 1921, 209–10; Gaudier-Brzeska 1918, 210; Seven & Five 1932, 230; Lewis 1937, 324; Nash 1938, 324 & 382 n47; Seven & Five 1931–4, 346–7; Nevinson 1919, 362 n41; Wadsworth 1920, 363 n14; Nash 1924, 364 n2; Epstein 1917, 367 n1
Leighton, Sir Frederick, 125
Lenin, V. I./Leninist, 252, 303
Levy, Simon, 346
Lewis, Percy Wyndham: and Fitzroy Street Group, 29; and Gilman, 29, 44, 131 & 361 n30; and Camden Town Group, 36; at Second Post-Impressionist Exhibition, 67, 79; and Omega Workshops, 72, 74; and Fry, 74, 118, 162 & 364 n23, 177; early years, 76, 90; as a writer, 76, 111–12, 117 & 359 n5, 162; work 1909–12, 76–80; and Epstein, 83; and Grafton Group, 84 & 356 n16; and London Group, 85, 156; and Bergson, 87, 356 n19; and Futurism, 90, 116–17; Introduction to the Cubist Room, 90–91; and Bomberg, 92–3; Hulme on, 97; and Rebel Art Centre, 100–101; and *Blast*, 101–2, 110–12, 116–17, 120, 126; and Vorticism, 102–5, 115–20, 125; and Wadsworth, 108–9, 129, 158; works 1914–15, 112–13 & 359 nn54–5; and Vorticist exh., 115–16; 'Review of Contemporary Art', 117–18; war service, 122; death of Gaudier-Brzeska, 125 & 361 n19; as war artist, 126–7, 129, 359 n12; 'Guns' exh., 127; Bell on, 146; supported during twenties, 147; on Grant, 149; and X Group, 156–60 & 363 n16; portraits, 160–63 & 363 n21; 'Tyros and Portraits' exh., 161–2; 'Thirty Personalities' exh., 162 & 364 n24; post-war influence, 163–4, 176, 209; on Seven & Five, 164; on the 'child-cult', 190–91; Grigson on, 278; on Surrealism, 302 & 379 n17; work in thirties, 324 & 381 n46; and McLuhan, 358 n52; political views, 358 n53; and Unit One, 373 n41; mentioned, 87, 121, 151, 152, 178, 232, 233, 250, 333, 356 n22, 358 n51, 361 n18, 363 n15
Works: *Creation*, 67, 79, ill. 25; Timon of Athens drawings, 67, 79; *Smiling Woman ascending a Stair*, 77–8 & 355 n4, ill. 30; *The Creditors*, 79, ill. 31; *Kermesse*, 80, 88 & 355 nn5, 6; *Composition*, 91, ill. 35; panels for the Countess of Drogheda, 100; *The Crowd* ('Revolution'), 112–13, 114, ill. 51; *Composition in Blue*, 113, ill. 50; *Plan of War*, 115–16, ill. 52; 'Vorticist' interiors, 115 & 359 n3; *A Battery Shelled*, 126–7, ill. 56; *A Canadian Gun-Pit*, 126 & 361 n23; *The No. 2*, 127, ill. 57; self-portraits, 160; *Girl Reclining*, 160, ill. 82; *Mr Wyndham Lewis as a Tyro*, 161, ill. 83; *Portrait of Edith Sitwell*, 162–3, ill. 84
l'Hote, André, 63, 183, 187, 346
Liberal party, 75, 147
liberalism (ideology of), 75, 208, 277, 303, 307–9 passim, 333, 381 n36; *see also* autonomy
Lightfoot, M. G., 36
Liley, William, 346
Lindsay, Sir Coutts, 348 n2
Lipchitz, Jacques, 225, 230; *Woman and Guitar*, 225
Lipps, Theodor, 95
Listener, The, 234, 241
Liverpool Post and Mercury, 250 & 372 n30
'Living Art in England' (exh.), 287, 316
Lloyd, A. L., 251, 305–6
Lloyd George, David, 147
London Artists Association, 184–5, 334
London Bulletin, 316, 333, 382 n49
London County Council, 339
London Gallery; exhs: 'Constructive Art' 1937, 287; 'Living Art in England' 1939, 287; 'Surrealist Objects and Poems' 1937, 316
London Group, 41, 85–6, 92, 94, 99, 115, 153,

154–5, 160, 184–5 & 365 n14, 187, 198 & 366 n29, 233, 345, 361 n18; *see also* Brighton Exhibition
'London Impressionists' (exh.), 25
Losch, Tilly, 239
Louvre, 176
Low, David, 379 n19
Lubetkin, Berthold, 371 n10
Lucas, Colin, 240
Lucas, F. L., 353 n32
Lucas, James, 251
Lurçat, Jean, 202
Lye, Len, 347

MacCarthy, Desmond, 49, 353 n32
MacColl, D. S., 47, 49–50 & 352 n11, 54, 60, 61, 64
MacKechnie, R. G. S., 347
Mackintosh, Charles Rennie, 238
Maddox, Conroy, 381 n41
Madge, Charles, 310
Magritte, René, 298, 309, 318–19
Maillol, Aristide, 80, 159, 367 n6
Malevich, Kasimir, 181 & 365 n11, 184, 261 & 375 n11, 284, 299, 377 n51; *Black Square*, 184
'Manet and the Post-Impressionists' (exh.), 36, 45–51 & 352 n7, 52, 54, 61, 64, 68, 76, 84, 86, 159, 177, 353 n35, 355 n1
Manet, Édouard, 20, 23, 36, 45, 50, 174, 320
'Manifesto of Futurist Painting', 86
'Manifesto of Vital English Art', 100–1 & 357 nn41–2
Manson, J. B., 29, 36, 85
Mantegna, Andrea, 320, 350 n9
Marchand, Jean, 60, 177
Marinetti, Filippo Tommaso, 86–7, 90, 100–1, 109, 126, 358 n53
Marlborough Gallery: Severini exh. 1913, 86
Marriot, Charles, 31–2 & 350 n18
Marsh, Edward, 84
Marshall, Frances, 353 n32
Martin, Leslie, 285 & 377 n53, 288–9, 377 n40
Martin, Sadie, 285
Marx, Karl, 284, 303, 305, 315; *see also* Marxism
Marxism/Marxist, 97, 252, 283–5 passim, 305, 307–8, 313, 315, 320, 382 n4; *see also* revolution, 'revolution', social function of art, Socialism
Masaccio, 224
Mass Observation, 310, 338
Massine, Léonide, 286
Masson, André, 236, 299, 309, 379 n10, 380 n30
Matisse, Henri, 45–6, 50, 61, 63–4, 65, 69–71 passim, 74, 100, 134, 153–4, 176, 185, 186, 195, 196, 198, 234, 291, 298, 334, 337, 353 n35, 354 n39; works shown at 'Manet and the Post-Impressionists', 63
Mayan art, 220
Mayor Gallery, 316, 371 nn14–15; exhs: Hitchens 1925, 183; reopening exh. 1933, 233, 240, 298 & 378 n7; 'Unit One' 1934, 243, 250, 294, 296; Ernst 1934, 298, 379 n11; Miró 1934, 298; 'Art Now' 1933, 298
McCullough, J. R. R., 346
McEvoy, Ambrose, 359 n12
McGrath, Raymond, 371 n9
McGuiness, Norah, 347
McLuhan, Marshall, 358 n52
McQuoid, Winston, 347
medieval art, 95, 218, 357 n31
Medley, Robert, 333, 347
Mednikoff, Reuben, 381 n42
Mendelsohn, Eric, 276
Mesens, E. L. T., 309, 316, 381 n42
Mesopotamian sculpture, 229 & 370 n34
Metaphysical painting, 200–2
Metropolitan Museum of Art, New York, 51, 351 n3
Metzinger, Jean, 97 & 357 n36
Meunier, Constantin, 307
Mexican art, 220, 225 & 370 n31, 384 n22
Michelangelo, 54, 222 & 369 n27, 224, 350 n9
middle class(es), 32, 56, 71, 73, 88, 89, 223, 238
Milhaud, Darius, 379 n17
Miller, Henry, 316
Millet, Jean-François, 26, 33
Ministry of Information, 120 & 359 n12, 124, 126, 129, 141 & 362 n41
Minotaure, 278 & 376 n38
Miró, Joan, 233, 236, 245–7, 255, 258–9 & 374 n4, 274, 298, 299, 304, 309, 380 n30
Modern Architectural Research Society (MARS Group), 239 & 371 n12
Modern Movement (in art, design and architecture), 13, 212, 234, 238–9 & 371 n9, 249, 253, 264, 268, 276, 280–81, 284–5, 288, 290
modern movement (in English art), 37, 46, 52, 60, 66, 237–9, 310
Modernism (as a critical position), 18 & 359 n11, 31, 46, 56, 168, 172, 176, 179, 208, 212, 221, 362 n2, 365 n12, 368 n18; *see also* autonomy, C. Bell, R. Fry, Hulme, 'purity', 'radical modernism', Read, universality, Wilenski
Moholy-Nagy, Laszlo, 249, 260, 274, 276, 286, 287, 304, 308, 321
Modigliani, Amadeo, 82, 92, 209, 298
Mondrian, Piet, 258 & 374 n5, 260, 261, 263 & 375 n14, 274, 275, 276, 286–9 passim & 377 n55, 292, 299, 304
Monet, Claude, 17 & 349 n7, 19, 20, 25, 26, 35, 46, 49, 50, 334–6 passim, 341; *Rouen Cathedral*, 335
Moore, G. E., 57–8, 122, 353 n34
Moore, Henry: and Epstein, 210, 222, 245, 355 n8; and Gaudier-Brzeska, 210–11 & 368 n10, 223 & 369 n28; and 'truth to materials', 213; and Gill, 213; and Royal College of Art, 217, 219, 223 & 369 n29, 245, 368 n18; and Greek and Renaissance art, 217; influence of Fry, 218–19; and British Museum, 219–20, 229; and the figure, 221–2; and Michelangelo, 222 & 369 n27; exh. at Warren Gallery, 224, 371 n11; early reclining figures, 224–6; and Picasso, 225 & 370 n32,

Moore, Henry *cont.*
230, 245–7 & 372 n22, 298, 319, 329; 'vernacular modernism', 226–30, 232; and Seven & Five, 230, 254, 271–4 & 376 n30, 344, 347; in 'Recent Developments in British Painting', 235–6; and Unit One, 239–40, 247–8, 294 & 378 n1, 326; work 1931–3, 242–8; exh. at Leicester Galleries, 245; and Brancusi, 247, 268, 273; and AIA, 252, 308, 379 n19; and Giacometti, 273, 298; and abstract art, 273–4; and *Axis*, 276, 278; Grigson on, 278; and Circle, 286; in 'Constructive Art' exh., 287; and Surrealism, 287, 298, 300, 302 & 379 n16, 316–19; and International Surrealist Exhibition, 309; drawings, 323, 329; 'Notes on Sculpture', 326–7; work and ideas 1935–9, 326–31; mentioned, 265, 303, 338, 344, 347, 369 nn20 & 24 & 30, 370 n34, 372 n29, 381 nn36, 39
Works: *Torso*, 210–11; *Dog*, 211; *Mother and Child* (Hornton stone), 222–4, ill. 115; *Reclining Figure* (Hornton stone), 224–6, ill. 116; *Reclining Figure* (Ancaster stone), 225; *Torso* (cast concrete), 225; *Head and Shoulders* (Verde di Prato), 225; *Half-Figure* (cast concrete), 225–6, ill. 117; *Mother and Child* (green Hornton stone), 226–7, ill. 118; *Reclining Figure* (carved concrete), 226; *Half-Figure* (veined alabaster), 229; *Head of a Woman*, 230; *Composition* (blue Hornton stone), 245–6 & 372 n22, ill. 129; *Reclining Figure* (lead, 1931), 246–7, 309, 327, ill. 130; *Composition* (carved concrete), 247, ill. 131; *Four-Piece Composition: Reclining Figure* (Cumberland alabaster), 272–3, 344, ill. 143; *Square Form* (green Hornton stone), 274, ill. 144; *Reclining Figure* (lead, 1939), 316; *Reclining Figure* (elm, 1936), 328, ill. 159; *Reclining Figure* (elm, 1939), 329, ill. 160; *Recumbent Figure* (green Hornton stone), 329–30, ill. 161; *Madonna and Child* (Northampton), 369 n25
Morgan, Pierpont, 51–2, 352 n17
Morley, Harry, 346
Morrell, Lady Ottoline, 145, 360 n12
Morrell, Philip, 145
Morris, William, 13–14 & 348 n1, 16–17 & 349 n5, 19, 24–5, 56–7, 71–3 passim, 212, 238, 281, 357 n31, 365 n15
Mortimer, Raymond, 339, 353 n32
Morton, Alastair, 287
Morton, H. T. J., 353 n32
Moynihan, Rodrigo, 334–7 & 383 nn9–11 & 14–16 & 384 n26, 339–42 passim, 383 n7, 385 n27; *Objective Abstraction no.1*, 336–7, 340–41, ill. 163
Mumford, Lewis, 286
Munich, 54, 66, 76, 357 n34
Munnings, Alfred, 40
Muntz, Betty, 184, 230, 347
Murray, William Staite, 184, 271, 344, 347, 376 n30
Museum of Modern Art, New York; exh. 'Cubism and Abstract Art', 286
Mussolini, Benito, 308, 358 n53
Nabis, 16 & 348 n4
Nash, John, 41, 85, 131 & 361 n31, 132, 198, 334, 359 n12, 383 n20; *Over the Top*, 131 & 361 n31; *Oppy Wood*, 131–2, ill. 62
Nash, Paul: on Tonks, 22 & 350 n4; on the Post-Impressionist exhs., 65; and Slade, 65–6 & 354 nn42 & 45, 135, 172; at Omega, 72, 135; and London Group, 85, 198; war service 113, 121, 136; and Vorticism, 119; early works, 134; as war artist, 134–41 & 362 nn39 & 41, 359 n12; exhs. of war work, 136; post-war 'struggles', 147; and Lewis, 163–4; in early twenties, 167–74 & 364 nn1–4; and B. Nicholson, 172–4, 375 n15, 376 n28; work in later twenties, 199–203 & 366 n32, 367 n36; and de Chirico, 200–2; exh. at Leicester Galleries, 201, 234; exh. at Warren Gallery, 224; and European art in early thirties, 232–4; writing on art, 234–9 & 370 n6; and Modern Movement, 238–9; and Unit One, 239–42 & 371 n16, 248, 250, 275, 286, 294–5 & 378 nn1–2, 300, 371 n7; work 1930–3, 244–5, 370 n3, 371 n20; and AIA, 252, 379 n19; and *Axis*, 275–6, 279, 300; and Surrealism, 233, 298 & 379 n11, 300–2, 309–10, 316–19, 324; work 1934–7, 294–8 & 378 nn3–6, 300; and International Surrealist Exhibition, 309–10; and *London Bulletin*, 316; in 'Living Art in England' exh., 316; M. Piper on, 320–21; and Romantic Revival, 322; work in later thirties, 324–6; mentioned, 175, 176, 177, 197, 254, 265, 288, 338, 350 n4, 362 n33, 371 n11, 376 n32, 381 nn39, 45
Works: *The Three in the Night*, 134, ill. 64; *The Landscape – Hill 60*, 136–7 & 362 n41, ill. 66; *Landscape – Year of our Lord 1917*, 138, 141, ill. 66; *The Menin Road*, 139, 141, 362 n39, ill. 67; *After the Battle*, 140–41, ill. 68; *We are Making a New World*, 140–41, ill. 69; *The Mule Track*, 141; *Wooded Hills in Autumn*, 169, ill. 86; *The Shore*, 170–71, ill. 87; *Dymchurch Wall*, 172–3, ill. 88; *Walnut Tree*, 199, ill. 104; *Cactus*, 200; *Autumn Crocus*, 200; *Dead Spring*, 200; *Landscape at Iden*, 200–1 & 366 n32 & 367 n36, ill. 105; *Northern Adventure*, 201 & 366 n33, 232, ill. 121; *Opening* ('Opening Abstract'), 202; *Wood on the Downs*, 202–3 & 367 n36, ill. 107; *Kinetic Feature*, 234–5, ill. 122; *Urne Buriall* illustrations, 244; *Event on the Downs*, 244, ill. 128; *Landscape of the Megaliths*, 295–6, 309–10, ill. 150; *Equivalents for the Megaliths*, 247, ill. 151; *Harbour and Room*, 297, 301, 309, ill. 152; *Voyages of the Moon*, 297; *Encounter in the Afternoon*, 309; *Mansions of the Dead*, 309; *Landscape from a Dream*, 317–18 & 381 n43, ill. 155; *Monster Field*, 325–6 & 382 n49, ill. 158; *The Lake/Chestnut Waters*, 364 n2; *Winter Sea*, 364 n4; *Monster Shore*, 382 n49
National Gallery, London, 50, 52, 320, 383 n6
National Gallery of British Art, *see* Tate Gallery
National Gallery of Canada, Ottawa, 120, 338, 361 nn18, 23, 25, 362 n41
Nature, 55, 57, 94, 97, 112, 117, 190, 240, 261, 292, 295–6, 326, 381 n46

Nazism/Nazi, 259, 276, 280, 281
NEAC, see New English Art Club
'Negro art', *see* African sculpture
Neo-Impressionism, 37
Neolithic art, 220
'neo-picturesque', 322
'Neo-Primitives', 65
'Neo-Realism', 41 & 351 n28, 43, 351 n30
'neo-romantic', 322
'Neo-Traditionism', 348 n4
Neutra, Richard, 286
Nevinson, C. R. W.: at Slade, 65–6 & 354 n45, 152; and Friday Club, 68; and Rebel Art Centre, 74; at Hulme's at homes, 84; and London Group, 85; and 'Post-Impressionist and Futurist Exhibition', 88; and Futurism, 88, 90, 123–4; 'Manifesto of Vital English Art', 100–1; and *Blast*, 101; war service, 113, 121; and Vorticist exh., 115; exh. at Goupil Gallery, 123; as war artist, 123–6, 131 & 361 n29, 135, 141, 359 n12, 362 n41; mentioned, 175, 355 n5
Works: *Departure of the Train de Luxe*, 88 & 356 n21; *The Arrival*, 89, ill. 34; *Returning to the Trenches*, 122 & 361 n18, ill. 53; *La Mitrailleuse*, 123, ill. 54; *Harvest of Battle*, 124–5, ill. 55; *Searchlights*, 361 n18; *The Food Queue*, 361 n29; *Paths of Glory*, 362 n41
New Age, 30, 84, 94, 95
New Burlington Galleries; exhs: International Surrealist Exhibition 1936, 309; *Guernica* 1938, 334 & 382 n3; Wood retrospective 1938, 382 n3
New English Art Club, 19–22, 25, 26, 28, 33, 35, 37, 47, 51, 53, 349 nn7 & 3, 352 n8
New English Weekly, 251, 336, 375 n25
New Gallery; Burne-Jones exh. 1893, 16
'new movement'; *c*.1910: 45–7 passim, 51, 56, 59, 61, 64, 73, 351 n30; *c*.1933: 238–9, 275, 294–5
New Realism, 236
New Review, 84
Newman, Barnett, 375 n22
Nicholson, Ben: at Slade, 65–6 & 354 n45, 172; and Lewis, 161, 164 & 363 n15; exh. at Patersons, 166; and Seven & Five, 166, 183–5, 190–91, 196, 198, 230, 254, 271–5 passim, 344, 346, 376 n28, 378 n1; in early twenties, 167, 172–83; and Cézanne, 177; and P. Nash, 172–4, 297–8; and Cubism, 177–81, 185, 198, 254–9; and Wood, 186, 187–91 passim & 365 n18 & 366 nn19–20 & 25; exh. at Beaux-Arts Gallery, 187; and Wallis, 188–90; landscapes 1928–30, 188, 190–92, 203; compatibility with sculptors in twenties, 218; and Hepworth, 230, 254–5, 258, 265–7; exhs. at Lefevre and Bloomsbury Galleries, 230; and European art in early thirties, 232–3; in 'Recent Developments in British Painting', 235–6; and Unit One, 240, 242, 248, 250, 252–3, 294 & 378 n1; work and ideas in early thirties, 254–66 & 375 n12; contacts with European artists 1932–3, 254–9; and Mondrian, 256, 261, 262 & 375 n14, 276, 288–9; and Abstraction-Création, 260–61; white reliefs, 263–5 & 375 n15, 271, 273, 276–7, 288, 290–91, 344, 372 n34; and abstract art in England, 271–7 passim, 299–300; J. M. Richards on, 276; Grigson on, 277; and *Circle*, 285–8 & 377 n53; and 'Constructive Art', 287–8; work in later thirties, 288–93; Martin on, 288–9 & 377 n55; and AIA, 308; in *London Bulletin*, 316; mentioned, 244, 304, 320, 338, 365 n10, 375 n24
Works: *Dymchurch*, 173–4, ill. 89; *Cortivallo Lugano*, 175–6 & 364 n5, ill. 90; *Trout*, 179–80, 182, 185, ill. 91; *First Abstract Painting*, 181–2 & 365 n11, 185, ill. 92; *Goblet and Pears*, 182, ill. 93; *Pill Creek, Moonlight*, 189, ill. 95; *Birch Craig*, 192, ill. 97; *Walton Wood Cottage no. 1*, 190; *Still Life 1933–5*, 242, ill. 125; *Au Chat Botté*, 255–6 & 373 n1, ill. 132; *Auberge de la Sole Dieppoise*, 256; *Guitar*, 256–7, ill. 133; *Composition in Black and White*, 257, ill. 134; *December 1933 (First Abstract Relief)*, 262, ill. 135; *2 Circles*, 263; *White Relief* (1934), 263, ill. 136; *White Relief* (1935), 264–5, ill. 137; *Painting* (1935), 289, ill. 147; *Painting* (1937), 289; *White Relief* (1939), 290, ill. 148; *Painted Relief* (1939, Stromness), 291; *Painted Relief* (1939, New York), 292, ill. 149; *Winter in Cortivallo*, 364 n5
Nicholson, William, 23–4, 66, 166, 185; *A Downland Scene*, 23, ill. 5
Nicholson, Winifred, 175–6 & 365 n7, 183–92 passim & 366 nn19–20 & 22, 254, 271, 275, 285–7 passim, 344, 346, 364 n5, 375 n12, 376 n30, 377 n55; *Seascape with Dinghy*, 192, ill. 96
non-figurative art, *see* abstract art
non-representational art, *see* abstract art
North American Indian art, 220
'North Staffs', *see* Hulme, T. E.

Oakley, A. J., 346
'Objective Abstractions' (exh.), 198, 334–7 & 383 n7, 341–2, 383 nn8 & 17
Oceanic sculpture, 105, 107, 218, 220
Omega Workshops, 71–4, 84, 85, 90, 100, 101, 104, 105, 135, 150, 180
Orage, A. R., 84
O'Rourke, Brian, 240
Orozco, José Clemente, 339 & 384 n22
Orpen, William, 40
Ozenfant, Amédée, 235, 321

Paalen, Wolfgang, 309
Pailthorpe, Dr Grace, 381 n42
Painter's Object, The, 321–2, 324, 326–7
paleolithic art, 107, 220
Palmer, Samuel, 134, 136, 320, 322–3
pantheism, 96, 223, 318–19
Paris: NEAC connections with, 19, 20; Gilman and Ginner in, 35; Camden Town Group and, 36–7, 41; Fry in, 52; C. Bell and, 54, 68, 146, 186; 'Quelques Indépendants Anglais' exh., 62; Grant in, 68, 69; Lewis and, 76; Futurist work shown in, 77; Epstein in, 80–83; sculpture in, *c*.1900–14, 80, 82, 209; Nevinson with Severini

Paris *cont.*
in, 88; Bomberg in, 92; Dismorr a student in, 103–4; hegemony of, 146, 321, 350 n20; Smith in, 152–3; prevalence of 'classicism' in early twenties, 156–7, 186; B. Nicholson visits to 1920–3, 176, 177, 178; Wood and, 185–8 passim, 193, 201, 231; Parisian painters in 1920s, 186–7; Hodgkins in, 196; London Group and, 198; Moore's visits to, 225; Wadsworth exh. in, 231; P. Nash in, 233, 275, 376 n32; Abstraction-Création, based in, 249, 259–60; B. Nicholson and Hepworth visits to, 254, 256, 262; Gabo in, 258; work seen by B. Nicholson in, during early thirties, 258–9; developments in art in, during later twenties, 258; Miró in, 258; Calder in, 258–9; émigrés in, 259–60; W. Nicholson living in, 271; interest in Unit One in, 275; M. Piper visit to, 275; and Surrealism, 302, 379 n10; Gascoyne living in, 302; Penrose living in, 309; Atelier 17, 310, 380 n30; text of 'Towards an Independent Revolutionary Art' sent from, 316; International Exhibition of Modern Decorative and Industrial Arts, 371 n10; Bateau-Lavoir, 376 n36; Luxembourg, 376 n9; Trevelyan in, 380 n30; *see also*: Barbazanges; Bernheim Jeune; Druet; Kahnweiler; Louvre; Percier; Père Lachaise; Rosenberg, Léonce; Rosenberg, Paul; Sagot; Salon d'Automne; Salon des Indépendants; School of Paris; Vollard
Parkes, Kineton, 368 n17, 369 n29
Partridge, Ralph, 353 n32
Pascin, Jules, 187, 193
Pasmore, Victor, 334 & 383 n6, 337, 339 & 383 n20, 341–2, 383 n7, 385 n27
Passchendaele, 138, 362 n39
Patersons Gallery; exhs: B. Nicholson 1923, 166, 183 & 365 n13, 364 n5, 365 n13; Seven & Five 1924, 166, 346–7; Seven & Five 1923, 346–7
Pears, Charles, 120
Pearson-Righetti, L. 346
Pellerin, 35
Penguin Club, New York; exh. of Vorticist works, 120
Penguin Modern Painters, 364 n23
Penrose, Roland, 277, 309–10, 316, 333, 347, 375 n25, 380 n28, 381 nn39 & 42
Penrose, Valentine, 381 n39
Percier, Galerie; Calder exhs. 1931–2, 259
Père Lachaise cemetery, 81
Persian art, 220
Peruvian art, 220
Pevsner, Antoine, 259, 260, 283–4, 285, 286
photography, 103, 120, 220, 239, 296 & 378 n5, 320, 382 n49
Picasso, Pablo: works seen by Gilman and Ginner, 35; in 'Manet and the Post-Impressionists', 45, 47, 50; parodied in Chelsea Arts Club, 47; older generation's response to, 50, 61; Sickert on, 50; in Second Post-Impressionist Exhibition, 63; Omega Seccessionists and, 74; Lewis and, 77, 116, 117; Epstein and, 82; Bomberg and, 92; Wadsworth and, 108; P. Nash and, 134, 234 & 370 n6, 325; B. Nicholson and, 176–81 passim, 254–5, 291; characteristics of Cubist work, 178–81, 291, 374 n4; Wood and, 186–7, 191, 193; Moore and, 225 & 370 n32, 230, 245–7 & 372 n22, 316–17, 318–19; Hepworth and, 230, 254–5, 266; Piper and, 273; representation of work in England, 298 & 378 n9; Read on, 299; in International Surrealist Exhibition, 309; C. Richards and, 311; in *Painter's Object*, 321; controversy over *Guernica*, 334, 382 n4; G. Bell on, 340; Greenberg on, 374 n4; mentioned, 41, 87, 185, 339, 357 n36, 380 n30
Works: *Tête d'Homme*, 63; *Demoiselles d'Avignon*, 77; *Trois Baigneuses, La Source*, 225; *Figure by the Sea* (7.4.29), 245; *Still Life with Classical Head*, 255; *Profile*, 298; *Girl with Tambourine*, 316–17; *Guernica*, 325, 334 & 382 n4
Pillico, Lena, 346
Piper, John, 271–3, 274–6 passim, 287, 308, 316, 319–22, 344, 347, 376 n30
Piper, Myfanwy, 231, 275, 277, 292, 319–22
Piscator, Erwin, 313
Pissarro, Camille, 25, 30, 50
Pissarro, Lucien, 28, 30, 36–7, 38
Poesia, 86
Pointillism, 37
Post-Impressionism/Post-Impressionist, English: Camden Town Group, 38; as a group, 51, 62; at Second Post-Impressionist Exhibition, 64–9 passim; 'community' of, 1910–13, 84–5; class and cultural character of, 88–90; and war, 120, 131; post-war hegemony of, 145, 148–9, 155; Gertler and, 150–51; and London Group, 155, 198; B. Nicholson distinguished from, 176–7; P. Nash and, 199; Aldridge, 236; *see also* C. Bell, V. Bell, Bloomsbury, Brighton Exhibition, Grant, R. Fry, London Group, Omega Workshops, Post-Impressionism (in general)
Post-Impressionism/Post-Impressionist (in general): Sickert and, 26, 28, 47–51 passim; Gore and, 28, 51; and Camden Town Group, 35–8; Gilman and, 42–3 & 351 n30, 51; C. Bell and, 46, 47, 64; controversy over in 1910–12, 47–51, 64; Fry's distinction between Impressionists and, 52–3; Fry's lecture on, 54; effects on Slade, 64–5; and furniture and decoration, 72–3, 100, 150; challenge to orthodoxy of, 74, 86, 88, 100; as 'Revolution in Art', 75; Futurism and, 88, 100; Vorticists distinguished from, 101, 102; P. Nash and, 136, 174, 234 & 370 n6; Seven & Five and, 184–5; London Group and, 184–5, 198, 233; close of era of domination by, 234; mentioned, 69, 82, 83, 97, 101, 279; *see also* C. Bell, Cézanne, R. Fry, 'Manet and the Post-Impressionists', English Post-Impressionism, Second Post-Impressionist Exhibition
'Post-Impressionist and Futurist Exhibition', 88
Pound, Ezra, 70, 80, 84, 100–3 passim, 110–11 passim, 117, 119–20 & 359 n10, 210–11, 357 n38, 358 n53
Power, J. W., 235, 240, 346
Poynter, Sir Edward, 30, 54

Pre-Raphaelite/Pre-Raphaelite Brotherhood, 51, 133, 134, 164, 168–9 & 364 n1, 185 & 365 n15, 240–41, 278, 357 n31
'primitive'/primitivism: Fry's and Bell's interest in, 49, 52, 59, 118, 218, 353 n35; 'Neo-Primitives', 65; Lewis's 'modern primitives', 76, 119; in tomb of Oscar Wilde, 82; in *Mud Bath*, 94; in *Rock Drill*, 99; B. Nicholson's interest in, 175–7 passim; Douanier Rousseau, 176, 190; Seven & Five and, 190; cult of in 1920s, 190; and sculpture in 1920s, 217–18, 223, 225; Moore and, 224, 225 & 370 n32, 369 n24; in late thirties, 293; *see also* African sculpture, child art, Italian Primitives, 'purity'
Principia Ethica, *see* Moore, G. E.
Pritchard, Jack, 276
Productivism, 283–5 & 377 n50
proletariat/proletarian, 303, 307, 313–16 passim
psychology, 95–7 passim, 241, 248, 273, 278, 300, 318, 329–30, 357 n31
Pugin, A. W. N., 281, 357 n31
Purism, 235, 238, 239, 263, 349 n11
'purity': and technical autonomy, 17; and aesthetic experience, 55, 56, 64, 176; increasing, in art, 56; as an aspect of form, 94, 308; of early Renaissance art, 176; in works of art, 271; in life and interior décor, 271; of abstract art, 300; *see also* autonomy, child art, 'primitive'

Quinn, John, 210, 355 n5, 359 n2, 362 n3

'radical modernism', 87, 96–100, 107, 118–21, 131, 162–3, 360 n16, 372 n26; *see also* Hulme, Lewis, Futurism
Raine, Kathleen, 380 n29
Ratcliffe, William, 36
Ray: art miscellany, 184, 379 n10
Ray, Man, 309
Rea, Betty, 251, 379 n20
Read, Herbert: writing for *The Listener*, 234; *Art and Industry*, 239, 248, 249–50, 279, 371 n9; and Unit One, 248–51 & 372 n23; 'Psychoanalysis and the Critic', 248, 379 n16; *The Meaning of Art*, 248–9 & 372 n24; *Art Now*, 248–9 & 372 n25, 279, 299 & 379 n12; introduction for *Unit 1*, 249–51, 261; on art and politics, 260 & 374 n7, 261–2; and *Axis*, 275–6; 'A Nest of Gentle Artists', 276; on abstract art and design, 279, 281–2, 304–5; *Art for Society*, 281–2; and *Circle*, 286, 379 n16; on Dadaism, 299; and Surrealism, 299, 304 & 379 n16, 309, 312–13, 316 & 381 n42, 333, 380 n33, 381 n42; on 'Revolutionary Art', 304–5; and International Surrealist Exhibition, 309, 312, 319, 380 nn28 & 31; and *London Bulletin*, 316, 333; and 'Realism', 333–4 & 382 nn2, 4; mentioned, 219, 233, 353, n27, 358 n43, 372 nn22, 26, 29, 373 n41, 377 n55, 379 n19, 381 n39
realism/'realism': of Camden Town painting, 41; pessimistic, of Lewis and Hulme, 112; professional, of Pears, 120; documentary, of J. Nash, 131; introspection and, in P. Nash, 169; heightened, in *Rock Drill*, 206; aspiration to, 278; lack of in abstract art, 305; idealized, in Surrealism, 306; heightened, in Hillier, 310; blurred, in Pasmore, 337; Coldstream and G. Bell and, 338; and Euston Road School, 339 & 384 nn22–3, 341–2; Moynihan, G. Bell and Tibble and, 340; 'documentary', as antithesis to technical autonomy, 343
Realism/Realist, 16, 26, 41, 43, 333–4; *see also* Neo-Realism, New Realism, Realistic Manifesto, Social Realism, Socialist Realism
'Realistic Manifesto', 284 & 377 n50
Rebel Art Centre, 74, 100–1, 103, 357 n40
'Recent Developments in British Painting' (exh.), 235–7
Renaissance (Italian), 51, 82–3, 96–7, 176, 217, 224
Renoir, Auguste, 20, 26, 35, 151
Revel, J. D., 346
revolution: in society, 13, 75; Russian, 206, 238, 259, 280, 282, 285
'revolution': 'in Art', 75; radical modernist fixations with, 87, 97; Lewis's painting known as, 113; 'revolutionary rich', 190; Gill on, 213; Modern Movement's aspirations to, 239; *Circle* and idea of, 287; Surrealism and idea of, 302–6, 312–17 passim; abstract art and idea of, 304–6; competing views on in thirties, 313–15, 337; *Guernica* and, 382 n4; Mexican muralists and, 384 n22; *see also* Communism, *Five on Revolutionary Art*, Marxism, Socialism, 'Towards an Independent Revolutionary Art'
Richards, Ceri, 311, 334
Richards, J. M., 276, 286, 375 nn24–5
Riegl, Alois, 95, 357 n31
Rimmington, Edith, 381 n42
Rivera, Diego, 316 & 381 n40, 339–40 & 384 n22
Roberts, William: at Slade, 66 & 354 n45; at Omega Workshops, 72, 355 n49; and London Group, 85, 198; and 'Manifesto of Vital English Art', 101; and Vorticist manifesto, 102; and Vorticism, 104–5, 115; and *Blast*, 111; and Vorticist exh., 115; war service, 122; as war artist, 122, 129 & 361 n25, 359 n12; and X Group, 156; work since 1920, 158–9; and Cubism, 178; and Unit One, 240; mentioned, 89, 175, 357 n38
Works: *The Toe Dancer*, 104 & 358 n47, ill. 42; *The Gas Chamber*, 129, ill. 59; *The Cinema*, 158, ill. 80; *The First German Gas Attack at Ypres*, 361 n25; *A Shell Dump, France*, 361 n25
Roberts, Winifred, *see* Nicholson, Winifred
Rodchenko, Alexander, 284
Rodin, Auguste, 209, 367 n6
Rogers, Claude, 334, 339 & 383 n20, 385 n27
Rogers, Gilbert, 359 n12
Romanesque art, 220
Romantic Movement, 174, 190, 312, 322
Romantic Revival, 174, 319–24
Rosenberg, Léonce, 233
Rosenberg, Paul, 178
Rosenberg and Heft Gallery; Sutherland exh. 1938, 382 n47

Rossetti, Dante Gabriel, 134, 136
Rothenstein, Albert, *see* Rutherston, Albert
Rothenstein, William, 26, 29, 223 & 369 n29
Roughton, Roger, 381 n39
Rousseau, 'Douanier', 35, 176, 190
Rousseau, Jean-Jacques, 190
Roussel, Theodore, 19
Rowe, Clifford, 251
Royal Academy/Academician, 17, 35, 47–8, 61, 64, 158, 216, 249, 278, 308, 320; exhs: work by war artists, 146, 359 n12; Ruskin Centenary 1919, 368 n13; 'British Art in Industry', 371 n9
Royal Academy Schools, 165
Royal College of Art, 217, 219, 223 & 369 n29, 228, 245, 368 n18, 371 n10, 385 n27
Royal Society of British Artists, 349 n7
Ruskin, John, 14 & 348 n2, 16–17 & 349 n5, 19, 55–7 passim, 71 & 354 n47, 73, 212 & 368 n13, 281, 348 n3, 352 n9, 357 n31
Russell, Bertrand, 87, 122 & 360 n16, 353 n32
Russell, William, 29
Russia/Russian art, 54, 62, 238, 251, 280–85, 313, 374 n8
Russian Ballet, 125, 186, 187
Russolo, Luigi, 86, 87
Rutherston, Albert, 29, 62
Rutter, Frank 29, 75, 88

Sackville Gallery; Futurist paintings exh., 86, 88
Sagot, 35, 351 n3
St George's Guild, 349 n5
St Ives, 188, 196, 264, 291–2
Salon d'Automne, 146
Salon des Indépendants, 30, 146
Sandham Memorial Chapel, *see* Burghclere Chapel
Sands, Ethel, 29, 351 n21
Sargent, John Singer, 19, 30, 47, 52; *Monet Painting at the Edge of a Wood*, 20, ill. 2; *Gassed*, 359 n12
Sartoris, Alberto, 286
Saunders, Helen, 102–4, 115, 359 n3
Schoenberg, Arnold, 357 n40
Schofield, Margaret, 347
School of Paris, 186–7
Schwitters, Kurt, 260
Scriabin, Alexander, 357 n40
Sealey, Colin, 346
Second Post-Impressionist Exhibition, 62–7, 69, 79, 87, 159, 183, 250, 349 n10, 370 n6
Seuphor, Michel, 374 n8
Seurat, Georges, 26, 35, 36, 42
Seven & Five Society, 164–6, 181 & 365 n11, 183–91 passim & 365 nn14 & 18, 195–9 passim, 230, 233, 240, 254, 261, 269, 271–5 & 375 n24 & 376 nn28 & 30, 276, 291, 334, 344–7, 371 n14
Severini, Gino, 77, 86, 87, 88
Sevier, Michael, 370 n1
Sewter, A. C., 381 n42
Shaw, George Bernard, 207
Shell Guide to Oxfordshire, 321
Shipp, Horace, 368 n11
Shove, Gerald, 353 n32
Sickert, Walter Richard: and NEAC, 19, 25–6, 35; early years, 24–5; relation to Impressionism and Post-Impressionism, 26; and Gore, 26–8 & 350 nn10–11; and Fitzroy Street Group, 28–30; as a writer on art, 30; on AAA, 30; on Whistler, 31, 34–5, 48 & 352 n10, 50, 341; Marriott on, 31–2; V. Woolf on, 32; work and ideas 1903–10, 32–5, 41; and Camden Town Group, 36–41 passim; Gilman and, 43; and Post-Impressionist exhs., 47–51 passim, 61; on Picasso, 50; and illustrative traditions, 54, 350 n9; joins Royal Academy, 61; and Renaissance, 83; and London Group, 85, 198; and Smith, 153; and Euston Road School, 339, 342–3; C. Bell on, 350 n20; mentioned, 66, 176, 279, 350 nn7 & 8, 352 n10, 356 n21
  Works: *The Juvenile Lead*, 24, ill. 6; *Mamma mia Poveretta*, 25, ill. 7; *Noctes Ambrosianae*, 27, ill. 8; *Portrait of Harold Gilman*, 29, ill. 10; Camden Town Murder series, 33 & 351 n21, 34, 38; *L'Affaire de Camden Town*, 34, ill. 11; *Ennui*, 40, ill. 16; *What shall we do for the Rent?*, 351 n21
Signac, Paul, 25, 30
'significant form', 64 & 354 n40, 94, 221, 307; *see also* C. Bell
Sims, Charles, 359 n12
Skeaping, John, 228, 230, 347, 369 n20
Slade School, 21–2, 24, 33, 35, 43, 47, 64–6, 72, 76, 80, 89, 92, 104, 105, 129, 133, 135, 152, 172, 177, 240, 334, 339, 350 n4, 354 n45, 385 n27
Slater, Montague, 308 & 380 n26
Smith, Matthew, 152–5; *Fitzroy Street Nude no.2*, 153, ill. 75; *Cornish Church*, 154, ill. 76; *Woman with a Fan*, 155, ill. 77
social function of art, 13, 57, 251–2, 261, 302, 308–9, 313–15, 338–43; *see also* autonomy, Marxism, realism, revolution, 'revolution', Socialism
Social Realism, 33, 313, 315, 322, 339
'Social Theme, The' (exh.), 252
Socialism/Socialist: Sickert and, 30; C. Bell and V. Woolf and, 57; at Hulme's at homes, 84; blasted, 111; authoritarianism and, 112 & 358 n53; Roberts and, 158–9; and Epstein's *Christ*, 208; Gill and, 212–13, 223; Modern Movement and, 212, 261, 284; Unit One and, 251; AIA and, 251–2; abstract art associated with, 252, 278–9, 287; Surrealism and, 312–15 passim; Fry's 'Art and Socialism', 352 n17; *see also* Communism, Marxism, revolution, 'revolution'
Socialist Realism, 131, 281, 302, 312
'Society of Anglo-French Painters', *see* NEAC
Society of Industrial Artists, 239
Sorel, Georges, 89 & 356 n22
South American sculpture, 107, 222
Spain, 77, 309, 322, 381 n39
Spanish Civil War, 308, 312
Spencer, Gilbert, 359 n12
Spencer, Stanley, 65, 66 & 354 n45, 120, 122, 133–4, 168, 359 n12; *The Nativity*, 66, ill. 24;

Burghclere Chapel, 133–4 & 361 n32; *Resurrection, Macedonia*, 133, ill. 63; *Travoys arriving with Wounded at a Dressing Station*, 133 & 361 n32
Sprott, Sebastien, 353 n32
Stalin/Stalinist, 252, 281, 313, 333
Steer, Philip Wilson, 19, 20, 21, 23–4, 47, 350 n20; *Walberswick, Children Paddling*, 21, ill. 3
Stendhal, 127
Stepanova, Varvara, 284
Stephen, Adrian, 353 n32
Stephen, Thoby, 353 n32
Stephen, Vanessa, *see* Bell, Vanessa
Stephen, Virginia, *see* Woolf, Virginia
Stephenson, Cecil, *see* Stephenson, J. C.
Stephenson, J. C. 276, 287–8, 347; *Painting*, 288, ill. 146
Stevenson, R. A. M., 349 n3
still life, 70, 71, 77, 151, 154–5, 167–8, 178–9, 182, 185, 194–9 passim, 203, 230, 254 9 passim, 289, 291, 335–7 passim, 365 n10, 383 n20
Stockholm Exhibition, 371 n10
Stokes, Adrian, 230, 233, 291
Stoop bequest, 233, 298
'Stormberg', 119
Storran Gallery; exhs: Rogers and Pasmore 1937, 339; work by teachers and pupils from the Euston Road School, 339
Strachey, Lytton, 67, 68, 353 n32, 360 n12
Stravinsky, Igor, 186
Strindberg, August, 80
Strindberg, Madame Frida, 80, 111
Studio, The, 263, 312, 371 n9
Sumerian art, 220
Summerson, John, 277
Superrealism, *see* Surrealism
Suprematism, 365 n12; *see also* Malevich
Surrealism/Surrealist: P. Nash and, 174, 233, 241, 295, 298, 300, 316–19; early showings in London, 233–4, 240, 245, 298, 300; Burra and, 236; influence in Unit One, 241–4, 248; *Axis* and, 277–8, 319–20; and abstract art as antitheses, 278–9, 299–302, 304–6; English isolation from, pre-1934, 298–9; Read and, 299, 304–5, 315, 319; Moore and, 300, 302, 316–19, 327, 329; 'English Manifesto of Surrealism', 302–3; *Short Survey of Surrealism*, 303–4; and spread of historical materialist ideas, 308; International Surrealist Exhibition, 309–12, 380 nn28–9; and competing views of progressiveness in later thirties, 313–15; activities in London 1936–9, 315–16, 381 nn41–2; and neo-romanticism, 321–5 passim; debate with 'Realists', 333; Surrealist periodicals, 379 n10; mentioned, 194, 258, 287, 293, 374 n8, 384 n23; *see also* Arp, Breton, Dali, Ernst, Giacometti, International Surrealist Exhibition, *London Bulletin*, Magritte, Miró, Picasso
'Surrealist Objects and Poems' (exh.), 316
Sutherland, Graham, 322–4 & 382 n47; *Welsh Landscape with Roads*, 323, ill. 157
Swingler, Randall, 382 n1
Sydney-Turner, Saxon, 353 n32
Symbolism/Symbolist, 16, 77, 261, 288

Tagore, Rabindranath, 111
Tanguy, Yves, 304, 309, 379 n17
Tate Gallery, 43, 47, 62, 71, 91, 92, 112–13, 153, 195, 200, 233, 234, 256, 264, 277, 289, 297, 298, 330, 335, 340
Tatlin, Vladimir, 283–5, 314–15
Tauber-Arp, Sophie, 260
Taylor, Basil, 347
Tchekov, Anton, 127
'Technical Manifesto of Futurist Painting', 87
'Thèse, Antithèse, Synthèse' (exh.), 286
This Quarter, 379 n10
Thomas, Edward, 121
Thompson, d'Arcy, 282 & 377 n45
Thornton, Alfred, 349 n2
Tibble, Geoffrey, 334–7, 339–42; *Reclining Nude*, 341–2, ill. 165
Times, The, 240–41, 295
Tomlin, Stephen, 353 n32
Tonks, Henry, 22, 47, 65, 240, 350 n4, 359 n12; *The Unknown God. Roger Fry preaching . . .*, 47 & 352 n8, 48, ill. 20
Tooth's Gallery, 240, 367 n36; exhs: de Chirico 1928, 200 & 367 n34; 'Recent Developments in British Painting', 235; B. Nicholson and Hepworth 1932, 255, 266; Seven & Five 1929, 346–7; Hitchens 1928, 366 n26; Wadsworth 1929, 367 n34
Torres-Garcia, Joaquín, 374 n8
'Towards an Independent Revolutionary Art', 316 & 381 n40
Townsend, William, 339
'traditional modernism', 96, 118
Transatlantic Review, 379 n10
Transition/transition, 379 nn10 & 17, 380 n29
Trevelyan, Julian, 310–11, 317, 321, 333, 380 nn28–30
Trotsky, Leon, 316 & 381 n40
Trotskyism, 333
'truth to materials', 213, 219
Tschichold, Jan, 276, 286
Turnbull, John, 156
Turner, J. Doman, 36
Turner, J. M. W., 196, 320, 337

Uccello, Paolo, 127, 176
Underwood, G. C. L., 346, 369 n20
unemployment, 147, 238, 306
Unit One, 224, 228, 230, 232, 239–43, 248–53 & 372 nn29–36, 265, 273, 286, 294–5 & 378 nn1–3, 302, 308, 310, 334, 371 n7
Unit 1: the Modern Movement in English Architecture, Painting and Sculpture, 249–51, 260–61, 265–6, 295, 300, 371 n16
universality: of appeal of art, 208; of 'sculptural experience', 210; of aesthetic rationality, 238; of 'right idea', 260; of abstract art, 261, 263, 268, 280; of distinctions, in modernist aesthetics, 264;

universality *cont.*
of understanding, 270; of 'language of colour and form', 270–71; of spiritual 'truth', 280; of style, 281; of shapes, 300, 327; of qualities of art, 305
University College, London, *see* Slade School
Utilitarianism, 58, 75, 130
utopia/utopianism, 97, 190, 238–9, 279, 299

van Dieren, Bernard, 367 n8
van Doesburg, Theo, 260, 374 n8
van Dongen, Kees, 63
van Gogh, Vincent, 26, 35, 36, 38, 42–3, 51, 127, 185, 187, 298, 307
Vantongerloo, Georges, 260
Vaughan, Father Bernard, 206
Velazquez, Diego, 20 & 349 n3, 127, 174
'vernacular modernism', 226–30, 245, 267
Veronese, Paolo, 350 n9
Vézelay, Paule, 198
Vkhutemas, 282–4
Vollard, Ambroise, 35, 351 n3
von Anrep, Boris, 62, 67
von Herkomer, Hubert, 13
von Hildebrand, Adolf, 95
Vorticism/Vorticist: and London Group, 41; *Blast 1*, 101–2, 110–12; signatories to manifesto, 102–5; Gaudier-Brzeska and, 105–8; Wadsworth and, 108–9; Pound and, 110–11, 119–20; Lewis and, 111–13, 115–19; Vorticist exh., 115–16; *Blast 2*, 116–17, 119; reactionary aspect of, 119; exh. at Penguin Club, 119–20; and war, 120, 124–30 passim, 145; Nash and, 141; and X Group, 156–7, 160; influence of, 163–4; fluctuating interest in, 355 n5; mentioned, 177, 210, 211, 381 n46; *see also Blast*, Lewis
Vuillard, Édouard, 25, 26, 35

Wadsworth, Edward: at Slade, 65–6 & 354 n45; in Second Post-Impressionist Exhibition, 67; and Friday Club, 68; and Omega Workshops, 72–4; and Brighton Exhibition, 85; and 'Post-Impressionist and Futurist Exhibition', 88; and Futurism, 90; and 'Manifesto of Vital English Art', 101; and *Blast*, 101–2, 108, 111; and Vorticism, 105, 108–9, 115; in Vorticist exh., 115, 127; war service, 121; as war artist, 127–9, 359 n12; supporting Lewis, 147; and X Group, 156–7; 'Black Country' works, 157–8 & 367 n14; marine still lifes, 201–2 & 367 n34; exh. in Paris, 231 & 370 n1; in 'Recent Developments in British Painting', 235–6; and Unit One, 239–40, 248; work 1931–3, 242–4; and Abstraction-Création, 260; in mid-thirties, 275; mentioned, 175, 254, 355, n5, 370 n6, 372 n29, 373 n41 Works: *Five Designs for the Omega Workshops*, 73, ill. 28; *L'Omnibus*, 88 & 356 n21; *Trees beside a River*, 108, ill. 47; *Study for a Vorticist Painting*, 109, ill. 48; *Enclosure*, 110, 127, ill. 49; *Combat*, 115 & 359 n2; *Dazzle Ships in Drydock at Liverpool*, 128–9, 359 n12, ill. 58; *The Cattewater, Plymouth Sound*, 156, ill. 79; *Ladle Slag*, 157, ill. 78; *Regalia*, 202, ill. 106; *Composition*, 236, ill. 123; *Dux et Comes*, 243, ill. 126; *Blackpool*, 359 n2
Walker's Galleries; Seven & Five exhs: 1920: 164, 346–7; 1922: 346–7
Wallis, Alfred, 188–91 & 366 n22, 194, 256, 347; *St Ives Harbour and Godrevy Lighthouse*, 188, ill. 94
Warren Gallery; exhs: P. Nash 1926, 224 & 371 n11; Moore 1928, 224 & 371 n11
Wedekind, Frank, 80
Weekend Review, 234, 239
Weimar/Weimar Republic, 238, 261, 280
Wellington, Hubert, 350 n8, 367 n8, 383 n8
Wells, H. G., 351 n1
Weltanschauung, 102, 168, 234
West, Alick, 305, 313, 333
West, Rebecca, 84, 111
Westminster School of Art, 66, 196, 354 n45
Westminster Technical Institute, 212
Whistler, James McNeill, 14–16 & 348 nn3–4 & 349 n6, 19 & 349 n1, 24–5, 26, 31, 35, 48 & 352 n9, 50, 51, 55, 57, 174, 179, 185, 341, 349 nn7 & 1; *Nocturne in Black and Gold: the Falling Rocket*, 14, 15, ill. 1
White, J., 346
Whitechapel Art Gallery; exhs: 'For Peace, Democracy and Cultural Development', 309; *Guernica*, 334 & 382 n3; 'Art for the People', 340, 381 n37
Wildman, W. A., 346
Wilenski, R. H., 205, 208, 217, 219–21, 233, 282
'will to form', 95, 97
Williamson, H. S., 346, 364 n25
Wolfe, Edward, 198, 346
Wolmark, Alfred, 356 n21
Wood, Christopher, 184–9 & 365 nn16 & 18 & 366 nn20–21 & 23, 191–5 & 366 n25, 198, 201, 203, 231, 254, 320, 347, 382 n3; *PZ 134*, 193, ill. 98; *Sleeping Fisherman, Ploaré, Brittany*, 193, ill. 99; *Building the Boat, Tréboul*, 194, ill. 100
Woolf, Leonard, 353 n32
Woolf, Virginia, 32 & 350 n19, 45 & 351 n1, 57, 65, 75, 147, 350 n20, 353 n32
Wordsworth, William, 372 n21
Woolway, G. R., 346
Worker, The (Daily), 322
working class, 13, 75, 89, 218, 252, 305–6, 313
Worringer, Wilhelm, 95–7 & 357 nn30–31, 34, 279
Writers International, 307

X Group, 156–60 & 363 nn14–15, 164, 176

Yeats, W. B., 80
Yorke, F. R. S., 371 n9
Yorkshire, 90, 210, 217, 221, 372 n29
Yorkshire Post, 372 n29

Zadkine, Ossip, 370 n1, 380 n30
Zwemmer Gallery (and bookshop), 240, 275, 298; exhs: 'Objective Abstractions', 198, 334, 337; Seven & Five 1935, 273–4, 276, 344, 346–7